READINGS IN

The Clinical Method in Psychology

READINGS IN

The Clinical Method in

PSYCHOLOGY

EDITED BY

ROBERT I. WATSON

WASHINGTON UNIVERSITY SCHOOL OF MEDICINE

HARPER & BROTHERS, PUBLISHERS, NEW YORK

Contents

Contents

viii   *Contents*

Preface

This volume attempts to demonstrate the clinical method of the psychologist, its nature and historical background, its application in various settings, its use in diagnosis and prognosis, and its use in treatment. The articles chosen for inclusion are considered the best available for the purpose of illustrating certain applications of this method of the psychologist.

The general plan of presentation follows this sequence. Six selections are devoted to a general orientation to the clinical method, its history, the present professional status of the clinical psychologist, the clinical method in general, its application in guidance, the relation of psychology and psychiatry, and varying approaches in clinical psychology. The functions of the clinical psychologist are illustrated by reports of eight experts on their work in various clinics and institutions, followed by a short summary of the way a psychologist works in other settings. Considerable attention has been paid to the functions of the clinical psychologist, since one cannot appreciate the significance of the clinical method of psychology without knowledge of the settings in which this method is applied. Diagnostic and prognostic methods are represented by nineteen articles from various journals. Articles concerning the construction or validity of a specific test are not included, nor does the summary of some of the other literature on diagnostic techniques that follows these readings attempt to deal with such matters. Some familiarity with this literature is presupposed. The eighteen articles in the section concerned with treatment represent a considerable variety of approaches. In the area of treatment men are working who are formally trained in several professional disciplines. Contributions included in this and other sections of the *Readings* are limited to those made by psychologists, i.e., members of, or other persons apparently eligible for membership in, the American Psychological Association. This plan, in part, is frankly exploratory. What a psychologist does in treatment, for example, is hard to establish. The pragmatic solution is to assume that he works in treatment in accordance with the methods which he describes in his publications. Admittedly this approach allows considerable gaps in the knowledge necessary either for conducting work in treatment or for working in collaboration with others who do so. However, these gaps are partially filled by inclusion of the contributions not merely of the psychologists but also of the psychiatrists, neurologists, social workers and other contributors in the summary of some of the remaining literature which follows the selected articles.

Inclusion in the Readings of reports by psychologists on various methods of treatment by no means implies that all psychologists are competent to use them either alone or in collaboration with other specialists. Special training and supervision are necessary for those temperamentally suited to apply them.

No one can select readings in this or any other field entirely without bias; views on the psychology of personality, the proper training and function of the psychologist, and many less important matters will affect the selection perhaps without the awareness of the influences of some of these tendencies. Insofar as his limitations permitted, the editor has chosen readings representing diverse points of view. This he has done though fully aware that the charge of inconsistency or even incoherence may be leveled at the collection as a whole. The editor is no system builder, and he views with equanimity and even perverse pride the probability that a certain amount of what he would consider to be healthy confusion will result. This, after all, is the advantage that a collection of readings has over a text or systematic treatise. Each reading stands alone, as originally published, not filtered through the lenses of some other person's interpretation. The reader may disregard the interpretation and opinions expressed in one article without affecting the value of the other articles.

To avoid misunderstanding, some mention must be made of that which was excluded or minimized. It was found that as selection proceeded, references appearing some years ago had been excluded, not because of any desire to minimize their importance—for without the contributions they represent, the later work could not have been done—but because they are often couched in terms of devices, techniques, and even purposes absent from present practice. Then, too, the results of those earlier publications which are still applicable are apt to be now firmly imbedded in the texts and consequently unnecessary of repetition. Also developments in the last few years have been so rapid that otherwise it might be difficult even to attempt to illustrate the full scope of present-day practice. Inspection of the names of the authors will, however, dispel any fear that these are exclusively the contribution of the younger generation of clinical psychologists.

This volume is not intended to supply background for certain other equally important, if not more important, phases of the education and experience of the clinical psychologists, the knowledge and understanding of the dynamics of human adjustment, and the training in the use of specific testing devices. Characteristically, then, there is no overlap with either that valuable compendium edited by Sylvan Tompkins, *Contemporary Psychopathology*, or the typical volumes on tests and rating scales. Research with the clinical method has also been minimized, not because of a disbelief in its importance, but rather because this volume centers around a different orientation. Without research, both fundamental and applied, any profession would wither and die. The paucity of material on this issue is by no means to be construed as grounds for disparagement. An appreciation and understanding of the work of the professional clinical psychologist through knowledge of the setting in which he applies his method and of some of the approaches he uses in his dual task of diagnosis and treatment are its more modest aims.

It is with pleasure that acknowledgment is made of the permissions so graciously given by the authors and editors to reprint these articles. Specific acknowledgments to the journals and authors are given in the text. In addition, acknowledgment is made to the American Council on Education, the American Orthopsychiatric Association, the American Psychological Association, the International Council for Exceptional Children, The Journal Press, G. Fredric Kuder, The National Committee for Mental Hygiene, the University of Chicago Press and Frederick C. Thorne for permission to reprint articles from journals published under their auspices.

July, 1948 ROBERT I. WATSON

I

The Clinical Method

1

The Clinical Method

C. M. LOUTTIT

Galesburg Division, University of Illinois

The Nature of Clinical Psychology[1]

American psychology, generally speaking, has not been greatly interested in practical problems of human behavior. There have been many brilliant individual exceptions to this generalization, but the attitude of the representative professional group is clearly evident in the Proceedings of the American Psychological Association, which have been summarized in Fernberger's history (47, pp. 42–53).[2] That the laissez-faire attitude of the Association was not shared by many of its Members is shown by the organization of the American Association for Applied Psychology (8, 43) in 1937. One of the fundamental reasons for the new organization is the ever-increasing opportunities, even demands, for psychological work in varied human affairs. Whether the practicing psychologists are working in schools, industry, business, hospitals, courts, or in private consultation, a large number of them are confronted with problems concerning specific individuals. It is in dealing with such individual problems that one of the most important services of psychology is to be found, and it is this individual work which constitutes, in a general way, the field of clinical psychology.

A statement such as the one last made is unsatisfactory because it is so general that it conceals many detailed problems which must be faced and solved if clinical psychology is to mean anything more than what each individual speaker uses it to mean. In other words, there is little or no actual agreement as to what clinical psychology is, except that it deals with individuals.

---

[1] Reprinted from *Psychological Bulletin*, 1939, 36, 361–389. Copyright 1939 by American Psychological Association.

[2] Bibliography begins on page 88.

A more specific definition of clinical psychology has been attempted by many writers during the past quarter of a century, but their statements do not always agree among themselves. There is no intent in writing this paper to present a new, and the final, definition. Rather, we shall be content with doing spadework furnishing data for such a formulation. In order to define this subject we should investigate at least 5 areas: (1) what it has been historically; (2) what people have said it was; (3) what is actually being done in its name; (4) the nature of the training required; and (5) what its relations are to borderline fields. A critical appraisal of material in these 5 directions should afford a more integrated basis for definition than has hitherto been possible.

I. History

The history of clinical psychology and psychological clinics is yet to be written. Interesting as such a history might be, we cannot undertake the task at this time. However, in order to understand present-day problems, it is important that we consider the main tendencies and influences that have shaped clinical psychology up to the present.

In 1896 Witmer (130, 131) presented to the meetings of the American Psychological Association a series of proposals concerning the practical investigation of problems of school children utilizing methods available from the psychological laboratories. The immediate occasion for these proposals was the examination of a child in the laboratory at the University of Pennsylvania. The study of this child and several others soon after gave birth to what Witmer later called "clinical psychology." There is little evidence that Witmer's proposals found response among the psychologists of that day. A decade later, in an editorial inaugurating his journal, the *Psychological Clinic*, Witmer (132) briefly described the occasion of his starting a psychological clinic and something of its subsequent history. In spite of Cattell's (30) recollection, at a much later date, that he had tried to start a psychological service for students of Columbia during "the middle of the nineties" and Fernberger's (46) statement that, if Witmer had not inaugurated clinical psychology, someone else shortly would have, it would appear that Witmer alone must be given the credit for the establishment of the clinical type of psychological application.

Because of the unique position of Witmer, it is necessary that his concept of clinical psychology be considered. While Holmes (65) described the clinic and its work as it was in 1912, Witmer himself has never described in any great detail the organization of his own clinic or the methods he used. The basic ideas of the originator of clinical psychology are to be found in a series of papers from 1907 to 1925 (132, 134, 146), in which are discussed certain details of clinical methods and the author's psychological systematization underlying clinical investigation. Essentially, Witmer was interested in the school child, and the task of clinical psychology was to describe and to evaluate the child's behavior according to certain analytic categories (136, 138, 144, 146), and to discover the reasons for deviations. Once this was done, special programs could be devised to improve the behavior. The techniques are illustrated in a number of cases by Witmer and his students published in the *Psychological Clinic*. Many of these are very short, and it would unduly expand our bibliography to list all of them, but one (142), illustrating the treatment of a case of arrested development, i.e. feeblemindedness, is typical. This case and its treatment would not be foreign to any modern child guidance clinic. In fact, both in Holmes's book and Witmer's papers there is much evidence that Witmer, and not Healy, first recognized the value of coöperation between psychologist, psychiatrist or physician, and social worker.

Essentially, Witmer's method was to study thoroughly the child as an individual; to use tests if they were indicated, but not to be bound by them; to make long-time observations in a teaching situation called diagnostic teaching; to evaluate social histories and findings from physical examinations; to keep always in mind that understanding of the child was the goal, not accumulation of data concerning him. This attitude minimized the values of formal case outlines (135) and too great dependence on standardized tests.

While the beginnings of clinical psychology must always be associated with Witmer, it is true that trends and events during the late Nineteenth and early Twentieth Centuries influenced its development. In fact it is probably true that Witmer's influence on present-day activities in the clinical field is rather small. In a large part this is to be regretted because he has always maintained a cautious attitude toward standardized procedures which, away from his influence, have frequently come to be synonymous with clinical activity.

An event of great significance for the development of clinical psychology was the publication of the Binet-Simon (10) scale in 1905. While the idea of measuring abilities was by no means new, Binet supplied a measuring tool that appeared to have more significance to the child's everyday life than any of the tests in earlier use. We need not consider the mushroom growth of tests of all sorts [Hildreth (61) lists about 3000, and Buros (28, 29) has added 868 more], as excellent treatises on the subject are available (53, 94, 95). It is necessary to point out one important result of this growth. Tests appeared to be universal and foolproof diagnostic tools—they were easy to administer; they gave definite numerical scores; they appeared to be easy of interpretation. Because of this, much dependence was placed upon tests; and while we never quite got to a stage of advertisements such as

BE A CLINICAL PSYCHOLOGIST
The Binet test in 20 easy lessons

we came near to it.[3] In 1913 Sylvester (119) pointed out that one adverse criticism of clinical psychology was that there was too great emphasis upon mental tests. He admits that the criticism is valid and accounts for the condition on the ground of psychological interest in tests, their quantitative nature, and the public demand. While neither Binet himself, nor any of the early clinical psychologists, ever claimed miracles for standardized tests, the inevitable result ensued, and persons with a knowledge of tests—or even 1 test—began to offer themselves for, and were employed in, positions where only sound clinical training and experience were really valuable. While to follow all the possible results of this attitude would take us too far afield, we must point out that this is the essential basis for the widely held belief that clinical psychology and mental testing are the same activity.

The psychological study of the feebleminded was another early contribution to clinical psychology. In 1906 the Training School at Vineland, New Jersey, started a laboratory for the study of feeble-

---

[3] In the Newsletter of the Pennsylvania Association of Clinical Psychologists, Vol. II, No. 1, February, 1939, attention is called to an advertisement offering essentially this!

mindedness (39). While research in feeblemindedness had produced a sizeable literature before this time, the Vineland laboratory
was apparently the first to be devoted primarily to the psychological
study of this condition. Under the original directorship of H. H.
Goddard (1906–1919) this laboratory soon demonstrated the usefulness of the Binet tests and investigated other types of measuring
tools. Under the subsequent directorships of Porteus (1919–1925)
and Doll (1925–to date) there has been constant attention to the
clinical problems of feeblemindedness. This work of Goddard's introduced psychological methods in the study of 1 large group of abnormal individuals. Work with the subnormal has been, and still
is, an important field of activity for psychologists, but again it must
be pointed out that such work is not coincident with clinical psychology.

A third name which appeared early and which has long been connected with clinical activity is that of J. E. Wallace Wallin. As long
ago as 1909, while at the East Stroudsburg (Pennsylvania) State
Normal School, Wallin (122) published a paper concerned with the
psychological and medical inspection of school children. This paper
pointed out the need for, and the excellent advances that had been
made in, the medical and dental inspection of school children. But,
he argues, this is not enough. There must also be systematic inspection and examination of mentally exceptional school children. In
1910 Wallin was director of a clinical laboratory for the National
Dental Association and by 1912 had established a psychoeducational
clinic at the University of Pittsburgh. His first specific paper on clinical psychology (123) was an extensive survey of existing clinics and
a detailed exposition of the nature of the work. These early papers
set the tone for all of Wallin's work, i.e. a specific interest in the
school child and problems associated particularly with academic and
social adjustment in the school.

Simultaneously with the activity in the strictly psychological field,
there were movements in psychiatry that were destined to influence
clinical psychology. During the last half of the Nineteenth Century
a psychological or functional point of view was being introduced
into psychiatry by such men as Charcot, Janet, Carpenter, Maudsley,
Weir Mitchell, and Freud. This point of view led to the modern
concepts of dynamic psychiatry, which is more psychological than it
is medical. Partly influenced by this movement in psychiatry, partly

from a more specifically psychological approach, and partly from the practical problem with which he was confronted, Healy (59, pp. 809 ff.), in 1909, started a behavior clinic to deal with juvenile delinquents in connection with the Cook County (Chicago) Juvenile Court.

This Juvenile Psychopathic Institute was at first financed by private endowment and in 1914 was taken over by Cook County. In 1917 it was taken over by the State of Illinois and in 1920 was renamed the Institute for Juvenile Research. Originally, attention was directed primarily to study of juvenile offenders, and this has remained an important part of its work, but its field of activity includes practically all types of children's behavior problems (68).

In 1909 Clifford W. Beers started the National Committee for Mental Hygiene as an agency to correct conditions in hospitals for · psychotics as he had experienced them. The introduction to his book, A mind that found itself (9), was written by William James, a psychologist, but the activities of the National Committee have always been controlled and directed by psychiatrists. By the early 1920's it was recognized that any efforts at prevention of behavior difficulties must start with children. For this reason the National Committee organized and operated, with funds from the Commonwealth Fund, 5 experimental child guidance clinics between 1925 and 1929 (115). The minimum standard personnel for such clinics includes a psychiatrist, a psychologist, and a psychiatric social worker.

The child guidance movement started and has operated under essentially psychiatric auspices although there are accepted child guidance clinics in charge of psychologists. Stevenson and Smith (115) ascribe the beginnings of such guidance work to Healy, who, they claim, introduced the social worker as an integral part of the professional staff. They, incidentally, say: "To some degree, the way had indeed already been blazed by Lightner Witmer's Psychological Clinic established in 1896 at the University of Pennsylvania" (p. 15). This sentence is essentially incorrect because Witmer's philosophy and actual clinic organization [as described by Holmes (65)] do not materially differ from the modern psychiatric child guidance clinic.

From this very brief historical survey of the beginnings of clinical psychology we may itemize the following common characteristics:

1. The interest was rather definitely with children.
2. Children with behavior deviations were the primary concern.
3. The methods used emphasized a well-rounded study of the child as a physical, social, and psychological individual.
4. Diagnostic study was not an end in itself, but a starting point in a reëducational, corrective, or therapeutic program.

The soundness of these characteristics cannot be questioned. They are the essence of Witmer's teaching, but they were lost sight of largely because of the misleading apparent simplicity of mental tests. For a decade and a half the things Witmer stood for were far from being the important elements in activities going under the name of clinical psychology. These earlier ideals were reintroduced from another angle by the child guidance movement, and the last decade has witnessed the efforts of psychologists to regain ground lost during the dark ages of mental testing.

II. Definitions

To search out all of the definitions of clinical psychology that have ever been published would be a tedious and unfruitful task. I have collected around 40, which should be a fair sample. These may be classified into 4 rather specific categories with a few remaining for the inevitable class, "miscellaneous."

The largest group of definitions characterizes clinical psychology essentially as the behavior study of the individual. In some cases the definitions explicitly include treatment, while in others it is implicit or ignored. An early statement by Witmer (132), when read in the light of his total position, expresses everything that subsequent definitions do: "For the methods of clinical psychology are necessarily involved whenever the status of an individual mind is determined by observation and experiment, and pedagogical treatment applied to effect a change, i.e., the development of such individual mind." Recent statements by 2 of Witmer's students elaborate the essence of his early formulation. Brotemarkle (22) has the following rather lengthy definition:

> Clinical psychology is the art which studies and applies itself to the inter-organized patterns of behavior in the human individual. Gathering its materials and techniques primarily from psychology, it also deals with the materials of education, the medical sciences, the social sciences, and all factors which influence individual personality; and is based upon the results of scientific research in human personeering. Its methodology is

the analysis of the competencies, efficiencies, and proficiencies of the individual through clinical diagnoses, tests, and diagnostic teaching. It proceeds through post-analytic diagnosis of the human personality to the prognosis of the future performance of the individual. Its outcome is the accomplishment of the highest level of individual perfectability through the corrective, directive, preventative, and creative production of patterns of preferred behavior in the integration of human personality (p. xviii).

More specifically he details the following 6 functions: (1) analyze the individual reaction patterns and capacities; (2) discover the etiology of these; (3) interpret their integration in the individual's behavior; (4) study the adjustment of the individual on the basis of the foregoing; (5) outline a program of readjustment; and (6) recommend, assist with, or, on occasion, direct the applications of these methods.

Much more concisely Viteles (121) says: "The complete study of the individual from the point of view of his adaptability in diverse situations has been the particular province of the clinical psychologist" (p. 34). This is elaborated on a subsequent page: "However, the point of emphasis in such clinical study is the individual—an individual looked upon as an integrated organization of behavior patterns—as a 'whole' personality against a background of objective conditions to which he is called upon to adapt himself" (p. 596).

Such definitions are not unique with students of Witmer. Doll (40) says that clinical psychology "attempts to combine all characteristics, mental, physical, and social, into a composite appraisal which is significant for purposes of individual adjustment in the normal relations of the individual to society and social institutions." In the compilation of statements concerning clinical psychology issued by the Clinical Section of the American Psychological Association (6), Gesell, Hegge, Maxfield, Paynter, Terman, Town, Wallin, G. B. Watson, and Wells all express the same ideas. Incidentally, the reading of this compilation is exhibit "A" for indicating the difficulties individual psychologists have in attempting to define the field which they consider to be the one in which they are working. From the material in the compilation and other investigations the Committee formulated a definition which was adopted as part of its report by the membership of the Clinical Section of the American Psychological Association, thus giving it a semiofficial status. This semiofficial definition is as follows:

Clinical psychology is a form of applied psychology which aims to define the behavior capacities and behavior characteristics of an individual through methods of measurement, analysis, and observation; and which, on the basis of an integration of these findings with data received from the physical examinations and social histories, gives suggestions and recommendations for the proper adjustment of the individual (5, p. 5).

This definition shows care in its formulation, and it serves as an adequate statement of the behavior study type.

A second class of definitions which has some reasonable basis in historical conditions, and which is popularly held today, emphasizes the methods of mental or intelligence testing or even makes psychometrics and clinical psychology synonymous. The most recently published definition of this sort has been promulgated by the Institute for Juvenile Research in Chicago (68). This Institute (let us hope not its psychologist) says that "the clinical psychologist is concerned with the evaluation of the child's innate abilities, educational achievements, and special aptitudes" (p. 81). David Mitchell (6) says: "Clinical psychology has to do with the examination of individuals to determine the mental level or ability. It is primarily a diagnosis of subnormal states" (p. 20). Bronner (6) says: "Clinical psychology . . . describes the field of giving and interpreting psychological tests as part of the study in the field of guidance" (p. 9). These quotations have precedence in Mateer's (82) claim that "the psychological diagnosis of psychopathy must be a diagnosis based upon psychological tests alone. In other words it must be a qualitative analysis of test finding" (p. 287). In a later book (83, p. 3), she makes clinical psychology, mental measurements, and intelligence testing synonymous, although, to be fair, we should point out that on a later page she says that the goal idea of clinical psychology is "more definitely understanding [the individual] and his behavior" (p. 22).

Psychologists who would adhere to such limited definitions of clinical psychology are extremely few, and, we may say, limited in their grasp of what clinical psychology may mean. The definitions would hardly be worth considering except that they appear to express the notions held all too frequently by psychiatrists, social workers, teachers, and laymen.

The third type of definition would limit the activities of clinical psychology to study of the subnormal or abnormal. This idea is included in Mitchell's statement quoted above. Goddard (54) said: "Clinical psychology should mean personal examination of some one who is mentally abnormal, or subnormal, leaving those psychologists who apply the science to determining what the special traits of a normal individual may fit him for, to form a representative group possibly called vocational psychologists" (p. 85). Wallin (124), in 1913, said: "Clinical psychology is concerned with the *concrete* study and examination of the behavior of the *mentally exceptional individual* (not groups), by its own methods of observation, testing, and experiment" (p. 896). It should be noted that these last 2 writers, in later statements (6), have not emphasized the abnormal or subnormal. Modern opinion would entirely agree with Witmer (132) when he says: "I would not have it thought that the method of clinical psychology is limited necessarily to mentally or morally retarded children . . . Clinical psychology, therefore, does not exclude from consideration other types of children that deviate from the average—for example, the precocious child and the genius. Indeed, the clinical method is applicable even to the so-called normal child."

In the fourth class of definitions we have those which place a medical emphasis on clinical psychology. The close association of clinical psychology to medicine was early recognized by Witmer (132), but he pointed out that it was equally close to sociology and pedagogy. As early as 1915 Haberman (56) defined clinical psychology as medical psychology and psychotherapeutics. In a later paper (57) he says: "It is for the clinical psychologist (who is physician and neurologist as well as psychologist) to determine: and it is for him likewise, in connection with the pedagogue to suggest the remedy" (p. 862). More recently another physician, Bisch (12), defined the field thus: "Clinical psychology is what the words imply—psychology based upon clinical experience. No person should consider himself a qualified clinical psychologist who has not had some medical training, nor should a physician qualify as such who lacks training in psychology" (p. xiii). Ethel Kawin (6), whose statement is a little confusing, seems to feel that the chief task of clinical psychology "should be limited for the most part to tests, measurements, and observations that serve as an integral part of a complete clinical examination and treatment that are basically medical or psychiatric in character" (p. 16). These definitions with a medical emphasis represent statements of too narrow bias, similar to the narrowness of the preceding 2 sorts. Such narrowing of the field represents either a personal bias or an unfortunate lack of insight into what clinical psychology really is.

In the fifth, miscellaneous, class of definitions are included a number which, if they had been expanded by their authors, might well be included in one of the other 4 classes. Thus when Pintner (6) says, "Clinical psychology is that type of psychology in which help to the individual is stressed" (p. 21), there is implied certain study of the individual. Among the miscellaneous definitions is the entirely useless circularity which Ackerson (6) takes from Webster's dictionary, that clinical psychology is psychology "of or pertaining to a clinic." As in its definition of so many technical terms, the dictionary offers no help with this pedantic etymology. (It is interesting to note that Warren's psychological dictionary does not include the term "clinical psychology.")

Any attempt to summarize these representative definitions of clinical psychology must first eliminate those which set too narrow limits. Clinical psychology is not psychometrics; it is not medical psychology, nor does it deal primarily with the subnormal or abnormal. The field includes all of these, but it is broader than any of them.

In the broader sense we can agree with Westburgh (128) that "clinical psychology is an art." As I have elsewhere pointed out (74, p. 3), each practical art is the application of one or two basic sciences, but in its successful practice many other sciences must be involved. The implications of the definitions classed in the first group above are in agreement with this. In these definitions psychological principles are primary, but it is evident that the contributions of sociology, education, and the medical and biological sciences are also important. The semiofficial definition, using the wording of Gesell (6), says that clinical psychology aims to define "behavior capacity and behavior characteristics." The former includes skills, knowledge, aptitudes, intelligence—in short, what the individual does and can do. The later phrase concerns how he does these things, *i.e.* question of motivation, inhibition, emotional disturbances, and so on. The methods of describing this behavior may come from the psychological laboratory, e.g. tests, or they may be borrowed from other fields, e.g. the case history. In any case, the final job is an understanding description of the individual's pattern of behavior. If these patterns are socially or personally unacceptable, an effort must be made to change them until they are acceptable.

III. Psychological Clinics and Their Work

Another approach to the problem of what clinical psychology is may be made by considering the nature and work of existing clinic organizations. Certain information can be secured by analysis of 2 published directories. Between 1931 and 1934 a committee of the Clinical Section of the American Psychological Association was working on the definition of clinical psychology and a survey of psychological clinic facilities in the United States. Their report, pub-

TABLE 1. Number of Psychological Clinics Reported in 1914 and 1935

	A		B		C	
	1914 Wallin	1935 A.P.A.	1914 Wallin	1935 A.P.A.	1914 Wallin	1935 A.P.A.
University and College.	15	7	4	1	30	6
Normal Schools.......	1	0	2	0	20	0
Medical Schools......	3	0	2	0	8	0
TOTALS...........	19	7	8	1	58	6

lished in 1935 (7), includes a directory of psychological clinics which apparently have in common the feature of being directed by a psychologist. In 1936 the National Committee for Mental Hygiene published a directory of psychiatric clinics, compiled by Clark (31), which included only those organizations directed by a psychiatrist or at least having a psychiatrist on the staff who was in attendance at specified hours. Together, these lists are probably fairly inclusive for their dates. However, the opening of new clinics continues, so that any list is soon out-of-date.

Some idea of the increase in the number of clinics may be gained by contrasting a list published by Wallin in 1914 (123, 125) and the first list mentioned above. Wallin circularized universities, normal schools, and medical schools in 1913 and received replies from 66, 33, and 25, respectively. He classified his respondents into (A) those having bona fide clinics, (B) those giving some attention to clinical psychology but only in connection with courses, and (C) those giving pertinent courses but having no practical clinical work. In Table 1 are shown the numbers in each of these groups and also the number of the same institutions which had clinics in the 1935 list.

According to Table 1 there were 19 bona fide clinics in 1914 operating under the auspices which Wallin surveyed; by 1934 only 7 of these were still in existence, although there was a total of 34 clinics under these auspices, as seen in Table 2. In Wallin's groups B and C there were 1 and 6 clinics, respectively, reported in 1934. Interestingly enough, the 1 normal school and 3 medical schools which were reported to have psychological clinics in 1914 were not reported at all in 1935. Wallin's figures are, of course, not comparable with the total number reported in 1935 because he surveyed only institutions of higher education; however, it is doubtful if there were many clinics under other auspices at the earlier date.

TABLE 2.   Auspices of Psychological Clinics 1935 (*65*)

University and Colleges	34
Public and Private Schools	17
Social Agencies	12
State Department	6
County Department	2
City Department	1
Self-supporting	2
Private Endowment	4
Institutions	9
TOTAL	87

The contrast between these 2 sets of figures does not present the total picture. In the time between the 2 studies the child guidance movement was initiated and grew to significantly large proportions. Essentially, this movement was under psychiatric guidance, but of a nature somewhat different from the psychiatric attention to adults. In the directory published in *Mental Hygiene* (31) there were approximately the number of clinics devoted to children and adults shown in Table 3 as compared with a similar distribution of the psychological clinics.

This brief summary of the data supplied by the 2 available published lists of behavior clinics indicates the very decided increase in this specialty since the first clinic of Witmer in 1896. It is also evident that children are the chief interest of behavior clinics. This is very probably wise, because all evidence indicates that adult behavior difficulties are based upon childhood conditions, and during

TABLE 3.   Age Clientele of Behavior Clinics

	Psychological	Psychiatric	Total
Children Only.....................	29	204	233
Children and Adults..............	46	391	437
Adults Only......................	4	81	85
TOTALS........................	79	676	755

childhood the chances of correcting damaging conditions and undesirable behavior are much greater than in adulthood.

Further analysis of the data from the directory of psychological clinics reflects the nature of problems dealt with and the relations of these clinics to other social institutions and agencies, as shown in the following list:

> Guidance: general, primarily for children.
> Guidance: general, children and adults.
> Departments of Education: school children.
> Juvenile delinquency: courts and institutions.
> Psychoeducational clinics: Schools of Education.
> Children's institutions: orphan homes, etc.
> University clinics: primarily for teaching.
> Hospitals: children's, psychopathic.
> Prisons.
> Social agencies: family and child welfare.
> Speech clinics.
> College student guidance.
> Vocational guidance.
> Family problems.
> Institutions for the blind.
> Institutions for the feebleminded.

This bare recital of the directions in which clinical psychologists are working serves to emphasize its broad usefulness.

Clark's (31) directory of psychiatric clinics includes 676 clinics operated in connection with hospitals, schools, and as independent community agencies. Among this total number were 116 specially designated as child guidance clinics and 34 which had seen at least 100 children during the year reported. According to the record there were over 225 psychologists on the staffs of these clinics. Louttit (77) reported results from questionnaires sent to the senior psychologists of these clinics. Our interest here is in the type of work the psychologists do. Among the 111 psychologists for whom data were received, the types of work shown in Table 4 were reported.

TABLE 4.   Types of Work Done by 111 Psychologists in Child Guidance Clinics

	No. Reporting	%
Psychometrics	96	86.5
Educational Guidance	81	73.0
Vocational Guidance	77	69.4
Diagnostic Interviewing	72	64.9
Remedial Teaching (speech, reading, etc.)	49	44.1
Psychotherapy (therapeutic interviewing)	39	35.1
Teaching	10	9.0
Administration	4	3.6
Social Investigation	3	2.7

In so far as these data are representative of the psychologists' work in clinics they indicate a variety of tasks, some purely psychological, others in the field of remedial education and in social investigation. They indicate the psychologist's concern with securing an integrated picture of the case on the side of diagnosis and his adaptation of many procedures on the side of treatment.

The types of activities engaged in by clinical psychologists may also be found in published descriptions of clinics. There are too many of these to attempt an exhaustive list, but several recently published ones will show the trend.

Witty and Theman (147) analyze a questionnaire survey of 34 psychoeducational clinics and describe practices in the Northwestern University clinic. McBee (84) describes a mental hygiene clinic in a high school, and Frith (51) reports how one city school system makes use of a part-time psychologist. Kelly (69) operates a traveling clinic which serves schools in all parts of Kansas. Sangren (107) demonstrates the use of a clinic as a teaching method in a teacher-training institution. All of these clinics have their primary interest in problems of the school child —retardation, special subject disabilities, social and personal adjustment.

Brousseau (25) and Nimkoff (90) both describe clinics organized to deal with problems of marital and family adjustments. Louttit (75) has reported on the work of a university clinic dealing primarily with children which has branches on the university campus and in a children's hospital. Kinder (70) explains the work of the psychologist in an institution for the feebleminded. Fenton (44, 45) and Martens and Russ (81) have described a method of the community coördinating council in child guidance work. This system is perhaps the best so far developed for dealing with behavior problems because it utilizes the services of all community agencies—school, welfare, health, police, etc.—in the study and treatment of the child. Link (72) describes the methods used in the Psychological Service Center operated by the Psychological Corporation.

In addition to these examples of specifically described clinics and clinic organization we may here mention the use of clinical psychology in other directions.

Brotemarkle (23) indicates its value in college student personnel work. Viteles (120, 121) and Rosenstein (103) apply it to industrial problems. Forbes (48) illustrates results from clinical studies of accident-prone automobile drivers. It is an integral part of the classification work in adult prisons (26) and in correctional institutions for juvenile delinquents. The work of the psychologists in connection with study and treatment of psychoses was discussed at a round table held in connection with the second annual meeting of the American Association for Applied Psychology.

Ridenour (101) has analyzed the membership of the A.P.A. and the A.C.P. in New York State and has found that 24% of the individuals included had positions essentially of a clinical nature in clinics, courts, schools, hospitals, and social agencies. She also reports that of 30 clinics in New York City organized for psychiatric service only 16 clinics employed a psychologist. Louttit (77) reported that 13, or 9%, of 150 psychiatric child guidance clinics had no psychologist. These 2 studies indicate that, in spite of the demonstrable value of psychologists in behavior work, there are many psychiatric clinics which feel that this professional group is not necessary.

From this very brief survey of the nature and extent of clinical psychological services as they actually exist today we may isolate the following trends:

(1) The emphasis appears to be largely directed toward children.
(2) Clinical psychology is employed in every type of charitable and humanitarian agency—schools, social welfare, health, institutions

for mental defectives, and those for social deviates, etc.—especially those which deal with children.

(3) There is an appreciable attention to adults (which is probably increasing) in the areas of family, industry, colleges, criminology, and psychoses.

(4) The work of the clinical psychologist in either child or adult directions is characterized by the individual being the center of interest.

(5) The possible avenues of psychological service are barely opened as yet. Even in the field of child guidance there are still a very considerable number of clinics which do not employ psychologists, and in the adult field only a beginning has been made.

IV. Training for Clinical Psychology

Poffenberger (96) suggests that "a clinical psychologist will be a person who can do, and does, what a certain prescribed academic and field training enables him to do." While there is an ideal reasonableness in this suggestion, it cannot be very meaningful in the near future. Only by knowing what tasks the clinical psychologist is called upon to do can we know what to prescribe for training.

As in so many other phases of clinical psychology, Witmer was the first to outline a program of professional training. In 1907 (133) and again in 1911 (134) Witmer described the curriculum at the University of Pennsylvania. This curriculum offered a background in general psychology and culminated in practical courses dealing with the problems of actual children. In essence this is the nature of all subsequent systems. Wallin (123, 126) emphasized the necessity of training in clinical procedures as distinct from purely academic psychology. He also held that work in education (including actual teaching experience) and in certain medical subjects was necessary.

In spite of the specific training needs pointed out by Witmer and Wallin many years ago, graduate schools have not advanced far in the direction of meeting these needs. The Ph.D. degree figures more and more in formal requirements, but, as has been pointed out by Hildreth (62), Louttit (76), and others, this degree varies greatly in the kind of work required for it. Therefore, it does not guarantee that its holder is qualified to do clinical psychological work. Greene (55) reports a study made by, and among the Members of, the Michigan Psychological Association. Respondents were asked to indicate courses which they felt were necessary in the training of a clinical psychologist. We cannot repeat the details of the findings, but a survey showing the trends in suggested number of hours (including undergraduate and graduate) in various major fields is given in Table 5.

TABLE 5. Summary of Hours Suggested for Training

Languages	24
Sciences	20
Sociology	17
Medical	12
Psychology	44
Speech	2
Education	16

While these data are merely suggestive, being based on the responses of a small group, they do indicate the trend toward a fourfold curriculum—psychological, medical, educational, and sociological—suggested by Louttit (73, 76) and implied much earlier in the work of Witmer and Wallin. Goodwin Watson, commenting on the report of a Subcommittee of the White House Conference (129), clearly points out the difficulties when he says: "I see no possible hope for training adequate personnel if we assume they must know everything the doctor has been supposed to know, and everything the psychologist, the educator, and social case worker have been supposed to know. The conclusion toward which the Subcommittee report seems to point in a constructive fashion is a reanalysis of those materials of training, a selection of the crucial and significant parts as rapidly as they can be determined and the reconstruction of curricula" (p. 57). To ask the clinical psychologist to be fully trained in all 4 directions is to ask the impossible. However, Burchard (27) has organized a detailed course of study which includes pertinent subjects in each area. Poffenberger (96), in briefly describing a proposed curriculum, takes a somewhat backward step by confining it entirely to psychology, although he does include a full year of practical internship.

Without doubt any program of training for clinical psychology should include a period of practical experience. Hildreth (62) points out that at the present time experience in actual clinic situations may be more important than academic course work. Shakow (111) has analyzed the values of an "interne year" which he feels should follow academic work. This author indicates 4 values of an internship, especially in an institution: (1) it improves facility in the use of techniques; (2) it saturates the student with clinical contacts; (3) it intensifies the experimental-objective attitude of psychology (which he feels is different from that of the psychiatrist or social worker); and (4) it develops insight and understanding of the attitudes of clinical colleagues.

In summary, we may point out that suggestions for professional training include (1) sound training in psychology, (2) work in medical, educational, and sociological fields, and (3) at least 1 year of practical experience under supervision comparable to the physician's internship. Such a program should be oriented around the individual.

V. Relations of Clinical Psychology to Bordering Fields

On the basis of evidence so far presented we may say that the clinical psychologist deals with adjustmental problems of individuals. His activities, of necessity, overlap those of several other professional workers, notably in medicine, education, and social work. This overlap has introduced a problem of differentiating clinical psychology from the work of the bordering fields. Because of the complex nature of the work, it is difficult to enumerate specific differentials, but we can survey important comments on the relations between clinical psychology and its nearest neighbors.

Medicine. With the medical profession, clinical psychology finds perhaps its greatest overlap and the most difficulty in attempting differentials. The *status quo* and the difficulties are easily understood. By and large, clinical psychology deals with people in trouble —in a sense they are behaviorally ill. For a long time it has been the province of the physician to deal with physical ills. He has had a background of clinical efforts and a legal position in relation to suffering man. Therefore, it has been a natural consequence that the physician should find himself faced with problems of behavior which have had no physical basis, and with a public demand that he do something about them. Unfortunately, physicians in general are not at all prepared to deal with nonphysical difficulties. This, of course, is not true of the psychiatrists and especially those with modern training and clinical experience in dynamic psychiatry. Nonetheless, the greater portion of behavior or psychological problems is essentially nonmedical, and most physicians are essentially untrained in dealing with behavior difficulties. This combination of facts has resulted in the growth of behavior clinics under medical and nonmedical auspices with a frequent conflict between different groups. While this has been unfortunate, it is probably due to professional jealousy engendered, as Woodworth (149) suggests, because "each group [psychologists, psychiatrists, social workers, etc.] feeling unsure of itself because in possession of only a modicum of relevant knowledge, has tended to overcompensate for this feeling" (p. 4).

As early as 1917 Cornell (34) wrote a very bitter article denying the psychologists any function in diagnosing feeblemindedness. While he admits that psychologists may give tests, he says that the physicians must make the diagnosis. He explains that tests, especially the Binet, are all right because Binet was a physician. (Actually he had his degree in law!) He then laments that physicians have allowed nonmedical men to usurp the field of mental testing. This paper, while only of historical interest, shows an early medical attitude toward clinical psychologists.

The currently accepted psychiatric notion of the function of the psychologist is shown in the definition of clinical psychology quoted previously from the book on procedures published by the Institute for Juvenile Research (68). Another, and more explicit, expression of this idea is made by Welsch (127), who says:

An understanding of human behavior requires the study of four aspects of the individual: (1) Physical status, (2) Emotional make-up (feeling, attitudes, loves, hates, jealousies, fears), (3) Intellectual endowment, with any special disabilities or abilities, and (4) Environmental factors. The study and understanding of the first two is the special contribution of the psychiatrist. The third is the realm of the psychologist, including any special vocational guidance or remedial work as indicated by the test results. The fourth is the special study of the social worker . . . (p. 12).

As a final—and the most naïve—example, we may quote from Sadler (106): "In recent years the general public, more especially psychologists and psychiatrists, have awakened to the fact that psychology deals merely with the phenomena of the intellect . . ." (p. 419).

The untenableness of this position is so evident to anyone who knows even a little about the history of psychology that it would hardly be worth discussing. However, it is so widely believed that some effort should be made to answer it. A quotation from an earlier paper (76) of the writer's states the logical position quite clearly:

(1) Human psychology—and here we are not concerned with any other kind—is the scientific study of human behavior. It must be noted here that the modern tendency in psychology is away from the behavior of an isolated organism and in the direction of the organism's—i.e., the psychological personality's—behavior in interaction with its environment. (2) Any sort of behavior, normal or abnormal, usual or unusual, good or bad, individual or group, is a legitimate field for psychological study. (3) The data and principles of psychology may be applied as are the data and principles of any science. (4) One application of such data and principles is to the behavior of an individual to the end of guiding that individual to satisfactory adjustment or of correcting an existing unsatisfactory adjustment. This is the field of clinical psychology.

It is in point to mention here that psychiatry itself has not had a ready acceptance by the other medical specialists. Before the War it was the Cinderella of the medical family; since then, while it has made considerable advance, it is still far from wholly accepted by the nonpsychiatric physician (16). In relation to pediatrics this problem was of sufficient importance for the White House Conference on Child Health and Protection to organize a special Subcommittee on psychology and psychiatry. Its report (129), prepared under the chairmanship of Dr. Bronson Crothers,

is a careful consideration of the relations of psychiatry and psychology to pediatrics. As only one member of the Subcommittee was not a physician (Dr. J. E. Anderson, a psychologist), it is to be expected that the claims of the physician should loom large. However, this is not a serious matter. The position taken, that the family doctor is closest to the family, and comes first into contact with the problems of the children, is well taken. While it would appear that the Subcommittee would desire all physicians to acquire some specialized training in psychology, they do not appear to feel that the psychologist might get a similar amount of medical training and do the job as well (74, p. 4).

The following statement made by the Subcommittee may be taken as a mild rebuke to those physicians who deny the psychologist a legitimate part in the study and treatment of behavior problems:

This Subcommittee believes that the study of an individual distress is the logical concern of the doctor. Those of us who are responsible for "child guidance" are obviously going to become involved with fields of effort where our status is not clear. Education and psychology are sciences or "disciplines" with definite traditions and techniques. "Social science" has a definite meaning to some individuals. When doctors enter these fields they have no right to attempt to lead or to dictate simply because their prestige as physicians gives them an advantage. The attempt to carry prestige beyond the field where it was earned is the cause of most of the confusion which exists. Doctors are flagrant offenders, psychologists have not been guiltless, and teachers and clergy have furnished their share of examples. The medical profession and its attitude are our direct concern. As physicians we can investigate the situation and make our own disclaimers of expert knowledge. At times we should be prepared to lay aside the mantle of authority and enter the field with all comers. There may be corners of domains of education, psychology, and social science where we can establish positions by earned prestige in a new field (129, p. 24).

The entire report bears the stamp of the same sound, critical attitude shown by Dr. Crothers in a later book (36). A quotation from this book nicely sums up the relation of the psychologist to the medical man and especially the pediatrician: "At worst, I think, the psychologist will be recognized as a reliable purveyor of intelligence quotients. At best, his advice will be sought and considered in problems as diverse as those connected with neurological diagnosis and those involved in arranging for convalescent supervision after contagious disease" (p. 167).

While we cannot finally decide the boundaries between psychology and medicine, we can vehemently deny the common psychiatric notion that the psychologist's function is to give tests. From the viewpoint of psychological history we can lay just and logical claim to all behavior problems—emotional, motivational, personality, intellectual, etc.—as long as such problems do not involve purely physical pathologies. At the present time the best method of dealing with behavior problems is probably the open professional coöperation of the psychologist, psychiatrist, social worker, or other persons who have something to contribute to the understanding of the problem. Ability to deal with these problems must be judged on personal qualification rather than on strictly delimited professional labels.

Social Work. The relations of clinical psychology to social work are much clearer than to medicine. While there are individual complaints of usurpation of authority from both psychologist and social worker, little has been written. Mary Richmond's (99) definition of social case work is essentially psychological in nature: "Social case work consists of those processes which develop personality through adjustments consciously effected, individual, by individual, between men and their social environment" (pp. 98–99). In so far as this definition represents actual case work—and I believe it does—the professional social worker should have some foundation in psychology. The importance of this is evidenced in Hagerty's (58) discussion of the social worker's training.

In 4 papers published in *The Family*, Acheson (1) and Ridenour (100) both state that the psychologist's greatest function in social work is in mental testing. Ridenour holds that even at the psychometric level a well-trained worker is absolutely necessary if test results are to be adequately interpreted. With this we agree, but we feel that the other 2 authors, Peters (93) and Regensburg (98), recognize a still greater value in the psychologist's services. Peters says that "although she [case worker] may express only a desire for diagnosis and prognosis in requesting an examination, she often wants further interpretation of the problem. This may vary from something of a very simple, obvious nature to a quite involved and complicated interpretation and discussion of the total situation" (p. 179). Regensburg goes still further by saying: "The clinical psychologist is not only a psychometrician. He is a professional consultant who must supplement this skill with such knowledge as enables him to understand the client as a total individual in whatever predicament the client finds himself" (p. 201).

Not only does clinical psychology have value for the social worker, but there is a reciprocal value in case work for the psychologist. Acheson (1) is essentially correct when she says that usually the psychologist coming to a social agency is well trained in psychological techniques, but that he lacks training in, and often an appreciation of, case-work techniques. It is just here that graduate training in psychology is lacking and it is from the social work curricula that psychologists must take their cue.

Education. Historically and practically education has been, and must be, concerned with the training of all children; it must deal with children in groups. This is the very antithesis of clinical psychology which, while it does use teaching as a therapeutic method, is concerned only with the individual child. While modern progressive education is based upon a "child centered school," it is the child in a group rather than the child in isolation. There is no real confusion between the teacher or educator and the psychoclinician. That education has accepted and used clinical psychology is shown in the reports of clinics operated by school agencies (51, 69, 78, 84, 107, 147).

VI. Summary

In this article we have tried, by surveying representative selected literature, to picture the present status of clinical psychology. The findings indicate that modern definitions, the work done in psychological clinics, and the curricula proposed for training are not greatly different from those given 20 or more years ago by Witmer and Wallin. Overenthusiastic dependence upon mental tests has diverted clinical work away from its broader aspects and has put the psychologist in the difficult position of being considered a mental tester by his nonpsychological, professional colleagues. If clinical psychology is to take its rightful place in the family of arts dealing with individuals' problems, its present adherents must achieve a broader concept of its nature, and the training of the student must compass much beyond the academic psychology of the present graduate schools.

In conclusion, we may enumerate certain specific points that have been frequently evident in our detailed discussion.

1. The interest of the clinical psychologist is in the individual considered as a physical, social, and psychological being in the matrix of his environment.

2. The individuals in whom the psychologist is usually interested are those exhibiting mild or severe deviations in behavior. However, there is a growing interest in the guidance of the nondeviating individual to the end of more successful adjustments—academic, vocational, marital, personal, or what not.

3. Historically, and at the present day, the interest is emphatically directed toward children. Nevertheless, there is an increasing number of clinical psychologists directing their professional attention toward the problems of adults.

4. The method of the clinical psychologist is primarily that of

an extensive, systematic case study. The emphasis on psychometrics has done harm, but appears to be waning.

5. The aim of clinical psychology goes beyond diagnosis to the planning and carrying out of a program designed to help the individual readjust or make a more satisfactory adjustment.

6. Present training facilities for clinical psychology are inadequate. There is too great an emphasis on academic psychology and too little opportunity for work in the medical, social, or educational fields. Also, the problems of intensive clinical experience have hardly been considered by the training centers.

7. In its relations with medicine, social work, and education, clinical psychology has suffered from academic psychology's aloofness from practical problems. Perhaps the most necessary activity of clinical psychology—and each individual clinical psychologist—is to demonstrate to the bordering professional disciplines and to the lay public that this field has a useful contribution far more valuable than psychometrics alone.

Perhaps in a final paragraph I may digress from the attempt to summarize others' ideas concerning clinical psychology and make my own suggestion concerning the future of this field of endeavor. Three premises may be stated as a starting point: (1) the interest is in the behavioral adjustment of an individual; (2) understanding of the individual requires knowledges of physical, educational, social, and psychological factors; (3) both diagnosis and treatment require the services of variously trained professional workers. If these 3 premises are critically considered, it is quite evident that the rôle of leader in the problems of behavior adjustment cannot be assumed by the psychologist, the psychiatrist, the sociologist, the social worker, the physician, or the educator, judged solely on the basis of their training. In the best operated clinics today the contributions of each profession are mutually discussed, and a treatment program coöperatively planned. Actually, such a coöperative ideal exists in very few places, and usually some one individual (most frequently a psychiatrist or a psychologist) integrates the various findings. Such an integrator or synthesizer is probably more efficient than a discussing group. It appears to me that for real professional dealing with problems of behavior the future must produce a new specialist. This behavior specialist will be the product of an entirely new curriculum which will include pertinent materials from psychology, medicine, education, sociology, and social work. It may even be necessary to establish a new degree as a symbol of the curriculum. This new professional man will not be expected to do all of the diagnostic and treatment work with behavior problems himself. His function will be to serve as coördinator—integrating the diagnostic findings of the physician, psychologist, social worker, or teacher on the one hand, and on the other using his integrated diagnosis to plan a treatment program in which he will be able to indicate the part to be played by the teacher, the social worker, the psychotherapist, the recreation worker, or others who may be necessary to bring the program into being.

ROBERT I. WATSON

Washington University School of Medicine

The Professional Status of the Clinical Psychologist[1]

Since 1939, when the review of the nature of clinical psychology by Louttit appeared, tremendous developments have taken place in the professional practice of psychology. It was already proceeding at a rapid pace at the outbreak of World War II, and the war served to increase the tempo and to introduce certain unanticipated changes. Most of the developments of those busy years from 1939 to 1945 can be understood as extensions of the trends emphasized in Louttit's review, since the conclusions reached have been borne out by present events. As Louttit points out, there was already a firmly established pattern of interest and activity in regard to the individual deviate using the case study method in its entirety rather than merely the psychometric approach. Although emphasis at that time was upon children as the subjects of attention and upon diagnosis as the task, Louttit considered the trend of the future to include more work both with adults and with treatment. Then, as now, the questions of training and *rapprochement* with academic psychology loomed large. It is to an examination of these developments and changes that attention will now be directed.

The American Psychological Association

The American Psychological Association, the major national professional organization of psychologists, was reconstituted in 1945. It was not a merger, as is sometimes mistakenly stated. Rather, it

[1] Prepared especially for this volume.

adopted the name of the American Psychological Association while accepting what was the essential organizational feature of the structure of the American Association for Applied Psychology. A quotation from Dael Wolfle (148),[2] the Executive Secretary, seems especially pertinent.

The purpose of the reorganization was twofold. One reason for the change was to give greater recognition to the individual interests, both scientific and professional, of specialized subgroups within the total membership. Several years ago a feeling that the APA did not give adequate attention to divergent interests led to the formation of the American Association for Applied Psychology and the Society for the Psychological Study of Social Issues. The broadened objectives of the APA and a structure which encourages special interests have brought both of these organizations into the APA.

The second reason for reorganization was a widespread belief that the association should pay greater attention to the professional problems of its members. The constitution formerly stated that the object of the APA was the advancement of psychology as a science. The corresponding statement in the new constitution reads: "The object of the American Psychological Association shall be to advance psychology as a science, as a profession, and as a means of promoting human welfare." This change is not an idle rewording of the preamble to the constitution; it reflects a real change in the purposes of the association (p. 3).

Thus the psychologist now has a stronger organization to further scientific and professional aims and a better instrument for facing collective problems. With a membership in recent years of over 5000, it speaks for the great majority of psychologists and is a truly national organization embracing all the manifold interests of the psychologist, academic and applied. Specific implementation by establishment of a permanent central office, the continuing of an office for dealing with personnel problems, a journal dealing with professional issues, and sponsorship of a certifying professional body are some of its present means of meeting these issues.

Psychologists in the Armed Services and Their Effect upon Psychology in the Post-War Period

About 1500 psychologists served in the Armed Services during World War II.[3] About one out of four psychologists thus were

---

[2] Bibliography begins on page 88.

[3] Only a few years ago there appeared in the professional journals many articles, perhaps 100 in all, primarily devoted to a description of the work of the

called upon to function in an applied field—that is, psychology applied to a very practical problem, war. Moreover, this group was predominantly young, averaging about 32 years of age (20). It thus included many individuals just reaching their professional maturity. It is not unduly optimistic to suppose that some of their experiences during these tours of duty carried over in attitude and practice in the post-war years.

To appreciate properly certain changes of attitude, it must be remembered that a considerable number of psychologists in uniform were products of an academic tradition whose isolationist tendencies in regard to professional application prior to the war they were quite willingly and even complacently furthering.

As a result of the process of learning to apply their psychological training to the military situation, later consideration revealed at least two major trends that have had, and will continue to have, a profound effect upon contemporary psychology. They discovered to their mild surprise and to the considerable amazement of their colleagues from other disciplines that their general training in psychological methods was capable of application to many problems which at first seemed utterly alien to their background. From aircraft instrument panel design to selecting underwater demolition teams, psychologists found that they, in collaboration with specialists from other fields, had something valuable to contribute. Realization was forced upon them that an experimental background in psychology is capable of transfer to intelligent and capable handling of many sorts of problems.

Paradoxically, however, they gained added respect for the clinical approach. In this connection it must be realized that almost half of the psychologists used clinical and counseling procedures during some part of their period in uniform (20). Many psychologists were placed willy-nilly in a position where they functioned in selection and assignment, sat as members of discharge boards, worked as members of clinical teams, conducted therapeutic sessions, both group and individual, and in these and many other ways used diagnostic and treatment methods. Concrete expression of this interest

psychologist in the Armed Services. Fascinating as these articles were to the contemporary reader, today almost all of the programs as they describe them have passed into limbo. Consequently, no attempt, either here or later, will be made to describe this voluminous literature.

can be found in an article by Britt and Morgan (20) concerning the results obtained from a questionnaire mailed to every psychologist in uniform. They conclude that there was an overwhelming interest in having post-war graduate training more practical in nature. Nearly 24 per cent of the suggestions for new courses for graduate study were clearly within the general clinical field. Only a little more than 2 per cent of the suggestions were for courses in psychometrics as such. None suggested the elimination of clinical courses from the graduate curriculum. At least some psychologists in the Services previously not particularly receptive came to understand and appreciate the contributions, past and potential, of the clinical method.

The Clinical Psychologist in the Post-War World

In 1944 Marquis (79), writing from the Office of Psychological Personnel, estimated that following the termination of World War II one-half of the psychologists would change employment. This prophecy has been more than fulfilled in the post-war years, although no exact figures are obtainable. There is a shortage in all fields, academic and applied alike, but it is intensified by a steady draining away from the strictly academic to the quasi-applied or applied fields. This shortage is counterbalanced to some degree by the tendency of more and more individuals to enter employment that embraces both teaching and application; many men and women now teach perhaps most of their time and spend the remainder in clinical or other forms of applied activity. The reverse emphasis exists: the number of mature clinical personnel without academic connections are without them almost accidentally, geographically or otherwise.

In any attempt to discuss the number of psychologists using the clinical method, the published reports of employment and employment prospects are difficult to interpret. The results of these studies are stated in terms of place of employment, e.g., colleges, schools, clinics, business, and government. Such an institutional approach, in so far as the present purpose is concerned, would not be helpful since obviously the clinical method is used outside "clinical" organizations.

Some information, however, may be gleaned from Hilgard's report (63) on psychologists' preferences, without regard to eligibility, for divisions under the reconstituted APA despite the fact that since his report several reorganizations in divisional structure have taken place. Of 6000 ballots mailed, 3680 usable ballots were returned. Of these, 53 per cent selected the clinical division either as a primary choice or as a choice among several other preferences. Nearly the same percentage, of course with considerable overlap, checked personnel psychology as a primary or secondary choice, while consulting psychology was a choice of 38 per cent. It is not implied that all individuals in these three interest groups use the clinical method either extensively or at all. Moreover, expression of interest does not guarantee use, but neither does failure to express interest demonstrate the contrary. Many using this method (for example, some school and industrial psychologists and even some working in the guidance field) would not feel it necessary to demonstrate their interest by affiliation. This may again be due in part to the confusion of subject matter, area of employment, or type of subject with what is essentially a method. Many, of course, would not call themselves clinical psychologists, either because of such confusion or because until recently it was not always politic to be so labeled, since in the not too distant past the term "clinical psychologist" in some circles approached the level of an epithet. It is certainly not going beyond the facts to conclude that over half of all psychologists replying to the questionnaire make use professionally of this approach to psychological phenomena. It would appear that at least 3000 psychologists are to some degree clinical practitioners, if we accept as the most probable approximation of the total of all psychologists the 6000 persons to whom ballots were mailed, and if we make the further assumption that those failing to return the questionnaire would have checked clinical psychology at least proportionately as often.

When the estimates by psychiatrists of just the number of those clinical psychologists eventually necessary to work in collaboration with them range from 10,000 to 20,000, it is evident that the number available is much less than that required to meet even today's more modest demands. According to Darley and Wolfle (38), the Veterans Administration programs alone will need 4700 clinical psychologists and vocational advisors. Many other articles stress the enormous number of personnel demands that are and will be made for clinical psychologists. Estimates of trends in specific institutions and positions are given in Shartle's comprehensive analysis of occupations in psychology (113).

These numbers are both exhilarating and disquieting—exhilarating because they represent a public recognition of need for psychological services, and disquieting because these demands are by no means certain of fulfillment without a lowering of standards or dilution of clinical personnel by individuals from other fields. Many of the positions are now open and will be filled regardless of competence or training.

Dazzling figures such as these should not blind us to a warning sounded by a leader in the clinical field, Edgar A. Doll (42). In discussing the divisional structure of the American Psychological Association, he warns that there may be confusion of "numerical size of a division with its academic, scientific, or professional significance. It is to be anticipated that the basic needs of psychology as a science may attract relatively few individuals compared to the useful exploitation of the instruction received in psychology as a discipline. A few theoretical psychologists may well influence the future of psychology more than hundreds of field workers. And experimental research may well continue to be pursued more vigorously in a few laboratories than in many institutes" (p. 344).

The Psychologist and the Psychiatrist

One of the present trends of interest in and application of the clinical method involves an increasing awareness of the importance of the relation of the psychologist to the psychiatrist. The relation between the two disciplines to be discussed is complicated by the dual way in which psychology is related to psychiatry. First, psychology is one of the sciences basic to psychiatry in the same way as biology, chemistry, and physics. As Menninger points out, ". . . the human being must be regarded as a physio-chemo-psychological unit capable of being studied, observed, interpreted, and treated from a physical standpoint, from a chemical standpoint and from a psychological standpoint, conjointly" (86, p. 89). Second, psychologists in dealing with their problems have developed certain techniques broadly subsumed under the clinical method, the value of which has become apparent to the psychiatrist. Psychology in the sense of a science of medical psychology may legitimately be considered outside the scope of the present discussion; in the second sense, the psychologist and the psychiatrist as clinicians will be the focus of attention.

Two trends of interest and application in present psychiatric practice must be sketched before discussion of the interpersonal relationship of practitioners in the two fields. From an earlier position of relative isolation the psychiatrist has made a closer *rapprochement* with other medical specialists, much psychiatric teaching and practice now finding its place in what is variously called psychosomatic, conjoint, or integrative medicine. In this development medical psychology has played no small part, although the contribution of the psychologist, as such, has been surprisingly small. The psychiatrist has also become increasingly concerned with individuals showing only relatively minor deviations from the normal rather than those showing grosser mental disturbances. Ministering to the needs of the total personality, he works with behavior problems of the child, the inefficiencies of the industrial worker, and the reactive problems of the college student. In these and other similar areas the psychologist has a legitimate interest. If an analogy including both trends may be permitted, the citizens of the psychiatric domain, achieving dominion status after a period as a less desirable protectorate, have now seen fit to establish reciprocal trade treaties with the homeland and have also expanded their frontiers to include territory the sovereignty of which other interested parties, including the psychologist, tend to dispute. It will be noted that the discussion is placed on a basis of interpersonal relationships. Dissension and strife, agreement and mutual respect do not take place between sciences; they take place between persons.[4]

The psychiatrists who are often most vocal about the lack of competence and what they consider to be the overweening pretensions of the psychologist are those who have had either no direct experience with the psychologist or experience only with those functioning at a psychometric level and perhaps representing that still rather sizable proportion of individuals in the profession not suited for anything but a subordinate technician's role. Some of the physician's condemnation of the psychologist is justified because of the psychologist's failure adequately to control the quality of

---

[4] R. A. Clark (32) offers some very practical advice on how the psychologist and psychiatrist might get along with one another.

personnel and techniques offered in the clinical field. A psychiatrist
with approximately eight years of graduate training and internship
is justified in objecting to the admission to professional equality of
someone whose training consists of several courses in undergraduate
psychology (67). A psychologist likewise objects to those physicians
who, since they are in a position of administrative authority, presume to dictate in regard to matters falling within the province of
the psychologist.

Occasionally a psychologist in his working relationships with
physicians, including psychiatric specialists, is unpleasantly impressed with what he considers to be a calm assumption of authority
on the part of the medical practitioner. This, however, when confined to medical matters, is an entirely proper procedure based both
on legal sanction for the practice of medicine and on the best
interests of the patient. Medical authority rests with the physician,
and workers in ancillary fields, including the psychological, must
adapt themselves to this situation when dealing with medical
matters.

The crux of the matter, of course, is the delimitation of what is
properly the medical man's sphere and what is properly the psychologist's, and what is the inevitable area of overlap. At this date
such delimitation cannot be set for the professions in general despite
the fact that in specific organizations, such as the clinics of the
Veterans Administration, considerable degree of concurrence seems
to have been reached. Further attention will be given to this issue
in the discussion of the psychologist and treatment.

The formation of the Committee on Clinical Psychology of the
American Psychological Association and a corresponding committee
of the American Psychiatric Association, both charged with the purpose of seeking a clarification of professional relationships, indicates
that both bodies officially recognize this matter as one needing a
mutually agreeable solution. A report of the Committee on Clinical
Psychology (80) officially accepted by the psychological society
marks an important step in regard to professional relationships.
Laurance Shaffer, chairman of the committee, discusses the various
points of agreement in his article in these *Readings*. Since the
problem of proper delimitation of spheres of interest and activity
connected with treatment occupies such a prominent place in these
discussions, attention will now be directed to this issue.

The Psychologist and Treatment

Those who question the right of the psychologist to engage in treatment or even to be conversant with such matters are, strictly speaking, starting from a false premise. Sargent (108) puts the matter succinctly.

Not only psychologists but deans, teachers, ministers, priests, and others are constantly confronted with problems which, from the practical stand-point, cannot always be referred for psychiatric treatment, even if we were to take the extreme view that this would be ideal procedure in every case, mild or severe. For this reason, the basic principles of therapy should be widely understood and applied. It must be generally recognized that diagnosis, consultation, and therapy cannot be regarded as separate and distinct functions, since the short, apparently superficial contact, as well as more thorough-going participation in an individual's problem, can be therapeutic or otherwise, according to their handling. Even if the psychologist were willing, or preferred, to act as a mere diagnostic technician, it would be essential for him to know both the dangers and the possibilities inherent in his contacts with clients. Furthermore, research in interpersonal relationship falls directly within the scope and training of the clinical psychologist (p. 47).

It would appear, then, that much therapeutic work is done by the psychologist, and rightly so, in many situations which by general agreement are of a non-medical nature. By training and position the psychologist is occupied in many varieties of treatment.

Occasionally, for purely tactical reasons created by the setting in which the work takes place and often as a face-saving gesture, a specious distinction is made between psychotherapy and counseling. For example, in the college guidance bureau the latter term is more acceptable, and in other situations some may find comfort in the fact that psychologists only do "counseling."

The elements common to "counseling" and "psychotherapy" make attempts at fundamental distinction unprofitable or even impossible, if one rejects that superficial and circular differentiation on the basis that the spheres of psychologist and psychiatrist are respectively counseling and psychotherapy. Even the briefest consideration of the common elements exhibited will demonstrate the point. Both involve a face-to-face relationship in which attempts to stimulate growth, understanding, and ability to cope with personal problems of adjustment are consciously carried out. All forms of such personal treatment merge into one another in such a fashion as to form a continuum or scale (116).

Of the several possible approaches to the nature of this scale, presumably one would be to regard the end of the continuum concerned with problems and techniques of treatment as the primary concern of the psychologist, and the other the concern of the medical practitioner, with an inevitable area of overlap which could be referred to as the medico-psychological or psycho-medical area. It is to this controversial area in which both psychiatrist and psychologist have some legitimate claim to an interest that attention will be directed.

Some few practitioners would insist that therapy in this medico-psychological area be conducted only by those possessing the M.D. degree. This is a stand which is contradicted by the present state of affairs, since all forms of such therapies, except those which for the sake of brevity may somewhat loosely be described as organic therapies, are practiced by workers whose professional degrees place them in various specialities. That specifically the psychologist works in many diverse variants of therapy is amply demonstrated by the articles appearing in the treatment section of the present *Readings*.

This situation is recognized by most professional workers today. The failure to possess an M.D. degree does not bar the individual from work in treatment in the borderland area. However, it is extremely important to bear in mind that acceptance of this position does not further imply that all forms of treatment are, forthwith, open to anyone who desires to conduct them, for many elements taught in the medical curriculum are still essential to a proper understanding of at least certain processes of treatment.

A solution acceptable to some representatives of all the professional fields concerned is the example set by the typical child guidance clinic approach. The conventional conception of the psychologist's position in treatment is that his training is such as to fit him particularly for working with problems stemming from the school situation. The psychologist is considered the most appropriate staff member both for maintaining contacts with the school and for carrying on the burden of treatment of problems centering around the learning process or school achievement. He is often recognized as the authority on reading difficulties or other subject matter disabilities.

Although one can say that this by no means holds true for all psychologists working in the clinical field, since sometimes familiarity with school problems is as remote as that of, let us say, the typical physicist, nevertheless it is a reasonable and essentially sound position. What is not sound is the unwarranted extension of this interpretation of the special fitness of the psychologist to deal with treatment problems of an educational nature as an argument that this is his only sphere of treatment. That he is often the most appropriate person to deal with a certain type of problem is hardly logical evidence that this is his only sphere of service.

Why has not the psychologist been more occupied with problems of treatment in the borderland area under discussion? First, his training in diagnostic procedure with particular emphasis on tests has created a definite and concrete position for him to occupy. It might be said that his tests have very often stood between him and more directly therapeutic endeavors. Second, and contrary to popular opinion, not all clinical psychologists by any manner of means are interested in active personal participation in treatment. The article by Shakow in these *Readings* dealing with the diversified approaches discernible among psychologists makes this point quite clear. Third, and most important, before appearing on the clinical scene the typical psychologist received no direct intensive training in this field. Consider the past curricula in psychology of the graduate schools and then consider how many of their products are trained for therapy in the medico-psychological field. Some few are now adequately prepared for such work and presumably increasing numbers will be trained in the future.

It would appear that whatever solution is accepted more or less generally, it will depend upon the adequacy of training and experience of the practitioners. It should not cause the surprise it sometimes does that in many instances social workers are entrusted with certain forms of treatment by the supervising psychiatrist. The crux of the matter is that the social worker has been trained for this work. Beginning as she did with environmental manipulation as her principal technique, she has obtained professional training and practice that have overcome the essentially artificial distinction existing between this and other forms of treatment to the benefit of the patient or client and the enhancement of her own professional position.

The situation at the present time permits of no blanket prescription. The position that a psychologist occupies in therapy in a medical institution typifying one of the extreme ends of the continuum previously referred to is dependent upon individual experience, training, acceptance by his colleagues, availability of other specialists, interest in participation, and many other factors. The position that the Veterans Administration has announced in regard to its medical services seems a healthily pragmatic one. Baldly stated, it amounts to this: the psychologist will be permitted to do the therapy he proves himself capable of doing, and no more. If we possess faith in our abilities, it is not too much to be expected to demonstrate it to those legally and popularly vested with authority in this field.

Whatever the solution in the medical or non-medical field, it follows from this discussion that there is no one "psychologist's" therapy. The psychologist plays a greater or lesser role in many therapies.

Daniel Blain, chief of the Neuropsychiatry Division of the Veterans Administration (14), makes an extremely important point when he chooses to remind us that the patient is somehow lost sight of in discussions of this issue. He goes on to indicate that perhaps the object should be stated in terms of what is best for the patient, not of what each of us can, would like to, or may be called upon to do. A certain amount of the heat engendered in discussions of rights and privileges would be dissipated if this were kept clearly in mind and we examined our talents, training, and experience in the light of this criterion. Although perhaps too much to expect, it is possible that if such a test were honestly and conscientiously applied, a certain number of psychologists and physicians would disqualify themselves from participation in some of the activities they now conduct.

The Psychologist and the Social Worker

Another co-worker and colleague that the psychologist meets under many circumstances and in many settings is the social worker, particularly the psychiatric social worker. The typical social worker is a graduate of a two-year course at a professional graduate school which combines class work and field instruction in the basic principles of social work theory and practice. Specific attention is given in the course of training to the development of the skills required in the variety of services afforded by social agencies. Some specialization is permitted in this training, of which psychiatric social work is an illustration. Many recent and some older graduates have received as a part of their training specific instruction designed to acquaint them with the methods and reports of the psychologist and to give some understanding of his position in the agency organization. This orientation to the work of the psychologist is in keeping with a recommendation by the national professional association of social workers that such training be included in the curriculum.

It should be obvious that the activities carried out by the psychiatric social worker would vary according to the agency setting, the degree of specialization within the agency, her personal competence, the attitude taken toward her proper sphere by the administration of the agency, the needs of the particular case, and many other factors. Nevertheless, certain essential tasks are present, the variation being in degree of emphasis. French (50) describes four distinct but interrelated functions in the treatment of the patient's social situation.

First, she analyzes the patient's social situation in relation to his present difficulty; such analysis is based upon a study of conditions in his home, family, and neighborhood, and his attitude toward them, and is utilized, with the psychiatric, physical, and psychological findings, in diagnosis and treatment. Second, she interprets to the family the patient's problem and the recommendations made by the psychiatrist, always keeping in close touch with changing conditions in the home and family life which may cause an adaptation in plans. Third, she aids the patient and family to work out a program for a more adequate social adjustment, working closely with the psychiatrist as treatment progresses. And, last, she interprets the diagnosis and plans for treatment to her coworkers or to members of other social agencies who may also be interested in the client and family (p. 17).

This same source (50) gives a thorough account of the field and function of psychiatric social work. The methods used by the social worker receive considerable attention as does the relationship of the social worker to the psychiatrist. There is curiously little mention of the psychologist. French refers to him as a member of the staff and then ignores his existence. Nevertheless, there is a wealth of material about the function of this partner in the clinic team, although, because of the omission just mentioned, nothing about the relationship of the social worker to the psychologist.

A committee on professional relations with social workers has been maintained by one of the psychological societies for a period of some years. According to the chairman of the committee (35) a certain amount of confusion has arisen among social workers as to what to expect from psychologists because of the great variety in duties on the part of psychologists who work for and with social agencies. Matters of policy, such as whether or not a specific I.Q. should be given to a social worker or agency, is one point on which there are considerable differences in practice. Some psychologists insist upon a certain type of social case history, others desire some social history but in an unspecified form, and still others accept cases without a social history. Another field in which psychological practice is diverse is that of the nature of the reports made to the agency; some psychologists confine themselves to issues lying exclusively within the educational field, whereas others interpret their function as going far beyond this aspect. Some confine themselves exclusively to recommendations; others include so much direct work with the client that some case workers complain that the psychologist has taken over case work responsibility.

Although the psychiatrist and the social worker are the colleagues most commonly met by the clinical psychologist in the course of his daily activities, in certain situations other co-workers may include probation officers, personnel experts, deans of men and women, occupational therapists, neurologists, psychiatric nurses, vocational counselors, speech specialists, adjustment teachers, rehabilitation experts, pediatricians, and reading specialists. Some of these will be primarily trained in psychology; all will have at least some acquaintance with this discipline which supplies both some of the understanding of dynamics and some of the technical tools used in their specialization. The relation, unfortunately, often will not be reciprocal; the psychologist is apt to have an amazing ignorance of and even disdain for many of these fields.

Ethics and the Professional Psychologist

In recent years increasing attention has been given to the ethical connotations of the professional practice of psychology. In 1944 Poffenberger (97) thought the problem sufficiently important to give it considerable attention in his presidential address before a professional society. It is worth while, then, to consider briefly the historical background of the issue, some of the reasons for the present interest, and the recent literature that has appeared concerning the matter. The academic psychologist in classroom and laboratory needed and found acceptable ethical principles based upon the credos of teaching and scientific research, and hardly distinguishable from the principles of ethical behavior considered desirable for scholarly persons in general. Outside academic walls the early clinical practitioner did not lack ethical principles; rather, he possessed a private *ethos* as high as that found in individuals in other professions. But his very obscurity in so far as the general public was concerned, the paucity of his fellow workers, the relatively low level of economic return for his labors, the fact that he was more than likely to be protected in an institutional setting and to be primarily concerned with psychometric activities—all united to keep his interest in verbal expression of the problem at a relatively low ebb. World War II served to accentuate certain trends already operating to change these conditions. Of recent years public and professional recognition of the clinician has been increasing and more individuals are now engaged in non-academic practice, in which salaries are apt to be higher. The clinician, not being as much confined to children or institutional inmates as in the past, is brought into more direct contact with all sorts of people; and, most important of all, his continuing development of techniques beyond the narrowly psychometric have all served to give prominence to ethical aspects of professional practice. Under such conditions the opportunist and the near charlatan within the profession are apt to make their presence felt. Then too, the discovery by the outright charlatan that pseudo-psychology pays has obvious dangers against which such a prominent professional leader as Brotemarkle (24) has warned.[5]

It is significant that many of the titles in the current literature refer to *codes* of ethics. As yet, the psychological profession lacks anything comparable to the code of medical ethics adopted by the American Medical Association (4). This document, incidentally, is

---

[5] In spite of ineptitude and ignorance, it is precisely because of his lack of ethical standards that the financial success of the charlatan is possible. Collectively, if not individually, his financial returns are phenomenal. Steiner's book (114) describing where people take their troubles contains many revealing anecdotes about psychological quacks and their unprincipled behavior.

worthy of careful perusal since some of the problems of clinical psychology have an intrinsic similarity to those of clinical medicine. The American Psychological Association, which has already acted in this field through its committees especially in regard to individual cases, will, it is presumed, eventually foster some code of ethics. A growing realization of the necessity for some form of licensing of psychologists reinforces this demand for codification.

The current literature will be examined briefly for indication of the direction that this codification may take. Although Sutich (118) unwarrantedly infuses a therapeutic approach of a non-directive character within the framework of his preliminary analysis of a professional code, it is, nevertheless, instructive to find that he is concerned with the relationship of the clinician to (1) the client, (2) other interested non-professional parties, and (3) other professional workers, while the client in turn is considered to have a lesser number of reciprocal duties and rights. A detailed but sympathetic critique of his position was made by Sargent (108), who offered certain needed correctives, staying, however, within the general framework of his presentation without attempting to offer a substitute code. Preliminary to the development of Sutich's presentation of a professional code he considered the obligation of the clinician to society. This responsibility, however, was not stated in terms of rights and privileges as were the interpersonal relations mentioned previously. Bixler and Seeman (13) stress this point by paying as much attention to the responsibility of the psychologist to society as they do to his responsibility to the individual or to members of the related professions. These articles may be said to show the trends of interest in ethical problems in so far as current publications reflect these trends. In one sense, however, the presentations of Sutich and Sargent might be considered as offering a misleading view of the matter. Writing, as they are, within a frame of reference of non-directive counseling, the authors describe a position presumably unacceptable to other psychologists. Meehl and McClosky (85) present a penetrating critique of this approach. Quite apart from the merits of either the directivist or the non-directivist position, it is safe to assume that any officially sponsored, certainly any generally accepted, code will have to rise above these or any other ideological positions.

Certification and Licensure

If the clinical psychologist is to reach maximum usefulness and effectiveness, legal professional status is essential. Certification on the basis of formal training and experience hardly needs defense of its desirability or even its necessity. A single illustration will suffice. It is a bit chastening to realize that as late as 1940 Doll (41), writing in the *American Journal of Mental Deficiency* on the needs of psychological personnel in the field covered by that journal, had to plead that a psychologist should have at least a bachelor's degree. The situation is becoming acute because of the rapidly increasing number of psychologists doing therapeutic work with widely varying degrees of competence. Suits for malpractice are not inconceivable; rather, they appear inevitable. It is no cause for surprise, then, to find considerable attention being paid to this problem by psychologists and psychological organizations.[6]

Before dealing with present accomplishments and future plans in the development of certification and licensure, it is appropriate to define broadly what is meant by these terms. Certification permits the use of the term "certified psychologist" only by those specified by the certifying professional body set up either by the state or by the professional organization. It does not restrict the practice of other individuals not so certified; it merely denies them the right to speak of themselves as certified. The situation in accountancy is comparable in that a distinction is made between a Certified Public Accountant and others without restricting the practice of accounting. There may be certification of a professional psychologist as a psychologist in general, or certification as a specialist in some branch of the field. In the medical profession, professional bodies certify the medical specialist. Any licensed physician may specialize in

---

[6] The closely related issues of standards and certification of psychological clinics and of standards for graduate training programs are also being vigorously attacked by committees of the American Psychological Association. It would take us too far afield to discuss the training of the clinical psychologist. However, it might be mentioned in passing that an especially valuable historical summary of internship is given by Morrow (88), while the status of training facilities is given by Sears (109, 110). An official committee report of the nature of training recommended under the chairmanship of Shakow (112) is also a very important document.

psychiatry; the American Board of Psychiatry and Neurology certifies him as a specialist in that field on the basis of examination, length of training, and nature of his experience. Thus is created what in the various medical specialities is referred to as a diplomate—i.e., a specialist certified by issuance of a diploma. In other professions as well, this has been the function of some professional body either state or national. A system of licensure, on the other hand, would deny the person without a license the right to practice psychology. Presumably this would be a state function, since it is difficult to conceive a license system not in some way a matter of statute. Anticipating the later discussion of the nature of current interest and activity, it would appear that certification will precede any serious attempt at licensure.

Although some states have given varying degrees of legal status to psychological practice, the situation in Ohio is unfortunately typical of the majority of states. An analysis of Ohio statutes (49) shows that psychologists are not licensed. One who is a member of a licensed or certified profession is generally and routinely accepted as an expert witness, which means he is allowed to give his opinion, not merely testify to factual evidence. Not so the psychologist in Ohio; to qualify he must prove sufficient education and experience to satisfy the judge. A psychologist cannot claim as privileged any communication given him, whether supposedly in confidence or not. Perhaps most important of all, psychotherapy, otherwise unidentified, is defined as a limited branch of medicine and for its practice requires a medical degree. It is not inconceivable that a psychologist may be brought into the Ohio courts for violation of the Medical Practice Act for carrying out duties accepted at least by the profession itself as falling within its province. Much of what a clinical psychologist does, except mental testing and certain forms of speech therapy, perhaps constitutes a technical violation of the statutes in Ohio.

Although some states have been active in this regard and may well continue to be so, a national organization for specialist certification is in the process of being implemented. This function is vested in the recently established American Board of Examiners in Professional Psychology (80), a corporate body legally independent of the American Psychological Association, its sponsor. This independence, a counterpart of which exists in the medical specialities, is necessitated by the fact that otherwise the Association would be liable in possible damage suits brought against the members of the certifying body. The by-laws of this Board are given in a 1946 issue of the *American Psychologist* (80, pp. 512–517). It proposed certification in the fields of clinical psychology, industrial psychology, and guidance, and calls for the doctoral degree, an examination, and five years of professional experience. The first diplomas have recently been issued.

The situation in certain states now fortunate enough to have certification in one form or another will be briefly examined. In Connecticut (60) a bill went into effect in July, 1945, which restricted the use of the title "certified psychologist" thereafter to those acceptable to a board of examiners appointed by the Governor. It provided further (1) for the registration of educational institutions which maintain acceptable standards of training in accordance with which the applicant for certification may satisfy the educational requirement of a Ph.D. or other training in lieu of that degree, (2) for the suspension or revocation of the certificate, and (3) for penalties for false representation of possession of such a certificate. After a year of operation, Miles (87), who served as Chairman of the Board previously referred to, expressed the opinion that favorable and useful results had accrued from its operation. Experience in New York with the problem of certification of clinical psychologists within the framework of a state professional association is described by Long (73) and Wulfeck (150). Peatman (92) has described how this same organization is working on the problem of legal certification of psychologists in general by the state legislature, the Connecticut State Law being used as a guide in their proposed formulation. As yet the bill rests in committee, but apparently the situation is hopeful. Both organizational and state certification are considered necessary, the former to certify specialists, the latter to certify psychologists as such. In Virginia, on the other hand, the state certification system is designed to operate for the clinical psychologist only, not for professional psychologists in general (104, 105).

Both self-certification by a professional group and legal certification by state action have their proponents and opponents. Representative discussions on this issue are those by Fryer (52), Britt (19), and Landis (71) in a 1941 issue of the *Journal of Consulting*

Psychology devoted to the topic of certification. In 1939, Britt (18) published a model "Certified Psychologists Act" which has excited considerable interest.

State certification of school psychologists is a somewhat different problem from that of other forms of certification. In many ways it is similar in intent to civil service requirements, for it sets up standards only in so far as work in a given city or state school system is concerned. According to a study by Horrocks (66), only seven states make provision for the certification of school psychologists. In view of its setting, it is not surprising that the requirements made of the psychologist are stated in a fashion drawn from prior experience with the certification of teachers. Course requirements are likely to be specific and detailed, although not necessarily complete or more than superficial. Most psychologists, no matter what their experience in other fields, would not qualify unless they had served in a school situation, since education courses loom large. The manner in which the Connecticut procedures for the licensing of school psychologists was developed is described by Cutts (37). In an article by Cornell (33) the New York certification system is examined.

FREDERICK C. THORNE

University of Vermont

The Clinical Method in Science[1]

Historical

Clinical psychology is entering a period of tremendous development at a time when the profession of medicine as dated from Hippocrates is over 2300 years old, the specialty of modern psychiatry as dated from Pinel is over 175 years old, and modern psychopathology as dated from the work of Freud is almost 50 years old. The significance of these facts is that clinical psychology has a rich medicopsychological heritage with which one must be familiar in order to gain historical orientation to current problems. Paradoxically, the history of medical psychology has not received the consideration it deserves in standard histories of modern psychology such as Boring (15)[2] or Murphy (89). A *History of Medical Psychology* by Zilboorg (151) is a necessary supplement to these.

In contrast with clinical psychiatry and psychoanalysis which are direct descendants of medical psychology dating back from the ancients, clinical psychology in America has its roots in experimentally-oriented academic psychology which is more closely related to philosophy, physics, and mathematics than to medicine. Lacking the orientation of the clinical method as evolved in medical science, many clinical psychologists have approached their problems from the viewpoint of laboratory science and have shown a lack of understanding of the basic prinicples of clinical methods as developed in medical psychology. The result has been a schism between many

---

[1] Reprinted from *American Psychologist*, 1947, 2, 159–166. Copyright 1947 by American Psychological Association.

[2] Bibliography begins on page 88.

clinical psychologists and medically trained physicians because of mutual failure to understand differing viewpoints. It is not desirable for psychologists to retrace the steps of generations of physicians and psychiatrists in discovering the principles of clinical science, or for physicians and psychiatrists to retrace the steps taken by modern psychology in applying the experimental method to the study of personality. In order to avoid a further waste of time and energy in rediscovering what is common knowledge to the older clinical professions, the study of the evolution of clinical science in general and medical psychology in particular should be a basic requirement in the training of all professional students in the psychological sciences.

Clinical Science

The Nature of Clinical Science.   Modern medicine is both a clinical science and a technology. The historical development of modern medicine has been characterized by increasing emphasis on the basic sciences of anatomy (gross, microscopic, and comparative), biochemistry, physiology (normal and pathological), and pathology (gross and microscopic). Both medical education and clinical practice are currently oriented about a thorough foundation in basic science which operates to introduce the experimental viewpoint wherever applicable. Although medical science has not utilized experimental and statistical techniques to the same degree as psychology, recent trends indicate that knowledge of these methods is rapidly becoming widely disseminated in medical science. In most modern medical teaching centers, there is as rigid adherence to experimental methods as may be found in psychology.

Similar comments are applicable to the clinical handling of individual cases. Formerly, clinical technology was mainly empirical, i.e. based on study and "experience" rather than experiment. To a certain degree, therapy must always be empirical since the primary consideration is the welfare of the patient rather than the conduct of a scientific experiment. Perhaps the most significant development, however, is the increasing application of the experimental approach to the individual case and to the clinician's own "experience." Ideally, diagnosis (description) and treatment of each individual case may be regarded as a single and well controlled experiment. The treatment may be carefully controlled by utilizing single therapeutic factors, observing and recording results systematically, and checking through use of appropriate quantitative laboratory studies.[3] In addition to the general scientific orientation to the individual case, there are frequent opportunities in clinical practice to conduct actual experiments to determine the validity of diagnosis or the efficacy of treatment. For example, a simple experiment may be set up in which a placebo and a specific drug may be administered according to a definite pattern such as ABBA with careful recording and mathematical analysis of results. In the most advanced medical center practice, experimental methods have largely replaced the intuitive methods formerly so commonplace. Individual clinicians are encouraged to apply experimental and statistical methods in the analysis of case results, and larger scale analyses are made of the experience of the whole clinic over a period of years. Thus, the clinician comes to regard each individual case as part of a larger sample.

Methods of Clinical Science. Although the primary emphasis is on the individual case, the basic methods of clinical science involve the same techniques of description, classification, and explanation as are standard in experimental laboratory science. The fact that description and classification in clinical science have the additional objectives of diagnosis and rational therapy does not detract from their essential validity and reliability, since all stages in the process may be objectively quantified by the same methods of analysis as are applicable to any other type of data. These points need to be clearly recognized as offering a rebuttal against the oft-repeated statement that clinical practice involves an art or a technology rather than a science. The increasing availability of scientifically validated tools and of clinicians whose judgments may be demonstrated to have high validity and statistical reliability is rapidly minimizing the necessity for the clinician to be an artist rather than a scientist. Both in medical practice and clinical psychology, "intuition" has long since been displaced by objective methods which may be taught and utilized by all who have adequate training in these fields.

Description in Clinical Science. Clinical medicine has slowly evolved a system for eliciting and describing the physical character-

---

[3] An example of the experimental therapeutic approach in modern medicine may be seen in the abandonment of older empirical "shot-gun" methods in which several drugs were included in one prescription in the hope that one would be effective. Current practice involves prescribing specific drugs singly so that the effect may be experimentally determined.

istics of the organism with special reference to pathological deviations. This description is technically known as *physical diagnosis*.
The subject of physical diagnosis represents the accumulated experience of many generations of physicians who have developed an objective system for describing every known sign; it can be taught to
medical students with such exactness that the results of the examinations of competent physicians show a very high reliability. In medical science, when a new sign is discovered, it is immediately investigated by the experimental sciences of physiology and pathology to
verify its aetiology and significance.

Techniques for objective description have been slower to develop
in psychological science because of the extreme complexity of personality. Psychiatry, however, has evolved the concept of *mental
status* which recognizes that personality characteristics are in constant flux so that any description can validly refer only to the moment at which it was made. Methods for objectively determining
mental status are outlined in all standard psychiatric textbooks. The
best examples of case history involve verbatim reports of the subject's actions and words with a minimum of interpretation by the
observer. Clinical psychiatry has developed methods for personality
study in the minutest details as evidenced by case reports of single
individuals totaling hundreds of pages.

Terminology of Clinical Science. The modern era of medicine
has been characterized by exacting attention to matters of terminology. The prescientific era lacked a uniform system of nomenclature and utilized personal names and popular terms to label new
discoveries. During the past two decades, the basic essentials of adequate terminology have been determined and made operative. New
syndromes of disease are described in terms of the basic pathological
processes. A standard nomenclature of disease has been accepted.
The metric system has become standard for describing the physical
attributes of objects. The use of personal names and popular terms
has been discontinued. The effect of these innovations has been to
standardize medical science throughout the world.

Validity and Reliability of Clinical Data. The basic validity and
reliability of the data collected in clinical science are determined by
the cumulative efforts of succeeding generations of observers trained
in the most advanced methods of their times. For thousands of years,
data have gradually accumulated and been transmitted through for-

mal education. The process was painfully slow until the modern era of scientific medicine. Within the last century, all data gathered in the prescientific era have been carefully rechecked with experimental methods to determine their validity, and an objective body of fact gathered which will probably stand the test of time.

In the United States alone there are over 150,000 registered physicians; the majority are graduates of grade A schools where they were exposed to objective methods of thinking and working. With such a large number of practitioners, every new discovery now receives an intensive clinical trial which quickly proves or disproves its validity. The psychologist will be interested in knowing that this mass clinical trial frequently results in disproving conclusions drawn from the most intensive preliminary experiments possible in the laboratory. In effect, the results accumulated by the entire profession constitute an experiment on a grand scale not possible in the laboratory. An interesting example of this general principle may be taken in the standardization of a new drug. Federal laws require extensive animal experiments to determine basic properties and toxicity. The drug is then released for preliminary human experiments. If the drug is safe and efficacious, it is finally released for general clinical use. In many instances, complete information has been obtained only after several years of clinical trials on a mass basis.

Prediction in Clinical Science. Extensive training under carefully controlled conditions provides the physician with a wide knowledge of clinical syndromes, the range of variation within a syndrome, and its typical clinical course. It is this ability to predict the clinical course of a single case, on the basis of data from an adequate sample of similar cases, which makes possible valid prognosis. Apart from its predictive values in understanding any particular case, accurate prognosis serves as a check on the validity of the rationale of the therapy. Given a wide experience concerning the range of manifestations of a disease, it is possible to predict eventual outcomes with genuine validity. Such accurate prognosis permits the anticipation of problems before they have developed and makes case handling more efficacious. It is in this respect, perhaps more than any other, that the older clinician is perceptibly more skillful than the younger, other factors being equal. In spite of the imposing complexity of theoretical knowledge as evidenced by impressive textbooks and medical center education, there is no substitute for experience in the translation of knowledge into practical case handling. With all the laboratory procedures available in the medical center, it is a significant fact that the experienced country practitioner utilizes the older methods of direct examination and prognosis to produce results in case handling which compare favorably with the best medical center practice.

Diagnosis in Clinical Science

In the following presentation, *diagnosis* refers to the description of the organism and its behavior by a variety of methods whose basic purpose is to discover the personality dynamics of each individual case. It is implied that the more complete the description, the more complete will be our understanding of why, when, where, and how the individual got that way. Once this information has been obtained it may be utilized for a variety of purposes outlined below.

Objectives of Diagnosis. Historically, the objective of diagnosis was principally to identify a disease. In modern medicine and psychiatry, however, diagnosis involves more than mastering the nomenclature of diseases and attempting to recognize a known syndrome of pathological phenomena. Psychodiagnostics has evolved beyond problems of classifications of "diseases" to the more mature objective of completely describing each individual case in order to demonstrate the aetiological factors whose dynamic interplay has produced the unique configuration of personality traits which is a person. Among the more important objectives of diagnosis are:

1. To demonstrate the aetiological factors.
2. To differentiate between organic and functional disorders.
3. To discover the personality reaction of the organism to its disability.
4. To discover the extent of organic damage with resulting functional disability.
5. To estimate the extensity or intensity of the morbid process in relation to actuarial data concerning type and severity.
6. To determine the prognosis or probable course.
7. To provide a rational basis for specific psychotherapy.
8. To provide a rational basis for discussing the case with the patient and relatives.
9. To provide a scientific basis for classification and statistical analysis of data.

Accurate diagnosis orients the clinician to many relevant facts relating to the pattern of disorder in general and to the particulars of the individual case which may determine the success or failure of the whole process of case handling. Brill (17) emphasizes that an inability to arrive at reliable diagnoses may threaten a psychiatrist's whole practice, particularly in cases where it is necessary to organize the resources of the whole environment to produce desired results. The beginner is primarily concerned with diagnosis as a method for identifying clinical syndromes. Identification is an important but preliminary step; the experienced clinician utilizes diagnosis as the foundation for all rational case handling.[4]

Principles of Diagnosis. Accumulated experience with problems of diagnosis has resulted in the acceptance of the following basic laws:

1. *The law of parsimony.* Lloyd Morgan's canon states that the simplest explanation involving the fewest possible causal factors is usually the most probable; an attempt should be made to explain all symptoms by one rather than multiple aetiological agents.

2. *Evaluation of the whole organism.* Disorders of parts or part-functions should be related to the whole organism. The psychobiological principles of Adolf Meyer represent an attempt to classify disorders as different patterns of reactions of the total organism as it meets the environment.

3. *Principle of differential diagnosis.* With complex diagnostic problems, it is necessary (a) to recognize the probability that a diagnostic problem exists, (b) to list the known syndromes which must be considered, (c) to weigh and evaluate the observed facts in the light of diagnostic possibilities and to reason from them to logical conclusions, and finally (d) to accept a diagnosis which explains all signs and symptoms.

4. *Laws of probability.* In the absence of pathognomonic evidence concerning the nature of a morbid process, mathematical prob-

---

[4] Compare with the viewpoint of nondirective counseling as expressed by Rogers (102). As emphasized by Super (117), nondirective methods are based on the diagnosis that all maladjustments are caused by emotional conflicts, which postulate in itself is questionable. Such a unidimensional cause for maladjustment is not only inconsistent with accumulated experience but leads to the therapeutic fallacy of treating every morbid process with a single panacea.

abilities favor those conditions for which there is actuarial evidence of higher incidence. Do not play the long shots.

5. *Evaluation of evidence.* The consensus of medical opinion is that the use of the senses is the most important factor in diagnosis, i.e. that there is no substitute for the careful and minute observation of the living patient. Where clinical findings from observation disagree with laboratory findings, the former have frequently proven to be more valid since human errors exist in laboratory work too. Where an apparent conflict exists between subjective reports of the patient and objective signs, the latter have greater weight.

6. *Cooperative studies.* The major contribution of modern medical center practice is the co-operation of specialists operating as a team in clarifying obscure diagnostic problems.

7. *Pathognomonic signs or symptoms.* Clinical data should be analysed to discover those pathognomonic signs which are of specific localizing value.

8. *Koch's postulates.* Although derived from bacteriology and not directly applicable to psychology, these laws state that in order to establish any agent as the definite aetiological cause of a morbid process, it is necessary to demonstrate that (a) the specific factor must always be associated with the disease; (b) when isolated in pure culture, and inoculated into a healthy susceptible animal, it must always produce the disease, and (c) it should be obtained again in pure culture. Some such criteria are needed in psychological science to establish definite standards for evaluating psychogenic factors.

Diagnosis must be a continuing process which can never be complete since the constantly evolving pattern of an individual life is not finished until death. The experienced clinician recognizes that the exploration of all the areas of personality is a lengthy process in which it is not unusual to carry a case for years before evidence vital to a valid diagnosis is discovered. In personality study, diagnosis concerns the description of a continuing process rather than the identification of a disease.

Different Diagnostic Approaches. Although complete description would ideally explain the dynamic personality configurations of each individual case, the practical situation frequently demands that the clinician construct a diagnostic summary of the dynamic factors operant in an individual case. Whether the objective is to identify a disease as in medicine or to describe the morbid characteristics of an organism-meeting-its-environment, it is necessary to make a valid analysis of clinical data and the following methods have classically been used:

1. *Inductive methods.* These involve reasoning from the particular to the general. Given a collection of signs, symptoms, and other data, an attempt is made to differentiate a more general pathological process capable of explaining all the clinical findings. This process may involve the following steps:
   a. Collecting all available evidence descriptive of the morbid process.
   b. Searching for pathognomonic signs.
   c. Postulating a pathological process to explain clinical data.
   d. Identifying the postulated pathological process with a known disease.

2. *Deductive methods.* These involve reasoning from the general to the particular, i.e. from premises or theories to concrete examples. Given a knowledge of pathology, an attempt is made to correlate clinical findings with standard patterns of disease according to the following steps:
   a. Listing all known syndromes even remotely related to clinical findings.
   b. Determining individually whether the data are congruent with a known syndrome.
   c. Various outlines may be utilized where obscure clinical findings cannot be immediately classified, i.e.
      i. In terms of aetiological factors such as heredity, infection, trauma, neoplasm, etc.
      ii. In terms of known disease entities, i.e. psychasthenia, etc. (This approach has been abandoned in the psychological sciences.)
      iii. In terms of dynamic personality processes, i.e. aggression, rejection, over-regulation, over-protection, etc.

3. *Diagnosis by exclusion.* Negative diagnosis by the careful exclusion of other diseases is notoriously invalid and generally unacceptable in modern clinical practice.

4. *Failure to diagnose.* Modern practice has discarded the older tendency to label a disorder as "idiopathic" when its cause was

unknown. Other "waste-basket" diagnoses such as "hysteria," are also no longer acceptable. The term "undifferentiated" is used in the absence of a definite positive diagnosis.

It is not the specific purpose of this paper to discuss in detail the various diagnostic methods which are currently available to implement the general approaches outlined above.

Role of Pathology. Psychologists in general have not shown understanding of the role of the basic science of pathology in modern medicine. Pathology is concerned with the aetiology and morbid processes characteristic of each syndrome of disease or disorder. The emphasis in gross or microscopic anatomic pathology concerns the morphology of disease; in pathological physiology, the primary concern is with the pathological functioning in disease; and in psychopathology, the emphasis is on a disorder in the total configuration of the individual meeting the environment. Pathology, whether morphological, physiological, or psychological, has reached its present important position in medical science because of the recognition that rational therapy depends upon valid diagnosis which depends upon an exact knowledge of the aetiology and dynamic nature of morbid processes. In medicine, pathology is (a) recognized as the basic course in preclinical basic science, (b) required for certification by the specialty boards, and (c) required in medical facilities for approved ratings.

The evolution of psychopathology as a formal subject has occurred more slowly. The methods of gross and cellular pathology are not directly applicable to psychological problems. Two important historical trends are demonstrable. *Abnormal psychology* contributed experimental studies of sensation, perception, memory, learning, thought, affective life and other more complex phenomena such as hypnosis. *Psychiatry* inherited the medico-psychological tradition which included major contributions from Virchow, Kraepelin, and Freud. Failure of these two historical trends to amalgamate is explained by the academic isolation of academic psychology and clinical psychiatry; an integration is long overdue. Whatever the subject matter comes to be called, it is basic to valid diagnosis and therapy.

A practical outgrowth of the subject of pathology is the *clinical pathological conference* which is a device for correlating and checking clinical findings with the results of gross, microscopic, laboratory, and other findings. In the CPC, the physician first makes a complete presentation of the clinical and laboratory findings in a case and then indicates his differential diagnoses, following which the pathologist presents his findings which prove the actual causes of the disease. In the psychological sciences, the conference might have a slightly different organization in which the clinician would present his analysis of the individual personality including evaluations of intelligence and personality dynamics following which objective evidence from psychometrics, projective testing, electroencephalography, etc., would be presented. The CPC is very effective in evaluating the clinical abilities of individual practitioners and in constantly rechecking the validity of diagnosis and treatment. Not only is the physician stimulated to perfect his diagnostic and therapeutic abilities, but there is a public discussion of his case handling by his colleagues. In contrast with older attitudes in professional ethics which tended to conceal and perpetuate error, the CPC operates to reveal and correct the causes of error and to improve the clinical abilities of all who participate in them.

Clinical Science and Therapy

Many of the observations which have been made in relation to scientific methods of diagnosis are also applicable to therapy but in lesser degree. In matters of diagnosis, scientific methods are almost universally applied within the limits of existing knowledge. In therapy, however, the major objective is to relieve or cure the patient and this sometimes conflicts with the systematic application of scientific methods. The modern era has been characterized by a constant revision of therapeutic methods in conformance with the latest discoveries of basic science. Wherever possible, experimental and statistical methods have been utilized in the evaluation of therapy both in individual cases and with large samples of clinical materials. Masses of data from large samples of a population have provided a validation of therapeutic methods far beyond that yet obtained from experimental laboratories.

Definition of Therapy. Formal therapy should be differentiated from common-sense techniques as applied by laymen. In its broadest connotations, therapy includes all forms of *case handling* derived from a scientific evaluation of the individual case by competent personnel. Rational therapy, whether directive or nondirective, proceeds logically from aetiological studies, clinical examinations, and laboratory studies from which a diagnostic formulation results. Depending upon therapeutic indications, case handling may range from the most superficial contacts as in counseling to the most intensive depth therapy as in psychoanalysis.

Principles of Therapy. Modern medical therapy is based upon a rigid adherence to materialistic concepts of the aetiology of disease. The prescientific dependence upon empiricism and trial-and-error methods has been displaced by a detailed knowledge of pathology, accurate diagnosis, and the rational formulation of a therapeutic plan which is specifically adapted to the individual case. In contrast with older irrational methods in which various combinations of methods were combined, modern practice emphasizes the selection of specific remedies utilized singly according to the latest scientific knowledge. Among the commonly accepted principles of modern therapy are:

1. *Adequate diagnostic study.* Except in emergency or to give symptomatic relief, the basic essential to rational therapy is a valid diagnosis.

2. *Detailed knowledge of limitations of methods.* The clinician should know the exact indications and contra-indications for each therapeutic tool. Choice of methods is determined only after a careful consideration of indications.

3. *Treating basic causes.* Treatment should be directed toward basic aetiologic factors rather than symptoms. Also, the whole organism should be treated rather than part functions.

4. *Plan of therapy.* Alexander (2) and others have stressed the importance of making a definite plan of therapy for each case with specific attention to individual needs.

5. *Specific therapy.* Where possible, methods known to have specific action should be chosen. Where symptomatic, palliative, or systemic therapy is indicated, these also should be prescribed specifically.

6. *Combinations of methods.* Where possible, the use of a single therapeutic agent at one time is indicated. This provides for more controlled variation of the experimental factor and facilitates scientific analysis of data. Where combinations are desirable as in the total push method described by Myerson, these should be prescribed rationally.

7. *Evaluation of results.* In the absence of experimental or statis-

tical proof, therapeutic results are evaluated with extreme caution.

8. *Scientific analysis.* Where possible, the latest scientific methods are to be utilized in the analysis of individual and group data.

9. *No miraculous panaceas.* The history of clinical science reveals that a true panacea has never been discovered in spite of claims made for new drugs and methods. Modern pharmacology has demonstrated that only a few of the thousands of known drugs have any specific effect. In the even more complex area of psychotherapy, it appears improbable that any one method has universal applicability.

10. *Eclecticism in clinical science.* The complexity of the human organism and its disabilities is so great, that methods of therapy must be equally numerous and complex. Adherence to any particular "school" of thought will usually limit the therapist's effectiveness to the situations for which his method is specific. Eclecticism is the keynote of modern science.

Objectives of Therapy. The rigid experimentalist sometimes overlooks the truism that the basic objective of therapy is to improve the patient's condition. There are situations in which the demands of scientific method and the needs of the individual patient are incompatible. Few patients desire to be scientific guinea pigs nor would their relatives condone this even though the patient desired it. Modern practice, therefore, usually represents a compromise between what is scientifically ideal and what is practically desirable. This conflict is not serious or insoluble in most cases since what is best scientifically is also best for the patient. Within the limits of this general orientation, we may consider a number of more limited theoretical objectives as follows:

1. *Prevention.* Even more basic than cure is prevention.

2. *Correction of aetiological factors.* Anatomical, physiological, and psychological factors are specifically treated.

3. *Palliation.* Symptomatic treatment directed toward the relief of subjective symptoms is of vital import to the patient.

4. *Systemic support.* Nonspecific measures are directed toward the improvement of the state of health of the total organism.

5. *Facilitating growth.* Treatment should ideally facilitate rather than interfere with natural developmental processes.

More specifically, psychotherapy seeks to achieve more limited objectives which are specifically corrective of various pathological syndromes which are dynamically related to the problems of the organism meeting the environment.

6. *Reeducation.* Since human behavior is regarded as being largely learned or acquired through experience, therapy seeks to reeducate and teach new modes of adjustment.

7. *Expressing and clarifying emotional attitudes.* From the cathartic method of psychoanalysis to current nondirective methods of counseling, major emphasis has been placed on methods of securing emotional release and expression in a permissive, accepting environment.

8. *Resolving conflict and inconsistencies.* Since conflicts and inconsistent attitudes threaten personality integration, therapy seeks to remove repression and ambivalencies in the mental economy.

9. *Catalysing maturation.* Recognizing that many morbid processes involve immaturity and regressive reactions, therapy seeks to catalyse maturation to the most complete state of development of which the individual organism is capable.

10. *Self-understanding.* All psychotherapy has the objective of stimulating the client to understand and accept himself, to develop genuine insight into feelings, attitudes, and motivations.

Conduct of Practice. The medical profession has always insisted that the patient be completely free to choose his physician. The physician is free to accept or reject the relationship, but once having accepted the patient for treatment, he is legally responsible for handling matters of diagnosis and therapy according to the highest standards existing in his locality until such time as the physician notifies the patient that he is withdrawing from the case. Once having chosen his physician, the patient is supposed to follow the directions of the physician who is no longer legally responsible if the patient fails to do this.

The ethical physician conducts his practice in accordance with the Hippocratic Oath and the recognized ethics of the profession. Errors of commission and omission caused by failure to observe ethical principles or to apply accepted methods of treatment make the physician legally responsible for malpractice. Since scientific medicine is now recognized universally as the basis for standard practice, it follows that increasing pressure is being brought upon the individual physician to conform to scientific practice wherever possible.

General Biological Orientation

The broad orientation of modern medicine is in the direction of biological science. It is significant that such recognized leaders as Sigmund Freud and Adolf Meyer had a genuinely broad and eclectic viewpoint based on intensive basic training in the biological sciences which are required in medical education. Psychologists have theoretically accepted the principle of the desirability of broad biologic training but in practice their training and experience have been much more limited. The factors which have kept psychology, psychiatry, and other specialties in scientific isolation are artificial and must soon be dispelled. Physicians will become better doctors when they are oriented toward the contributions of psychology, and psychologists will become more effective as they acquire a more general biological and medical orientation.

Summary

The history of medical psychology has great significance for the development of clinical psychology; it can profit from the long experience of medicine. Medical practice has evolved over a period of more than 2300 years with a resulting accumulation of general principles and methods of thinking which are significant for all clinical specialties. It is particularly important to integrate the contributions of the modern era of scientific medicine with clinical psychology to break down artificial barriers of isolation which have impeded the mutual development of medicine and psychology. The evolution of the clinical method in science has been reviewed with special reference to problems of diagnosis and therapy.

DONALD G. PATERSON

University of Minnesota

The Genesis of Modern Guidance[1]

My topic is the Genesis of Modern Guidance. Emphasis should be placed on the word *genesis* and the word *modern*. In using the word modern I refer to the 1930–37 streamlined version since guidance models prior to 1930 are disappearing even in the hands of the second-hand dealers through junking rather than resale. This suggests that guidance is in a state of transition—guidance workers everywhere seem to be groping for what is sound and worthwhile in the newer developments. But this idea of transition takes us back to this matter of genesis. We must have a proper historical perspective if we are to keep our feet on the ground. One of our foremost American historians in discussing the present era of rapid change recently intimated that the genesis of such change is quite old; in fact this historian goes back to the Garden of Eden, pointing out that Adam said to Eve, "Things seem to be in a state of transition."

We need not go back to Adam and Eve, however, in discussing the origin of modern guidance. We need merely to go back to 1909 and review briefly the classical "bible" for guidance, *Choosing a Vocation*, by Frank Parsons. It is significant that Leonard Ayres discovered Retardation in Education and Magnus Alexander discovered Labor Turnover in Industry at about the same time. Ayres' discovery was revolutionary leading to intensive inquiry into the causes of retardation, one of the chief being the enormous range of individual differences in mental ability found in any random sample of school children. Alexander's discovery of excessive labor turnover rates in

---

[1] Reprinted from *Educational Record*, 1938, 19, 36–46. Copyright 1938 by The American Council on Education.

American business and industrial concerns led to the attempt to find causes too, and this in turn led to the development of employment management and industrial personnel work. At about the same time G. Stanley Hall invited Sigmund Freud to a conference at Clark University, and America discovered psychoanalysis. All of these beginnings have given us vigorous movements designed to bring about better adjustments of the individual. Employment Management, Industrial Personnel Work, Vocational Guidance, Student Personnel Work, and Mental Hygiene are all organized attempts to provide ways and means of facilitating the adjustment of the individual to the demands of the environment whether it be in school, in the home, in social activities, or in the world of work.

At the outset I would like to suggest that every guidance worker should read and from time to time reread Frank Parsons' book. It outlines the proper steps to take in choosing a vocation. Briefly put, it advocates that vocational guidance should provide for a scientific analysis of the individual as a basis for vocational choice. The guidance counselor then presents the individual with needed knowledge of occupations so that an intelligent choice of life work can be made. The formula is simple, man analysis on the one hand, job analysis on the other, and the bringing of the two together in the interest of an intelligent choice.

Parsons knew what was needed, but when he went to the psychological laboratories for techniques he found that the cupboard was bare. The psychology of individual differences was almost unknown and adequate techniques for the analysis of the individual were conspicuous by virtue of their absence. But Parsons had developed a sound idea and he was determined to meet the demonstrated need for guidance. He and his followers began occupational studies so that youth could be provided with occupational information. And from that day to this we have had a steady stream of occupational pamphlets, books, and an occasional monograph. But he and his followers steered clear of the man analysis phase of guidance with the result that the vocational guidance movement became characterized by a technique which stressed the interview, self-analysis, and occupational information.[2]

---

[2] Vocational counselors who have continued to follow this pattern of activity until the present time may be characterized as being arrested in their professional development on the level of occupational information.

The failure of the vocational guidance movement to make any noteworthy progress in the development of improved methods of analyzing the individual has undoubtedly prevented the movement from making as great a contribution to American education as its founder had a right to expect. The newer approach to modern guidance attempts to remedy this deficiency by developing adequate techniques for the analysis of the individual. It is the clinical method and since 1931 it has been tried out extensively in a variety of situations with noteworthy success. This newer approach, it is important to note, also makes use of sources of occupational information but shifts the emphasis to a study of the individual in relation to occupational adjustments—his capacities, abilities, interests, and character traits in relation to occupational requirements. It is an attempt to individualize guidance service to meet specific life needs.

The development of the clinical method is a result of the research efforts of applied psychologists who for the most part were not concerned with the guidance movement as such. Reference is here made to the establishment of a research center in applied psychology at the Carnegie Institute of Technology just prior to the World War under the leadership of Walter Dill Scott and Walter V. Bingham. These men and their colleagues and students addressed themselves primarily to the baffling task of developing ways and means of measuring vocationally significant mental traits. The development of intelligence testing prior to and during the World War, together with the widespread application of intelligence testing in schools and colleges after the war, represents a major contribution. The development of a full-fledged personnel system for the United States Army during the World War by Walter Dill Scott and Robert M. Yerkes and other applied psychologists likewise constitutes a major contribution. Here we witnessed the wholesale application of the idea of the qualification card as a basic personnel technique which has since been developed into the cumulative record card as a basic guidance tool in education. The Army personnel work also developed detailed occupational specifications, trade tests, rating scales, and the group intelligence test to supplement the interview.

Following the war and as a result of the impetus provided by the personnel work in the Army there were a variety of developments. The Division of Anthropology and Psychology of the National Research Council held a series of meetings devoted to a consideration of the possibiilties of initiating a scientific vocational guidance program at the college level. As an outgrowth of these conferences, the American Council on Education sponsored a cooperative intelligence test program directed by L. L. Thurstone. In 1923 the American Council on Education also organized its Committee on Cooperative Experiments in Student Personnel. The work of this committee stimulated tremendous interest throughout the country in the desirability of undertaking student guidance programs in high schools and colleges. Of more importance is the fact that the committee provided workers in the field with instruments for making student guidance work more effective. The committee contributed the cumulative record card, the simplified rating scale for students, aided and encouraged E. K. Strong, Jr., in his work of measuring vocational interests, and encouraged experimentation in constructing adequate vocational information monographs from which have come Crawford and Clement's *The Choice of An Occupation*, and W. E. Parker's bibliography entitled *Books About Jobs*. The committee also developed adequate and reliable achievement tests at the secondary school level as well as at the junior college level. Out of this have come the batteries of objective and comprehensive achievement tests by the Cooperative Test Service directed by Ben D. Wood. All of these developments are described in the report entitled "Measurement and Guidance of College Students" published in 1933. It is also noteworthy that the American Council on Education is continuing its work actively in this field through its recently established Committee on Measurement and Guidance and its new Committee on Student Personnel Work.

While these activities were taking place, other significant developments were under way as an aftermath of the Army personnel work. The Scott Company's work in business and industrial personnel work (Scott and Clothier, Personnel Management), the organization of the Personnel Research Federation, the Psychological Corporation, the Vocational Service for Juniors in New York, the Educational Records Bureau, the Institute of Educational Research at Columbia and similiar research bureaus in other universities, the scholastic aptitude test program of the College Entrance Examination Board, the comprehensive Pennsylvania study of student guidance techniques, the Progressive Education Association study now in progress, the Minnesota Employment Stabilization Research Institute, the Rochester Employment Project, the Cincinnati Employment Center, the Adjustment Service in New York City, the Occupational Research Program of the United States Department of Labor, the National Occupational Conference, the University of Minnesota Testing Bureau—all these and others have made distinct contributions toward the development of a more scientific methodology in guidance. Indeed, the vocational guidance movement has been almost completely dependent upon these sources for its I.Q.'s, achievement tests, cumulative record cards, rating scales, aptitude tests, vocational interest tests, and personality measurements. As a matter of historic fact, the direct connection between Frank Parsons' outline and the newer approach is to be found in the Army, business, and educational personnel detour rather than in the highway of orthodox vocational guidance.

This newer approach could not have been developed had it not been for the slow and steady progress made by psychologists in dealing with the psychology of individual mental differences. That sufficient theoretical and technological progress has now been made to warrant intensive application in this admittedly difficult field is the thesis underlying the presentation of principles, point of view, methods, and results constituting modern guidance as an important branch of student personnel work. In short, this is the clinical method.[3]

Permit me to stress the fact that educational and vocational guidance is only a branch of student personnel work. Student personnel work itself is a broader field of action involving the narrower aspects of mental hygiene work (psychiatrist, psychologist, and social worker cooperating in the adjustment clinic); problems involving the proper housing of students and the maintenance of satisfactory home adjustments of students, the control and educational utilization of extra-curricular activities—fraternities, athletics, intramural sports and recreations, publications, literary societies, dramatics, etc.; services to provide part-time and full-time employment for students and graduates; programs to provide scholarships and other financial as-

---

[3] Strangely enough, the clinical method of guidance does not seem to be a direct outgrowth of the work of the clinical psychologist primarily because clinical psychologists all too frequently became arrested in their professional development on the level of the I.Q.

sistance including the N. Y. A.; and control of those environmental influences that directly and indirectly affect the morale, mores, and morals of the student body. Administratively there are, therefore, two phases of student personnel work, one dealing with the adjustments of individual students and the other dealing with student group life. These two phases should be intimately related and coordinated. A well-rounded personnel program for any organization must encompass both points of view and must provide facilities that will insure that both approaches are fully utilized. This is why student personnel work requires the closest possible cooperation between administrators, department heads, classroom teachers, registrars, deans of men and women, speech clinic specialists, educational research workers, clinical guidance specialists, psychiatrists and medical officers, and employment placement men. The lone worker in personnel work who attempts to perform all of these functions not only spreads himself too thin but he works under the handicap of a "Jehovah complex."

From the foregoing discussion it is clear that the pressing problems of guidance forces the professionalization of the guidance worker in the best sense of that term. Mere knowledge of industry and of vocational information books and pamphlets is not enough. The modern guidance worker must be thoroughly grounded in psychology, in research and statistics, and in clinical procedures. An M.S. degree in psychometrics or its equivalent would appear to be a minimum essential. The Ph.D. degree or its equivalent would appear to be a desirable qualification. It goes without saying, of course, that this newer type of guidance worker as well as the older type must also possess the personality traits that characterize those who are successful in dealing with people in face-to-face situations.

In contrast to such technical training demands, one may now look with amusement at the training program proposed by Frank Parsons in 1909. He described his school for vocational counselors, consisting of lectures, conferences, and laboratory practice.

At least three hours a week are given by each member to this laboratory practice examining applicants for vocational advice and formulating the counsel believed to be appropriate for the solution of the specific problem presented by each case. . . . To enter the vocational course a man must have excellent character and ability, good manners and address, *at least a high school education or its equivalent*, and a satisfactory experience of two years or more. . . . He must have attained the age of twenty-five years, unless very mature at an earlier age. . . . *The time required will be one, two, or three terms,* according to the ability and previous preparation of the student.

And still more astonishing is the description of what this type of student so trained will be able to do for the guidance movement as may be seen from the following:

A certificate of proficiency will be given at the end of any term in which the practical results achieved by the particular student justify his enrollment as an *expert, qualified to test the abilities and capacities of young men,* apply good judgment, common sense, and scientific method to the various problems a vocation bureau has to deal with, and give appropriate counsel with the insight, sympathy, grasp, and suggestiveness the service calls for.

Many persons have recognized the desirability for a more scientific approach to guidance work. But they raise objections whenever anyone proposes to utilize scientific techniques in an actual guidance situation. They seem to fear science when it touches the individual. The belief persists that psychology is far too tentative and nebulous to be applied here and now. Aptitude testing is regarded as theoretically desirable but available tests and measurements are believed to be too crude, unreliable, and not sufficiently valid to warrant serious use. These attitudes exist not only among many laymen, but among some psychologists as well. And then there are the mathematical statisticians who learn about the standard error of estimate and straightway contend that no test or measurement should be applied until its validity is such as to guarantee a minimum of error. They desire to reduce the error of prediction to negligible amounts *before* countenancing the practical use of a mental test. They are uncomfortable unless the error of prediction is reduced at least 60 per cent.

But some of us are even more uncomfortable in the presence of educational maladjustments and vocational maladjustments that involve large numbers of students and workers. Hence, we would be bold enough to risk error in order to provide a type of guidance that the complexities of modern life demands.

Strangely enough, those who demand perfect tests are the very ones who are complacent in the face of the far larger errors being committed daily in school and shop through sole reliance upon traditional methods. Classroom grades, interviews, self-estimates, diplomas, chronological age, recommendations, encouragement of unbridled ambitions—these are the traditional methods that Hollingworth has shown to have validities of 3 or 4 or 5 per cent better than chance (64).[4]

Our perfectionists however show another strange symptom. They survey with hypercritical eyes existing tests and measurements and find them wanting when tested by the severe standard of perfect validity. They impulsively throw the baby out with the bath and then in the next breath admit a host of street urchins by the side door without even a superficial inspection. I refer to those who reject tests and measurements but parade before the public an array of guidance techniques that are far less reliable and valid. What is the reliability and validity of a guidance interview? Of an occupational pamphlet? Of a lad's earnest but misguided desire to study medicine?

The way out of this dilemma is not for the pot to call the kettle black but for guidance workers to redouble their efforts through research and practice to provide a synthesis of all available guidance techniques with a view to obtaining the maximum service possible from our present methods. This has been done by the University of Minnesota Testing Bureau and follow-up studies indicate that 90 per cent of the students who carried out Bureau recommendations wholly or partly made satisfactory adjustment or progress toward adjustment, whereas only 22 per cent of the students who failed to follow Bureau recommendations made a satisfactory adjustment. This follow-up study of 987 students who have been subjected to the clinical method of guidance supplies the answer to the perfectionists who want to wait for perfect validity before venturing to put tests and measurements at work in the service of students.

The practice of medicine furnishes us with a deadly parallel. Should medical practice wait upon a completed and perfect science of medicine? Should the treatment of cancer be postponed until a cancer cure is discovered? Should we continue to rely on home remedies and patent medicines until scientific medicine can provide us with perfectly valid tests of the endocrines, of metabolism, of allergies, or of a legion of other problems confronting the practitioners of medicine today?

One other word needs to be said before we conclude this analysis

---

[4] Bibliography begins on page 88.

of the origins of modern guidance. I refer to the problem of methodology underlying clinical diagnosis in guidance. We cannot as yet reduce guidance predictions to a series of multiple regression equations. Nevertheless, the guidance clinician is dependent upon a background of statistical methods and a knowledge of statistical facts. Personnel research lies back of the clinical approach. Intimate acquaintance with the research data or the lack of research data supporting claims in behalf of this test or that test must be assumed. Otherwise, the clinical guidance counselor will be unable to judge the worth of the hundreds of tests now on the market. Critical appraisal of existing techniques must be used in the selection of the best available so that one may separate the wheat from the chaff. Knowledge of when to use a given test or type of test is essential if the most appropriate batteries of tests are to be administered to a given individual. In other words, through training and research we must implement our guidance counselors so that they will be able to provide the best possible type of scientific guidance service. For this reason it is significant that this guidance conference begins its working sessions this afternoon with a consideration of what research can contribute.[5]

In closing permit me to make a prediction. From developments and achievements to date and from the widespread interest one finds in scientific guidance work here in California, in the Midwest, in the East, and in the South, I am confident that we are on the threshold of a rapid expansion of guidance services in high schools, colleges, and universities, and in adult adjustment clinics attached to public employment offices. Another prediction is also safe, namely, we are on the threshold of a tremendous acceleration of testing programs everywhere as a result of the introduction at this very moment of an electrical scoring machine that will reduce costs to a negligible figure. I refer to the International Test Scoring Machine which has been perfected and is now being produced by the International Business Machines Corporation. This machine has been put to severe tests in the Regents' Inquiry in New York state and in the state-wide survey in Connecticut. In brief, this machine permits test booklets to be used over and over again by means of special answer sheets.

---

[5] The attention of counselors is directed to W. V. Bingham's *Aptitudes and Aptitude Testing* (11) and the handbook by D. G. Paterson, G. Schneidler, and E. G. Williamson (91).

These answer sheets containing as many as 200 items can be run through the machine at the rate of 975 an hour. The Strong Vocational Interest Tests, Thurstone's Tests of Primary Mental Abilities, Intelligence Tests, and Achievement Tests will all be rearranged to permit machine scoring. The machine will do the work of twenty scoring clerks and thus permit continuous testing of large numbers of individuals at very little expense. The machine will rent for $300 per year and it is safe to predict that most of the high schools, colleges, and universities in the United States will eventually be equipped with these machines.

For all these reasons I make bold to predict the immediate rapid development of educational and vocational guidance programs that would bring tears of joy to the Father of Guidance, Frank Parsons. Progressive educators everywhere will welcome this newer type of guidance program because it will break down the mass errors of mass education and will individualize education in a thorough-going manner. This newer type of guidance, therefore, stands as a challenge to educational traditionalism.

LAURANCE F. SHAFFER

Teachers College, Columbia University

Clinical Psychology and Psychiatry[1]

This meeting commemorates the founding of the first psychological clinic by Lightner Witmer, a psychologist. Without detracting from the honor paid to Witmer, it might be noted that another early and influential clinic was established by a psychiatrist. In 1909, 37 years ago, William Healy opened the Chicago Juvenile Psychopathic Institute, now the Institute for Juvenile Research. Ever since that time, psychiatrists and clinical psychologists have been drawn into increasingly complex relationships, because of their common aims and similar principles and methods.

The feeling tone of the relationship between clinical psychology and psychiatry has varied greatly during the past fifty years. From the very beginning there have been examples of cordiality and effective collaboration, as seen in the association of William Healy with Augusta F. Bronner, and that of Aaron J. Rosanoff with Grace H. Kent, partnerships that dated from before 1910. These classic relationships have set a pattern for many other collaborations that are less well known but equally fruitful. When two especially competent people are thrown into continued and intimate contact, they develop mutual respect, and this is true of a psychologist and a psychiatrist, as well as of other persons.

We would only be blinding ourselves if we asserted that the relation has always been so harmonious. Many psychiatrists and psychol-

---

[1] An address delivered at a symposium in honor of fifty years of clinical psychology, at the University of Pennsylvania, September 3, 1946. Reprinted from *Journal of Consulting Psychology*, 1947, 11, 5–11. Copyright 1947 by American Psychological Association.

ogists have regarded each other with mutual suspicion and distrust. This antagonism is itself of psychological interest. It is well recognized that we are more irritated by the blemishes of our closest relatives than we are by the derelictions of strangers. Psychologists and psychiatrists give evidence of a family feud. In extreme instances they have hated each other with an intensity equalled only by a pair of middle-aged sisters who are engaged in a law-suit over their father's will. Our professional case of sibling rivalry should be studied with a view to therapy!

Let us examine some of the bases of discord between psychiatrists and psychologists. Many examples of it seem to originate from dramatic individual instances. Sometimes these are clashes of personalities in which one man feels that another is arrogant, or conceited, or avaricious, or not entirely honest, or just personally unpleasant in an undefined way. More frequent are anecdotes concerning the professional incompetence of particular individuals, of the stupid mistakes made by this psychologist or by that psychiatrist. A fair-minded observer, of course, has to admit that these individual shortcomings are true. There are unpleasant persons in both professions, and both make mistakes from time to time. These particular cases seem to mold the attitudes of one profession toward the other, but, as psychological research has found in the case of other inter-group attitudes, dramatic instances are often not the fundamental determining factors. Something must make a psychiatrist want to believe that all psychologists are like the one whom he dislikes or distrusts. We must therefore search for a deeper source of the disharmony.

A very significant difficulty arises from the differences between the training of psychologists and the training of psychiatrists. The divergence of their educations is astonishing. Although they perform similar professional functions, it is possible for them never to have had a single semester hour of identical common instruction since Freshman English. It is frequently observed that persons tend to believe that their own professional preparation is the most appropriate and beneficial; in fact, some surveys of the opinions of graduate engineers, psychologists, and others, indicate that this viewpoint is held widely. A basic cause of distrust, therefore, is that no member of either profession can quite believe in the competence of another person whose background is so different from his own.

In addition to the very general source of suspicion, there are particular inadequacies that tend to be emphasized. They hurt because they are true. Psychiatrists complain especially of the variable* and unstandardized training of psychologists. One clinical psychologist may have a doctoral degree and a year of internship, but another person, also called a clinical psychologist, may have only a year of graduate work, with meager training beyond elementary testing. In fact, a survey not many years ago showed that two-thirds of the psychologists in child guidance clinics had only the Master's degree. Psychiatrists may well say that they have no means for identifying a really qualified clinical psychologist. This trouble is aggravated by psychology's unique semantic difficulty. In spite of attempts to name the specialties within psychology by adjective modifiers, most clinical psychologists are known simply as psychologists. Other psychologists poll public opinion, select employees, run rats, and conduct intricate experiments on the psychophysiology of vision. These are all psychologists too, but are not clinicians. Psychiatrists, who are always medical doctors and almost always practitioners, cannot understand this diversity clearly, but see only that even the doctoral degree is no evidence of competence in clinical psychology.

Another matter of legitimate concern to psychiatrists is the ignorance of many clinical psychologists in the area of medical diagnosis. In helping human beings solve their problems, we deal with the whole organism. Physiological conditions may play a large part in the determination of behavior, and few psychologists have the training and experience to detect them reliably. Physicians make mistakes in medical diagnosis too, but their education has prepared them specifically for this task.

The proper complaints that psychologists make against psychiatrists are well known and do not require detailed enumeration. Many psychiatrists, especially those trained some years ago, are acquainted only with the diagnosis and care of the psychoses, and are as helpless as laymen in dealing with lesser problems of human misery. More than one college psychologist has despaired when this kind of psychiatrist has sent back an anxiety-ridden student who was referred to him, with only a statement that there is nothing wrong, and that the youngster should engage more in social affairs and forget his troubles. Psychologists also see that psychiatrists lack a sound knowledge of experimental psychology, so that they are loose in terminology, and are easily attracted to grotesque theories. Psychiatrists usually do not appreciate the values of quantitative study, and have little knowledge of research methods or of the design of experiments. Therefore, sound research is lacking in many areas of psychiatry, and not a few published studies are seriously faulty.

These broader or corporate clashes between psychology and psychiatry, which transcend the more annoying but trivial ones of personalities, are not unlike the conflicts of the international political world. Individuals of various nations can get along together. An Italian and a Jugoslav, to select a contemporary example, can become real friends. Their countries cannot, because of the attitudes of nationalism and sovereignty which hold that nations must not compromise or extend full co-operation, lest they lose some transcendent quality of their selfhood. In international affairs conflicts of sovereign powers are met by armed truce, by open warfare, or by the development of a dominance-appeasement relationship. The futility of these methods for settling international conflict is still fresh in our minds. We hope for a democratic co-operative relationship among nations as among individuals, whereby the welfare of all is enhanced by the surrender of part of the sovereignty of each unit.

But who are we to urge co-operation among nations until we can cope with the smaller and closer concerns of our professional conflicts? Fortunately, a beginning has been made in this direction.

In the spirit of the development of a democratic–co-operative relationship, the two APA's—the American Psychiatric Association and the American Psychological Association—appointed committees to study the joint concerns of the professions. After a year of groundwork by correspondence, the two committees met in June, 1946, in an atmosphere of mutual acceptance and good will.

The keystone of the solution proposed by the joint committees arises from a frank recognition of the truth of the major causes for distrust that have already been cited. It is true that clinical psychology lacks uniform standards of training and competence. This can be remedied by actions already under way, in the establishment of the Board of Examiners in Professional Psychology. It is true that some psychiatrists lack skill in dealing with the lesser disorders, short of the psychoses. This defect can be overcome by training.

In addition to the obviously remediable handicaps, there are others not so easily cured. It is true that most psychiatrists lack a background in normal and experimental psychology, and are deficient in quantitative and research methods. It is also true that very few psychologists have the medical training that is essential to the detection and understanding of physiological disorders that may underlie mal-adaptive behavior. These weaknesses in the two professions cannot be overcome so easily. It might be suggested that a new profession should emerge, requiring the training of both psychiatry and psychology. This might mean ten years of graduate study, which seems impracticable at the present time. Furthermore, other professions have additional claims. Social work contributes to the whole understanding of an individual, and a demand might be made that the thoroughly trained clinician must know not only psychiatry and psychology, but social work as well. This is too large an order. Are we then at an impasse? Is there any recourse except to continue our inadequacies and our conflicts?

No, we are not at an impasse. There is an obvious solution to the problem of the professional relationhips of clinical psychology and psychiatry. This solution was a major point of agreement reached by the joint committee.

Neither profession is adequate in itself. As a principle and an ideal, the joint committees recognize the mutual dependence of the two disciplines, in the complete description of human personality, or diagnosis; in the handling of persons with deviations, or therapy; and in research on problems of human behavior. A full diagnosis of each person involves at least medical, psychological, and social contributions. The same basic considerations apply to the area of treatment. The interdependence of the professions is achieved most fully by emphasis upon the concept of team work, both in professional practice and also in training. This is the proposed solution. Since neither is self-sufficient, the only possible course of action is to join forces, so as to provide the most effective and the most widely available services for human welfare.

Does this basis for agreement surrender some of the sovereignty of psychology? If so, it involves some surrender of the sovereignty of psychiatry as well. The postulate of team work recognizes that professions as well as nations cannot realize their full development in isolation. The relationship that is sought, and that seems possible to achieve, is not one of conflict, and not one of dominance-appeasement, but one of democratic co-operation.

In beginning to apply the concept of co-operation, the joint committee discussed a number of matters relating to certification, training, practice, and research.

The problem of the identification of persons who can properly be regarded as well-trained clinical psychologists was of special interest to the psychiatrist members of the joint committee. The qualifications of psychiatrists have been standardized for some time by the American Board of Psychiatry and Neurology, so that anyone who can read a list of requirements may know the minimum standards of an accredited psychiatrist.

Up to the present time, the qualifications of clinical psychologists have not been defined at all clearly. The committees recognized that before there could be any discussion of what a psychologist is prepared to do, there must be a more definite conception of what kind of man or woman we are talking about. What a clinical psychologist can do depends on what a clinical psychologist is. The committee therefore gave their unqualified endorsement to the steps now being taken toward the certification of clinical psychologists by an American Board of Examiners in Professional Psychology. It was recommended that only one grade of clinical psychologist should be certified, and that this certification should require the highest standards of training and competence.

The certification of psychologists is inseparable from their training. If we are to maintain the desired equality with the medical profession, the standards of education should not be lower than those for medicine. Applicants for certification as clinical psychologists should have completed a standard University program for a doctorate, plus one year of internship. To gain the greatest benefit from the training program, the committee believed that the sequence should include two years of graduate work at the University with considerable direct contact with clinical problems, then an internship in the third year, and then a return to the University to complete the doctoral requirements in a fourth year. There were no more detailed recommendations for courses of study, as the time is not ripe for the crystallization of exact curricula. Variation and experimentation are desirable in our present imperfect state of knowledge, and the exact content of programs should be left to the several Universities.

Many competent clinical psychologists now in practice do not meet these new requirements. It is especially true that very few of us indeed who received the doctorate more than ten years ago had an opportunity to serve an internship. The committees gave realistic attention to the certification of those who have already completed their training. This became known as the matter of the "grandfather clause," although some of the grandfathers concerned may now be at the ripe old age of thirty! It is acknowledged that competent clinical psychologists now practicing may be certified, even though they do not meet the specific requirements to be demanded of new persons, as professional standards are raised. The psychiatrists did the same thing only in 1934, and they have no objection to our doing it now.

It has been noted that a major cause of distrust between psychiatrists and clinical psychologists is the radical difference in their training, and the isolation caused by infrequent contacts. The committees therefore believe that a basic concept in the preparation of both psychiatrists and psychologists should be that of team work between the two professions. This stresses the limitations of each discipline, and the necessity for the insights that each offers to the total problem. To achieve this end, and to insure that future generations of psychiatrists and psychologists are not strangers to each other, they should be trained together.

There are immediate and serious problems in the provision of proper training facilities for new members of both professions, especially at the internship level. The psychiatrists' committee has therefore recommended to its parent body that the American Psychiatric Association should refuse to certify any center as adequate for the training of psychiatrists if it does not have one or more certified clinical psychologists on its staff, and provision for the training of internes in psychology. This co-operative move should increase our facilities for internship training greatly, and should insure the common contact that is desired. In turn the American Psychological Association may well refuse to certify any center as adequate for the internship training of clinical psychologists if it does not have one or more psychiatrists who are diplomates.

These steps are directed chiefly toward the improvement of training in clinical psychology, but psychiatric education also has its shortcomings. Psychology has had an overbalance of formal training and a lack of supervised practice. Psychiatry has suffered from the opposite fault, as its postgraduate training has been almost entirely on an apprenticeship basis, with little classroom instruction. To rectify this, the committees recommended that psychiatric training should be supplemented by a greater amount of formal and planned education. Psychologists with backgrounds in both experimental and clinical psychology should participate in this training, by giving instruction in the newer trends of objective psychology specifically related to an understanding of learning, motivation, adjustment, and conflict.

The greatest hope for the future development of co-operation between psychology and psychiatry lies in the mutual respect to be cultivated by joint training. In this plan each profession contributes its greatest strength to the training of both groups, and men learn to work together by studying together.

In addition to the most significant principle of team work, the committees reached some other agreements on matters relating to the practice of psychiatry and psychology. In hospital practice, the primary responsibility for the patient's care and well-being is easily defined as medical. In other areas, including educational institutions, clinics, and private practice, the responsibilities are not so clearly defined. In these areas, both psychiatrists and clinical psychologists accept some degree of responsibility, according to their competences acquired through training. When either psychologists or psychiatrists work alone in these fields, it is good practice to use all available resources of the other professions that can contribute to the welfare of those who are served.

The problem of the administrative control of facilities other than hospitals was approached realistically by the committees. The rapid rise of community clinics, educational counseling centers, and the like, has resulted in a wide variety of patterns of administrative organization. In various places, a psychiatrist, a psychologist, a social worker, or an educator may be the responsible administrative officer. The committees recognized that there is no essential relationship between professional function and administrative responsibility, and that there is no need for changing the present diversity.

In the area of practice, the committees viewed most unfavorably a prevalent tendency to regard what is called "personal counseling," or the handling of the so-called "mild" psychoneuroses, as areas so simple that they can be served by persons with little or no psychological training. This type of service requires the highest degree of preparation and competence on the part of either a clinical psychologist or a psychiatrist. It is handled most fruitfully with a recognition of the interdependence of the medical, psychological, and social aspects.

The problem of research in clinical psychology and psychiatry is a basic one. Both are pioneer fields, seriously hampered by limitations in basic knowledge and in practical techniques. In the past we have thought of controlled and quantitative research as the primary domain of psychology. Yet during the past three years, what psychologist has produced basic research as significant to clinical psychology as the work of Gantt on experimental neuroses, or of Masserman on not only the induction but also the therapy of behavior disorders in cats? Both of these men are medical doctors. In the striving of clinical psychology to become a service profession, we must not neglect graduate training in experimental psychology, in research design, and in the sound background of general theoretical psychology that is essential to research. A clinical psychology without constant active research would stagnate into a cult, its frontiers unexplored or left to others.

Many important problems of the relationships between psychiatry and clinical psychology remain to be solved. The team work concept is adequate for hospitals and clinics, but what of the individual practitioner? Should a clinical psychologist ever practice alone? Is it enough that he work with a physician, or require that all of his clients first have a good medical examination? Or, should he always be associated with a psychiatrist? Should a psychiatrist in private practice always have a psychologist as a collaborator? If so, what are his responsibilities?

The problem of psychotherapy has also not been clarified sufficiently. In diagnosis, it is easy to see the relationships of a team of physician, psychologist and social worker. Each contributes elements of understanding not readily supplied by the others. Psychotherapy is a different matter. It is difficult, or even ridiculous, to imagine an individual with problems of personal adjustment being treated by any team of collaborators. Psychotherapy, as best conceived today, is a personal relationship, and the troubled individual can form this subtle association only with one therapist at a time. Perhaps a pattern will emerge in which the joint efforts of the several professions will be directed primarily to the diagnosis, and the individual to carry on the psychotherapy will be selected from the team, not because he is a psychiatrist or a psychologist or a social worker, but because he is the most suitable human being to form the therapeutic relationship with a particular person who needs help.

Might it be appropriate to conclude with a brief clinical report on the corporate therapy of psychiatry and psychology? The patients are not yet entirely cured of their aggressions, but some progress has been made. Rapport has been established, and mutual counseling has taken place in a most permissive atmosphere. Dependences and aggressions have been recognized, accepted, and even reflected! Considerable extinction of old anxieties has taken place. The prognosis is hopeful and with further treatment the patients, psychiatry and psychology, may look forward to the expectation of a happy and useful life together.

DAVID SHAKOW

University of Illinois College of Medicine

Training in Clinical Psychology—
A Note on Trends [1]

Fundamental to the current discussions of the problem of training in clinical psychology must be a recognition of the roles to be played in the process by the varying approaches now prevailing in clinical and abnormal psychology. An examination of these reveals that in relation to the two major emphases represented, that concerned primarily with the individual subject and that concerned with groups of subjects, at least four main trends can be differentiated.

The first may be characterized as advocating a *dynamic* approach to the problems in the field. The group representing this point of view is primarily interested in the understanding of the genetic development of motivation and personality organization, both in their structural and contentual aspects. It sees the problems of clinical psychology as one of research on the individual case directed at obtaining data about the individual both for generalizations about him and about the group of which he is a member. It frequently uses these data for therapeutic purposes. The affiliations of this group are largely with a dynamic psychology, psychiatry and psychoanalysis.

The second may be characterized as a *diagnostic* approach to clinical problems. The group representing this point of view is primarily concerned with the use of test devices which investigate the structural aspects of personality, e.g., in relation to intelligence and other

---

[1] Reprinted from *Journal of Consulting Psychology*, 1945, 9, 240–242. Copyright 1945 by American Association for Applied Psychology.

capacities, aptitudes and skills. Its interest is in the light which these devices throw on the person's adjustment with a view towards making recommendations for disposition which are usually carried out by others. The affiliations of this group are mainly with educational and vocational workers.

The third may be characterized as the *diagnostic-therapeutic* approach. This group has certain affinities with each of the two former groups but differs from them in several respects. Although it has an interest in the use of tests for the understanding of the presenting problems it is mainly interested in the therapeutic implications of test results for the individual person. In contrast with the first group there is here not so fundamental or systematic an attack on the problems of human motivation nor is the therapy involved generally of such a searching and extended type. Its major interests are in diagnosis and certain specific types of therapy. Two sub-groups may here be distinguished: One of these accepts the principle of the psychiatrist–psychologist–social worker triad as the most desirable clinic organization; the other takes the view that this type of organization is not essential and that other affiliations may be equally satisfactory, e.g., those of psychologists with teachers, pediatricians, or social workers.

The fourth may be characterized as the *experimental* approach. Its major interest is the study of clinical material from the experimental point of view. Here, also, two sub-groups may be distinguished. The main concern of one is with problems involving the cross-sectional structural characteristics of the deviant organism under varying conditions; the main concern of the other is with problems of a more dynamic kind, mainly cross-sectional but to some extent also longitudinal. Neither is interested in therapy per se—in fact, both generally take the view that therapy is not intrinsically a field for the psychologist. They are not interested in test devices as they relate to the individual case. Their concern is rather with the establishment of laws about types of deviants very much as certain groups of workers in normal psychology are interested in establishing laws about normal people. The individual deviant subject is considered by them merely as a means to such an end.

The above descriptions have attempted no more than to epitomize the essential nature of these differing points of view. In practice, obviously, there exists no such sharp distinctiveness—the overlapping among them is considerable and the shifts in emphasis with the passage of time pronounced.

All of these points of view should be reflected in a program of preparation for clinical psychology since they all have a contribution to make. An examination of the field, however, reveals that certain of these trends are gaining ground faster than others and we must therefore anticipate corresponding changes of emphasis in the nature of the preparation which the clinical psychologist will be expected to undertake.

The major change which seems to be taking place lies in the increasingly greater attention which is being given to what has been termed the "dynamic" approach. Psychologists, in the past, have been rather slow in occupying themselves with this field—a field which to the layman is definitely that of the psychologist and to psychologists themselves becoming increasingly so. The historical factors, deliberate and accidental, personal and impersonal, which have deflected the interest of psychologists from the complicated problems of motivation and personality development need not be gone into here. But that there has been such a lack of interest until fairly recent years cannot be denied. Psychoanalytic psychology slowly boring its way through the rather resistant skin of a non-personal psychology organized largely on a physical model, has finally been able to reach deep enough to meet burgeoning long-repressed inner yearnings. The juncture of the two has resulted in the recent remarkable growth of interest in personality dynamics and genetics. It is reasonable to suppose that no field of psychology will be more influenced by this development than will be clinical psychology.

If I am not wrong in the evaluation of this trend, it seems desirable for psychology to place more emphasis than it has on the aspects of the program of preparation for clinical psychology which the trend represents. In this connection the increasing concern of psychologists with the problems of psychoanalysis and its techniques should be encouraged. There is perhaps no better introduction to the complexities of human motivation than through some form of psychoanalysis. For this reason serious thought should be given to the desirability of encouraging persons about to enter clinical psychology to undergo a psychoanalysis. The pros and cons of this problem for psychologists are perhaps best stated in the symposium of analyzed psychologists edited by Gordon Allport (3).[2] If a psychoanalysis is deemed advisable as part of a program for clinical psychologists special care will have to be taken to select analysts who are relatively free from doctrinairism and who have an interest in psychological theory as well as in therapy. Although a Freudian type of analysis, because of its relative completeness, is perhaps generally preferable to other types of analysis, any detailed self-examination under competent guidance might serve as well for most candidates. In this connection, even Freudian psychoanalysts are beginning to recognize the desirability of broadening the base of psychoanalytic training to include non-Freudian approaches. It is understood, of course, that the purpose in proposing such a step is not to advocate the acceptance of a particular theoretical point of view; rather, it is to suggest the consideration of a technique which many have found valuable for the acquisition of insight into the complexities of personality dynamics.

Whatever the reaction may be to the last suggestion, it is clear to those who have given thought to the subject of trends in clinical psychology that no program of preparing clinical psychologists can be considered adequate which does not recognize the need for providing the student with a back-ground which takes cognizance of the various points of view described. The relative emphasis will for the present presumably have to depend upon the personal philosophy of the instructor and upon his sensitivity to growing trends in a rapidly developing field.

[2] Bibliography begins on page 88.

Bibliography

1) Acheson, E. M. Studies in co-ordination of effort between psychologists and social workers. *Family*, 1935–1936, 16, 205–209.
2) Alexander, F., and French, T. M., et al. *Psychoanalytic Therapy*. New York: Ronald, 1946.
3) Allport, G. W. (ed.). Symposium: psychoanalysis as seen by analyzed psychologists. *J. Abnorm. Soc. Psychol.*, 1940, 35, 3–55, 139–225, 305–323.
4) American Medical Association. Principles of medical ethics. *J. Clin. Psychol.*, 1945, 1, 336–342.
5) American Psychological Association, Clinical Section. The definition of clinical psychology and standards of training for clinical psychologists. *Psychol. Clin.*, 1935, 23, 2–8.
6) American Psychological Association, Clinical Section. Compilation of statements concerning the definition of clinical psychology and standards of training for clinical psychologists. (Mimeographed) 1934.
7) American Psychological Association, Clinical Section. Guide to psychological clinics in the United States. *Psychol. Clin.*, 1935, 23, 9–140.
8) (Anon.) The proposed American Association of Applied and Professional Psychology. *J. Appl. Psychol.*, 1937, 21, 320–341.
9) Beers, C. *A mind that found itself: an autobiography*. New York: Longmans, Green, 1908. (25th anniversary ed. New York: Doubleday, Doran, 1935.)
10) Binet, A., and Simon, Th. Methods nouvelles pour le diagnostic du niveau intellectual des anormaux. *Année Psychol.*, 1905, 11, 191–336.
11) Bingham, W. V. *Aptitudes and aptitude testing*. New York: Harper, 1937.
12) Bisch, L. E. *Clinical psychology*. Baltimore: Williams & Wilkins, 1925.
13) Bixler, R., and Seeman, J. Suggestions for a code of ethics for consulting psychologists. *J. Abnorm. Soc. Psychol.*, 1946, 41, 486–490.
14) Blain, D. The psychiatrist and the psychologist. *J. Clin. Psychol.*, 1947, 3, 4–10.

15) Boring, E. G. A *history of experimental psychology*. New York: Century, 1929.

16) Brennemann, J. The menace of psychiatry. *Amer. J. Dis. Child.*, 1931, 42, 376–408.

17) Brill, A. A. *Lectures on psychoanalytic psychiatry*. New York: Knopf, 1946.

18) Britt, S. H. Model "Certified Psychologists Act." *J. Consult. Psychol.*, 1939, 3, 123–127.

19) Britt, S. H. Pending developments in the legal status of psychologists. *J. Consult. Psychol.*, 1941, 5, 52–55.

20) Britt, S. H., and Morgan, J. D. Military psychologists in World War II. *Amer. Psychologist*, 1946, 1, 423–437.

21) Brotemarkle, R. A. (ed.). *Clinical psychology: studies in honor of Lightner Witmer*. Philadelphia: Univ. Pennsylvania Press, 1931.

22) Brotemarkle, R. A. Introduction. In Brotemarkle, R. A. (ed.), *Clinical psychology: studies in honor of Lightner Witmer*. Philadelphia: Univ. Pennsylvania Press, 1931. Pp. xiii–xxi.

23) Brotemarkle, R. A. College student personnel work. In Brotemarkle, R. A. (ed.), *Clinical psychology: studies in honor of Lightner Witmer*. Philadelphia: Univ. Pennsylvania Press, 1931. Pp. 103–106.

24) Brotemarkle, R. A. The challenge to consulting psychology. *J. Appl. Psychol.*, 1940, 24, 10–19.

25) Brousseau, K. Psychological service at the Los Angeles Institute of Family Relations. *J. Consult. Psychol.*, 1937, 3, 49.

26) Brown, R. R. A survey of psychometrics in state and federal penitentiaries for adult males. Unpublished report, U. S. Publ. Hlth. Serv., August, 1934.

27) Burchard, E. M. L. The reform of the graduate school curriculum in psychology. *Psychol. Exch.*, 1936, 5, 7–20.

28) Buros, O. K. Educational, psychological, and personality tests of 1933, 1934, and 1935. *Rutgers Univ. Stud. Educ.*, 1936, No. 9.

29) Buros, O. K. Educational, psychological, and personality tests of 1936. *Rutgers Univ. Stud. Educ.*, 1937, No. 11.

30) Cattell, J. M. Retrospect: psychology as a profession. *J. Consult. Psychol.*, 1937, 1, 1–3.

31) Clark, M. A. Directory of psychiatric clinics in the United States, 1936. *Ment. Hyg.*, 1936, 20, 66–129.

32) Clark, R. A. Psychologist and psychiatrist. *J. Personality*, 1946, 15, 101–104.

33) Cornell, E. L. Certification of specialized groups of psychologists: school psychologists. *J. Consult. Psychol.*, 1941, 5, 62–65.

34) Cornell, W. B. Psychology vs. psychiatry in diagnosing feeblemindedness. *N. Y. St. J. Med.*, 1917, 17, 485–486.

35) Cowan, E. A. Correspondence. *J. Consult. Psychol.*, 1945, 9, 64–65.

36) Crothers, B. *A pediatrician in search of mental hygiene.* New York: Commonwealth Fund, 1937.

37) Cutts, N. E. Development of a certification for school psychologists. *J. Consult. Psychol.*, 1943, 7, 45–49.

38) Darley, J. G., and Wolfle, D. Can we meet the formidable demand for psychological services? *Amer. Psychologist*, 1946, 1, 179–180.

39) Doll, E. A. (ed.). *Twenty five years.* A memorial volume in commemoration of the 25th Anniversary of the Vineland Laboratory, 1906–1931. (Publ. Ser., 1932.)

40) Doll, E. A. Fields of clinical psychology. *Psychol. Exch.*, 1934, 3, 134–137.

41) Doll, E. A. Psychological personnel. *Amer. J. Ment. Def.*, 1940, 45, 167–169.

42) Doll, E. A. The divisional structure of the APA. *Amer. Psychologist*, 1946, 1, 336–345.

43) English, H. B. Organization of the American Association of Applied Psychologists. *J. Consult. Psychol.*, 1938, 2, 7–16

44) Fenton, N. Child guidance in California communities: Part 2. The Co-ordinating Council in Child Welfare. *J. Juv. Res.*, 1937, 21, 26–43.

45) Fenton, N. *State child guidance service in California communities.* Stanford Univ.: Stanford Univ. Press, 1938.

46) Fernberger, S. W. The history of the psychological clinic. In Brotemarkle, R. A. (ed.), *Clinical psychology: studies in honor of Lightner Witmer.* Philadelphia: Univ. Pennsylvania Press, 1931. Pp. 10–36.

47) Fernberger, S. W. The American Psychological Association: a historical summary, 1892–1930. *Psychol. Bull.*, 1932, 29, 1–89.

48) Forbes, T. W. Age performance relationships among accident-repeater automobile drivers. *J. Consult. Psychol.*, 1938, 2, 143–148.

49) Fowerbaugh, C. C. Legal status of psychologists in Ohio. *J. Consult. Psychol.*, 1945, 9, 196–200.

50) French, L. M. *Psychiatric social work.* New York: Commonwealth Fund, 1940.

51) Frith, G. D., and Jones, J. The functioning of a psychological clinic in South Bend. *Amer. Sch. Bd. J.*, 1935, 90, No. 3, 41.

52) Fryer, D. Introduction: contributions of certification to unified professional status in psychology. *J. Consult. Psychol.*, 1941, 5, 49–51.

53) Garrett, H. E., and Schneck, M. R. *Psychological tests, methods and results.* New York: Harper, 1933.

54) Gesell, A., Goddard, H. H., and Wallin, J. E. W. Field of clinical psychology as an applied science. *J. Appl. Psychol.*, 1919, 3, 81–95.

55) Greene, E. B. What courses are essential for work in psychological diagnosis and treatment? *J. Consult. Psychol.*, 1938, 2, 43–45.

56) Haberman, J. V. Psychic therapy, clinical psychology, and the layman invasion. *Med. Rec.*, 1915, 87, 680–683.

57) Haberman, J. V. Clinical psychology in its relation to the school and to social medicine. *Med. Rec.*, 1915, 88, 861–864.

58) Hagerty, J. E. *The training of social workers.* New York: McGraw-Hill, 1931.

59) Healy, W. *The individual delinquent.* Boston: Little, Brown, 1915.

60) Heiser, K. F. Certification of psychologists in Connecticut. *Psychol. Bull.*, 1945, 42, 624–630.

61) Hildreth, G. *A bibliography of mental tests and rating scales.* New York: Psychological Corporation, 1933.

62) Hildreth, G. Psychology as a career. *J. Consult. Psychol.*, 1937, 1, 25–28.

63) Hilgard, E. R. Psychologists' preferences for divisions under the proposed APA by-laws. *Psychol. Bull.*, 1945, 42, 20–26.

64) Hollingworth, H. L. *Judging human character.* New York: Appleton, 1923.

65) Holmes, A. *The conservation of the child: a manual of clinical psychology presenting the examination and treatment of backward children.* Philadelphia: Lippincott, 1912.

66) Horrocks, J. E. State certification requirements for school psychologists. *Amer. Psychologist*, 1946, 1, 399–401.

67) Hunt, W. A. Editorial comment. *J. Clin. Psychol.*, 1947, 3, 108–109.

68) Institute for Juvenile Research. *Child guidance procedures, methods and techniques employed at the Institute for Juvenile Research.* New York: Appleton-Century, 1937.

69) Kelly, G. A. A state-supported child guidance clinic for Kansas school children. *Kansas Teach.*, 1936, 43 (June), 6–7.

70) Kinder, E. F. Psychological work at Letchworth Village, Thiells, N. Y. *J. Consult. Psychol.*, 1937, 1, 76–80.

71) Landis, C. Certification of psychologists by the state as contrasted to certification by psychological organizations. *J. Consult. Psychol.*, 1941, 5, 56–58.

72) Link, H. C. Practices and principles of the Psychological Service Center. *J. Consult. Psychol.*, 1938, 2, 149–154.

73) Long, L. Professional status and training of psychologists; report on annual meeting of N.Y.S.A.A.P. *J. Consult. Psychol.*, 1946, 10, 104–108.

74) Louttit, C. M. *Clinical psychology.* New York: Harper, 1936.

75) Louttit, C. M. The Indiana University Psychological Clinics. *Psychol. Rec.*, 1937, 1, 449–458.

76) Louttit, C. M. The place of clinical psychology in mental hygiene. *Ment. Hyg.*, 1937, 21, 373–388.

77) Louttit, C. M. Progress report on psychologists in child guidance

clinics. Unpublished paper presented at the 2nd Annual Meeting of the A.A.A.P., Columbus, Ohio, Sept. 6, 1938.

78) Madden, R. Organization and practices of the psycho-educational clinic in State Teachers Colleges. *Educ. Admin. Super.*, 1937, 23, 707–712.

79) Marquis, D. G. Post-war reemployment prospects in psychology. *Psychol. Bull.*, 1944, 41, 653–663.

80) Marquis, D. G. Proceedings of the Fifty-Fourth Annual Meeting of the American Psychological Association, Inc., Philadelphia, Pennsylvania. *Amer. Psychologist*, 1946, 1, 493–532.

81) Martens, E. H., and Russ, H. Adjustment of behavior problems of school children. *U. S. Off. Educ. Bull.*, 1932, No. 18.

82) Mateer, F. The future of clinical psychology. *J. Delinq.*, 1921, 6, 283–293.

83) Mateer, F. *The unstable child*. New York: Appleton, 1924.

84) McBee, M. A mental-hygiene clinic in a high school. *Ment. Hyg.*, 1935, 19, 238–280.

85) Meehl, P. E., and McClosky, H. Ethical and political aspects of applied psychology. *J. Abnorm. Soc. Psychol.*, 1947, 42, 91–98.

86) Menninger, K. A. Clinical psychology in the psychiatric clinic. *Bull. Menninger Clin.*, 1943, 7, 89–92.

87) Miles, W. R. A year of state certification of psychologists. *Amer. Psychologist*, 1946, 1, 393–394, 401.

88) Morrow, W. R. The development of psychological internship training. *J. Consult. Psychol.*, 1946, 10, 165–183.

89) Murphy, G. *Historical introduction to modern psychology*. New York: Harcourt, Brace, 1929.

90) Nimkoff, M. F. A family guidance clinic. *Social Soc. Res.*, 1934, 18, 229–240.

91) Paterson, D. G., Schneidler, G., and Williamson, E. G. *Student guidance techniques: a handbook for counselors in high schools and colleges*. New York: McGraw-Hill, 1938.

92) Peatman, J. G. Legal certification of psychologists in New York State. *Bull. N. Y. St. Assoc. Appl. Psychol.*, 1947, 10, No. 2, 1, 2.

93) Peters, M. W. What the social worker expects from the psychologist. *Family*, 1934–1935, 15, 179–183.

94) Peterson, J. *Early conceptions and tests of intelligence*. Yonkers, N. Y.: World Book, 1925.

95) Pintner, R. *Intelligence testing*. New York: Holt, 1931.

96) Poffenberger, A. T. The training of a clinical psychologist. *J. Consult. Psychol.*, 1938, 2, 1–6.

97) Poffenberger, A. T. Psychology: academic and professional. *J. Consult. Psychol.*, 1945, 9, 1–7.

98) Regensburg, J. Contribution of the social worker to clinical psychology. *Family*, 1935–1936, 16, 201–205.

99) Richmond, M. E. *What is social case work?* New York: Russell Sage Foundation, 1922.

100) Ridenour, N. A. What can the psychologist offer to the social workers? *Family*, 1934–1935, 15, 173–179.
101) Ridenour, N. A. Notes on the status of clinical psychology. *J. Consult. Psychol.*, 1938, 2, 137–142.
102) Rogers, C. R. Significant aspects of client-centered therapy. *Amer. Psychologist*, 1946, 1, 415–422.
103) Rosenstein, J. L. *Psychology of human relations for executives.* New York: McGraw-Hill, 1936.
104) Rymarkiewiczowa, D. (chm.). Certification of clinical psychologists in Virginia. *J. Clin. Psychol.*, 1946, 2, 308–309.
105) Rymarkiewiczowa, D. (chm.). The certification of clinical psychologists in Virginia. *Amer. Psychologist*, 1946, 1, 395–398.
106) Sadler, W. S. *Theory and practice of psychiatry.* St. Louis: Mosby, 1936.
107) Sangren, P. V. The psycho-educational clinic as an aid to teacher training. *Educ. Admin. Super.*, 1936, 22, 523–527.
108) Sargent, H. Professional ethics and problems of therapy. *J. Abnorm. Soc. Psychol.*, 1945, 40, 47–60.
109) Sears, R. R. Graduate training facilities: I. General information. II. Clinical psychology. *Amer. Psychologist*, 1946, 1, 135–150.
110) Sears, R. R. Clinical training facilities: 1947. *Amer. Psychologist*, 1947, 2, 199–205.
111) Shakow, D. An internship year for psychologists: with special reference to psychiatric hospitals. *J. Consult. Psychol.*, 1938, 2, 73–76.
112) Shakow, D. (chm.). Graduate internship training in psychology. *J. Consult. Psychol.*, 1945, 9, 243–266.
113) Shartle, C. L. Occupations in psychology. *Amer. Psychologist*, 1946, 1, 559–582.
114) Steiner, L. R. *Where do people take their troubles?* Boston: Houghton Mifflin, 1945.
115) Stevenson, G. S., and Smith, G. *Child guidance clinics: a quarter century of development.* New York: Commonwealth Fund, 1934.
116) Strang, R. Criteria of progress in counseling and psychotherapy. *J. Clin. Psychol.*, 1947, 3, 180–183.
117) Super, D. E. Book review of Rogers, C. R., and Wallin, J. L., *Counseling with returned servicemen. J. Appl. Psychol.*, 1946, 3, 565–568.
118) Sutich, A. Toward a professional code for psychological consultants. *J. Abnorm. Soc. Psychol.*, 1944, 39, 329–350.
119) Sylvester, R. H. Clinical psychology adversely criticized. *Psychol. Clin.*, 1913–1914, 7, 182–188.
120) Viteles, M. S. Industry. In Brotemarkle, R. A. (ed.), *Clinical psychology: studies in honor of Lightner Witmer.* Philadelphia: Univ. Pennsylvania Press, 1931. Pp. 117–133.
121) Viteles, M. S. *Industrial psychology.* New York: Norton, 1932.

122) Wallin, J. E. W. Medical and psychological inspection of school children. West. J. Educ., 1909, 2, 434–436.

123) Wallin, J. E. W. The new clinical psychology and the psycho-clinicist. In Wallin, J. E. W., The mental health of the school child. New Haven: Yale Univ. Press, 1914. Pp. 22–120. (Reprint with alterations from: J. Educ. Psychol., 1911, 2, 121–132, 191–210.)

124) Wallin, J. E. W. Clinical psychology: what it is and what it is not. Science, 1913, 37, 895–902.

125) Wallin, J. E. W. The mental health of the school child. New Haven: Yale University Press, 1914.

126) Wallin, J. E. W. The field of the clinical psychologist and the kind of training needed by the psychological examiner. Sch. & Soc., 1919, 9, 463–470.

127) Welsch, E., and Griffin, L. Welfare program includes child guidance as part of State Service. Publ. Welf. Ind., 1938, 48, No. 4, 12.

128) Westburgh, E. M. Introduction to clinical psychology. Philadelphia: Blakiston, 1937.

129) White House Conference on Child Health and Protection. Sect. I. C. Subcommittee on Psychology and Psychiatry. Psychology and psychiatry in pediatrics: the problem. New York: Appleton-Century, 1932.

130) Witmer, L. Practical work in psychology. Pediatrics, 1896, 1, 462–471

131) Witmer, L. The organization of practical work in psychology. Psychol. Rev., 1897, 4, 116–117.

132) Witmer, L. Clinical psychology. Psychol. Clin., 1907, 1, 1–9. (Also in (21), pp. 341–352.)

133) Witmer, L. University courses in psychology. Psychol. Clin., 1907, 1, 25–35.

134) Witmer, L. Courses in psychology at the Summer School of the University of Pennsylvania. Psychol. Clin., 1911, 4, 245–273.

135) Witmer, L. Clinical records. Psychol. Clin., 1915, 9, 1–17.

136) Witmer, L. The relation of intelligence to efficiency. Psychol. Clin., 1915, 9, 61–86.

137) Witmer, L. Diagnostic education—an education for the fortunate few. Psychol. Clin., 1917, 11, 69–78.

138) Witmer, L. Performance and success, an outline of psychology for diagnostic testing and teaching. Psychol. Clin., 1919, 12, 145–170.

139) Witmer, L. Problem of educability. Psychol. Clin., 1919, 12, 174–178.

140) Witmer, L. Efficiency and other factors of success. Psychol. Clin., 1919, 12, 241–247.

141) Witmer, L. Training of very bright children. Psychol. Clin., 1919, 13, 88–96.

142) Witmer, L. Orthogenic cases XIV. Don: a curable case of arrested development due to a fear psychosis, the result of shock in a three-year-old infant. *Psychol. Clin.*, 1920, 13, 97–111.

143) Witmer, L. Intelligence—a definition. *Psychol. Clin.*, 1922, 14, 65–67.

144) Witmer, L. The analytic diagnosis. *Psychol. Clin.*, 1922, 14, 129–135.

145) Witmer, L. What is intelligence and who has it? *Sci. Mon.*, 1922, 15, 57–67.

146) Witmer, L. Psychological diagnosis and the psychonomic orientation of analytic science. *Psychol. Clin.*, 1925, 16, 1–18. (Also in (21), pp. 388–409.)

147) Witty, P. S., and Theman, V. The psycho-educational clinic. *J. Appl. Psychol.*, 1934, 18, 369–392.

148) Wolfle, D. The reorganized American Psychological Association. *Amer. Psychologist*, 1946, 1, 3–6.

149) Woodworth, R. S. The future of clinical psychology. *J. Consult. Psychol.*, 1937, 1, 4–5.

150) Wulfeck, W. H. The program of self-certification in the specialties. *Bull. N. Y. St. Assoc. Appl. Psychol.*, 1947, 10, No. 3, 1, 3.

151) Zilboorg, G. A history of medical psychology. New York: Norton, 1941.

II

The Functions of the Clinical
Psychologist

DAVID WECHSLER

Bellevue Psychiatric Hospital and New York University

The Psychologist in the Psychiatric Hospital[1]

In discussing the place of the psychologist in the psychiatric hospital it will be useful to remember that hospitals called psychiatric may differ considerably both as to setup and function. An important difference to be borne in mind is that between the observation and custodial type of hospital.[2] An observation hospital is one in which patients are referred primarily for diagnosis and are kept only for a minimal amount of time, usually less than two and seldom as much as four weeks, after which they are either discharged or committed to a state institution.[3] An example of an observation hospital is the Psychiatric Division of Bellevue Hospital in New York City. A custodial hospital, on the other hand, is one to which mental patients are committed for an indefinite period for care and treatment. All state (mental) hospitals are of this sort, but many of them also serve as observation hospitals at the same time. An example of a hospital rendering this combined service is the Psychopathic Hospital in Boston, Massachusetts. In addition, some mental hospitals, whether custodial or observation, also have outpatient departments which function in the same way as any general mental hygiene clinic.

The main differences, so far as the psychologist is concerned, be-

---

[1] Reprinted from *Journal of Consulting Psychology*, 1944, 8, 281–285. Copyright 1944 by American Association for Applied Psychology.

[2] In some states, hospitals for mental observation are designated as psychopathic hospitals.

[3] Under a New York State law, effective October 1, 1944, patients may be kept for observation as long as sixty days.

tween working at an observation and a custodial hospital, are that at the observation hospital he will probably have less time for extensive testing, be required to dispose of patients more expeditiously, and in most instances also have less time for research. On the other hand, he will see a much greater variety of cases, including large numbers who are not psychotic; and, in general, he will be able to acquire techniques and training which will be more useful to him in other clinical fields or in private practice. Again, in states where mental care is limited, the psychiatric hospital may be run in conjunction with an institution for mental defectives or a colony for epileptics. In such places the psychologist is frequently called upon to divide his time between psychiatric and other services. The remarks to follow, however, will be confined to the role of the psychologist in hospitals which, whatever their title, concern themselves primarily with diagnosis and care of mental cases.

Duties of Psychologists in Mental Hospitals

In most psychiatric hospitals the primary function of the psychologist is to appraise the patient's intellectual functioning. The psychologist is expected (1) to define, as an expert, the patient's intellectual level and to indicate whether the I.Q. obtained represents the true or merely the present level of functioning; (2) to call attention to the presence of any special abilities or disabilities, particularly as they may be related to, or diagnostic of, the patient's clinical picture. From here on the role of the psychologist varies greatly from institution to institution. In many places he or she is called upon (3) to help in psychiatric diagnosis in terms of psychometric functioning. This may be achieved either by (4) analysis of intelligence test results, or by the use of supplementary test procedures involving special intellectual function or, more increasingly, by the use of (5) personality tests. In the latter instance, the advent of (6) projective techniques, particularly the Rorschach test, has greatly increased the diagnostic role of the psychologist.

In some institutions the psychologist is called upon to take case histories and in still others to interview patients. In such institutions the psychologist may, and generally does, participate in staff conferences on the basis of which the patients are assigned to different wards, and when up for parole and discharge, to offer suggestions as to disposition. In some institutions where vocational and special therapies are available, the psychologist will also be called upon to administer educational and vocational tests, and to make recommendations regarding them. This is true particularly of mental hospitals which have large adolescent and children's wards.

In addition to the above duties, the psychologist in a mental hospital often does a certain amount of teaching either of the institutional staff (nurses and interns) or in connection with the training program of intern psychologists and of psychology students from nearby universities. As regards the latter much can be said in favor of a more intimate tie between psychology departments in universities with mental hospitals as well as mental hygiene clinics. There are, however, a number of factors which tend to retard the association. One of these is that it has tended to be a one-way affair, namely, psychology departments like to send their students for practical work to mental hygiene clinics and hospitals but have been slow in adding members to their staff who have had practical experience in the field. In recent years, however, there has been a growing trend toward appointing psychologists working at the mental hospitals to at least part-time teaching at the university. This is a desirable trend and it is to be hoped that it will increase with time.

Research in Mental Hospitals

Except for institutions which have special research psychologists attached, and these are few, the opportunities for research depend largely upon the initiative and zeal of the individual psychologists working in them. Most of this research has to be done on one's own "free" time, but as the free time in paid positions is relatively small, actual facilities have been correspondingly limited. Nevertheless the amount of research emanating from psychologists working in hospitals has been considerable. Most of it has dealt with psychometrics, particularly intelligence testing of various psychotic groups. Recent examples are studies by Shakow (51),[4] Rabin (43), Jastak (25) and Wittman (71). Another field of psychiatric research by psychologists has been the general problem of mental deterioration (2, 53, 24) and in recent years a considerable number of studies by psychologists in mental hospitals have appeared on the effects of shock treatments in therapies (42, 72, 66).

A field which has been relatively neglected, however, is that deal-

---

[4] Bibliography begins on page 176.

ing with sensation and perception. Interestingly enough, the most original work done in this realm has been done by psychiatrists and neurologists (45, 5, 21). One of the main reasons for this is the limited training which most psychologists going into work in mental hospitals have received in advanced experimental and physiological psychology. The emphasis of recent years has been on psychometrics and statistics and while both of these are important, particularly the former, original work is more likely to be produced by individuals who have had thorough grounding in the basic psychological facts and processes than in applied specialized courses.

Relation of the Psychologist to Members of the Psychiatric Staff

As aforementioned, the role of the psychologist varies widely in different hospitals and opportunity for professional contact with other staff members likewise varies. In some places the psychiatrist prefers to look upon the psychologist as a technician. The psychiatrist wants an I.Q. report very much as he would call for a blood Wassermann or an electroencephalogram. Most clinical psychologists do not like either the restricted type of work or the status implied by this type of position. Many positions that are available in mental hospitals call for routine psychometrics and a certain percentage of psychologists wishing experience in psychiatric hospitals must expect this type of work, at least at the beginning. It is, however, equally true that psychiatrists in many places are learning that psychologists have more to offer. Any thorough psychological report makes this apparent to the psychiatrist. This is almost inevitable, as in most psychiatric cases the subject's I.Q. is just one of the factors, and often not the most significant one, for the appraisal of the patient's problem. It is here that the supplementary and special diagnostic techniques have served to reveal the special contributions which the psychologist can make to the understanding of the total problem. It is not an uncommon experience now to hear the psychiatrist inquire, "Does the patient show mental deterioration?" or, "Does he show a schizophrenic pattern?" and so forth instead of just asking, "What is his I.Q.?"

Scope of the Psychological Examination

What should be the scope of a psychological examination in a mental hospital is a problem which is not easily solved. The difficulty resides not only in the fact that the psychologist is called upon to do a variety of jobs; but also in the fact that the psychological techniques as presently developed are very time consuming. Consider, for example, what might constitute a relatively modest testing program, say for subjects aged 15–30. This would ordinarily include (1) an individual general intelligence test; (2) a personality inventory; and (3) a short battery of educational tests.

The time required for such an examination in the case of mental patients will ordinarily take about two hours, not counting write-up of the report and analysis. If to these latter, one adds as is often desirable—a projective technique such as a Rorschach or Thematic Apperception test, plus some tests attempting vocational appraisal, the time required for a complete study is easily doubled. This means that a psychologist can see at most one patient a day, a situation which even if feasible is not only too costly but also contrary to the time consumed by other professions in their examinations. Psychiatrists and physicians, even if not complaining, are continually asking why a psychologist needs so long a time to do an examination. At present this problem is met in part by having an intern or graduate student do some of the routine testing and in part by cutting down the testing program to a bare minimum. A more satisfactory approach would be the development of shorter examination techniques and the increasing use of the diagnostic interview. Unfortunately neither is as yet available to any considerable degree.

Training of the Psychologist

The training of the psychologist planning to work in a mental hospital setup varies in different parts of the country. Generally this variation depends not so much upon theoretical ideals as upon practical opportunities. In most cases the young psychologist is not guided but allowed to drift into this field. Very few universities offer a program preparing the student for a job as psychologist in a mental hospital.

Some part training, however, is often afforded by work at psycho-educational clinics which are now attached to a number of colleges and education departments in various parts of the country. Other areas for practical instruction are state and municipal employment and vocational services. But apart from these most of the specific training of psychologists hoping to enter the psychiatric field is being achieved through internships that have been established at various mental hospitals. These internships are usually for six months to a year and carry a very small, if any, stipend beyond general maintenance. In this respect they resemble the medical internships except that the psychology students are often less pre-pared to begin full-time work than are medical interns. Usually the psychological intern will require considerable elementary instruction in the administration of most of the standard tests, acquaintance with which is likely to have been more theoretical than actual. Such examinations as are done by the intern on patients are usually done under supervision of the psychologist-in-charge. Cases are gone over and considerable attention is paid not only to interpretation of re-sults but to the proper ways of writing up a psychological report. As in other fields, the intern will often have to do a bit of un-learning.

This brings us to a consideration of the desired preparatory cur-riculum for students going into mental hospital work while at the university. It would be easy to list the types of courses by title but obviously what is important is what the course actually consists of rather than under what title it appears in the catalogue. For ex-ample, all recommendations would include as prerequisite a course in abnormal psychology. But if the course in abnormal psychology only includes the reading of a general text and instruction by a person who has never had contact with mental patients, its value would be very limited. The point here is, of course, that the training of people preparing for psychological work in mental hospitals as well as clinical psychology in general, should be by individuals actually in the field. This holds for other applied subjects.

Apart from the introductory courses in general and an elementary course in experimental psychology, the most important preparatory courses are undoubtedly those in psychometrics. By psychometrics is meant not a theoretical discussion of tests and techniques but actual mastery of the administration and evaluation of standard clinical tests. Second, a course in the interpretation of results and instruction in report writing. Third, a course in abnormal psychology given in conjunction with a mental hospital or mental hygiene clinic. Courses in child development, and subject disabilities are desirable. So also is a course on projective techniques, especially the Rorschach. For those planning to go into research, advanced experimental, statistics and physiological psychology should be added.

In addition to his educational training the student planning to enter the field of clinical psychology should also meet a number of personality requirements. These requirements include first, emotional maturity; second, an ability to deal with and get along with people; third, an ability to utilize one's formal knowledge in practical situations. In addition, one might add a facility to express oneself clearly in writing. This is perhaps a good deal to ask for a position which generally pays less than college teaching, but the requirements are indispensable not only because they are necessary for the personal success of the individual psychologist but for the prestige of psychology itself. In more ways than one the psychologist in the field represents the practical achievements of psychology, and the individuals to whom this representation is entrusted should so far as possible be the most capable individuals available.

HELEN M. CAMPBELL

Mental Hygiene Service of the Ray Clinic, New York Regional Office,
Veterans Administration

The Role of the Clinical Psychologist in a Veterans Administration Mental Hygiene Clinic[1]

The New York Veterans Administration Mental Hygiene Clinic opened on May 10, 1946. Within the first few days several hundred patients sought admission to the clinic for treatment and through subsequent months about forty to fifty new patients were requesting treatment each day. The necessity of a continued increase in staff, space, equipment, and expansion of special activities retarded the expected rate of achievement of smooth organization and stabilization of procedures. Initially, only general principles and policies were established pertaining to such matters as handling of patients and delineation of the role of the various professional groups; specific procedures and most implementing details were left to be determined pragmatically. This tentative approach proved comfortably conducive to the rather constant, and usually unforeseen, changes necessary during the shake-down period which will probably characterize the first year.

The work of the clinical psychologist will be described as presently in operation, though, as suggested by the overwhelming demand for out-patient psychiatric treatment, techniques for the handling of large numbers of patients simultaneously may have to be developed in the future.

[1] Reprinted from *Journal of Clinical Psychology*, 1947, 3, 15–21. Copyright 1947 by Frederick C. Thorne.

Diagnosis. Team relationship between psychiatric social workers, clinical psychologists and neuropsychiatrists is emphasized as essential. A feeling of collaboration is promulgated, each professional group maintaining an equal attitude of responsibility for the patient. Social workers and psychologists are in no sense merely technical assistants to psychiatrists: they do not wait to see a patient by referral from a psychiatrist, and they assume full responsibility for a patient so long as the patient is in their charge.

A patient who comes into the clinic for the first time is directed immediately by the receptionist to the Admitting Room where he is interviewed briefly by a social worker and a psychiatrist. Two objectives are accomplished in this screening interview. An initial impression is gotten of the patient's difficulties and presenting symptoms, so that he may be assigned to the proper examining psychiatrist in the clinic, or it is determined that he should be sent to one of the several private clinics in New York which has a contract with the Veterans Administration to treat veterans. A patient admitted here for treatment is seen the same day by an examining psychiatrist if his condition is serious, or if not, given the earliest possible appointment on a subsequent day. While it is considered desirable that all patients next be seen by a social worker and psychologist so that each of these workers can contribute in his respective area to the total diagnostic picture, this has not been possible, because of the overwhelming load, and because the number of psychiatrists on the staff has so far been in excess of the number of social workers and psychologists. When the clinic is fully staffed, there will be one psychologist to one psychiatrist to two social workers. Psychologists have been primarily collaborating in the diagnostic work-up of patients referred from Advisement and Guidance Division with a question of present medical feasibility for vocational rehabilitation or prior treatment in the clinic, of patients under consideration for electro-shock treatment, and of patients being studied by the resident psychiatrists.

The contribution of the psychologist toward the total diagnostic picture consists in offering information relevant to the following main questions: (a) Does the patient show mental or personality deviations? (b) If so, what is their significance for determining the nature and degree of the patient's illness? (c) What psychogenic factors appear to be contributing to the patient's illness? (d) What steps should be taken in treatment? In his effort to answer these questions, the psychologist has available (a) the social, psychiatric and medical history, (b) reports of psychiatric examination, and (c) medical, neurological, and laboratory reports. He then examines the patient through informal interview and through the use of whatever diagnostic tests are required to answer, with a fair degree of assurance, the broad diagnostic questions or other special problems pertinent to the case under consideration. In order to maintain an acceptable standard of validity, the psychology staff has agreed on a minimum battery of tests for use, generally, with each patient. Since deviations in test performance must be observed as a differential pattern if they are to have fullest significance for answering the diagnostic problems, it follows that many areas of functioning must be observed in order that significant patterns of deviation emerge with fair validity.

The minimum battery of tests used in the examination of a patient consists of: Wechsler-Bellevue, Rorschach, Thematic Apperception Test, and a Projective Sentence Completion Test. There are occasionally exceptions when less than the battery is used, when, for example, patients are examined on a consultation basis and are not to be admitted for treatment in the clinic. Also, of course, very often testing beyond the battery is desirable, for example, the Goldstein-Scheerer or Bender Gestalt and other tests may be used if there is suggestive but not conclusive evidence of organic deterioration revealed on the other tests.

After the psychologist concludes his examination of the patient he writes an interpretation of the findings oriented toward the problems of diagnosis, prognosis, dynamics, and recommendations for treatment. There is then an informal conference with the psychiatrist and social worker who have collaborated in the diagnostic work-up to discuss the total findings and to agree on the appropriate steps in treatment.

For the purpose of emphasizing the exact role of the psychologist as a collaborator on the diagnostic team, a brief amplification of the principles implied by the foregoing description of procedure is offered. The psychologist is neither a technical (or laboratory) assistant to the psychiatrist, nor is he a consultant on special psychological problems deemed emergent during examination by the psychiatrist or social worker and posed by them to the psychologist for specific solution. As technical assistant or special consultant, the psychologist unnecessarily restricts his investigation to spheres far short of what he is in actuality able to accomplish. Moreover, he is almost certain either to arrive at conclusions unwarranted on the basis of his narrow approach, or report only very tentative findings frequently inappropriately utilized by the social worker or psychiatrist. In addition, the particular questions posed by the psychiatrist or social worker may turn out to be not the most crucial. In the interest of contributing to the full limit of which he is capable and of achieving optimal validity, the psychologist considers himself responsible for properly investigating all psychological functions (as distinguished from somatic) which may conceivably have bearing on the case of the patient to be treated. It is in this sense that the psychologist is a collaborator with the other professional groups forming the mental hygiene team.

In addition to the informal diagnostic conferences already mentioned, there are three regularly scheduled seminars each week where a case is presented by a resident psychiatrist. The social worker and psychologist who have collaborated in the diagnostic work on the patient present their findings. These are essentially teaching seminars, and they provide an opportunity for the exchange of ideas; in addition to those regularly attending as students or teachers, other members of the staff attend from time to time.

There are, also, two formally constituted diagnostic boards with psychologists as participating members. One is the Electro-shock Board which must review and approve all patients recommended for electro-shock therapy. A psychologist serves on this Board. He furnishes a thorough psychological work-up on each patient to be presented to the Board and participates in the discussion re presence of criteria which have been established to govern suitability of a patient for electro-shock. Another board in which a psychologist participates is the Medical Rehabilitation Board. This is an intramural board receiving patients who need total rehabilitation: medical, occupational and psychiatric. All patients who have been declared infeasible for vocational re-training by some division in the Veterans Administration are received by this diagnostic board. If infeasibility is established then treatment objectives are planned to render the patient ultimately feasible for vocational training. The Board is composed of doctors and other personnel from the Advisement and Guidance Division, Education and Training Division, Medical Rehabilitation Service and Mental Hygiene Service. Many of the patients appearing before this Board show the residuals of organic brain damage. The psychologist who serves on this Board collaborates with the psychiatrist from our clinic on the diagnostic problem. The Board meets twice weekly. The psychologist attends and participates in the total discussion.

Psychotherapy. Psychologists participate in both group psychotherapy and individual psychotherapy under the supervision of a qualified staff psychiatrist. In group therapy, the psychologist may act as the leader with a psychiatrist and social worker collaborating to form a team endeavor. The social worker is present during sessions to answer any questions which may arise in his area and to be ready to solve, concurrently, on an individual basis, any therapeutic problems that may be revealed in the environmental area. The psychiatrist acts as a general consultant, answers any medical questions, and is ready to arrange individual treatment sessions for patients as such need occurs. Group psychotherapy is variable in approach, depending on the composition of the group, and because it is regarded in general as still in the experimental stage. It may consist of mental hygiene talks to patients with mild somatization reactions and may be supportive, informative and inspirational, or it may involve active patient participation where a patient ventilates his problems to others in the group, receives their comments and attempts at interpretation, and has recourse to the therapist for only a minimum of information or interpretation. Visual aids are employed, particularly in explaining the relation between emotions and somatization reactions. In group therapy, the utilization of audio-visual aids will be greatly expanded in the future. Dr. Elias Katz, who has recently joined the psychology staff, is interested in work in this area, and has described his audio-visual aids program in another paper in this journal.

Through the cooperation of the American Woman's Voluntary Hospital Corps it has been possible to provide various adjuncts to group therapy: dances, and picnics are arranged frequently for patients. The psychologist takes an active part in planning and participating in these socialization and recreational projects. While we have not yet explored the use of psychodrama, we intend to do so just as soon as our theatre is completed. Group therapy sessions are recorded by sound recording equipment. This provides the means for a critical review of each session and for obtaining clues to guide subsequent sessions into the most productive channels. It provides information about patients for the use of the therapist who may be carrying the patient on an individual treatment level concurrently or subsequently. It also provides a teaching medium for the psychologist through self-criticism and consultative advice from a more experienced group therapist.

Psychologists carry out, under the supervision of a qualified psychiatrist, individual psychotherapy with patients who have minor or superficial psychoneurotic problems or problems in reeducation of habits, such as speech retraining. Each psychologist carries four or five such patients.

Research. Plans have been projected for research programs involving a cooperative endeavor with psychiatrists, and for research more exclusively in psychology concerning such problems as the development, refinement or validation of testing techniques. Two large problems of the first type are well under way, and a third problem has been formulated by one of the psychiatrists and is at present awaiting a psychologist who has time and interest to collaborate. One problem being studied is that of convulsive disorders. The psychologist is studying the psychological concomitants, and personality structure, before and after adequate treatment, and the psychiatrist is interested in EEG correlatives, and in the development and refinement of new treatments and an evaluation of their relative efficacy. Another cooperative research endeavor is in the study of patients before and after electro-shock treatment. The psychiatrist and social worker are concerned with adequate evaluation .of emotional and social adjustment subsequent to treatment. The psychologist is interested in evaluating particular and relatively circumscribed mental and personality changes, such as memory, affect, attitudes, etc. A comprehensive program in the study of patients whose major or presenting symptom is headache has been recently started by one of the psychiatrists and he is eager to have the collaboration of psychologists on the study.

Several staff psychologists intend to complete their doctoral dissertations through the use of research opportunities provided at the clinic. This will benefit their own professional advancement and at the same time promote the progress of knowledge essential to continued improvement of medical services for veterans. Rich research opportunities are available to the graduate student trainees and it is expected that more research will be under way eventually, by them, and by regular staff members.

The psychologist is frequently better trained than the psychiatrist in rigorous experimental procedures and, hence, can contribute effectively not only in adequately designing and carrying through his own projects, but can assist in insuring careful experimental design on cooperative projects, or even serve to advise on research procedures being conducted exclusively by psychiatrists, and on the gathering, collating, and analysing of statistical data.

Teaching. Responsibilities in teaching involve continued in-service training for psychologists on the staff, participation in the teaching program for resident psychiatrists, and specifically, the clinical teaching of psychology interns.

We have felt it essential to preserve two hours a week for a psychology staff seminar largely devoted to matters of a nature to promote our professional improvement. The subjects discussed in these seminars rotate among (a) diagnostic analysis of cases selected to demonstrate relatively obscure problems, (b) problems in therapy, (c) reports from the literature, and (d) reports on research in progress. Because of considerable initial differences between us in experience with certain psychological techniques, much time has been profitably spent in learning from each other in seminar discussion and also in informal consultation whenever the need arose.

Psychologists participate in teaching of resident psychiatrists by giving lectures, by taking part in case presentation seminars, and by informal discussion and dissemination of information whenever particular questions are raised.

There are eleven graduate students from three universities who are receiving intern training in psychological practice at the clinic. They vary widely in level of academic training and in experience. For this reason it was necessary to set up training objectives for each one individually. After an intern's background had been analysed and evaluated, specific training objectives were established for each. Training objectives are divided into the following three general classes:

(a) Development of satisfactory psychologist-patient relationships and of clinical sense or judgment. While progress in this area is continuous and develops in proportion to the number of different types examined, there are certain experiences which more particularly emphasize this objective. These are, chiefly, the development of interviewing techniques and of case history taking, and some formal training in clinical psychiatry through demonstration, discussion, presentation of typical case histories, and other adjuncts.

(b) Development of team relationship with social workers and psychiatrists. This objective is attained through familiarization with the approach and techniques of these workers and through active participation in team endeavor. Social workers and psychiatrists have cooperated in the teaching program to the fullest extent, providing lectures, discussions, demonstrations of such neuropsychiatric techniques as electroshock, electroencephalography, narcosynthesis, neurological examinations, etc. Teaching case seminars are held where there is collaboration between social workers, psychiatrists and psychologists in diagnostic conference on individual patients.

(c) Development of the specific techniques used by psychologists in both diagnosis and psychotherapy. The emphasis is placed on intensive training in a few major techniques, with the gaining of familiarity with others. Each intern is assigned to a supervising staff psychologist. The intern collaborates with the supervising psychologist on examination of a patient and carries out that part of the diagnostic process in which he has been, or is being, trained. Or, if he is at a stage of experience where he can handle the total diagnostic problem, he has full charge of the patient under only general supervision. In addition to constant teaching and discussion by the supervising psychologist, there are case seminars attended by all the interns and several of the staff psychologists, also, frequently by one of the special consultants in psychology. Specific training in psychotherapy comes only when an intern has achieved considerable skill in other areas. He must first have a thorough acquaintance with approaches and techniques from the theoretical point of view. He begins with observation (through one-way screens) of the performance of others, and his first assignment of a patient is, naturally, one involving only superficial handling. By the time he is ready for formal training in psychotherapy considerable experience has already been gained informally incidental to his other relationships with patients.

Teaching devices, not always available in the past, are used to major advantage. These are one-way screens, sound recording equipment, and audio-visual aids. For example, training in psychotherapy, whether group or individual, is aided remarkably by having an exact recording of all sessions for subsequent review, criticism, and guidance.

Summary

The work of the clinical psychologist in a Veterans Administration Mental Hygiene Clinic in operation for several months has been described. Plans formulated on the basis of a regulated admission rate have not met the realistic situation of an overwhelming number requesting treatment, and of an unfavorable proportion of psychologists to psychiatrists. The psychology staff has been increased three-fold since the clinic opened but there is naturally a limit to help in this direction. Psychologists have from the beginning engaged in the functions of diagnosis, therapy, research and teaching. These four functions have been described in some detail. We have considered our primary function that of aid in diagnosis and have to date preserved adequate standards to insure optimum validity in this service but at present are failing to handle the large patient load. It appears probable that sufficient professional personnel to examine and treat by traditional methods will not be obtainable. This situation is almost certainly not unique in this clinic nor in other clinics treating veterans. There is a probability that in the future clinical methods of diagnosis will have to be somewhat curtailed and the expedient of group testing explored. Until the patient load drops considerably, group therapy will have to be the primary method in therapy with many therapists participating. It may be regarded as a challenge to both psychologists and psychiatrists.

JOHN G. DARLEY

University of Minnesota

DONALD G. MARQUIS

University of Michigan

Veterans' Guidance Centers: A Survey of Their Problems and Activities[1]

The guidance centers operated by universities and colleges under contract with the Veterans Administration will carry considerable responsibility for the rehabilitation and readjustment of service personnel in the transition to civilian life. Since this responsibility is in part discharged by use of a wide range of psychological methods generally subsumed under the term "guidance" it is appropriate to review the clinic programs as examples of professional psychology in action. In May, 1945, and again in October, 1945, the *Office of Psychological Personnel* conducted a questionnaire survey of contract clinics listed by the Veterans Administration. Some of the results of that survey are reported herewith.

A general description of the contractual arrangements is pertinent to an understanding of the study. The institution contracts to provide either testing services alone, or testing and counseling services, to individual veterans referred by a regional office of the Veterans Administration. The contract may include provision for the housing and feeding of the clients during the testing or counseling process.

[1] From the *Office of Psychological Personnel*, Washington, D. C. The authors gratefully acknowledge the assistance of Lt. C. C. Bennett, USNR and Mrs. Jane D. Morgan in both the tabulations and the procedures of the survey. Reprinted from *Journal of Clinical Psychology*, 1946, 2, 109–116. Copyright 1946 by Frederick C. Thorne.

Applicants for vocational rehabilitation under Public Law 16 (disability cases) and for education or training under The Servicemen's Readjustment Act, Public Law 346 (the 'G. I. Bill') are referred to the center by the appropriate regional office of the Veterans Administration. The guidance center makes its reports on prescribed forms, and in the case of full counseling services, the educational-vocational plans are reviewed with advisors and training officers of the Veterans Administration.[2]

The individuals referred to the centers represent only part of the

TABLE 1. Classification by Institutional Enrollment of All Centers with Contracts Approved Through September 1945, and Tabulation of Respondents to OPP Questionnaire Survey

1943–44 Enrollment	Centers: Contracts Approved to 5/45	Respondents to 5/45 Survey*	Centers: Contracts Approved 5/45 to 10/45	Additional Respondents to 10/45 Survey*	Total Centers	Total Respondents
Below 1000.........	26	12	31	4	57	16
1000–2000..........	16	9	11	1	27	10
2000–5000..........	21	14	9	1	30	15
5000–6000..........	5	2	0	0	5	2
Above 6000........	14	8	8	1	22	9
No data...........	3	1	7	2	10	3

* An additional 20 centers in May and 5 in October replied to the OPP letter, but stated they were not in operation at those dates.

guidance load actually carried by the Veterans Administration. Advisement and training officers in hospitals, in regional offices, or in sub-regional offices will still deal with large numbers of men and women who need this service in order to return to satisfactory civilian status. The guidance center is the method adopted by the Veterans Administration to augment and improve its guidance services by seeking the most competent assistance the colleges and universities can provide. While the Veterans Administration still needs hundreds of trained individuals in professional classifications for counsel-

---

[2] Detailed procedures are described in the *Manual of Advisement and Guidance*, by Ira D. Scott (47). This is the official procedural and policy reference.

ing work, it has recognized the impossibility of carrying the full load of guidance within its own structure and is seeking, through the contract plan, to extend its services and to guarantee that an adequate professional job will be done. It is in this setting that psychology must view the programs of the guidance centers.

Table 1 classifies all institutions holding contracts by 1943–44 enrollment figures; it also includes a tabulation of the centers replying to the questionnaire survey. Enrollment size is used here as a crude index of the probable adequacy of psychological services available at the institution, both in terms of staff and past experience with guidance programs at the institutional or community level. If it is assumed that the larger institutions are in a better position to provide adequate services of a professional nature, the heavy concentration of clinics in smaller institutions (below 2000 enrollment) does not augur well for the level of professional services. The contracts have in part been approved on a criterion of population coverage, but population coverage and the problem of competent services may not be reconcilable.

Qualifications of Personnel. Another aspect of this situation may be seen in an analysis of the institutional personnel employed by the guidance centers. The 55 centers submitting replies listed approximately 225 full-time or part-time staff members doing either counseling or psychometric work for veterans. The names of these staff members were checked against the most recent *American Psychological Association* directory and the most recent membership list of the *American College Personnel Association*. Table 2 indicates the professional connections of the 210 people who could be traced from the identification given:

TABLE 2. Professional Connections of Guidance Center Personnel, Full-Time and Part-Time

	Counselors	Psychometrists	Total
Total Number...............	132	78	210
Member, APA..............	13	1	14
Associate, APA..............	22	8	30
Member, ACPA.............	3	0	3
Number with connection.....	38	9	47
% with connection...........	29%	12%	22%

In general, it appears that the personnel assigned to work with veterans are not closely associated with the field of psychology, using the APA membership requirements as a guide.

Since so many of the guidance centers are expanding and currently using part-time staff in the absence of full-time employees, the data on professional staff were adjusted to a full-time basis whenever possible in order to give a clearer picture of staff in relation to case load. For the 48 centers in which this adjustment was possible, approximately 142 full-time staff members are operating. Data regarding degrees obtained were accurate enough in 118 cases employed by 34 clinics to permit tabulation. Table 3 shows the result:

TABLE 3.   Educational Attainments of Guidance Center Personnel, Based on Adjusted Full-Time Professional Staff

	Counselors		Psychometrists		Total	
	N	%	N	%	N	%
Ph.D. or Ed.D......	16	19	0	..	16	14
M.A...............	42	49	11	34	53	45
B.A...............	27	31	17	53	44	37
No degree..........	1	..	4	12	5	4

The modal class of degree is the Master's in these data. At the psychometric level, the bachelor's degree is typically the highest degree reached. In establishing the college contract services, the Veterans Administration hoped that they would become centers for the professional training of additional counselors. Although graduate student enrollment is still much below pre-war levels, some of the guidance centers in the larger universities have begun to make effective use of advanced students as paid interns or assistants. This practice affects the figures given above on the educational level of staff employees.

Another approximation to the quality of services likely to be found in the guidance centers is afforded by the institution's past experiences with personnel and counseling procedures. One item of the questionnaire asked if testing and counseling services were available to people other than veterans. Forty-seven of the replies were in the affirmative. A follow-up question called for the number of years 'such organized counseling services' had been available. Thirty-seven of the clinics specified the number of years and the average number of years for this group was 9.8. In the main, however, the 'organized counseling services' referred to were student advisory programs which are known to vary widely in coverage and professional adequacy, all the way from a compulsory faculty advisory program for freshmen to the highly centralized technical services of some of the larger universities.

A composite picture of this sample would show the modal center operated by an institution whose student enrollment is under 2000. The center presently employs approximately four part-time workers, or three full-time workers; in this latter adjustment, two of the staff members are counselors and one is a psychometrist. The counselors will ordinarily have the master's degree, and the psychometrist will have the bachelor's degree. Usually the professional staff will not hold membership in the APA or in the ACPA, but they will be attached to institutions claiming about ten years of experience with some level of organized counseling services. The typical charge per case in those centers doing both testing and counseling is twenty dollars billed to the Veterans Administration. No such picture can do justice to the range or variability among the respondents in this study; it is generally true, for example, that the bigger schools have more, and more experienced, personnel assigned to this function. It is further true that the serious shortage of trained personnel has thrown the burden on institutional staffs, with whatever part-time arrangements can be worked out locally or whatever personnel can be found in the labor market.

Case Loads. Analysis of the case load is based on figures reported for the month preceding the receipt of the questionnaire. These figures do not necessarily reflect typical or ultimate loads; they tend to represent the size of operations near the start of the contract relationship. For 36 centers doing both testing and counseling, the average case load in the preceding month is as follows:

Number of veterans tested................ 43.1
Number of veterans interviewed............ 57.5
Number of veterans counseled............. 61.4

The above averages are markedly influenced by the presence of 4 guidance centers in urban areas with large staffs. In each of these cases, the loads were above 100 for the preceding month, and are not typical of the remaining respondents. For example, the averages resulting after the elimination of these four clinics are as follows:

> Number of veterans tested................... 33
> Number of veterans interviewed 44
> Number of veterans counseled 39

Total returns in this study were insufficient to permit a breakdown of the results by size or type of center, but as may be seen in Table 1, the sample that replied is somewhat overweighted toward institutions with enrollment from 2000 and up. The results need to be interpreted with this sampling bias in mind. For 13 centers doing testing only, with no counseling responsibility, the average number of veterans tested was 27.9.

Among the 36 centers carrying on both testing and counseling, 12 make an administrative separation between their veterans' service and their regular clinic program for students and others in their community. Thus 24 of the clinics have a distributed case load covering both veterans and other student or community groups. Twenty of these 24 provided usable figures regarding proportions of service load represented by veterans and by other cases. For these 20 centers, the services to veterans represented approximately 60 per cent of the work, and services to students and other groups represented approximately 40 per cent of the work. Since the institutions reporting these consolidated loads tend to be the smaller institutions, it appears that the work with veterans had come to loom larger than any service to local students. If the local personnel program is strong it is doubtful that services to veterans would exceed services to regularly enrolled students; these data may, therefore, represent another indirect check on the status of the personnel program in the institution maintaining the contract with the Veterans Administration.

Testing Programs. Forty-eight of the centers reported the number of tests used per case in the work with the veterans. No difference in the resultant averages appears between the clinics doing testing only and those doing both testing and counseling. The average for the 48 reporting was 4.95 tests per case. In a supplementary question calling for the names of tests that had proved most valuable in the various areas of behavior, 51 clinics named a variety of tests as follows:

17 tests of general academic ability
17 tests of educational achievement
5 tests of vocational interests
16 tests of personality
30 tests of specific aptitudes

Using the base figure of 51 clinics as the denominator, it is possible to index the most frequently mentioned tests by percentage of times mentioned. The results are given in Table 4.

TABLE 4. Incidence of Use of Various Tests in Testing of Veterans

	% Index
General Ability:	
The Otis Series...............................	73
Bellevue-Wechsler............................	69
American Council Psychological....................	67
Ohio State Psychological..........................	37
Educational Achievement:	
The Cooperative Test Service Series................	59
United States Armed Forces Institute Tests..........	38
Iowa Placement and Achievement Tests.............	27
Stanford Achievement Tests......................	24
Vocational Interest:	
Kuder Preference Record.........................	94
Strong Vocational Interest Blank..................	67
Personality:	
Minnesota Multiphasic Inventory..................	55
Bell Adjustment Inventory........................	35
Bernreuter Personality Inventory..................	29
Special Aptitude:	
Minnesota Vocational Tests for Clerical Workers......	61
Bennett Mechanical Comprehension Test............	53
Revised Minnesota Paper Form Board..............	43
Minnesota Spatial Relations Test..................	37
Detroit Mechanical Aptitude (MacQuarrie)..........	27
O'Connor Finger-Tweezer Dexterity Test............	43
Purdue Pegboard................................	39
Minnesota Rate of Manipulation Tests..............	29
Meier-Seashore Art Judgment Test.................	22

These are the tests most likely to appear in the group of 5 given on the average to each veteran referred for service. With the exception of the special achievement tests developed for the United States Armed Forces Institute they are in general the same measures that would be used with any young adult population. The significant problems—kinds of norms used and skill in interpretation of results —unfortunately cannot be probed at this time from the results of the questionnaire study.

Administrative Problems. The last broad area of the questionnaire survey dealt with the kinds of problems and attitudes encountered in the day-to-day work with veterans. Questions on these topics were generally in free-response form and the replies have been roughly classified for the frequency counts given below. Since case work of the contract clinic doing counseling must receive the final approval of officials of the Veterans Administration, the possibility that educational or vocational objectives first recommended may not be accepted by VA representatives exists. However, in response to a specific question on this topic, the 41 centers doing full counseling state that such cases are few or non-existent. Generally speaking, VA advisers and training officers are accepting the plans that the individual veteran works out with the guidance center counselor.

To a general question regarding the kinds of conflicts experienced with local Veterans Administration personnel, either stationed at the center or in the regional office, 31 centers indicated that relations were generally harmonious and straightforward. Twenty-three of the respondents itemized 41 complaints that fall approximately in 12 categories. The relationships cited with a frequency of four or higher as conflict situations are as follows:

	Frequency of Mention
1. Inadequately trained VA personnel assigned	8
2. Too much emphasis on records and forms	6
3. Poor scheduling of case load or erratic load	6
4. Insufficient time for case work	4
5. Poor liaison with VA training officers	4
6. Legal and procedural aspects of service poorly defined	4

The remaining complaints are too scattered to present any particular pattern.

A general question regarding conflicts in the community was used on the assumption that many local agencies are being set up to help

the returning veteran and that such multiplicity of service may breed
conflict and jurisdictional squabbles. Thirty-seven of the respondents
indicated no community conflicts in their work. Seventeen centers
had specific problems in the community setting, and they are
classified as follows:

Frequency
of Mention
1. Too many agencies acting for the veteran.................... 3
2. Misleading or unrealistic advice given by community agencies.... 9
3. Competition or non-cooperation among agencies............... 4
4. Community lack of understanding of function of contract clinic... 4
5. Lack of neuropsychiatric referral service..................... 1

There is some likelihood that these community problems will
multiply as greater numbers of veterans return to their homes and
as the employment problems and living problems become more
pressing. So far the guidance centers have not suffered from community criticism or conflict, but they are in a position to suffer
criticism if the situation in any locality becomes bad.

Free responses to a question regarding the attitudes of individual
service men and women indicate no great difficulties; 44 respondents
specifically state that the attitudes of the veterans indicate appreciation for the services of the guidance center, whereas only 2 of the
clinics find unfavorable attitudes toward the testing and counseling
service. Twenty replies mention the lack of any antagonism towards
civilians, while only one clinic finds this antagonistic attitude.
Among 17 replies classifiable as bearing on individual levels of motivation, 15 state that the veteran is well motivated toward the
problems of readjustment.

On one count the replies are less favorable: 27 centers mention
the nature of the plans the veterans hope to carry out, and of these
27, 18 replies indicate that the veterans are considering unrealistic
or impractical goals in terms of their own abilities and interests. No
great opposition seems to be encountered in setting up more realistic
goals, however.

No claim can be made that this particular survey is sufficiently
intensive to elicit all the problems involved in the contract relations
between institutions and the Veterans Administration as they both
embark upon a significant social experiment. The legal recognition
and status given to guidance by these arrangements and by the
legislation which brought them into being represent a serious chal-

lenge to psychologists in this specialty. To make sure that the job is properly done, at least two types of investigation are necessary; a field study, probably by the VA itself, of the men and women who have been served at the guidance centers; a continuing and more intensive study of the operations of the clinics by personnel of competence in the techniques of guidance. But pending such investigations, this interim report supplies some basis of generalization.

Summary

This report does not reflect an encouraging outlook regarding the services of psychologists in this program. When the VA turned to the colleges and universities for help, many institutions responded and more will probably accept contracts. But in the main the operating staff seems to have minimum training in the psychological specialties basic to good guidance work. The institutions under contract are experienced primarily in smaller-scale personnel programs for their own students and the VA load even now is running ahead of the local load from which sound clinical experiences are derived. Although the conflicts and problems faced to date are not excessively difficult, the service loads giving rise to these problems have not yet reached a maximum figure. Increased service loads will require additional staff member appointments, but the source of new staff members is questionable, since colleges, Civil Service and industry are bidding for the same types of personnel.

Again it appears that psychology is being called upon to supply more persons than are available. This is not the first time; during the war years this was also true and the small supply of trained people did yeoman service in many areas. The shortage will continue to exist until graduate schools start to make up the deficit of recent years. But even with the possibility of increased graduate enrollments the emergency is immediate and the job of assisting in reconversion must be done now. To meet the need, personnel of more or less tenuous connection with psychology will have to be employed, even though the success or failure of the work will be charged primarily to psychology as a profession. Thus it is incumbent upon psychologists to concern themselves with the guidance center program of the Veterans Administration, and to assist in any way possible in the task that faces these centers.

W. MASON MATHEWS

Merrill-Palmer School, Chicago, Illinois

Scope of Clinical Psychology in Child Guidance[1]

The role of clinical psychology in child guidance is not consistent from one area to another. At no time is there a very clear delimitation of the psychologist's function. His duties may range from those of a psychometrist, responsible only for the administration of tests, to the full responsibility in psychological areas for diagnosis, planning, therapy, research, community education, and all that these imply. At present it is difficult to determine at what point between these two extremes any given psychologist can and should function.

Perhaps some of the difficulty is due to the unawareness on the part of related professions of what clinical psychology has to offer. However, it seems more likely to assume that it is due chiefly, first, to the clinical psychologist's own slowness in recognizing and accepting his field as professional, and second, to his inertia in establishing his profession on an equal basis with psychiatry and psychiatric social work.

Proper orientation of the psychologist as a professional is approaching realization, but the establishment of his profession in its proper setting is still in the initial stage. An appreciation of the usefulness of clinical psychology in a child guidance clinic should provide a starting point for a clearer understanding of its place and importance among allied professions.

Clarification and delimitation of the scope of clinical psychology

[1] Reprinted from *American Journal of Orthopsychiatry*, 1942, 12, 388–392. Copyright 1942 by American Orthopsychiatric Association.

in child guidance may prove less difficult if it is first confined to a specific clinic. The following attempt at clarification and delimitation will be purely in the light of my own experience.

The clinic with which I am associated has been in existence for the past three years, starting with a basic staff consisting of one psychiatrist, one clinical psychologist and one psychiatric social worker. Later another psychiatric social worker was added. The number of cases admitted to service (1052) has been too large in comparison to the size of the staff to permit much intensive treatment or research.

Like the other members of the staff, the psychologist has carried a few selected cases. These cases were chosen mainly for their teaching value to the staff and other professional groups. Naturally, the need of the patient was not neglected. It was evident that the selected cases emphasized two important trends—service to the individual and service to the community. The individual is, of course, most important to all of us, but it appeared that he could ultimately be best cared for through emphasis on general service to the community. There were two reasons for this decision: first, the smallness of the staff; second, the request for community service was greater than for individual patient treatment.

As the initial period of time progressed it was felt that the community service could best be administered through the use of cases as demonstration material. Other educational services were offered but they were recognized mainly through the use of this demonstration material. The clinical psychologist in dealing with these cases, because of the very nature of his training, placed the most emphasis on measurement and evaluation of intelligence, school achievement and special aptitudes. This does not mean that emotional problems were considered outside the sphere of clinical psychology, but merely that they were considered only as they influenced intellectual function, educational achievement, or the satisfactory use of special aptitudes.

There were, however, instances where the problem was primarily emotional in nature and, because of certain indications, the clinical psychologist was preeminently indicated as the staff member to carry them. The first of these included cases where the older child or parent could tolerate initial treatment only if the problem were kept on an intellectual or educational achievement basis. The second group consisted of those who for individual reasons, either on the part of the staff member or the patient, could maintain a better relationship with the psychologist. Being the only male member of the staff, he had a small additional group of patients who could relate themselves best to this sex.

In our clinic diagnosis and interpretation have been of primary importance. This has been true whether the patient was selected for more intensive treatment or whether the findings and recommendations were to be used by another agency. Initial procedure entails a careful evaluation of the social history in order to review all reasons for referral, to gain a general picture of the patient's needs, and recognize what service the referring source expects. The psychologist can then determine what psychological tools will best aid him and the other clinic personnel in more thoroughly understanding the patient and, at the same time, be most useful in planning for ensuing treatment. Here the psychologist should spend as much time as is necessary to render the maximum aid in the final diagnosis.

As this procedure was carried out it became evident that the initial period with patients would serve as a starting point for much of the clinic's service to the patient and to the community. Care must be taken if this time is to be well spent. To use psychological tests to best advantage one must do more than administer and score them according to standardized directions. We all know that tests are not infallible, but this fallibility can be reduced to a minimum through subjective as well as objective evaluation of test responses.

Subjective evaluation of individual test findings was useful in two ways: first, through careful scrutiny of behavior reactions such as the interest, attitude, cooperation and other behavior characteristics; second, by thoughtful examination of the quality of the thinking as shown by the amount of orderliness, the ability for good self-criticism, and the way of meeting reality situations.

It is not always easy to evaluate these reactions to mental examinations particularly where certain types of cases are concerned. Many juvenile delinquents, reading and speech disabilities, and similar cases are adept at consciously or unconsciously deceiving the examiner into thinking that their cooperation, interest and general attitude are adequate. Strangely enough, a casual estimate of this false front will frequently agree with obtained scores and all will seem well. Agreement with the score can be explained on the basis that these patients set a low standard of performance for this type of situation and so maintain it and nothing more. Bright individuals are more adept in these circumstances than dull ones; hence the very group most in need of accurate evaluation is misjudged.

The thorough study of the various subjective findings, the combination of these findings with objective scores, and the orientation of test results with respect to general living situations provide the best possible evaluation of the individual's intelligence.

The interpretation of the diagnostic material can have a variety of uses. It serves to convey diagnostic findings to the school, other agencies, professional people and parents so that adequate planning for a particular case can be made. In addition, interpretation can be used as a teaching procedure for other professional groups, for students in all three services, and for specific lay groups. If interpretation is to be successful it is important that it be suited to the group for whom it is intended. A clear, detailed description of the test findings, relation of conclusions to as much objective material (both in the test and in the history) as possible, the frank admission that tests are not infallible, these are all in order and important, but they are not enough. Experience has taught us that the method of presentation to a given group will determine the success or failure of the whole interpretive procedure. It is essential to carefully evaluate the person or group for whom a report is intended and to keep in mind whether it is to be given orally or in writing. On the basis of this evaluation one can determine the amount of detail, length of time, and type of language presentation which has the best chance of conveying the intended meaning. It is as absurd to formulate a report to a psychiatrist or a general practitioner in language suited to the less informed lay person as it would be to formulate the same report to this lay person in scientific language appropriate for these special professional people. It is the psychologist's ability to describe his findings in terms of a reality situation which is most essential.

Diagnostic service divides cases into various groups. Two of these classifications were especially useful in demonstrating the psychologist's contribution in child guidance. One of them consisted of cases showing educational disabilities; the other contained cases referred for a study of special aptitudes as relating to vocational training or placement. The first group was composed chiefly of reading disabilities. Of all school subjects, reading was the most fundamental and for this reason treatment of children with reading retardation is a valuable demonstration to the community. Since all the children selected were carried in conjunction with other clinic services it was important to select only cases with hopeful prognosis and those which illustrated the relationship of the reading disability to the total personality. Rarely did the psychologist teach the reading itself. His function was that of selecting the special teacher, in supervising her contacts with the child, and in cooperating with her in determining what special reading techniques would have the best chance of success. Through special conferences between the teacher, psychologist and social worker the reading could be presented as a part of a total situation. This proved to be very important because without considerable readjustment on the part of the child and his parents methods of teaching seldom produced the best results.

With certain children treatment involved relatively simple procedures. Sometimes the interpretation of the child's limitations, his special interests, his reaction to success and failure, together with plans to meet these, was enough to permit the reading to progress. With other children the problem was more severe. Seriously maladjusted family situations with accompanying emotional instability on the part of the child necessitated much more careful and detailed planning and supervision. Frequently one or both of the parents had to be carried for long periods of time by the psychiatric case worker. Initial management of these children often placed more emphasis on treatment than on specific remedial reading techniques.

The second group of cases contained mostly adolescents who had been referred for study of their special aptitudes. Inadequate personal and group adjustment was found in a majority of them, and general treatment aimed at improvement was indicated. Except for diagnostic service and continued contacts with the psychologist, most of these individuals were carried by other agencies. These agencies were interested in obtaining a complete diagnosis and subsequent interpretation of the findings in order to more satisfactorily plan for the individual. The intelligence, emotional balance, and amount of social maturity were as important in planning for vocational training and work placement as they were in any other area of living, a fact many times overlooked.

The two groups of cases just discussed serve to illustrate two areas where the need for special service from the psychologist was urgent.

As the community became more aware of his function in child guidance a number of additional requests for his time were made. Some special projects growing out of these requests were: (1) a consulting and testing service for a pre-school group, (2) consulting and testing service for a school of nursing, and (3) periodical testing service for a boys' home. In all of these projects the usefulness of the psychologist increased as the staff members became oriented as to his function and could better relate this to their institution's needs.

No discussion of the work of clinical psychology would be complete without reference to research possibilities, and unquestionably there should be more emphasis upon collaborative research within guidance clinic services. Several interesting possibilities for investigation which presented themselves in our clinic were: (1) an evaluation of methods for diffusing various tested concepts through other community agencies and institutions; (2) the relation of psychological to sociological determinants of behavior in case treatment; (3) the differentiation of workable and unworkable theories of personality, particularly with respect to their usefulness in actual practice; and (4) a systematic evaluation of personnel and personnel relations in community agencies.

To summarize, the scope of clinical psychology in child guidance should be determined on the basis of community needs for service. The clinical psychologist can best show his usefulness both to his profession and to his practice by adapting his skills to meet these needs. A résumé of the activities in a specific clinic shows that the demands for his service increased in direct proportion to the extent that diagnosis and interpretation was translated in terms acceptable to other professions and to lay groups, irrespective of the type of case concerned. Whether the patient's problems were primarily on an emotional basis, or primarily on an intellectual and educational achievement basis, had little to do with their value for demonstration. All provided an opportunity for the psychologist to clarify and delimit the scope of his profession.

This very brief description of clinical psychology in a child guidance clinic should stimulate a more detailed survey of the duties and functions of the psychologist in other child guidance clinics, and from this to determine how best to select and train future workers in the field.

ETHEL L. CORNELL

New York State Education Department

The Psychologist in a School System[1]

In a one-room school, the teacher performs the necessary administrative services, does the janitorial work with volunteer pupil assistance, tries to recognize and exclude cases of contagious diseases,
becomes acquainted with the family background of all her pupils,
keeps track of illegal absences, teaches all the *subjects* that are
taught, as well as all the *children* from five to fifteen years of age who
attend, and gives the best counsel she can concerning future educational plans or vocational expectations. In a city of a million inhabitants, school services may become so specialized that the teacher
teaches only one subject in one grade. In such a system, in addition
to a specialized teaching and supervising staff, there is a central
administrative force which also has specialized responsibilities. For
example, there may be a health service including doctors and nurses,
and often dentists and oral hygienists; an attendance service staffed,
in a modern school system, by social workers; a guidance service
responsible for educational counseling, vocational guidance, placement, and follow-up; a research service, responsible, among other
things, for the administration of standardized tests, the evaluation
of instruction, and continuous revision of the curriculum; and some
provision for the study and special treatment of children who are
special problems—either scattered through the various other services
or coordinated in a bureau known as "special education," "child
study," "child development," "child guidance," etc. This last mentioned service, when complete, includes special classes for various

[1] Reprinted from *Journal of Consulting Psychology*, 1942, 6, 185–195. Copyright 1942 by American Association for Applied Psychology.

types of physically and mentally handicapped; special teachers for remedial work needed by some pupils in the tool subjects; and clinical provision for the diagnosis of social, psychological, and neuropsychiatric difficulties and their treatment, which requires the services of a psychiatrist, a psychologist, a psychiatric social worker, and perhaps a pediatrician.

Degrees of Specialization in School Services.   Between the one-room school and the city of a million, we have a great diversity of practice regarding the division of responsibilities, the combinations of specialized functions, and the overlapping of personnel. Examples of this diversity are numerous. The school nurse may in some cases perform the functions of attendance officer or visiting teacher. The guidance counselor may be responsible for the testing program of the high school, while in elementary schools the principals may or may not use standardized tests, according to their individual interests. Cases needing psychological or mental hygiene study may be referred to private or public clinics, or may be given casual Binet tests by someone on the staff. Remedial teaching may be given, if at all, by regular teachers in special periods set aside for the purpose by the administration, or after school by interested teachers on their own initiative, or by the elementary supervisor or the school psychologist. The health examinations of pupils may be under the jurisdiction of the city health department instead of the school, while the program of physical education remains with the school.

Examples of this sort could be continued indefinitely. They indicate clearly that we have no basic principles which determine school practices in caring for the individual problems of children in the most adequate and effectual manner, nor in providing the kinds of specialized services which would serve particular localities most adequately and economically.

It is not surprising that this is so. For the greater part of our history American schools have been trying to develop methods which would provide for rapidly increasing numbers of pupils. These were "mass" methods, aimed in theory to give everyone an "equal opportunity." In the last twenty-five years the concepts of individual differences, mental hygiene, emotional adjustment, personality integration have been making steady inroads upon the traditional concepts and practices of education, but their implications have not always been fully recognized even by their advocates, and consequently the school services developed to meet the differentiated needs of pupils have been uneven and sporadic.

Varieties of Clinical Services Available for Schools.   In the opinion of the writer, a distinction should be made between an educational psychologist and a school psychologist. The functions of the former are concerned with teaching general principles of psychology and child development to prospective teachers and with research on problems of psychology in its application to education. The functions of the latter are primarily the functions of a clinical psychologist, in a setting, however, where the adjustments needed are closely related to local and particular conditions affecting the general theory of the educational process. The clinical psychological services available for school children are not, of course, limited to communities that employ school psychologists. In some of the large cities child guidance clinics under psychiatric auspices provide psychological services also available to at least some school children. There are both community and traveling clinics of this general character, but very few of them have been organized directly under educational jurisdiction. On the other hand, there are "school psychologists" whose functions are limited entirely to giving routine "psychometric tests" in communities where complete clinical psychological and psychiatric services are not available. In short, there is so much confusion in the employment of terms and in the functions performed by persons of various levels of training and experience, that a definite effort is needed to clarify the functions and purposes of these various groups.

It probably would be expected that few school systems would be able to maintain a "child guidance" clinic in the sense in which this term has been used widely as a "psychiatric clinic that includes psychologists and social workers; . . . that deals primarily with behavior problems of children ranging fairly normally in distribution; . . . characteristically . . . equipped to dovetail psychiatric, psychological, and social services into a single diagnostic statement and a single plan of treatment." (58)[2] In the 1940 Directory of Psychiatric Clinics in the United States, which lists 745 clinics, 19 are found to be conducted directly under public school auspices. It is interesting to note the range in the size of the communities having

---

[2] Bibliography begins on page 176.

TABLE 1.   Comparative School Costs in Cities of Various Sizes With and Without Psychiatric Clinics[1]

Cities (Ranked According to Number of Pupils in Average Daily Attendance)	Average Daily Attendance (approx.)	Total Current Expense (approx.)	Current Expense per Pupil in Aver. Daily Attendance[2]	Clinic with Psychiatric and Psychological Services
A Population of 1,000,000 or more				
New York City.............	1,014,000	$164,559,000	$162	Yes
Chicago...................	424,000	50,453,000	129	Yes
Los Angeles..............	252,000	34,345,000	136	Yes
Philadelphia..............	243,000	28,697,000	118	No[3]
Detroit...................	242,000	27,079,000	112	No[3]
B Population 500,000 to 1,000,000				
Cleveland.................	130,000	15,300,000	118	No[3]
Boston....................	119,000	16,961,000	143	No
Baltimore.................	105,000	10,162,000	97	No
St. Louis.................	95,000	11,518,000	121	No
Pittsburgh................	92,000	12,680,000	138	No[3]
Buffalo...................	82,000	11,371,000	139	No[3]
Milwaukee.................	76,000	9,912,000	130	No[3]
San Francisco.............	65,000	9,827,000	151	No
C Population less than 500,000 maintaining clinics				
Minneapolis (492,000)........	75,000	8,085,000	108	Yes
Newark, N. J. (430,000)......	66,000	9,473,000	144	Yes
Indianapolis (387,000)........	54,000	5,601,000	104	Yes
Rochester, N. Y. (325,000)....	45,000	7,049,000	157	Yes
Jersey City, N. J. (301,000)....	40,000	6,231,000	156	Yes
Portland, Oregon (305,000)....	42,000	4,405,000	105	Yes
Providence, R. I. (254,000)....	38,000	4,479,000	118	Yes
Syracuse, N. Y. (206,000).....	32,000	4,220,000	132	Yes
Gary, Indiana (112,000).......	19,000	1,750,000	92	Yes
Spokane, Washington (122,000).	17,000	1,833,000	108	Yes
Schenectady, N. Y. (88,000)...	15,000	2,102,000	140	Yes
Berkeley, California (86,000)...	11,000	1,821,000	166	Yes
East Chicago, Indiana (55,000).	9,000	802,000	89	Yes
South Orange, N. J. (37,000)...	6,000	1,018,000	170	Yes
Orange, N. J. (36,000)........	6,000	705,000	118	Yes
Winnetka, Illinois (12,000).....	1,600	291,000	182	Yes

[1] Figures for 1937–38, taken from "Biennial Survey of Education. Statistics of City School Systems, 1937–38." U. S. Office of Education. Bulletin 1940, No. 2.

[2] Average current expense per pupil in average daily attendance for same year was $119.50 in cities of 100,000 or more.

[3] Known to have organized psychological services.

school clinics, from Winnetka, Illinois, with a school population of about 1,500 to New York City, with a school population of more than 1,000,000. It is also interesting to note that three of the five largest cities of the country (those with a total population of over a million) have so-called psychiatric clinics under the Board of Education, while the other two have organized psychological services;

that one of the three clinics is under the direction of a psychologist rather than a psychiatrist; and that among cities between half a million and a million population not one school clinic is found, although it occurs in much smaller places (see Table 1). This is an indication of how varied organization may be and to how small an extent size appears to be a factor.

Neither does cost seem to be a determining factor. The per-pupil current expense among cities of five hundred thousand or more varies without relation to the provision of clinical services (Table 1). It is relatively low in Chicago, which maintains clinical services, and relatively high in San Francisco, which does not. Among the cities of less than five hundred thousand population which do maintain clinics, the per pupil cost varies from much below average to much above. The implication is not to be drawn, of course, that only those places with school clinics have adequate services, either of a psychological or psychiatric kind; it is simply that we find organized services under a wide variety of conditions and costs.

Variations of Psychological Services in Schools. Moreover, the fact of organized school clinics tells us little about the adequacy of the services rendered, particularly the psychological services, either in terms of the training and experience of the staff, the number on the staff in relation to pupil enrollments, or the kind of contribution made to the growth and welfare of pupils. While fourteen of the nineteen school clinics listed were under the direction of a medical officer, presumably a psychiatrist, there were five under the direction of a nonmedical officer, possibly a psychologist. However, the names of only two of the five appear in the membership lists of either the American Psychological Association or the American Association for Applied Psychology. This is evidence, not necessarily of a lack of qualifications, but of the general lack of requirement—or even recognition—of professional status. The training of the psychologists employed by clinics and by schools which do not have clinics is no doubt likewise variable.

The United States Office of Education attempted to clarify these issues in a bulletin describing various types of organization for clinical service (31). It is there pointed out that the trend in cities of moderate size is toward a more comprehensive guidance program in the schools, in which "guidance is interpreted, not in the narrow sense of vocational counseling but as a broad service for the personal adjustment of all types of individual problems within the scope of school consideration . . . 'Problems of educational adjustment, problems of attendance and behavior, and finally various social problems are the sphere of the guidance bureau or clinic activity.' "[3]

The psychologist in a school system may, it is evident, function under a variety of organizations: there may be a child study bureau under the direction of a psychologist; there may be a child guidance clinic under the direction of a psychiatrist; there may be a general guidance bureau under the direction of an educator (usually a vocational educator), of which clinical psychological services are a part.

Definition of a School Psychologist. The development of any clear-cut concept as to the functions of school psychologists has been hampered in part by the various administrative organizations under which psychologists work and the various concepts of vocational educators, psychiatrists and school superintendents; but even more so (although probably as a consequence of this) by the varying kinds of training and preparation possessed by persons who are called school psychologists.

A more definite concept is now, however, beginning to emerge. It still needs some clarification, but it has been given a certain amount of definition by certification requirements in New York and Pennsylvania and possibly some other states. In New York State, for a permanent certificate (valid for ten-year periods upon evidence of further study or educational leadership during each ten-year period), a master's degree in psychology is required, together with not less than 52 semester hours' credit in theoretical, physiological, and experimental psychology, educational psychology and methods of instruction, educational principles, statistics, psychology of learning and growth, psychology of adjustment problems, clinical tests and procedures and supervised experience in clinical testing. Pennsylvania's requirements are comparable, though differing in details.

After these regulations had been in effect in New York for about six years, an attempt was made to discover how many schools were receiving any type of psychological service, either by the employment of school psychologists, by using other persons on the school staff, by utilizing child guidance clinics, or otherwise. It was found that much confusion still exists in the minds of school principals

---

[3] Martens (31, p. 3) quoted from Miller (35).

as to what or who a school psychologist is. Principals were asked, through a preliminary questionnaire, to give names of persons employed by the school who were performing psychological services. Outside of the cities of New York, Buffalo and Rochester, the names of 165 persons were submitted, but when these were followed up, it appeared that not more than 63 could be regarded as doing more than occasional and desultory psychological work. Of these, 50 had titles indicating that they were employed to administer individual psychological tests (at least part time) and 42 were certified as school psychologists by the State Education Department.[4] This is not a large proportion of the 165 mentioned by their principals! The 63 persons were working in 41 communities varying in size from eight places which employed a total of less than 50 teachers each to five places which employed over 200 teachers each. As in the case of clinics, size of school seemed to have little to do with the organization of facilities, at least above a certain minimum. The one common characteristic of these persons, the activity that determined whether they were included in the group, was the fact that they all used individual psychological tests to some extent. The first crude definition of a school psychologist is, then, one who uses individual psychological tests. This definition excluded many whose activities were concerned with "pupil adjustment," but it did not exclude anyone whose training was in psychology and who was acting as a psychological counselor.

Duties Performed by School Psychologists. The major activities of these 63 persons are shown in Table 2. All of them gave individual psychological tests, 54 of them as a regular part of their job, and 9 occasionally. Conferring with teachers about individual pupils, administering group tests, and making contacts with parents were either regular or occasional functions of 90 per cent or more. Writing diagnostic case reports, interviewing pupils, making contacts with outside agencies, and planning remedial instruction were functions mentioned by at least 75 per cent. The actual giving of remedial instruction was less common, and was mentioned by less than half of the group.

There were 42 persons whose whole time was devoted to psychological work or testing, of whom 38 were called school psychologists

---

[4] This number has since increased to about 50.

and 4 (who probably did not meet the certification requirements) were called psychometric or mental examiners. There were two part-time assistants to the school psychologists, and the remainder did psychological work in addition to their regular jobs. Their regular jobs varied from superintendents, principals, supervisors, and guidance counselors to school nurses, school physicians and school librarians.

Table 2.   Major Activities of School Psychologists

Activities Performed	Number Performing Activities			
	Regularly	Occasionally	Total	Per Cent
Individual Psychological examining.................	54	9	63	100
Conferring with teacher or principal regarding individual pupils.............	49	11	60	95
Conducting group tests.......	42	15	57	91
Making contacts with parents.	36	21	57	91
Writing diagnostic case reports	41	14	55	87
Individual interviews without examination..............	33	17	50	79
Contacts with agencies.......	16	32	48	76
Planning remedial instruction.	23	24	47	75
Giving remedial instruction...	8	20	28	44

A list of the miscellaneous activities engaged in by these psychologists reminds one a little of the functions of the one-room teacher with which this article began. The list ranges from teaching and supervisory work to participation in community mental hygiene programs, administration, research, vocational placement and social work. These activities (see Table 3) are all related to the needs of individual pupils and indicate how wide the scope of the psychologist's work may be in school systems that are not large enough to have many specialists. While the techniques required for many of these services are not necessarily part of the professional clinical training of the psychologist, nevertheless the well-trained clinical psychologist with sufficient maturity and educational experience can bring to bear on these phases of school work a point of view which has sometimes been sadly lacking. The psychologist who has also an educational background and is in daily contact with the particular school system can be far more effective than the visiting clinician not only in working out the best disposition of individual cases but also in grasping opportunities for enlightenment of the school staff and of community groups as to specific school practices which are not in the best interests of pupils' mental health or intellectual growth.

Utilization of Clinical Psychological Techniques. Is it then possible to define the psychologist's function, or to state explicitly what his techniques are or how the psychologist's use of these techniques differs from that of others? In the list of functions enumerated in Table 2, there is not one that is not sometimes performed by persons who are not psychologists. Only two could probably be regarded as *specifically* the province of psychologists: giving individual psychological examinations and writing diagnostic case reports. The others are equally and logically the province of teachers, administra-

TABLE 3. Miscellaneous Activities of School Psychologists

Psychological: Interpreting results of group tests in elementary school, in secondary school; using and interpreting rating scales; devising tests for reading readiness; interpreting needs revealed by readiness tests; participating in case conferences in school, or with social agencies; giving individual tests for other agencies such as traveling child guidance clinic; serving on committee for mental hygiene conference; talks on mental hygiene to junior and senior high school pupils; leading child study groups; speaking to P. T. A. groups and adult study groups.

Administrative: Supervising general testing program; giving group tests; making statistical reports of test results; grade and group placement of pupils; adviser in planning testing program; devising record blanks and forms for cumulative or permanent pupil records; assisting in formulation of administrative policies.

Research: Study of recreation program; evaluation of radio programs; study of ages in first grade.

Supervisory (curriculum): Demonstration testing of reading readiness; instructing teachers in administering group tests; serving on curriculum committees; supervision of special classes for mentally handicapped.

Advisory, counseling, visiting teacher: Group and individual guidance counseling; vocational and educational counseling; job placement (especially for part-time jobs); visiting local occupations to find job opportunities; making contacts for the school with social agencies; serving on community welfare committees; visiting homes to get better understanding and adjustment and to follow up pupils' progress; checking attendance and visiting absentees as attendance officer and to discover problems; chaperoning student activities.

tors, or social workers. How does the psychologist's use of these techniques differ? Does he contribute something that the others do not?

The answer, of course, depends in part upon how "psychologist" is defined. There are "psychometric examiners" in schools who examine individually, with Stanford-Binet tests, one thousand or more children a year. (This would be five cases a day, five days a week, for forty weeks.) No matter how competent they may be, individually, the pressure of testing of this kind makes mere technicians out of them. Individual children cease to be treated as individuals with specific problems other than those of grade or special class placement. The cues afforded by the incidental comments of the subject or by particular patterns of response cannot be followed up. The art of diagnosis, in short, is lost and the result is merely a quantitative score which could be obtained with only slightly less reliability by using group tests.

There are other people working as special teachers or supervisors or guidance counselors who sometimes give individual tests (or use test results of outside agencies) as aids in discussing educational needs or personal pupil problems with parents or with pupils or as evidence of remedial needs. Tests of this kind are also likely to give only quantitative scores, which, when given by inexpert examiners, may be no more reliable (or may be even less so) than group tests.

This seems to be a deplorable situation. The use of the individual psychological test as a controlled situation for observation has values for qualitative interpretation that should not be lost. The writer has pointed this out before (12) but believes that it needs re-emphasizing. It needs attention particularly in training courses in which students are learning to "interpret" their results. Too often the student's "analysis" of a test is no analysis at all but merely a summary of passes and failures at successive age levels. To discover from a Stanford-Binet test record that John Jones "fails the verbal absurdities at the eight-year level but passes them at the nine-year level" does not require psychological training. If the psychologist has found no clue in his examination to explain this discrepancy, either he or the examination is inadequate. Too often, also, even a competent psychologist expects the individual test to give only a general indication of the subject's intellectual level, and copies the techniques of social investigation, psychiatric interview, and group rating-scale devices to get an interpretation of the "whole child." It is the writer's conviction from her own experience that this sometimes yields a less valid interpretation than a more adequate use of the psychological test itself, partly because the former are more piecemeal and partly because they are more direct and permit the subject to infer to some extent what sort of reaction is expected. In the course of a psychological examination in which the subject's attention is directed toward the solution of specific problems, particularly if these problems vary over a wide range of content, there is ample opportunity for observation of patterns of response which the subject is unaware are being observed. Not only may intellectual patterns be thus observed, but also emotional patterns are often suggested, as well as indications of social background, all of which may be of unique importance for the best adjustment of the particular individual. Self-absorption, extreme ego-centeredness, lack of insight into one's own abilities—indicating misplaced self-confidence or inferiority feelings, vagaries of attention due to emotional blocking, tendencies toward perseveration, intellectual methods of approach to a problem, the kind of content that catches the subject's spontaneous interest, the social framework (or mores) which limits his thinking—all these are readily enough discoverable in the course of a psychological examination, as by-products of the tests used. For this reason they may have greater validity than when a more direct approach is made to them, although, of course, they have less objectivity and do not yield quantitative scores. These, however, are the things that should enter into the psychologist's diagnosis of the situation, and so far as the program of the school can affect the readjustment or the rehabilitation, the re-education or the reorientation of the subject, these are the most important things. For in order to be practical we must recognize that the school is only one of our social institutions and alone cannot alter the social conditions that may prevent adjustment in individual cases. It can alter, however, the school program of individuals, if it has the necessary understanding, in such a way as to develop individual habits of thought and of reaction most likely to lead to the adjustment of the individual in the situations in which he is likely to find himself. The psychologist's techniques should not only provide the diagnosis of the difficulty but should indicate the direction that remedial or adaptive procedures should take.

Functional Relationships of the Psychologist. This suggests that the psychologist should be in reasonably close contact with the individual teachers, or the parents, or the social workers, or the school nurses, or whoever may be in the most strategic position to give the necessary help to the pupil who needs readjustment. Sometimes, particularly in small communities, or with a pupil who needs to get a reorientation of his own attitudes and insights, the psychologist himself may be the person to give the direct help. In other cases, the direct help can best be given by the teacher, or the school nurse, or the parent.

For example, the child of eight or nine years of age, who is seen by his teacher as a child who "can't concentrate" and "doesn't remember what he learns" and is "very restless and nervous," may show these symptoms from a variety of causes. The restless, inattentive behavior so often reported by teachers of elementary school children may be evidence of an essentially unstable emotional makeup (or at least of a pattern of behavior so fixed in early childhood that it seems to be inherent). This possibility cannot be ignored by the psychologist, although it is probably the least frequent cause of such behavior. The same symptoms may, on the other hand, be the result of an inappropriate learning situation, which in turn may be due to the formality of the classroom, or to the failure of the school tasks to challenge the ability of the child, or to the fact that the progress of the class group is just a little beyond his ability to keep up with, or to a specific pupil-teacher antagonism or tension, or to a slight loss of hearing in the conversational range of tonal frequencies, or to a lack of adequate hygiene in the home, or to a combination of various items none of which is significant in itself. The behavior of a child during a psychological examination that lasts an hour or more will ordinarily reveal the difference between inattentiveness or restlessness which is due to deep-seated causes and that which is superficial or related to specific situations—provided the psychologist knows how to interpret his observations and has adequate time to pursue the clinical clues revealed.

Pursuing these clues may mean discussing with the teacher the possible causes of this particular child's inattentiveness in the classroom, in the light of the psychological factors revealed in the course of the psychological examination. This process should have reciprocal values: both illuminating the diagnostic process, for the psychologist, and clarifying the child's needs, for the teacher. The clues may lead further into the home or to the child's neighborhood companions. The investigation of such clues is primarily a social work technique and would naturally fall to the visiting teacher or to the school nurse, in the school system having qualified personnel in those fields. Whoever may gather the information, the psychologist should make his contribution in interpreting its particular importance for the particular child. The *uniqueness* of interpretation is essentially the psychologist's job and yet, it is to be feared, is often missed, either because the psychologist has not had the intensive clinical training necessary or because the school administration fails to appreciate the importance of this sort of contribution and to provide for the necessary administrative relationships.

After the interpretation of the child's needs has been made, the remedial procedures necessary may vary all the way from half a dozen remedial reading lessons, planned to give a particular pupil a new method of attack in "reading for ideas," to removing a child from his home for a while to reduce the emotional tension between his mother and himself. Sometimes the procedures may be concerned with overcoming specific obstacles to learning, in which case the psychologist, or the psychologist and the teacher together, may plan a procedure for the teacher to carry out. Sometimes they will involve co-operating with a social agency to create a better understanding at home or to provide more wholesome recreation.

Thus, although the psychologist may perform many functions that can be performed as well or better by persons with other kinds of training, the difference between his approach and that of others lies in bringing to bear upon the whole situation the interpretation of a problem from the clinical study of the child's psychological patterns of reaction.

Problems for the School Psychologist. The school psychologist, then, deals with children in a school setting. Occasionally a child will be found who does not belong in the school setting: imbeciles, psychotics, epileptics, for example, are problems for other social agencies than the school. The school psychologist, in co-operation with the school physician, is able to locate these cases and refer them to the proper agencies.

Other types of children can be handled in the school setting but not in the usual curriculum. Much depends, of course, upon how flexible the "usual" curriculum is, whether it will serve the needs of 50, 75, 90 per cent or more of the school population. There is fair agreement both among educators and psychologists, however, that those in the lowest 2 or 3 per cent of the intellectual range require a definitely specialized curriculum. There is less agreement about the best program for the highest 2 or 3 per cent but general agreement that some special educational provisions for gifted children are needed. ("Gifted," however, is variously interpreted to mean anywhere from the highest 2 or 3 per cent on general intelligence tests to the highest 25 per cent; or, with a different connotation, to mean talented children—those with some special ability markedly superior to the average.) It should be part of the school psychologist's job to find such children, to point out the educational implications of their assets and liabilities and to assist in planning a school program which will be appropriate for them.

Even when special provisions have been made for the intellectually most exceptional children, there remain wide individual differences in intelligence, in interest, in speed of learning, in rate of growth, in ability to acquire generalized concepts and to apply them to particular situations, in emotional maturity, in emotional stability, in persistence, in courage, in ability and willingness to take responsibility and to co-operate with others, in creativeness, originality and independence, and in all the characteristics which are part of the developing personality of a child and which are amenable, in theory, to educational influences. At the present time, teachers and school administrators are struggling to find out how to make this theory work in practice. The well-trained school psychologist can make a distinct contribution to the development of curricular and extracurricular programs that will be adapted to the wide range of capacities of "normal" children. One of the most convincing ways in which this can be done is by continuing to point out the possibilities of changes which can be made to adapt the *particular* school practices to pupils whose specific needs have been revealed by psychological study. An outstanding example of this type of service is in the field of primary reading, in which the psychologist's emphasis on the need of a certain degree of maturity as readiness for learning and of methods appropriate to varying aptitudes has had considerable effect on teaching.

The general area of behavior and personality problems is also an area in which the school psychologist has a contribution to make. The division of labor between psychiatrists and psychologists in this field should not present much difficulty since psychiatrists are rare in school service. Cases suspected of psychopathy should, of course, be referred to the psychiatric resources of the community. This is a field in which the inadequately qualified person can do more harm than good if he attempts to delve into the more subtle causal relationships of behavior. Nevertheless, the attempt to deal with problems of personality and behavior is made and has to be made daily by teachers and principals, and even the moderately trained psychologist may throw some light on such problems, particularly on those types of behavior and personality that are produced or aggravated by inappropriate school programs. To speak from personal experience again, the writer has found that teachers and administrators often fail to recognize the relationship between the school program and the personality problem, although they appreciate it when it is pointed out. When the causal factors appear to lie outside of school, the school psychologist should perhaps tread more warily. The school's relation to the child's home is different from that of an agency to which the parents voluntarily take the child. One can go, therefore, only so far as one is assured of co-operative attitudes. Co-operation grows, however, by the evidence of success, and parent-child relationships (clinically considered) may become a field of service for the school psychologist.

Participation in the general program of explaining the school program to the community and of interpreting to parents or to other social agencies the changes taking place in education as well as the needs of children which schools must try to meet is also part of the job of the school psychologist. This may involve public speaking to large groups, conducting small study groups, working as a liaison officer with social welfare agencies, stimulating the use of the case conference as a method of educating teachers and parents, assisting in preparing report cards or pupil records that will be more meaningful to parents and to guidance officers, and other methods for increasing the general understanding of children's needs. The extent to which the school psychologist participates in this program depends largely upon his own capacity for leadership.

Instead of regarding the school psychologist as a luxury few schools can afford, we may come to the point of regarding the school psychologist as one of the most important specialists for even small school systems to have. To reach this point, however, the well-qualified school psychologists now employed need to be alert to grasp every opportunity to make their contribution most effective. This contribution should not be isolated nor designed only for the benefit of exceptional or problem children. Even for these children, however, the effort will be more effective if it is part of a co-operative effort of forces both within and without the school which are struggling to build a better school program. The psychologist's contribution is greatest when he is an integral part of a school program directed not only toward individual development but toward the co-ordination of each individual's activities with all the others', in order to attain the civic and social as well as personal competence now more than ever emphasized as an essential objective of schools, if we are to attain and preserve the "democratic way of life."

E. G. WILLIAMSON
University of Minnesota

Coordination of Student Personnel Services[1]

The psychologist has made or may make a distinctly important contribution to the following phases of college personnel work:

1. The role of psychological testing in admissions procedures is so well known that it need not be reviewed at length. For the past two decades psychologists have contributed to the construction of scholastic aptitude tests, validation of those tests against the criterion of grades, derivation of critical scores for the determination of "good scholastic risks" and the development of group and individual procedures in the identification and selection of applicants for admission. The actual admissions procedures themselves have, in most colleges, been delegated to persons not trained in psychology. Consequently the psychologist largely continues to function in the capacity of psychometrist and statistician. In reviewing the experience of these two decades it is apparent that merely turning over to admissions officers test scores and validity coefficients, as well as critical minimum scores, has not always resulted in improved admissions procedures. The day is past when admissions may be based solely upon a single test score or even a battery of tests. It is now clear that interviewing and counseling procedures must be used in admissions interviews and decision-making to derive the maximum validity from psychological techniques. The perfection of these extra-testing procedures is a real task confronting the psychologist. An even more dif-

[1] Reprinted from *Journal of Consulting Psychology*, 1940, 4, 229–233. Copyright 1940 by American Association for Applied Psychology.

ficult task awaits the training of admissions officers in the use of these educational techniques.

2. In an increasing number of colleges a new type of psychological service has been developed during the past decade. Essentially this is an adaptation of clinical methods earlier developed in work with children and now applied to problems of the college adolescent. These clinical services include the diagnosis and remediation of reading, problems of study methods and preparation for class examinations, special counseling of students who do not make satisfactory progress in their class work and including the perplexing problem of inadequate scholastic motivation coupled with adequate aptitude, and the many types of speech disorders and milder cases of worry, fear, and social maladjustment which are not of a psychiatric nature.

3. This intensive cultivation of a new type of clinical work was preceded by two decades of efforts to make trained counselors out of faculty members trained in their own teaching specialties but without psychological background. Even today some college administrators seem to expect that the mere appointment of teaching specialists as counselors will serve to institute an adequate program of counseling for the many types of adjustment problems faced by college students. In the light of history it is interesting to read Paterson's early discussion of the nature of student counseling (40).[2] Although experience indicates that faculty members will always play a vital part in counseling students about their adjustments to college life, we now realize that many of these adjustment problems are of such a complex nature that counselors, professionally trained in clinical psychology, are required to supplement the simpler types of student counseling performed by faculty members. The development of a central staff of specialists working coordinately with faculty members is a perplexing problem of administration and coordination. For the most part these faculty members performed what has been called a "first aid" type of assistance which in itself may prove sufficient for certain types of problems but totally inadequate for other types. The delineation of what problems need what types of counseling assistance awaits intensive analysis of a large number of actual case histories.

Moreover, the training of faculty counselors in the performance of

---

[2] Bibliography begins on page 176.

their special type of counseling remains a perplexing problem despite widespread attempts to develop in-service training programs. The mere instituting of a psychological testing program to provide counselors with test scores does not in itself guarantee adequate use of those test scores in the counseling of students. Many teachers experience difficulty understanding such simple concepts as the meaning of a percentile rank and a validity coefficient. An amazing number of faculty members and administrators continue to have difficulty in not expecting that test scores will predict scholarship perfectly for every student. The case of a student with low test scores who achieves a satisfactory level in his class work continues to embarrass the college psychologist in his conferences with the untrained faculty counselor. When present day teachers who did not experience counseling and other personnel services in their own under-graduate days are eventually replaced by younger men with such experiences, perhaps this function of training teachers in the performance of their own teacher-counselor functions will prove to be a simpler task.

4. A new type of psychological service is being evolved in some colleges as a result of the demands of an increasing number of progressive employers who ask for aptitude, interest and personality test scores on college seniors who apply for positions. The college psychologist has an opportunity to provide this new type of service for placement officers in colleges. It is to be hoped that these psychologists will not make a similar mistake as noted above in the case of admissions officers but will provide a clinical interpretation of test scores along with the numerical values themselves.

5. A vast new field of psychological services may be opened up to the psychologist when he develops new types of relationships with college administrators in charge of group recreational programs and activities. Numerous possible contributions come to mind from the psychologist's experience with problems of mental hygiene, group adjustments, and problems of learning applied to social situations. The coordination of individual and group work is a challenging problem for future exploitation of psychological services.

6. The psychologist needs to explore the contributions he may make to the development of an adequate financial aid service to college students. At the present time financial aid officers are not in agreement as to whether this aid should be distributed in terms of the scholastic promise of students or solely on the basis of financial

need. Under either or both policies the psychologist may contribute to the improvement of financial aid counseling because of his experiences in the diagnosis of aptitude, interests and personality traits. At the present time this is largely an unexplored field.

7. The psychologist continues to face the opportunity and obligation to perfect his methods of diagnosing and predicting scholastic grades since this criterion continues to be, in the faculty mind, the dominant test of the adequacy of students' adjustments. Gradually the psychologist may introduce new methods of diagnosing other types of capacities, such as social adjustments, if and when the faculties are persuaded to recognize the value of other than intellectual outcomes of college experiences. When the impact of progressive movements is felt in higher education, the psychologist may be called upon to assist in setting up new types of educational programs which will produce new types of outcomes.

With these seven types of psychological services in mind we may now outline briefly the nature of the task of integrating these services with the strictly instructional problems of the college and with the many other types of personnel services not performed by psychologists (13, 14, 29). The coordination function in student personnel work is many-sided. At the present stage of development neither the nature of the function nor the underlying structure of organization are clearly discernible. Several types of structures have been tried in colleges beginning with the first formally organized personnel bureau at Northwestern University. In those early days testing, interviewing and research on scholastic adjustments apparently were the dominant services. Today there is a tendency to supplement the work of a central organization by means of other coordinating agencies.

At the present time the following phases of coordination of psychological services are in various stages of development in different colleges:

1. Informal education of faculty and administration through interviews, conferences, bulletins and over-the-luncheon-table-talks in the use of the available psychological techniques and tools. Since faculty members and administrators will undoubtedly continue to advise students as long as there is a college, then the psychologist faces the responsibility, often neglected, of keeping these lay counselors (7, pp. 49–50) informed of possible improvements in the tech-

niques they use. The only alternative to this instructional function is the rigid centralization of all psychological counseling in a departmental organization manned by professionally trained counselors. In the case of health services in colleges this latter form of structure has been evolved. For a number of reasons which need not be outlined here rigid centralization is impossible as well as unwise. One of the chief objections to centralization is the need for improving teaching techniques and changing teachers' attitudes toward students through the experience of counseling even though that counseling may not be of a professional grade. If, for this and other reasons, centralization is unwise, we must attempt to perfect better methods of educating the faculty to discharge the lay type of counseling.

2. Similar informal education must take place with regard to use of results of many decades of research and experience with interviewing and counseling methods. To the psychologist, interviewing calls for a high degree of skillful use of techniques which are often obscure but which nevertheless have evolved from years of experience and research. To the lay faculty member, interviewing is something which may be done casually by almost anyone without training. The college psychologist faces a real task in translating the results of his research into simple descriptions and in using such information in the informal training of faculty members in the use of improved techniques.

3. Just as counseling should be decentralized, in a similar manner personnel research should take place wherever there is a qualified staff member to do it. Therefore, a vital part of coordination is the informal stimulation of use of research facilities throughout the college. Members of education, psychology, and sociology staffs need to be stimulated and encouraged to work separately and independently on the many problems of adolescents which await experimental study.

4. A most important phase of coordination is the discovery of new sources of data and services on each campus and the persuasion of personnel workers, faculty members and administrators to use these new sources. One might conclude that it is inherent in the nature of higher education that various forms of assistance to students should develop in isolation of each other and without members of the staff being informed. Sometimes this isolation is insulated by legal rules and guarded by jealous administrators who want to work alone. On

every campus an active coordinating agent may discover scores of types of psychological services which have been developing unknown to the rest of the campus. At Harvard, Wisconsin, Northwestern, and Minnesota (67, 69, pp. 82–83) formally or informally organized councils of personnel workers hold periodic meetings to learn about what is going on on their own campus in the way of personnel services. Years of use of this type of educational technique must precede the actual developing of lines and methods of cooperation. Before personnel workers may use local resources to improve assistance to students they need to know the nature of those resources and to study in detail the actual methods of collecting and exchanging new information. At Minnesota this exchange is facilitated by a central registration of counseling contacts, the actual case information being decentralized in the offices where that information has first been collected (68, 69, pp. 22, 83). In other colleges a complete central file of information about each student is being collected to which any and all personnel workers may refer by telephone or in person.

5. A more difficult phase of coordination has to do with the clarification of fields of work and functions. Various types of personnel services have evolved not only in isolation but in confusion sometimes because of the rigid administrative structure inherited from the past. Anyone who has worked with colleges knows how difficult it is to change structures which have been legalized. Personnel functions may change as personalities change and as our knowledge of adolescents increases but structures are more rigid and resistant to change. Consequently coordination becomes difficult when structures interfere with proper discharge of personnel functions. Informal discussions leading to understanding by all must precede any attempt to readjust the structure of personnel work in terms of new functions and services. This is particularly true since personnel workers for the most part do not hold membership in those administrative bodies which determine structures.

A discussion of these phases of coordination of psychological services in college leads one to the conclusion that personnel work is not a function of higher education which can be rigidly centralized but one which will always be performed in various parts of the campus. Therefore, the problem becomes one of stimulating exchange of information and case data among many agents and the cultivation of a desire to work cooperatively together rather than in isolation. The problem is further one of how to perform systematically these coordinating functions without centralizing the actual services themselves. Coordination is, therefore, a staff function rather than an administrative one. By staff function is meant a supervisory relationship rather than rigid control over personnel services themselves. Coordination is comparable to the type of supervision of teaching developed in large schools and in the personnel departments of industry. Few other functions in higher education are similar in organization and administration, except possibly certain phases of decentralized graduate instruction and research.

ELAINE F. KINDER

Rockland State Hospital, Orangeburg, N. Y.

Psychological Work at Letchworth Village, Thiells, N. Y.[1]

The psychological work at Letchworth Village is intimately a part of the institution as a whole, and can be understood only in terms of that relationship. A brief summary of the purpose, organization and history of the research department in particular, is a necessary introduction to an account of the psychological service.

Letchworth Village is one of five New York State institutions for mental defectives under the Department of Mental Hygiene. It was established in 1911 and has been of especial interest to those in medical and scientific fields on account of its rather unusual construction and organization as well as because of its early and continued recognition of the importance of research.

As far back as the Fourth Annual Report of the Board of Managers (1913) there was a record of this interest in research possibilities with mention of the need to provide "for special phases of the work."[2] The following year, when the inmate population was still less than one hundred, the Annual Report included a "Report of the Advisory Medical Board's Special Committee into the Cause and Prevention of Feeblemindedness" which recommended a research

---

[1] Reprinted from *Journal of Consulting Psychology*, 1937, 1, 76–80. Copyright 1937 by American Association for Applied Psychology.

[2] "Such, for instance, is the creation of endowment for carrying on scientific investigation, which may produce no present returns, but will be invaluable for studying causes and in determining facts leading directly or indirectly to the solution of some of the problems which have made the existence of these state institutions necessary." *Fourth Annual Report of the Board of Managers of Letchworth Village,* 1913.

program that is still forward-looking today. This report was signed by men whose vision has influenced many fields of investigation; L. Pierce Clark, August Hoch, Walter Fernald, H. H. Goddard, Charles B. Davenport, and William G. Lyle.

It was not until 1921, however, when the population of the institution had reached nearly two thousand, that research work was established as a part of the institution program, a development made possible by the generosity of Mrs. E. G. Harriman, who provided funds for the employment of a full-time scientific director. Dr. Howard Potter was appointed "to organize and direct the research work," Miss Grace Taylor was appointed psychologist, and Miss Ruth Liddle, social investigator, but until 1924 there was no laboratory and very little equipment. In 1924 the basement of one of the cottages and a small adjacent office building were turned over to the research department with its staff of five members. Miss Minogue, who had succeeded Miss Taylor, had undertaken the task of providing necessary test equipment, and, with Dr. Potter's support and assistance, had established the psychological service as an integral unit of the research department.

In 1925 the entire responsibility for the laboratory was taken over by the institution. At this time the position of psychologist was given civil service status, although it was not until 1928 that the position was listed in the Annual Report. The resignation of Dr. Potter in 1929 to accept appointment as director of research, at the Psychiatric Institute, closed this initial organization period.

Following Dr. Potter's resignation, the research department was under the supervision of Dr. Eugene W. Martz, clinical director, until 1933 when Dr. Edward J. Humphreys was appointed director of research. Under Dr. Humphreys' direction there has been a reorganization of the work of the department, providing for closer integration of the activities of its various divisions: psychiatry, neurology, psychology, and an affiliating unit in dentistry. The reorganization has also included the general division of labor into the clinical, educational and research responsibilities of the department; and the formulation of a program for development of these activities under the general direction of a research council representing various scientific and clinical fields.

The psychology division, therefore, functions as a unit of the research department of the institution; and its work, like that of the department as a whole, is organized under three heads: clinical service, educational activities, and research investigations. Its regular staff includes a research psychologist, a clinical psychologist and two resident intern assistants, with additional provision for students-in-training.

Since the fall of 1935 when the research department was moved to new quarters, the psychology division has had adequate office and laboratory space for its work. Equipment includes a relatively wide range of test materials, and a fair reference library. Equipment for research projects is added as needed.

Clinical Service

An institution whose inmate population is nearly four thousand, representing practically all forms of mental deficiency, and with a chronological age range from infancy to over seventy years, inevitably presents a wide variety of clinical, educational and custodial problems. These problems dictate the direction and extent of the clinical service, which is planned with three objectives in mind: first, to meet the needs of the institution; second, to furnish clinical material for students-in-training; and third, to provide data for research studies. The clinical work therefore must meet as fully as possible the rigid requirements of the research field, at the same time that it considers the more immediate problems which are a primary responsibility of the institution.

The major load is the examination of new admissions. The annual rate of admission has increased steadily during the twenty-five years of the institution's existence, having this year reached a peak near the six hundred mark. Each new patient is examined as soon as possible after admission, the preliminary survey consisting of a physical examination and brief psychiatric note, both by the physician, and a psychological examination. The latter includes a Stanford-Binet test, where this is practicable, with supplementary examinations, in most cases the Goodenough Drawing Scale and some performance tests. A preliminary report of the psychological examination including both quantitative and qualitative findings is sent to the physician in charge of the child, to the school, and to the social service department.

As soon as the social service record of the case is complete the child is presented at a consultation clinic, at which the psychiatrist, neurologist and psychologist together review the case record and the symptomatologies, and examine the patient with the idea of diagnoses which will include neurological, medical, psychiatric and psychological factors.

In addition to the study of new admissions the clinical work includes retests, special examinations requested by the doctors, teachers or staff members in other departments, and battery examinations which are part of the program for all high grade children, and are given within a few months after their admission to the institution. For the battery examinations wide range testing is employed with a view to determining special abilities or disabilities. Detailed reports of these examinations are sent to the physician in charge of the child and to the school.

Consultations with the parole staff, and with the physicians, are another aspect of the clinical service.

Educational Activities

The educational activities include the intensive training of intern members of the staff and special students; demonstrations in clinical psychology to physicians recommended by the Public Health Department of Washington and to visitors from other institutions; as well as presentation of psychological work at clinics given for visiting students.[3] These activities carry out one of the traditions established by Dr. Charles S. Little, who, during the twenty-five years of his superintendency at Letchworth Village, was most generous in providing opportunities for students who wished training in the field of mental deficiency.

The most important part of the training program is the work with the junior psychologists in intern positions. Since 1935 internships in psychology have been available for advanced students who are interested in having clinical training for a period of six months or a year. The work of these interns is planned to present a general course in psychological techniques, especially test techniques, with particular emphasis upon their application to problems of mental deficiency. In addition, it provides experience with the interrelation-

---

[3] During the year 1935–36 over seven hundred students visited the institution. Although the presentation of clinical material to these students is regarded as incidental to the regular work of the department, the effort and time involved is considerable.

ships within an institution, and opportunity to become acquainted with psychological work as correlated with the work of other members of the institution staff.

Interns have the privilege of attending staff meetings and clinical presentations in the allied medical fields of psychiatry, endocrinology and neurology, and of consulting with all other members of the research staff. They also have access to clinical material for research studies. Interns are expected to devote a certain amount of their time to the general routine work of the department, and to participate in such special work as may be assigned to them. Time allotments are arranged to give opportunity for independent work. This may emphasize the acquisition of psychological techniques, intensive psychological study of various features of cases, or the investigation of specific problems, depending upon the student's interests, earlier training and experience.

In brief, then, the educational activities of the psychology division are directed toward offering intensive practical experience in the application of psychological training to problems of mental deficiency and related fields.

Research

The research investigations in psychology, like the educational activities, have been closely related to the clinical service, and also, insofar as possible, to the work of other units of the research department, especially to the work in neurology and psychiatry. A list of papers and reports of studies in psychology from the institution was prepared. This list indicates that, particularly since 1935, there has been considerable interest in the study of tests and test techniques. Tests have been administered to selected groups of subjects within the institution, with a view to investigation of some of the assumptions underlying test performance, and to the possible extension of the clinical application of these measures.

A second group of studies has been concerned with the investigation of abilities of groups of subjects who have become expert in specific vocational tasks.

A third series of studies deals with inquiries into the behavior of mentally defective subjects in a free situation using a one-way-screen observation method. Other research in progress is not sufficiently advanced to warrant report at this time.

In addition to studies made by members of the staff, the courtesy of the department has been extended to research workers from other institutions: from the psychology department of the New York State Psychiatric Institute; the psychological department of Bellevue Hospital; and the research department of the Manhattan Industrial Trade School. Also, research opportunities are afforded for student members of the department whenever possible.

An important and most constructive influence in all of the research work at the Village has been a working relationship over a period of years with the Department of Genetics of the Carnegie Institution of Washington. Dr. Charles Davenport, a member of the Special Committee established in 1913, and still a member of the Letchworth Village Research Council, over this long period has not only himself carried on studies of children in the institution, but has also assisted most generously both officially and unofficially in the development of its research program.

In conclusion, it may be said of the psychology division that the clinical service represents primarily the work of the division in its relation to the institution, while the educational and research activities involve, in addition, a relationship to the community at large, and especially to professional and scientific fields. Taken together they represent the effort of this division to support a cardinal principle of the organization of the research department, namely, collaborative work dependent upon close clinical relationships with other divisions of the institution, and the establishing of avenues of exchange with educational and research interests outside the institution toward facilitating study of problems of human deficiency.

Functions of the Prison Psychologist[1]

Some two hundred thousand people at this moment are confined in the United States in correctional institutions such as jails, penitentiaries, reformatories, and prisons. According to a recent estimate (30)[2] there are eighty psychologists employed by correctional institutions, although there are certainly at least twenty more who are not members of professional groups. The ratio is therefore, for the country as a whole, one prison psychologist for every two thousand prisoners. These hundred psychologists probably would be best represented by the Medical Correctional Association, an affiliate of the American Prison Association, but less than twenty actually do belong.

Psychology in prison, of necessity is a recent innovation, since clinical psychology may be said to have begun after the first world war. As far as the author knows, no one has written a history of prison psychology, which is certainly excellent material for a master's thesis in social psychology or sociology.

In this paper the following topics will be discussed briefly:

1. What are the standards for prison psychologists?
2. What do prison psychologists do?
3. What forms of organizations do they function within?
4. What special training is indicated?
5. What is the probable future in this field?

---

[1] Reprinted from *Journal of Consulting Psychology*, 1945, 9, 101–104. Copyright 1945 by American Association for Applied Psychology.
[2] Bibliography begins on page 176.

I

For the most part, prison psychologists operate under civil service regulations, appointment being made on the weighted basis of clinical experience and training. In the state of New York the grades of Junior Psychologist and Psychologist exist. For the first grade a master's degree in psychology plus one year's clinical experience is required; for the higher grade, three years' clinical experience plus sixty graduate credits is needed. The requirements for psychologist closely correspond to the requirements of the Department of Mental Hygiene's standards for certification for qualified psychologist. While, in terms of the salaries, hours of work, and desirability of work as found in the State Prisons of New York, such standards are high, it may be said that standards should be raised higher, requiring the Ph.D. and five years' clinical experience for the higher grade.

II

The work in a prison may be said to fall under three broad headings:

1. Psychometric. To have a minimal amount of psychometric information for each individual. To compile periodical statistics of these findings. To administer other tests, such as personality tests, aptitude tests as needed. To measure academic progress.

2. Guidance. To give educational, vocational, and personal guidance, usually on the basis of request. Naturally, due to the unfavorable ratio of psychologists to inmates either minimal guidance to many or adequate guidance to relatively few is possible. While the problems of prisoners in terms of educational and vocational needs are similar to those of free adults, various limitations, such as educational facilities, institutional rules, and problems of outside adjustment, in terms of parole limitations must be taken into consideration.

3. Total evaluation. To act as a "penologist" in the total personality evaluation of the individual in terms of prognosis. Gives opinions, based on evaluation of the global individual, to the warden, classification board, parole board, etc. . . .

Personal guidance, which is perhaps the most valuable of any of the psychologist's functions, is hampered by the fact that the clients cannot enter into good rapport with the therapist since he is a prison official, and on the other side of the fence. Fearful that frank disclosures of personal problems may mean additional punishment keeps the great majority of men from complete rapport. To counteract this phenomenon which has been commented on by various writers such as Brancale (8), it has been suggested by Barnes and Teeters (3) that all therapists such as teachers, chaplains, doctors, psychiatrists and psychologists be employed by outside agencies, rather than by the correctional institution.

The third aspect of a prison psychologist's work refers to his relationship with the line and staff officers in a prison. He may be sent men who are observed to have peculiarities or are not adjusting to routine. He will make routine and special reports to various officers and departments. He may evaluate the individual's attitudes and personality as well as his more static mental processes for the board of paroles; furnish valuable information to the principal keeper who will assign the inmate to work; measure learning ability and mechanical aptitude of the inmate and make educational and vocational recommendations for the educational director; and make reports which will become part of the inmate's dossier for favorable action by the Governor in commutation cases.

III

Psychologists may function as relatively independent entities, loosely collaborating with other staff officials, or may be part of a closely integrated team or teams of workers. In the New York City Penitentiary under Warden R. A. Magee and Commissioner Austin H. McCormick, psychologists, psychiatrists, social workers, and physicians made separate reports, which were integrated by a classification expert into a master report. This was read to a classification board composed of ten or more prison officials who attempted to set up a plan of rehabilitation for the inmate following an interview.

In some institutions, the psychologist, and the psychiatrist are the permanent members of the classification clinic, doing the spade work for the fuller classification board where a high-ranking uniformed member, chaplain, director of industries, educational supervisor and others will sit in.

The best method of work seems to be a rather flexible system which allows the psychologist to function both in a team, and independently. Various experimental approaches have been tried in the federal prisons and in states such as New York, New Jersey, Connecticut and Texas, which, penologically speaking, are relatively advanced.

IV

The social value of rehabilitating felons is so great that the highest possible standards in all branches of personnel should exist. Such standards become unrealistic if pay is not commensurate, since any specialist, teacher, physician, or psychiatrist undoubtedly would prefer to work elsewhere than in a prison, other conditions being equal. In various states a 200 per cent increase in pay for keepers has resulted chiefly through pressure and information supplied by various prison associations as to the necessity of having high-type personnel. Using the keeper's salary as a guide, it might not be unrealistic to suggest that since equal danger exists, a psychologist's as well as other professional men's pay should begin at double a keeper's salary. Surprising as it may seem, in some states, there are prison teachers and prison psychologists who earn less than prison guards.

The special training and background of a prison psychologist may be broken into three areas: educational qualifications, experience, and personality. As previously indicated, the Ph.D. or equivalent of sixty graduate points in psychology, a majority in clinical and applied aspects, together with concentration in sociology (juvenile delinquency, criminology, penology), economics and the biological sciences is needed.

The greater variety of experience the psychologist can accumulate both in and out of psychology, the more valuable he will be. Work in a mental hospital, child guidance clinic, adult guidance clinic, is particularly helpful. Experience in teaching, leading adolescent groups and social welfare is also valuable. Work in factories, farms, menial labor work of all sorts should be considered an essential part of the prison psychologist's background, also close intimate contact with depressed groups especially in high delinquency areas on an equality basis is imperative.

The personality of the prison psychologist is valuable. A man may be an excellent psychologist, have a good knowledge of his techniques, but if he cannot enter into good rapport with the widest variety of individuals, in the age group from 16 to 80, Negroes and whites, mental ages 6 to 20, former annual incomes nothing to a million dollars, his other abilities come to naught. He must be able to repress his own moral standards, and evaluate the individual on the basis of his particular background, never sermonizing or evaluating the crime. Paraphrasing Clarence Darrow, he must love the criminal but hate the crime.

V

The immediate future for the prison psychologist is poor, and the present condition is difficult. This does not seem like a good field for the average young man trained in clinical psychology to enter, except for experience. Psychology in prison is generally dead-end work, especially, paradoxically, in the more progressive penal systems. All penal work is conducive to relaxation of standards. There has been an extremely high turn-over rate for psychologists in this field, and at the present time prisons are finding it very difficult to recruit personnel in psychology. Men who tend to remain in prisons are generally unqualified, do not keep up their professional contacts, do little reading and research. This is due to the unfavorable effect of prison work, which is generally conducted in professional isolation, without competent professional supervision, in a hostile or at least suspicious environment. Petty intrigues, unbending discipline, chicanery, deadening routine, and the general attitude of defeat do not help in keeping morale up to a high pitch. The psychologist always finds that he must consider his loyalties to his "clients" and to his institution, for often they conflict.

The long-range future for prison psychology is bright. Despite the fact that there were probably more psychologists working in prisons in 1928 than in 1948, the influence of prison psychology appears to be growing. Prisons which have resisted the impact of human engineering are beginning to bend with the stream of scientific thought. The emergence of the Reception Center Idea, the re-organizations of some prison systems with scientific psychology as a central core, and the growing influence of such men as Doll and Yepsen in New Jersey, Lindner in Maryland, Fenton in California and Giardini in Pennsylvania are signs of a new period in penology.

Prisons are often called correctional institutions. By and large they are mostly punishment institutions, but the change towards a stronger correctional policy is to be hoped. The reason for the enormous lag between actual policy in a prison and penological thought may be the inertia of such institutions, the caliber of governing officials, and most of all the indifference and misinformation of the public. The caliber of personnel in some prison systems such as New York is definitely improving, and although there have been backward slips, penology in practice has advanced considerably in the last forty years.

In concluding, we may briefly look at this matter from the eyes of the prison inmate. On the average, he is a young man, emotionally unstable, vocationally untrained, a product of an environment economically, socially, morally impoverished. He is usually a "rebel without a cause" (28), torn by conflicting values. He finds himself in a new, highly artificial environment, surrounded by criminals who, by and large, represent a concentration of the worse elements in his old neighborhood. Basically moral and law abiding, despite the fact that he is a convicted criminal, wearing a mask of indifference and a false bravado, he is actually a puzzled, hurt, lost human, without direction. His hopes and fears both vague, his ego alternating between excesses of rationalizations and self-punishment, stewing in an atmosphere of indolence conducive to grandiose day dreams, he is in a most excellent frame of mind for positive thoughts of good or evil.

This is the moment when a wise society should take this deviate, study him as an individual in terms of his personal background and endeavor to reconstruct with him a new realistic goal. The prison psychologist should be qualified to do this, and some bright day prisons may have more psychologists than keepers.

ROBERT I. WATSON

Washington University School of Medicine

Functions of Other Clinical Psychologists[1,2]

A considerable number of psychologists who use the clinical method are employed in agencies similar to those described in the previous *Readings*. Furthermore, the importance of this approach to human problems has found recognition in the employment of psychologists in a great variety of other areas, some closely related to those previously described, others very different in nature. The present account will deal briefly with some of these fields of employment and cite some of the literature on the remainder.

Psychological Clinics

Certain clinical organizations defy attempts to place them in any pattern because of differences in services rendered, the age groups seen, the nature of their sponsorship, and other factors. Since the only points in common are that they are organized to render "psychological service" and are headed administratively and professionally by psychologists, they will be referred to simply as psychological clinics. The University of Pennsylvania Psychological Clinic, whose history is described by Louttit in the *Readings*, is an instance. However, attention will be directed here to other clinics.

Rutgers University in New Brunswick, New Jersey, maintains a psychological clinic whose functions have recently been described by

---

[1] Prepared especially for this volume.

[2] An especially valuable summarized description of occupations in psychology, clinical and non-clinical in nature, appears in an article by Shartle (52).

Anna S. Starr, its director (57).[3] No restriction is placed because of the nature of the problem facing those who apply for its services; anyone requesting an appointment is seen in his proper turn. Its services are primarily diagnostic with specific interpretations and recommendations including suggestions for further referral being made to the person who referred or accompanied the case. All ages are involved, although 70 per cent of its recent clientele have been of school age. Schools refer a considerable number, but there has been an increase in self-referrals which is interpreted as an increasing public awareness of psychological services. The reasons given for referrals most commonly center around a determination of mental status either as a problem in itself or as a contributing factor in some behavior problem.

The Wichita Guidance Center of Wichita, Kansas, has been in operation for over fifteen years, during which thousands of clients have been seen. Jerry W. Carter (11), its director, has published an account of its program, which comprises psychological service in regard to vocational guidance, social adjustment, personality problems, inacceptable social behavior, and foster home placement. It uses as methods of study, preparatory to interpretation and remedial assistance or referral, a physical examination, the responsibility for which is assumed by the referring agency or person, and a social history and psychological study by the agency itself which involves interviews and tests appropriate to the situation. The staff at the time of publication included the director and two other psychologists, a psychological examiner, a remedial teacher, and a social work consultant.

So far examples have been drawn from general psychological clinics under either university or community auspices, which place no specific restriction whatever upon the nature of the clientele to be seen initially. Many other very similar organizations limit their attention to the child, as in so-called psycho-educational clinics connected with universities, colleges, and teachers' colleges, e.g., the Harvard Psycho-Educational Clinic and the Fort Hays State College Psychological Clinic.   •

College Mental Hygiene Services

Certain colleges maintain mental hygiene clinics or departments. In such a department the emphasis is by no means placed upon deal-

---

[3] Bibliography begins on page 176.

ing with the psychotic, psychoneurotic, or psychopathic individuals. True, the department serves as a clearing house for disposing of the cases of this sort that do arise, but such cases by no means constitute the bulk of practice. Rather, emphasis is placed upon dealing with so-called normal persons with the result that the clientele of a mental hygiene clinic often can be said to form almost a cross-section of the college population. The problems that cause a student to seek the help of the mental hygiene service are those attendant upon his adjustment, both to his stage of growth and to the special environment of a college.

In some instances the clinic is under the direction of a psychiatrist with a staff that includes a clinical psychologist. Relatively little has been published about the duties of the psychologist in such programs, but that which has appeared creates the impression that frequently there is a combination of the duties typical of a psychiatric clinic team member with those conducted by college counselors who work with vocational matters, study habits, and reading disabilities. Such is the case reported in incidental comments in the very valuable book of Fry and Rostow (19) on mental health activities at Yale University.[4]

Mental hygiene clinics may have, instead of a psychiatrist, a psychologist carrying the principal diagnostic and treatment load. McKinney described his operation of the "Personality Clinic" of the Student Health Service of the University of Missouri (33, 34). Housed in, and with access to, the full physical and personnel facilities of the Health Service and hospital, the clinical psychologist uses their records before counseling the student. In a sample of 200 cases thoroughly studied, McKinney found that in 39 per cent the complaints centered around social situations, though often such emotional factors as adjustment to fellow students, shyness, and lack of self-confidence were also involved; that in 38 per cent, motivational issues, such as problems of philosophy of life and self-evaluation, were present; that in fully 69 per cent, emotional issues with the social factor not predominant, such as emotional instability, irritability, depression, and worry appeared; while such issues as those centering around familial, sexual, disciplinary, academic, and financial problems were present in a considerably smaller percentage. In

---

[4] A shorter report of the same service is also available (18).

general, he found that multiple rather than single problems troubled the members of this group.

Problems coming to a student personnel counseling service embrace all of these mentioned, but focus of emphasis is shifted in college mental hygiene clinics. Much more reliance is placed upon short therapeutic sessions and the creation of attitudes and much less upon test interpretation and giving of information in these mental hygiene clinics, whether conducted by psychiatrist or psychologist. Although the student personnel and mental hygiene approach are complementary and equally desirable, the overlapping that occurs breeds the belief in college authorities that they have met the needs of their students with regard to problems of adjustment when one or the other is established. The name given, the auspices under which it is installed, the personnel staffing it, and publicity released about its work, all lend themselves to production of one emphasis or the other.

Psychiatric Clinics

The psychiatric clinic is primarily concerned with pre-psychotic and non-psychotic individuals who exhibit personality problems of varying severity. Their aim is to work with persons not requiring institutionalization and to make it possible for them to continue to remain active members of the community. This emphasis on prevention of more severe difficulties requiring institutionalization has given rise to the use of the term "mental hygiene clinic" for this sort of activity. Despite this aim, at least some of the patients seen must be institutionalized, and the original visit to the clinic is merely the first step in this process. Often such clinics limit their clientele to adults with the associated or independent agencies for children commonly referred to as child guidance clinics. Since Mathews describes the organization of one of these clinics for children in an article in the *Readings*, attention will be centered upon those serving adults.

Administratively, such clinics are connected with a variety of organizations.[5] Numerically they are most often outpatient clinics of state mental hospitals or some other agency of the state government. Clinics conducted as departments of general or psychopathic hos-

---

[5] A valuable national directory of psychiatric clinics is published by the Na-

pitals, or sponsored by city, county, federal, or private agencies, make up the remainder. In one sense this numerical preponderance of the state mental hospital clinic is misleading, for the large majority are traveling clinics appearing in a given community only at stated intervals, in some instances as infrequently as once a month. Not only does this make clinics organized under other auspices relatively more important, but it also introduces certain distinctions in operation.

The traveling clinic can allot a given community only a limited amount of time, often no more than a few hours a month. All services then are directed toward doing only that portion of the task that no one in the community is capable of doing. Almost always, single visits are all that can be allowed a patient. The session then becomes primarily diagnostic in nature. Treatment and follow-up are arranged with the referring agencies, if any, or with interested persons, friends, relatives, physicians, or nurses. Personnel of the clinic drawn from the sponsoring hospital, although almost invariably including the psychiatrist, may or may not include both the psychologist and the social worker. If it includes but one of these team members, the one available carries out the functions of the others. If the diagnostic testing and interview load of the psychologist permits, he is apt to assist in outlining the suggested treatment procedures to the referral source. The social worker is often the clinic manager arranging appointments and securing whatever social history the local agencies have available. Her case work contact with relatives or patients in the home is often relegated to the background or is even non-existent. In some few clinics the psychiatrist works alone collecting such social history and doing such testing as time, inclination, and skill permit. There are, of course, some traveling clinics where the personnel is adequate for the patient load, in which cases more time is given to diagnosis and much more attention is paid to treatment. In many such instances the procedure followed resembles that of the child guidance clinic (70).

The policy of an out-patient clinic attached to a general or psychopathic hospital in the community where the hospital is located is apt to stress treatment although some strictly diagnostic work unaccompanied by local treatment is carried on. If the psychological staff of the hospital is small, and the psychologist is called on to function only on referral, his duties are apt to be confined almost exclusively to testing, his report being included as part of the record for the use of the physicians just as is a report from a worker from any other special department in the hospital. On the other hand, if the out-patient staff in general is limited and the time of the psychologist is available he is more likely to be called upon to work on school and social problems directly with the patient (*41*).

Physical Rehabilitation Agencies

The term "rehabilitation" is capable of varying degrees of breadth of interpretation. Indeed, it is sometimes used to cover practically any sort of effort to restore some degree of physically or mentally healthy functioning to those individuals who have been deprived of it. Even after allowance has been made for a rather broad interpretation of the term, the review of Novis (*38*) shows that many public and private rehabilitation facilities are now in operation for both veteran and civilian. Dabelstein (*15*) points out that for every disabled soldier there are five disabled civilians and goes on to indicate that the National Health Survey immediately prior to World War II revealed that there are "approximately 23 million persons handicapped to some extent by disease, accident, and other sources" (p. 237). Even with allowance for the fact that many of these disabilities are comparatively minor, the potential magnitude of the task of rehabilitation is apparent. That many difficulties which these individuals face, especially those of a vocational nature, could be surmounted with the aid of the methods of the clinical psychologist is equally apparent. To avoid overlapping with other discussions, present consideration will be limited to the functions of the psychologist in program devoted to the rehabilitation of civilians whose disabilities are primarily physical in origin.

A federally supported state program for the vocational rehabilitation of the civilian physically disabled has been in operation since 1920 (*15*). In earlier years emphasis was almost entirely upon vocational training, with little attention given to diagnosis and prognosis. This emphasis, coupled with lack of interest on the part of the psychologist, probably accounts for his almost complete absence from the activity. Personnel was recruited primarily from the educational field. In 1943 the program was given new impetus by the passage of Public Law 113, which shifted the focus of attention from training to diagnosis as a prior step along with a general broadening of the entire activity.[6]

In this program most psychological activities are conducted with varying degrees of competence by so-called rehabilitation counselors, not professionally qualified as psychologists. There is provision for a psychologist as consultant in the federally sponsored organizational plan for the state rehabilitation agency. He is charged with state-wide responsibility in developing standards for the use of psychological techniques, a high level of clinical and administrative skill evidently being expected. Counselors, or, in the large local offices, psychometrists, actually carry out these activities (16). With the number of individuals employed by the states in the field of rehabilitation increased from 314 in 1940 to 967 in July 1945, and with an additional 409 positions remaining unfilled, a representative of the Federal Office of Vocational Rehabilitation (15) estimates that eventually 2100 professional personnel will be needed. Psychologists in considerable numbers, including those trained in clinical methods, will be in demand, both on a private individual or agency fee basis and as full-time employees. The position of the clinical psychologists in this program is not yet firmly fixed and, indeed, is a matter for pious hope rather than for description in terms of present accomplishment.

Institutions and Agencies for the Delinquent

It would appear that somewhat less than half the training schools for juvenile delinquents in the United States have the full- or part-time service of a psychologist (22, 23). What the psychologist does in these institutions is described in an investigation by a committee of one of the professional associations (20). The report shows that the superintendents expected the psychologist to help the staff and administration gain an understanding of the inmates, to aid in the treatment of behavior problems, to make vocational and educational recommendation, and to aid in the selection of parolees. The psychologist, it was found, attempted to carry out these services by means of various intelligence and achievement tests, collection of

---

[6] The program was also increased in scope to include mentally or emotionally handicapped persons. Since today there is some confusion as to what this change means (65) and thorough implementation remains in the future, this phase will be ignored.

case histories, and interviewing for the purpose of helping the child make an initial institutional or later parole adjustment. In about 75 per cent of the institutions the psychologist interviewed every child. His recommendations were made at staff conferences through written memoranda or to individual staff members. Rogers, Symonds, and Shakow (44) in commenting on the report of this committee viewed the findings as indicative of an inevitable stage of development of a professional field in which inadequately trained personnel are in the process of exploring the confines of a relatively new area of function. They point out that standards of professional competence are not high; utilization of the newer devices of personality, such as the projective techniques, seems non-existent; research is not mentioned; and the treatment techniques utilized are primarily of an intellectual supportive symptomatic type. It could also have been mentioned that the salary standards found are not such as to attract very many of the most adequately trained or alert members of the profession.

Despite the findings suggested by the previous articles, Habbe (23), as the result of a further questionnaire study, concluded that the treatment programs in training schools for delinquents are relatively effective. Reception interviews, tours of the building, orientation talks, a cottage program, sports, and social events are described by him as treatment techniques in common use. In some schools the reports prepared on a new arrival by various persons are routinely reported to those in direct contact with the boys; in others such procedure is followed only in exceptional cases. Some attention, especially by example, is given to the development of good character. Both individual and group treatment by varied personnel, ranging from Boy Scoutmasters to vocational counselors, are rather generally described.

The fact that a great variety of techniques such as these are used and accepted by their practitioners to bring about social and personal adjustment does not, however, prove either that they are effective or that more effective methods might not be appropriate if more adequately trained personnel were available. It would be fair to conclude that psychological services in training schools for delinquents are at a low level of professional development at present.

Another agency in which the psychologist works with the delinquent is the juvenile court. The work in California is illustrative

(10). Not only juvenile delinquents but neglected and mentally defective individuals under 21 years of age may be made wards of the court, which may provide for them in a manner best suited to their needs, as through a foster or boarding home, a psychiatric hospital, an institution for the mentally deficient, an orphanage, a training school, or by placement on probation. The probation officer serves the judge as counsel with regard to appropriate steps, and may in turn use the services of a psychologist or a psychiatrist. In the case of the defective psychopath, epileptic, or mentally deficient, it is mandatory that the individual be certified by two clinicians who may be psychologists. Otherwise, the employment of the psychologist is discretionary with the probation officer. A questionnaire sent to 58 county departments with returns from 44 to 76 per cent showed that half of these had some sort of psychological service. Two-thirds of those having none replied that they felt a definite need for some service, although there was confusion as to what it might be.

Miscellaneous Psychological Services

In spite of the diversity of function and locale of the clinical psychologist, there remain a considerable number of less common areas where he functions as well. The only thread of consistency in the list that follows is that, the clinical method of psychology as described by a psychologist is used in the following institutions: general hospitals (46), neurological hospitals (59), hospitals for the tuberculous (48, 49, 50), nursery schools (39), pre-schools (4), child health centers (17), family consultation centers (6, 9), case work agencies (54), psychiatric units for children (26), schools for the deaf (36), agencies working with the alcoholic (62), and old-age counseling centers (32). Psychologists are employed in various capacities in the U. S. Public Health Service (63) and the U. S. Employment Service (1), whose programs are in a state of rapid growth as yet uncrystallized.

Problems in dealing with reading difficulties are the concern of both educational specialists and certain psychologists. Most children's clinics are equipped to deal in some fashion with reading difficulties (27). Reading clinics, as such, are affiliated with some colleges and universities (55, 56, 60, 61).

Surprisingly little has been published in recent years about the psychologist in individual private practice. This is probably a reflection of interest and emphasis on socialized practice, since the number primarily engaged in this type of activity is very small (30, 64). Of course many psychologists do a certain amount of consulting work, but their major allegiance is elsewhere. Vernon (64) sent a questionnaire to those listing themselves as consulting psychologists and found that some were in general practice, while the others in varying degrees engaged in specialized practice, particularly with children or with school problems. In regard to matters of professional activity, such as methods of getting oneself known, fees, relationship with the medical profession, and legal problems, they showed surprising agreement of opinion.

Bibliography

1) Alexander, L. S. Employment counseling program of the United States Employment Service. *J. Clin. Psychol.*, 1946, 2, 123–126.
2) Babcock, H. An experiment in the measurement of mental deterioration. *Arch. Psychol.*, 1930, No. 117.
3) Barnes, H. E., and Teeters, N. *New horizons in criminology.* New York: Prentice-Hall, 1943.
4) Baruch, D. W. *Parents and children go to school.* Chicago: Scott, Foresman, 1939.
5) Bender, M. B., and Sairtsky, N. Micropsia and teleopsia limited to the temporal fields of vision. *Arch. Opthal.*, 1943, 29, 904–908.
6) Bennett, M. W. The psychologist in family consultation service. *J. Consult. Psychol.*, 1942, 6, 85–88.
7) Bragdon, H. D., et al. *Educational counseling of college students.* Series IV, Student Personnel Work, Vol III, No. 1, American Council on Education, 1939.
8) Brancale, R. Psychotherapy of the adult criminal. *J. Crim. Psychopath.*, 1943, 4, 472–483.
9) Brousseau, K. Psychological service at the Los Angeles Institute of Family Relations. *J. Consult. Psychol.*, 1937, 1, 49.
10) Burton, A. Functions of clinical psychological service in California juvenile and adult courts. *J. Psychol.*, 1946, 22, 93–96.
11) Carter, J. W., Jr. The Wichita Guidance Center. *J. Consult. Psychol.*, 1944, 8, 27–30.
12) Cornell, E. L. Taking the dogma out of the I.Q. *Ment. Hyg.*, 1927, 11, 804–810.
13) Cowley, W. H. The disappearing dean of men. *Proc. 19th Ann. Conf. Nat. Assoc. Deans, & Adv. Men*, 1937, 85–103.
14) Cowley, W. H. The strategy of coordination. *Occup.*, 1938, 16, 724–727.
15) Dabelstein, D. H. Counseling in the rehabilitation service. *J. Clin. Psychol.*, 1946, 2, 116–122.
16) DiMichael, S. G., and Dabelstein, D. H. The psychologist in vocational rehabilitation. *J. Consult. Psychol.*, 1946, 10, 237–245.
17) Frankl, A. W. Mental hygiene work in a well-baby clinic. *Amer. J. Orthopsychiat.*, 1945, 15, 103–111.
18) Fry, C. C. Mental hygiene and freshmen counseling. *Ment. Hyg.*, 1939, 23, 268–276.

19) Fry, C. C., and Rostow, E. G. *Mental health in college*. New York: Commonwealth Fund, 1942.
20) Giardini, G. I. (chm.). Report of the Committee on Psychological Work in Institutions for Delinquent Boys and Girls. *J. Consult. Psychol.*, 1942, 6, 157–162.
21) Goldstein, L., and Steinfeld, J. I. The conditioning of sexual behavior by visual agnosia. *Bull. Forest Sanit.*, 1942, 1, 137–145.
22) Greco, M. C. Clinical psychology and penal discipline. *J. Clin. Psychol.*, 1945, 1, 206–213.
23) Habbe, S. Treatment program in American training schools for delinquents. *J. Consult. Psychol.*, 1943, 7, 142–159.
24) Hunt, W. A., Wittson, C. L., and Harris, H. L. Temporary mental impairment following a petit mal attack. *J. Abnorm. Soc. Psychol.*, 1942, 37, 566.
25) Jastak, J. The manual-minded child. *Del. St. Med. J.*, 1942, 14, 126–129.
26) Kinder, E. F. Work of the psychologist in a psychiatric unit for children. *J. Consult. Psychol.*, 1944, 8, 273–280.
27) Kopel, D., and Geerdes, H. A survey of clinical services for poor readers. *J. Educ. Psychol.*, 1942, 33, 209–220.
28) Lindner, R. M. *Rebel without a cause: the hypnoanalysis of a criminal psychopath*. New York: Grune & Stratton, 1944.
29) Lloyd-Jones, E. M., and Smith, M. G. *A student personnel program for higher education*. New York: McGraw-Hill, 1938.
30) Marquis, D. The mobilization of psychologists for war service. *Psychol. Bull.*, 1944, 41, 469–473.
31) Martens, E. H. Clinical organization for child guidance within the schools. *U. S. Off. Educ. Bull.*, 1939, No. 15.
32) Martin, L. J. *A handbook for old age counsellors: the method of salvaging, rehabilitating and reconditioning old people used in the Old Age Counselling Center in San Francisco, California*. San Francisco: Clare deGrucy, 1944.
33) McKinney, F. Four years of a college adjustment clinic: I. Organization of clinic and problems of counselees. *J. Consult. Psychol.*, 1945, 9, 203–212.
34) McKinney, F. Four years of a college adjustment clinic: II. Characteristics of counselees. *J. Consult. Psychol.*, 1945, 9, 213–217.
35) Miller, J. The function of the child guidance personnel bureau. *Educ. Meth.*, 1937, 17, 118–120.
36) Myklebust, H. R. Functions of a psychologist in a residential school for the deaf. *J. Consult. Psychol.*, 1945, 9, 236–237.
37) National Committee for Mental Hygiene. *Directory of Psychiatric Clinics in the U. S. and Other Resources*. New York: National Committee for Mental Hygiene, 1946. 7th ed.
38) Novis, F. W. Developments in human adjustment and rehabilitation. *J. Clin. Psychol.*, 1946, 2, 1–12.

39) O'Shea, H. E. A psychologist in a university nursery school. *Ment. Hyg.*, 1939, 23, 40–48.

40) Paterson, D. G. A program for student counseling. In Hudelson, E. (ed.), *Problems of college education.* Minneapolis: Univ. Minnesota Press, 1928, 265–287.

41) Pierce, H. O. The function of a psychologist in a psychiatric clinic. *Ment. Hyg.*, 1946, 30, 257–276.

42) Piotrowski, Z. A. The Rorschach method as a prognostic aid in insulin shock treatment of schizophrenics. *Psychiat. Quart.*, 1941, 15, 807–822.

43) Rabin, A. I. Test-score patterns in schizophrenia and non-psychotic states. *J. Psychol.*, 1941, 12, 91–100.

44) Rogers, C. R., Symonds, P. M., and Shakow, D. Comments on the report of the Committee on Psychological Work in Institutions for Delinquent Boys and Girls. *J. Consult. Psychol.*, 1942, 6, 163–164.

45) Schilder, P. *Mind: perception and mind in their constructive aspects.* New York: Columbia Univ. Press, 1942.

46) Schott, E. L. The psychologist in the general hospital. *J. Consult. Psychol.*, 1944, 8, 302–307.

47) Scott, I. D. *Manual of advisement and guidance.* Washington, D. C.: U. S. Government Printing Office, 1945.

48) Seidenfeld, M. A. The psychological care of the tuberculous. *J. Consult. Psychol.*, 1938, 2, 176–179.

49) Seidenfeld, M. A. The psychological reorientation of the tuberculous. *J. Psychol.*, 1940, 10, 397–405.

50) Seidenfeld, M. A. The psychologist in the tuberculosis hospital. *J. Consult. Psychol.*, 1944, 8, 312–318.

51) Shakow, D. Deterioration in schizophrenia as reflected in performance on a variety of psychological tasks. *Psychol. Bull.*, 1942, 39, 508.

52) Shartle, C. L. Occupations in psychology. *Amer. Psychologist*, 1946, 1, 559–582.

53) Shipley, W. C., and Burlingame, C. C. A convenient self-administering scale for measuring intellectual impairment in psychotics. *Amer. J. Psychiat.*, 1941, 97, 1313–1325.

54) Shirley, M. M. The function of a psychologist in a case work agency. *Smith Coll. Stud. Soc. Work*, 1943, 13, 207–223.

55) Sievers, C. H. The University of Wichita reading clinic diagnostic and remediation program. *Univ. Wichita Bull.*, 1939, 14, 7–36.

56) Simpson, R. G. The reading laboratory as a service unit in college. *Sch. & Soc.*, 1942, 55, 621–623.

57) Starr, A. S. Patterns in clinical services. *Train. Sch. Bull.*, 1946, 43, 110–116.

58) Stevenson, G. S. Community clinics as training centers for psychiatrists. *Ment. Hyg.*, 1934, 18, 353–361.

59) Tallman, G. The psychologist in a neurological hospital. *J. Consult. Psychol.*, 1944, 8, 308–311.

60) Triggs, F. O. Remedial reading. *J. Higher Educ.*, 1941, 12, 371–377.

61) Triggs, F. O. Remedial reading programs: evidence of their development. *J. Educ. Psychol.*, 1942, 33, 678–685.

62) Trowbridge, L. S. The psychologist works with alcoholics. *J. Consult. Psychol.*, 1945, 9, 178–185.

63) United States Civil Service Commission. Standards for clinical psychologists in the Federal Government. *J. Clin. Psychol.*, 1946, 2, 126–130.

64) Vernon, W. H. D. Some professional problems of the consulting psychologist. *J. Consult. Psychol.*, 1946, 10, 136–142.

65) Wallin, J. E. W. The psychological aspects of the problem of vocational preparation and rehabilitation of mentally and physically handicapped civilians. *Amer. J. Ment. Def.*, 1945, 49, 290–299.

66) Wechsler, D., Halpern, F., and Jaros, E. Psychometric study of insulin-treated schizophrenics. *Psychiat. Quart.*, 1940, 14, 466–476.

67) Williamson, E. G. Minnesota's program for coordination of decentralized student personnel services. *Rep. 16th Ann. Meet. Amer. Coll. Pers. Assoc.*, 1939, 101–116.

68) Williamson, E. G., and Paterson, D. G. Coordinating counseling procedures. *J. Higher Educ.*, 1934, 5, 75–78.

69) Williamson, E. G., and Sarbin, T. R. *Student personnel work in the University of Minnesota.* Minneapolis: Burgess, 1940.

70) Witmer, H. L. *Social work: an analysis of a social institution.* New York: Farrar & Rinehart, 1942.

71) Wittman, P. Psychometric efficiency levels for psychotic and age classifications. *J. Abnorm. Soc. Psychol.*, 1943, 38, 335–350.

72) Zubin, J., and Berrera, S. E. Effect of electric convulsive therapy on memory. *Proc. Soc. Exper. Biol.*, 1941, 48, 596–597.

III

Diagnostic Methods

JERRY W. CARTER, JR.

Wichita Guidance Center

A Note on Psychodiagnosis[1]

Perhaps our difficulty in formulating a satisfactory curriculum for the training of clinical psychologists and in coping with other professional problems such as standards for membership in the Clinical Section of the A.A.A.P. grows out of confused and inadequate notions of what we expect of psychoclinicians (155).[2] In a field so intimately concerned with that of test construction, it is understandable how many of us would tend to confuse psychodiagnosis with psychometrics even to the point of attempting to quantify the case history method (9, 119) and how others might compensate for this limitation by emphasizing psychotherapy somewhat to the neglect of its basic and correlate subject, psychodiagnosis (218). It is with these considerations in mind that the writer attempts the following description of psychodiagnosis.[3]

Psychodiagnosis is the evaluation of an individual's behavior equipment preparatory to helping him adjust better in the future. By behavior equipment we refer to those classes of organized responses commonly called personality traits such as abilities, skills, achievements, habits, attitudes, ideals, temperaments, fears, etc. (134, pp. 121–126). Before the treatment or handling of a case, the clinician's first job is to weigh the individual's personality traits and determine their asset and liability values.

Essentially, the method of psychodiagnosis is one of interviewing.

---

[1] Reprinted from *Journal of Consulting Psychology*, 1940, 4, 137–139. Copyright 1940 by American Association for Applied Psychology.

[2] Bibliography begins on page 428.

[3] The writer has offered elsewhere a more extensive outline and description of psychodiagnostic procedure (43, 158).

In the diagnosis of children's behavior pathologies, it is necessary as a rule to interview parents or other informants as well as the child himself. In the main, there are two general types of interview techniques: (a) standardized interview-tests such as the Binet and other psychometric tests; and (b) unstandardized interviewing which may vary from casual conversation to more systematic questions and answers. Both are directed towards the same end, namely, of trying to discover in a psychodiagnostic sense "Who is this child and what are his problems?" With few exceptions, neither the standardized techniques by themselves nor the unstandardized interviewing alone will satisfy the requirements of good clinical practice; both are required in the great majority of cases.

When both of the above types of interviewing are effectively employed, they yield a behavior picture of the child and his problems in two dimensions. The first or cross-sectional dimension is secured by the clinician directly from his own observations of the child's behavior, by means of both psychometric aids and unstandardized interviews, and indirectly, from the informants' descriptions of the child's behavior as it is at the time, in the home, school and elsewhere. The second or longitudinal dimension is concerned with the historical antecedents of the behavior exhibited by the child at the time he is seen in the clinic. Unlike some of those in the cross-sectional, there are no standardized interview techniques for getting at the longitudinal or developmental dimensions of a child's behavior because of the myriad complexity of his reactional biography (134, Chapter III). Rather, the clinician has to rely upon parents and other sources for information about the child's behavior development. Each of these two dimensions is a necessary complement to the other in any adequate picture of the whole personality of the child. It is only when the circumstances, conditions and events that have contributed to the child's present behavior are known, that the latter appears in its true perspective.

While diagnostic interviewing is inclusive of the field of clinical psychometrics it is in no wise synonymous with the latter. Psychometric tests are tools which may aid the clinician in obtaining cross-sectional samples of a child's behavior. By means of them one is able to compare certain features of a given individual's behavior equipment with statistically derived norms. In the best clinical sense, tests are more controlled interview techniques. Their value depends upon their statistical reliability, their applicability to the individual case and upon the circumstances of administration (Kent 135, 136, Mitrano 183). Therefore, all the assumptions implicit in the testing situation must be satisfied before the behavior sample can be considered a valid one. Since one can never be certain how well these requirements are met, the clinician cannot afford to be content with numerical test scores alone. Moreover, behavior, other than that required by the test, may be exhibited which is frequently of more clinical value than the test scores themselves. Furthermore, the experienced clinician will recognize that no one test nor any battery of tests can completely describe the whole of the individual's personality or behavior equipment. For one thing, tests are usually designed to "measure" only particular achievements, skills, abilities, etc. On the other hand, despite their number and variety, there are not enough tests with which to "measure" all the behavior equipment of every individual. However, in recognizing these limitations, one should by no means minimize the usefulness of tests but accord them their properly proportioned share of importance among other techniques used in diagnostic interviewing.

Although there are no standardized interview techniques for obtaining an adequate longitudinal view of behavior development, this type of interviewing can be none the less objective (7, 43, 133, 154). It depends entirely upon the availability of information, the examiner's skill in obtaining it, and upon his ability to evaluate information secured. Success with this type of interviewing is largely a matter of the adequacy of the clinician's own personality make-up. He must avoid being that kind of an expert whom Stromberg defines as ". . . one who avoids the trivial errors that he may speed on to the grander fallacies." Instead, he must seek a real understanding of the child and his problems. Because there are no exact rules to follow he must rely upon a rigorous clinical discipline based upon sound training and experience if he is to remain free of those "expert" ways of thinking which variously relate all behavior pathologies to either glandular dysfunctions, special brain centers, focal infections, mental complexes, hereditary factors, or what not. Instead of these over-simplified short-cuts of dubious clinical value, he must think in more realistic terms of the child's behavior history.

The behavior of every individual whether subnormal, normal, or abnormal has a history. No clinician can hope to understand a case adequately without knowing its history.

Psychodiagnosis as a clinical procedure usually involves some such program of interviewing as outlined below (43, 154, 158):

1. The securing of the complaint history and other information as may be more or less spontaneously told by informants.

2. A more systematic inquiry into the child's developmental history.

3. An investigation of familial interpersonal relationships and home conditions.

4. An interview with the child to secure his version of his difficulties and any other information he may give.

5. The psychometric examination of the child.

6. The clinical interpretations and synthesizing of all the information obtained into a diagnostic formulation of the problem as a basis for prognosis and treatment or handling of the case.

If some such notion of psychodiagnosis as the one stated above is, in principle, an acceptable partial definition of what is to be expected of clinical psychologists,[4] its implications for many of our professional problems are important. For example, the educational objectives as well as the course content of a curriculum for the training of clinical psychologists might be operationally defined, instead of relying upon surveys of opinion as to the already existing courses which should be included in such a curriculum. Again, much the same thing might well be applied to formulating a conception of our professional standards for clinical practice. Even though it may not be possible at present to set up standards in terms of what a clinical psychologist ought to be able to do, it is important that we conceive an adequate and desirable goal as a basis for future action.

---

[4] Although the correlate subject of treatment is omitted here, it should not be ignored by the reader in an operational consideration of the field of clinical psychology.

EDGAR A. DOLL

The Training School, Vineland, New Jersey

Psychometric Pitfalls in Clinical Practice[1]

It has sometimes been said that clinical psychology is an art which employs scientific procedures. The observation is sometimes made proudly and sometimes disparagingly. Yet there is no inconsistency in the statement, for as an art clinical practice leans heavily on the support of science. But as a science, clinical psychology has not yet transcended its artistic antecedents.

This anniversary of the founding of the first formally organized psychological clinic in this country marks more than the mere passage of years; it marks the turn of an era. Present indications suggest that clinical psychology has come of age. Born under somewhat dubious circumstances as the outcome of an early romance between psychology and education, this infant prodigy of our time dates the first flirtation of psychology in the fields of application. Our patrician forefathers viewed the liaison askance and repeatedly sought to disown the offspring. This is perhaps not the place to review the childhood and youth of clinical psychology in the orthopsychiatric clichés of paternal rejection, sibling rivalry and traumatic episodes. Rather this is an occasion to welcome this promising youth into the company of his academic elders along with those professional siblings whose careers, while somewhat less stormy, have profited materially from the mutual association.

[1] An address delivered to a symposium in honor of fifty years of clinical psychology, at the University of Pennsylvania, September 3, 1946. Reprinted from *Journal of Consulting Psychology*, 1947, 11, 12–20. Copyright 1947 by American Psychological Association.

Yet few will deny that clinical psychology has been something of a problem child. Nor has the stripling yet achieved a fully mature adjustment. It seems pertinent to indulge in some self-analysis of our present status with due reference to anamnestic background and prognostic trends. Perhaps in doing so we shall discover some suggestions for therapy and regimen which may facilitate a more favorable outcome than would otherwise be the case.

I first became acquainted with clinical psychology some years ago as undergraduate laboratory assistant to Guy M. Whipple in his years at Cornell when his *Manual of Mental and Physical Tests* was the only standard materia psychometrica for the study of individual differences. It was one of my functions to assist in a realistic demonstration of the errors of individual measurement. The opening exercises in Whipple's manual, as some of you will recall, dealt with physical measurement as a preliminary to mental measurement. It was one of my functions to serve as the Vp, or subject, of these measurements and to make such a simple task as the measurement of height as susceptible to error as I could. Accordingly with the first observer an unnoticed bending of the knee, for the second a stretching of the neck, for the third a slump of the spine, and so on, served to disturb the accuracy of the measurement. The observers, meanwhile, absorbed in the novelty of applying a new technique, were characteristically more concerned with the measurement than with the person measured. Imagine the astonishment of the class when the diversity of measures was arrayed. This led into a statistical treatment of the measures for central tendency and dispersion, which, if I was successful, proved to be sufficiently erratic to point a moral.

To emphasize the unreliability of measurement, or shall we say its probable error, the measurements were then repeated. With increasing alertness on the part of the observers it was only somewhat more difficult to continue to evade accuracy of measurement.

You will readily understand that here was an object lesson designed to reveal the pitfalls of measurement. While this illustration reflected only intentional dissimulation, the moral was readily apparent. Whipple would then point to the motto on the east wall which read, "You can tell by trying." The class would then about face and read the second injunction, "But don't monkey with the method."

Here were the beginnings of precision attitudes toward measurement. This lesson was carried over into the more subtle phases of psychometric effort with two major principles at issue, first that of always keeping the subject before the examiner, and second that of emphasizing the variables inherent in personal appraisal. For example, in the measurement of weight it was my task to see that the scales were out of balance before I was weighed, thereby encouraging the examiners to insure the accuracy of their instruments before putting them to use.

I recall an episode which illustrated the uncertainties of inference in the detection of guilt. On a certain occasion I was asked to inspect one of two boxes in the adjoining room. On my return it was the task of the class to see if they could determine, by means of the association technique, which box I had opened. In this little plot I had opened the box which contained a revolver but not the box which contained an ace of diamonds. As the experiment proceeded I was already sufficiently hardened in my career of dissimulation to evade detection. But all stimulus words cued for diamonds proved too romantically cathectic. Imagine the chagrin of the class in falsely convicting me of having viewed the ace of diamonds; the verdict lacked the ring of truth!

These personal experiences no doubt influenced my later and continuing concern for errors of measurement and for errors of inference based on measurement. Meanwhile clinical psychology was outgrowing its infancy and with the advent of the Binet scale may be said to have entered its later childhood. This preadolescent spurt in growth and development marks the second epoch in the history of our turbulent hero who was now sufficiently stalwart to carry arms in the first World War. The callow youth survived this episode not only with astonishing credit, but with a very marked accession of adolescent maturity. He could even complacently accept his infant sibling rival of 1920, child development, on whom he has since attempted to bestow brotherly affection, though not perhaps with the degree of success that might have been anticipated.

As a vigorous young man in the second World War, clinical psychology attained a stature and an association with other relatively novitiate fields of psychological application, including even his critical sire, experimental psychology, with such success that today we have new promise of honorable status in the parental house.

Those here present who assisted during the confinement, nursed the infant, nourished the child, and were the boon companions of its adolescence, may well view with pardonable pride the recognition now accorded this vigorous stripling. Hail, Pennsylvania!

This pride is not unmixed with concern for the future history of a career which might easily be gravely impaired unless the integrity of its character is soundly established in the world of scientific moral values. We may well view with alarm as well as satisfaction the extraordinary future which lies ahead, and we shall do well to moderate our pride with misgivings centering around the sense of trust and mission which confronts us.

In one sense all science begins as art, namely, the art of observation which precedes measurement. We agree with McCall that whatever exists exists in some amount, and that these amounts are susceptible to measurement. But we must first observe what exists before we can proceed to its measurement. That existence may even be only hypothesized and the real proof of existence may perhaps not be attained until adequate measurement has been accomplished.

The clinical psychologist is, or at least should be, first of all a *psychologist* concerned with the phenomena within his professional framework. Psychometry is the technician aspect of clinical psychology. The more successfully objectification, standardization and categorical definition are achieved, the more completely does the field become subject to the use of technical assistance. This is remarkably witnessed in the experience of Manson and Greyson in the evolution of the psychological clinic of the disciplinary training center in the Mediterranean theater of operations of the U. S. Army, where the technician aspects of clinical psychology were highly systematized and reduced to the level of nonprofessional operation. The first pitfall for the clinical psychologist to avoid is this reduction of his status from clinical *psychologist* to psychometrician. The bait in this trap is the scientific ideal offered as a substitute for the professional art. To avoid this the clinical psychologist must not yield his patrimony of psychology for the blandishments of psychometry.

As we consider the practice of clinical psychology in its overall aspects, with an orientation toward psychometry as only one of the means by which the ends of practice may be achieved, we start with Propbst's concept of the patient as the unit of practice and Wells' definition of the mental test as a standard situation in which the subject may be psychologically observed. Such client-centered study and such test-centered observation derive from a consideration of the total clinical problem, the precipitating complaint, or the guidance-oriented attitude. Hence it is necessary first of all to clearly set forth the purposes involved in the clinical-psychological consideration of the individual client. And it is necessary to establish an explicit bill of particulars as to the issues to be resolved. This specification of the problem immediately leads into an estimate of its ramifications based on insightful consideration of the history of the problem and the various stages and concomitants of its development. Coincidentally, the clinical psychologist indulges in reasonable speculation regarding the etiological origins, the behavioral manifestations, and the situational circumstances attending the matter under consideration.

At this point the technique of interview is at maximum operation since it provides not only the orientation toward the problem, but also affords background information essential to the development of explanatory hypotheses. Yet it is particularly in this field that clinical psychology has not yet been successful in establishing more than meager procedures of the order of scientific merit. Bingham and Moore's *How to Interview* is a helpful guide, and Paul W. Preu's *Outline of Psychiatric Case-Study* affords a useful manual. The recent literature shows some tendency toward interview standardization, and such an instrument as the Vineland Social Maturity Scale offers a specific technique which is useful for laboratory instruction in interviewing. Yet the range of knowledge and skill required for successful interviewing even in narrow areas of practice poses a serious obstacle to the successful development of standardized interview methods. Likewise, the scope of potential coverage makes the interpretation of interview data almost inevitably artistic rather than scientific. If we can develop the technique of interviewing to the present level of psychometry it is not to be doubted that fifty years from now we shall write a different chapter not only on this topic but on clinical practice in general.

The second pitfall in psychometric measurement is that of selecting the tests that may most advantageously be resorted to in given clinical situations. Is the subject infant or senescent? Male or female? Literate or nonliterate? With or without sensory or motor handicap? Gifted or feebleminded? Adjusted or disturbed? Of what race, color or nationality? Of what social background? And so on? These circumstances will obviously influence the choice of tests in respect to which some will be impracticable, others irrelevant, and still others misleading. Here again, the clinical psychologist is an artist selecting the brushes and pigments most appropriate to his canvas.

There are almost no standard operating procedures which definitively outline with scientific warrant the particular battery of tests most likely to prove successful in a given case. Nor do we have multiple regression equations or other satisfactory means for their scientific evaluation. Perhaps this is the reason why some psychologists rely completely on some single test which happens to be conventionally fashionable. Obviously the selection of the most practicable and most relevant tests will be determined in large measure by the clinician's speculative orientation toward the case, derived from the hypothetical consideration of the most probable or most plausible resolution of the clinical problem. Yet if in respect to a particular case study one asks the clinical psychologist why he employed a particular test rather than some other, one too often encounters a hurt rejoinder, or an ingenuous astonishment rather than a rational explanation. "It's in our routine," they say. But it is one thing to use a test for frankly exploratory purposes and quite another to select a test with clear design as specially relevant to the problem under consideration. Here, too, we may anticipate that the next half-century will reveal marked advances in the systematic planning of test batteries (or SOP's) scientifically standardized in relation to specific clinical issues. Indeed as early as twenty-five years ago at least one clinical laboratory, that at Ohio State University, was seriously engaged in the development of differential clinical syllabi systematically oriented to particular types of clinical problems.

But assume that a suitable battery of tests has been agreed upon as representing demonstrated scientific merit. It is evident that today we have no common standardization of these batteries in respect to the same subjects, so that cross-reference from one test to another may be had in respect to the same standardization samples. Undoubtedly a serious task of the future is such multiple standardization of test batteries on identical subjects for equivalence of norms and correlational interpretation.

For simplicity of exposition we may therefore confine ourselves to the consideration of single tests, scales, or systems. Here the clinical psychologist in his psychometric endeavors is faced with many problems, each of which presents a series of pitfalls besetting the steps of the unwary. Let us consider some of these hazards.

1. Has the test been normatively standardized, and if so on what kind and how large a sample? Does the norm of central tendency represent a general or a particular norm? How has the sample been selected? What variables are reflected in it? To what extent can these variables be allowed for in respect to subjects from less generalized samples?

Californians present will not be reluctant to admit that the inhabitants of that fair state reflect superior social-economic selection. Many evidences support this conclusion. And no doubt the citizens of Palo Alto will modestly recognize that a university community generally contains a somewhat more superior population (from at least the standpoint of intelligence) than do most industrial or geographically isolated areas. It is not therefore too surprising that the mean I.Q. of 100 established for most age levels of the 1916 Stanford has not been duplicated, but rather that the mean I.Q. for wider selections of the population proved to be closer to 85. But the citizens of Millville, New Jersey, are at a disadvantage in comparison with those of Palo Alto, and consequently it would not be strange if the early mean quotient score of 100 established at successive ages for the Porteus Maze might prove to be 115 in other population samples. If these differences in samples are not recognized, the individual subject who achieves a quotient score of minus one sigma on the 1916 Stanford and plus one sigma on the early standardization of the Porteus Maze should have this difference attributed not to a Stanford–Porteus difference but rather to a Palo Alto–Millville difference.

Here again we foresee future resolutions of these difficulties; indeed the 1937 Binet specifically attempted to achieve a standardization based on a national rather than upon a local sample. But what allowance should one make in local case studies? Perhaps the techniques of market research and opinion polling will be much more widely used in the future than in the past in the determination of normative samples. In any case we may certainly expect that the populations employed for test standardization will in the future be much more adequately described than in the past and by such means as will permit some more effective translation of equivalent scores than has heretofore been practicable.

2. Whatever the sample, and whatever the test, the results will show both a floor and a ceiling, the former reflecting the minimum effective age or level of ability at which the test may be successfully employed and the latter the optimum age or asymptote of the maturational standardization. Both floor and ceiling will depend upon the range and functions of the test in question and upon the selectivity reflected within the sample according to the availability of normative subjects. The practice of obtaining ceiling samples based on school achievement is definitely to be deprecated in view of the school mortality of the intellectually or linguistically inferior subjects, which results in artificial ceilings above those of the total population. Witness again the ceiling standard of the 1916 Stanford which logically represents the upper quartile rather than the median of unselected populations. When this ceiling was validated for more random samples at the fourteen-year level, that validation was not generally accepted. Although now validated for the 1937 scale at the fifteen-year ceiling, some states continue the legal requirement of employing the sixteen-year ceiling. Maturation ceilings will vary from test to test, and this constitutes a serious difficulty in the comparison of scores above the lowest ceiling in a given test battery. Moreover, in the measurement of adults there is apparent need for recognizing the regression of such ceilings to lower levels for the period of mental involution.

3. A corollary of the test ceiling is evident in the compression effects on test performance resulting from the limitations of a testing instrument beyond its average maturation ceiling. This restricts the attainment of superior scores as age advances, since the range at the upper limit of most tests or scales reflects progressively diminishing return. Consequently the interpretation of ceiling scores cannot ignore the subordinate ages or performance levels at which the compression effects are observable. Therefore each test system must be considered not only with reference to its total range but also its effective range since the interpretation of scores at either extreme of the scale is more or less hazardous.

A further aspect of the ceiling score is the question of how to express scores beyond the normative ceiling. Some test systems employ arbitrary systems of weighting these post-ceiling scores. Others resort to extrapolated scores based on the distribution of measures in the ceiling sample. Such scores are sometimes expressed in sigma units, sometimes as percentiles, sometimes as extrapolated age scores based on evidence or assumption of a symmetrical distribution.

These difficulties materially embarrass the interpretation of compared scores derived from tests with unequal ceilings. They affect not only test-age differences and test-quotient differences, but also the deviation differences since the normative ogives for different tests and test-systems may not be unequivocally comparable at all points. It is probable that these difficulties will be resolved by ingenuities of statistical manipulation. But such manipulation does not always completely resolve all the issues involved. They are too often comparable to methods of resuscitation which maintain breathing but leave the victim somewhat waterlogged.

4. Another hazard is that of test-retest reliability. This measure of reliability should not be confused (as it so often has been) with the split-half method of estimating test reliability. Whereas the former gives a measure of dependence on the stability of test scores under repeated measurement, the latter gives only a measure of consistency for one-half of the scale compared with the other. Each measure has its place but they serve different purposes. It is to be expected that in the future no test will be considered adequately standardized until both these estimates of reliability have been employed. Obviously a test which yields unstable scores under repetition must be employed with definite reservations.

5. One of the widest pitfalls in psychometric measurement is that of the probable error of the measure. This expression usually includes the variability of measurement due to minor sources of error both within and without the subject's control. First among these is the personal equation of the examiner whose personality, clarity of speech, facility in test administration, and so on, materially affect the subject's responses. Factors emanating from the subject himself such as degree of health or fatigue, amenability to examination, facility of response, and the like, materially influence the *entre-nous* relationship between subject and examiner. It may be assumed that all psychologists are familiar with the phenomenon of the probable error of the measure and that they do not confuse this with the

probable error of the distribution. Yet our literature is replete with publications on comparative test performances which wholly ignore this source of error, the consequences of which are self-evident in any attempt to fix specific cutting scores, especially when such classification scores are confused with diagnostic implications. The attempt to use specific I.Q.'s as limiting points for mental deficiency is extraordinary witness of the failure to observe the significance of the probable error of the measure. We ignore here the probable error which attends gross errors of measurement due to faulty examination, dissimulation, unresolved effects of various handicaps, and so on.

6. Akin to this difficulty is that of the use of deviation scores based on generalized distributions. It is regrettable that many test standardizations are not even reported in such a manner that deviation scores can be successfully employed. But even where deviation scores are available, there is a notorious failure to employ them in comparing the results of one test with those of another. There is a tendency to employ constant cutting scores from one test to another regardless of the deviation significance of such scores. The indiscriminate use of quotient scores is a prime source of error unless the significance of such scores in terms of some equivalent of standard deviation is rigorously adhered to. This is reflected at its worst in the indiscriminate averaging of age scores, quotient scores, and percentile scores without regard for the nature of the respective distributions. It is therefore incumbent upon the clinical psychologist when employing psychometric methods to be thoroughly familiar with the distributive aspects of specific test standardization.

7. Closely allied to the statistical interpretation of scores is their relation to the validity of cutting scores in terms of differential standardization, especially where diagnostic symptom-complexes are at issue. This error has been conspicuously apparent in the attempts to employ critical scores for the determination of mental deficiency in the use of particular test systems without reference to the validity of such critical scores in relation to the criteria of differential clinical diagnosis. It should by this time be almost axiomatic that a test has not been sufficiently standardized for clinical use until it has also been validated in terms of the clinical significance of the deviations from its central tendencies. Many clinical symptom-complexes show marked overlap in relation to the uncritical use of critical scores. Witness for example the complete overlap between the moron

degree of mental deficiency as feeblemindedness and the lower limits of intelligence in the normal continuum. There are relatively few critical scores which are clinically pathognomonic and it is difficult enough to set up multiple pattern scores which are consistent with the criteria of differential mental diagnosis. Obviously a particular problem here is the determination of suitable criteria for the assignment of critical scores with respect to their clinical validity. This problem involves a progressive resolution of the issues as our knowledge advances both in respect to the clinical symptom-complexes and the optimum use of psychometric devices.

8. And what shall we say of the practice effects from repeated administration of the same test? Some standard tests are almost immune to practice effects, including both the incidental effects of repetition and the effects of deliberate coaching, while other tests show a marked consequence of such influences. The validity of test interpretation will be materially affected by the extent to which repetition of the same test shows practice effects. The interpretation of practice effects must also reckon with the size of the effect in relation to the time interval between repeated administrations of the same test, and for that matter the effect of practice in test situations as such in a succession of different tests, or what has sometimes been called the "test-wiseness" of the subject. The influence of practice needs also to be determined in relation to age and in relation to the deviation scores themselves. The validity value of a test may also be influenced by its repeated use. On the other hand, the repetition of a test may be an index of ability to learn and might in this way become clinically useful under sufficiently sophisticated interpretation.

For clinical purposes it is not sufficient that a given psychometric score be reliable and valid pro tem. In clinical practice, psychometric results are used not only to evaluate the present status of the subject but also to predict his future status. The clinical psychologist must therefore be concerned with the prognostic value of his psychometric scores. Life would be so simple if the I.Q. were really constant for purposes of individual prediction! At the race track one is not so much interested in the average horse as he is in the one on which he has placed his bet. Moreover, such a race is often won or lost by a nose rather than by a length. Shall we place our bets any less cautiously on the human race? If the individual has an I.Q. of 69 today, what are the chances of his having an I.Q. of 71 later in life if I.Q. 70 is to be used as a critical score for mental deficiency? Obviously such predictive values would have a relation to the probable error of the measure as well as to clinical validity for purposes of diagnosis. Here too as experience evolves in the years ahead, we shall if sufficiently alert have no particular difficulty other than that of time for amassing the evidence in establishing far more accurate criteria for prediction than is possible at present. But we should not be too surprised if our colleagues in the field of medical diagnosis show some amusement at the ingenuousness with which we now alter our diagnoses from day to day.

It is as painful to reassert these obvious dangers in the field of psychometric measurement as it is to listen to their repeated recital. You know these hazards and no doubt you present them forcefully in your instruction of students. But what shall we say of the observance of these difficulties in the laboratory as opposed to the classroom? How genuinely are we concerned to insure that these sources of error shall not vitiate our practice? To paraphrase a well-known observation, "The fault is not in our tests but in ourselves." Fifty years ago the clinical psychologist was in command of his tests: today the tests threaten to dominate him. So much has been learned in the meantime that, if our tests do not suffice to meet our needs, at least we have better ideas as to what those needs are and how the tests can best be made to serve them.

Assuming that the clinical psychologist in his use of psychometric measurement is clearly alert to these pitfalls and wary in their avoidance, there yet remains the problem of interpretation. There is no evidence at present, or at best only dubious evidence, that psychometry can replace clinical psychology. At best psychometry is only a stand-in for the clinical psychologist. The psychologist as clinical artist must still conceive his goal as an achievement in respect to which mental tests can only be the hammer and chisel, but not the sculpture.

We have suggested the difficulties of relevant test selection and use. We may now deal with their incompatibility for interpretation. This immediately raises the question of the test patterns for different aspects of total clinical consideration. These patterns have reference to the clinical syllabus or SOP in relation to particular complaints. But they have an internal significance in relation to different parts of that syllabus. Thus the distinction between mental level (or quantity) and mental type (or quality) is far from being achieved. Yet it may be clinically more important to decide whether a person is fluid or crystal in mental operation than to estimate the level of such operation. Likewise a clinical diagnosis may fairly be considered as incomplete except as it accomplishes an etiological as well as a therapeutic interpretation of the evidence.

Such orientation is of relatively recent date and may be expected to command highly profitable attention in the years ahead. Yet Witmer in his earliest days was an advocate of diagnostic teaching. And the Psychological Clinic of this University still employs response to learning as a highly useful means of mental diagnosis.

We have only begun to capitalize clinical psychology for psychological therapy, but the rush of events of the past five years has set goals and techniques for evaluating the dynamics of personality structure and expression which open vistas only dimly foreseen in the past. One ultimate test of the successful practice of clinical psychology is the outcome achieved through successful treatment. This includes not only therapy but also disposition and regimen. The extraordinary, not to say alarming, demand for clinical psychology in the Veterans Administration is only one evidence of the distance we have gone in the past fifty years. If we can meet those demands effectively we may look forward to a second half-century in our field even more promising than the pioneering years behind us.

It is fitting to close these observations with a tribute to The Psychological Clinic of this University, not only for its historical role in the development of clinical psychology but also for its very survival during the unsettled period behind us. Such a tribute recognizes not only the forceful personnel associated with this Clinic throughout its history, but also witnesses the inherent native strength and continuing needs of clinical psychology itself.

And perhaps a word is in place respecting the courage and vision of those other pioneers—Terman, Huey, Wallin, Pintner, Goddard and the rest—who sowed the seed the reaping of whose harvest lies immediately ahead of us. Our best work is yet to be done. The tasks seem clear and the available tools not too badly fashioned. The market is waiting. Our task is to recruit promising personnel and to insure sufficient skill and competence to capitalize the opportunities that so obviously confront us.

ARTHUR E. TRAXLER

Educational Records Bureau, New York City

Case-Study Procedures in Guidance[1]

Origin of Case Studies

The case-study technique, which has recently begun to assume an important place in educational procedures, is of ancient origin. It is reported that the oldest known case study is a record of child placement presumably made about 4000 B.C. (253, p. 33).[2] From that time down to the present, case-study procedures have occasionally been employed, but it was not until the latter part of the nineteenth century that case studies were placed on a well-organized basis in connection with certain professions.

One of the most important developments of the case-study method was in the field of law. About 1870, case studies were initiated in the Harvard Law School as a device for training students to think about fundamental principles. In the nineteenth century the medical profession began to develop a literature of medicine based on the accurate observation and recording of cases. The case study has now become a fundamental aspect in the training of medical students. Case-study procedures, because of their obvious value in social investigation, were soon adopted by sociologists. Psychologists were slower to take over the case-study method because until recently they have seldom been interested in the whole personality. The case study is now a basic method in both psychology and psychiatry.

Schools did not begin to adopt case-study practices until the

---

[1] Reprinted from *School Review*, 1938, 46, 602–610. Copyright 1938 by the University of Chicago Press.

[2] Bibliography begins on page 428.

method had been tried out extensively by several of the other professions. As long as teachers were mainly interested in teaching subject matter to groups of pupils, they had no real need for case studies. However, the recent tendency to redirect education to take account of individual differences and the emphasis on mental hygiene and on guidance have brought into sharp focus the need for understanding each pupil. Consequently an increasing number of schools are turning to the case-study method as an indispensable aid in making adequate provision for their pupils, particularly for pupils who deviate from the average in any important respect.

What the Case-Study Method Is

The term "case study" has been employed in two types of investigations. A study in which real or assumed situations are presented for discussion as a means of arriving at basic principles in a given field has been called a case study. Law case studies are of this sort. A detailed study of an individual conducted for the purpose of bringing about better adjustment of the person who is the subject of the investigation is also known as a case study. It is in the latter sense that the term will be employed in this article.

In a case study of this kind all available data about an individual are surveyed, and the significant items are assembled, organized, and studied in order that the nature and the causes of difficulties may be discovered and that treatment designed to remove the difficulties may be planned and carried out. Thinking will perhaps be clarified if a distinction is made between case studies and case histories. A case history presents the story of an individual in as complete and as objective a form as possible. It does not interpret the data, and it does not, in itself, bring to a focus the information on the present problems faced by the individual. If the school maintains a complete cumulative-record system, it has a continuous and an up-to-date case history for every pupil in the school.

Since the first task in making a case study is to obtain the facts about the individual, the initial stages of the case study are almost identical with the case history. Thus, if the school has a cumulative-record system, a great part of the arduous work of gathering data for a case study is cared for as a matter of routine. The case study, however, goes far beyond the case history. A case history is largely a clerical task, but keen intelligence and insight are called for in making a case study. The facts available in the case history are marshaled and interpreted, and a diagnosis is made which will serve as a starting point for treatment.

The question may be raised whether the treatment of the case is a part of the case study or is a procedure that follows the case study. The case studies and the case-study outlines appearing in recent educational and psychological literature exhibit no uniformity in this respect. Some case studies end with the diagnosis; others report extended treatment and the results that attended the treatment. Notwithstanding the fact that treatment is not included in some case studies, it should be clearly understood that every case study implies treatment; otherwise there would be no point in making the study. After the facts have been analyzed and a tentative diagnosis has been formulated, treatment should follow and, if possible, should become a part of the case-study record. Whether the treatment is recorded as a part of the case study will depend, to a large extent, on how the case is handled. If the person who initiates the case study also applies the treatment, a record of the treatment will ordinarily be added to the case study. If the case is referred to another person for treatment (for example, if a case of personality adjustment is referred to a psychiatrist), it may not be practicable to report the treatment in the case study. In cases treated by a specialist in psychiatric problems, facts are sometimes discovered which are of such a confidential nature that they should not be set down in writing. In cases of learning difficulty treated in the school, the case study will be much more valuable if it is concluded with a report of the nature of the treatment and of the progress of the pupil during treatment.

Assembling and Organizing Data in a Case Study

In a case study of a pupil usually the first step is to collect from the school records all important information pertaining to the pupil. The question of whether a given item is important will depend on the nature of the case. If the purpose of the study is to discover the causes of, and to prescribe treatment for, an observed difficulty (for example, inability to deal with situations involving number), only those items in the records which may contribute to an understanding of the difficulty are of immediate importance. However, even in a specialized case of this kind it is desirable to get a complete picture of the pupil, since a particular difficulty can best be interpreted against the background of the whole personality.

If the study is undertaken, not for the purpose of alleviating a special difficulty, but for the purpose of arriving at a thorough understanding of the pupil so that he may be assisted to better adjustment wherever need may manifest itself, every item of information may be important, and the whole record of the pupil should be carefully scrutinized. In schools maintaining cumulative records, including data on the social history, aptitudes, achievement, and personality, the first step of the investigation will be concerned mainly with the pupil's cumulative-record card.

Although the school records should supply much helpful information, even the best of records will not provide complete data. As a rule, the data are entered at regular intervals, and there will usually be a period of several weeks between the time of the last entry on the record and the time of making the case study. The case investigator will, therefore, find it necessary to interview the persons who have contact with the pupil, including classroom teachers, home-room teacher, physical-education instructor, librarian or study-hall supervisor, adviser, and possibly the parents. Notes should be made after each of these interviews, or, better still, each of the teachers and other school officers who are in contact with the pupil should be asked to write out a brief statement concerning the child's attainments, growth, and personality.

A third step is to interview the pupil himself and perhaps to give him additional tests. The school records will sometimes provide all the test data necessary, but, if the case is one of learning difficulty in a certain subject, it is improbable that the survey-test scores in the school records will furnish an adequate basis for diagnosis. For example, if the case is one of reading disability, a diagnostic silent-reading test and an oral-reading check test should be employed as a minimum. If the difficulty seems to be in the field of personality, one of the more promising personality inventories, such as the Bernreuter test or the Bell test, may be given, not so much for the purpose of record as for the purpose of securing responses which will form a convenient starting point for interview.

When reasonably complete data about the pupil have been collected, the case should be written up, and a tentative diagnosis and plan of treatment should be formulated. Although a case study could conceivably be conducted without making a written record, the necessity of putting the study into writing provides excellent training in stating, organizing, and interpreting the facts. Even though the plan is to include the progress of treatment as a part of the study, the case should be written up before treatment starts, and, when treatment is applied, this record should be amplified from time to time. When a written record has been made, it will be helpful to present the case study to the pupil's teachers and to secure their reactions and further suggestions before proceeding with a plan of handling the case.

Outlines for Case Studies

There is no set way of making a case study. The outlines will vary with the nature of the case and with the preferences of the person conducting the study. If the school maintains a cumulative-record system in which comparable data for a pupil are recorded in organized fashion from year to year, it may be desirable to have the outline of the case study up to the point of diagnosis agree with the outline of the cumulative record.

One of the most detailed and useful outlines for the case-study method available anywhere was published by Morrison (185, pp. 644–666). The outline is too long to reproduce here, but teachers contemplating case studies will find it worth their while to look up this outline. The main headings are:

Symptoms	Social history and contacts
Examination	Diagnosis
Health history	Treatment
School history	Follow-up
Family history and home conditions	

Strang (253, pp. 38–40) has classified and discussed the content of case histories under the following headings.

Family history	Vocational and educational plans
Developmental history	Objective data from tests and observation
Home and neighborhood environment	Introspective reports
School history	

This outline is simple and clear, and it includes one feature that is omitted from some of the other published outlines, namely,

"Vocational and educational plans." However, if this outline be adopted, it might be advisable to add a section for diagnosis and suggested treatment.

The following outline was set up recently by a school psychologist as a guide for teacher-advisers in making case summaries, which may be regarded as abbreviated forms of case studies.

Introductory statement	Attitude toward work
Physical condition	Interests and special abilities
Mental ability	Personality
Achievement in school	Summary
Study habits	

In connection with the work of a laboratory school, a school psychologist and a psychiatrist co-operated some time ago in a series of case studies. The psychologist carried on the initial stages of each study and provided a tentative diagnosis. The psychiatrist then took the case over, basing his treatment on a more adequate diagnosis than the psychologist was prepared to make. The outline used by the psychologist in reporting the cases to the psychiatrist could readily be applied to case studies by a classroom teacher. The outline included the following steps.

Introductory statement—identification, age, school grade, etc.	Social history
	Health history
Intelligence	Personality problems
Scores on achievement tests	Observation of pupil
School progress	Summary
Summary of teachers' statements	Tentative diagnosis
Learning defects	

Among the valuable illustrative case studies appearing in educational literature are those by Reavis (214), Smithies (248), Brewer (28), McCallister (176), and Hawkes (112). The publication by Hawkes should be of special interest to schools maintaining cumulative-record systems, for it contains two significant case studies based on cumulative records.

All case-study outlines have many elements in common. The specific type of outline to be used is not important. Presumably each teacher will wish to formulate his own outline. The main thing is to present the major facts in an orderly fashion and to formulate a plan for using the facts in understanding and helping the pupil.

Points to Be Observed in Making a Case Study

Planning the Case Study. The following suggestions are offered to persons who are contemplating the making of a case study for the first time.

1. Select a case in which you are really interested both from the standpoint of the nature of the case and the personality of the individual concerned.

2. If possible, choose a pupil from one of your classes who, you feel, needs attention and help and who will probably co-operate well with you.

3. When considering various pupils, give some thought to the shy, quiet, retiring pupils. Pupils of this type are sometimes more suitable subjects for case study than pupils whose difficulties or behavior causes them to be noticed.

4. Plan only as much as you feel that you can accomplish. If you contemplate a thorough case study, including treatment, it will probably be best in the first year to confine your study to one pupil. If you prefer merely to make case summaries, you can perhaps do several summaries or even summaries for an entire class if it is small.

Collecting the Data. Some of the main points with respect to collecting the data have been set forth earlier in this article. In addition it may be said that, when a pupil is being interviewed and tested for the purpose of securing more data about his difficulties, care should be used not to place him on the defensive. He should not be made to feel that he is a culprit or that he is in any way an extreme deviate from his fellow-pupils. The meeting ground of the case investigator and the subject should be one of sharing in the solution of the pupil's problems. If the case investigator can enlist the interest of the pupil and can bring him to take the initiative from the beginning, the prognosis for successful solution of the pupil's problems is excellent.

Writing up the Case. As already indicated, there is no single pattern for writing up the case, but certain general principles should probably be observed.

1. Write objectively, simply, and with directness. Although you should be vitally interested in the case, your report should not reflect personal bias. The description of the case should be as objective and the intrepretation should be as impersonal as possible. This rule does

not mean that you should avoid interpretation and inference but that you should distinguish meticulously between the facts which you have discovered and the interpretation or the diagnosis based on those facts.

2. In the report of the case use both general statements and specific illustrations. General statements about intelligence, achievement, and personality are much more convincing if they are supported with some definite data.

3. Eliminate irrelevant items; confine the case report to a few typewritten pages.

Applying and Evaluating Treatment. Persons who are inexperienced in making case studies often find that the study moves along smoothly until they reach the stage of applying treatment but that this stage presents problems which seem baffling. The observation of a few suggestions may help to clarify these problems.

1. A case investigator should not attempt to apply treatment for difficulties that are entirely outside his experience. If he makes such an attempt, it is probable that he will become involved in an embarrassing situation and that he may do the pupil more harm than good. If the problem is one of learning in his own or a related field, the teacher should be able to handle it. If the problem is one of reading or study difficulty, as so many cases are, he should be able to offer the pupil valuable help in reading and studying the content of his own special field and perhaps of other fields. The case investigator can also handle many problems which are volitional, which are caused by lack of interest, or which are of a minor behavior character. If, however, the case involves learning adjustments that are entirely foreign to his experience or if it includes obscure personality disorders, the investigator should frankly recognize his inability to meet the situation and should conclude his report with a recommendation for referral.

2. During the period of treatment the case investigator should keep a careful journal record of the progress of treatment. He should not depend on his memory but should write up each interview with the pupil and each significant observation just as soon as possible. Not all of what is written in the journal will find its way into the case report, but a complete journal record is of inestimable help in making a final report at the end of the period of treatment.

3. If the case lends itself to measurement (for example, if it in-

volves achievement in a certain skill or school subject), comparable tests should be administered at the beginning and the end of the treatment. Such tests will take the evaluation of the treatment out of the realm of speculation and will sometimes reveal significant progress under conditions where no conclusions about growth could be made on the basis of observation alone.

4. After a pupil has been released from treatment, he should be followed up and kept under observation for a few months to make sure that a relapse does not take place. Follow-up is especially important in cases involving skills, such as reading, spelling, and arithmetic. Some pupils who make marked gains on tests during a period of teaching will tend to return to their old habits unless they are carefully supervised.

5. Throughout the study the case worker should constantly keep in mind the whole personality development of the pupil. Every case study, regardless of its immediate purpose, has implications that are much broader than the acquisition of a limited area of subject matter or the mastery of certain skills. In the last analysis, each case study must be evaluated according to the contribution that it makes to the better adjustment of the pupil in his school environment and in his out-of-school relationships.

JOHN G. DARLEY

University of Minnesota

The Structure of the Systematic Case Study in Individual Diagnosis and Counseling[1]

Much of the difficulty in judging the quality of case work in college personnel programs results from lack of agreement about the structure of case work and the quantity of data necessary within the structure. Therefore, any personnel worker or administrator may say that diagnosis and counseling are done in his institution, without fear of criticism, rebuttal, or evaluation. Programs involving any form of faculty-student interviewing, regardless of available types and amounts of case data, are of equal stature in questionnaire surveys with counseling programs based on extensive information about the individual student. As in many other fields of therapeutic work, the label for the function—in this case "diagnosis and counseling"—tends to subsume a wide range of practices and malpractices, rather than to identify a grouping of agreed-upon procedures.

Admittedly the structure of case work and the minimum quantity of data within the structure are not perfectly correlated with *effective* diagnosis and counseling of the individual student. The skill of the competent practitioner is still indispensable as a vitalizing force to make the data meaningful and patterned for the individual. But it is safe to say that without a defined minimum of case material and without a structure to give it coherence, case work is either impos-

[1] Reprinted from *Journal of Consulting Psychology*, 1940, 4, 215–220. Copyright 1940 by American Association for Applied Psychology.

sible or inadequate, even though case work may still be inadequate when a poor counselor is operating with essential data.

While there can be no final answer, in the present state of student personnel work, to questions about an ideal case work structure for individual diagnosis and counseling, there can be "touchstones," as Matthew Arnold defined the concept for literary criticism, against which case work practices may be assessed. In an effort to provide graduate instruction in clinical work with college students, we have evolved such "touchstones" as a teaching device. As anyone familiar with clinical work will realize, a case history or a series of case histories may, in the process of case reading, be analogous to the trees obscuring the outlines and characteristics of the forest. A more systematic organization of the clinical processes is not only an aid in teaching, but should also be valuable in approaching the problem of quality in case work.

Williamson and Darley (297, chap. 6)[2] first classified and described six steps in clinical work with individual students: analysis, the collection of pertinent data by a variety of tools and technics; synthesis, the mechanical and graphic organization of the data in such a way that the counselor was ready to draw a meaningful picture from them; diagnosis, the interpretations of the data in terms of problems to be cured, prevented, or alleviated; prognosis, the projection or prediction of events for the student under alternative courses of action which were possible or desirable in the light of the diagnosis; treatment, the modification of the individual or the environment necessary for the desirable outcomes listed in the prognosis; follow-up, the process of evaluating total effectiveness of the previous steps and checking on the progress being made.

Later, Williamson (296, chaps. 3, 4, 5) rephrased these steps into four broader groups: the use of analytic tools and technics; diagnosis, including prognosis and the presentation of alternative courses of action for the student; counseling, standing for five clearly-defined technics and procedures of treatment for purposes of alleviation, prevention, or cure of maladjustment; follow-up, again defined as a progress check and research evaluation procedure.

The present article emphasizes the analysis-synthesis steps in the first reference, and the use of analytic tools and technics in the sec-

---

[2] Bibliography begins on page 428.

ond reference. In addition, it is essential to break down these steps into their respective elements if a structure of case work is to emerge. The structure rests first on five assumptions, which may be briefly stated.

(1) In the "bandwagon" state of student personnel programs today, the issue is not a contrast between clinical work and no clinical work, but is rather a continuum of bad clinical work to good clinical work. An institution's location on such a continuum is largely conditioned by the adequacy and range of the judgment-taking devices it uses in its case studies, and the skill of the counselors using the devices.

(2) The most frequent deterrent to effective case work is the tendency of new case workers and old alike, to "abridge" the case study, as Symonds states, at the point of a clinical "taking-off place" rather than completing the case study before beginning treatment or counseling.

(3) There is absolutely no a priori basis for assuming that the student's stated problem or complaint excludes a different problem or a greater number of problems in addition to the stated problem and its ramifications. Therefore a systematic, or inclusive, case study must be made, even though certain data will prove to be irrelevant.

(4) From available research and clinical experiences, a range of areas relevant for systematic case study can be identified and labelled as a touchstone, even though problems of the most effective judgment-making devices in each area are not yet solved in basic research studies.

(5) If clinical work is to be buttressed by effective research on procedures, hypothesis, and results, not only must the presence of problems be clearly stated, but also the absence of problems and the possible problems on which no data are available must be equally explicit. Bacon's *Novum Organum* contains an aphorism on the tables of presence and absence which should be required reading for clinical psychologists.

Based on the fourth assumption, the systematic case study should start with a systematic case analysis. Included in the analysis will be nine areas of the behavior of the individual student, for the reasons stated.

(1) *General Scholastic Ability.* College students are competing in a situation placing a premium upon this type of "intelligence."

Each institution enrolls students from a known range of this characteristic and each individual's chances of success in the institution are definitely conditioned by his location within this range. The judgment-making devices for this characteristic—scholastic aptitude tests—are inexpensive and widely available; they provide a more accurate and purer judgment than inferences about ability derived from grades and other measures. Even though past achievement measures show higher correlations with college achievement, the clinician must make his analyses of scholastic aptitude as directly as possible in the process of tracing down reasons for deviation from predicted performance.

(2) *Achievement to Date.* In general, past achievement is the best single index of future achievement (240). Past achievement, estimated from grades and course patterns, is the traditional focus of attention in admissions procedures and the administration of academic regulations. It is a basic point of reference in the reiterated phrase about getting students to "work (achieve) up to capacity." In the systematic case study, grades, standardized achievement test scores, reports from employers and reports from supervisors of extracurricular activities are minimal judgment-making data permitting an analysis of strong and weak points, differentials, and disabilities.

(3) *Aptitudes.* While the theoretical literature of psychology affords no final definition of these narrower segments of behavior, the clinician pragmatically must deal with them in relation to mechanical, clerical, dexterity, motor, artistic, or musical potentialities, since various curricula may require such characteristics *in addition to* specified levels of general scholastic ability. The judgment-making devices in a systematic case study include not only the relatively small number of so-called "aptitude tests," but also inferences from achievement differentials, avocational activities and their products, and differential successes in work experiences.

(4) *Disabilities.* These characteristics, the reverse of aptitudes, are recognized as important determinants of discrepancies between predicted and actual achievement. Reading disabilities, speech handicaps, study deficiencies, arithmetic, and language or English disabilities exist in various proportions of college students to impede academic progress. The clinician must make one of two broad decisions: the disability is remediable within the time available for a specific curriculum; the disability is sufficiently severe to indicate the

advisability of a curricular change that will permit the student to avoid the disability situation. Judgment-making devices basic to diagnosis and counseling in these problems comprise diagnostic tests, questionnaires, direct interview investigation of study technics and conditions, inferences from consistently poor grades in one area (when accompanied by average or better than average general scholastic ability for the institution's competitive standards), and markedly deviate performance on standard aptitude or achievement tests.

(5) *Interests.* Probably the most frequent and least accurate item of information collected from students is the expression of their curricular and vocational choices. A close second in this area is the request on the institution's records for expressions of avocational, cultural, or recreational interests and activities. Seldom is any question raised about the validity of these claimed choices, even though they determine the curricular channel into which the student is directed at the college level. A good share of college mortality and withdrawal can be attributed to discrepancies between claimed vocational choices and measured interest patterns (61). In addition to the student's expression of occupational choices, interest tests, subject-matter preferences, avocational interest patterns, and discrepancies in these data are available as judgment-making devices to elucidate or explicate problems of patterns of interest and their place in guidance (62).

(6) *Attitudes.* These characteristics of the individual still lie mainly in the realm of publicity material in college bulletins, as a hoped-for outcome of education by some process of transfer. Yet, as a phase of the total personality of the individual, even though they shade off into other aspects of personality measurement, they are illuminating in clinical work. Not only are tolerance and "open-mindedness," for example, desirable outcomes of intellectual activity in the class-room, but also the degree of possession of these same traits *prior* to class-room exposure tends to determine how much the student will get from the class. Thus in the systematic case study, judgments about attitudes are definitely pertinent. Judgment-making devices include the general and specific attitude scales available from the research of Thurstone, Likert, Remmers, Rundquist and Sletto, and others. In addition, inferences may be drawn by use of the interview as a technic of investigation in this area.

(7) *Personality.* Again, while psychologists may not agree on the

definition and range of this area of behavior, the clinician constantly faces more or less severe deviations in personality characteristics which upset the relation between earned and predicted achievement, or which may have no effect on grade-getting, but have tremendous effect on placement after graduation. Pencil-and-paper tests, anecdotal records, psychiatric and other interview technics, and rating scales are the available judgment-making devices foundational to diagnosis and treatment of student problems. The issue of clinical maladjustment versus tested maladjustment has been discussed elsewhere (60); the important point here is that the systematic case analysis must contain minimal data on this phase of the individual, even though the research problems in this field of measurement are elusive and difficult.

(8) *Physical Status.* It is by now axiomatic that a case study must include data on the physical well-being or deviations of the individual. Health service facilities are available in some form in the majority of institutions where psychological services will be found. The judgment-making in this area is to be done by the technics of the medical practitioner. The problem, however, is twofold: to have these diagnoses so phrased that their relation to the educational behavior of the individual is explicit; to get the cooperation of medical men in making relevant parts of their diagnoses available to the personnel worker.

(9) *Socio-economic Status.* Education must reinforce the adequate phases of the home background and counteract the inadequate phases. Futhermore since educational opportunity for the individual is so closely related to ability to pay, familial status is requisite knowledge in this regard. Judgments here may be made by a variety of questionnaire forms, socio-economic scales, and interview technics. The usual application for admission contains data of this type.

If this be accepted as the structure of a systematic case analysis, it must immediately be obvious that some data are usually available, in varying degrees of reliability, in each of the nine areas. The registrar's office, the admissions office, the medical service, the special testing facilities, the casual interview records of the institution house, or entomb, such data. But they are seldom regularly available in advance to those who can counsel competently and who attempt two things: helping the student choose an educational or vocational goal group where his chances of successful competition are greatest;

helping to alleviate, prevent, or cure the individual problems which may cause the student to work below capacity.

Once such data are available, the counselor can use his skill and interpret his judgment-making devices in diagnosis and counseling. A second structural step here is the classification of types of problems. Six problem types may be defined: financial, educational, vocational, family, health, personal-emotional. Williamson and Darley (297, chap. 7), and Williamson (296, Parts II–VI), have described in detail the etiology, symptoms, and treatment technics for specific problems within each type.

A third structural procedure is necessary in effective diagnosis and counseling, and this deals with the organization of case records. Starting from the premise that it is difficult if not unwise to attempt to standardize the clinical interview itself, we have arrived at a method for standardizing case notes and case records to achieve a basis for evaluating quality of case work. The technic, described in detail by Sarbin (231), permits presence of problems, absence of problems and problems regarding which no data are available to be explicitly stated in the record for future clinical or research work.

Within these frameworks, case work with students demands greater, not less, clinical skill. Referrals to other personnel agencies, consultations, staff clinics, subsequent interviews, and follow-up procedures follow normally as the data intrude upon the complacency that exists when case work is done without a clear awareness of its structure.

For those who will accept this "touchstone," it becomes possible to evaluate clinical work in each of its major steps: analysis, diagnosis, counseling, and follow-up. Are the technics of analysis the most reliable and valid obtainable in each area? Are enough areas of the individual's behavior covered? Can those who interpret the data in making diagnoses handle them competently? What does follow-up work reveal about previous case work?

Out of this structuralization has developed our final outline of the basic research problems underlying the analysis of the individual, again on the assumption that without a good analysis, the remaining clinical steps are ineffectual. These problems are:

(1) What rates of growth and amounts of change or development characterize each of the nine areas of the individual student's behavior which we must analyse?

(2) What general correlational values may be expected among these nine areas? We know that all nine are intercorrelated, but we cannot set limits on these correlations yet.

(3) Within each area, what specific behavior elements are to be subsumed and labelled? For example, Thurstone's seven primary mental abilities may be seven out of N specifics in the area of general scholastic ability.

(4) For any area, what are the most economical, reliable, and valid judgment-making devices? Tests, rating scales, questionnaires, the interview, the grade record, anecdotes, the casual question—all have inherent in them factors of reliability and validity. What, in over-simplified form, is the relative ranking of available judgment-making devices within any area in regard to economy, reliability, validity?

A little reflection should indicate that these four problems are also included in the basic problems of theoretical psychology. And thus we come full circle back to the discipline upon which individual diagnosis and counseling rely so heavily. In summary, if case work is approached by these four "touchstones," it will inevitably improve in quality:

(1) In systematic case analyses, does the institution cover all nine areas adequately?

(2) Can diagnoses be made of specific problems within the six problem types?

(3) Are the case records structuralized to indicate presence and absence and no investigation in the diagnosis?

(4) Does the case worker keep clearly in mind the four basic research problems in case analyses?

As theoretical psychologists and educational administrators become increasingly aware that the clinical problems of students are also basic problems of differential psychology, we may expect to see the quality of case work improved by the employment of clinical psychologists well-grounded in basic psychological theory.

THEODORE R. SARBIN

Beverly Hills, California

The Case Record in Psychological Counseling[1]

I. Introduction

Few who have read case notes written by psychological counselors will disagree with Whitehead's statement that "the success of language in conveying information is vastly over-rated, especially in learned circles." Perhaps one of the most difficult forms of expression is that of writing meaningful case notes. In trying to record material, psychologists have variously employed three general forms: (a) the one-phrase or one-line digest, (b) attempts at photographic reproduction, and (c) selection and interpretation.

The one-phrase or one-line digest crams into a small space the counselor's[2] analysis, diagnosis and treatment. This method is usually employed where cumulative record forms or other prepared forms are the sole instruments for the recording of case data. A full

---

[1] Adapted from a paper read before the 17th Annual Meeting of the American College Personnel Association, February 21, 1940, at St. Louis, Missouri. This paper is primarily concerned with the structure of the case record in the psychological counseling of college students. The writer's experience with social work and child guidance records suggests the adoption of a similarly designed method of recording case data. Reprinted from *Journal of Applied Psychology*, 1940, 24, 184–197. Copyright 1939 by James P. Porter.

The case material in this article is illustrative of a method of recording interview notes and does not necessarily represent the point of view of the author in so far as counseling is concerned (personal communication from author).

[2] The expression "counselor" or "clinical counselor" in this paper has as its referent an individual trained in clinical psychology and allied fields. See Williamson, E. G., *How to Counsel Students* (296).

hour interview might be recorded as follows: "12–1–39. Cannot make up his mind about vocation. Discussed scientific fields." Obviously this over-simplification and over-compression provides hardly any information on which to make an adequate diagnosis. If the student were subsequently to be interviewed by another counselor, he would have to repeat his entire history and complaint.

The reproductive method, on the other hand, attempts to reconstruct the whole interview from beginning to end photographically; that is to say, the counselor tries to include, usually in chronological fashion, *everything* that happens without regard for utility, significance, or relevancy. Thus the material in the case record is all-inclusive, unselected, and entirely dependent upon the memory and fluency of the counselor. This method calls to mind the attentive student whose lecture notes missed nothing, not even the professor's "Good morning."

The third method, that of selecting and interpreting elusive interview data and objective test results, requires a considerable degree of skill. One is repaid for developing this skill, however, in that the results have meaning and utility for both the counselor and the clinic. Few will deny that much of the counseling process has no relevance for the real or imagined problems of the client or patient. Establishing rapport, for example, is a necessary part of every interview, but it need not be described in detail unless it is specifically related to the complaint or problem. In constructing the case notes this material is culled out, and only that which has meaning in terms of the individual's problems is retained. Not only does the clinical counselor sift out the relevant from the irrelevant, he also interprets and gives meaning to otherwise meaningless test scores and interview data.

The first method, that of the one-phrase or one-line digest, is rapid and economical, but is to be eschewed in clinical counseling because it adds nothing to our knowledge of the patient. The second method, complete and unselected reproduction, is undesirable because of the difficulty of conveying photographic images by the hurriedly written word, and further, because of the inefficiency of recording a mass of irrelevant data. The third method, although subject to errors of judgment, is considered the most desirable in terms of the functions to be served by case notes.

II. Functions of Case Notes

Our preference for the third method is based upon a consideration of the purposes or objectives of these records of counselor-counselee relationships. Recording the events of the interview without guideposts in the form of objectives of case notes lacks significance for the counselor and for the clinic. In writing or dictating case notes, the counselor should be guided by the functions that are to be performed by his record. Case history notes, then, should be functional, fulfilling certain clearly defined objectives.

We can establish the objectives of recording counseling procedures by seeking answers to this question: what uses are made of case notes? Once we have answered this question, we shall have before us definite objectives which may serve as silent presuppositions, as conceptual sifting devices, in recording the counseling process. At least six answers may be given to our question.

First, the case record serves as a point of departure for the counselor in interviews subsequent to the initial contact. The counselor saves time for himself and for the student by reviewing the events of previous interviews before the student's re-appearance. Furthermore, he is able to identify the student by means of the case notes. It is not uncommon to find counselors who disdain case notes, treating one student for another student's problems simply because no adequate record is available of the earlier diagnostic interview.

Second, case notes serve to acquaint a second counselor with the case when the first cannot continue the treatment. In the event of a counselor's separation from the clinic, it is obviously necessary to have a record of his relationships with the student. In some cases it is necessary for one counselor to transfer a student to another counselor because of failure to maintain rapport or because of inability to cope with certain problems. Thus, case notes should serve to tell the new counselor what happened in interviews with previous counselors.

Third, understandable case notes are prerequisite to the supervisory functions in the psychological clinic or counseling bureau. In order for the director or supervisor to know what the counselors are doing and the details of the counseling procedures, he must have some form of record available. From the examination of case notes, the director may compare the work of one counselor with another and the work of the counseling staff as a whole with the major objectives of the clinic.

Fourth, case notes are used in the training of counselors. One of the most frequently used educational techniques for acquainting interns with procedures of diagnosis and treatment is the careful analysis and study of counselor's case notes.

Fifth, case notes are often employed to correct erroneous impressions left by the student in relating the events of the interview to others. Psychological counselors are often called upon by school officials, psychiatrists, social workers, employers, and parents because of errors or inconsistencies in the student's report. Not infrequently, he may distort or misinterpret the information or advice given by the counselor. For example, an irate parent calls upon the counselor with this question: "Why did you tell my boy to quit school?" The case notes—the significant parts of which are read to the parent— tells that the counselor advised that the boy drop only one of his courses. The documentary evidence satisfies the parent. A psychiatrist suspects the student's report that "The counselor said I had a bad personality." The counselor saves his professional reputation by showing the psychiatrist the case notes which read: "I told the student that his personality traits were not like those of students in the Engineering college, that he would fit into the Arts college group much better."

The most carefully given advice is sometimes subject to misinterpretation, misquotation, and distortion. The only means whereby the counselor can protect himself from the consequences of such inaccurate reporting is adequate documentation. By employing case notes to protect himself against such contingencies, the psychologist builds and maintains his professional reputation.

Sixth, case notes are used in the facilitation of personnel research. Increasingly, case records are serving as the raw data in research. At the present time two research problems are paramount in counseling work. One is the problem of evaluation. Clearly written case notes, intelligently interpreted, serve as the first step in evaluation studies. The second research problem is the isolation and description of treatment or counseling techniques. The literature of clinical psychology is replete with discussions of analytic and diagnostic techniques, but not many treatment techniques are described in detail.

Case notes may serve as an excellent vehicle for describing the treatment phase of the interview. To be sure, it is often difficult to transform a gesture or an inflection of the voice into the written word, but we must try to record these so-called intangibles if we are to make progress in psychological counseling.

To recapitulate, six major purposes of case notes are listed:

(1) Recording of the counseling process for the counselor's future use in treatment.

(2) Recording for continuation of treatment by other counselors.

(3) Supervision of counseling staff.

(4) Training of interns.

(5) Protection against misinterpretation and misquotation.

(6) Research in clinical psychology.

III. Characteristics of Good Case Notes

Having established six objectives of case recording, it is in order to discuss what goes into the record and what characteristics are necessary to fulfill our objectives. Before discussing the actual content of the counseling record, we first consider what characteristics good case notes should possess to carry out the previously designated functions. At least these five characteristics are essential: accuracy, brevity and conciseness, relevancy, ease of reference, and uniformity.

Accuracy. The record must provide an accurate account of the counseling process. It must reduce the inaccuracies which would follow from mere dependence on the counselor's memory. Inaccuracies are usually the result of the lapse of time between making an observation and recording it. "Other things being equal . . . the longer the time has elapsed between your conversation and the recall of it, the less complete and the less trustworthy will be that recall" (290).[3] At the University of Minnesota Testing Bureau we try to reduce to a minimum inaccuracies due to lapses of time by providing each counselor with a dictaphone. The moment the student leaves the consultation room, the counselor records his case notes on the dictaphone cylinder.

Brevity and Conciseness. The record should not be so long as to approach a novel in length. Service to the client or patient, not literary achievement, is our aim. We are concerned with a problem

---

[3] Bibliography begins on page 428.

that must be solved, not with story telling. This means that minutiae and insignificanta must be omitted. The interpretations that the counselor makes will reduce the amount of material to be recorded, although they cannot substitute for concrete, factual data. The amount and kind of data will, of course, depend upon the objectives of the clinic or bureau.

It is not always necessary to write grammatically complete sentences. Many times just a phrase will carry the meaning intended, such as, "Cooperation poor on Stanford-Binet," "Performance on all ability tests in the 90's," or "Poor risk for college work." It is also considered advisable to use parenthetical remarks, which, to be sure, may interfere with an accurate chronology but which give added meaning to the content. Here is an example:

John has low scores on the spellng sub-test of the Coop. English Test and on the reading test battery. (Later I learned that at 6 years of age his handedness was reversed—he had been a natural sinistral before. His halting speech patterns and low scores on spelling and reading tests suggest referral to Speech Clinic.)

Relevancy. This characteristic calls for skill on the part of the counselor in determining what is relevant and what is irrelevant. If a student's problem is, let us say, definitely one of study habits and uncomplicated, it is unnecessary to include such irrelevant data as kind of magazines read or performance on an unreliable test of art appreciation. If an individual's problem is solely one of choosing a vocational goal, it is unnecessary to write about his living arrangements. A recitation of health history is unnecessary when a simple problem of social skills is the diagnosis. Careful selection of items will insure that the finished record will be a meaningful and integrated psychological document.

Ease of Reference. In the usual narrative case record adapted from social work methods, no paragraphs or identifying headings are given. Ordinarily the whole record must be read in order to discover the stated problems, the analysis and diagnosis, and the treatment. For more efficient reading, the style should be that of short paragraphs with underscored side-heads. This technique makes for rapid perusal of the record and many times will obviate the reading of the entire record when the reader is interested in finding only one particular item. Consider the usual narrative record dictated with no paragraphs or identifying side-heads. A reader interested in isolating, let us say, parental problems, would have to read through the whole record before he could discover whether such a problem was involved. If, on the other hand, a short paragraph is devoted to family or parental relationships, introduced with an appropriate side-head, then the reader would have merely to glance through the sideheads until he came to the one marked *Parental Relationships*. If the director had received a call from another agency and wanted to see if any reference had been made to the family situation, he would not be forced to digest the whole record, but could spot the paragraph immediately.

This procedure is a time-saving device in training interns in specific treatment and diagnostic techniques. If an intern seemed to be weak in knowledge or handling of family problems, he could study cases which showed diagnoses and treatments of family problems. Instead of reading every case in its entirety, however, he could isolate by means of the underscored side-heads those records which were especially pertinent to his training needs.

Uniformity. This characteristic does not mean rigid adherence to a standard form. Rather it calls for all counselors to organize their case notes and their case thinking along certain functional lines. Research especially would be facilitated if all counselors in the same clinic adopted a uniform method of case recording.

IV. A Satisfactory Method of Recording Case Notes

To fulfill the functions outlined before, case notes should begin with the student's statement of his problem—in medical terms, the patient's "complaint." This will include the individual's reason for coming to the bureau or clinic. Here are two examples:

Tom Jones, a junior in the College of Education, came to the Bureau with the problem: "I am not making satisfactory progress in my work." He wants the Bureau to help him discover the cause of his self-diagnosed under-achievement and to help him make the necessary adjustments.

Mary Brown was referred to the Bureau by Professor X because of her persistent anxieties arising from lack of finances and from failure to make normal social adjustments.

Taking the counselor's expression of his problem or the referring agency's suggested diagnosis as the point of departure, we make an analysis to discover the cause of the complaint. Beginning with the phenotype, we search for the genotype. The analysis is made not only from test results, but from clinical data gathered in the interview and from information contained in the individual record forms. These forms usually provide such data as socio-economic status, occupation of father, work experience, and social activities, which may or may not have a bearing upon the problem at hand. Those items that have no relation to the case as diagnosed by the counselor are omitted from the notes.

Since the interview data are the most fleeting and elusive, the counselor must dictate or write as soon as possible whatever relevant material he has collected. For ease of reference, this is given the side-head *Clinical Data*. An example follows:

Clinical Data: On the individual record form the student has checked several items on the health record sheet—exhaustion, nervousness, easily fatigued, headaches, and backaches. Questioning revealed that these symptoms appear only during the school year. The headaches were especially severe when Elmer had to study. Physician's report shows "no pathology nor recommendations. . . ."

Following the recording of significant data collected in the interview, the counselor refers to the test profiles or psychographs. What data are taken from this source? A routine listing of test scores is obviously wasteful. It merely duplicates material that is already easily accessible. Suppose three tests of academic ability have been administered to a student and the results on the psychograph are contradictory. The counselor interprets the contradictory findings in terms of his knowledge of the validity, reliability, norms, etc., of the tests in question. For facilitating reference, this discussion of the test results may be divided into the following categories: *General Ability, Achievement, Special Disabilities, Special Aptitudes, Interests,* and *Personality.* The following illustrates one treatment of test results:

Test Analysis:

General Ability—Three tests of college aptitude show this boy to be poor material for college. Only on the arithmetic sub-test of the ACE test does his performance exceed the median.

Achievement—High School achievement rather high according to report card. Mostly A's and B's. Standardized achievement tests, however, show no percentiles higher than 60, mostly below 40 for freshman norms. High school grades probably a result of very pleasant, outgoing personality.

Special Disabilities—Reading speed and comprehension, average. Spelling very weak.

Special Aptitudes—Clerical test placed him in upper decile on clerical worker norms. Other special tests administered but considered irrelevant.

Interest—Claimed interest, medicine. Strong Vocational Interest Blank shows only one primary pattern—Group VIII—Business Detail occupations. Occupational level is low, only 31 percentile. This contraindicates professional training, especially in view of general ability scores. No verification for claimed interest in medicine.

Personality—Bell Adjustment Inventory reveals no deviate scores. Social scale indicates an aggressive lad. (Clinically verified.)

It often happens that in the process of dictating or writing the test analysis, certain clinical material comes to light which was omitted from the *Clinical Data* paragraph. This may be dictated after the test analysis. Suppose, for example, the personality tests indicate a neurotic invididual. The following notation might be appropriate:

Additional Clinical Data: While the interview was in progress, Elmer continually toyed with an ashtray that was on my desk. He frequently twitched his shoulders, bit his upper lip many times. His movements were quick and jerky; he spoke in a nervous, hurried manner. This would tend to verify the scores on the Bell Adjustment Inventory.

Having analyzed the test results and other data in terms of the student's problem or complaint, we are ready for a diagnosis. The counselor's statement of the problem may or may not agree with the student's statement. The student may make, let us say, a diagnosis of under-achievement where the counselor will write:

Diagnosis: Emotional problem. Probably a result of level of aspiration which is much too high for level of ability. No real disjunction between ability and achievement.

Another example of a counselor's diagnosis follows:

Diagnosis: Under-achievement. Probably due to lack of motivation, lack of study habits, too much social life. Parental involvements. (No identified problems in health area or financial area.)

It is important to know whether the counselor has investigated other possible areas of diagnosis. If he has inquired into the health status of the individual and learned of no positive findings, the case notes should contain a brief statement to this effect. Thus, the absence as well as the presence of problems is noted. This statement (under *Diagnosis*) further illustrates the point:

No problem identified in health area. Physician's report enclosed.

Having stated a diagnosis, what is the next step? Logically, the treatment (or counseling) phase of the total process. This area requires especially careful reporting. The counselor must try to delineate the techniques that he used in treating the student for his problems. He should state what he tried to do, and the methods he used to achieve his purposes. If he tried to modify the individual's attitudes, he will mention what facts were brought up, what emotionally colored words and cliches he used and so on. If he listed a series of facts for the student to consider, these should be summarized in the record. The plan of action accepted by the counselee should be reported, if possible, in 1–2–3 order.

If treatment is directed at more than one problem, the notes should be organized accordingly. As an illustration suppose the diagnosis indicates an emotional problem arising out of a history of social backwardness, and an educational problem of unwise curricular choice. The case notes would be organized as follows:

Counseling: (or Treatment)

Emotional Problem: Part of the treatment was centered around catharsis. Frank seemed to get relief in talking out his problems to an interested and sympathetic listener. He told me of numerous occasions where he had been miserable and unhappy because he never had learned how to meet people (more of this under Clinical Data). My first step was to have him state that this personality trait was undesirable for life adjustment and that steps should be taken to correct it. My question was: "Do you want to remedy this defect in an otherwise pleasant personality?" He answered in the affirmative. I outlined the following steps for rehabilitating him socially: (1) Register in the Social Skills Course of the Y. M. C. A. (2) Attend meetings of the Cosmopolitan Club where he could use his knowledge of world events. (3) Participate in the Y. M. C. A. mixed group activities. (Letters were sent to the appropriate officer of each group to insure a personalized reception.)

Scholastic Problem: My job was to dissuade him from continuing in pre-business and in having him accept a substitute program of general education. First I pointed out the standard of competition in the professional School of Business. This made no dent in his armor. He still maintained that his D+ average would come up to a C this year. Knowing his dislike of courses involving math, I showed him the courses as catalogued in the professional business curriculum: statistics, finance, money and banking, theoretical economics, insurance accounting, and so on. (With silent apologies to my friends who teach these courses)

I told the student that these courses were "highly theoretical and abstract" and considered "very dry." On the other hand, courses in general education were practical and interesting; no economics or math prerequisites were necessary. I described some of the interesting features of the Orientation Courses. He finally agreed to think it over. I outlined this plan of action: (1) see the counselor in the general education unit for further information (I arranged an appointment); (2) discuss the matter with his folks; (3) secure transfer blanks from the Registrar's Office.

The next step follows logically, what is the prognosis, the expectation? What results may we reasonably expect if the student accepts our advice? if he acts contrary to our advice? A prognosis should be stated for each major alternative open to the student. For example:

Prognosis: In General College, good. About C+ or B average for year. In pre-medicine, failure after one or two quarters. Prognosis reserved on emotional problem.

Frequently a prognosis is stated conditionally. For instance, if a family problem complicates the case, the prediction of adjustment in another area is stated with a proviso:

Prognosis: Educational adjustment satisfactory providing mother's attitude can be changed, or student moved to a campus residence.

Finally, in order to verify the diagnosis or to continue with the treatment, and to learn the effectiveness of our counseling, as well as the accuracy of the prognosis, we arrange for a follow-up. The case notes should state clearly the follow-up plans of the counselor:

Follow-up: Send notice to return for further counseling in two weeks. Determine whether student has attended group activities; inquire about parents' reactions; get grade report.

The same general procedure, with modifications, is used in recording subsequent interviews. Counselors should dictate progress reports as new data come to light in the development of the case.

Progress Report: Three time distributions show study hours of 20, 24 and 31 respectively for the first three weeks of the quarter. Waste time is reduced from 18 to 10 to 6 hours. His comment, "Now there is so little time in which I can do nothing." I encouraged him to continue the good work. He says he enjoys chemistry very much.

Additional Clinical Data: I asked Frank what was driving him to do such good work. He analyzed it after several halting attempts in this way: (1) for the first time he was interested in school; (2) he feared that he would have to return to the pattern-maker's bench if he failed; (3) he felt he owed me something for the trouble I had gone to in getting him re-admitted.

V. *Conclusion*

From the foregoing it may appear that counseling follows a prescribed routine. This is far from true. In the actual counseling situation, a shifting attack generally prevails. Now the counselor is interpreting test data, now he asks a question, now he gives advice, now he makes a diagnosis, and so on. The counseling process is a dynamic, fluid process. Case notes cannot adequately reconstruct the counseling process. No matter how facile the interviewer with the spoken or written word, he can never reproduce the events of the counseling situation so that the reader will perceive the same total situation. Photographic and chronological reproduction being impossible and demonstrably unnecessary, we should recognize that verisimilitude must serve as an appropriate standard for reporting.

To summarize: We have presented six functions of case notes in psychological counseling. We have briefly described the characteristics of desirable case notes which meet our stated objectives. And finally, we have demonstrated the form and content of case notes now in use at the University of Minnesota Testing Bureau.[4] Our method provides for a statement of the problem as perceived by the client or referring agency, meaningful clinical data, interpretation of test results, diagnosis, treatment, prognosis, and follow-up. Psychologists will immediately recognize these as the major steps in the clinical method.

---

[4] The steps in clinical counseling which precede the recording process are described in Williamson, E. G., and Darley, J. G., *Student Personnel Work* (297).

EDWARD S. BORDIN

Washington State College

Diagnosis in Counseling and Psychotherapy[1]

In the last ten years there has been considerable ferment in the thinking about counseling and psychotherapy with normal individuals. This period has been marked by great strides toward converting an unverbalized art to a carefully delineated practice based upon the results of empirical studies. Books and articles have been published which dealt with concrete descriptions of practices and which presented theories of treatment.

Within the groups turning toward more definitive discussions and descriptions of treatment, two somewhat divergent points of view have been discernible. Rogers and his students have been the primary source for the presentation of a nondirective theory of counseling and therapeutic procedures, and Williamson, Darley, and more recently Thorne have been the most vocal exponents of conceptions which have been labeled directive by the first group. Williamson (296)[2] made a pioneer contribution by presenting a rich compilation of the kinds of individuals with whom the student personnel worker will deal and the procedures he might use in attempting to aid them. Rogers (219) has contributed an integrated description of a treatment process. Further, he has distinguished his treatment as nondirective and has questioned the validity of directive methods used by personnel workers and others concerned with individualized

---

[1] Reprinted from *Educational and Psychological Measurement*, 1946, 6, 169–184. Copyright 1946 by G. Fredric Kuder.

[2] Bibliography begins on page 428.

treatment. Thorne (265), while conceding the contribution of non-directive techniques, has contended that it is not the only method which has value and has attempted to describe situations in which directive types of processes would be more effective.

Thus the psychological practitioner is faced with a choice of treatments. He is faced with a choice which will be difficult to make unless he is already prejudiced in favor of one or the other. He is faced with a difficult choice whether he is undecided as to the relative validity of the two or accepts Thorne's thesis that they are not incompatible. In the latter instance he still must decide the proper time to use each one.

Before this decision can be made in an adequate and final manner, there is still one more element to be added, namely, diagnosis. There can be no completely definitive demonstration of the differential validity of treatment without knowledge of what we are treating. True, one could say that we are treating human dissatisfaction and unhappiness, but could the great strides in medical therapy have been made if medical scientists and practitioners had been willing to stop at the level of diagnosing patients as such? Guthrie makes the same point when he says:

It (psychotherapy) must be restricted to those efforts at treatment which are consciously (in so many words) based on a knowledge of the ways of the mind, those treatments in which we are aware of the psychological explanation of the distress and the principles of adaptive habits we are establishing as a cure (104, p. 372).

We must be able to distinguish the behavioral characteristics which will accompany one type (source) of dissatisfaction from those that will accompany another type of dissatisfaction. From classifications based upon specific sets of characteristics we must be able to predict other characteristics which will be found either at the same time or with the progression of time; as, for example, by knowing the species of a bird we are able to predict its mating behavior, its migratory habits, etc. In this way we can set the stage for the most important prediction, from the practitioner's standpoint, that is, the prediction of the effect of one treatment as compared to another (or as compared to no treatment).

It is the purpose of this paper to explore the diagnostic concepts which have been used and to attempt to contribute toward the development of a series of diagnostic constructs which will make possible definitive studies of treatment hypotheses. Since most counseling and psychotherapy is being directed toward the psychological problems found within the normal range of individuals, and due to limitations of the writer's own experience, the constructs developed will have primary reference to problems as they appear in counseling and guidance services in colleges and universities and other educational institutions. Both Williamson and Rogers have tended to address themselves to this type of setting.

Desired Characteristics of Diagnostic Constructs

It has been suggested that substantial progress in the validation of psychotherapeutic treatment processes cannot be made without the postulation and validation of constructs or "causes" of psychological problems. Let us consider the characteristics by which a potentially valuable set of diagnostic constructs can be recognized.

1. One of the most important characteristics of such a construct is that it enables the clinician to understand more clearly the significance of the individual's behavior. For example, this kind of understanding would appear to play an important role in the therapist's ability to respond adequately to feelings expressed by the client in a nondirective treatment process. Diagnostic constructs should sensitize the clinician to respond to significant characteristics of the client's behavior that might otherwise have been overlooked. The degree of understanding fostered by the constructs will be reflected by the comprehensiveness of the predictions which can be made about the individual by assigning him to a class. This is the operational significance of understanding. We perceive a distinctive and familiar pattern which is part of a larger pattern the characteristics of which are then predictable from our perception of the smaller pattern. This is the secret of the medical diagnostician's success, namely, that from a few symptoms he is able to predict the other symptoms. In fact, he checks his diagnosis by seeing whether the additional symptoms do conform to expectation.

2. The more a set of diagnostic constructs vary independently, the closer they are assumed to be to the status of "true" causes and the farther from the status of surface symptoms. That is, the more independent a set of constructs, the more sharply focused the prediction yielded. If, for example, fever, coughing and sneezing, blood counts, skin condition, etc., were used as basic constructs in the medical

field, it would soon be found that they do not vary independently—that they form patterns—and that the predictions provided by any one construct are very limited. The medical practitioner would explain to us that these characteristics do not predict much because they are symptoms, not causes. To state it another way, a set of constructs based upon the patterns of these limited classifications will provide a basis for a more comprehensive set of predictions. From this point of view the most desirable statistical characteristic of a set of diagnostic classifications is that they vary not only independently but are also mutually exclusive. However, we could no more expect this than we should expect that there will be no individuals who have measles and whooping cough or any other combination of diseases at the same time. By setting a criterion of statistical independence we ask only that various combinations of categories do not occur more frequently than would be expected by chance. We can become most suspicious of the comprehensiveness of a set of categories when we find greater than chance incidence of combinations of three or more of them.

3. From the theoretical as well as from the applied point of view, but particularly from the latter, the most vital characteristic of a set of diagnostic classifications is that they form the basis for the choice of treatment. This means that there should be some understandable and predictable relationship between the characteristics which define the construct and the effects of treatment processes. From the therapist's point of view diagnosis will be of little value unless it points to treatment. Part of the definition of a diagnostic construct should include some statement as to how the condition can be modified, and its validity will depend in good part on whether this prediction can be verified.

Present Status of Diagnosis

In the area of normal psychological problems the concept of diagnosis presented above has been used rarely. Rogers treats the question of diagnosis, but he does so as though there was only one possible type of interview therapy. He confines his discussion to listing two sets of criteria, one for the use of treatment by manipulation of the environment and the other for determining whether the individual can take interview therapy.

For a long time there has been current among counselors, working in the educational and vocational guidance setting, terminology for describing their clients' problems which centered around the difficulties about which they complained. Williamson and Darley (297) and later Williamson (296) developed these ideas into an attempt at a systematic set of diagnostic categories. Only a summary will be presented with no attempt to reproduce Williamson's extensive description of the five suggested categories:

Personality Problems. Included in this grouping are difficulties in adjusting in social groups, speech difficulties, family conflicts, and infractions of discipline.

Educational Problems. These include unwise choice of courses of study and curricula, differential scholastic achievement, insufficient general scholastic aptitude, ineffective study habits, reading disabilities, insufficient scholastic motivation, overachievement, underachievement, adjustment of superior students.

Vocational Problems. Descriptive subdivisions of this category are uncertain occupational choice, no vocational choice, discrepancy between interests and aptitudes, unwise vocational choice.

Financial Problems. These include difficulties arising from the need for self-support in school and college and the correlated questions of student placement.

Health Problems. This category refers to the individual's adjustment to his health or physical disabilities, or both.

Examination of this diagnostic system indicates that primarily it represents an attempt to describe the individual in terms of his adjustment to the demands of his environment. It places its emphasis upon the aspects of his social environment with which he appears to be unable to cope to his satisfaction or to the satisfaction of society (which assumes eventual dissatisfaction for the individual). This type of description might be termed a sociological description of the individual to distinguish it from a psychological description of the individual which starts at the individual describing the organization of his behavioral characteristics and predicting what his reactions will be to his social environment.

Let us consider the adequacy of these sociologically rooted diagnostic classifications by applying the criteria suggested above.

First, do they point the way to treatment? Since Williamson does not attempt a clearly structured description of treatment processes, the answer must be inferred from his discussions of specific procedures in specific situations. Such analysis leads us to the conclusion that treatment is not indicated by the problem classification but by other factors. Williamson does state that "the effective counselor is one who adapts his techniques of advising to the personality of the student" (296, p. 138). Some individuals who present vocational problems or educational problems or financial or personality problems might be helped by giving them information. Yet others who present difficulties in the same areas must be dealt with in terms of their feelings. Thus, the assignment of the individual's difficulties to one of this set of classes of difficulties does not provide a basis for prediction of the relative success of different treatments.

Second, to what degree do these classifications vary independently? To answer this question there are data available on some two thousand cases who came to the Student Counseling Bureau at the University of Minnesota, between 1932 and 1935.[3] These cases were classified according to the above diagnostic system. The resulting distributions showed a high degree of patterning in the occurrence of the problem categories. For example, there was only one category, vocational problems, which exhibited any appreciable occurrence by itself. Approximately twenty-three per cent of the total number of individuals were classifiable as having only vocational problems. The next highest occurrence of a single problem was only 1.6 per cent for educational problems. Similarly, the distributions of combinations of two of the problems were far removed from what would be expected by chance. The highest frequency of a combination of two problems was vocational-educational which was represented by 27.7 per cent of the total population as compared to the next highest frequency of 5.8 per cent for the combination of vocational and personality problems. Similar non-chance distributions are found in the occurrence of combinations of three and four problems. Further, there were more individuals who presented all five problems (1.1 per cent) than there were individuals who presented single problems of either financial (0.2 per cent), personality (0.2 per cent), or health (0.0 per cent). These results would appear to suggest strongly that there is a deeper level of analysis than is represented by these categories. It suggests that these categories would appear in the relation

---

[3] Taken from an unpublished report by E. G. Williamson and E. S. Bordin.

of surface symptoms to a set of categories representing a deeper level of analysis.

What of the third criterion, the amount of understanding conveyed by the classification, that is, its predictive value? The same study, cited above, produces data on this question. It was found that various characteristics of the individuals were not predicted so much by the single classifications, except for vocational, as by various combinations. In other words, again it looked as though there was some more basic classification which might be somewhat reflected by the present ones.

A Suggested Set of Diagnostic Constructs

Because analysis of the type presented above indicated that the present system of diagnostic classification far from fulfilled the desired characteristics of diagnostic categories, the writer felt it necessary to search for some more adequate system. Williamson's treatment of these categories seems to reflect a recognition of their incompleteness and offered one useful source of inspiration. For each category and the subdivisions of it he gives considerable time to a discussion of the causes of the problem. Here much of his analysis is at the psychological as well as the sociological level. In other words, he considers the organization of the individual's life history which leads him to his present status and its significance for other forms of behavior.

This source and others were consulted, but the main basis for the set of diagnostic constructs which will be presented below is the actual observation of clients over a period of about six months. As each client talked about his difficulties in making a vocational decision, or about the fact that he felt that he needed help in working out a method for financing his education, etc., the writer asked himself, and attempted to answer, the questions, "Why cannot this individual work this thing out himself? What is stopping him from being able to find a satisfactory solution? How is he different from his fellow students who appear to be facing the same problems and working them out successfully for themselves?" Certain types of answers began to appear. They were answers which suggested ways in which the client could be helped. They were answers that gave the counselor the feeling that he could predict how the client would react to various possible verbal stimulations. They were answers which seemed to have antecedents in other psychological observation and experimentation.

Having considered the method of search, we are ready to look at the resulting diagnostic constructs.

Dependence. This concept is common currency in child and adolescent psychology where it is usually discussed under the rubric "psychological weaning." The client comes to the counselor for help because he has not learned to solve his own problems. The client is used to playing a passive role. He has been dependent upon his parents or parent-surrogates to solve his problems for him. His progress beyond the infant stage is reflected by the fact that he has learned how to ask for help more explicitly and is more discriminating as to where he directs his requests for aid. Usually he has come to the counselor because someone has taken the responsibility to suggest it. The counselor will find that this type of client resists accepting responsibility. He will be anxious to continue his contact with the counselor. If given the opportunity, he will wear a path to the counselor's door, coming in for help with every decision that faces him: how to plan his time, how to find a part-time job, whether to take Psychology this quarter or wait until next? The unwary counselor will feel that he has established a good relationship (rapport) with this client, but it would appear that he is fostering the further development of an unsatisfactory behavior pattern (from either the social or individual viewpoint). The treatment of individuals presenting this kind of problem would appear to include aid in insight and acceptance of the fact that they do feel inadequate to cope actively and responsibly with their everyday problems and aid in obtaining the experiences that will enable them to work out their own problems. Merely solving their problems for them will perpetuate the state which will bring them back to the counselor or to someone else as each new problem presents itself. Yet in the early stages, but after the client has gained insight into his dependent feelings, it may be necessary for the counselor to partially guide the client as he makes his first tentative steps toward independent action, much as, at earlier stages, we keep youngsters from harm as they learn to cross streets by themselves.

Lack of Information. Many individuals face situations for which their experience has not prepared them. The individuals who would fall in the lack-of-information category are individuals who are used to accepting the responsibility for making their own decisions, but who face a decision involving information or special skills out of the realm of their experience. In a university that draws students from small rural schools there will be many such individuals, bewildered by the organizational details of a complex educational instrument or by social customs foreign to their experience. These individuals lack the opportunities to compare themselves with representative groups necessary to accurate judgments about their learning abilities, relative weaknesses or strengths in their background of knowledge. They lack sufficient information about the occupational world to set their sights realistically. Sometimes they lack knowledge of appropriate social behavior causing them to feel insecure and ineffectual in attempting to achieve social goals. While the counselor should beware of motivated ignorance, he must also recognize that ignorance may also arise as a function of restriction in opportunity to learn. The types of lack of information which have been mentioned can arise from all types of environmental restrictions in experience which make this ignorance plausible. He needs to beware of excessive ignorance or unusual combinations of ignorance which is insufficient to account for the perplexity displayed. Yet, if he is working in a situation where large proportions of a student body are aware of the counseling service, a sizable proportion of the individuals who come to him will be classifiable as lacking information. The treatment of such individuals would appear to be quite direct. They should be given information, referred to books or other individuals, and so on. Where the individual is seeking to avoid responsibility care must be exercised to avoid giving him the information in such a manner as to foster his potential dependence.

Self-Conflict. The fact that there appears to be sharply differentiated organizations of individuals' behaviors toward themselves as stimulus objects has been receiving renewed and extended attention in the recent psychological literature. This factor has been discussed under the topic of ego, by Allport (4); ego involvement, by Edwards (75, 76), and Wallin (280); role and self, by Guthrie (104); and self-concept, by Raimy (210) and Bordin (26). From clinical observation it appears that many of the obstacles in the individual's ability to cope with his problems arise from the conflict between the response functions associated with two or more of his self-concepts or between a self-concept and some other stimulus function. Guthrie takes a similar position when he cites the "conflict between role and actuality" as a source of students' breakdowns. He cites as an example:

a docile girl who received good marks throughout grade and high school. Modern schools grade their pupils according to effort and docility and not according to actual achievement. . . . When she reaches the university there is keener competition and more objective grading. As a result she manages to receive only average grades in spite of increased effort. She cannot reconcile herself to average grades or face her family where her record has always been a matter of pride and comment. She begins to lose sleep, to become despondent, to find herself unable to study. (*104*, p. 351.)

The description is a familiar one. It has been duplicated in the experience of most college clinicians. In addition to such familiar instances of conflict between a self-concept and the ability to behave in a manner consistent with that self, there are instances where two self-concepts come into conflict. Take, for example, the instance of the son of a doctor who has developed considerable identification with his father. Through the years they have shared many activities, hunting, building motors in a shop, attending athletic events. But the activities shared were not necessarily those intimately related to the practice of medicine. The development of the son's experience is such that one of his dominant self-concepts is that of a forester. At the same time, the son's close relationship with his father and his father's evident desire for him to become an M.D. makes for a competing picture of himself, but one which is not as closely allied as forestry to the majority of his behavior patterns. The basis for conflicting motives is largely unverbalized. The student can only say that he cannot seem to make up his mind as to what to do.

The nondirective treatment process described by Rogers (*219*) appears to apply most completely and most directly to this type of psychological problem. It can be assumed that individuals presenting problems of self-conflict must be aided to recognize and accept their conflicting feelings before they will be able to arrive at the positive decisions involved in resolving the conflict.

Choice Anxiety.[4]   In 1941–42 when these concepts were being

---

[4] The writer is indebted to Mr. Harold Pepinsky for the suggestion of the name for this category.

formulated, large numbers of students in colleges and universities were grappling with the problem of their relationship to the national emergency. This was the period of the Army Enlisted Reserve Corps, the Navy V-5 and V-12 programs, and the deferment of students in certain scientific and technical fields. The nature of the psychological problem represented by the students who came to the writer with their quandary can be represented by an analogy to the experimental neurosis experiments reported by Maier (165). In these experiments rats were trained to jump from a platform toward the correct one of two doorways. If the correct doorway was discriminated, it swung open as the animal hit it and a reward of food followed. If the wrong discrimination was made, the door did not swing open, the animal bumped its nose and fell into a net below, presumably a very dissatisfying experience. After the animals had learned to make the correct discrimination, experimental neurosis was induced by the punishment of either choice. Maier noted that not all of the animals developed neurotic behavior. Those that may be said to have accepted their plight, as evidenced by abortive jumping, did not develop neurotic symptoms. On the other hand, those animals that continued to "expect" to find a rewarding choice were the ones that did develop the symptoms. The analogy to the plight of the students seeking help was striking. These individuals were faced with alternatives, all of which were unpleasant in that all would involve a disruption of their life plans. The student talking to the counselor was fully informed on all of the alternatives open to him. He appeared to be coming to the counselor in the hope that he would be able to find some other alternative that would represent a way out without unpleasant consequences. These students were under considerable tension, indecisive, and tending toward physical exhaustion. The state could be characterized as approaching psychasthenia. It could be said to differ from psychasthenia in that it depends more on sudden disorganizing crises of a type that can lend themselves to procrastination and are not as clearly a part of a long-term behavior pattern of the individual. Perhaps one of the essential differences would be that of degree and amenability to therapy.

It can be expected that problems of this type will increase in incidence during any period of social upheaval and rapid change. The writer has since encountered the same psychological state in returning veterans. One example is that of an ex-serviceman in his middle twenties, married and trying to make up his mind whether he should go to college or accept immediate employment. If he goes to college he realizes his fondest dreams, tries out his new-found confidence in himself, and makes it more possible to set his occupational aspirations at a higher level. But also, if he goes to college, his wife has to work to contribute to their support. This postpones having children, raises uncertainties about his wife's satisfaction, because she too would like to go to college, and postpones his own economic independence. On the other hand, accepting immediate employment, even with some opportunity for on-the-job training, means resigning himself to a lower level of aspiration and giving up the chance for a college education. Neither alternative is free of unpleasant results.

That this psychological problem is not confined to situations arising out of rapid social change can be illustrated by still another problem of choice anxiety. This is a case of a woman in her early thirties whose husband decided that marriage is too confining for his catholic sexual tastes. She comes to the counselor, presumably to obtain help in deciding what occupation she should train for in anticipation of the need to be independent. However, she appears unable to decide, while expressing concern about the need for decision and exhibiting symptoms of continuous tension. It is evident that her alternatives are both punishing, one to submit to the insecurities of life with her husband or the other to submit to the insecurities of life without a husband.

The treatment that appears to be indicated for individuals with this type of problem is to enable them to face and accept the fact that they are "in for it." It is here assumed that once the individual has accepted the fact that he is in a situation from which there is no escape without unpleasantness, the psychasthenic symptoms will disappear and the individual will be able to make a decision. It is further assumed that many such individuals will be able to accept this statement of their problem when it is given to them directly after some "talking out" process. In the cases of the woman cited above, of students thinking about themselves in relation to the draft, and of the returning serviceman, the resolution of their problems seemed to follow that course.

No Problem. To keep his perspective, the clinician should recognize that, if he works in a widely publicized and widely accepted agency to which individuals have easy access, a considerable proportion of the individuals who seek him out will not present definitely classifiable problems. For the most part they will be individuals who come to the counselor in the same spirit in which we might visit our doctor once a year for a physical checkup. In other words, they are playing safe. In an agency like the Student Counseling Bureau of the University of Minnesota, which is widely known throughout the state and favorably recommended by high-school educators, it is to be expected that many students will visit it as a safety measure at the time of entrance to the university which means a time of educational and vocational decision. These students are likely to say to the counselor, "I know what I want to do, but I wanted to see what you would say." True, this statement could also be a reflection of a defensive reaction against a feeling of self-conflict or dependence, and there is no attempt to suggest that such a statement should be accepted as indicating no problem. It is cited, however, as illustrative of the fully revealed reaction of the individual. Such individuals will usually be very relaxed about taking tests. They will probably want to take a considerable number of them. When they have completed testing and have heard an interpretation of them, they will take the initiative very readily and terminate the interview in a short time. Another type of case that might be listed under this category is that of the student who uses his interviews, with or without testing, as the occasion for making up his mind. Other than furnishing the occasion, the counselor, if he realizes it, does not need to play any role in the process.

In addition to the hypotheses about treatment specific to each of the diagnostic categories which have been presented above, a word should be said about certain general treatment implications. Since there is general agreement that therapy starts with the first contact between the client and the counselor, there cannot be a clear temporal demarcation between the diagnostic and treatment processes in the interview. This raises the problem of what treatment processes are most effective in that period when diagnosis and treatment are developing together. It is suggested that during this introductory phase of the treatment process, the counselor's objective should be to enable the client to clarify his conception of his problem, to develop insights into his own role and the counselor's in the treatment process, and, where necessary, to give immediate release to dangerously pent up feelings. This points to the need for fostering client initiative and the exercise of alertness and insight in responding to client feelings, embodied in the treatment processes so well described by Rogers.

Does the suggested set of diagnostic categories meet the criteria more effectively than the set it is designed to replace? At this time only a partial answer is possible. There seems to be a firm basis for saying that the suggested set of categories are more clearly linked to differential treatment. Further, these categories are more closely linked than their predecessors to fundamental psychological concepts. However, the adequacy of this or any such set of categories cannot rest upon common-sense judgments alone. Their ultimate acceptability must be based upon actual demonstration that: (a) there is a reasonable degree of agreement among counselors making a diagnostic judgment on the same client; (b) there is a greater degree of randomness in the occurrence of various combinations of categories and a greater frequency of occurrence of clients who can be diagnosed as belonging to only one category than is true of the previous set; (c) the diagnoses do in fact point to differentially effective treatments; (d) a greater degree of understanding of clients' results, as indicated by a more comprehensive set of predictions being associated with the new than with the old set.

One final point should be made. Even though the rationale upon which this set of diagnostic categories should be substantiated, it appears unlikely that all of the specific categories will prove to be the most effective and most complete ones. It is hardly likely, assuming the validity of the general concept, that the writer's experience and insight would have been broad and deep enough to have taken into account all of the possible psychological problems that could fall within this framework. It is more likely that further observation within this framework would reveal additional categories or more methodology for such processes may possibly contribute to the qual-present ones.

Summary

This paper has presented an analysis of the place of diagnosis in counseling and psychotherapy. It has attempted to demonstrate that diagnosis is a necessary process in treatment and in the types of research that will provide the basis for the improvement of treatment. Diagnostic concepts now used by counselors in educational institutions were examined in terms of criteria of meaningfulness, statistical characteristics of independence, and relation to choice of differential treatment. This examination suggested that the present diagnostic concepts based on environmental or sociological constructs are not adequate, and a new set of concepts based upon psychological constructs was suggested.

JOSEPH L. TAYLOR

Veterans Administration, Regional Office, Cincinnati, Ohio

ARTHUR TEICHER

Veterans Administration, Regional Office, New York, New York

A Clinical Approach to Reporting Psychological Test Data[1]

Introduction

This paper is directed toward a methodology in recording and reporting the test data of the clinical psychologist in order to achieve an expression of that wealth of material obtainable through psychological tests which gives a sensitive, dynamic understanding of the patient and his problems. The paper is offered also as an attempt to orient the written statements of the practitioner in terms of professional needs and relationships with professional associates.

The raw data obtained from psychological examinations are quite meaningless to persons other than the examiner and, even to the examiner, the original, unassembled data assumes greatest significance only when sifted, interpreted and organized. In customary practice, and particularly where the psychologist is a member of a clinical team, the final organization of test data emerges in a formal report which serves to provide a record of the test situation and to communicate the findings to interested professional persons. Since the very act of formulating a written statement of findings makes it imperative to sift, interpret and organize the data to a high degree, a

---

[1] Reprinted from *Journal of Clinical Psychology*, 1946, 2, 323–332. Copyright 1946 by Frederick C. Thorne. 2

methodology for such processes may possibly contribute to the quality of the end product.

Clinical psychology, unlike allied practices which are directed toward the understanding and treatment of the individual, appears to have given little systematic study to the manner in which test findings are organized and formulated to provide necessary records and to render the data easily and fully understood by professional associates. The many well-written, well thought-out psychological reports found in current practice appear to stem from individual intuition or individual study of the problem of recording, rather than from a commonly accepted system. Social case work, for example, after long struggle with the problem of recording, has evolved its concepts of "process recording" and "summary recording" as the most effective means of stating observations and findings. Psychiatrists, too, observe an ordered scheme in preparing formal statements of their data and the fact that such schemes differ from setting to setting is only a reflection of singular need or purpose and in no way denies the existence of generally accepted principles in psychiatric recording. In all allied fields the matter of recording involves much more than maintaining an historical record of the situation. More important, the task of recording provides a reasoned statement in a commonly understood structure of the important facts which emerged in a specifically oriented clinical relationship. There exists a need for standardized methods among clinical psychologists in the recording of test data. It is conceivable that the psychiatrist or social worker who relies upon the work of the clinical psychologist may frequently be confused or frustrated because methods of reporting data are so varied and lacking in central philosophy and direction.

Theoretical Considerations

If any central direction to the reporting of psychological test data may be established, it seems that the specific orientation of the clinical relationship, e.g., the "function," might serve as a basic frame of reference. By "function" is meant the job which the psychologist sets out to do which serves as the basis from which all subsequent practice follows. An awareness of function would, by definition, cause the clinical psychologist to take cognizance of the specific objective of a particular examination and to frame his report in terms of that objective. Thus, a conscious utilization of the concept of function in recording would assist the psychologist in thinking clearly about what to include and what to omit in the report; would avoid introducing irrelevancies to the problem under investigation; would help in preventing the inner needs, the focus or particular school of thought of the psychologist from dominating the findings and from robbing his written statement of the broader perspective required to achieve a dynamic understanding of his patient. As a final corollary, a more conscious utilization of the concept of function would increase the possibility of making available to interested professional persons the best that the clinical psychologist has to offer in a given situation.

Stated broadly, the function of the clinical psychologist is that of obtaining a general abstract picture of the patient's intellectual resources under specified conditions, his intellectual patterns of abilities, his adjustment styles in conventional self-management, and his basic personality needs and mechanisms of reaction in self-expression —all in the context of a situational variable represented by his immediate environment. It is rare, however, that the source who refers an individual to a clinical psychologist for testing needs or desires such a complete abstract picture of the patient. Usually, even when the referral is made in vague, over-all terms, such as with a request for a "psychological work-up," the referral source has a specific question, or set of questions, for which he seeks clarification through testing. Ideally, since the referral source usually desires a specific job of the clinical psychologist, it would seem that his needs could best be met if he were to present the psychologist with a definition of the service desired. Experience suggests that requests for psychological services, however broadly or vaguely expressed initially, upon further inquiry devolve essentially into one of three main groups of services desired. The psychiatrist or social worker was interested either in the patient's "level of mental functioning" (commonly and inadvisedly referred to as an "I.Q. examination"); or they desired clues from psychological techniques in arriving at a "differential diagnosis"; or they were interested in a "personality evaluation" of the patient.

Since the problem presented is different for each of the above referrals, the psychologist has a different focus for each situation and may employ different instruments to obtain the necessary data. Employing different instruments with varying focus and intent, it is evident that the findings in one type of case will differ in major aspects from findings in the other types of cases. Therefore, should not the purpose, or function, of the examination play a significant part in the psychologist's recording of his findings? Do not the various levels towards which psychological examinations may be directed require that pertinent and fundamental features of each be observed in a formal statement of results? For that reason it is recommended that a distinct and characteristic method of summarizing the data for each of these three groups of examinations be employed, yet in a manner which permits flexibility in evaluating each individual. Such a characteristic framework for the written statement would point up the main problem under investigation and make it easier for the psychiatrist or social worker to grasp the particular information he is looking for.[2]

Indirectly, another advantage might accrue from organizing the act of recording which is not an easy one. Considerable mental effort is required to formulate clearly and meaningfully the mass of data which the examiner accumulates. Supervisors and administrators are well aware of the inertia and even blocking which comes upon workers in relation to dictation schedules, and many of the more recent discussions about recording in various fields have been concerned with evolving simpler, time-saving techniques without sacrificing content. Thus, a guide in recording, such as a methodology offers, may be a helpful tool. Such a guide might be particularly helpful to new practitioners who seek assistance in evaluating and formulating their findings.

Methods

The following material presents and briefly discusses outline guides for the preparation of records with reference to the three main groups of services commonly requested of clinical psychologists. The outlines suggest a common approach to analyzing and or-

---

[2] It will be readily granted that the results of a practice such as clinical psychology which, by its very nature defies stereotypy and which, on the contrary, frequently gains its chief effectiveness from the unique style or personality of the practitioner, cannot be recorded under a rigid, inflexible scheme. The written word must necessarily reflect the uniqueness of the individual in his approach, his perspective and professional skill, and any attempts to formulate recording schemata need not be construed as inevitably imposing stereotypes or inhibitions upon the individuality of the practitioner. Indeed, the unique approach, style and skill of the psychiatrist or social worker is readily apparent despite the popular framework of his recording.

ganizing test data, but comparable areas within each are differentiated in degree of intensity, according to the needs presented by the
specific referral. These outline guides are most applicable to evaluating test findings from individual examinations of adults, but with
appropriate modifications not here discussed they might be adapted
to the examination of children. Further, the procedures developed
in the outlines are based upon the assumption that, to perform adequately the explorations required, the psychologist utilizes a battery
of tests which includes, at the minimum, an intelligence test which
lends itself to diagnostic interpretation and any additional techniques, projective and non-projective which are helpful in analyzing
intellectual and emotional functioning.

The psychologist's statement of findings can not go beyond what
he perceives or comprehends. The matter of clinical sensitivity and
understanding is so intimately connected with any thinking about
organization of data into a written statement that the former must
receive simultaneous consideration. Hence the suggested outlines for
recording also imply a tentative clinical approach to analyzing test
data. This discussion assumes a working knowledge of the clinical
concepts employed and the paper is not concerned with a presentation of such concepts.

The clinical approach involves an analysis of the quantitative and
qualitative aspects of test results, the language organization and quality of verbal responses and finally the observations and interpretations of behavior and adjustment traits which emerge during the
examination. Each outline for recording attempts a development of
data from one sub-area to the next to achieve a logical, interlocking
and progressively deepening understanding of the problem being
explored. Although the outline guides attempt to present a comprehensive approach to evaluating and preparing test data, the various
sub-areas in each outline need receive explicit treatment in reports
only when the findings of a particular situation are relevant.

Level of Mental Functioning. Under this heading we find those
psychometric examinations whose specific purpose is a measure of
general intelligence. The recording is oriented to the recognition
that a statement of "I.Q." is inadequate in such situations inasmuch
as cultural, emotional and motivational forces are integral factors in
intellectual functioning. Hence any statement of general intelligence must also concern itself with the inter-relationship of environ-

mental and psychodynamic factors in order to describe intelligence in its functioning as an attribute of a unique personality. The reporting is further oriented to the recognition that a specific, defined service is requested of the psychologist and that any findings which pertain to deeper levels of understanding are not pertinent to the service requested.

In reporting investigations on *Level of Mental Functioning*, the following outline is suggested:

Outline of Content of Report for Level of Mental Functioning

1. Reason for referral.
2. General observations.
   a. Note adjustment to test.
      1. Cooperation.
      2. Effort.
      3. Attention.
      4. Adaptability.
   b. Note behavior which characterized adjustment.
      1. Social maturity.
      2. Self-criticism.
      3. Self-confidence.
      4. Introversion-extroversion.
      5. Dominance-submission.
      6. Attitudes.
      7. Insight.
   c. Note unusual appearance or speech patterns.
3. Intelligence.
   a. State intellectual functioning level in terms of I.Q., M.A., percentile ranking and classification as "defective," "dull normal," "average," etc.
   b. If results are not representative or valid, give evidence and show reasoning.
      1. Variability in mental functioning.
      2. Distorted results because of adjustment difficulties.
      3. Educational or cultural factors.
   c. Indicate best and poorest abilities when they merit attention.
4. Other test analysis.
   a. Use other tests as supplementary material to aid in determining intellectual level or to indicate the presence of disturbing elements which interfere with an adequate presentation of the individual's intellectual level.
   b. When supplementary tests contradict general findings, attempt to explain contradictions and integrate them into the understanding of the patient.

5. Summary.
   a. Answer problem in light of psychological findings.
   b. Incorporate general interpretations in summary fashion or by recapitulation.
   c. Suggest need, if indicated, for re-examination or further study.

Beginning the above report with a statement of the reason for referral provides an early orientation to what follows and indicates the examiner's frame of reference for his work and conclusions. The next section of the report offers a picture of behavioral factors emerging during the examination against which the patient's utilization of his intelligence may be understood. Because of the inadequacy of such derived symbols as I.Q. and M.A. in expressing the dynamic nature of intelligence, the statistical expression of intellectual level is immediately followed by a statement of the existence of any factors which suggest that the derived symbols are not valid or not representative of optimum capacities. Other tests administered receive comment in terms of additional light shed upon intellectual functioning and, to emphasize succinctly and pointedly the significant findings, the report concludes with a brief summary.

Differential Diagnosis. If it is granted that "every activity of the individual bears the stamp of his individuality," then, with the proper skills, any behavior can be interpreted and "will serve as an indicator of the individuality and its adjustment or maladjustment" (212, p. 3).[3] Thus, the unique personality and the manner of his relating to his world can be inferred out of his activities observed under the controlled conditions of a psychological examination.

As distinguished from the general approach utilized in investigations of *Level of Mental Functioning,* study of *Differential Diagnosis* becomes more intensive in terms of sensitivity to qualitative peculiarities, efficiency of various mental functions and depth of psychological exploration. With these remarks as a frame of reference, the outline for studies of *Differential Diagnosis* contains:

Outline for Recording of Study of Differential Diagnosis

1. Reason for referral.
2. General observations.
   a. Pattern of adjustment to testing situation.

---

[3] Bibliography begins on page 428.

b. Note atypical behavior, attitudes and feelings.
c. Describe symptomatic mannerisms.
3. Intelligence.
   a. State functioning level; express in terms of I.Q., M.A., percentile rank, and descriptive groupings as "average or superior."
   b. If results are not representative or if they are invalid, give evidence and show reasoning.
4. Analysis and intensive investigation of following areas for clues of psychodynamic forces determining behavior as revealed by psychological data.
   a. Quantitative analysis: Analysis of test patterns: Study of "Scatter" measuring the depth of the maladjustment and the specific point of vulnerability using as many of the following techniques as feasible.
      1. Discrepancies between performance and achievement on verbal and non-verbal tests.
      2. Inter-test variability.
         a. Central tendency deviation on both verbal and non-verbal test groups.
      3. Inconsistency in mental functioning.
         a. Uneven performance on one test, failure on easy items and success on more difficult items.
      4. Vocabulary deviation.
         a. Tendency of sub-test scores to drop below or rise above the vocabulary level.
      5. Range deviation.
         a. Extent of the scatter from the lowest to the highest scores.
      6. Sub-test relationships.
         a. Analysis in terms of the relation of one type test to another type test.
         b. "Pairs technique" (212, p. 31).
            1. Relation of block design and object assembly test (of neutral emotional content) to other non-verbal tests and to picture completion and picture arrangement.
            2. Relation of digit span to arithmetic ("out-of-pattern") relationship when arithmetic is more impaired than digit span.
   b. Qualitative analysis.
      1. Evaluation of test in terms of its "rationale."
         a. Understanding of the meaning, scope and limitation of each test and the functions underlying test achievement. It is on this understanding that an appraisal of qualitative peculiarities can be made, that an assessment of the functions which are impaired can be discerned. It is the relationship of scores and the understanding of how they are achieved or attained that reveals patterns of efficiency of different functions. Such method allows for insight into the forces of dynamic be-

havior, its quality and direction, that resulted in such a pattern.

2. Evaluation of patient in terms of relevant developmental-social history.

   a. Testing procedure is an integral part of clinical examination and thus should be evaluated in terms of patient's educational and cultural background, his lingual facilities, and his temporary emotional reactions to the stimuli, for valid interpretation. The core of diagnostic evaluation revolves about an understanding of the factors that create discrepancies and cause inconsistencies and unevenness in test results that are contrary to expectations when examined against the background of life history data.

3. "Item analysis."

   a. Establishing groups of items on the same sub-test in which accumulation of failures is a pathological condition; easy items and difficult items.

   b. Differentiation of the underlying causes of failure.

      1. "lack of attainment.

      2. temporary inefficiency.

      3. impairment.

      4. deterioration" (212, p. 60).

   c. Content ideation of responses indicate the cause and level of failure.

      1. Coherence of thought patterns.

      2. Bizarreness of response.

      3. Irrelevancy of response.

   d. Concept formation.

      1. Level of organization.

         a. Concrete.

         b. Functional.

         c. Abstract.

      2. Use of stereotypes.

         a. Conventional modes of expression used to conceal individual variation.

         b. Deviation from stereotypes.

      3. Difficulty in planning, organizing and synthesizing.

         a. Use of substitutions or simpler levels of accomplishment.

c. Language organization and quality of verbal reactions.

   1. Quality of response.

      a. Terse.

         1. Reticent, extremely difficult to elicit response.

         2. Unwilling to discuss pertinent data, responds only to direct questioning.

      b. Adequate, concise and well-planned.

         1. Speaks freely and volunteers information.

        a. Deliberately or without deliberation.
        b. About self or about others.
    c. Verbosity.
        1. Talks profusely but offers relevant comments, speaks to the point.
        2. Talks profusely.
            a. Introduces extraneous conversation: tangential.
            b. Generally irrelevant, redundant, bizarre.
            c. Associated material, bizarre phrases such as "gamble . . . . speculate to accumulate."
            d. Deliberately changes subject, evasive.
            e. Lies or malingers.
        3. Misuse of words and word meanings.
  2. Type of response.
    a. Answers before question is finished.
    b. Answers impulsively.
    c. Deliberates before answering.
  3. Anticipatory reactions.
    a. Shows over-confidence, braggard, grandiose.
    b. Fairly confident.
    c. Anticipates failure.
        1. Says he cannot do it.
        2. Afraid or unwilling to try.
  4. Awareness of difficulties and problems.
    a. Insight or lack of insight into difficulty.
  5. Fluency.
    a. Unusual fluency.
    b. Some hesitation in speech.
    c. Halting speech.
    d. Speech defect.
  6. Emotional reactions in speech.
    a. Gross display of emotionality, "gushing."
    b. Complete lack of emotionality, "poker face."
    c. Appropriate affect and remarks.
5. Other test analysis.
  a. Observation of and interpretation of adjustment under controlled conditions and situations of a different nature.
6. Summary.
  a. Answer problem of referral in light of psychological data in summarized manner.
    1. Intellectual functioning.
        a. Current functioning level.
        b. Potential optimal level.
    2. Areas of impairment and statement of symptomatology of specific disease entity described in lay language.
    3. Resultant conclusion if clearly indicated; otherwise, only description of psychodynamics of adjustment.

Again the report opens with a statement of reason for referral to provide an orientation to what follows and to indicate the examiner's focus for his investigation. The "general observations" are intended as a description of behavior in adjusting to the test situation which lends itself to psychiatric evaluation. The report presents the patient's intellectual functioning, first in the conventional terms of derived symbols. If the test performance is not representative of the individual's intellectual capacity, a statement of his reduced mental efficiency leads into a quantitative "scatter" analysis to indicate depth of maladjustment, degree of deterioration and specific points of intellectual and emotional vulnerability. It is not intended to assume that unevenness in mental functioning is unnatural or abnormal, for unevenness of mental abilities found in psychological test results is an expression of particular developmental patterns. An increasingly dynamic understanding of the test results is given by a qualitative evaluation in terms of "rationale," "item analysis," language organization and quality of verbal responses—thus pointing up the real nature of internal disorganization and emotional reactions viewed against the background of the patient's educational and cultural milieu. A wider cross-sectional view of the patient's personality is obtained by evaluating the data from other tests administered which yield clues as to behavior and adjustment. The summary serves to answer the question posed in the referral, recapitulates the patient's current and potential level of intellectual functioning, areas of intellectual and emotional disturbance and psychological evidence of symptomatology of specific disease entity.

Personality Evaluation. The appraisal of test results in *Personality Evaluation*, while developing basically from the same techniques utilized in studies of differential diagnosis, does differ in some important aspects of orientation, degree of skill and clinical insight required of the examiner in understanding and integrating his findings. In personality evaluation the focus of the examination is insight into all the forces which integrate the behavior of the patient into a unique entity; it embraces the whole system of dynamic life history forces which differentiate one individual from the other.

The purpose of a personality evaluation is no longer a psychological study of part activities of the individual, such as intelligence, nor is it a description of the sum of an individual's traits, nor of behavior which can be conveniently translated into nosological groups. A per-

sonality evaluation probes more deeply into the depths of functioning to determine the patient's conflicts, frustrations, unconscious
motivations, ego organization and the particular systems connecting
his basic personal drives to their manifestations in behavior and adjustment. It serves as a description of what a person is, why he is
that way, what types of etiological factors are responsible for his
present mode of adjustment and what direction the forces operative
within him may take in the future. This total analysis of the psychodynamic forces molding the individual's pattern of life adjustment
may very well be significant for prognosis and also may serve as a
guide in psychotherapy.

With such thinking about the nature of *Personality Evaluation* in
mind, the outline for recording cannot contain the specific suggestions found in mental evaluation and differential diagnosis, but
rather offers a framework for a sensitive organization of data.

Outline for Recording of Personality Evaluation

1. Reason for referral.
2. Behavior observations in testing situations.
   a. Pattern of adjustment in testing situation.
      1. Initial orientation.
      2. Effort.
      3. Work habits.
         a. attention.
         b. persistence.
         c. adaptability.
         d. tempo of work.
         e. accuracy.
         f. reactions under speed pressure.
         g. comprehension.
         h. self-reliance.
         i. self-criticism.
      4. Physical adequacy.
         a. movement of hands.
         b. body movements.
         c. perceptive abilities.
      5. Final adjustment.
   b. Evaluation and interpretation of behavior.
      1. Emotional stability.
      2. Social maturity.
      3. Critical powers.
      4. Confidence.
      5. Introversion-extroversion tendencies.
      6. Dominance-submission tendencies.

3. Intelligence.
    a. Statement of intellectual functioning as measured by "intelligence tests," expressed in terms of I.Q., M.A., percentile rank, and descriptive groupings, e.g., "average," or "superior."
    b. If results are not representative or invalid, give evidence and show reasoning.
    c. If impairment of mental functioning is indicated, show statistical, quantitative and qualitative evidence.
4. Utilization of all techniques and skills enumerated in "Differential Diagnosis Outline."
5. Evaluation of psychological data accumulated from all tests.
    a. Most important consideration is the individual, not the test, nor the test results, nor the mental disorder. Attention is to be focused on individual by revealing the following as evidenced in psychological test data.
        1. To what situation is he adjusting inadequately?
            a. Reasons for inadequate adjustment.
            b. Survey of basic emotional drives, ego strengths and resources at the individual's disposal in meeting life problems.
        2. By what means is he making a partial adjustment?
            a. Personality mechanisms being utilized to handle his reality and himself.
            b. The conflicts or clashes between his manipulation of reality and himself.
            c. The relationship between the ego and reality.
        3. What factors in his experience and training or development led to the present pattern of adjustment?
            a. Evaluation of psychological test results against selected life history data.
        4. How can he be guided to a better degree of adjustment?
            a. What types of forces or influences can help him achieve different types or levels of adjustment?
    b. Classification plays a subordinate role in personality evaluation.
        1. The individual should be considered as a unique human being, not "a type of case."
    c. Organizing the data obtained from psychological examination so that answering these four preceding questions leads to a thorough understanding of the individual and his problems without the need of classification labels. The existence and frequency of maladjustment and non-adjustive states that do not fit into a preconceived scheme of classification throws doubt on the validity of utilizing and relying on nosological (242, p. 277) terminology in personality evaluation.
6. Summary.
    a. Answer problem in light of psychological findings in summarized, brief manner.
        1. Intellect.

      a. Functioning level.
      b. Potential optimal level.
      c. Abstraction of impairment of intellectual processes and possibly etiology.
    2. Other interpretations.
      a. Emotional adjustment.
      b. Attitudes and feelings.
    3. Suggestions for further study.

The sections on reason for referral, description of behavior in adjusting to test situation, statistical expression of intellectual functioning, and quantitative and qualitative "scatter" analysis are based on the same reasoning found in above discussion of "differential diagnosis." The remainder of the report is concerned with a discussion of combined test findings, oriented to the total functioning of the individual rather than to specific test results, psychological functions or symptoms of mental disorder. Included in the report are the inferences and implications which may be significant for the psychiatrist in terms of prognosis and cues for psychotherapy. The report concludes with a summary which recapitulates, in the light of psychological findings, the answer to the problem posed in the referral.

Discussion

The best writing, in all media, is characterized by simplicity of language and clarity of expression. These generic tenets, combined with a specific dignity and feeling tone which derives from the fundamental nature of clinical psychology, namely, the human relationship involved, should be the keynote of style in psychological reporting. The writer need not be overly concerned with making his report "professional." A studied attempt at being "professional" or at being "scientific" not only robs psychological reporting of the dynamic qualities which distinguish a human relationship from an experiment with test tubes, but, more seriously, invariably reflects a basic attitude in the psychologist which will prevent him from establishing a warm, genuine, friendly rapport. The opposite, an overemotional, gushing report, also bespeaks a lack of mature professional development. Apart from technical considerations pertinent to a particular media, one's manner of relating to others and the way he feels and thinks will creep into his writing and thus the major problems about "tone" in psychological reporting are part of the broader problem of personal growth as a mature, sensitive practitioner. If any concrete suggestions can be made, it would seem that excessive informality, or slang, which detracts from a proper amount of professional dignity should be avoided, as should pseudo-scientific jargon which is understood only by an esoteric few, which vitiates the human element inherent in a testing relationship, and which too often is used to hide a poverty of thought.

Summary

A method for reporting psychological test data in terms of the specific function of given clinical relationships has been presented. It is felt that a method for psychological test reporting may be useful in communicating and interpreting clinical test data to professional associates who share in a study or treatment plan. The function of the clinical test examiner is broken down into three levels of intensity and outline guides for reporting psychological test studies on each level are suggested. The clinical approaches utilized in investigations on these three levels overlap in certain areas but this is felt to be an unavoidable consequence of a practice which seeks to study circumscribed but nevertheless inter-related areas of a personality.

LAWRENCE K. FRANK

Caroline Zachry Institute of Human Development, New York City

Projective Methods for the Study of Personality[1]

An initial difficulty in the study of personality is the lack of any clear-cut, adequate conception of what is to be studied. The recent volumes by Allport (3)[2] and by Stagner (249), and the monograph by Burks and Jones (34), may be cited as indicators of the confusion in this field, where as they show, there are so many conflicting ideas and concepts, each used to justify a wide variety of methods, none of which are wholly adequate.

A situation of this kind evokes different responses from each person according to his professional predilections and allegiances. Obviously pronouncements will be resisted, if not derided, while polemics and apologetics will only increase the confusion. The question may be raised whether any light upon this situation can be obtained by examining the *process* of personality development for leads to more fruitful conceptions and more satisfactory methods and procedures.

A.

Specifically, it is suggested that we reflect upon the emergence of personality as an outcome of the interaction of cultural agents and the individual child. In the space here available only a brief summary statement is permissible of the major aspects of this process in which we may distinguish an individual organism, with an organic

---

[1] Reprinted from *Journal of Psychology*, 1939, 8, 389–413. Copyright 1939 by The Journal Press.
[2] Bibliography begins on page 428.

inheritance, slowly growing, developing, and maturing under the tutelage of parents and teachers intent upon patterning him to the culturally prescribed and socially sanctioned modes of action, speech, and belief.

As elsewhere stated (84, 86), the child is not passive clay but a reacting organism with feelings, as are the parents, nurses, and teachers who are rearing him. He therefore receives training in the prescribed cultural and social norms of action, speech, and belief, according to their personal bias and feelings, and he accepts this training with varying degrees of observance, always idiomatically and with feelings toward these instructors. What we can observe then is the dual process of *socialization*, involving sufficient conformity in outer conduct to permit participation in the common social world, and of *individuation*, involving the progressive establishment of a private world of highly idiosyncratic meanings, significances, and feelings that are more real and compelling than the cultural and physical world.

The foregoing does not imply any subjective duality or other traditional dichotomy; it is an attempt at a simple statement of the well-known and generally accepted view that in all events we may observe both similarities or uniformities and also individual deviations. We may concentrate upon the larger uniformities and ignore the individual components that are participating, as we do in measuring the temperature, pressure, and other properties of a gas or we may look beyond the aggregate uniformities to the individual, discrete molecules and atoms and electrons which, as we now are realizing, are highly erratic, unpredictable, and far from that uniformity of behavior described statistically. Thus, we may observe a similar antithesis between the group uniformities of economic, political, and social affairs and the peculiar personal conduct of each of the citizens who collectively exhibit those uniformities and conformities.

Culture provides the socially sanctioned patterns of action, speech, and belief that make group life what we observe, but each individual in that group is a personality who observes those social requirements and uses those patterns idiomatically, with a peculiar personal inflection, accent, emphasis, and intention (12, 16, 179). Strictly speaking, there are only these individuals, deviating from and distorting the culture; but with our traditional preoccupation with uniformities we have preferred to emphasize the uniformity of statistical aggregates of all activities as the real, and to treat the individual deviation as a sort of unavoidable but embarrassing failure of nature to live up to our expectations. These deviations must be recognized, but only as minor blemishes on and impediments to the scientific truths we seek!

Those ideas flourished in all scientific work up to about 1900 or 1905 when x-rays, quantum physics, relativity, and other new insights were developed that made these earlier ideas obsolete, except in a number of disciplines which still cling to the nineteenth century. Thus it is scientifically respectable, in some circles, to recognize that uniformity is a statistical group concept that overlays an exceedingly disorderly, discontinuous array of individual, discrete events that just won't obey the scientists' laws! It is also respectable to speak of organization and processes "within the atom," although it is recognized that no direct measurements or even observations can be made within the atom; inferences being drawn from activities and energy transformations that are observable and frequently measurable.

For purposes of discussion it is convenient to see individuals (a) as organisms existing in the common public world of nature, (b) as members of their group, carrying on their life careers, in the social world of culturally prescribed patterns and practices, but living, (c) as personalities in these *private worlds* which they have developed under the impact of experience. It is important to recognize these three aspects of human behavior and living because of their implications for scientific study.

As organisms reacting to the environmental impacts, overtly and physiologically, human activity presents a problem of observation and measurement similar to that of all other organisms and events. The human body moves or falls through geographical space, captures, stores, and releases energy and so on. As members of the group, individuals exhibit certain patterns of action, speech, and belief that may be aggregated into larger categories of uniformity or cultural and group norms; at least we find certain pronounced, often all inclusive modes in their observed activities in which they tend to conform to social and cultural prescriptions.

When we examine the personality process or *private worlds* of individuals we face a somewhat peculiar problem, because we are seeking not the cultural and social norms of the uniformities of organic activity, but rather the revelation of just that peculiar, individual way of organizing experience and of feeling which personality implies.

In this context we may emphasize then that personality is approachable as a process or operation of an individual who organizes experience and reacts affectively to situations. This process is dynamic in the sense that the individual personality imposes upon the common public world of events (what we call nature), his meanings and significances, his organization and patterns, and he invests the situations thus structured with an affective meaning to which he responds idiomatically. This dynamic organizing process will of necessity express the cultural training he has experienced so that until he withdraws from social life, as in the psychoses, he will utilize the group sanctioned patterns of action, speech and belief, but as he individually has learned to use them and as he feels toward the situations and people to whom he reacts.

If it were not liable to gross misunderstanding, the personality process might be regarded as a sort of rubber stamp which the individual imposes upon every situation by which he gives it the configuration that he, as an individual, requires; in so doing he necessarily ignores or subordinates many aspects of the situation that for him are irrelevant and meaningless and selectively reacts to those aspects that are personally significant. In other words the personality process may be viewed as a highly individualized practice of the general operation of all organisms that selectively respond to a figure on a ground, by reacting to the configurations in an environmental context that are relevant to their life careers (83).

It is interesting to see how the students of personality have attempted to meet the problem of individuality with methods and procedures designed for study of uniformities and norms that ignore or subordinate individuality, treating it as a troublesome deviation which derogates from the real, the superior, and only important central tendency, mode, average, etc. This is not the occasion to review these methods and the writer is not competent to assess them critically, but it is appropriate to point out some aspects of the present methodological difficulty we face in the accepted quantitative procedures.

Since individuals, as indicated earlier, learn to conform to the socially sanctioned patterns of action, speech, and belief (with individual bias and flavor of their own), it is possible to establish the social norms appropriate for groups of like chronological age, sex, and so on and to construct standardized tests and to calculate statistically their validity, i.e., do they measure or rate what they are expected to measure or rate for each group, and their reliability, i.e., how well or reliably do they measure or rate the performance of the groups (85)?

While standardized tests are generally considered to be measurers of individual differences, it would be more appropriate to say that they are ratings of the degree of likeness to cultural norms exhibited by individuals who are expected, as members of this society, to conform to those group patterns. In other words, the standardized test does not tell very much about the individual, as an *individual*, but rather how nearly he approximates to a normal performance of culturally prescribed tasks for which a more or less arbitrary, but internally consistent, scheme of quantitative ratings is utilized (136). By the use of an all-over total figure for an individual it becomes possible to assign numerical evaluations to individuals in various categories of achievement, skill, conformity, and so forth, such as accelerated, average, or retarded mentally; manual or verbal proficiency, etc. Having assigned him to a rank order in a group or class according to the standardized test, the individual is disposed of and adequately explained.[3] The history of the use of standardized tests shows how they are used to place individuals in various classifications that are convenient for administration, for remedial work and therapy, or for segregation for purposes of social control, with little or no concern about understanding the individual so classified or placed, or discovering his characteristics *as an individual*.

It would seem fair to say, therefore, that standardized tests offer procedures for rating individuals in terms of their socialization and how nearly they approximate to the acceptance and use of the culturally prescribed patterns of belief, action, and speech for which statistical norms can be calculated from actual observations of performance of groups of individuals, according to age, sex, etc.

In order to apply these and more recently developed quantitative methods to the study of personality it has been necessary to adopt

---

[3] *Cf.* Lewin, K., *A Dynamic Theory of Personality* (150). (Especially Chapter I on Aristotelian and Galilean modes of thought, and the class theory of investigation.)

a conception of the personality as an aggregation of discrete, measurable traits, factors, or other separable entities which are present in the individual in differing quantity and organized according to individual patterns. But since the personality is more than overt activity, some way of getting at the underlying personality is necessary. The need, for quantitative data has led to the use of the culturally standardized, socially sanctioned norms of speech and belief and attitudes in and through which the individual has been asked to express his personality, as in questionnaires, inventories, rating scales, etc.

If time allowed, it would be desirable to examine more fully the implications of this procedure which attempts to reveal the individuality of the person by using the social stereotypes of language and motives that necessarily subordinate individuality to social conformity, emphasizing likeness and uniformity of group patterns. This point becomes more significant when we recall that almost identical actions and speech may be used in extraordinarily different senses by each individual using them; while conversely the widest diversity of action and speech may have almost identical sense and significance for different individuals exhibiting them. Moreover the conventional traits and motives and objectives derived from traditional concepts of human nature and conduct, carry meanings often alien to the investigator using them as data. Words are generalized symbols, are usually obscuring of, when not actually misleading about, the individual idiomatic personality using them (298).

It should be further noted that many procedures for study of personality rely upon the subject's self-diagnosis and revelation of his private world of personal meanings and feelings which the social situation compels the individual to conceal, even if, as is unusual, he had any clear understanding of himself. When we ask an individual to tell what he believes or feels or to indicate in which categories he belongs, this social pressure to conform to the group norms operates to bias what he will say and presses him to fit himself into the categories of the inventory or questionnaire offered for self-diagnosis (279). Moreover, as Henry A. Murray has observed, the most important things about an individual are what he cannot or will not say. The law has long recognized testimony as unreliable, to be accepted only after many checks and tests as formulated in the law of evidence.

At this point there may be a feeling of dismay, if not resentment, because the discussion has led to a seeming impasse, with no road open to study the personality by the accepted methods and procedures of present-day quantitative psychology. Moreover, the insistence upon the unique, idiomatic character of the personality appears to remove it from the area of scientific study conceived as a search for generalizations, uniformities, invariant relationships, etc. It is proposed, therefore, to discuss a few recent developments in scientific concepts and methods and the new problems they have raised in order to indicate a way out of this apparent impasse.

B.

It is appropriate to recall that the uniformity and laws of nature are statistical findings of the probable events and relationships that occur among an aggregate of events, the individuals of which are highly disorderly and unpredictable. Theoretical physics has adjusted itself to the conception of a universe that has statistical regularity and order, and individual disorder, in which the laws of aggregates are not observable in the activity of the individual making up these aggregates. Thus quantum physics and statistical mechanics and many other similar contrasts are accepted without anxiety about scientific respectability. The discrete individual event can be and is regarded as an individual to whom direct methods and measurements have only a limited applicability. We can therefore acknowledge an interest in the individual as a scientific problem and find some sanction for such an interest.

Another recent development is the concept of the *field* in physics and its use in biology. The field concept is significant here because it offers a way of conceiving this situation of an individual part and of the whole, which our older concepts have so confused and obscured (40). Instead of a whole that dominates the parts, which have to be organized by some mysterious process into a whole, we begin to think of an aggregate of individuals which constitute, by their interaction, a field that operates to pattern these individuals. Parts are not separate, discrete, independent entities that get organized by the whole, nor is the whole a superior kind of entity with feudal power over its parts, e.g., a number of iron filings brought close to a magnet will arrange themselves in a pattern wherein each bit of iron is related to the other bits and the magnet and these relations constitute the whole; remove some bits and the pattern shifts as it does if we add more filings, or bits of another metal. Likewise, in a gas, the gas may be viewed as a field in which individual molecules, atoms, and electrons are patterned by the total interactions of all those parts into the group activity we call a gas. Ecology studies this interaction of various organizations in the circumscribed life zone or field which they constitute.[4]

This field concept is highly important because it leads to the general notion that any "entity" we single out for observation is participating in a field; any observation we make must be ordered to the field in which it is made or as we say, every observation or measurement is relative to the frame of reference or field in which it occurs.

There are many other far-reaching shifts in concepts and methods that should be discussed here, but the foregoing will suffice to indicate that the study of an individual personality may be conceived as an approach to a somewhat disorderly and erratic activity, occurring in the field we call culture (i.e., the aggregate interaction of individuals whose behavior is patterned by participation in the aggregate). Moreover, the observations we make on the individual personality must be ordered to the field of that individual and his life space. We must also regard the individual himself as an aggregate of activities which pattern his parts and functions.

Here we must pause to point out that the older practice of creating entities out of data has created many problems that are unreal and irrelevant and so are insoluble. In by-gone years it was customary to treat data of temperature, light, magnetic activity, radiation, chemical activity, and so on as separate entities, independent of each other. But the more recent view is to see in these data evidences of energy transformations which are transmitted in different magnitudes, sequences, etc., and so appear as heat, light, magnetism, etc. This has relevance to the study of personality since it warns us against the practice of observing an individual's actions and then reifying these data into entities called traits (or some other discrete term), which we must then find some way of organizing into the living total personality who appears in experience as a unified organism.

---

[4] Cf. du Nouy, P. L., *Biological Time* (72). (Other part-whole fields are a candle flame, a fountain jet, a stream of water, etc.)

With this background of larger, more general shifts in scientific procedures, let us examine some more specific developments that are relevant to our topic.

Within recent years new procedures have been developed for discovering not only the elements or parts composing the whole, but also the way those parts are arranged and organized in the whole, without disintegrating or destroying the whole. The x-rays are used, not merely for photographs or to show on a fluorescent screen what is otherwise invisible within an organism or any object, but also for diffraction analysis, in which the x-rays are patterned by the internal organization of any substance to show its molecular and atomic structure. Spectrographic analysis reveals the chemical components qualitatively, and now quantitatively, and in what compounds, by the way light is distributed along a continuous band of coarse and fine spectral lines, each of which reveals a different element or isotope. The mass spectroscope offers another exceedingly delicate method for determining the composition of any substance that gives off radiations whereby the electrons or their rate of travel can be measured and the composition of the substance inferred.

X-rays, however, are only one of the newer methods whereby any complex may be made to reveal its components and its organization, often quantitatively, when approached by an appropriate procedure. Recently, it has been found that the chemical composition of various substances, especially proteins, can be ascertained by the reflection of a beam of light upon a thin monomolecular film of the protein substance spread on a film of oil on water over a metallic surface. Again it has been found that metallic ores and coal may be analyzed, i.e., be made to reveal their chemical composition and other properties by the "angle of wetability," the angle of reflection, or the color of the light reflected from a liquid film that adheres to the surface of the unknown material.

Polarized light has also become an instrument for revealing the chemical composition of substances without resort to the usual methods of disintegration or chemical analysis. Electrical currents may also be passed through substances, gaseous, liquid, or solid, and used to discover what they contain and in what form. Indeed, it is not unwarranted to say that these indirect methods that permit discovery of the composition and organization of substances, complexes, and organisms, seem likely to become the method of choice over the older destructive analytical procedures, because these methods do not destroy or disturb the substance or living organism being studied.

In this connection reference should also be made to the development of biological assays, whereby a living organism, plant, or animal, is used for assaying the composition of various substances and compounds and determining their potency, such as vitamins, hormones, virus, drugs, radiation, light, magnetism, and electrical currents (including electrophoresis for separating, without injury or change, the different sub-varieties of any group of cells, chemical substances, etc.). In these procedures the response of the living organism is utilized as an indicator, if not an actual measurement, of that about which data are sought, as well as the state, condition, maturation, etc., of the organism being tested. It is appropriate to note also that physicists are using such devices as the Wilson Cloud Chamber and the Geiger Counter to obtain data on the *individual* electrical particle, which reveals its presence and energy by the path traced in water vapor, or by activation of the Counter, although never itself observable or directly measurable.

These methodological procedures are being refined and extended because they offer possibilities for ascertaining what is either unknowable by other means or is undeterminable because the older analytic methods destroyed part or all of that which was to be studied. They are being accepted as valid and credible, primarily because they are more congruous with the search for undivided totalities and functioning organisms and are more productive of the data on organization on which present-day research problems are focussed. They are also expressive of the recent concepts of whole-and-parts and their interrelations, which no longer invoke the notion of parts as discrete entities upon which an organization is imposed by a superior whole, but rather employ the concept of the field. Finally they offer possibilities for studying the specific, differentiated individuality of organized structures and particulate events which are ignored or obscured by the older quantitative determinations of aggregates.

Since the threshold task in any scientific endeavor is to establish the meanings and significances of the data obtained by any method of observation and measurement, it should be noted that these indirect methods for revealing the composition and organization of

substances and structures rely upon experimental and genetic procedures to establish reliability and validity, not statistical procedures.
That is to say, these newer procedures establish the meaning of any
datum by employing the procedure upon a substance or structure
of known composition, often made to order, so that it is possible to
affirm that the resulting bending, patterning, arrangement of light,
radiation, and so on, are reliable and valid indicators of the substance or structure when found in an unknown composition. These
methods for establishing reliability and validity are therefore genetic
in the sense of observing or tracing the origin and development of
what is to be tested so that its presence or operation may be historically established: they are also dependent upon the concurrent use
of other procedures which will yield consistent data on the same
composition which therefore are validated by such internal consistency and congruity of findings.

Psychology developed the statistical procedures for establishing
reliability and validity because the only data available were the
single observations or measurements taken at one time on each subject. Since no other data were available on the prior history and
development of the subjects, reliability had to be determined by
statistical manipulation of these test data themselves; also since no
other data were available on the subject's other functions and activities only statistical validity could be established. It would appear
that these tests of reliability and validity devised to meet the difficulty presented by absence of other data now act as barriers to the
use of any other procedures for personality study in which reliability
and validity for each subject is tested through these other non-
statistical methods.

Methods of *temporal validation* offer great promise because they
permit testing of the validity of data for a *specific subject* over a
period of time, and the method of congruity among data obtained
by different procedures from the same subject offer large possibilities
for testing the reliability of any data for a *specific subject.*[5] It is
appropriate to recall here that the accepted methods for testing
reliability and validity of tests, inventories, etc., offer indices only
for the *group*, not for any individual subject in that *group.*

We may therefore view the problem of personality in terms of

---

[5] Cf. Bateson, G. *Naven* (12), in which appears a discussion of diachronic
and synchronic procedures.

these more recent ideas and conceptions and consider the application of these indirect procedures for revealing the composition and organization of substances and energy complexes.

As indicated earlier the personality may be viewed as a dynamic process of organizing experience, of "structuralizing the life space" (Lewin) according to the unique individual's *private world*. This conception may be made precise and operational by seeing the individual and his changing environment as a series of fields which arise through the interaction of the individual personality with his selective awareness, patterned responses, and idiomatic feelings, with the environmental situations of objects, events, and other persons. A field organization or configuration arises out of this interaction wherein, as suggested, the personality distorts the situation, so far as it is amenable, into the configurations of its *private world*, but has to adjust to the situation in so far as it resists such distortion and imposes its necessities upon the personality. What we have called personality and fumblingly have tried to formulate as the total responses of the whole individual and similar additive conceptions becomes more understandable and approachable for investigation when conceived as the living process in this field created by the individual and the environing situation.

The objective world of objects, organisms, and events likewise may be seen as fields of interacting object-situations, upon which cultural patterns operate in the conduct of human beings who, by very reason of behaving in these learned patterns, create the cultural fields of interacting human conduct. What is highly important to note is that every observation made must be ordered—given its quantitative and qualitative interpretation—to the field in which it occurs, so that the idea of pure objectivity becomes meaningless and sterile if it implies data not biased, influenced, relative to the field in which observed. Likewise the conception of a stimulus that may be described and measured apart from the field and the organism in that field is untenable.[6] The "same" stimulus will differ in every

---

[6] Cf. Vigotsky (279). "The investigator who uses such methods may be compared to a man, who, in order to explain why water extinguishes fire, analyzes the water into oxygen and hydrogen and is surprised to find that oxygen helps the process of burning and hydrogen itself burns. This method of analyzing a whole into elements is not a true analysis which can be used to solve concrete problems" (p. 29).

field, and for every field and for every organism which selectively creates its own stimuli in each situation. Indeed, this dynamic conception of the personality as a process implies that there are no stimuli to conduct (as distinct from physical and physiological impacts) except in so far as the individual personality selectively constitutes them and responds to them in its idiosyncratic patterns. In other words the stimuli are functions of the field created by the individual interacting with the situation.

Thus the movement in various areas of scientific work is toward recognition of the field concept and the devising of methods that will record not merely data but the fields in which those data have been observed and find their significance. Those who are appalled by the seeming anarchy thus threatening scientific work may be reminded that the present-day standards of scientific work and of methods are part of a development that will inevitably make today's ideas and procedures obsolete. It is well to recall how proud (justly so) chemistry was to achieve quantitative determinations of the composition of substances and now, how crude those early quantitative methods and findings now appear, when they now are seeking to find out not merely what and how much, but the spatial arrangement of the constituents as in stereochemistry where the same atoms in the same quantity produce different substances according to their spatial arrangement. It is likewise worth recalling, that about 1900, young physicists could find no problems except the more precise measurement of the pressure, temperature, etc., of a gas and were content with such crude quantitative findings. Furthermore, biologists today are accepting as common-place that the same nutritive components, amino-acids, carbohydrates, fats, minerals, and vitamins are selectively digested, assimilated, and metabolized in different ways by each species and by each individual. Moreover, it is conceded that the proteins of each species are different as are those of each individual with the possibility of an almost unlimited number of different protein molecules, in which the same basic elements are organized into unique spatial-temporal configurations appropriate to the organic field of the individual organism.[7]

---

[7] The concepts of individuality and of individuation are being used by biologists because they find themselves confronted with individual organic activities and idiomatic processes (25, 51, 52).

C.

Coming directly to the topic of projective methods for personality study, we may say that the dynamic conception of personality as a process of organizing experience and structuralizing life space in a field, leads to the problem of how we can reveal the way an individual personality organizes experience, in order to disclose or at least gain insight into that individual's *private world* of meanings, significances, patterns, and feelings.

Such a problem is similar to those discussed earlier where indirect methods are used to elicit the pattern of internal organization and of composition without disintegrating or distorting the subject, which is made to bend, deflect, distort, organize, or otherwise pattern part or all of the field in which it is placed—e.g., light and x-rays. In similar fashion we may approach the personality and induce the individual to reveal his way of organizing experience by giving him a field (objects, materials, experiences) with relatively little structure and cultural patterning so that the personality can project upon that plastic field his way of seeing life, his meanings, significances, patterns, and especially his feelings. Thus we elicit a projection of the individual personality's *private world* because he has to organize the field, interpret the material and react affectively to it. More specifically, a projection method for study of personality involves the presentation of a stimulus-situation designed or chosen because it will mean to the subject, not what the experimenter has arbitrarily decided it should mean (as in most psychological experiments using standardized stimuli in order to be "objective"), but rather whatever it must mean to the personality who gives it, or imposes upon it, his private, idiosyncratic meaning and organization. The subject then will respond to *his* meaning of the presented stimulus-situation by some form of action and feeling that is expressive of his personality. Such responses may be *constitutive* as when the subject imposes a structure or form or configuration (Gestalt) upon an amorphous, plastic, unstructured substance such as clay, finger paints, or upon partially structured and semi-organized fields like the Rorschach cards; or they may be *interpretive* as when the subject tells what a stimulus-situation, like a picture, means to him; or they may be *cathartic* as when the subject discharges affect or feeling upon the stimulus-situation and finds an emotional release that is revealing of his affective reactions toward life situations represented by the stimulus-situation, as when he plays with clay or toys. Other expressions may be *constructive* organizations wherein the subject builds in accordance with the materials offered but reveals in the pattern of his building some of the organizing conceptions of his life at that period, as in block-building.

The important and determining process is the subject's personality which operates upon the stimulus-situation as if it had a wholly private significance for him alone or an entirely plastic character which made it yield to the subject's control. This indicates that, as suggested earlier, a personality is the way an individual organizes and patterns life situations and effectively responds to them, "structuralizes his life space," so that by projective methods we are evoking the very process of personality as it has developed to that moment.[8] Since the way an individual organizes and patterns life situations, imposes his *private world* of meanings and affectively reacts upon the environing world of situations and other persons and strives to maintain his personal version against the coercion or obstruction of others, it is evident that personality is a persistent way of living and feeling that, despite change of tools, implements, and organic growth and maturation will appear continuously and true to pattern.

When we scrutinize the actual procedures that may be called projective methods we find a wide variety of techniques and materials being employed for the same general purpose, to obtain from the subject, "what he cannot or will not say," frequently because he does not know himself and is not aware what he is revealing about himself through his projections.

In the following statement no attempt has been made to provide a complete review of all the projective methods now being used, since such a canvass would be beyond the present writer's competence and intention. Only a few illustrations of projective methods are offered to show their variety and their scope, in the hope of enlisting further interest in and creating a better understanding of, their characteristics and advantages.[9]

---

[8] *Cf.* Dunbar (71). An individual may express his feelings, otherwise blocked, in illness or physiological dysfunctions.

[9] *Cf.* Horowitz and Murphy (120) for further discussion of different procedures and their use.

The Rorschach ink blots, to which the subject responds by saying what he "sees" in each of a number of different blots, are perhaps the most widely known of these procedures. They have been utilized in Europe and in the United States, frequently in connection with psychiatric clinics and hospitals, for revealing the personality configurations and have been found of increasing value. In so far as life histories and psychiatric and psychoanalytic studies of the subjects who have had the Rorschach diagnosis are available, the ink blot interpretations are being increasingly validated by these clinical findings. Such comparative findings are of the greatest importance because they mutually reinforce each other and reveal the consistency or any conflicts in the different interpretations and diagnosis of a personality.

Another similar procedure is the *Cloud Picture* method, developed by Wilhelm Stern, to evoke projections from a subject upon more amorphous grounds, with advantages, he believed, over the Rorschach blots. The more amorphous or unstructured the ground, the greater the sensitivity of the procedure which however loses in precision as in most instruments. Hence the Rorschach may be less sensitive than *Cloud Pictures* or clay but more precise and definite. Both the ink blots and the *Cloud Pictures* offer a ground upon which the subject must impose or project whatever configural patterns he "sees" therein, because he can only see what he personally looks for or "perceives" in that ground. The separate detail of the responses, however, are significant only in the context of the total response to each blot and are meaningful only for each subject. This does not imply an absence of recurrent forms and meanings from one subject to another but rather that the same letters of the conventionalized alphabet may recur in many different words and the same words may be utilized in a great variety of sentences to convey an extraordinary diversity of statements, which must be understood within the context in which they occur and with reference to the particular speaker who is using them on that occasion.[10]

Play techniques are being increasingly employed for clinical diagnosis and for investigation of the personality development of chil-

---

[10] *Cf.* since each personality must use socially prescribed cultural patterns for his conduct and communications he will exhibit many recurrent uniformities but these are significant only for revealing the patterns or organizations or configurations which the personality uses to structuralize his life space.

dren. As materials almost any kind of toy or plaything or plain wooden building blocks may be presented to the subject for free play or for performance of some designated action, such as building a house, sorting into groups, setting the stage for a play or otherwise organizing the play materials into some configuration which expresses for the subject an affectively significant pattern. In children, it must be remembered there are fewer disguises and defenses available to hide behind and there is less sophisticated awareness of how much is being revealed in play. The investigator does not set a task and rate the performance in terms of skill or other scale of achievement, since the intention is to elicit the subject's way of "organizing his life space" in whatever manner he finds appropriate. Hence every performance is significant, apart from the excellence of the play construction or activity, and is to be interpreted, rather than rated, for its revelation of how the subject sees and feels his life situations that are portrayed in the play constructions and sequences. The question of how to decide whether a particular activity is or is not meaningful is to be decided, not by its frequency or so-called objective criteria, but by the total play configuration of that particular subject who, it is assumed, performs that particular action or uses that specific construction, as an expression of his way of seeing and feeling and reacting to life, i.e., of his personality. But the degree of relevance is to be found in the context, in what precedes and what follows and in the intensity of feelings expressed. If these criteria appear tenuous and subjective and lacking in credibility, then objections may be made to the use of various methods for discovering the composition and structure of an unknown substance through which light, electric current, or radiations are passed, to give patterned arrangements or a spectrum photograph in which the position, number, intensity of lines and the coarse and fine structure indicate what the unknown substance is composed of, how organized internally, and so on. Personality studies by projective methods have not, of course, been as extensively studied nor have the patterns used by subjects been so well explored. The important point is that the way is open to the development of something similar to spectroscopic and diffraction methods for investigation of personality.

If the foregoing appears far-fetched it may be recalled that the lines on the spectroscopic plate were established, not by statistical procedures, but by experimental procedures through which a known chemically tested substance was spectroscopically tested so that its identifying line could be precisely located and thereafter confidently named. In much the same fashion it is being established that a child who is known to be undergoing an affective experience will express that feeling in a play configuration that can be so recognized. Thus, children who have lost a beloved parent or nurse, who have been made anxious by toilet training, are insecure and hostile because of sibling rivalry, etc., will exhibit those feelings in their play configurations. Experimentally produced personality disturbances can be established and their severity investigated by subsequent play forms and expressions. Moreover, the insights derived from play configurations yield interpretations that are not only therapeutically effective but often predictive of what a child will show in the near future.

Not only play toys and objects are utilized but also various plastic amorphous materials such as modelling clay, flour, and water, mud and similar substances of a consistency that permits the subject to handle freely and manipulate into various objects. In these play situations the subject often finds a catharsis, expressing affects that might otherwise be repressed or disguised, or symbolically releasing resentments and hostility that have been long overlaid by conventionally good conduct. Dolls, capable of being dismembered, can be used to evoke repressed hostility and aggression against parents and siblings. Dramatic stage play with toy figures and settings have also provided occasions in which a subject not only revealed his personality difficulties but also worked out many of his emotional problems. Clay figures are modelled by child patients in which they express many of their acute anxieties and distortions. Reference should be made to eidetic imagery, which, as Walther Jaensch in his constitutional studies has shown, indicates one aspect of the subject's way of expressing what enters into his personality make-up or way of organizing his life space.

Artistic media offer another series of rich opportunities for projective methods in studying personality. Finger-painting has given many insights into child personality make-up and perplexities. Painting has been found very fruitful for study of personality make-up and emotional disturbances. Other clinical uses of painting have been reported that indicate the way paintings and drawings supplement the clinician's interviews and evoke responses, that are exceedingly revealing, often more so than the verbal responses. Puppet shows elicit responses from child patients that are both diagnostic and therapeutic because the intensity of the dramatic experience arouses the child to a vehement expression of his feelings toward authority and toward parents and of his repressed desires to hurt others. Rôles have been assigned to individuals who are then asked to act out those rôles impromptu, thereby revealing how tangled and repressed his or her feelings are and how release of pent-up emotion leads to insight into one's personality difficulties. Dramatic teachers are finding clues to personality in the way individuals portray the characters assigned them in a play. Music offers similar and often more potent possibilities for expression of affects that are revealing of the personality. It is interesting to note that as psychotherapy proceeds to free the patient, his art expressions, painting, modelling, music, and dramatic rendition become freer and more integrated.

As the foregoing indicates, the individual rarely has any understanding of himself or awareness of what his activities signify. In the Thematic Perception methods this unawareness offers an opportunity to elicit highly significant projections from subjects who are asked to write or tell stories about a series of pictures showing individuals with whom they can identify themselves and others of immediate personal concern. Likewise the subjects project many aspects of their personality in the completion of stories and of sentences, in making up analogies, sorting out and grouping objects, such as toys, and similar procedures in which the subject reveals "what he cannot or will not say."

Expressive movements, especially handwriting, offer another approach to the understanding of the personality who reveals so much of his characteristic way of viewing life in his habitual gestures and motor patterns, facial expressions, posture and gait. These leads to the study of personality have been rejected by many psychologists because they do not meet psychometric requirements for validity and reliability, but they are being employed in association with clinical and other studies of personality where they are finding increasing validation in the consistency of results for the same subject when independently assayed by each of these procedures. In this group of methods should be included observations on tics of all kinds and dancing as indications of tension, anxiety or other partially repressed feelings.

If we will face the problem of personality, in its full complexity, as an active dynamic process to be studied as a process rather than as entity or aggregate of traits, factors, or as a static organization, then these projective methods offer many advantages for obtaining data on the process of organizing experience which is peculiar to each personality and has a life career. Moreover, the projective methods offer possibilities for utilizing the available insights into personality which the prevailing quantitative procedures seem deliberately to reject.

Here again it may be re-emphasized that the study of personality is not a task of measuring separate variables on a large group of individuals at one moment in their lives and then seeking, by statistical methods, to measure correlations, nor is it a problem of teasing out and establishing the quantitative value of several factors (129). Rather the task calls for the application of a multiplicity of methods and procedures which will reveal the many facets of the personality and show how the individual "structuralizes his life space" or organizes experience to meet his personal needs in various media. If it appears that the subject projects similar patterns or configurations upon widely different materials and reveals in his life history the sequence of experiences that make those projections psychologically meaningful for his personality, then the procedures may be judged sufficiently valid to warrant further experimentation and refinement. In undertaking such explorations the experimenter and clinicians may find reassurance and support in the realization that they are utilizing concepts and methods that are receiving increasing recognition and approval in scientific work that is today proving most fruitful.

JEAN WALKER MACFARLANE

University of California, Berkeley, California

Problems of Validation Inherent in Projective Methods[1]

Spreading with the rapidity of a virulent infection is the use of a large array of clinical devices which are loosely labelled "projective techniques." These are, in short, devices to obtain from a patient or research subject "what he can not or will not" disclose directly about his private world of preoccupations, feelings, attitudes, and the meanings that his inner and outer world have for him. They are devices which, at their best, aim to tap in action the very *processes by which* and the *patterns through which* an individual selects and organizes his life experiences. They throw light on his areas of sensitivity or vulnerability, and his methods of defense. There has developed a mushrooming literature on such devices which includes the use of spontaneous drawing, painting, modeling, writing, psychodrama, and voice productions, as well as those using standard stimulus equipment, such as Rorschach ink blots, Stern clouds, Murray pictures, play materials, etc.

It is highly appropriate at this exploratory stage in the use of these devices, that this round table is called to take stock of where we are and whither bound. In fact, it is mandatory, if the present epidemic use of such tools is to yield substantial and trustworthy results, that we face the difficult conceptual and methodological problems they present. For not only is there a mushrooming litera-

---

[1] Read at a round table on projective techniques; American Psychological As-ican Journal of Orthopsychiatry, 1942, 12, 405–410. Copyright 1942 by American Orthopsychiatric Association.

ture on a large array of such devices, but projective techniques are used by persons of varying clinical experience and insight, by persons of varying degrees of appreciation of the laws basic to scientific method, and those with varying conceptual habits and terminologies. It this were not confounding enough, the real Achilles heel of these techniques is that the meaning obtained through them rests upon interpretation by these variously trained, experienced and conceptualizing users. Interpretation in the hands of the clinically inexperienced, the doctrinaire, or the methodologically uninformed, easily degenerates into nothing but one more projective tool—to wit, one which discloses the organizing dynamics of the interpreter rather than the organizing dynamics of the research subject.

If the picture presented is black, it is not to add to the confusion, but to point out the needs of a coordinated and articulated attack upon the strategic problems of method inherent in the use of these tools which tap projective or expressive material. If used with sound method, they promise a welcome and fruitful future after our long period in psychology of highly respectable but often sterile quantification of that abstraction known as the "single variable." In fact, part of the present chaos in the literature on "projective techniques" is due to a new (and as yet undisciplined) vitality born of sensing possibilities for significant understanding of two major problems of human psychology. The first concerns one facet of the problem of the selective responsiveness of the individual to the multiplicity of potential stimuli of his inner and outer world; the second concerns the organization of his responses, overt and implicit, into the ordered patterns we call personality, on into the erratic responses we call personality disorganization.

There are two major areas which projective techniques serve, namely, therapy and research. Logically, research should precede therapeutic usage, but actually, the therapist, confronted with a baffling patient, cannot wait until detached scientific clarity is established, but will in practice avail himself of any tools which offer hope of supplementing his ordinary approaches of measurement, observation, and interview; especially when his established tools do not readily yield the essential clues of the meaning *to the patient* of his own anxieties, preoccupations, and behavior. The therapist must depend upon the trial and error judgment of his interpretive artistry until science has caught up with him and made more explicit or has modified these judgments. Further, in the therapeutic situation which extends through time, he can check his intuitions and hypotheses and discard the inappropriate ones providing, of course, that he is not wearing blinders imposed by doctrinaire rigidity.

This paper concerns itself not with the therapeutic, but rather with the research aspects of projective techniques and with only one sub-heading of research, namely, validation. In view of the time limitations, it is so over-condensed that it may sound both dogmatic and over-critical, since taking for granted the importance of projective protocols, it stresses certain major methodological pitfalls in their use as research instruments. It discusses the three *sine qua nons* of validation: I. concepts; II. samples; and III. specific validation procedures.

Concepts

It is not the function of this paper to discuss or to evaluate the varieties of conceptualization, implicit and explicit, fluid, fragmentary, or systematized which flood the field of personality research and therapy, important as that topic is. However, inasmuch as *all* validation rests on concepts and hypotheses, and since as yet (in the writer's opinion) we have no universally accepted scientific terminology which does justice to the richness and diversity of personality and at the same time adequately orders this richness and diversity, it becomes clear that an articulated conceptualization is basic. When one further considers that validation of the Gestalting process we call subjective interpretation rests uniquely upon the concepts, theories, and experience of the interpreters, it is evident that we should formulate certain basic rules. The writer suggests three. The reader, who has had experience with personality literature, will think of others.

One, it should become part of the scientific mores in this pioneering, unstructured stage that the first step in projective research should be an explicit statement of concepts used, and an orientation with respect to theoretical biases. Further, such a statement should appear on page one of any article, instead of leaving it to the inference of the reader.

Two, the investigator should constantly be on the alert that his concepts remain his tools, rather than that he become the tool of his concepts and thus lose his flexibility and openness of mind. He should remember that concepts are *not empirical data* and that their only criteria of merit lie in their usefulness: (a) in inducing non-spurious ordering of empirical data; (b) in leading productively to verification procedures; and (c) in leading to increasing accuracy in prediction.

Three, he should constantly check himself lest his concepts become little more than sheer magic. For with the heritage of "trait" and "instinct" tradition from psychology, psychoanalysis, and psychiatry, the classificatory words first used to describe processes easily become reified into god-like or devil-like entities which are then used like magic, as if they caused the behavior or fantasy they seek to classify. The whole literature of personality, including psychoanalysis (a rebel against classificatory psychiatry), even with its emphasis on dynamic theory, fairly reeks with this pervasive fallacy of reification of instinct and trait labels with its bastard offshoot—inferred causality. This fallacy is one which beclouds analysis and validation, since it confusedly lumps inferred-drives-from-which, goals-toward-which, and processes-by-which. Historically, in any discipline classification is an essential step, but if a discipline jells at the classificatory level and then weakly infers causality, it stagnates. The writer suggests that our classificatory constructs be sentences which emphasize processes rather than nouns which slip so easily into magic reification. Word-economy, the *raison d'être* for substantives, far too frequently leads merely to economy in observation and discriminative judgment, with pigeon-holing displacing scientific fertility. Since there is no more complex problem in science than personality research, we cannot afford to economize in disciplined and productive thinking.

Samples

The second basic factor in validation concerns samples studied. It should be obvious that valid generalization is limited by the nature of the samples on which either interpretive or statistical judgments rest. Clinicians, from whom the rich possibilities of the projective and expressive hypotheses have sprung, are conspicuously subject to faulty over-generalization due to restricted sample experience. Each interpreting clinician should make for himself (and his readers) a tabulation showing what his sample experience has been

—how much and what proportions of his experience with and without projective tools have been with normal adults, adolescents, or children, with special organic or psychopathological adults, adolescents, or children, how much with different cultural and different intellectual levels. He should then be able to be cautious about generalizations concerning individuals outside of groups with which he has had rich experience, or about which adequate second-hand experiences through literature are lacking.

Present intensive attempts at objectification of the criteria for interpretation, essential steps toward communicability, will be, however, pseudo-scientific steps unless generalizations explicitly stay within samples, or unless samples are sufficiently large and distributed as to be really representative. This last is a job which necessitates sample planning and the coordinated execution by workers using normals and special groups of various age and maturity levels, and a clearing house of information for each projective tool which is to have wide and scientifically valid applicability.

The basic need of control or contrasting groups cannot be overlooked if differential criteria are to be established. Two types of comparisons appear essential. One type of comparison should look to the similarities and differences in the projective protocols from such contrasting groups as pre-adolescents and post-adolescents, clinical diagnostic groups and normals, etc. The other comparison should look to clinical correlates of similar and contrasting protocols.

Validation Procedures

Inasmuch as the aim of the projective techniques is to get at selective responsiveness and at organizational processes, expressive or projective, it becomes clear that ordinary statistical devices used in clear-cut measurement studies do not meet our needs. Let us look at available methods of validation.

1. *Correlation with outside criteria* is the most common method of validation. What can our outside criteria be, since it is the organizational processes of *individuals* which we are attempting to assess? Obviously, comparisons of the projective productions of many individuals via the same technique give us orienting and normative material and point to the frequencies of certain patterns from which some generality of statement is possible. Such normative material makes possible the comparison of an individual's picture

with that of a similar age or sociological group, but it does not give us a picture of validity for individual dynamics. For example, a verbalized fantasy of a given individual may, on a manifest level, be similar to those of his group and yet have for him a highly special and idiosyncratic meaning.

Comparisons of the projective materials from the same individual via an array of "projective" techniques furnish a check for consistencies and disagreements. If consistencies seem absent, those with systematized concepts may be able validly with their conceptual tools to subsume under one embracing concept, material which on the surface looks incongruent. But, on the other hand, by interpretive classification they may produce a pseudo and non-valid congruence merely because they interpretively stick everything into a few categories. The congruencies they report may be due to the stability of their concepts and not to the congruencies of the material. Internal consistency alone does not establish scientific validity, for what has more internal consistency than a paranoid's delusional system?

2. Another approach toward validation lies in the comparison of projective material with life history material. This is an essential check but it also offers difficulties, as life histories, too, must be organized according to concepts, and if the concepts used are the same, the congruencies again may be an artifact of simplicity and stability of concepts rather than consistency of the material. Or, the material from each source may, in point of fact, actually be highly congruent. How to sift pseudo congruencies from valid congruencies is the problem to be tackled. Let us look at a frequently encountered situation. A 10 year old boy on the overt level is reported by parents, teachers, clinic interviewers, and peers to be a very docile, well-mannered conformist, yet consistently discloses via all sorts of projective tools, a fantasy full of brutal action. Can either the projective material or the overt material be ignored because they do not agree? Is the projective material to be considered invalid because it is in violent opposition to the child's persistent overt behavior? Obviously not! It is equally obvious, too, that overt behavior cannot be ignored because it is at variance with fantasy production. For it is by taking account of both aspects—overt behavior and fantasy—that we will understand these interlocking patterns we call dynamics. It is clear that a simple correlation between overt behavior and fantasy mate-

rial is a tool completely inadequate to show the important organizational patterns involved in such combinations of explicit and implicit behavior. It may even mask dynamics discerned by other approaches. For a docile, well-mannered child may have fantasy (1) that shows a docile hero who receives kudos for docility; (2) fantasy that is neutral in this conformity aspect; (3) fantasy where the hero is belligerent and hostile and escapes unpunished; or (4) is caught and punished.

3. Another attack at validation is the search for through-time consistencies. Especially important is this in the study of pre-adult personality where personality patterns are less firmly entrenched. Longitudinal studies lend themselves to this approach to validation, since trends over time may be inspected without the distortion involved in retrospective reconstruction.

4. Collateral experimental approaches, too, should clarify the meanings of certain aspects of the protocols. Time precludes further discussion of this approach.

5. In the last analysis, the criterion *sine qua non* of validation is the degree of success in prediction. It is a criterion which in this complex and difficult field of personality research the writer would hazard is the only one which will settle the arguments of the productivity of the various conceptual schools with their varying techniques of approach, and throw into relief, at least in studies where long through-time records are available, the significant tools of validation. This is the task for the future. The task for the present is to have many skilled but diversely conceptualizing clinicians and experimentally and statistically trained scientists attack jointly this complex and promising field.

The writer's opinion is that the utilization of the interpretive and predictive judgments of widely experienced clinicians later checked for predictive success, will offer at this stage the most productive leads. If an experienced clinician is able to predict with considerable success, then the data on which he bases his correct intuitive predictions can be inspected and validly weighted configurations can be established, quantified, and made available to less experienced people. Also, his wrong and partially right predictions in conjunction with the correct ones can serve for finer and more differentiating criteria.

In conclusion, may I make a plea that responsible university teachers discourage the untrained and inexperienced people from this field until they have acquired experiences with other tools of science and clinical practice so that the whole future of a productive lead will not be prejudiced by incompetents. May I urge that all working in this field commit themselves openly with respect to their conceptual notions; that they shun concepts which are in the realm of the reified or mystic; that they adopt those which provoke procedures for verification; and that they become both conscious and articulate about what statements are permissive from their samples. And further, may I urge that they try the several approaches to validation and remember with some degree of humility that the ultimate criterion of validation is success in prediction, which requires a study covering a rather protracted period of time. When a single projective technique is used without the validating tools of measurement and case history, and without methodological responsibility, it becomes a charlatan's tool. There are no get-rich-quick schemes in the field of personality research.

SAUL ROSENZWEIG

Western State Psychiatric Institute and Clinic, Pittsburgh, Pennsylvania

Fantasy in Personality and Its Study by Test Procedures[1]

The Power of Fantasy

If truth be stranger than fiction the reason must undoubtedly be sought in the fact that truth is often an unavowed expression of fantasy just as fiction avowedly is. That it is stranger than fiction indicates that those who compose fiction set conscious limitations to their productions of which the realm of fantasy itself knows nothing. The strangest aspect of the matter concerns the possibility that an individual may unwittingly translate into reality fantasies which have been rejected by and carefully hidden from consciousness.

These propositions are the tentative result of one of the distinguishing trends of modern psychology. Even William James, as we learn from a recent book of a former student (109, p. 77),[2] was capable of beginning a lecture one morning with the question: "Why is it that a perfectly respectable man may dream that he has intercourse with his grandmother?" Such questions were, however, not characteristic of Jamesian psychology. They are, needless to say, more natural in that Freudian psychoanalysis the "complexes" of which he was somewhat skeptical. One conjectures that in the rest of James's lecture which began with the quoted question he referred to what was in his time even more than in our own the first indica-

---

[1] Reprinted from *Journal of Abnormal and Social Psychology*, 1942, 37, 40–51. Copyright 1942 by American Psychological Association.
[2] Bibliography begins on page 428.

tions of this new approach to the psychology of the unconscious. For only with the advent of psychoanalysis has the importance of fantasy been duly stressed and made the subject of careful investigation by psychologists.

After Freud, Adler's voice, even while dissenting, carried on the tradition that fantasy wields great power—he formulated the concept of "guiding fictions"; and Jung, though again diverging from Freud in other matters, even deepened this emphasis by pointing to the possibility of collective fantasies—the so-called archetypes—inherited through successive generations.

Despite these protagonists it may at first glance seem frivolous to delve into the realm of fantasy when faced with the grave problems of mental disorder. Not that the psychiatrist has failed to recognize delusions and hallucinations as fantastic in nature—fantasy at this diagnostic level has always been appreciated. But about the dynamics of fantasy and its possible role as an etiological factor skepticism is still fairly general. The reason is not far to seek. The disciplined modes of scientific thought are naturally antagonistic to such vague and irrational stuff. Trained as we are to exercise restraint in our own thinking—sometimes even to the point of naïve materialism—it is but a short step for us to turn a deaf ear to the patient's aberrations. To do this is, however, to prove more faithful to our formal training than to our duties as objective investigators of whatever presents itself.

A good part of the impediment to a recognition of the power of fantasy may be supposed to have resulted from the startling novelty of the conception and the almost revolutionary demands which it makes upon the sober investigator. Freud has more than once put on record his own bewilderment at finding some completely infantile imaginative construction at the basis of a patient's symptoms. Thus he has written in one place:

A . . . peculiarity of the analysis has only increased my difficulty in deciding how to make a report upon it. . . . Many details . . . seemed to me myself to be so extraordinary and incredible that I felt some hesitation in asking other people to believe in them. I requested the patient to make the strictest criticism of his recollections, but he found nothing improbable in his statements and adhered closely to them. Readers may at all events rest assured that I myself am only reporting what I came upon as an independent experience, uninfluenced by my expectation. So that there was nothing left for me but to remember the wise saying that there are more things in heaven and earth than are dreamed of in our philosophy. Any one who could succeed in eliminating his pre-existing convictions even more thoroughly could no doubt discover even more such things (91, pp. 478–479).

The existence of such statements is seldom appreciated by critics who upbraid Freud for introducing nonsense into the domain of science and who, instead of reading carefully such reports of clinical material as do exist or open-mindedly examining the similar data of their own patients, have been satisfied with the easier solution of characterizing the whole of psychoanalysis as fantastic.

That the characterization applies cannot be denied. The *data* of psychoanalysis are usually fantastic. But this truth has hardly registered in the critic's mind before he escapes its full appreciation by extending the characterization to the *concepts* and *methods* of psychoanalysis—which, for all their shortcomings, are only occasionally that bad. In other words, the critics of analysis have sometimes made the mistake of blaming the analyst instead of the analysand, and of taking the former less seriously instead of taking the latter more so. In the end we shall undoubtedly have to acknowledge our debt to them both—to the analysand for providing the data and to the analyst for taking his patients more seriously than has ever before been their lot in the history of psychopathology. The upshot will be that instead of calling Freud's views fantastic we shall begin to study the nature and habits of fantasy itself.

The Nature of Fantasy

As already implied, the first and foremost feature of fantasy is its infantility. Fantasy is a characteristic mode of the child's adjustment —his way of getting immediate satisfaction despite adverse circumstances in the environment. It is, of course, not always gratification which fantasy provides; anxieties are also thus envisaged. In the latter case one may suppose that some defensive function is served when the organism anticipates a danger which might otherwise overwhelm it unexpectedly. But gratifying or defensive in function, the fantasies of infancy are in either event a mode of adjustment to frustration. Whether, having once occurred, they may in some fashion get fixed in the personality so as to interfere by repetition compulsion with later adjustment is the crucial problem for psychodynamic research.

A corollary of the infantile nature of fantasy is the great serious-ness with which the child treats it. The play in which he expresses it is quite as important to him as are the working duties of an adult. Since, however, it is the adult who is responsible for the child's up-bringing, one of the chief functions of education consists, as already suggested, in inhibiting the fantastic mode of adjustment and in-culcating instead a healthy respect for reality as defined in social terms. This transition is one of the most difficult in the individual's existence—so difficult that nearly every mythology and religion has taken it into account, as witness, for example, the story in the Book of Genesis of man's expulsion from Eden into the world of adult labor. Moreover, this inhibitory process is hardly ever completely successful. There are moments when even the most normal individ-ual relaxes to indulge a reverie and practically all of us can remember the nocturnal fantasies which we call dreams. Occasionally, too, the failure of such inhibition is manifested in overt behavior of an erratic or bizarre kind.

The ground is thus prepared for recognizing a second main fea-ture of fantasy—its possibly unconscious character. While in early childhood fantasy plays a more or less accepted consciously domi-nant role, education gradually inhibits it. In adulthood, disciplined as it is to social adaptation, fantasy can eke out only a marginal ex-istence. The fantasies of the adult are hence usually repressed and are sometimes traceable to infantile experiences which have never been completely surmounted or mastered, i.e., they are "uncon-scious."

A third characteristic of fantasy, concerned now less with its func-tion in behavior than with its qualitative nature, lies in its irration-ality and illogicality. The same thing which now means black may at the next moment or even simultaneously mean white as well. One is reminded of Humpty Dumpty in Alice's looking-glass world:

"When *I* use a word," Humpty Dumpty said, in rather a scornful tone, "it means just what I choose it to mean—neither more nor less."

"The question is," said Alice, "whether you *can* make words mean so many different things."

"The question is," said Humpty Dumpty, "which is to be master—that's all" (42, p. 214).

Needless to say such a cavalier attitude in the land of fantasy holds out little hope for a purely logical appreciation of its language.

A fourth characteristic of fantasy is its affinity for concrete *pictures*. This feature is, of course, cousin to the illogical and irrational nature of it. The language of fantasy practically never employs abstract terms; in it everything, including even complex relationships, finds expression in some concrete form.

Fortunately, however, it is just this feature of fantasy which at last rescues us from what might otherwise be a hopeless attempt to decipher the vague and codeless thing it must by this time surely appear. That is to say, it is the very concreteness of fantasy which indicates its determined character. The language may be primitive, but the things expressed in it and even the very way in which they are expressed at any particular time can with striking regularity be traced to some direct previous experience of the individual. Let the individual who has reported the fantasy relax and follow the psychoanalyst's instruction to associate freely, *i.e.*, without criticism or censorship, and it is usually possible to trace the evoked pictures to their origin and to recognize how they have been determined. For paradoxical as it may appear, it is *free* association which reveals the *determinism* of fantasy, the fact being that one of the chief functions of disciplined thinking is to defeat the determinism of that impulsive life which is characteristic of the child but taboo in mature adulthood.

This method of investigating fantasy by free association is, now that the genius of Freud has put it into our hands, appreciated as a very natural one. It involves the use of a tool which by its very lack of restriction is adapted to the kind of data to be studied. If fantasy is in its very nature opposed to the disciplined forms of logical thinking, it is, of course, necessary for a subject whose fantasies we wish to understand to adopt a mental set which is equally free and untrammeled. Since, moreover, we may expect from the postulate of psychic determinism that everything in human behavior has been produced by a definite condition of previous experience, such free association should lead to the source of the fantasies studied.

In summary, then, these characteristics of fantasy—its infantile origin, its inhibition by education and its subsequent unconsciousness, its disregard of logic and reason, its concrete pictorial quality and its determinism—must be kept clearly in mind if any method for studying it is to be pursued with success.

The Language of Fantasy

If, having recognized the importance of fantasy and having surveyed its chief characteristics, we next examine the possible ways of studying it, the first method to be considered is, as already anticipated, psychoanalysis itself. The psychoanalytic procedure generally means two things: the technique of free association and its especial application to the dreams of the analysand. From the historical fact that Freud's first independent psychoanalytic work was on the interpretation of dreams may be gleaned the insight that his approach was from the outset a method for studying fantasy. That free association was for the first time elaborated in relation to dream interpretation and was thus initially expounded in the book on dreams further corroborates this view.

There can be little doubt that the highly personal and continuous approach to fantasy in which psychoanalysis consists is still ideally the method of choice. It is also unfortunately clear that it is far too expensive of time and labor for general utilization. There have accordingly sprung up more recently certain alternative methods which are much shorter and which, though necessarily less complete and perhaps in some respects less reliable, are proving themselves well adapted to certain psychological ends that emphasize measurement and diagnosis rather than therapy. These new devices also have the merit of providing a kind of objective experimental validation of psychoanalytic concepts.

The techniques in question have collectively come to be called "projective," since they all depend upon the subject's objectification of his subjective processes. Each of them encourages the individual in the presence of an unorganized neutral stimulus medium—whether visual, auditory, plastic, etc.—to let himself go and render it meaningful. He may, for example, be shown an ink-blot and asked to tell what objects it resembles or he may be given some modeling clay and requested to fashion it into something or other.

An interesting problem is involved in the comparison of such a general approach with the psychoanalytic method of dream interpretation. While it is not difficult to appreciate how dreams as material for analysis are equivalent to fantasies elicited by the projective devices, from this point on the comparison is more hazardous. Most knotty of all aspects of the problem is that concerning the role of free association, for, while in dream interpretation free association occurs after the dream is reported, in the projective methods it enters—and then only in a very modified way—in the actual process of creating the fantasies. One might at first glance suppose that the distinction is not vital since dreaming is itself a kind of free association but this solution turns out to be imperfect. Fortunately, however, these finer theoretical difficulties are of little moment here. It suffices to note certain essential resemblances between dream interpretation and the projective procedures as follows: The reported dreams are equivalent to the projective products or fantasies; the same inner tensions that lie behind the dreams are presumably back of the fantasies, too; the immediately present stimuli of the dream (e.g., the buzzing of a fly near the bed) correspond to the neutral stimuli of the test procedures, and memory fragments have an equal opportunity for expression in both; free association is encouraged in post-dream interpretation—even if not strictly involved in the process of dreaming itself—and *freedom* of association is urged upon the subject in the test procedures for eliciting fantasies.

It is thus expected that the projective techniques will give the personality an opportunity to cast up its own—whether as regards the content of specific fantasies or as regards particular modes of functioning. Some of the tests, as will appear subsequently in more detail, favor the contentual aspects of fantasy; others elicit more readily the formal aspects of mentation; but all of them include a measure of each complement.

The brief survey of actual procedures for which there is time may conveniently follow, though only approximately, the chronological order of their development. Preference in selection will be given to those methods which have in general been broadly adopted as clinical aids and have in particular been successfully and consistently used at the Worcester State Hospital.

1. *Word Association Test.* This first method is the oldest and the most widely known. Adapting a technique which had been introduced into experimental psychology by Galton and elaborated by Wundt, Kraepelin, and others, Jung (132) around 1900 attempted to corroborate and extend psychoanalytic theory by means of the word association test. That this is a projective device has been convincingly shown by Wells (287) in an instructive paper in which the Rorschach test has been compared with word association. Since

the words with which the subject is stimulated may produce any of an unlimited number of possible responses, it is easy to appreciate that one is here dealing with a technique in which the subject perceives the word in his own way. Where complexes dependent upon repressed fantasies are involved, unusual associations as indicated by the nature of the response word, delays in the reaction time and other cues are available for observation. The method has had extensive application both in clinical practice and in research, as, for example, in the Kent-Rosanoff norms and in connection with the Luria technique (126, 161).

2. *Rorschach Test.* More obviously concerned with fantasy and its elicitation is the method which Hermann Rorschach developed from 1911 on and introduced in his 1921 monograph *Psychodiagnostik* (220). This technique has since been elaborated by Beck (14), Klopfer (139), Hertz (114), Rickers-Ovsiankina (216), and others. In it ink-blots, colored or gray, are presented to the subject with the instruction that he is to report what he sees—in much the same way that he might do if he were looking at drifting clouds or gazing into an open fire.

One rather significant difference between the word-association procedure and this one lies in the latter's greater emphasis upon formal categories of interpretation rather than contentual ones. It is true that the Rorschach tester notes any special content which appears insistently or in some unusual context but greater reliance is placed in the scoring on, say, the number of colored parts which are reacted to, the number of movement responses given and the precision with which the forms reported are perceived. In the word-association technique, on the other hand, the accepted meaning of the stimulus word plays a more determinative role in the interpretations, such as when a delayed response to a word which is easily taken in a sexual significance appears in the record.

3. *Play Technique.* The method of play technique, though conceived by Vernon (276) to represent a prototype to which the Rorschach test is assimilable, resembles the word-association procedure even more closely in that it emphasizes content more than form. There is also a new feature to note here for in play technique we come for the first time in this survey upon a procedure which very directly aims at revealing complete fantasies with plot structures. The method probably had its origin in Freud's "Analysis of a

Phobia in a Five-Year-Old Boy," published in 1909 (91, pp. 194–195), where he wrote: " 'For some time Hans has been playing horse in the room: he trots about, falls down, kicks about with his feet, and neighs. Once he tied a small bag on like a nose bag. He has repeatedly run up to me and bitten me.' " Freud interprets these observations, reported by the child's father, as follows: "Thus he was the horse, he bit his father, and in this way he was identifying himself with his father."

Hug-Hellmuth (123) later elaborated his casual use of play spontaneously manifested by the child into a more deliberate attempt to elicit such behavior, and Melanie Klein (138) has within recent years taken the final step by systematically and consistently applying play technique with toys as a substitute for free association with words in work with children. As can be readily appreciated, this procedure is particularly suitable for the study of very young subjects—with whom it had its origin—but it has also been significantly applied to adults, among them schizophrenic patients (224).

4. *Thematic Apperception Test.* In 1935 Morgan and Murray (184) of the Harvard Psychological Clinic introduced a method which resembles play technique in being designed to elicit full-fledged fantasies but which is more readily applicable to adult subjects. Here the aforementioned clue from literary fiction—that truth is stranger than fiction but derives from the same psychological source—has been taken quite seriously for the stimulus material is a set of pictures which are individually presented to the subject with the instruction that he is to regard them as illustrations in a story book. He is requested to build up plots around the pictures, identifying the people represented, explaining what they are doing, how they got there, and what the outcome will be. From the stories thus elicited Murray, Morgan, and their co-workers have found it possible to reveal highly significant facts about a subject's personality (194). Masserman and Balken (10, 172, 173, 174) in Chicago, Rotter (226) and Harrison (111) at the Worcester State Hospital, and others who have subsequently attempted to validate the procedure with groups of neurotic and psychotic individuals—the original subjects at the Harvard Clinic were normal—have reported promising results.

5. *Tautophone.* A final technique which may be mentioned employs an instrument designed in 1936 by B. F. Skinner (247) and

named by him the "verbal summator." The instrument is a phonograph which repeats recorded patterns of vowels until the subject who is reclining at some distance from the machine and has been instructed to report what the man on the record is saying gives a response. Thus, a subject given the stimulus pattern ŭ ŭ ē ū replied "a hoodoo," while to the vowel pattern ŭ ah ŭ ī he responded "about a pint." To ī ŭ ŭ ū another said, "I was born on a square piece of land," and to ŭ ī ū ŭ still another responded, "Goodbye, Hoover!" Shakow and I (244) have adapted this device as an auditory apperceptive test and have re-christened the instrument "tautophone" to avoid the theoretical implications of Skinner's term. Thinking of the role of audition in delusions of reference and the high frequency of auditory hallucinations as compared to those of other sensory modalities, it was our notion that this test might supplement such visual ones as the Rorschach or the Thematic Apperception significantly. As developed thus far it resembles the former of these more than the latter because of its relatively greater emphasis upon formal than upon contentual scoring categories. A scoring system which takes into account the complexity of the structure of the response—syllables, words, etc.—the similarity of the response to the stimulus sample, personal reference in the response, as well as certain relational indices has been developed on the basis of material from a group of normal and another of schizophrenic subjects. It appears at present that the method may, after more experimentation, provide a further useful technique of a projective sort.

In view of the fact that these tests are all attempts to study fantasy either with reference to form or content the question may well arise as to whether more than one of them is necessary. The answer which practice gives is that because they favor form or content to a different degree and, moreover, appeal to subjects in diverse ways from the standpoint of the stimulus material, they usually complement each other significantly. While it is obviously not worth while to use all of those procedures with every individual, it has been found that, for example, the combination of the Rorschach test, emphasizing formal features of interpretation, with the Thematic Apperception, which stresses meaningful content, is unusually fruitful in results.

It is noteworthy that such projective methods for studying personality as have just been reviewed are in the spirit of some of the most recent tendencies of modern scientific work, as L. K. Frank (87) has shown. He has particularly called attention to such parallels as are found in spectrographic analysis (to reveal the chemical components of compounds) and in biological assays, in both of which an organized unit can be studied as to its composition without being destructively broken down. Frank notes that such techniques, whether in chemistry, biology, or psychology, have the great advantage of respecting the organization of the individual and of revealing it without annulling it. Thus in the projective psychological procedures the personality of the subject is evaluated by observing the way in which he organizes a field in which he has been encouraged to react as freely as possible. For if the individual responds, not to some predetermined meaning imposed upon the stimulus by the experimenter, but in terms of his own subjective experience, it is possible from noting with sufficient skill the ways in which he configurates, organizes, or distoits the material to trace the content of the fantasies and the formal functions which have participated to produce the result.

Another advantage of the projective devices is their relatively high proof against the subject's ability to conceal or deliberately modify the facts about himself. In other words, these test procedures are *behavioral* in nature—they instruct the subject to do something instead of asking him his opinion about what he might do under given circumstances. The pitfalls of such devices as the personality inventory—from which one learns little else besides a person's misconceptions about himself—are thus obviated. Since the subject is, moreover, usually unaware of the purpose of a projective test, he is again less able to dissimulate.

It is nonetheless necessary to admit that these projective techniques also have their pitfalls. Considerable skill is involved in the interpretation of the data obtained and this represents a serious limitation. In uncritical hands the invocation of fantasy to explain behavior can become so far-fetched as to be itself fantastic. The only safeguard against such a misapplication of the procedures is a sound background in scientific parsimony and a thorough acquaintance with specific alternative factors underlying behavior—physiological, neurological, and psychological. Besides this quantitative danger there is, moreover, a qualitative one. It is easily possible in making intepretations of projective material to project one's own fantasies in the process. The psychoanalyst would undoubtedly maintain that for most persons who are to use these procedures, just as for prospective psychoanalysts, a preliminary period of self-analysis is necessary in order to prevent reciprocal projection; and, since it appears that the outstandingly distinctive result of a didactic analysis is a real appreciation of the power of fantasy, this suggestion is not unreasonable. These drawbacks to an able use of the techniques may not in a collaborative set-up like a mental hospital be as formidable in practice as they sound in generalization but they must be squarely recognized for what they can be at the worst if abuse is to be avoided.

Conclusion. The present discussion of procedures for studying personality by educed fantasies has been necessarily selective. Other devices as, for example, cloud pictures, finger painting, and modeling clay might have been described in addition to those given— Word Association, Rorschach Ink-blots, Play Technique, Thematic Apperception, and the Tautophone. But these omissions are of minor importance provided that the general significance of fantasy in psychodynamics has been made clear and some impression as to its nature and its availability for study by projective techniques has been conveyed.

SAUL ROSENZWEIG · ROBERT A. CLARK

Western State Psychiatric Institute and Clinic, Pittsburgh, Pennsylvania

The Personality of a Psychotic Ex-Soldier[1]

At the request of the Editor the present paper is being prepared to illustrate the role of the psychologist in the process of psychiatric collaboration. To make clear the nature of the presentation it should be stated that the case—that of a man discharged from the Army on neuropsychiatric grounds—has been selected not because of its clinical unusualness but rather because it represents the usual problem that invites collaboration. Since, however, the present discussion is intended primarily for the psychological student, less emphasis will be placed upon the psychiatric approach than upon the contribution from psychological procedures. Paralleling the actual method of study followed in this as in our other ex-soldier research cases, the results of the psychological examination will be presented on a minimal anamnestic background. The part contributed by psychological tests may in this way perhaps be more readily distinguished. The projective techniques, constituting, as they do, the most significant recent advance in clinical psychology, figured saliently in the investigation and have an accordingly prominent place in the account which follows.

Identifying Data

The patient is a 34-year-old Roman Catholic single male, born in a small Ohio town, the youngest of six siblings. He was educated

---

[1] Reprinted from *Journal of Abnormal and Social Psychology*, 1945, 40, 195–204. Copyright 1945 by American Psychological Association.

through the ninth grade and is a printer by occupation. His father, a pottery-maker, died ten years ago. His mother is living and well. Both parents are native-born. There are two older sisters and three older brothers, all married. The patient enlisted in the Army in December 1940, but after serving for only a few months became mentally ill and was given a medical discharge.

Psychological Examination

The patient was given ten psychological tests[2] of which eight—the most productive—will be discussed here. The tests were selected to evaluate intelligence and other aspects of capacity and, more especially, to elicit information about psychodynamics. For the latter purpose the projective techniques, including particularly the Rorschach and Thematic Apperception Tests, were employed.

SUMMARY OF PSYCHOLOGICAL TEST RESULTS

WECHSLER-BELLEVUE INTELLIGENCE SCALE
Verbal Scale: I.Q. 89
Performance Scale: I.Q. 103
Full Scale: I.Q. 96
Interpretation: Average intelligence. Not optimal.

WELLS MEMORY TEST
Memory Quotient: 76
Interpretation: Memory loss. Not optimal.

SHIPLEY-HARTFORD RETREAT SCALE
Vocabulary Age: 12.3 yrs.
Abstraction Age: 11.5 yrs.
Mental Age: 11.5 yrs.
Conceptual Quotient: 92 (unreliable)
Interpretation: Qualitative results indicate efficiency loss in vocabulary and abstraction.

RORSCHACH METHOD OF PERSONALITY DIAGNOSIS
Interpretation: Introversive (autistic). Disturbance of conceptual thinking. Disappointed ambitions.

THEMATIC APPERCEPTION TEST
Interpretation: Maternal domination. Pseudo-artistic inclinations. Disappointment in life. Sexual maladjustment.

WORD ASSOCIATION TEST
Group Contact Score: 53 per cent (good contact)

---

[2] The technical assistance of Lourene Bundas, Kelly Lumry, and Helen Davidson in the administration and interpretation of these tests is gratefully acknowledged.

ROSENZWEIG PICTURE-FRUSTRATION STUDY
Extrapunitive: 25 per cent
Intropunitive: 42 per cent
Impunitive: 33 per cent

Interpretation: Exaggerated intropunitive tendency. Trend from impunitiveness to intropunitiveness.

DAVIS PERSONAL PROBLEMS TEST
Interpretation: Conflictful insight regarding sexual maladjustment.

ATTITUDE. The patient was passively cooperative in attitude during nearly all of the tests. Attention, however, was variable and persistence irregular. He was frequently preoccupied and was slow to respond. He grimaced without external cause again and again, shook his head as if in response to his own thoughts, and occasionally sighed. He spoke with a certain affectation resembling an educated British accent. He sat in a slouched position, kept one hand in his pocket most of the time, and was probably masturbating during some of the tests. Nevertheless, the results may be considered representative of the patient's best efforts at the present time since variability of attention, preoccupation, and slowness are constant factors in his condition.

INTELLECTUAL FUNCTIONS. The results of several tests in this area point to a present functioning level of average intelligence. Loss of efficiency is indicated. On the Wechsler-Bellevue Scale this loss is brought out by the inconsistencies within as well as among the various subtests. The Shipley-Hartford Scale confirms the presence of deterioration. The Wells Memory Test shows a clear memory loss noticeable chiefly in respect to new associations. The Rorschach findings, discussed in the next section, support and extend the foregoing interpretation of the subject's capacity.

1. *Wechsler-Bellevue Intelligence Scale.* The Full Scale I.Q. of 96 indicates a present functioning level of average intelligence. There is a significant difference between the ratings of the Verbal (I.Q. 89) and the Performance Scales (I.Q. 103). A difficulty in conceptual (verbal) thinking may be present. Although there is wide scatter within and among all the subtests, there is less variability in the Performance Scale, and this fact may account in part for the higher performance rating. The inconsistencies in the various subtests indicate moderate loss in efficient functioning. The original intelligence level was probably somewhat above average.

The Information Test score is above the average score range. The long-range memory required in this test has been better preserved than any of the other verbal functions but some inconsistencies and illogicalities occurred. Although the performance on numbers forward was adequate, he had considerable difficulty with reverse digits because of a perseverative trend and short attention span. A significantly low total score for Digits Memory resulted. The Similarities Test score was also low. Here again the performance was erratic and confusion of thought was evident. Both the Picture Arrangement and the Object Assembly scores were high and show good grasp of social relationships and essential details, respectively. However, the awkward position of the subject's fingers and the slight tremor of his hands interfered with the fitting of the blocks in the latter test. An inferior result on the Digit Symbol Test indicates poor visual-motor coordination. On Block Design his score was high.

2. *Wells Memory Test* (*Worcester Revision*). The Memory Quotient of 76 reflects considerable variability. His scores were above the current norms for school knowledge, repetition of the alphabet, counting backward from 20 to 1, and repetition of numbers forward. He achieved at the average level for sentence memory. His scores were very low for "old" personal information, new learning, repetition of numbers backward, and naming of common objects. His difficulty in the latter groups of items was chiefly a matter of retardation rather than inability to recall. His attempt to learn new associations, however, was almost a total failure. As a result he became somewhat facetious and lost the idea of the test completely. In their entirety the findings indicate more inefficiency in present memory function than any actual loss of memory and confirm the Wechsler-Bellevue indications.

3. *Shipley-Hartford Retreat Scale.* On this test the patient was very slow and finished neither the vocabulary nor the abstraction sections within the time limit. The vocabulary results are inconsistent, containing a number of early failures among the successes. These inconsistencies, as well as slowness, strongly suggest an original vocabulary level above the present rating of 12.3 years. Thus, the Conceptual Quotient of 92 cannot be considered reliable. The mental age of 11.5 years is, however, consistent with the rating on the Wechsler-Bellevue Verbal Scale. Loss in functioning efficiency is clearly implied.

PERSONALITY STRUCTURE AND DYNAMICS. Tests in this area indicate marked intellectual and emotional disorganization much of which centers in sexual conflicts and disappointed aspirations. The Rorschach Test does not yield a completely typical psychotic picture but the indications of maladjustment are, nevertheless, numerous. Some superior intellectual ability is suggested but this is largely dissipated in fantasy. Intellectual disorganization, affective repression and disappointed aspirations are indicated. Active conflict with a compensatory trend seems to be present. The Thematic Apperception Test emphasizes the part which family relationships have played in the patient's faulty personality development. The mother is represented as a crude, dominating, and censoring figure who has influenced both his sexual and vocational adjustments unfavorably. The father, with whom he appears to have identified, is represented as weak. A clear tendency toward homosexuality is revealed. The patient has apparently been driven, though almost completely in the realm of fantasy, by high aspirations few of which he has been able to realize. He now attempts defensively to deny ever having had these ambitions. Another way in which he reacts to his failures is by withdrawal, guilt feelings, and a strong sense of inadequacy.

4. *Rorschach Method of Personality Diagnosis*. Interpretation of this test must be made with particular caution because of the patient's underproductivity (15 responses). The protocol reflects an individual of good intelligence, probably of superior level. Intellectual control is fairly adequate (high percentage of good form-clarity) but is maintained with difficulty. The introversive orientation is marked (movement responses) and is strongly autistic. Intellectual ambitiousness, probably disappointed, is suggested (comparison of whole and movement responses). Vague anxiety of a "free-floating" type appears to be present (shading responses). Repression of affectivity was manifested in the almost total lack of color responses. Although an unusually long reaction time for all cards was found, the especially long delay for the color cards suggests color shock with implied emotional conflict. Features of the record which correspond to the pattern usually found in schizophrenia are as follows: loss of contact with reality (low number of popular responses, insufficient normal detail responses, and the presence of vague abstractions); difficulty in conceptual thinking (pseudo-abstractions, contamination tendency, inconsistent poor form-clarity, whole and unusual

detail responses exaggerated); irregularity in tempo and in number and quality of responses; affective blocking. The presence of anxiety responses, the suggestion of color shock and, in some measure, the number and type of the movement responses indicate an active restitutive process.

5. *Thematic Apperception Test.* The patient sat in a huddled position throughout the test and spoke in a low voice. He reacted strongly to the stimulation of the pictures, perhaps because they nourished his already existing preoccupations. At times he seemed to be so carried away by his emotions and thoughts that it was necessary to recall him to the task at hand. There was evidence to indicate that he was secretly masturbating and this behavior seemed to vary according to the emotional stimulation of the particular picture. His facial expression was then one of absorption, his eyes were staring, and he failed to answer the examiner's questions.

Analysis of the stories, card by card, follows. *Card I* (1—boy with violin)[3] reveals a tendency toward self-absorption and self-directed criticism. Insight is indicated in the subject's statement that emotions may interfere with practical adjustment. *Card II* (2—country scene) brings out attention to unusual details and a tendency to characterize reality in a symbolic way. The family is described as intellectually disappointing. The story expresses conflict among the "mental, emotional and physical aspects of life" and, by implication, in the subject. The relationship between mother and father is not smooth and the father plays a relatively minor role in the family conflicts. *Card III* (6 B M—elderly woman and young man): army life is described as disturbing. There is recognition of the hero's lack of self-discipline. Feelings of guilt with a need for punishment are expressed. The hero shows impulsivity, rebelliousness, and an inability to face problems rationally. The son is a disappointment to his mother, and she cannot understand him. The relationship between them is problematic. (At this juncture signs of increased preoccupation were manifested.) *Card IV* (14—silhouette of man in dark room against bright window) indicates the repression of anxiety. The matter-of-fact treatment and relative brevity of the response support this interpretation. However, in *Card V* (10—woman's head against a man's shoulder) the repressed anxiety becomes partly

---

[3] Numbers in parentheses indicate, with one self-explained exception, the relationship of the pictures to the now published TAT series.

manifest. The patient includes the death of a son in the story. The subject's own guilt and need for punishment may be here involved. Although the woman is being comforted by her husband, she is the dominant figure. The man "is gaining strength from the mother's weakness." (Evidence of tension in the subject became more pronounced at this point.) In *Card VI* (3 B M—huddled form of boy on floor, head against couch), the anxiety is openly expressed in a suicide theme. The figure portrayed in the picture is usually described as a boy. The subject speaks of "a girl who has had a child." A defensive dissociation may be indicated; or a possible homosexual trend. Sexual problems and unhappiness are coupled in the narrative. Art is presented as a possibility for sublimating unacceptable sex drives. (Preoccupation here markedly increased. The patient seemed to have difficulty in responding to the examiner's questions.) The *Blank Card* yields what seems by available criteria to be largely autobiographical material. Heterosexuality is rejected. Platonic friendship and art are goals to be pursued. The hero's emotional turmoil, fear, self-disgust, feelings of inadequacy, and need for punishment are reflected. Disillusionment is expressed, and some insight by the subject into his own state of mind is shown. *Card VII* (Picasso painting of nude figures, contained in an early, unpublished Harvard Psychological Clinic series): (The obvious sexual aspect of this picture seemed to rouse the subject from his preoccupations. He became more alert, perhaps defensively.) An initial effort to minimize the sexual aspect appears, but presently an incestuous situation is described. The nude figures are characterized as brother and sister. The ego-ideal maternal figure is chastizing and censorious. *Card VIII* (7 B M—grey-haired man and adolescent boy): Restlessness and conflict concerning the choice of an occupation are revealed. The son expresses rebelliousness but submits finally to the father's authority. The subject's identification with the father is suggested. *Card IX* (18 B M—man clutched from behind by three hands): (The subject again gave evidence of preoccupation.) The story describes a very dissipated individual who has strong guilt feelings. The word-choice suggests a homosexual theme. *Card X* (8 B M—adolescent boy in scene of surgical operation): The difference between aspiration and achievement is stressed.

In summary, the impression of somewhat superior intelligence is conveyed by the vocabulary used by the subject in his stories. The extent of his subjective participation in the responses is shown by the way in which his total behavior seemed to vary with his productions. The mother figure is described as having very high standards. She is concerned about her son but does not understand him. She represents the "emotional" aspect of the family situation. She is characterized as dominant and disapproving. The patient is critical of the relationship between his father and her. The father is described as weaker than the mother. He is reserved and unconcerned about the family, although he dominates in the father-son relationship. The son is more or less identified with him. There is a suggestion of incestuous inclinations towards a sister. Heterosexuality is rejected as leading to trouble and unhappiness. A homosexual trend appears. Lack of success in life is ascribed to sexual excesses and unconventional behavior. Aggression is turned inward with accompanying emotions of guilt, self-blame, and remorse. Frustration is met by indecision, withdrawal, and thoughts of suicide. The need for punishment is clearly expressed in the endings of the stories and in the constant themes of discouragement, despair, submission, and dissipation. High but disappointed aspirations are revealed. Introspective self-criticism, suggestive of insight, is outstanding. He recognizes his own emotional instability. He sees salvation in sublimation through art.

6. Word Association Test. The patient was slow in understanding the directions for this test. Additional explanation, however, resulted in his full cooperation. The reaction time to the words varied from 1 to 15 seconds with a median of 3.5. Reaction times of 7 to 10 seconds were found for the words command, attack, smooth, tongue, luck, hard, cottage, pity, thirsty, couple, and different. Extremely long response times were found on the words love (15 seconds) and blame (14 seconds). Unusual responses which may be of significance are as follows: fruit-children, justice-unjustice, month-Mississippi, suck-honey, swallow-man, home-soon. The complex indicators suggest a definite sexual problem, possibly homosexual (love, swallow, tongue, suck, different, couple, hard, etc.). Anxiety and guilt are also indicated.

REACTIONS TO FRUSTRATION. Information regarding adjustment to stress has, among other things, been presented in the discussion of the three foregoing projective techniques, but for the specific purpose a relatively new device was employed. Since the test in question is not yet adequately described in the literature, a brief account may be helpful.

The Picture-Frustration Study is a limited projective technique for assessing an individual's characteristic modes of reaction in everyday situations of stress. Stereotypes of response are elicited. The test material consists of 24 cartoon-like drawings each of which represents an everyday situation of frustration. Two individuals are always involved, one of them usually frustrating the other. Facial expressions and features are purposely not sketched. The frustrating person is shown saying certain words which either help to describe the frustrating situation in which the other person finds himself or which of themselves actually frustrate the other person. The subject is asked to look at the pictures one at a time, read the statement given for the articulate character, and then write down the very first reply which comes to his mind as appropriate for the other character. The responses given by the subject are scored as to the manner in which aggression is employed: turned outward onto the frustrating person or some other aspect of the situation (extrapunitive); turned in upon the subject himself in the form of guilt or remorse (intropunitive); or evaded altogether by attempts to gloss over the situation without blaming anyone or anything (impunitive). The aggression scores are totalled. The trend, if any, revealed in the sequence of the responses is noted; e.g., a subject who begins with a high degree of extrapunitiveness may shift in the latter portion of the record to a predominance of intropunitiveness. Identification of the subject with the frustrated character in each pictorial situation is assumed to have occurred. Percentages of total intropunitive, extrapunitive, and impunitive responses are construed to indicate the degree to which the subject employs these modes of reaction in his everyday behavior. From the trend analysis a tentative interpretation may be made regarding the subject's own reaction to his previously expressed aggressive patterns.

7. *Picture-Frustration Study.* From the total scores for extrapunitiveness, intropunitiveness, and impunitiveness it would appear that the patient characteristically turns aggression upon himself (42 per cent) in situations of frustration with accompanying feelings of guilt and remorse. He is particularly limited in his capacity to exter-

nalize aggression. While his record begins with seemingly characteristic impunitive responses, he soon has recourse to the intropunitive mode which is presumably more ultimate for him.

INDICATIONS OF INSIGHT. Evidence of the patient's insight into his condition can be obtained incidentally from several of the foregoing tests, e.g., the Thematic Apperception Test. From such findings he appears to have considerable awareness of his problems and may in fact be morbidly preoccupied with them.

In order to evaluate insight more directly a personality inventory was administered. The present use of this device proceeds on the assumption that, while the evidence from the responses cannot be accepted as a description of the subject, they yield a self-estimate for comparison with the more objective evidence at hand. Such use of personality inventories in a sense places them in the category of projective techniques: The subject is permitted by this means to project his self-opinions.

8. *Davis Personal Problems Test.* To indicate his worries, in accordance with the instructions, the patient underlined only a few words, all of which he evaluated by an intensity number of 1. Nevertheless, he constantly referred in conversation to the other intensity numbers. Once he asked the meaning of "acute anguish." The words underlined were: *temptation, cravings, excesses, nervousness,* and *unnaturalness.* Anxiety concerning sex and mental illness are thus evasively admitted. He has some awareness of his difficulties but is not able to face them straightforwardly.

Psychiatric Findings

The family history of the patient contains no other example of nervous or mental disease except for a temporary facial tic in one sister. The father was a steady worker, sociable and sober, who died in 1934 of "cirrhosis of the liver and spleen." His mother, still living, is inclined to drink too much. All the siblings are in good health.

The patient's early development was normal except for a fracture of the right forearm at four and of the right femur at five. While he was in the seventh or eighth grade at school a tic developed in the muscles around the right eye, which has persisted since. Not caring for school, he was often truant during the last few years. He went to work in a printing shop and continued this work until his enlistment, except for short periods during the depression when he delivered groceries or worked for the CWA. He was not ambitious nor was he greatly concerned about the amount of money he earned. He went to Mass nearly every Sunday. In his spare time he was content to sit with his friends talking and drinking wine, or to read newspapers and current magazines such as *Reader's Digest* and *News Week*. Always quiet, he preferred reading to company, and liked to keep neat and clean. He had little interest in moving pictures, was not athletic, never traveled, and had no hobbies. Although he enjoyed dancing, he had no steady girl friend and never contemplated marriage. According to his mother, one girl who liked him called him up and wrote to him but he paid little attention to her. He states that the sex relations he had, mostly with prostitutes, did not give him much "kick." Neither venereal diseases nor homosexual contacts are reported.

On December 16, 1940, the patient volunteered for service in the U. S. Army. He did not wait to be inducted because he wished to choose his own branch of "defensive" service. At first there was no complaint from his instructors in the Engineer School Provisional Battalion, where he was working in the printing shop. However, on January 28, 1941, he came to the orderly room demanding to see the Major. He said he was a conscientious objector and wanted transfer to the infantry. When on KP over the week-end, he thought spies had been posted to watch him. After a few days in the Station Hospital he seemed quieter and was returned to duty. On February 17 he reported for sick call, bringing a post-card to "Dr. Quack of the Quack Quack Hospital." Again admitted to the Station Hospital, he stated that since discontinuing sex relations three years ago from fear of syphilis, he had striven toward "intellectual intercourse." He wanted to be a man but wished to avoid hurting his mother, to whom he was very close, although he had never kissed her. He was afraid that when he had spoken in one of his letters of being a "tower of strength" he may have been misunderstood. His mail, he thought, was being intercepted and read. He believed he had a mission in reference to Negroes, who should not do menial work. The Army had in his opinion a "spiritual function." He expressed the fear that his friends would think him a pervert because after paying a prostitute he did not have intercourse with her. On June 14 he was given a medical discharge from the Army and sent home.

At home he stayed in the house most of the time, frequently sitting and laughing to himself and slapping his knee with his right hand. Although untidy about his appearance, he took showers so often at all hours of the night that the water had to be shut off. He gradually became more and more preoccupied, talking to himself and being suspicious of everyone.

On February 17, 1942, he was admitted to a State Hospital in Pennsylvania, his mother having meanwhile established residence in that state. There he was quiet and cooperative but asocial and preoccupied, with a speech mannerism resembling an English accent. He claimed to have been commissioned by the Virgin Mary to travel throughout the world and report conditions to her. He conversed continually with the Virgin by means of a generator ray, which made him irritable and weak. He was able to have sexual intercourse by air or telephoto. Realizing he had been mentally sick, he attributed his illness to poisoning. Not liking Army life, he said, he could not adapt himself to it. He now thought himself to be well. A diagnosis of paranoid schizophrenia was made. Electroshock treatment produced no improvement.

He was transferred to the Western State Psychiatric Hospital on September 3, 1943. Here he was observed to be asthenic in body build. He sat with his arms and legs folded as though to take the smallest possible space; walked close to the walls of the corridors, and often stood, jiggling rhythmically, and peered with an empty smile into a vacant room. He replied to questions politely, in a pompous, vaguely evasive manner, getting fleetingly irritable when asked about his mannerisms. His florid delusions were no longer evident. He admitted only that he felt a warm ray continually playing on his back, which he believed was put there by the doctors in order to help him. Although he denied hallucinations, he was seen talking to himself at times. He ate poorly and paid no attention to his personal appearance. In spite of good memory for past events, he did not keep track of the date or care about current events. He was indifferent to his present condition and to his future.

Physical examination showed no contributory pathology, and his urine, blood, and serological tests were normal.

Concluding Integration

From the psychiatric findings and the psychological test results a more or less intelligible portrait emerges in the following terms. The patient has always been a withdrawn personality, indulging in fantasies and preoccupied with himself. This schizoid trend, seen through the life course, may be regarded as the developmental background of the present psychosis.

He appears to have experienced little in the way of normal family life. He felt dominated by his mother whose place was sometimes taken by his oldest sister. The mother was undependable and frightening. The father was a weaker person with whom the patient may have identified in terms of submission to the mother. The sister's temporary facial tic and the patient's persistent one may have either a physical or psychological relationship but further information on this point is lacking. Socially the patient's life was that of the average small-town fellow. His adult recreations consisted in drinking and lounging around on the street corners. He did not have much to look forward to and was not completely satisfied with so unpromising an existence.

Conflict over sexual adjustment appears to have existed perennially. An undercurrent of homosexuality was probably present. Most of his recreations were with men, even his visits to prostitutes in the company of other fellows without his ordinarily having intercourse. His drinking with the boys may also have expressed some latent homosexuality and his artistic inclinations and present affectations are probably to be interpreted in the same way. Domination by the mother is possibly to some extent responsible for the sexual maladjustment.

While military enlistment may to some extent have represented an effort to break away from his drab and unhopeful existence, in another sense it was an escape from anxiety about the Army itself. He states that he enlisted in preference to being drafted because he believed he would in that way have some choice regarding his branch of service. He could not tolerate the thought of being assigned to an "offensive" rather than "defensive" line of duty. His statement at the onset of the psychosis that he was a conscientious objector is thus understandable. The enlistment which might therefore at first glance seem to be an assertive act becomes instead a form of escape. It is little wonder that on this basis army life proved to be intolerable and precipitated a mental breakdown in which loosely organized delusions of grandeur autistically compensated for his almost equally autistic former ambitions. The erotic content of his delusions may indicate the part which his unsolved sexual problems played both before and during his military experience.

While the interpretation up to this point has been largely developmental and psychiatric in emphasis, it is desirable now to stress the present personality picture. The psychological tests have at points confirmed or supplemented the foregoing account. Their distinctive contribution stands out more clearly in the following.

Taken in their entirety, the tests reveal an individual who was originally of somewhat superior intelligence but had ambitions that extended far beyond his possibilities of achievement. He is functioning now at the level of average intelligence so far as his test results indicate but a significant degree of deterioration appears to have occurred. The decline is evidenced particularly by impairment in memory function and by defects in the ability to think in abstract terms. His emotional problems center largely around disappointed ambitions and profound sexual conflicts. Both these sources of maladjustment seem to have been unfavorably influenced by his early family situation. His mother appears to have dominated him; his father represented a weak model with which to identify. That he never managed to make an adequate sexual adjustment may have been to some extent due to confusion by homosexual conflicts which he found it impossible to resolve without anxiety. His typical reaction to frustration and failure is one of self-blame and withdrawal from reality, and he at times even goes so far as to entertain thoughts of suicide. He has a high degree of insight into his present maladjustment and is attempting to preserve his personality integration with some slight measure of success. That he is also failing appears from the manneristic affectation of his voice, the grimacing and other lapses of attention noted during the tests, and by the more objective indications of deterioration in the various findings.

It would seem from these studies that the Army represented for the patient a challenge to which he was not equal—an opportunity for comparing himself with other men that left him with an increased sense of inadequacy; a disciplinary life which interfered with his acquired habits of daydreaming as a substitute solution for unsolved problems; and, perhaps, an excessive strain on his homosexual tendencies which in a more mixed civilian environment received less stimulation. With his originally better-than-average intelligence and his present insight it is possible that reeducation could restore him to at least a moderate degree of successful adjustment, but counter-indications are the long-standing faulty habits of withdrawal, the marked sense of failure and patterns of excessive self-blame, and the evidence of existing intellectual impairment.[4]

---

[4] For another illustrative case study with similar expository aim see: S. Rosenzweig, B. Simon, and M. Ballou (225). (Bibliography begins on page 428.)

ESTHER KROOP SARASON

SEYMOUR B. SARASON

Clark University and The Institute of Human Relations,
Yale University

A Problem in Diagnosing Feeblemindedness[1]

The purpose of this paper is to examine the clinical methods employed by the psychologist in helping to make a diagnosis of mental deficiency. Criteria for the evaluation of the clinical psychologist's findings will be given and an illustrative case presented.

The psychologist occupies an assured role of importance in the field of mental deficiency by virtue of the fact that a diagnosis cannot accurately be made without psychological tests. It is true that in cases of idiocy and low-grade imbecility, where there are usually clear neurological signs of extensive brain damage, the physician's diagnosis need not be corroborated by the psychologist's findings. However, in the vast majority of cases the physician must fall back on "impression" and "observations," the unreliability of which bitter experience has exposed, unless he has a psychological report.

If the conclusions of the clinical psychologist are to be decisive, it is important that he subject his methods and approach to careful scrutiny. The implications of a diagnosis of mental deficiency are far reaching, and in cases where commitment is being considered the entire course of the person's life may be altered. Committing defectives to an institution is not always an unmixed blessing and it is

---

[1] Reprinted from *Journal of Abnormal and Social Psychology*, 1945, 40, 323–329. Copyright 1945 by American Psychological Association.

much less so when one is concerned with individuals whose capacities are of a nondefective nature. The individual of nondefective capacity who is functioning defectively may well remain a functioning defective as a result of commitment. It becomes the obligation of the clinical psychologist to use and interpret the techniques at his disposal in a way that gives as complete a picture of the individual as possible. At this stage of his field's development the clinical psychologist must use freely his critical powers if he is not to be lulled into easy acceptance of his tools as precise measuring instruments.

Several criteria have been formulated by means of which any clinical report can be judged. Several of these criteria have been set up by others many times before and may appear to be commonplace. They have been brought together to emphasize their importance in the diagnosis of mental deficiency, to investigate to what extent they are utilized in practice, and the consequences that result from their neglect. When one is trying to evaluate the functioning of an individual brought up in a more or less normal manner, the violation of these criteria is by no means as serious as when one is examining a child who, as is the usual case with subnormals, has been subject to a number of environmental pitfalls from early childhood. The criteria are:

1. A psychological examination should include several measures of intelligence of the individual type of test. The tests should be chosen so that an adequate picture of verbal, conceptual, visual-motor, and memory functioning can be obtained. The status of academic achievement should also be ascertained.

2. The personality organization should be carefully evaluated by means of projective techniques such as the Rorschach or Thematic Apperception Tests. The relation in each case between intelligence and personality should be sought. The importance of the Rorschach test as a clinical tool should be stressed since one can obtain from it a picture of intellectual functioning. In some cases the Rorschach findings are in closer agreement with the behavior of the individual than the standard test of intelligence.

3. Each test should be analyzed to see to what extent there is an internal consistency in the results and to determine, if possible, to which clinical picture the test pattern shows most resemblance. Since any given mental age may be compounded of numerous com-

binations of successes and failures of the items which comprise the test, an internal analysis is indicated. Two individuals with the same MA and CA may show very different internal test pictures.

4. Test results should be interpreted in the light of the outstanding features of the past or present environment which might have affected functioning and are reflected in the examination. One can safely assume that the behavior of the individual during test stems from the same personality roots as behavior before testing. Functioning during a test is not functioning in a vacuum and is part of a continuous behavioral sequence.

5. All the foregoing information should be brought together so that one gets a total picture in which all features of the examination are related.

In order to study to what extent these criteria were met in practice, the case histories of all high-grade boys in a cottage at the Southbury Training School were examined. Since these boys were admitted at different times from different places, and all the boys in the cottage were included, it can be assumed that no selection factor is present and that this group is representative of the school's high-grade (moron) population. Of the 36 boys in this group 28 had their commitment based upon one test (25 Binet and 3 Wechsler-Bellevue); eight were given more than one test, in three cases of which a paper-and-pencil test of personality was administered. In no case was a projective technique utilized. There was a psychological analysis of test results in less than 25 per cent of the cases. In most instances the MA and I.Q. were merely reported with a negligible accompanying psychological report.

It is clear that the criteria for evaluating a psychological report have not been adequately met. There can be little doubt that in many of these cases more intensive testing would not change the diagnosis of mental deficiency. However, in some instances, there would seem to be doubt about the diagnosis. It is in these doubtful and near-borderline cases that one must be careful not to accept numerical scores as a true indication of functioning, but rather to interpret them in the light of the individual's background.

The case to be discussed was chosen for presentation because a subsequent psychiatric appraisal was obtained which corroborated the main psychological findings. This case was a girl referred to the

Southbury Training School out-patient clinic. The complete report follows.

Psychological Report

Interview with Parents. Mary Smith was brought directly to the school by her father and step-mother without an intervening social agency. It was their impression that the child was not behaving normally and, after being told by a physician that there was nothing wrong with her physically, they took her to the School for an intelligence test which the physician suggested. The father, who is a farmer at present, gave the history, and his account was devoid of the concern end emotions usually displayed by parents who love their children. It also revealed ignorance about the child's activities and upbringing, which suggests that the child had been neglected by him. The step-mother was very cold and distant throughout, smiling cautiously only when the interviewer turned to her with a smile. She commented only when asked to do so by her husband, and usually these referrals were made by him at crucial points. In their relationship it appeared as if her opinion carried much weight and she was not likely to yield easily to her husband's wishes.

The father indicated that his first wife died when the child was three months old. The child was taken to the maternal grandparents in another town and lived there until a few days before Christmas of 1943. After the father mentioned the fact that the child was taken by the grandparents at three months, he went into great detail about his inability to care for a tiny baby and why it was natural for the maternal grandparents to take her. Mary came to live with her father and step-mother because within a few months before Christmas of 1943, her maternal grandmother, great aunt, and uncle died, thus depriving her of a home. He was vague about the child's relationship to the grandmother and her activities with other children. He admitted that he saw her infrequently because he worked constantly.

The father remarried five years ago. Mrs. Smith commented readily when the attitude of her husband's first wife's people toward him was discussed. She said that they felt that he was not doing enough for the child and that he did not see her as often as he should. She added angrily that whatever Mr. Smith did for the child was never considered by his first wife's people to be enough. She also corroborated her husband's statement that they could not break away from the farm to visit the child.

The child was described by the father laughingly as "very foolish and lacking in common sense." He said that she stands in front of the mirror and makes faces at herself and behaves like a two-year-old with strange people who come into the house. He could not substantiate her childishness very well, giggling being the only characteristic he would give. (This might well be due to the man's own difficulties with description.) He added that she does not know the first thing about arithmetic and is not capable of doing fourth-grade work. Mr. Smith was unable to inform the interviewer whether he noticed any peculiarities in Mary's behavior at her grandparent's home. He did say that he heard from his first wife's cousins that the grandmother forbade the child to engage in activities enjoyed by children because she felt that the child had a weak heart like her uncle. The father said that, according to his knowledge of the child's health, Mary had only an occasional cold. Mr. Smith said that he was informed that the grandmother used to admonish Mary not to do wrong or else her father would beat her. He feels that this explains the strange attitude of the child toward him when he used to visit. Mrs. Smith indicated that the child wets the bed at night unless she is tripped. She also said that Mary's memory is very poor as she cannot remember simple, household tasks which Mrs. Smith thinks every girl should know. Mrs. Smith added that the child could read and spell well.

Though rejection of his child, probably at the instigation of his wife or even on his own volition, was sensed at this point, it was not overtly expressed. It was overtly expressed when the examiner inquired about their plans should the child be found normal intellectually. Then Mr. Smith explained that he was in a predicament. He said that they had sold their farm, had to evacuate it by April 1, and were making plans to go to California to live. They did not want to take the child along because she would prove to be an added burden in their efforts to find work and a place to stay. Mrs. Smith's sinus trouble was given as a reason for leaving for California. Mr. Smith felt it would be shameful to deprive the girl of schooling during that period. When asked if he would take the child when he finally settled, he said that would depend on her condition at the time and whether his wife wants to have the girl. Then Mrs. Smith spoke up and said that the girl gets on her nerves and that she loses sleep when she trips Mary at night to prevent her from bed wetting. Mrs. Smith's attitude toward the child seemed more clearly defined when Mr. Smith was asked if he would bring the child back again should it be impossible to finish the examination at one sitting. He looked at Mrs. Smith who exclaimed that it would be difficult since movers were calling for a bedroom set which they had sold.

When the examiner's conclusion of "not feebleminded" was offered to the parents and the recommendation of psychiatric therapy suggested, the parents asked if she could be boarded out while the treatments were going on. Mr. Smith elaborated on his reasons for wanting to go to California. He claimed that he no longer wanted to be a farmer, that he wanted more relaxation, and he felt that the opportunities for doing carpentry work were greater in the West. When the possibilities of staying in Connecticut were discussed, Mr. Smith reiterated that the child makes his wife nervous. Mrs. Smith said that she has been under the doctor's care for "nerves" and the child aggravates her. In another breath she explained that she treats the child as she would her own and wants to do what is best for her. Although the parents agreed that the child needs parental security and affection, it is doubtful whether they will yield to the needs of the child and modify their plans.

General Observations. Mary, a cleanly dressed, immature-looking girl with sparkling, brown eyes and a broad, affectionate smile, was seen on three different days. The first day, when the Binet and Rorschach were presented, she seemed too preoccupied to concentrate, staring blankly and silently several moments after directions were given without any apparent effort to respond. This made testing difficult for it was frequently impossible to contact the girl. Even when contact was apparently good she responded impulsively and incorrectly with what seemed to be the first thought that came to her mind. When asked to reconsider her answers and pay closer attention to directions, surprising insight and judgment were revealed. It was necessary to prod her constantly and caution her frequently, since she feared to assert herself and needed reassurance, which was also inferred from her concern about the correctness of her answers. During this session she grinned and laughed inappropriately. She was in good contact, however, when questioned about her personal matters and was capable of carrying on an excellent conversation. Her verbal usage was good and she was able to carry an idea through without confusion. She spoke in a soft voice and her social manner, though childish, was charming and delightful.

During the second session Mary seemed more friendly and the social distance which existed the previous day did not seem present. She was very spontaneous, laughing and talking without any apparent restraint. After her initial resistance of withdrawn silent behavior was broken at the beginning of the period, she responded promptly without coaxing. She was thoroughly at ease and the appearance of her face seemed softer and glowing with happiness. At first it was felt that the informal character of the material presented had this effect since the test used was the Thematic, but the fact that her disposition was similar during the administration of the achievement tests speaks in favor of the interpretation that the child recognized that she was being accepted and reacted more securely. The spontaneity continued on the third day when the Arthur Point Scale was administered. During this test tendencies to be careless and to respond impulsively were also present but not to the extent observed on the Binet.

Careful examination of the child's behavior for three days revealed, on the one hand, withdrawn peculiar behavior evident in a strange situation; and, on the other hand, warm, affectionate, and spontaneous reactions when security was seemingly experienced. In both situations a good deal of silliness was apparent, consisting of odd grimaces and seemingly unprompted laughter. Her emotional reactions were quite childish. It is felt that this girl's behavior cannot be explained on the basis of her age alone, although her physical development does not seem in keeping with her chronological age.

Another outstanding characteristic which impressed the examiner was the girl's rather shallow, emotional reactions. Although she manifested at times different emotions in varying degrees, it seemed that none of her reactions had any genuine depth. In one instance when the conversation turned to the fact that three of her closest relatives, with whom she lived, had died within several months of each other, there did not seem to be the affective reaction one would have expected. On the contrary, she spoke of these events in a rather perfunctory manner. In general, this girl's manifestations of withdrawn behavior seemed to be in part compounded of apathy and phlegmaticness.

Tests. Tests and results are presented in Table 1.

TABLE 1

Tests	Results		
Terman-Merrill (L).............	MA—7–9	I.Q.—62	CA—12–6
Arthur Point Scale..............	MA—11–4	I.Q.—91	CA—12–6
Metropolitan Achievement—Inter-			
mediate Complete (A).........	Reading		Grade 5.5
	Vocabulary		Grade 4.9
	Arithmetic Fundamentals		Grade 4.7
	Arithmetic Problems		Grade 4.0
	English		Grade 7.5
	Literature		Grade 5.2
	History and Civics		Grade 4.2
	Spelling		Grade 7.6
Rorschach.....................	(See text)		
Thematic Apperception Test.....	(See text)		

Discussion of Test Results

Terman-Merrill (L). Mary earned an MA of 7 years and 9 months with an I.Q. of 62 which if strictly interpreted would place her within the mentally defective range. The scatter and the total test picture, however, do not warrant such a classification. As was described previously, the child seemed too preoccupied to concentrate. This was clearly visible on memory and reasoning items where poor attention and impulsiveness were apparent. The basal was lowered from VI to IV–6 years because of failure on memory for sentences at V. The memory pattern on succeeding items is variable. For example, memory for stories is failed at VIII and memory for sentences is failed at VIII and IX, but four and five digits are reversed correctly at IX and XII, while six digits are not repeated correctly at X. Difficulty in recall was striking at X, where Mary read a passage beautifully in good time, but could not give an adequate account of it from memory. That variability in memory was probably due to inadequate concentration was even more apparent at XIII, where Mary was able to remember the general pattern of a bead chain but carelessly substituted cylindrically shaped beads for square ones and vice versa. In her work on memory items which involve immediate recall, it is felt that her slow, phlegmatic attitude might also have interfered. On reasoning problems the girl responded impulsively and without deliberation. When directions were repeated and prodding ensued, surprising insight was revealed. Surprisingly poor judgment was revealed on relatively simple, social problems as on comprehension at VII and VIII, and on finding reasons at X. These failures are more or less inconsistent with her work on similar and more difficult, practical reasoning problems at XIII, where credit was received. It is noteworthy that on these reasoning problems Mary grasped the main ideas but elaborated each with difficulty, and showed more than ever before her hesitancy to respond and a tendency to interpret a request to qualify a statement as a sign that her responses were completely incorrect. Inconsistencies were also apparent on items which involved abstract thinking. For example, credit was received on similarities and differences at VIII but no credit was received at VII on determining the similarities of two things.

The degree of irregularity can be seen at a glance in the unusual scatter of successes. Mary bases at IV–6 after passing all at VI; then fails all at X, but achieves her highest success at XIII. In addition she was able to do the last part of the induction series at XIV, but did not receive credit because she was unable to give the principle involved in the solution. This total performance is very unusual and definitely uncharacteristic of a feebleminded child. The results obtained are more indicative of an unstable, disturbed child, and are at most a minimal representation of what she can do intellectually. The results of the achievement tests, obtained when the child was in better contact, corroborate this contention. If the mental level as obtained on the Binet is the true measure, the child would never have been able to do the work she did on the achievement tests.

Metropolitan Achievement—Intermediate Battery—Complete (A). According to this battery of tests Mary did best on English and spelling, reaching grade 7.5 on the former and 7.6 on the latter. Her lowest grades were 3.8 on geography, 4.0 on arithmetic problems, and 4.2 on history. Reading received a grade of 5.5 and vocabulary 4.9. Considering her low scores on history, geography, and arithmetic problems, difficulty in the sixth grade, her present placement, can be readily understood. Coaching in these subjects is indicated. It is noteworthy, however, that a feebleminded child of similar MA would not have achieved the level that Mary did.

Arthur Point Scale. On this performance test which was administered when Mary was friendlier, an MA of 11 years 4 months with an I.Q. of 91 was obtained. The carelessness evident here was slight by comparison with that seen on the Binet. Good motor coordination and average planning and organizing ability were observed. The tendencies to seek help and to blame the examiner when frustrations were encountered were apparent. Variability on the Porteus Mazes from trial to trial is an indication of the effects of instability.

Rorschach.[2] On the Rorschach record the manner in which the amorphous blots were shaped and organized indicates that the girl is not mentally deficient, but is at least of average intelligence. This estimate is approximate in that it was not always possible to obtain a fine description of how she saw things. The variability noticed within and among the other tests administered is also present in the sequences of responses of this record. On the one hand, there are childish and bizarre responses, and, on the other hand, there are very well-perceived ones. When asked to examine her concepts, however, she sometimes recognized the irrational elements and refused to accept them. In this frame of mind, the girl became confused and more insecure, and tended to adopt an overcritical attitude toward good concepts so that they too were no longer acceptable to her. There was an emphasis on movement responses without the rational control necessary for a healthy balance. This suggests an inability to handle social and emotional situations effectively. It would seem as if a good deal of her responsiveness has been turned inward and phantasy has been given full sway as a substitution. Mary is not completely withdrawn from reality but there is evidence to suggest that when she does respond to emotional situations, her reactions are tactless, uncontrolled, infantile outbursts. The variability evident

---

[2] The writers are indebted to Mrs. Ruth Wolfson for her help in the interpretation of the Rorschach.

within and between tests is understandable in light of the girl's disturbed personality makeup. It is safe to say that she has the intellect to do the work of her grade, but emotional difficulties are interfering. The saving graces in this girl's record are her ability to detect the irrational features in her concepts when her attention is called to them, and the capacity to think along the lines of other people.

Thematic Apperception Test. A surprising feature of this girl's stories was the strong aggression displayed by the characters with whom she had identified herself. In many of the stories people are being killed, murdered, or crippled. Mary's narratives contain many illogicalities and lack an inner consistency so that it is difficult at times to determine the object of the hostility and aggression. There are indications, however, that her father and step-mother are the ones against whom these feelings are pointed. In one story, for example, the central character is lying on the floor asleep while the "stepfather" points a gun in his direction. A fear of rejection is evident in the story where a married couple are looking for an intruder whom they think has entered their house; and in a story where the central character is "caged in" and occasionally given freedom of movement —the autobiographical elements in these stories being noteworthy. Revelation of past events and feelings emerges strongly in a story about a baby who is left by the mother when two weeks old, becomes sick, is sent to the hospital, and dies—causing the parents to be sad. That ambivalence toward the father exists in this girl becomes clear in the story where a girl dreams that her father is sleeping with her and when she awakes finds that he is in bed with her.

Most outstanding was the unusualness of her stories, and the contrast between the main body of a story and the ending—several of the endings not being in harmony with the mood of the story and generally introducing a strong note of hostility. It is important to note that there is a surprising discrepancy between the outward manner of this girl and her inner feelings and desires as revealed in the stories.

On the basis of the behavior of the girl and the test results obtained, it was felt that an independent, psychiatric appraisal be secured in order to determine the best disposition of the case. The psychiatrist's conclusions were:

Impression: This child does not give the impression of being feebleminded or moronic. I believe in time, when her neurosis has been worked out with her, that her true intellectual capacities can only then be tested. The child does not present a picture of psychosis. At present, there is no evidence of schizophrenia. There is no real peculiarity of affect, no real disassociation of thought. She makes a quick and good rapport, and is surprisingly well in touch with the reality of a very difficult life situation. In my opinion, this is a very sick child in terms of a severe emotional disturbance. She is suffering from a neurosis in which I imagine the conflict of her father may be the main theme. The child is and feels rejected. She copes with anxieties in a passive, conforming fashion.

Recommendations: The parents have already considered placement in a community center. This child is very much in need of intensive psychotherapy over a long period of time. Just now I think she is not a suitable candidate for foster home placement.[3]

In view of the psychological and psychiatric findings this girl was not admitted to the Southbury Training School. This case is instructive in that it demonstrates how fallacious a strict interpretation of an MA or an I.Q. would have been, and also emphasizes the necessity of evaluating personality organization by projective techniques. It is felt that the criteria presented for the evaluation of the clinical psychologist's report will, if followed, increase the value, depth, and accuracy of the psychological examination.

---

[3] The writers are indebted to Dr. Helen G. Richter, Psychiatric Consultant and Assistant Clinical Professor of Pediatrics at the Yale University School of Medicine, for her cooperation in this case and for permission to quote this section of her report.

EDGAR A. DOLL

The Training School at Vineland, New Jersey

The Social Basis of Mental Diagnosis[1]

The text for this homily is found in the following words: "It is only in the heart of society that man can attain the preeminent position which is his natural destiny." With these words Itard closes the opening sentence of his first report on the Wild Boy of Aveyron (127).[2] In this statement he epitomizes the social philosophy and guiding purpose of the clinical experiment from which we today trace so much of the modern movement for the care and treatment of the mentally handicapped.

The present paper is constructed on Itard's thesis with reference to the role of mental diagnosis in assisting man to attain his social destiny. For those who practise mental diagnosis are concerned to assist men as individuals to accomplish that type and degree of social adjustment which affords the most expressive fruition of their native endowments.

We may begin, then, with the premise that the immediate occasion for any mental diagnosis is always some social circumstance, and that the ultimate purpose of such a diagnosis is directed toward the solution of some individual social problem. This observation is so obvious as not to receive the attention which it merits as determining both the point of departure and the point of arrival in casework. Too frequently the clinical examination begins too far down the road from the original problem and stops too far short of its real solution.

---

[1] Read before the Section on Clinical Psychology of the International Council for Exceptional Children, Pittsburgh, February 23, 1940. Reprinted from *Journal of Applied Psychology*, 1940, 24, 160–169. Copyright 1939 by James P. Porter.

[2] Bibliography begins on page 428.

This is not to say that all mental casework is concerned with deficiency, defect, maladjustment, or individual failure in self-expression. Increasingly today the clinical psychologist is faced with the more positive problems of prophylaxis and guidance designed to foster normal aptitudes rather than to overcome deficiencies. On the negative side the clinician is concerned with disability and disorder of behavior as handicaps to be corrected or compensated. On the positive side we are concerned with the optimum exploitation of normal talent, normal conduct, and normal aptitudes. But in either case the basic origin as well as the ultimate goal of mental casework is one of social concern for individual welfare. We deal with man in relation to his environment. In the total disposition of a given case they are inseparable, however specifically we may analyze the component elements or their interaction.

As a second premise we may observe that mental diagnosis as generally practised today by clinical psychologists reveals an exaggerated reliance on mental tests. We may further note that this false confidence is aggravated by limited discretion in the selection of such tests as to scope and variety. Nor can one escape the conclusion that clinical-psychological mental diagnosis is too often unsound because of limited sophistication in the interpretation of such mental test data as are obtained. The tests employed are too frequently selected without specific regard to the original problem and purpose of the examination, and reveal a random or routine choice of tests for their own sake rather than for their peculiar fitness in the given situation. There is, in short, too little analysis of the clinical problem as a whole in terms of social origin and social outcome, with the result that the individual may undergo examination by devices which resemble the shotgun prescriptions of proprietary medicines.

If on the contrary the clinician begins with the fundamental social problem and proceeds from that base through the maze of secondary and more remote problems to the clinical analysis of the individual in relation to his developmental history, he will then be in a more sound position to determine the nature and course of the mental examination most likely to clarify those problems for purposes of treatment. To this end the clinician needs to employ some over-all appraisal of the individual which stresses no single aspect of his personality but rather assays the whole. From this point of vantage he may then proceed with a more detailed analysis of the relevant variables which compose the aggregate. And with such a method the clinician is able more successfully to evaluate the success of treatment.

As a third premise we may then state that mental diagnosis is well-advised when directed toward an evaluation of the individual as a whole in his social milieu. This bio-social emphasis now receives more attention in principle than in practise for the simple reason that no satisfactory over-all method of individual appraisal has been available. Consequently, in spite of the acknowledged precept, the clinician finds it impracticable to study the entire organism except by way of its parts. He therefore is compelled to dissect the individual for detailed analysis and then as best he can reassemble him by some new synthesis of elements.

It is this very dilemma which we sought in some measure to solve by constructing the Vineland Social Maturity Scale (68).[3] This scale is founded on the assumption that nothing that the individual is or does is significant except in terms of its ultimate social import. There are, to be sure, exceptions from this principle with reference to the inner soul or private life of the individual, but even these are sooner or later reflected in some social impact. This principle of social competence serves as a point of reference for evaluating all detailed aspects of individuality since each of these is ultimately capitalized for some social end. Thus the individual's appearance, his health, his racial or national derivation, his sensory acuity, intelligence, motor coordination, skills, attainments, personality, in short all his attributes, are ultimately significant in terms of their contribution to his personal-social welfare.

From this it follows that the clinician concerned with mental diagnosis must go beyond the mere mentality of the individual and include his total individuality. All these aspects of the unique personality are reflected in the total diagnosis as a clinical picture, syndrome or symptom-complex.

As a fourth premise, it is obvious that every individual grows in various respects as his age increases. This growth is initially determined from the potentials inherent in the fertilized cell, the final fruition of which is modified by environmental circumstances. As the organism grows in structure it develops in function. The indi-

---

[3] An annotated bibliography of investigations and experience with this scale has appeared (69).

vidual also matures in living as he grows in size and develops integrated organization. In this process of maturation the organism profits from environmental stimulation and opportunity through the spontaneous capitalization of experience as well as through formal instruction.

Social competence may therefore be considered in terms of its maturation at successive life ages or progressive developmental stages. An immediate problem is to determine the nature and course of this maturation, and in the specific case to measure it in terms of the over-all concept of individual adjustment. This social aspect of growth and development may be conceived in terms of individual responsibility (self-sufficiency) and group responsibility (social participation). That is, each person as he matures acquires increasing degrees of personal independence and exercises an increased sharing in the social order as a whole.

In constructing a scale for the measurement of social competence in terms of maturation we may employ two different approaches. The first consists of an inventory of those relatively universal forms of social expression which are characteristic of given age periods as successive stages of development. Or we may employ the alternative of analyzing social behavior into certain gross categories of behavior and delineate the evolution of successive degrees of aptitude within these categories. In constructing the Vineland scale both methods were used. It is further necessary to designate specific modes of behavioral expression and to define these in such a way as to afford distinctive stages of their progression.

In formulating these item performances it proved desirable to employ only those details of behavior which are relatively universal in a standard environment so that departures from the norm might be interpreted either in terms of individual aptitude or in terms of environmental opportunity and convention. To this end it was necessary to select items which are relatively free from the influence of intelligence as such, as well as of those other personal traits and environmental conditions which might affect a given item too heavily in the direction of specific variables of less universal distribution. The categories selected as reasonably representative of total behavior include such universal performances as self-help, locomotion, occupation, socialization, communication, and self-direction. All individuals mature in each of these respects in any environment. The specific mode and tempo of expression in these respects may be peculiar to a given environment, but are relatively universal within that environment with due regard for individual differences. Indeed the influence of the environment may itself be evaluated by observing those modifications of the scale which are necessary in alternative environments.

This scale has been released in experimental form for professional experimentation. It has not yet been published as an instrument for general use justified by ample details of standardization and validation. During the experimental period, however, many studies have been made with different types of individuals designed to explore the technical advantages and weaknesses of the method and to provide an ample experimental foundation for ultimate release of the scale as a practical instrument. In the meantime, many clinics and individual clinicians are finding the scale useful at the same time that they are evaluating its limitations. Much subsequent work will be necessary before the scale can be considered adequately standardized or reliably proved. Yet those employing the scale in its present form give many assurances regarding its scientific value and practical usefulness.

This scale affords an immediate means for determining the present, and under some circumstances even the past, social competence of the individual in terms of individual maturation. Its use is most apparent as affording an initial appraisal of the individual on the basis of his total traits and their capitalization in the environmental situation. Because of the composite capitalization of abilities reflected in the items of the scale the examiner is enabled to obtain a more comprehensive understanding of the person under examination than is otherwise practicable. Questions of health, special handicap, special aptitude, general ability, educational attainment, occupational proficiency, and the like, are broadly revealed in a manner which affords direct suggestions for specific clinical elaboration of detail. The scale also affords a means for subsequently interpreting these details in terms of a total criterion. It also affords a means of measuring the improvement of the individual as an outcome of treatment recommended as a result of the total mental diagnosis.

The argument may be made specific by an illustration. Consider the problem of mental deficiency, regarding which there is so much confusion today because of the ill-advised confidence in mental tests, or more specifically, in various I.Q.'s. Mental deficiency has traditionally been considered a social problem. If the feeble-minded were capable of managing their affairs with ordinary discretion, or if they were capable of sustaining themselves in society without the aid of others, our interest in this condition would be only academic. As a matter of fact, the problem of mental deficiency is one of vital social concern because of the social inadequacy of the feeble-minded. They come to our attention because of this inadequacy and our mental diagnoses are designed to indicate those modes of disposition which will best conserve the social interests of the individual, the family, and society. Feeble-mindedness is initially defined on the basis of the essential social incompetence of the individual so affected. This incompetence is variously expressed at different life ages in terms of behavior, adjustment, profit from instruction, occupational proficiency, and social-economic independence. These basic concepts of feeble-mindedness have not previously been very clearly defined nor adequately measured. This difficulty of clearly expressing the social incompetence of the feeble-minded in standard modes and degrees of behavior has led to a current disregard for the basic significance of social competence as the first consideration in the authoritative recognition of this condition.

Binet and others before and after him made clear that the social incompetence of the feeble-minded was a consequence of their mental incompetence, and the success of Binet's scale for measuring intelligence led to the gradual, and now almost total, relegation of the social criterion to the background of diagnosis. Binet and others demonstrated that the socially incompetent who are feeble-minded are also mentally incompetent. But neither Binet nor any one since has demonstrated that the mentally incompetent are inevitably socially incompetent, or that all of the socially incompetent are feeble-minded. In short, to avoid these logical errors of the obverse the concept of feeble-mindedness requires not one but three criteria, namely, social incompetence, mental incompetence, and arrested development. The socially incompetent who are not feeble-minded include many insane, epileptic, ne'er-do-wells, physically handicapped, and so on, among whom intelligence may or may not be subnormal, and among whom intelligence if subnormal may be due to deterioration or dysfunction, or to limited expression rather than to genuine developmental deficiency.

Hence it is not permissible to diagnose mental deficiency in terms of intellectual retardation alone. Before a person can be considered feeble-minded his low intelligence must be shown to have been arrested in development and it must also be shown that the low intelligence is accompanied by submarginal social competence. Every psychologist knows, or should know, that many of those with low I.Q. as measured by Stanford-Binet are not necessarily of correspondingly low degrees of intelligence as measured by other tests. Many of these individuals are above the limits of social competence which may properly be designated as feeble-mindedness or mental deficiency. Hence it becomes obvious that the determination of social competence is a *sine qua non* of the diagnosis of mental deficiency, and if this principle were accepted in practise it would go far toward obviating the confusion now prevailing in both the scientific and the public press that individuals may be altered from genius to deficiency or from deficiency to genius by environmental circumstances. The current turmoil on the relative influence of nature and nurture is much more clear when confined to mental test data than when expressed in designations which are clinically conceived as diagnostic symptom-complexes. This confusion can readily be clarified by employing a measurement criterion for the social factor in mental diagnosis just as it can be clarified by using batteries of mental tests as opposed to single scales.

The same issues are reflected only in different manner and degree as the illustrations are drawn from the fields of general and special talent, delinquency, behavior problems, special disabilities, or social adjustment and maladjustment of any type. We may safely stand by the position that no mental diagnosis is complete which does not begin with a sound estimate of social competence or which does not end with the prediction or confirmation of social competence following prognosis or treatment.

This argument applies with even greater force in the case of those exceptional children and adults who are affected by handicaps of vision, hearing, speech, or motor coordination, or in short any of the groups encompassed within the interests of the International Council for Exceptional Children.

In support of the observations that current mental diagnosis frequently employs an ill-advised selection of test procedures, places too much reliance on mental tests, and is inclined to unsophisticated interpretation of such data, we may now more logically reassert that every case study originates in some social situation. This is commonly referred to as the immediate problem or the "complaint." Sound casework requires that this immediate problem be formulated as explicitly as possible, and that it be verified in fact as may be practicable by objective procedures before proceeding with the clinical analysis of the problem. The delineation and verification of the initial problem requires a review of the individual's history in all aspects and this review is most serviceable when obtained prior to the use of test procedures. One of the most serious errors in current clinical-psychological practise is to proceed with test devices long before the immediate problem is specifically assured and before the antecedent history of the individual has been adequately explored. We may suggest with confidence from our own experience that the use of the Vineland Social Maturity Scale serves greatly to illuminate the immediate problem and sheds critical light on its antecedent origins as it also indicates the most profitable lines of clinical exploration for purposes of diagnosis and treatment. The only sound position that can be taken by any competent clinician is to hold fire on test procedures until these preconditions of a satisfactory mental diagnosis are well established. Only by this approach can the clinician decide which tests are relevant in a given case and how many or of what variety. Only under these circumstances can he economically and quickly determine the direction of test analysis. And only from this base can he properly interpret the data derived from applying clinical-psychological test procedures with assurance of a harmonious coordination of these data with the entire clinical picture. And we might add that only in this way can the psychological clinician also anticipate the desirability or necessity of referring a case for consultation with other specialists outside his own field.

We may conclude as we began with a reiteration of Itard's thesis, namely, that "It is only in the heart of society that man can attain the preeminent position which is his natural destiny." The role of the clinical psychologist in facilitating the attainment of that destiny consists in a harmonious evaluation of all the circumstances, both in the individual and in the environment, which are thereto related. This requires a final integration of mental diagnosis based on evaluation of the individual within his social circumstances. It requires a clear understanding of the immediate reasons for a given examination and its ultimate purpose. This point of view particularly demands a clear understanding of the social setting within which the problem has developed, that is, the immediate social circumstances which precipitate the examination. And it particularly involves clear concepts as to the social outcome of the mental diagnosis to be accomplished through treatment as indicated by the total clinical analysis.

RUTH M. HUBBARD

Family Service Society, Detroit, Michigan

What Constitutes a Psychological Examination?[1]

This paper is a development from some questions turned in at the Clinical Psychology booth at the National Conference in 1937 and from comments made in discussion at various sessions at that Conference. Though clinical psychological studies of individuals have much in common under whatever auspices they may be made, we will consider especially psychological examinations as a part of the work of a social agency.

Working in a social agency, the psychologist contributes her specific techniques for evaluating abilities and personality, and her habits of thought, as these were described at the Conference by Dr. Carl Rogers (217);[2] she borrows from the social worker certain techniques for interpreting test findings to a client in such a way that he can accept them emotionally and make use of them. These functions make up the psychological examination and are the material for this discussion.

I. What tests are given in social agencies? What are the specific techniques used by psychologists in agencies for evaluating abilities and personality traits? This Clinical Psychology Section has for several years asked various agencies; family and child-caring, institutions for the feeble-minded and insane, child guidance clinics, courts and others, to send for exhibition at the conference, sample copies of

---

[1] Presented at the National Conference of Social Work, 1938. Reprinted from *American Journal of Orthopsychiatry*, 1940, 10, 152–162. Copyright 1940 by American Orthopsychiatric Association.

[2] Bibliography begins on page 428.

psychological reports written by them for the use of social workers. From these reports we may gain an idea of the types of tests used in the agencies and the variety of tests given to any one client. All agencies used some scale, measuring general intelligence, for every client examined; either the Stanford Binet or a specialized scale for work with preschool children. Such a scale is given individually, requires an hour or more, hence is expensive in time but is a highly reliable indication of the client's general ability. From studying particular items passed or failed in the scale, one may also gain clues that suggest particular abilities or lines of difficulty.

Rarely, group (or pencil and paper) tests of intelligence were substituted for the Binet in testing adults. Since these may be given to several persons at a time, they require less time per client, but they also are somewhat less reliable than individual examinations.

There is much variation in individual abilities and some persons, because of language handicap and foreign background or because of factors within themselves, cannot function adequately in situations so largely verbal as these tests of general intelligence present. Hence most of the social agencies sending in reports, gave some performance tests, aimed at measuring the individual's adjustment to concrete situations. An immense variety were used, depending upon the client being studied, the functions of the agency, and its resources for specialized psychological study.

For children being studied by social agencies it seemed important to learn their educational level. Tests of school subjects are differentiated from tests of general intelligence by the fact that they test knowledge, not ability; they cover material specifically taught in school. Scales covering the whole range of school subjects were used; intensive diagnostic studies of particular subjects were also used, e.g., in the case of a child who had difficulty in reading, tests for the specific functions involved in reading would be given, tests for mirror-image reversals, auditory perception, discrimination and memory, visual perception, discrimination and memory, blending and sounding of individual letters. Special functions connected with reading, eyedness, binocular fusion and muscle balance were tested. Tests for other school subjects were usually less varied and less intensive but included some diagnostic effort to learn, if possible, the mental hurdles the child was facing in acquiring academic knowledge.

One very important purpose in testing either adolescents or adults in social agencies is to learn their vocational possibilities so they may be placed at suitable work. A variety of tests for mechanical ability were given, tests for clerical and selling abilities, and for artistic ability. The selection of vocational tests depended on the general intelligence of the client, his occupational aspirations and the evaluation of his probable capacities by the psychologist. Realizing the importance of interests as well as abilities in placing people occupationally, these agencies used a variety of interest questionnaires suited to the different ages of clients.

Personality tests were used less often than general intelligence, achievement or vocational tests and almost exclusively with adults. In this realm an exceedingly important addition to test results were descriptions of clients' personalities as they appeared during the testing period. The test ratings are objective estimates of abilities or aptitudes based on performance in certain standardized situations. Personality reactions occurring in those same standardized situations have a validity from which probable response in life situations may be predicted; for example, the individual who constantly requests assistance during the tests is probably dependent and uncritical in life situations; the person who resents assistance when it is necessary or who thinks the examiner is trying to put something over on him, is likely also to be resentful and suspicious in real life. The psychologist's observation of these traits during the testing is of help to the case worker, especially if the test is being given rather early in the agency's contact with the client, as a method of evaluating the client's possibilities both for himself and for the case worker. If the client has been known to the agency for some time, personality observations from the standardized test situation are still valuable for the distinctive point of view they offer, for the clearness with which personality traits stand out during the test in contrast with the worker's feeling that in life situations there are always extenuating or confusing factors.

These reports did not mention a further diagnostic service which the psychologist is equipped to provide; that of showing change in mental status from time to time. For the normal person, one estimation of intelligence by means of an individual test represents adequately his present ability, predicts with fair accuracy his future mental level and indicates fairly well his ability in the past. The rate of mental growth of a normal person is fairly predictable. Under some circumstances and for some people, however, repeated examinations are wisely used in order to point out losses in particular capacities or in general efficiency which may appear as concomitants of head injuries or operations, infections of the central nervous system, or functional mental illnesses. A short scale has also been devised by Babcock for determining present mental efficiency or deterioration in relation to the client's previous level of mental ability. This may be used in the many situations arising in social agencies where repeated examinations over a period of years cannot be obtained. Repeated examinations may also be of value in determining for children the benefit or hindrance to mental growth provided by certain environments.

In the four years during which reports were sent for exhibition at the Conference, 96 agencies in the United States sent reports. These agencies reported giving at least 1221 tests to 395 persons, or an average of 3 tests per person. This means that each client tested took at least an hour of the psychologists' time, most of them took two to three hours, and a few who were given exhaustive educational tests or diagnosis of reading disabilities, took from seven to ten hours for the testing alone. The amount of time given to testing and the variety of tests actually used, shows in a rough way how important psychological testing may be in the total functions of an agency and the variety of lines from which understanding of a client may be gained. A client is tested not merely in general intelligence but in several other special capacities, the selection of capacities depending upon the client's age and plans and upon his purposes in having a test.

II. In speaking of the function of the psychologist in a social agency, the administering of tests is the most tangible, most easily described and most easily taught part of the work. However, more important than the mere giving of the tests, is their interpretation to the worker and their integration with the case work program for the client; even more important still is the relationship developed between examiner and client during the test, the evaluation of himself which the client takes with him from the tests, and the effect this whole experience has on his attitudes and behavior afterwards. The writer (122) has previously discussed the interpretation of psychological results for social workers. It is, therefore, the relationship between examiner and client, such intangible and yet exceedingly important aspects of the psychological testing situation, which we shall now consider.

Case work has become very self-conscious about its relationship aspects. Clinical psychology has been less so, but relationships are no less important parts of the testing situation than of the case work situation. As clinical psychologists we have been taught that to get the best possible work from a client we must put him at ease, have good rapport. We have learned from case workers certain definite techniques for gaining a rapport more subtle than that obtained by conversation about sports, reading, etc., a rapport dependent not upon words but upon emotional attitudes. What specific techniques do we use?

A large part of the client's acceptance of the test situation rests in the explanation given to him and the manner of the giving. A preschool child is always eager to "play games," if the emphasis is on the games, not on the examiner or the strange surroundings. A school child almost inevitably likens the test to school; if he likes school, this makes cooperation for testing easy; if he dislikes school the explanation may be given that certain things are hard for him in school and we want to find out why so we'll be able to help him get them; though he dislikes school and teachers and may even say they are "picking" on him, still he is almost sure to have under this projection the real wonder as to why he cannot do as well as others. This explanation then reaches his real feeling about school rather than his expressed feeling. For older children and adults the making or re-making of vocational plans are real reasons for testing. Probably no test should ever be given unless the client (or his parent if the client is a child) has requested it; this means a consideration of the client's real wishes and following them rather than following some case work goal the agency may have in mind. Frequently the worker enlarges very small openings given by the client in order to lead him to an interest in having a test. The crux of getting a psychological test successfully accepted by a client is the worker's sincere feeling that the test will offer the client something, that it will be an aid to therapy, that, like a medical examination, it is of direct benefit to him.

When the child or adult arrives for the test any conversation beyond the amenities necessary in greeting and removing wraps is a distraction, all the more so if the client is in any degree apprehensive. He has come for a definite purpose and a business-like beginning of the matter in hand is an aid to his feeling of ease. Conversation about school and occupational history is a natural introduction the appropriateness of which is readily apparent to the client. It has the additional value of being familiar ground and, to the client, appears as factual rather than emotional material. This suggests one contrast between the interview of a psychologist and that of the case worker. An objective atmosphere is more easily maintained by the psychologist because the interest of both examiner and client is centered on certain concrete data, namely, tests, and because a certain tangible progression in the material is evident. In the case worker's interview, interest must, as a rule, center on the two persons involved and progression may be very difficult to see except over long periods of time. The psychologist has a certain security within her test materials, specified questions to ask, specified ways of proceeding. Beyond these specific procedures she uses interviewing techniques that will center interest on facts which, though they are objective to the client, still by their description portray attitudes to the psychologist. The school and occupational information elicited at the beginning of the interview is of this sort. The psychologist asks, "In what grade are you?" and the child answers "Well, I'm in 6th but I should be in 7th. I stayed back last year but it was because I was sick with a broken leg." Another child may answer "I'm in 6th; my sister is in 5th, but I'll get to Junior High before she does." Or the psychologist asks, "What kinds of work have you done?" and the 23 year old client proudly lists a dozen kinds of work since he left high school, each of which he has done for a short time only. Another client might answer, "I haven't really worked at all. I want an office position but wherever I've tried to work the girls were so gossipy and chewed gum and didn't tend to business so I wouldn't work in such a place." Answers like these appear spontaneously in response to ostensibly factual questions and point the way toward valid personal and vocational counselling.

As the test begins the examiner maintains a cooperative relationship with the client by constantly meeting unconscious as well as conscious attitudes. She may explain as a preliminary that the tests are of all sorts, some easy and some difficult, that no one ever does all of them, that we are interested in finding out what things he

himself does best. The mere fact that an adult is giving a child undivided and interested attention for two hours serves to raise that
child's estimate of himself. That attention need not always be
approval; comment about errors may be made where it is called for
in test administration. Occasionally also, an over-confident child
does not criticize his own work, or a spoiled child seems to think
that anything he has done is good just because he did it; the examiner then needs to call attention to some small slip, or remark
that she is sure he can do better so that in later tests he will be more
careful. The show-off is frequently showing off because he is unsure
of himself; here critical friendly attention serves to bring out his
best work. A shy child may need more overt approval to bring his
confidence to the point where he can answer questions readily.

The experienced examiner rarely encounters actual refusals in preschool children because she centers attention on the test activities
rather than on herself or the child. She allows the child to choose
activities, accepts his way of doing tests so far as is consonant with
standard test conditions, and where negativism is encountered does
not force the issue but seems to accept his objection, returning to
the refused test at a later time. Negativism in older children or even
adults is rarely a specific rejection of examiner or test but is rather
a reaction to some other situation or person with which the child is
identifying them. The examiner may begin with performance tests
or some non-scored items to allow the child time to accept her and
the situation, at the same time that her own attitude of acceptance
of him and his surliness helps to dissociate this occasion from his
earlier unhappy experience. For the purpose and duration of the test
we try to prevent a flare-up of hostility by saying "That's a hard one"
when the child fails, or by other expressions of what we may think he
is feeling. These remarks not only make him feel his effort is appreciated but dissipates hostility by taking the responsibility for
stating it ourselves. One exceptionally bright adolescent expressed
her hostility in facetious fashion, "Who invented this game?" The
examiner knowing she did not really want to know the name of the
man who originated the tests answered casually "Oh, a lot of psychologists; they spend their time inventing things like this." The
girl remarked emphatically, "Well, it's a waste of time," perhaps
expressing her feeling about the value of the tests for herself. The
examiner accepts some domination from clients who show a need to

control the situation. She accepts new information, criticism of the tests, quibbling over the meaning of words. Her acceptance and continued friendly interest throughout show-off, dominating, surly, hyperactive and other kinds of behavior, constitute a kind of protected situation in which the client quickly finds he is free to express himself. As a result he feels less need to express the undesirable traits and can more freely give all his energies to the tests. This adjustment to the individual which is made by the psychologist is not at all a matter of altering test instructions or standards to suit a particular person; the child has, usually before reaching the test room, accepted the idea that certain rules will be in operation, just as there are rules to every game. The freedom consists in the examiner's complete acceptance of the standards and rules and abiding by them strictly at the same time that she accepts his efforts (possibly ineffectual) to meet the standards, and the legitimacy of his wish to evade the rules.

It is probably possible to administer tests without being aware of the unconscious meanings of the client's behavior, but it is a question whether we obtain his best performance when we are not alert to these attitudes and dealing with them as they appear. Every tone of the examiner carries her attitudes of objectivity and acceptance to the client regardless of her words, and a very short inventory of school or work history before beginning the test is entirely sufficient for setting this attitudinal stage so that he will feel a security with the examiner and even with the test situation itself. Security may show itself in his willingness to admit he does not know, his freedom in comparing test items and, more important still, it may appear in his ability to evaluate himself and to state that evaluation in terms of plans for the future.

III. The client who comes for psychological testing usually comes because he has reached a point where he is willing to take inventory, to evaluate his abilities in relation to those of other people, to the educational or occupational world and in relation to the particular goals he has set for himself. This gives the psychological interview a strategic position so far as the client's facing of reality is concerned. The test results may be discussed with him later by the worker but his evaluation is clearer, based on more exact instances and more inescapable if it can develop directly out of this relationship with the psychologist and be a part of the interview with him. Also, if results can be discussed with him directly he is more apt to believe the test was given for his benefit rather than for the agency's or the worker's, he is more ready to accept professional recommendations and to take responsibility for decisions based upon the findings (changes of school curriculum, choice of less difficult work).

An important part of the discussion of test results with the client is pointing out his strengths and balancing them against his weaknesses or disabilities, of which he may be only too well aware. If these come to him later through a third person he is apt to have difficulty facing them and, like an adolescent boy we once tested, demand another appointment with the examiner in order to thrash out the matter.

In contrast to the field of medicine we have found that, in the field of personality, specific recommendations frequently cannot be accepted. In spite of this fact, it is sometimes wise for a psychologist, because of her position as an expert, to make rather definite suggestions. The skill in such a situation is represented not so much by knowledge as to what should be done as by a presentation to the client in such a way that he can accept and carry out. For example, the psychologist may wish to recommend that an enuretic boy should make a chart of his dry nights; this suggestion has greater validity if made to the boy himself with its implication that he is a self-governing person and that he can have dry nights, that his wish to be independent of his mother is justifiable and accepted. The psychologist may feel that a girl should stop school and hunt work but the girl can carry out such a recommendation only when her worry that she might be unable to finish school has entered at least tacitly into the situation. The examiner may suggest placement of a child at the institution for the feeble-minded but the parents can carry out the suggestion only if it is given after the reasonableness of their ambivalence has been recognized. When parents come to discuss with the psychologist the ratings of a child, they frequently need to express both their disappointment and their pride in the child before any recommendations are given them. Probably the best situation is where no recommendations are made by the psychologist, a deliberate policy with validity in terms of relationship; she would merely give test results (not in terms of I.Q. but in general classifications) and educational ratings, leaving the parent to state the recommendations himself. They are then a part of his own thinking, not something pressed upon him by another; also this insures the using of only such test findings as are comprehensible to him and does not require the acceptance of all the implications immediately. It sometimes happens that the parent is still unready for any professional recommendations and must be left to grow toward these with the social worker's help.

The giving of vocational advice is another situation in which many factors other than test results need to be considered. We base a vocational prognosis on information about the client's age, appearance, physical condition, cultural background, educational level, his tested abilities, intelligence, motor skills and other vocational aptitudes, his interests as stated spontaneously or as recorded on blanks, personality traits observed or possibly tested, and upon his emotional stability and maturity as observed during the time the agency has known him and during the test. This last category (emotional stability and maturity) is probably the least objective but of the greatest single importance of all. Upon the client's emotional maturity depends his ability to accept and integrate all the other data. Some who come for vocational advice need merely intellectual help; need to be told what occupations are available, what abilities and traits are necessary for reasonable success in them (so far as we know them) and in what way their abilities and traits fit into this scheme. With such people test material can be discussed very freely and the individual is mature enough to accept and follow the indications. In the case loads of social agencies, however, these people are very rare. Most of them find suitable occupations without psychological advice; they use employment agencies and industrial personnel offices.

The majority of persons known to case working agencies are there because of some emotional need which shows itself in the variety of symptoms known to case workers, and also in an inability to adjust occupationally. For these people vocational advice, given directly and intellectually, is of no help whatever and may be a hindrance. They may follow it and follow it so literally or in such a way as to prove the advice false; or they may go exactly opposite to the advice. To consider a few individuals in this group, there is the man who has no preference whatever. Do we dare give him one—any more than we make any other choice for such people? Sometimes the occupational world and its demands temporarily decide for him but a permanent and satisfactory choice must arise from his own development. The man with a very definite preference of his own will go his own way regardless of our advice, and perhaps learn limitations by trying himself out. Some persons' apparent preferences are determined by their family. The way seems marked out for these people but we must be especially careful about giving them advice because no one, least of all themselves, may know what they really want. As an example of this there was the 16 year old son of a milkman; his father was extremely clean about himself and about the housekeeping, and the older brother who brought John for his test was a student in college, an exceedingly dapper student, slick haired and well-groomed. John himself was excessively untidy, even odorous. The report from home was that when his dirtiness would reach a point the family could not tolerate they would force him upstairs to put on a clean shirt, only to find later that he had put the clean shirt over the clothes he was already wearing. He was of high average intelligence. His suggestion for future jobs for himself was "a job that keeps your muscles alive." He would not want something that uses brains. He had thought of coal shoveling; rejected our suggestion of road building. As preparation for coal shoveling, he felt his college preparatory course in high school with a specialty in languages was the best selection he could make. His behavior and choices seemed to be as definite a contrast as he could achieve with that of his older brother, the good, responsible, clean son. This boy was on the verge of psychosis but the situation dramatizes the need to learn a boy's own choices as distinct from his resistance to or acceptance of family standards and aspirations. Another individual is the girl with a perfectionist drive; no matter whether she is reasonably successful or not, any job is unsatisfactory to her either because she thinks she does not do it perfectly or because it does not offer her complete satisfaction. In the same way any friend, any dress, any husband is unsatisfactory to her; the perfectionist vocational drive is a concomitant of her total personality, that is, not isolated as a specific vocational problem.

What can we do for these people by way of vocational advice? We can discuss with them their abilities, with examples from the test situations to make clear what we mean. We can discuss the general fields of activity these abilities suggest, and the worker can arrange for the client to try out particular jobs he chooses, so far as resources of the community permit. However, he must make his own choice, must achieve his own occupational adjustment just as he achieves any other kind of emotional growth.

Since the test is a time for evaluation of abilities it is very apt to become also a time for evaluation of personality traits. This is especially true when personality tests have been given but may occur anyway as a concomitant of educational or vocational planning with the client. The client may mention personality traits or fears that he feels stand in the way of his success at some occupation suggested by the tests; or in reporting test results the examiner points out methods of working which may lower a prognosis made on the basis of test scores alone. This opens the way for a personality or emotional evaluation, fitting into the general purpose for which the test was being given.

The psychological interview may have a further evaluative function, this time in relation to the worker, which is well illustrated by a case from our experience. A girl of about 20, who strongly desired the material things of life, had taken a short-cut method of attaining them, writing begging letters to wealthy persons and appealing to their sympathies. She had been moderately successful. The social worker to whom she was sent after one of these letters helped her to progress, small step by small step, toward procuring economic success for herself; the worker supervised her shorthand practice, arranged an opportunity for her to practice typing speed, obtained an opening for her to do office work without pay to gain experience in the demands an office makes and was on the point of finding her a real job when the psychological test was given. Incidentally the test had been delayed because at the beginning the girl would have seen no need for it and would have been greatly threatened by it. These other steps had been partial attempts to evaluate the girl's efficiency in lieu of tests. During the psychological interview she expressed the feeling that one cannot obtain one's goal in a hurry, that she used to be impatient to get somewhere, but that she now realized one goes farther by taking it one step at a time. This attitude had never been discussed with her by the social worker but here appeared an excellent verbalization of the actual experiences she and the worker had shared. It is in this way that the psychological interview may give opportunity for the client to clarify his progress and, by so doing, indicate how much growth has taken place.

IV. The case worker has one main function in her contacts with people, that of therapy; all the varieties of work she does are subsidiary to the main purpose of helping people grow to a point where they can solve their own problems. Her contacts hold the expectation that they shall need to be continued for a period of time in order for that growth to take place. The psychologist has a double function, that of diagnosing, securing from a client his very best work in order to measure adequately his abilities; and secondarily the function of therapy, helping the client to accept the implications of the specific test findings. Her contacts, because of the diagnostic function and the specificity of the direction of treatment are ordinarily limited in time. They have many characteristics of the "short-contact" therapy, the occasion for which, is the client's having reached a crisis and being in need of re-evaluation and re-orientation. The progressive effects of the re-orientation are ordinarily not apparent in the psychologist's short contact.

The training of psychologists has included methods of putting the client at ease; we have felt successful when a previously apprehensive client returned to her worker and reported that the test was "not bad at all, it was like talking to an old friend." This feeling of comfort has been one of the desiderata for successful diagnosis. In order to obtain the client's best work we have surrounded him as it were with an envelope of cottonwool, warming him with approval and protecting him for the duration of the test, from comparisons with the outer world, from the bitterness of his memories of failure, and from any apprehension over a readjustment to life which may soon need to be faced. When, however, we consider the second, more therapeutic, function of the testing we realize that in order for the evaluative experience to become integrated with the rest of the client's life we must open the envelope and admit reality and its demands into our interview. We may open the envelope bit by bit, or in certain areas only, but outside comparisons must eventually enter into our relationship if the experience is to have meaning for his development. The client's limitations are discussed with him frankly but with assets counter-balancing them and pointing out what may be done about the situation. It is as if he receives a complete report of medical findings from the physician; such a report is "hard to take" but is acceptable because it gives him data with which to work and is accompanied by suggestions of steps to take toward improvement. The client takes comfort in its scientific validity and often, too, in the fact that it is not so bad as he had feared. A frank report of the findings from the psychologist is a surer foundation for the continuing therapy of the case worker than an entirely protected testing situation could be. Thus the therapeutic function of the psychologist is not contrary to, but develops directly out of the diagnostic function which has always been her primary concern. Treatment is somewhat foreshortened in time because the client usually comes at a time of crisis and is emotionally ready for re-evaluation.

The psychologist deals with attitudes as they are expressed within the testing situation, usually without a conscious concern for their effect on *later* adjustment. However, her acceptance of the client and his statements about himself, together with the evaluation to which test results give rise, seems to have a therapeutic value that carries beyond the interview itself. An adolescent came in for vocational testing because she could not hold a job, was resentful of the world, refused criticism and tried to boss fellow-workers. The testing interviews included a discussion of her high average intelligence and vocational possibilities, but no promise of definite help and no referral to a specific job. As she left the second interview she remarked, "The world's a hard, practical place—but kind when you begin to get used to it." This statement of a changed attitude was not due entirely to the interviews with the psychologist but appeared as a crystallization from the one or two interviews she had had with the worker as well as from the testing. Her situation had become no less intolerable but she had become better able to meet that situation. This is an example of a therapeutic function arising from the psychologist's diagnostic function. When the psychological interview looks toward the future, with a discussion of the client's plans and desires, not only is our evaluation of the client more complete, but a therapeutic effect on later behavior may be seen.

V. To summarize: the clinical psychologist's service to the client of a social agency is usually of short duration in point of time as compared with the prolonged treatment given by social worker and the possibility of prolonged treatment by psychiatrist. It is primarily diagnostic in function, including the administration of a wide variety of standardized reliable tests in such a way as to obtain the client's optimum performance. It involves discussing with the client his abilities, vocational assets and liabilities, personality traits, and habits of work in such a way that he can evaluate and accept these realities. As a by-product of these functions a change in attitude toward co-workers, teachers, siblings or the world in general, may appear. These services of the psychologist are an integral part of the case work service offered the client and have their greatest strength in the continuity of follow-up service which case workers are equipped to provide.

These things, then, constitute a psychological examination.

PHYLLIS BLANCHARD

Philadelphia Child Guidance Clinic

The Interpretation of Psychological Tests in Clinical Work with Children[1]

The extensive use of intelligence tests has been a rapid development within a comparatively short period of time. Binet's tests were not described in the psychological literature until 1905, and were not organized into the form of a scale until 1908, although Binet and Simon had been working upon the project for some years before that. Goddard observed the Binet tests in actual use when he went to Europe in 1908. In December of that year he introduced them into this country by publishing a translation and a brief description of them. In 1911 Binet's revised version of his scale appeared, and in 1916 a translation of this work was published (21).[2] Meanwhile, Terman revised and enlarged the 1911 Binet scale, standardized this revision on the basis of the results from testing 905 American children under fourteen years of age and a smaller group of adolescents and adults, and published an account of this work in 1916 (261). Kuhlmann made another revision and extension of the original Binet, which was published in 1922 (145). The Kuhlmann-Binet was the first scale to provide a series of tests for infants;[3] it included tests for three, six, twelve, and eighteen

---

[1] Read, in part, at a meeting of the Philadelphia Pediatric Society, May 9, 1939. Reprinted from *Mental Hygiene*, 1941, 25, 58–75. Copyright 1941 by The National Committee for Mental Hygiene.

[2] Bibliography begins on page 428.

[3] Gesell's *Mental Growth of the Pre-school Child* (96) was published in 1925, and Stutsman's *Performance Tests for Children of Pre-school Age* (255) in 1926.

months and for two years, while Terman's earlier revision began with the three-year level. But for school-age children, Terman's revision, known as the Stanford-Binet, was probably the most widely used in clinical practice from the time of its appearance in 1916 until 1937, when Terman and Merrill published a new revision of the Stanford-Binet, which was better standardized than the old Stanford-Binet and also had a wider age range of tests.

The new Stanford-Binet starts at the two-year level and provides tests at half-year intervals for the ages from two to five years; the old scale had tests only at yearly intervals for the ages three to five. Furthermore, the new revision provides tests for eleven, twelve, thirteen, and fourteen years, while the old scale offered no eleven- or thirteen-year tests, having two-year intervals between the ages ten to fourteen. The new Stanford-Binet also has a larger number of tests at what are called the average and superior adult levels (above fourteen years) than the old one.

A corrected table for the calculation of intelligence quotients (I.Q.'s) for children over thirteen years of age is furnished for use with this new Stanford-Binet scale. The old method of calculating the I.Q.—by dividing the mental age obtained on the test by the exact chronological age up to sixteen years and thereafter using sixteen years as divisor—had been called into question, some psychologists claiming that fourteen or fifteen years, rather than sixteen, should be the point at which the exact age should no longer be used as divisor. As a result of these differences of opinion as to the best method of calculating the I.Q., some variations of method arose in clinical practice with the old Stanford-Binet, when I.Q.'s were computed for children over fourteen years of age. The corrected I.Q. table for the new revised Stanford-Binet presumably meets this situation by providing a more acceptable method for calculating the I.Q. for older children.[4]

As might be expected with so many changes in the scale and with some change in the method of calculating I.Q.'s, the results of testing with the revised Stanford-Binet tend to differ somewhat from those obtained with the old Stanford-Binet. Hildreth, for instance, comparing the results obtained with the old and the new

---

[4] For a more detailed description of the new revised Stanford-Binet, with directions for giving and scoring the tests, I.Q. tables, and so forth, see Measuring Intelligence, by L. M. Terman and M. A. Merrill (262).

scale in a group of Lincoln School children whose central tendency was toward an I.Q. of 120, states that a greater increase in I.Q. was found when children were retested by the new Stanford-Binet than when they were retested by the old Stanford-Binet. Hildreth also notes that with the new revision there was a tendency toward a larger increment in score between the age levels of ten and sixteen than with the old revision (117). However, there are correlations from .64 to .80 between retests with the old and the new Stanford-Binets, according to Merrill's report on test-retest data with the two scales in a group of 1,517 elementary-school children (181).

Not long after Terman's original revision of the Binet scale was made available for individual testing, the group tests began to appear. During 1917 and 1918, the army Alpha and Beta group tests were devised by psychologists working with army personnel problems (305). It was not long before other group tests were devised for use in educational guidance work with children. These group tests for children now include intelligence tests, tests for educational achievement, tests for the diagnosis of reading disabilities, tests for the measurement of aptitude for mechanical work, tests for the measurement of artistic talent, and so on.

The group tests have the obvious advantage that a large number of children can be tested in less time than if the tests were given separately to each child, but there is the disadvantage that personal observations, which are a valuable contribution when testing is done individually, cannot be secured when tests are given to children in a group. Therefore even those tests that were devised for group testing are more satisfactory when applied in an individual testing situation, where the responses of the child may be observed and the test results interpreted in the light of the observations. The following illustration from clinical case material indicates how individual observations may provide information that cannot be obtained in the group testing situation.

A twelve-year-old girl was having trouble with school work, especially with arithmetic. She had done very poorly on the group achievement tests in arithmetic at school and was failing her daily work in that subject. There was a question as to whether she might be mentally deficient and should be transferred to a special class, or whether she was normally intelligent, but had a special disability in arithmetic and needed tutoring in that subject.

When she was given form L of the revised Stanford-Binet, she made an I.Q. of 92, which indicated that she was but little below the average intellectually. The achievement test in arithmetic that was used at the clinic was similar to the achievement test that she had previously had with the rest of the pupils in her school class. Her score on this test was very poor and she did most of the examples incorrectly, just as on the test given at school. But at the clinic, where she was taking this test alone instead of with a group of children, it was possible to observe her method of working on arithmetic problems. It then became evident that her method of doing arithmetic could never, except by chance, enable her to obtain any correct solutions, for she invariably began to add, subtract, or multiply starting with the left-hand column of figures and working from left to right, instead of starting with the right-hand column and working toward the left.

Thus the tests could be interpreted on the basis both of the numerical scores and of these observations. We could say that this girl needed special teaching in arithmetic rather than placement in a special class for mentally deficient children and, since our observations revealed the chief source of her difficulty with arithmetic, we could pass on this information to the teacher who was to tutor her. The girl's erroneous method of working on arithmetic could not be observed in the group-testing situation, nor would it have been easy for a teacher to detect it in her daily work. In looking over the girl's tests or her daily papers in arithmetic, all that would appear would be that her solutions to problems were almost always incorrect, but the method of work that made them so would not be evident.

It is necessary to interpret psychological tests not only on the basis of the numerical scores, but also in the light of our understanding of the child from information that may have been supplied by parents and others and from his own reactions and conversation during the testing interview. In group testing, this personal material cannot well be secured, for in that situation there is no opportunity to observe the responses of an individual child or to enter into personal conversation.

The group tests have a real usefulness in a school testing program because they are a time-saving device. The ideal program for the psychological testing of school children, however, would provide adequate facilities for supplementing the group tests with individual testing and case studies of pupils who rate low on the group tests or who are having serious trouble with some particular school subject.

In the early days of psychological testing, it was believed that the I.Q. obtained from a single test furnished not only a diagnostic picture, but also a prognosis of the child's capacity for mental development. Studies of groups of children who were tested and retested did not confirm the assumption that the I.Q. obtained from the first tests would almost invariably remain constant and stable through the later years of the child's life. Florence Goodenough has summarized data on the constancy of the I.Q. from a number of the studies published prior to 1933 (99). Most of the studies of school children who were retested after a lapse of time indicate that in about half of the cases the I.Q. on successive tests will not vary by more than five points; but in the remaining half of the cases the variation will be greater than five points, and in approximately 4 per cent there will be a change of 20 or more points in I.Q. on a second test as compared to the first test. The change in I.Q. may be in either direction, higher or lower. The figures just quoted are for data obtained when the old Stanford-Binet was used both for the first tests and for retesting. In studies reporting similar data when group tests were used, the constancy of the I.Q. was even less and a greater variation appeared between I.Q.'s on first and second testings.

Research data indicate that the I.Q. tends to be less constant if the children were first tested under the age of six years than if they were over six years old when first tested. In one group of more than 400 children, only 4.3 per cent of those first tested when more than six years of age varied by more than 20 points in I.Q. on the second test as compared with the first test, while of those first tested under six years of age, 19 per cent varied by 20 or more points in I.Q. upon a second testing (115).

Another study indicates even less constancy and stability of test ratings for very young children. Dr. Hallowell tested 436 children between the ages of three months and four years, then retested the same children from one to two years later. Although the test ratings remained constant for about half of the children, there was greater variation between the two tests for those children who had first been tested under two years of age than for those first tested between the ages of two and four. Of the entire group of 436 children, 30 per cent did better on the second test while only 17 per cent rated lower on the second test. This finding seems particularly significant, since it suggests that the test results with very young children are more likely to underrate than to overrate their intellectual capacities (106).

That the greatest inconstancy of test ratings appears in the testing of pre-school children is quite understandable, for it is often very difficult to secure as good coöperation on tests from very young children as can ordinarily be expected from children of school age. Young children are very apt to be either timid and shy or exceedingly negativistic. The negativistic reactions of young children are especially likely to invalidate test results. In one study of 277 pre-school children, negativistic reactions to the tests were prominent between the ages of two and a half and four years, reaching a peak around the age of three, and the children who were negativistic and resistive made a lower mean rating on their tests than those who were less negativistic (175).[5]

Although the research projects were undertaken in an effort to discover how much mental development may be affected by the child's environment, the data from certain recent studies from the University of Iowa Child Welfare Station suggest that variations in I.Q. upon successive tests may be expected if marked changes in the child's living situation have occurred in the interval between tests (102, 246).

Certain studies on the variability of the I.Q. indicate that the longer the interval between test and retest, the greater is the probability of variation in I.Q. R. L. Thorndike reports that the tendency toward constancy of the I.Q. decreases as the time interval between tests increases. R. R. Brown states that an interval from five to nine years between two Stanford-Binet tests increases the variability of the I.Q.'s to nearly twice that when the interval between tests is less than two years, and the chances are about 25 in 100 that the I.Q. will vary by more than 15 points when there is a seven-year interval between tests (32, 264).

In devising psychological tests, the aim was to provide objective

---

[5] See also The Effect of Resistance on Intelligence Test Scores of Young Children, by M. M. Rust (229).

and reliable methods of measurement, independent of the subjective judgment of the person giving the tests. But although this purpose was partially achieved through the provision of instructions for giving the tests and crediting success or failure according to well-defined rules, such factors as the personality of the examiner, the background and experience in giving tests and in working with children, and skill in evaluating and interpreting the test results in the light of other information about the child and his reactions during the testing, cannot be excluded from the testing situation. Psychologists, like the members of any other profession, differ individually in native aptitude for their work and in the amount of experience and professional skill that they have acquired. In a recent study, it was found that the same child might differ by as much as 30 or more points in I.Q. when tested by two different psychologists, even though the two tests were given within a short period of time (44).

If the personality and experience of the psychologist who gives the tests sometimes influence the results, it is equally true that the personality and emotional state of the child who is taking the tests may affect the ratings. We have learned, from clinical experience, that when there is an opportunity to retest an emotionally disturbed child at a time when there is less emotional disturbance, the rating on the second test may be substantially higher than on the first one. This point is of such importance that it may well be illustrated by several cases in which the gain in I.Q. upon retesting seems to be related to the change in the child's emotional state.

Our first illustrative case is that of a child of six and a half years who was first tested shortly after he entered school. He was one of those children who find it very difficult to adjust to the partial separation from home and mother that is involved in going to school. This particular boy cried every morning because he did not want to leave his mother and go to school; at night he had dreams about school from which he awakened with fear and in tears. At school he was often tearful, and did not seem to comprehend any of the first-grade work, so that the teacher raised a question as to his intelligence and referred him to the school psychologist for tests. When he was tested, in the state of emotional stress described above, he made an I.Q. of 79. He was then placed in a special class.

Two months after the placement in the special class, the boy had become better adjusted to the separation from his mother and had even begun to like school. His nightmares had ceased and he was beginning to learn the school work. The special-class teacher felt that he was, in fact, learning at a rate that would be expected of a child of good intelligence. It was at this time that he was brought to the clinic for retesting. He made an I.Q. of 97, which confirmed the special-class teacher's impression that the results of the first tests had been affected by the emotional disturbance he was undergoing at the time when he had taken them.

Another illustration is the case of a boy who was brought to the clinic for treatment because of many emotional and personality problems. He was the only boy in a family of girls. His father had died when he was a baby, and thereafter the mother had become very protective of this boy. She did not allow him to enter school until he was seven years of age, but kept him closely at home and permitted him to play only with his sisters. Even after he was in school, his mother still insisted that he play with his sisters because she considered the other boys in the neighborhood too rough and dangerous as playmates for him. The boy made a very poor adjustment to school. He could not compete with the other boys in games and was called a "sissy." He often complained of being sick during school hours, refused to eat lunch, and asked to go home. He was not able to do any of the work. At the age of nine, after two years in school, he had only reached second grade, after having spent three terms in first grade. He was then referred to the school psychologist for testing, and made an I.Q. of 79. He was transferred to special class on the basis of this low I.Q. and the history of poor school progress.

A year later, when he was ten years old, his mother brought him to the clinic for treatment, complaining that he still was not learning at school, even in the special class, could not get along with the other boys, was very effeminate, and was suffering from enuresis. There was an eight-months period of treatment with the boy and case-work with the mother. During treatment, the boy changed from the fearful, inhibited, passively feminine kind of personality that he appeared to be when first seen at the clinic. He became more aggressive in his behavior and more masculine in his interests. He played with other boys and no longer had enuresis. His mother had stopped restricting his companionship with other boys. At this time, he was retested at the clinic, and made an I.Q. of 99, which was 20 points higher than the I.Q. of 79 on the tests given elsewhere twenty months before.

There was as great a difference in his responses to the two tests as in the I.Q. ratings. At the time of the first test, he was described as slow in all his responses, unable to express himself well, lacking in initiative and energy. At the time of the second test, he was rapid in his responses, energetic, expressed himself freely, and seemed mentally alert and possessed of an ordinary amount of initiative. The change in his responses at the time of the second test obviously corresponds to the change in his personality that took place through the treatment. However, at the time of the second testing, it was discovered that he had a severe reading disability and would need remedial teaching in that subject before he could be expected to make any normal progress in school.

The low rating on the first test, the reading disability, and the continued failure in school, all seem quite explicable on the basis of the boy's serious emotional problems and his personality difficulties. Yet at the time of the first testing by the school psychologist, it was only natural that his low I.Q., his slowness and seeming dullness in responses, and his school failures should be interpreted as evidence of mental deficiency. Even for the most experienced psychologist, it is not always easy to judge whether a low I.Q. and retarded responses are due to mental deficiency or whether the child is emotionally inhibited or resistive to the testing.

Since there have been studies that indicate some tendency for test results to vary when the testing is done by different psychologists, the question might be raised as to whether this may be the chief factor in the variation of I.Q. in the two cases just described, rather than the emotional state of the child at the time of the tests. We can answer this question only inferentially by data from cases in which this factor of the influence of different examiners is ruled out. Similar changes in I.Q., with changes in the child's emotional state, appear when the tests are repeated by the same psychologist.

Take the case of a child first tested at the clinic when he was three years old. He was then resistive and negativistic, throwing the test materials around the room or trying to destroy them, and it was difficult to secure any coöperative response from him. His negative, destructive reactions were greatest, however, at the start of the testing, when his mother was in the room. After she left him alone with the psychologist, he was a little more coöperative, but even so he made an I.Q. of only 70 on the Kuhlmann-Binet. However, this rating could not be accepted unreservedly as evidence of mental retardation, since the boy's responses indicated that it might well be his resistiveness, rather than lack of intelligence, that was responsible for his making a low I.Q.

Although the boy's mother complained that his behavior at home was as destructive, negativistic, and disobedient as his behavior in the testing situation, she did not care to consider treatment for him at that time. Four years later, she brought him back to the clinic for treatment. He was then seven years old, and was doing very well in the second grade at school, so that his teachers had no complaint about his behavior, but at home with his mother he was as disobedient, rebellious, and negativistic as ever.

Before treatment was started, the boy was retested. He worked well and coöperatively on the tests and made an I.Q. of 105, which was 35 points higher than the I.Q. of 70 obtained when he was tested at the age of three. At the time of the first test, he had apparently responded to the psychologist with the same negative, destructive attitudes that he had toward his mother at home, but when he came for the second test, he responded coöperatively to the psychologist as he did toward his teachers at school. These differences in his attitude toward the psychologist probably accounted for the difference in the I.Q. ratings.

In the case just described, the possible factor of influence of different examiners upon the test results is excluded, since the two tests were given by the same psychologist. But in view of studies which indicate that when the first testing is at a very early age, there is greater probability of variation in I.Q. in retesting, and other studies which suggest that a long interval between test and retest increases the probability of a marked change in the I.Q., there might be a question as to whether the fact that this child was three years old at the time of the first tests and seven years old at the time of the second tests should be considered significant in explaining the divergent I.Q. ratings. However, our emphasis on the significance of the child's attitudes toward the testing is in accord with studies of negativistic reactions of young children to testing, which indicate the tendency of such reactions to result in lower test ratings. In this particular case extremely negativistic responses were prominent during the first testing, so that it seems that the more probable explanation of the 35-point difference in I.Q. is the change in the boy's attitude toward the psychologist and the testing situation, rather than the age at which he was first tested or the four-year interval between the two tests.

In the next two case illustrations, all such factors as different examiners, a long interval between tests, or testing at a very early age are excluded, for the testing was done by the same psychologist, the children were beyond pre-school age, and the time interval was fourteen months in one instance and four months in the other.

The first of these cases was a boy who came to the clinic at twelve years of age because he was in trouble over truancy from school. His truancy began when he entered sixth grade and at the same time was transferred to a new school. His own explanation of his truancy was that he stayed away from school because he feared the other boys, who teased him about his foreign accent and mannerisms and "beat him up" when he tried to fight them in outbursts of anger at their teasing. He could not go to school because he feared these boys, he stated, but he was worried about staying away from school lest he be sent to a reformatory as a punishment for truancy.

While the boy was, by his own admission, in this state of conflict about his school situation, he was given tests at the clinic. On the old Stanford-Binet, he made an I.Q. of 87, and the Stanford achievement tests gave him only a fifth-grade score, although he was in sixth grade at school. These test ratings raised the question whether inferior intelligence and inability to do sixth-grade work might be contributing to his truancy. But there was also a question as to whether the I.Q. could be considered reliable as a measure of the boy's real intellectual ability, since he had taken the tests under great emotional stress. He had constantly interrupted the tests to talk about his worries, and had even said that he would run away from home or kill himself rather than go back to school, where he would be at the mercy of the other boys or run the risk of being sent to a reformatory because of his continued truancy. With his mind so full of his personal feelings and problems, there was a possibility that he was unable to give sustained attention to the testing and that he obtained a low I.Q. because he was unable to work efficiently rather than because he was actually dull. There was also a question whether the low educational-achievement test scores were due to intellectual limitations which prevented him from mastering the work of his school grade or whether his failure to master the sixth-grade work was a result of having missed a part of it through his continual truancy and his inability to concentrate upon it when he was in school, because of his preoccupation with his own problems.

These diagnostic questions could be answered only later, when he could be retested under more favorable circumstances. Meanwhile, a way out of his unhappy situation was offered him through the opportunity to go to a boarding school for truant boys. Although some boys took being sent to this school as a punishment, this boy was eager to go. In his first year there, he did so well in his school work that retesting was requested, to determine whether the first tests had been inaccurate.

Fourteen months after the first tests had been given, the boy returned for retesting. He was alert, cheerful, and able to concentrate on the tests, working very efficiently. He made an I.Q. of 113, when the old Stanford-Binet was repeated. This I.Q. was 26 points higher than the I.Q. of 87 on the earlier test. On the Stanford achievement tests, he made an eighth-grade score, whereas on those tests fourteen months previously he had made only a fifth-grade score.

The boy's own words, at the time of the second testing, indicate how differently he was feeling than at the time of the first tests, when he was talking of running away from home or of suicide as an escape from what seemed to him an intolerable situation. After being told that he had done much better on the retesting, he stated that he had expected to do better because this time he could keep his mind on the tests.

"When I took the tests before," he said, "I just couldn't keep my mind on them. That was when my father was trying to make me go to school and I couldn't go because I was so afraid of the other boys. I like boarding school. I get along all right with the boys there. I can keep my mind on my work now."

It may be of interest to add that after the boy had had another year at the boarding school for truant boys, he returned home and attended high school, doing satisfactory work and graduating in the usual length of time.

The second case of this kind was that of a boy who was brought for treatment at the age of eight and a half years. He had been excluded from school after two years in the first grade. He had not been able to learn any of the work and had disturbed the class by his restlessness. He had never played voluntarily with the other children and if a supervising teacher made him join their games, he retreated from play as soon as this supervision was relaxed.

When first seen at the clinic, he looked, talked, and acted so much like a mentally deficient child that it seemed advisable to give him tests. It was surprising to have him make an I.Q. of 84 on the old Stanford-Binet, since this rating ruled out the possibility that he was mentally deficient. In the treatment interviews immediately following the testing, it became evident that he was a repressed, inhibited, fearful child, who was afraid to undertake any activity, even play.

Burnham calls this kind of child "pseudo-feebleminded," and states that such a child resembles a mentally deficient child in behavior, but is shown by adequate tests not to be actually mentally deficient. Burnham further states: "One of the most serious causes of pseudo-feeblemindedness is the inhibition of fear" (35, chap. 18). Anna Freud describes such children as neurotically inhibited, with severe restriction of ego activities. She speaks of them as intelligent, but not taking part in the regular games or lessons and behaving as as if they were intimidated (90, chap. 8).

Whether we use Burnham's concept of pseudo-feeblemindedness due to fear inhibition or Anna Freud's of neurotic inhibitions with restriction of ego activities, as a diagnostic classification for the boy in our case, the fact remains that at the time he came to the clinic, he was afraid to do anything, even to play. After four months of treatment, during which time he was seen two hours weekly, he was learning to read and to do arithmetic with a private tutor, was playing in a normal manner with other children in the neighborhood, and no longer looked or acted like a mentally deficient child. He himself spoke of how he had been afraid of people when he first came to the clinic and said that he was glad he was not afraid any more. Preparatory to his return to school, the Stanford-Binet was repeated, in order to secure an up-to-date report for the teachers. In this retest, at the end of his four months of treatment, he made an I.Q. of 99, which was 15 points higher than the I.Q. of 84 on the first test given at the beginning of treatment. This I.Q. of 99 rated him as of normal intelligence. When he was told that he had done better on the second test than on the first, he spontaneously offered the explanation: "When I first came, I was afraid to talk to you, so I didn't answer as many of the questions."

When the Stanford-Binet was first made available in 1916, Terman stressed the necessity of giving intelligence tests in a quiet room, without distracting influences, and stated that the presence of other persons was one of the most disturbing influences. Terman was indeed so definite on this point as to say:

> If accurate results are to be secured, it is not permissible to have any auditor, besides possibly an assistant to record the responses. Even the assistant, however quiet and unobtrusive, is sometimes a disturbing element. . . . If the examiner is experienced, and if the child is not timid, it is sometimes possible to make a successful test in the presence of a number of auditors, provided they remain silent, refrain from staring, and otherwise conduct themselves with discretion. But not even the veteran examiner can always be sure of the outcome in demonstration testing (261, chap. 8).

This warning as to the unreliability of tests given in the presence of observers is not always heeded, and on the basis of an I.Q. obtained under such unfavorable circumstances, a child is sometimes diagnosed incorrectly. Our last illustrative case shows what the response of a sensitive child may be when examined in the presence of observers.

A mother came to the clinic asking for help with her twelve-year-old son. He was not doing well in school and had become somewhat of a behavior problem. The school was suggesting that she send him to a school for mentally retarded and problem children. Two years before, the boy had been tested at a hospital clinic and had obtained an I.Q. of 78, and a diagnosis of border-line mental deficiency had been made and reported to the school. A group of students had been present as observers during the testing and afterward the boy had complained about how nervous their watching him had made him. When the mother suggested returning to the hospital clinic for another test, the boy refused; his memory of his previous visit made him feel that it was an ordeal too painful to be repeated. His mother thought that she could persuade him to go to a different place, however.

Knowing of the boy's unpleasant and painful experience with testing, it was possible to plan for a few informal interviews with him before any retesting was done. In these interviews, he was able to talk about his feelings with regard to coming to another clinic, after his past experience, and also to enter into a somewhat positive relationship with the psychologist. The necessity of repeating the tests was explained to him realistically in terms of what school plans could be made for him. He agreed to take the tests again, but he spent the rest of the interview in talking about his feelings at the time of his first testing two years before.

The clinic to which he had gone then was at a hospital where "crazy" people were kept. He had not liked the place and had hated to go inside. There had been a lot of "doctors" around, watching him do the tests, and finally he had felt so nervous and angry that he would not answer any more of the questions, but had just said he didn't know, whether he really knew the answer or not. He supposed that had caused him to get a poor mark on the test, but he had not cared about that—he had only wanted to get out of the place, and he had thought that he could get out quicker by saying that he didn't know instead of answering any more questions.

In spite of having said that he would be willing to take the tests again, when it came to the actual testing, he was resistive. Soon it became necessary to interrupt the testing to have him talk further about his feeling with regard to it. When the psychologist said that he probably felt angry at being made to take the tests, just as he had felt angry when he had had to take them before, he replied that it did remind him so much of the first time he had them that he felt angry all over again. But he would try to do the tests this time, he added.

He then worked very well until the tests began to be somewhat difficult for him, when he began to hesitate in his replies and to confuse the instructions for one test with those for another. Again the tests were interrupted while it was suggested that perhaps he was afraid that he might not be able to do any better than he had on his previous tests and was worrying about that. He replied that he was very much worried about it. He was informed that he need not worry; he had already done enough of the tests to make a higher score than the one he had made before. Thus encouraged, he put forth good effort again and was able to work efficiently until the tests were completed. In contrast to the I.Q. of 78 which he had made two years before, when tested in the presence of observers, he now made an I.Q. of 100, which classed him as of normal intelligence.

He was so pleased to find that he was not "dumb," as he called it, that he was eager to continue interviews at the clinic, and became optimistic about succeeding in school work in the future. The tests had revealed not only that he was of normal intelligence, but also that he had a slight reading disability which was handicapping him in his school work. He was transferred to a school where he received special instruction in reading. He made good use of his treatment interviews at clinic and of the special teaching at school, so that within a few months he was doing much better in his school work than ever before and there were no longer any problems so far as his behavior was concerned. The treatment was terminated, with his agreement, at this time.

He came back for single visits toward the end of each school year for the next three years. When he came for the first two visits, he was worried about passing the final examinations for the year, but could see that this anxiety was because of his past experiences in failing. At the end of the third year, he came without any anxiety, reporting that he had just passed the year's final examinations successfully. He had wanted to make this visit in order to express his thanks for the help he had received at the clinic, he explained. He has not asked for a visit in the two years since that time, so that in expressing his gratitude he was also apparently severing his connection with the clinic, feeling no further need of even occasional support.

It is impossible, within the scope of a single paper, to describe the large number of tests now available, or to survey all the literature that has a bearing upon the use and interpretation of tests. It has been necessary, therefore, to limit the discussion to those tests most frequently used in our own clinic, to report only samples of studies in the literature, and to draw upon clinical experience for individual case material to illustrate some of the important points to be considered in the use and interpretation of psychological tests.

Psychologists have devoted considerable research to the question of the reliability of psychological tests. Outside of the psychological profession, the evaluation of tests often seems to be largely a matter of personal opinion, with an all-or-none attitude. The results of tests tend to be accepted too unquestioningly by some, while others have considered them of little if any value. The truth seems to lie some-where between these two extremes, for tests are reliable in the majority of cases, and it should be possible for the experienced examiner to evaluate the situation in individual testing so as to detect many of the cases in which there is sufficient question as to the reliability of the test results to make retesting advisable at a later time before giving anything more than a tentative diagnosis, or even before giving any diagnosis at all.

If we are thus cautious about interpreting test results for diagnostic purposes, it follows logically that we are also cautious about making any prognosis. We have indeed departed from the original concept, in the early years of testing, that the chief usefulness of tests was to classify the child in some category that could be expected to remain fixed and permanent and to furnish a basis for prediction of the child's development for his whole life span. We may say, instead, that the most valuable and the most legitimate use of tests is as a measurement of the efficiency of the child's mental functioning at any given time, with the realization that at another time, with the changes that may have occurred within the child or in his living situation, the same tests may show more or less efficiency in his mental functioning, depending upon whether the changes in his life have been favorable or unfavorable for his growth and development.

ANNI WEISS FRANKL

United Jewish Social Services, Kansas City, Missouri

Diagnostic Methods in Child Guidance and Psychological Counseling[1]

A large part of the diagnostic work in psychological counseling at the present time is being done by interview and test. In many cases it is extremely difficult for the counselor to gather from the material thus gained the particular information he needs in order to understand the specific problem presented. This paper will review the procedures in use and will outline a supplementary method which, with the aim of securing more insight into the problem and the implications for guidance, is concerned with the informal behavior of parents and children and the utilization of the child's play for diagnostic purposes. For the most part, this method can easily be interwoven into the routine procedure of psychological counseling.

We will take up first the values and limitations of the common clinical case-work in child guidance, as evident in interviews with parents, visits to home and school, and psychological examination of the child.

Interviews with Parents. In almost every case, when a mother seeks advice about a problem child, it may be assumed that she is somewhat out of balance.[2] Something in the child's development or his relationship to others is wrong or seems wrong to her, and this fact not only weighs on her, but makes for a specific relationship be-

---

[1] Reprinted from *Mental Hygiene*, 1937, 21, 579–598. Copyright 1937 by The National Committee for Mental Hygiene.

[2] The discussion that follows holds true, of course, for the father as well as for the mother, or for any person responsible for or concerned with the child.

tween herself and her child, herself and her environment, and the child and his environment. Something about the situation can be learned from the interview; at least we can conclude from it how the mother sees the problem, and we can form some first hypothesis about the child's status within his environmental field.

It must always be remembered, however, that the information that a parent gives us about herself and her child is seldom a definite body of facts that will hold true continuously. Personality and behavior problems are not static, but dynamic; they are part of complicated individual developments influenced by and, in turn, influencing the whole environmental field. An interview cannot give the psychologist much more than a random cross section of the situation; it reveals what seems important to the mother at the moment —if she is willing, and is given a chance, to speak out freely—and what seems important to the interviewer, in as much as he is taking the lead in discussion and questioning.

Usually, then, the information given is somewhat biased, and, besides, is mixed up with a certain amount of more or less controlled interpretation. The popularity of various educational philosophies and modern interpretative psychologies—more or less well understood—adds to the entanglement. Thus, the information is but a small sample of a developmental stream, made up of many currents interconnected with one another and working upon one another in various ways, and, furthermore, changing according to the time, place, and situation in which the information is given. The psychologist is supposed to solve a complicated equation in which practically all the factors are either hypothetical or entirely unknown to him.

Every interview has, however, one definite value no matter how distorted the material presented and how completely puzzled the psychologist may be at first: the individual who is being interviewed is always a real person acting in a concrete way and thus making a positive contribution toward a solution of the problem, viewed from the standpoint of the whole field of action around herself and the child.

Of course, if the psychologist is experienced, he gains a general impression of the person interviewed and of the situation around her, especially after he has seen her several times. This enables him to evaluate her information and to select from it what seems to be pertinent for an understanding of mother and child while he is securing additional information.

Visits to Home and School. If a visit to the home is made, and possibly one to the child's school, the picture becomes somewhat more rounded. But this procedure may have many of the same limitations as an interview, especially when the child in question is beyond the pre-school age and is well aware that the visitor has some purpose in coming to see him. The same is often true for the family and the school. The mere fact of the visitor's presence may change the psychological situation and affect the validity of the study. Of course, skilled case-workers are able to overcome most of these difficulties and to draw highly important material from one visit or repeated visits. But some of the factors that later on prove to be responsible for the conflicts and problems may show up only vaguely or not at all. On the other hand, certain family patterns that are easily recognized—such as dominant behavior of one member of the family, extremely high standards for behavior and achievement, fears and over-solicitude, or neglect and lack of affection—may impress the visitor as the evident cause of the trouble, though later on it may become clear that they are merely contributory factors. Or the psychologist may feel that school discipline, as observed during his visit, is so rigid that a sensitive child could not be expected to adjust, or that the teacher does not understand the child.

However obvious causes and effects may seem to be in the data secured by this type of observation, the fact remains that the psychologist has to make his interpretation on doubtful evidence. He knows that similar or even worse family and school set-ups do not necessarily result in problem behavior like that of the child in question. There are great individual differences in the matter of what children can endure and overcome, and, on the other hand, in what causes them to suffer and fail in life. We do not know exactly what it is that makes for maladjustment, although we do know that, in general, more so-called unfavorable factors are found in families with maladjusted children than in those with children who are well adjusted. A comparison of the behaviors of different children in their natural environment can be only tentative in its findings, because almost no factor can be satisfactorily controlled, and, for the present at least, our methods of examining the non-overt factors that enter into behavior are far from adequate.

Nevertheless, clinical practice based on present-day observation and interpretation is successful in many cases, although we often do not know specifically the "what" and the "why" of the success. Naturally, the next step is to try to become more conscious of what is really happening in and to the child and his environmental field, and what effect the psychologist is having upon both. We must realize that his work often passes the border line between scientifically controlled procedure, on the one hand, and "mere commonsense," "intuitive," or "artistic" work on the other side. This intuitive work is often said to be dependent upon the special ability of the person who uses it. The two arguments against it are that it cannot be taught in the same way as other subjects in psychology and that its scientific reliability has not been established. We should not, however, drop a method that has proved successful to some degree merely because of certain difficulties in its present state of development. Rather we should study the method with the purpose of making it more communicable and scientifically sound. Clinical child-guidance needs increasing integration with psychology and particularly with child-development research.

To come back to our problem of what is really going on psychologically during our case-work, our plan should be to analyze the procedure and to devise a better control for the factors that are at work around the child. Methodological suggestions will be outlined in the second part of this paper.

Psychological Examination of the Child. The values and limitations of psychological tests in the pracice of child guidance need not be discussed in detail in this paper. Modern psychologists agree to a certain extent that good tests, competently administered, are more or less indispensable for clinical work. At the same time they realize that the tests can be only one of several tools in the study of the child.[3]

We do not find the same agreement about interviews with children, and, accordingly, practice varies considerably. The present

---

[3] In "Qualitative Intelligence Testing as a Means of Diagnosis in the Examination of Psychopathic Children" (285) I have discussed a supplementary method of test evaluation for the study of the personality of the child.

writer holds to the opinion that information gained from an interview with a child, if taken alone and at its face value, must be considered even more questionable than that secured in the adult interview. We know that many children who are referred for study do not understand or realize at all that they are "problem children." Even if they do realize it to some extent, they can seldom be expected to give detailed information about themselves in an interview. This does not, of course, imply that talking to a child about personal matters is without value. But it is important always to remember that children react in very different ways and that we must gain some understanding of the reaction of the particular child who is being interviewed before drawing conclusions as to the information given. A child who is being interviewed in a sympathetic way may repeat certain rules as to what his behavior should be; he may show reluctance, anger, or irritation when painful problems are touched; he may take an interest in telling about agreeable or disagreeable events and experiences; he may begin by defending himself if he feels that he is being blamed for his behavior. He may be pleased at being taken seriously and getting so much individual attention, and, consequently, be very eager himself to please; this may induce him to say what he believes the interviewer would like to hear. Again, he may be self-conscious and try to retire. No matter how the child responds to the interview, we are not necessarily justified in concluding that he will behave in the same way in the actual situations that are being discussed with him. On the whole, the interview situation calls for reactive behavior rather than spontaneous activity in the child, and the interviewer more or less gets the response he is expecting and stimulating.

The various possible reactions of the child are always revealing to the experienced counselor, but at the same time they may be misleading unless he has some other, less artificially gained, information about the same child to assist him in evaluating the material of the interview. In other words, the interview does not reveal how the child really behaves in the situation to which a stated problem refers. The fact that a child is troublesome at home, does not get along well with other children, does not work up to capacity, or is becoming delinquent can hardly be explained by the child in such a way that the counselor will understand exactly where the difficulty lies. A six-year-old girl who was shy and unhappy at school gave as her only reason for this behavior the fact that the teacher had too loud a voice. There was no evidence of her being oversensitive to loud noises in other situations, however. A boy, referred for study because of his asocial behavior at school, rated among the highest in his class in a test of social intelligence. He knew perfectly well how one should behave, but he could not make use of his knowledge in his own actions; nor was he able to give any explanation as to how or why he misbehaved. A young delinquent may give or accept many motives for his conduct; yet none of them can be taken as a final explanation as to why he acted in this or that particular way. Only if we know how the child behaves in actual, everyday situations, and how he reacts in crucial moments, can we interpret with some certainty the information given by him in the interview.

Recommendations Based on Interviews and Tests. The beginner in psychological counseling can hardly believe that a child who behaves perfectly while with him really causes the difficulties people complain about. He will accept willingly any plausible explanation of the circumstances around the child that are brought forth as responsible for the trouble. Optimistically, and certainly with some right, he expects the problem behavior to vanish if only the unsatisfactory conditions are changed for the better. As a rule, he is inclined to believe that parents and teachers are mainly to blame, and he gives, according to his knowledge, recommendations as to how the child should be handled. Often, of course, this simple method works, although we cannot always be sure which particular item of procedure has been effective. Merely the fact that some one has taken a serious interest in the problem may influence favorably both parents and child or teacher and child. Sometimes the very fact that the parents come for help and are ready for a discussion of their problem means that they have begun to face it and to work on it, and the counselor's interest encourages them to continue in the course already adopted. In other cases, success is less evident. Old emotional patterns of relationship resist the changes recommended, and the counselor concludes that the family is not coöperative. One can express the same fact in a different way by saying that the counselor has not found the right way to make them coöperate, or that the family is not ready to coöperate in the present situation. It requires a considerable amount of experience and of insight into the whole dynamic situation around the problem to know in advance what may happen during the work with a problem child and his parents and to conduct the work accordingly.

My own opinion is that insight and foresight can be acquired more satisfactorily by observing the child's behavior and the environmental situation in as natural a set-up as possible. This might be accomplished through a thorough study of the child and his environment in a number of visits to home and school. Growing familiarity with the psychologist would then free the members of the group from constraint in his presence, and he would have a chance to see all the situations in which they behaved or failed to behave in a desirable way. But it is obvious that such a study as this would take far too much time, and, moreover, would remain on the level of individual case-work, with little or no opportunity for an exact comparison of problems in different families.

The suggestion is offered, therefore, that in addition to interviews and casual school and home visits, less formal techniques of investigation be utilized. The psychologist needs somewhat controlled situations for observation of behavior and relationships, situations in which parents and child are not so much aware that they are being studied. At the same time, the time spent on each person should be limited somehow. It is suggested that the additional observation be made an integral part of the procedure from the moment the application for study of the child is made, use being made of the time during which mother and child are waiting for their appointment, or when one of them is waiting while the other is seeing the psychologist. According to the individual set-up of the clinic and the organization of the staff, various standard situations can be developed, and an experimental play group may be added.

The following paragraphs will outline some of the situations that the writer has found helpful in her work.[4] It will be noted that paramount use is made of play material, both for direct experimental use and as a bridge toward good and free contact with the counselor. These techniques have been used successfully for children between two and ten years of age and, in a limited number of cases, for younger and older children, too. There is no definite rule for the sequence of the different situations in the progress of the case study,

---

[4] They are based on experience from the child-guidance department (*Heilpädagogische Abteilung*) of the pediatric clinic at the University of Vienna, Austria.

nor is every situation a necessary requirement for every study. As to the attitude of the counselor, one very general rule can be formulated: he has to be active all the time in the sense that he must be quick to observe and react to all that is happening; he has to show his friendly and intensive interest without giving evidence of becoming emotionally involved; he has to keep back his own opinion about the problem until he knows his subjects well enough to evade major misunderstandings. In other words, his attitude must encourage his clients to express themselves without interference. Beginners are sometimes worried lest this apparently passive attitude may interfere with their authoritative position. They feel that they should impress their clients with their knowledge and competence. They do not realize that quiet, intensive interest, with casual replies and remarks, during the beginning of a new contact serves their purpose better than early interpretation and recommendation. This attitude helps them to become part of the developmental stream in which the child and his problem are moving.

Situation I: Introductory Observation of Mother and Child. As a rule, when a mother comes to see the psychological counselor for some problem with her child, a short play observation, preceding the interview and taking place in the presence of the mother, is revealing for the counselor in the following ways: it shows the relationship between mother and child, particularly the degree of dependence of the child and the dominance of the mother; the mother's idea about good behavior with strangers and her methods of making the child behave according to her ideals; the mother's standard of behavior for the child; the child's approach to play materials, and his skills and knowledge in using them, his play persistence, his emotional patterns in attacking play problems and overcoming difficulties, the quality of his work as such and the quality of his work in relation to satisfaction with his achievement, his spontaneity and curiosity in the use of the play material available, and his method of becoming acquainted with the counselor's quarters, the play equipment, and the counselor himself; and, finally, the mother's attitude toward the child and the counselor during this whole procedure.

If a psychologically trained receptionist is available, she can observe and record inconspicuously from the start the behavior of the two. This observation might be developed into a waiting-room service with selected material serving as a stimulus. Much regarding the behavior patterns and routine relationship of the family would be revealed. In a clinic with a large out-patient department and a staff of counselors, a waiting-room service would be mainly a matter of well-planned organization, requiring little additional time. Several families could wait together under the supervision of staff members while registration is taking place, and the development of contacts of various kinds could be observed. Most children, during that time, would get sufficiently acquainted with the new environment. Thus the field would be well prepared for the individual contact with the counselor, so that this contact could be shorter than it would have to be without the preparation in the waiting room.

During the preliminary contact with the counselor, it has proved helpful to ask mother and child a few questions regarding such matters as the name, address, and age of the child, his school and grade, and the status of the immediate family. These questions should be asked in a routine way and without emphasis upon their importance. Usually this short conversation will give additional information as to the relationship between parent and child and possible tensions between them. Either the mother or the child or both will answer, and sometimes the one who proved less active at first will correct or contradict what the other has said.

To illustrate by some examples, a mother came to consult the psychologist about her eight-year-old boy, who did not get along well at school and was stubborn and disagreeable at home. For one of the conferences, the mother came with the boy and his four-year-old sister. While before that the boy had been very talkative during contacts, unless his mother had quieted him, this time the little girl led the conversation, no matter whether she, her mother, or her brother were addressed. On other visits the mother had shown annoyance when the boy spoke and tried to send him out of the room in order to speak to the counselor. Now she kept quiet and smiled at everything the girl said. During another contact with the same family, father, mother, and boy came. This time, neither the father nor the boy had much chance to talk, and an incidental observation disclosed that they were well aware of this fact and took it with resigned humor. This observation was the more important because the mother had reported that the father was deeply annoyed by his son and often spanked him.

A very different kind of relationship was demonstrated in the case of a six-year-old boy and his mother. He was the only child and was very close to his mother. However, from time to time the mother was alarmed by his outbursts of independence and even expressions of hatred toward her. When they came to see the counselor, the boy was immediately attracted by the play material in the room. The mother watched him closely and interfered with almost everything he did, either giving him directions as to how to handle the material or forbidding him to play with it, with the argument that he would dirty his hands with the clay or that perhaps the counselor would not like him to take the blocks. She seemed to try desperately to give the counselor a good impression of her son. When, later on, the counselor discussed with her her problem with the boy, it was evident that she did not realize at all that she was continually building up barriers around her child and interrupting almost every one of his activities. The counselor might have inferred this situation from the mother's reports, but he could hardly have discussed it with her successfully without this actual and detailed evidence; for the mother's subjective impression was that she was giving the boy a great amount of freedom.

Thus the counselor may witness a conflict between mother and child as to how the child should behave during the contact with him. In this way both the counselor's person and his play material become active factors in the observation of mother and child and, at the same time, constant factors in the psychological experiment organized through this situation. That is to say, the counselor can compare the behaviors of different mothers, fathers, or children, and their standards and values. During this conversation, the counselor usually finds an opportunity to indicate to the mother that he will discuss the actual problem with her later and that he wants to become acquainted with the child first.

Situation II: Solitary Play of the Child During the Mother's Interview with the Counselor. If the child is fairly independent of his mother, he can be persuaded to wait in another room with some of the counselor's play material which he has chosen himself. It seems that the most successful technique for this situation is just to tell the child that he will have to wait in another room and may play there. Usually he will enjoy choosing material from the selection in the counselor's room and will take it to the waiting room. Variations from this technique should be used only on the child's initiative; that is to say, if the child wants to be reassured as to where his mother will stay and where he can find her, the counselor will repeat and emphasize this information. The child may raise other questions which should be answered. The counselor's purpose is to create the most favorable background for spontaneous behavior of the child. The more rules and limitations he insists upon as to what the child may or may not do, the less opportunity is left to the child to act spontaneously. Almost anything may happen, then, during the interview with the mother, from one extreme—namely, that the child remains in his room until called for, no matter whether he is enjoying it or not—to the other extreme—that he keeps going from one room to the other with continuous questions or requests of some sort. In addition, the mother's reaction to what the child does is revealing. In case of misdemeanor, she will start to explain and to describe behavior conflicts at home, and with the evidence going on before his eyes, the counselor will have a vivid picture of the home situation.

In the case of a seven-year-old boy who had never been away from home, the counselor witnessed a perfectly tragic love scene, with many tears and kisses from both mother and child, when the boy was invited to play in another room. This performance was utilized afterwards to explain to the mother that her own excitement had made the parting very difficult for the boy. In fact, only the decided and assuring attitude of the counselor had made it possible. Toward the end of the interview, the mother was able to smile at her own foolishness, although there were tears in her eyes, and the reunion was celebrated happily, although still with a great display of emotion. In this case, it was possible to start therapy from the very beginning of the contact, because the main difficulties in the parent-child relationship were evident at once. Diagnostically, however, the situation was not clear at all. No recommendations could have been given before the counselor knew just how much strain he could put on both mother and child. That is why he had to start and control the "weaning" process himself. Both the mother and the boy proved to be extremely sensitive, and a very gentle and gradual increase of recommendations toward independence was essential in the progress of this case.

In the case of a four-year-old boy who had always been with his mother, there seemed to be a similar psychological situation. But this boy himself proved to be considerably more independent. He was sent to play in a distant corner of the large room where the interview took place, and was immediately attracted by some play material. The mother watched him nervously and commented to the counselor that she was sure the boy would cry for her. The child, in his excitement, called, "Mother!" several times, and she would jump up and move toward him; but every time, when she was on her way to him, he said, "Stay where you are." Apparently all that he needed was to point out to her from time to time how happy he was, while she thought (and probably wished) that he needed her. Again, this gave a better insight into the mother-child relationship than the interview alone could have given. At the same time, it could be used as the starting point for constructive work with the mother.

Furthermore, as in Situation I, the child in his solitary play shows his attitude toward play material, his likes and dislikes of games, his ability, persistence, investigative and constructive power, his resourcefulness, and so on, but during a longer period than in Situation I.

A four-year-old girl, who was of superior intelligence, was given an opportunity to play in the psychologist's room while another counselor talked to her parents. Her behavior toward the psychologist was charming and well-balanced. However, she was at a loss as to what to do with any of the material offered, such as clay, blocks, paper and crayons, and the like. This observation brought out much more clearly than the interview with the parents that the child's all-around activities had been neglected in favor of her intellectual development.

According to the set-up of the laboratory, the child in his solitary play can be observed either secretly from behind a screen or openly, but inconspicuously, by some one apparently occupied with something else in the same room. Other workers of the laboratory with whom the child comes in contact may contribute their observations. Even if none of these factors can be arranged for, the counselor can get some information about this solitary play from the child's behavior when he reappears in the counselor's room, from his reports about what he has done, and from the evidence given by the products of his activities. The discussion above has shown that this kind of observation can be carried on within the same time span as the interview. Of course, it is an advantage if a trained psychologist is available for this service. In a number of cases such observation might permit us to dispense with a home visit.

Situation III: Play Interview. With the contact established between psychologist and child by means of an objective tool such as the play material, the next step can be taken easily. The child at this stage has seen and talked to the counselor several times and has become accustomed to being in the laboratory. The mere fact that he has entered and left the room more than once without having the notion that some unknown danger or unwanted familiarity may follow may have helped him to get acquainted. Even a shy and fearful child usually will be ready by this time to accept a positive attitude on the part of the counselor. There still remains the danger that the child may shrink back or assume an artificial attitude as soon as his private affairs are discussed, and that his behavior will lose its spontaneity. The counselor does not desire to place the child's problem of adjustment in the center of his conscious attention for more than a few moments, unless the child is already full of it from the start. Distortions in the child's interpretation of the situation are less likely to occur if he does not feel that the psychologist is particularly interested in it. And before the psychologist, in the therapeutic procedure, makes the child feel what he considers important, he must—very inconspicuously—find out what the child considers important. This cannot, in many cases, be found out on an intellectual and highly linguistic level of communication. But much can be revealed by having the child do something he likes in the presence of the psychologist, who, part of the time, keeps in the background and does not impose his influence noticeably upon the child. The situation becomes natural, then, if the psychologist is working at something himself, and casual conversation takes place. That releases the child from the "tell-mother-everything" pressure. He may tell less in amount, but what he tells will be integrated with the whole field of his experience and his attitude toward his experience, as his play and contact with the psychologist will be included in his natural environment instead of being outside of it and, one might say, of different quality.

Of course, such a play interview will vary greatly according to the child's age and sex, his problem and its present state, his personality, and various other factors. Different kinds of relationship to authority will develop, from that of the submissive child, who waits for the counselor's direction in every detail of his activity, to that of the aggressive one who takes the lead from the start.

A seven-year-old girl, who had been referred because of her apparent unhappiness at home as contrasted with her leading rôle in a group of neighborhood children, was extremely shy and retiring when her mother first took her to see the counselor. She was unable to enjoy the play material offered to her, although she tried to use it. However, from the moment her mother and the counselor left the room, leaving her with the counselor's assistant, she became active and happy, and used liberally and with good imagination the same clay, drawing paper, and crayons which she had fingered listlessly before. She delighted in assigning tasks to her companion and dominated over her in a decided, although charming, manner.

The same child, observed in an experimental play group (which will be discussed later in this paper), behaved passively and quietly again. For the most part, she followed the directions of a somewhat older girl and smiled at the advances made to her by a very active boy, without joining in his activities. The shyness was observed at the beginning of every subsequent contact, although she liked to come and was always looking forward to her visit.

A few contacts were planned with this child so as to show her in a variety of situations. At the same time, both parents discussed the family's problem in a series of interviews, with increasing confidence in the counselor on the part of the mother. These revealed just what were the social difficulties of the child within her family and her whole environmental field, and the family's social difficulties, too. If the counselor had paid a visit to the home, which, incidentally, was distant, the parents would probably have been so self-conscious as to make the situation most artificial.

A nine-year-old boy who came to the counselor for a series of play interviews gradually developed an extensive, well-organized construction project, for which he used the Erector set, clay, pieces of wood, cardboard, and so on. He would start out at every new period where he had stopped at the end of the preceding one. He soon began to dramatize his activity, talking, singing, whistling, and making all kinds of noise for the different characters who played a part, no matter who might be disturbed by his noisiness. The counselor, working and writing in the same room, gave him just as much attention as was necessary to make him feel at home.

During his play and interwoven with it, most of his personal experiences of the day came up in some way, and, in reaction to that, the counselor could ask him a few questions. The reason for his difficulty—failure to adjust socially at school—became very evident during these play interviews. Obviously, his activities meant so much to him and captured his whole person so entirely that he forgot all the persons around him and their needs. Thus his extremely egocentric and asocial behavior, which had, of course, been most irritating at school, could be understood from the standpoint of his individual needs, and it was possible to institute an educational program aimed at establishing a balance between those needs and socially acceptable behavior.

In following the principle that the situation during a play interview should be natural, the psychologist will react to these various types of behavior in an individual way, encouraging the shy and passive child and resisting the domineering attitude of the aggressive child. He will experience within himself the emotional reaction of anger, irritation, disappointment, and so on, or feel pleased, charmed, and attracted by the child's behavior. This will help him to understand the parents' or teachers' reactions, no matter whether or not he can approve of them. At times, he will find it wise to join the play; at times, to leave the room and give the child some opportunity to continue without any outside influence. At times, he will ask concrete questions, perhaps more for the purpose of stimulating the child's thoughts than for immediate clear-cut answers. If a series of play interviews are taking place, certain individual patterns will develop. The child may report each time what happened at school or at home; he may discuss his experience with other children; he may reveal what he is hoping and dreaming or what he is worried about. While, gradually, the counselor will display a more active interest, the child will always have the chance for some spontaneous talk. There should always be natural periods without talking.

Practically, we cannot draw a precise border line between diagnostic and therapeutic procedure during play interviews. Therapy sets in gradually as the contact develops, and the psychologist gains insight into the whole situation around the child's problem. There may be a therapeutic influence at work from the beginning. Usually during the first contacts the diagnostic purpose predominates, while later on therapy takes the more important rôle. But, according to the assumption that the problem that is being attacked is part of a constant development, the counselor will always have to readjust and to bring his knowledge up-to-date, concerning not only outside events, but also the development of attitudes in the persons involved. Thus the diagnostic work—in the broadest possible sense— never comes to an end completely.

The play interview, with child play as an important tool, has some points of similarity with psychoanalysis of children as described by several authorities in this field. There are, however, fundamental differences in purpose and procedure, based on differences in the underlying theories. Although the scope of this paper does not allow a detailed discussion, the main differences may be stated briefly as follows:

1. The psychoanalyst establishes a contact that is in most respects different from all other contacts in the child's life. The psychological counselor attempts to establish the kind of contact he wants to teach the parents to have with the child.

2. In psychoanalysis the child is allowed and even stimulated to do and say things that he may not do and say in his home and school environment; this behavior is expected to help him become free from suppression, which in turn is supposed to have caused his maladjustment. In the play interview the psychologist does not stimulate so-called objectionable behavior. He accepts it when it occurs and tries to find out what it means for the child, but he does not believe that it is essential in every child's development.

3. In psychoanalysis the child's play and his behavior in general are considered as symbolic and are interpreted mainly as such. The sexual side of life is stressed in these interpretations. In the play interview, the actual content of the play is considered of primary importance. Likes and dislikes, abilities and disabilities, various kinds of attitude in connection with play material are studied and analyzed. Care is taken to give only such interpretations and explanations to the child as are in accord with clear evidence and with the child's actual needs. Emphasis is placed upon various aspects of life according to the individual differences of the children studied and their problems.

Situation IV: Play in a Group of Children. If children do not feel comfortable when alone with the counselor, or if they are being studied mainly because of their difficulties in getting along with other children, observation in a small experimental play group may give valuable information as to the specific obstacles in the way of social adjustment. By varying in a controlled way the different factors that accentuate the relationships in the group, the psychologist can find out, approximately, the situations for every child in which he is a useful member of the group and the situations that are crucial or too difficult for him. In addition to that, the specific part that the individual child is able to play in any of the various groupings can be ascertained. One variable factor in the set-up of the group is the play material offered—whether it invites the children mainly to coöperative, parallel, or solitary play, or whether it sponsors clashes and fights. Another factor is the space available for the various types of activity. The selection of the children in the group, involving such factors as similarity or diversity in age, sex, interest, social background, educational background, and personality traits, may also have important bearings on the behavior of each individual child. Another factor that can be varied is the rôle of the psychologist— whether he joins the group as a member or as the leader, whether he supervises it actively or less conspicuously or disappears in the background.

This situation offers us an opportunity to study the individual child in a more controlled social group setting than the individual family or school can offer. If a mother states that she is obliged to supervise her eight-year-old boy intensively lest he come home extremely dirty, the psychologist's first reaction may be to blame her for too high a standard of neatness. But when this same boy, in a group occupied with finger painting, soils his clothing much more than some of the younger members, and, in addition, delights in wiping his fingers on the others' faces, we begin to see him with his mother's eyes. When the nine-year-old who has been mentioned before is blamed for appropriating all the play material with no consideration for the other children, we certainly agree with his tutor that he acts egocentrically and asocially. But when we observe him becoming enthusiastic about some new material, and find out that, no matter what is offered to him, he sees *all* materials in connection with one another and has at once "wonderful" constructive ideas about how to use them, we begin to understand his point of view. Even though the findings will be highly specific and may vary from one day to another for the same child under similar conditions of the play group, certain general behavior trends and attitudes toward the other children—or toward the adult when the child is associated with other children—will persistently show up in the individual child. In addition, we are able to secure information as to the emotional threshold of the individual child for certain social stimuli and its changes under various conditions.

Again, as we realize that the child is constantly, although slowly, developing, we cannot expect our findings to be absolutely true. They merely suggest possibilities and perhaps limitations for the child's development; and they help us to discriminate between more or less favorable environmental conditions which are influencing the individual child's development.

Summary

I have tried to outline the various steps in the procedure of child guidance and to describe their values and limitations. Those methods which are particularly recommended in this paper tend to give an insight into the individual child's actual behavior. The psychologist wants to see the behavior, not merely to hear reports on it. He wants to learn through his own experience how the child may impress the persons of his environment, and in somewhat the same way, he wants to study the parents. This has, of course, been attempted before, mainly by means of visits to the child's home and school environment. But such studies have frequently proved to be unsatisfactory because of lack of time or complete coöperation, or for other reasons. Furthermore, one can never be sure whether a sample taken from school or home life during a visit will be representative for the specific environmental field of the child and helpful in solving the specific problem.

For a study of the dynamics of behavior and problem behavior, it is suggested that use be made of natural situations for observation arranged in the laboratory. From these, specific findings will be secured about the personalities of the child and his parent and their relationship within and outside of the family. Furthermore, as a matter of experience, these situations lead to a more sincere and more realistic contact with the family. The psychologist has entered their field, acting and reacting in it instead of watching it from the outside. This may affect favorably all the other steps of the guidance work. The interview may be based in part upon situations that have actually been experienced by both the parent and the counselor. Other situations that come up for discussion can be derived from and compared with those that the two have shared. Thus, there is a fair chance that both the counselor and the parent will know exactly what they are talking about. For an evaluation of test findings apart from their quantitative results, the study of the child will be helpful. In addition, visits to home and school can be planned with specific questions and problems in mind, derived from the laboratory observation.

A last word should be said about the time spent on such a study, although it is hardly possible to lay down any definite time span. Satisfactory results have been secured in a number of cases in one or two two-hour sessions. In many cases, however, more time will be needed. Just which kind of study should be stressed and which items may be omitted will depend upon the individual problem; it is generally possible to decide such questions during the first contact. If a group of psychologists are working together, they may save much time by having joint waiting groups and play groups. In general, the greater the experience of the worker, the more he may dispense with some of the procedures that are usually considered as necessary items in the diagnostic process.

ANNI WEISS FRANKL

United Jewish Social Services, Kansas City, Missouri

Play Interviews with Nursery School Children[1]

Introduction

Child guidance work, in recent years, has been enriched by the widespread use of play interviews. The method shows a wide variety of trends, varying with the background and philosophy of the therapist and the problems offered by the children. One of the most important features of the present development seems to be the tendency of the psychiatrist to renounce premature hypotheses about the causes underlying maladjustment in all those cases where they cannot readily and overtly be found; instead he concentrates upon the present manifestations of the child's difficulties and problems. Thus, after having considered the information from parents, teachers, or social workers about the child's background and history, he starts his work by utilizing the child's spontaneous activity for both diagnostic and therapeutic purposes.

For some time it has been considered indispensable for successful play therapy that the child be made to realize his need for help. Such a preparation for the therapeutic experience, it was thought, would motivate the child to give active cooperation to the psychiatrist. In the case of young children, this prerequisite has been dropped by some workers. They felt children were too young to be made aware of their problems. Experience seems to have proved

---

[1] Presented at the 1940 meeting. From the Winnetka, Ill., public school nurseries. Reprinted from American Journal of Orthopsychiatry, 1941, 11, 33–39. Copyright 1941 by American Orthopsychiatric Association.

that this omission did not affect the therapeutic success of the play interview method. Thus it seems justifiable to start by establishing rapport with the child and giving him opportunity to express himself through play. This procedure serves two purposes: one, to give the child the satisfying experience of a free play period with the sympathetic attention of the therapist; and the other, to give the therapist an opportunity for studying the child in action.

Purpose of Present Experiments with Play Interviews

In this paper no attempt will be made to review development and varieties of the method. This has been done competently in the American Journal of Orthopsychiatry and elsewhere. Only one particular way of using play interviews will be described. In the investigator's own work with this method at Columbia University, she has tried to develop it into an objective tool for the study of child personality. The present research was planned and carried out in connection with a more general observational study of the personality development of young children in the Winnetka and Chicago Nursery schools.[2]

In playing with these children, the writer was interested in finding out what the method would reveal about a child's personality, particularly his social and emotional characteristics. The focus was not so much upon the content of what the child had to say, verbally or through play, but upon his way of behaving, his behavior patterns. The child guidance worker, when asked for advice, is confronted with problems of the child's way of behaving that are frightening, puzzling or irritating to parents. It seems almost too matter-of-course to be mentioned that he should try to study how the child actually behaves when acting in the manner described as problematic. This is precisely what we are trying to study by means of play interviews. It will be shown how this method of approach for the study of behavior patterns can lead to increased understanding of the child as an individual, and how it can be used to advantage in educative guidance work with parents and children.

An exploration in the direction indicated can be done only by

---

[2] The study was greatly enriched by the valuable cooperation of the staffs of the Winnetka Public School Nurseries and the Chicago W.P.A. Nursery Schools. Grateful acknowledgment is made to Rose H. Alschuler, Director of both school units.

studying the child in an environment equivalent to a real life situation, that is, equivalent to what the child is experiencing every day in his play activities and social contacts. The nursery school offered a convenient setting. Here the worker could meet children informally and give opportunity for repeated individual interviews.

Preparatory Arrangements and Contacts

It has always been one of the writer's leading principles in psychological examinations to combine a controlled situation with the greatest amount of opportunity for spontaneity and freedom of expression by the children. Consequently, the stage for the play interview experiments was set so as to allow them to have the major initiative for action at all phases. The worker was an unobtrusive visitor for several days and let the children discern that she had some toys with which they could play. After that, the chief stimulation for play interviews was simply her presence and availability at school. The principle of spontaneity was applied even to the scheduling of interviews. Instead of having formal appointments, children could volunteer momentarily for play turns. Any child could come and have his turn immediately or was told he could come after the child who was playing at the time was through.

The study was not limited to the actual play interview but included all preparatory contacts and interactions between children and worker, and between different children in connection with the play interviews. In fact, it turned out that much illuminating information about a child's way of handling situations, and about his desires and the way he goes after them, could be obtained from these preparatory happenings. The attraction value of the play interviews rose and fell, for certain children, with certain events at school, behavior of other children, and other factors within or without the actual play interview situation. Some seemed little attracted by what the worker offered; for other children the opportunity for individual play sessions appeared to be an important event, and they tended to take as much advantage of it as they could. Most of them were at least curious. Each child approached the worker and her toys in his own way. The arrangement permitted the worker to observe how the different children reacted to the situation, what it meant to them in relation to other situations within their life span, how they made decisions and went after what they wanted.

Primarily, opportunities for play interviews were equal for all children. However, because of the worker's somewhat passive attitude, the children developed the situation and, in so doing, met certain characteristic constellations to which they had to adjust. At times, when a child wanted to play, the experimenter was not available for him. Sometimes, when she was free, the child preferred to do something else. The records show that some children frequently volunteered for play turns when it was obvious that they had no chance; others tended to pick the right moment for asking to be admitted. Some came from time to time to see if they could have a turn, and apparently were prepared for either alternative. They would leave again without being upset when they found that another child had come first; or else they decided to wait. Other children, however, came with nothing in mind but a wish to play, and resented finding themselves barred.

In this way, the experimental situation created problems for many of the children which, for some, grew into serious conflicts. Both teacher and worker were ready to help them overcome somewhat painful decisions or adjustments, such as postponement of a desired play period, or to let another child have their bicycle while they went with the worker. In that way, creation of lasting disappointments was avoided, but the conflict situation was sufficiently developed to offer valuable material concerning the individual child's attitude in it and his ability to cope with it. It was amazing to witness the enormous differences in problems and conflicts, both quantitatively and qualitatively, for different children in this basically similar situation. The program allowed the display of problems characteristic of the individual child and gave insight into his character.

Thus far, the writer has described how a real life situation was created in the setting of an experiment, just as real as the nursery and the home situation, with features of both of them, such as personal relationships, real contact with people, routine, privileges and limitations. The advantage of this set-up over an entirely free situation lay in the fact that a fair amount of knowledge about the children's physical and emotional conditions, their interests and experiences during the day was available to the investigator. A further control was effected by the arrangement that all activities connected with play interviews revolved around the worker who was prepared to observe and record them immediately.

The Play Interviews

With our aim at diagnosis and educative therapy in mind, we will now discuss some of the details that all play interviews had in common and to which the children reacted in their individual ways. They were free to choose play materials from a representative selection which had been provided, and could do with them as they pleased. There were blocks, crayons and paper, clay, dolls, cooking utensils, cars, trucks, stuffed animals, and some rags and scarfs. Care was taken not to offer materials directly suggestive of a single exclusive use, as is frequently done in play therapy with materials such as guns, beds, etc. Shooting, sleeping, etc., could be played with little imagination, with materials selected for the experiments; and, as a matter of fact, some of it was done by a number of children. The worker was more interested to see what the children would do with a variety of flexible materials than with materials offering restricted possibilities.

A few rules were always introduced during the first and second play interview. Most children are accustomed to rules and expect them, so that rules usually help to make a situation familiar. At the same time, reaction to the rules gave the observer a chance to find out a child's attitude toward them, and study the problems resulting from the child's attempt to conform to, or resist or ignore regulations. The child was taught that the toys belonged in a bag and that after the play period, they must go back into it. The worker did not insist on having the child put them back himself if he did not want to. Instead, she volunteered to help or do it herself. All she wanted him to realize was that the materials belonged in the bag. For the older children, another rule was introduced: the child was invited to select the toys he wanted to play with and put those he did not need at the time in a special place.

Children's reactions to these rules varied to a considerable extent. Some definitely asked for rules; they wanted to be sure they did things "right," and seemed at a loss when they did not get more definite instructions. They would ask a variety of questions, such as, "What is this supposed to be? How do you do this? What is this

for? May I take this? Where shall I put this? May I make noise?"
Other children accepted the rules given and did not actively seek
more. They took it as a matter-of-course that they could take from
the bag what they liked, and that, after the termination of the interview, everything had to go back. Some children indicated they had
had enough by putting the materials back in the bag. Others, after
having indicated they wanted to go back to the nursery room, hesitated and glanced at the toys, apparently reluctant to put them back
themselves and at the same time uneasy lest the toys would not get
back ino the bag. Some made an issue of it, defying the worker and
saying, "I'm not going to put them back; I hate it," or the like. Or
others, with more poise and diplomacy, "You put them back, I'm
in a hurry. I'll watch you put them back in the bag, I want to see
how you do it," or, hesitantly and worried, "You better do it, I
wouldn't do it right." Similarly, the separation of the needed from
the not-needed toys was reacted to in various ways. Most of the
older children were very much interested. Some would change frequently during one play session, while others would stick to the
same toys thoroughout one or even several periods. For some children, the rule did not seem to stand; they wanted to have everything
around in case they would need them. One boy kept the rule efficiently and conscientiously. In repeated play interviews he would
start by himself, "Now where are we going to put the things I don't
need?" He almost always put the dolls in that place, but several
times inspected them there in a playful, casual manner.

It will be noted that the rules, as they were introduced, imposed
only a minimum of restrictions. They were more or less impersonal
regulations that helped organize the play sessions. Yet the children
showed quite personal reactions to them, some feeling uneasy and
wanting more directions, others almost the opposite. It follows that
here, again, was valuable information as to how children tended to
react to environmental influences. One could discern what the directions meant to them, what they did with them, and, in visualiz-
ing the child's home situation as far as rules and regulations are concerned, could also determine how a specific environment influenced
a particular child and how he reacted to it.

As far as possible, the signal for termination of the play interview
was left to the children. Some tended to settle down for good and,

sometimes after more than an hour, had to be told it was time to go back to the nursery room. Other children investigated the materials, and when they believed they had seen everything and handled all, they announced they were through. Others again, after a more or less extended period of intensive play and maybe some conversation, became slightly uneasy and expressed their intention to go back, or readily accepted the worker's suggestion to leave. Others would come and start some play, then get tired of it and leave again. A few were keenly aware of the routine events at school, some of which they did not want to miss. For them, the termination of the play interview was dependent on the events outside of it. Extremely sensitive children would discontinue their activities when something went wrong in their play or when some noise or happening outside disturbed them. They apparently were so discouraged by the failure, or upset by the disturbance, that the whole play interview situation lost its attraction for the time being.

The toys were used, as would be expected, in many ways, varying with a child's age, interests, abilities, and other factors. The present paper will not enter into a discussion of the content of the children's activities with the experimental play materials. It will point out only some of the activity patterns which became evident during play interviews. For almost all children there was a developmental sequence as to treatment of the materials. First they explored, took the toys out, looked at them, eventually asked the worker or told her about them. This was followed by experimentation with the materials, and gradually a child would settle down with one or several things, and would use them again in subsequent play interviews. Then variations of these activities and more complex projects followed. Different materials were used together, and again, these projects would undergo changes, variations and developments. While the sequence became distinct in most children's activities, individual differences and peculiarities occurred to an amazing degree. Some children skipped certain phases of the sequence or ran through them so quickly they could hardly be noticed. Some children did not explore; they would play with the first thing that came to their hands or even wait to have the worker give them something. Others did not enter the stages of experimentation or variation. They would determine what the use of each object was and play with it in a stereotyped manner. These children rarely reached the project stage; they did not create anything but seemed satisfied to repeat what they had done or seen done by others.

The manner of work of individual children also varied at the different stages. Exploration was done gently and carefully by some, with an observable system of organization of the materials. For some, such a system of organization became a project in itself. They would set up everything neatly and put things together according to some principle, such as size, function, or similarity. Some children arranged materials into a decorative pattern; others would dump everything out more or less carelessly. In experimetation the taking apart and putting together of materials played an important role. Realistic and fanciful experimentations and projects were attempted and enjoyed. Some children, in their plans, would surpass the limits of what they could do or what could be done with the materials. They would give up altogether, or try again and again with increasing irritation, switch to something easier, or come to the experimenter for help. When she also was unable to do it, it was interesting to observe how some children were satisfied to know it could not be done, while others were keenly disappointed. They would blame her or the materials, and some gave evidence that they were distressed mainly because of their own inability to succeed.

The Interviewer's Attitude

So far we have dealt mainly with the description of the children's behavior. Now the interviewer's own attitude during the experimental period deserves some discussion. She was a psychological observer taking a diary record of a child's behavior in a controlled although complex situation. She differed from most psychological observers in that she was in the situation instead of outside. She took the place of the educator, the mother, or companion, according to what the child made her. She played with him if he wished, helped, admired, praised, answered, interfered when absolutely necessary. In other words, she did what a non-aggressive, friendly person in charge of a child would do. The one definite rule she had for herself was to be as little suggestive and as little interfering as was possible, while keeping up the few rules that had been introduced, and reacting to each child in the way suitable to his individuality.

Through this attitude a relationship was allowed to develop that had much reality for the child, and did not differ in quality from other relationships the child was having. The worker stepped into the role of one of the child's adult companions, and learned how they experience this individual child's behavior—what delights, disappoints, worries or puzzles them. Sooner or later she was bound to observe something in the child's behavior that would throw light upon his problems or the educator's problems with him. And, knowing the parents too, she could get an idea as to the particular way their child would impress them and be impressed by the environment they offered him.

At this point, the worker could begin to experiment by making slight variations in her overt responses to the child. She might help a fearful and insecure child with his play project and thus prevent him from giving it up before obstacles that impressed him as too difficult. She might give quiet, undivided attention to a restless child who was in danger of becoming more and more irritated by his own restlessness. She might pay less attention to a child who abandoned his play and tried actively to tease and annoy her, or she might join his play in a not-too-personal way and arouse his curiosity for exploring materials he had not yet seen. Such experimentation gave the worker a chance to find out conditions under which the individual child was able to be happy, to play constructively, and under what conditions his mood changed, in what situations he needed help, and when it was better to leave him alone.

Such an attitude makes possible a diagnosis of the child's personality in a dynamic sense. It allows insight not only into his abilities and traits but also how and under what conditions he is able to function. At the same time, it is the beginning of educative therapy, a form of therapy that can be explained and handed over to the parents and teachers. The term "educative therapy" has been used several times before and, at this point, its specific meaning in this paper will be illustrated by some examples. By taking cues from the child's behavior and his reactions to the adult during the observational period, the worker can use her influence on the child in a soothing, stimulating, or encouraging way. She can help him stabilize his mood, or open up new resources for interests and activities, or help him revise over-rigid taboos. She can be friendly and helpful in an impersonal way with a child who displays embarrassment when approached directly and closely. These are only a few examples which may serve to illustrate the method and its therapeutic possibilities.

Conclusions

By going through these various experiences with a child, one is gradually able to get a many-sided picture of him—of his likes and dislikes, his sensitivities, his abilities and shortcomings, his picture of the world as disclosed by the content of his conversation and activities, his questions, and the problems he sets for himself. One learns what tends to upset him, what gives him security, and what he seems to avoid or pursue. The result is more than an inventory. It is a live portrait of the individual, developing child. With this in mind, it is easier to visualize and understand what teachers and parents tell about the individual child. According to the writer's experience, it is one of the few satisfactory preparations for a worker in child guidance who is called upon to consult in matters of behavior difficulties. It provides a common basis for a discussion of the child between worker and parents. Both have had somewhat similar experiences with the child; so the worker, after his examination, has nothing to tell the parents that is entirely new to them. Instead he can start out describing the child as he has seen him and reacted to him, and, in an understanding way, encourage the parents to take part in the description and interpretation of the child's behavior. Many things the parents had known and to which they had paid little attention can be brought out in a new and significant light. Beliefs based on more or less well understood generalizations about children's behavior can be modified. In this way the parents themselves can be guided to use their own experience with the child constructively. Their intimate knowledge of him and their common sense can be called upon, so that the consultant does not have to instruct them in treating the child in a manner strange to their thinking. Instead he can lead them a step further on their own path by helping them understand the child's personality and adjust their treatment of the child accordingly.

WILLIAM A. HUNT

Northwestern University

The Future of Diagnostic Testing in Clinical Psychology[1]

Psychological testing has firmly established itself as a diagnostic procedure in clinical practice. The tests employed and the diagnostic uses to which they are put are well known and it is not proposed to review them here. Rather let us face the fact that diagnostic testing is at present in a state of relative stagnation. Anyone surveying the tremendous development of clinical psychology during the last ten years, and the major importance that psychological testing assumes in such clinical practice, cannot help but be struck by the small amount of progress we have made in developing our psychological tests as diagnostic instruments. Our advances have been in the expansion of physical facilities, in the extension of clinical services, rather than in the improvement of our existing diagnostic techniques and the discovery of new ones. This paper will offer a possible explanation of our lack of progress and suggest certain lines of attack upon our problems that may help to move us out of the present doldrums.

To do this it is necessary to return to fundamentals. My suggestions will stem from two basic premises concerning the fundamental nature of testing:

1. The main contribution of the psychological test is that it offers an opportunity of sampling a subject's behavior in a standard situation.

[1] This paper is based upon some remarks delivered before the Chicago Psychology Club and the University of Minnesota chapter of Psi Chi. Reprinted from *Journal of Clinical Psychology*, 1946, 2, 311–317. Copyright 1946 by Frederick C. Thorne.

2. The main contribution of the individual test (as opposed to the group test) is that it offers the tester an opportunity personally to observe such behavior as it takes place.

It follows from the first premise that the primary datum offered by the psychological test is the subject's raw behavior in the test situation. The mathematical symbols into which this behavior can be translated are secondary instruments of convenience and should not be allowed to conceal the primary datum, the actual behavior. That our mathematical measures, ranging from the simple use of numerical units in scoring to the use of symbolic measures such as the mental age and the intelligence quotient, do obscure the richness of the behavioral data upon which they are based would be admitted by any psychologist, but the point needs constant reemphasis.

Let me illustrate it by quoting some actual answers to two questions on the Information sub-test of the Wechsler-Bellevue Intelligence Scale. In response to the question, "How far is it from Paris to New York?" a subject may answer "About 3,000 miles"; but I have had another subject say "Unfortunately I cannot be as exact as I would like to. No, I don't know exactly. For an approximation —about 3,000 miles. Sorry I can't answer more definitely." Both these answers are correct and count the same in the scoring system, with the numerical symbols concealing the diagnostic richness of the second answer. In response to the question, "Where is Egypt?" a subject may answer "In South America"; but I have had a schizophrenic answer "In a manner of speaking it may be said to be in an oasis—plenty surrounded by sand." Both answers are wrong and in scoring are represented by the same symbol, zero. Not only is the pathological significance of the second answer lost, but I would submit that a real difference in intelligence is overlooked.

A further example may be offered from one of Kent's brief tests of Mathematical Reasoning. One of the questions is "If 8 boys club together and pay 2 dollars for the use of a room, how much should each pay?" Any answer other than 25¢ is scored as incorrect, but a careful examination of the various "wrong" answers shows some interesting differences among them. The most frequent responses for those mental deficients who attempted this question were 4 and 16. Apparently the mental deficients were able to isolate the necessary mathematical elements of the problem (8 and 2) and also to comprehend vaguely that something more "complex" than addition or subtraction was called for. Unable to divide 2 by 8, they fell back either upon multiplying 2 by 8 or upon dividing 8 by 2. On the other hand, a group of malingerers tended to answer 23¢ or 27¢ with a range of answers through the twenties. They grasped the fundamental procedure but selected an error in calculation as their response, something the mentally deficient did not show. The examination of test responses on this question thus enables us not only to subject the reasoning processes of the mental deficient to further analysis but also to differentiate true mental deficiency from malingering (125).[2] All this would have been lost had we not carried our examination back beyond the numerical scores to the original test behavior.

Many individual clinicians do not overlook such data. They are not content to base their judgment upon the mere test score or profile of scores but carry their interpretation back to the subject's original performance. This is done somewhat shamefacedly, and is referred to apologetically as the exercise of "clinical judgment" or even more apologetically as "clinical intuition." This is not intuition in the mystical sense. It is the same sort of intellectual process of judgment that ensues when a psychologist considers a test score in the light of the known validity and reliability of the test used before making an interpretation, and in many cases the mathematical data upon which such an interpretation is based are no more reliable than the observational data upon which we base our clinical "intuitions."

Our standard test manuals, however, give little space to any discussion of the quality of test responses and their interpretive significance. The Wechsler-Bellevue manual (284) devotes only 22 pages to criteria for scoring. The Terman-Merrill manual (262) is much better, but both manuals limit their treatment of test responses to the problem of translating the response into the particular numerical symbols used in their respective scoring systems. Nor is the professional literature more helpful. Our journals are filled with articles on the mathematical treatment of test scores, but only rarely does one find any discussion of actual test behavior and its significance. Behavior as such, seems to be viewed as a necessary evil, justified

---

[2] Bibliography begins on page 428.

only by the fact that it will yield us a numerical symbol with which we can then embark upon a flight of mathematical abstraction.

There is no necessary antithesis between the observation of the subject's test behavior and the expression of this behavior in convenient numerical symbols which lend themselves to statistical manipulation. The two approaches are complementary. Actually some return to the observation of test behavior is a necessary precursor to further numerical "objectification." In a recent paper on "An Analysis of the Concept of Clinical Intuition," Cofer (50) has attempted to identify some of the actual test behaviors upon which our clinical judgments are based. Once such behaviors are identified they can be translated into numerical symbols. If they prove valid diagnostic indicators we then extend our objective scoring system to include them.

We can use the Kent item mentioned above as an illustration. At present the response "25¢" contributes one point to a score for intelligence. Any other answer contributes nothing. An examination of these "other" answers, or errors, however, reveals reliable differences between the mistakes made by the truly mentally deficient and those made by malingerers. It is then possible to extend our scoring system, and say that any answer not 25 but within the range of the twenties will also count one point on a scale for malingering.

The purpose of the present paper, however, is not merely to encourage clinical psychologists to look beyond test scores to the underlying test behaviors, nor to suggest the stimulation and new research ideas that might result from such contact with the raw materials of clinical diagnosis. The value of such an approach is accepted in psychology. Rather we would call attention to two consequences which follow logically from the acceptance of this view and which have implications for the development of our diagnostic techniques.

Since we are all agreed upon the diagnostic richness of actual test behaviors, and since most of us, however apologetic we may be in practice, do use such behavior as a basis for our clinical judgments, let us face this fact in the development of new tests. Individual test items as well as types of sub-tests differ in the amount of such clinical material that they offer. Let us rework our present tests and throw out those items that do not offer it. In constructing new tests let use select items that are deliberately chosen not only to allow a

numerical measure but also to provide the subject with an opportunity for revelatory clinical behavior even though it goes beyond
the present potentialities of "objectification." Without losing the
objective efficiency of our present tests we can increase their clinical
utility by such deliberate selection of diagnostically rich test items.

If we are to encourage the use of such test material, we must face
the fact that only trained clinicians can use it. We need as psychological tests trained observers and interpreters with a wealth of clinical experience behind them, not untrained cashiers to operate an
automatic scoring cash register. These last may be left to the field of
group testing which is frankly committed to the limitations of the
exclusively objective approach. Group testing is essentially nomo-
thetic. In the individual test, however, we can add to the nomo-
thetic all the flexibility of the idiographic approach.

This leads us to the second premise stated at the beginning of
our paper—that the main contribution of the individual test (as
opposed to the group test) is that it offers the tester an opportunity
personally to observe the subject's test behavior as it takes place.
There are other contributions. A wider range of test materials can
be presented. Moreover, the standard conditions assumed in the
group testing conditions assumed in the group testing situation can
more definitely be assured. The opportunity for the observation of
test behavior, however, remains the primary value of the individual
technique.

This second premise has an implicit corollary that is often overlooked. It is that in the individual testing situation the tester is expected to contribute to raising the level of prediction. This is not to
say that the tester in the individual test situation *does* succeed in
raising the level of prediction. A poor tester may even lower it. The
fact remains, however, that his participation is based either implicitly or overtly on the belief that his presence will increase the efficiency of the testing. In this connection we might cite the practice
of some clinical psychologists in administering group tests on an individual basis. Such a contribution might come about through the
wider range of materials that can be presented, or through the extra
care which is possible in administering the test and the extra attention which can be given in assuring the desired standard conditions.
It may also come about through the deliberate intervention of the
tester in changing some of the "standard" conditions to fit some

special requirement of the subject or of the testing situation, as well as through the clinical interpretation of the resulting score or the addition of a further clinical judgment based upon the observation of test behavior which is not amenable to translation into standard scoring measures. Such procedures may be frowned upon officially, but they are used by most practicing clinical psychologists, who seem willing both to accept them and to attempt their justification. Unless the tester in the individual testing method is expected to make some such contribution toward better prediction it is difficult to justify his participation.

At the risk of being accused of making an artificial or erroneous distinction between group testing and individual testing, I should like to bring out what seems to me to be an underlying and tacit, though seldom consciously realized, difference in fundamental philosophy between the two approaches. The accepted goal of both is perfect prediction. I would submit, however, that in general, group testing is used in situations where a certain amount of error is acceptable, and that psychologists using group tests operate acquiescently and even contentedly in many situations in which the test prediction is far below the level of perfection. On the other hand, it seems to me that the individual tester never openly accepts the margin of error inherent in the test, but always strives consciously and definitely toward perfect prediction. I am not saying that the individual test actually does come closer to perfection, nor denying the value of group tests and their necessary use in many situations, but merely suggesting a difference in the fundamental motivation of the people using them. My point is that group tests are used with full acceptance and understanding of the test error involved, whereas the individual test is used in an attempt to lessen the inherent test error, with the clinician striving through personal supervision and the addition of clinical interpetation to achieve better prediction than can be attained with the mass methods of group testing. Whether or not he is successful is another question.

This difference in philsophy between the group test and the individual test was evident in their military uses. In general group tests were used in selection procedures where the manpower pool from which the selectees were drawn was large and where failure on the test did not unduly stigmatize the individual. Thus in the Navy, group tests were used in classification for selecting candidates for the various trade schools, specialized services where the manpower reserve from which the candidates were taken was sufficiently large so that the loss through test error of some potentially acceptable men was not serious, and where men rejected by the test were not lost to the Navy but were passed on to some other branch of the service. Moreover, while the failure to make a certain trade school may have seemed important to the recruit involved, his failure to do so did not entail any serious social stigma. The same was true of the use of group tests in selecting aviators. As opposed to this, individual tests plus clinical interpretation were used in the neuropsychiatric examination where the manpower reserve being tapped (the military manpower potential of the country as a whole) was low, where rejection meant the loss of the man to the military services, and his return to society with the social stigma attached to a discharge for psychiatric reasons. The same general trend is reflected in civilian practice where group tests are used for such things as selecting insurance salesmen, admission to college, selecting students for special classes, etc., while the individual test with a clinical interpretation is relied upon in cases such as commitment to an institution, where the social consequences for the individual are particularly severe.

We have already advocated the frank and open acceptance of the importance of the clinical psychologist in the individual testing situation and the admission as a valid clinical instrument of his use of clinical intuition or, as I would rather phrase it, professional judgment. Such acceptance, however, cannot be based upon faith, hope, and professional charity toward one's clinical colleagues. It must be based upon a sound body of scientific evidence. It will be necessary to consider the clinician objectively as a testing instrument and to submit him to the same objective processes of validation that we would use in evaluating any test. The validity and reliability of his judgments are as open to experimental verification as are the validity and reliability of our tests, and such verification must be carried out.

The objection is often raised to the clinical approach that, while many clinicians can make valid clinical judgments, many cannot, i.e., that there are bad as well as good clinicians. The same thing is true of psychological tests. There are bad tests as well as good tests. When we discover that a test is bad, we do not hesitate to discard it. Just so, when we find that a clinician is "bad," or cannot make valid professional judgments, he, too, should be discarded, or limited in his activities to those fields where the value of his contribution can be demonstrated. Such evaluation of clinicians has been lacking in the past, nor will it be easily installed in the future, although the present interest of the American Psychological Association in certification for applied psychologists is a hopeful sign.

In evaluating clinical performance we must be careful to avoid committing the "isomorphic" error that has marked our previous thinking when we have assumed that there is a direct, one-to-one correlation between the performance of the individual clinician and the excellence of the training program which he has undergone. We have limited our critical inspection to a survey of the thoroughness of the curriculum, excellence of the teaching staff, and breadth of clinical experience available in those institutions which offer training programs, assuming that a good training program assured a good clinician. Unfortunately this is not always so, and it will be necessary to supplement our evaluation of training programs by a further professional examination of the clinicians they produce. The evaluation we are suggesting, however, goes well beyond the original selection of clinical workers for the field. We would propose a continuous evaluation of clinical performance as an integral part of administrative practice in any clinic.

Such evaluation may be difficult to obtain on an individual clinician working independently, but is relatively easy if the clinician is functioning as one of a team in an organized clinic. In this latter case it is easy to have an individual's judgment checked by a colleague or by further testing. In most clinics the patient is usually seen by more than one professional worker and the record will contain test scores and case history material which offers a further check. Adequate follow-up material on each case could also be obtained. In fact, if an adequate system of clinical records is established, the checking of each worker's efficiency becomes merely a matter of clinical bookkeeping which can be done with little extra work, and provides a continuous, running evaluation of clinical performance for any staff member.

Such a system was in practice at the Psychiatric Unit at the Newport, R. I., Naval Training Station during the last war whenever the exigencies of the war emergency left time for its use. It was thus possible to make a direct comparison of the relative efficiency of the psychiatric interview administered by the staff personnel and the group paper-and-pencil test as neuropsychiatric selection procedures (300). It developed that both procedures were about equal in their detection rate for potentially unfit personnel but that the false-positive rate (number of fit recruits falsely identified as unfit) was much higher for the test. As a result, the paper-and-pencil test was used as a preliminary coarse screen to select men for subsequent psychiatric interview, and it was possible to cut down the number of personnel engaged in interviewing by two-thirds without loss in the efficiency of the screening procedure. It also developed that there were large individual differences in the ability to handle the brief psychiatric interviewing technique, with the result that specialization was introduced with some members of the staff being assigned to interviews and others being given the task of working up cases on the ward where the pace was more leisurely and a more detailed, painstaking investigation of each case was necessary. Moreover, differences in the ability to handle certain types of case were discovered. Some men were good at handling psychopathic personalities; others were not, but might excel with schizophrenics, epileptics, or homosexuals. These differences were taken into account in assigning cases, and more efficient teamwork was the result.

On the testing side, differences were revealed in the ability to handle the abbreviated intelligence testing techniques used to supplement the original screening interview. Some men were very proficient with these, others did better with the longer tests such as the Wechsler-Bellevue scale. Some clinicians were excellent with the Rorschach test, some with the Minnesota Multiphasic, while others produced adequate judgments of personality structure as a secondary product of administering individual intelligence tests. The demonstration of such individual differences in clinical performance made an efficient allotment of duties possible. The continuous nature of the check provided by such clinical bookkeeping even made possible the detection of the "staleness" and operational fatigue which developed inevitably in a group which was being driven dangerously close at times to the limits of physical capacity. It was a compliment, not merely to the professional caliber of the staff at Newport but to the professional motivation and integrity

of psychiatry and psychology as a whole, that such evaluation procedures were actively welcomed and willingly participated in by the
individual staff members.

What we are suggesting here is the application of the principles
of applied psychology to the field of clinical practice itself. Psychology has long been a leading proponent of efficient personnel procedures in industry and has produced many important studies in the
field of motor skills and the efficient organization of work habits.
It is fitting now that it turn its attention on itself, and there is no
better field in which to begin than clinical psychology. Efficiency
engineering is as appropriate in the clinic as it is in industry, and if
the volume of future clinical practice turns out to be anywhere near
our present estimates it will be not only appropriate but necessary.

Summary

This paper opened with the observation that diagnostic testing
in clinical psychology was in a state of developmental quiescence
with little evidence at present of any very effective solution of its
many problems. After considering certain premises concerning the
basic nature of testing, some suggestions were made for progress
within the field. These suggestions may be summarized as follows:

1. As clinical psychologists we should pay more attention to the
subject's raw behavior in the actual testing situation and not concentrate exclusively on the resulting numerical scores.

2. We should rework our tests to obtain items which will yield
diagnostically rich observable material as well as convenient numerical measures.

3. We should accept the importance of the clinician as a contributing element in the test situation.

4. We should consider the individual clinician as a clinical instrument, and study and evaluate his performance exactly as we study
and evaluate a test.

ROBERT I. WATSON

Washington University School of Medicine

Diagnosis as an Aspect of the Clinical Method: A Review[1]

Psychological procedures directed toward acquiring knowledge about the origin and nature of the conditions affecting the adjustment of the individual under consideration have been described in the previous articles in this section of the *Readings*. The present review is concerned with some of the other literature that should be of value in diagnostic methodology. No attempt will be made to describe the material in detail; rather, information sufficient only to identify the nature of the topic under consideration is given.

On examination of the sources which form the basis for this review, it was decided that they could best be presented through a consideration of the literature concerned with various kinds of diagnostic techniques, followed by an account of the references on these and other techniques more specifically directed to some particular class of individuals for whom they were developed. Accordingly, the plan of presentation includes discussions of clinical prediction, the case study, tests, ratings, observation and word association as techniques in general, and then an examination of accounts of diagnostic procedures specifically directed to work with mentally deficient persons, with children showing behavior difficulties, with guidance activities in the narrower sense, and with patients exhibiting severe personality disorders. Although these latter four categories do not coincide with those adopted in connection with the previous

---

[1] Prepared especially for this volume.

section of the Readings, which was concerned with the various functions of the clinical psychologist, it was found that the studies considered valuable could be presented in terms of such categories without either artificiality or incongruity. Despite the placement in a setting of one or another of the four areas of specialization, certain articles are included in the general discussion of a given technique. Since they are considered to have an obviously broader significance, these references are not repeated in the later discussions of the literature concerned with specialized groups. Thus, certain publications of Williamson and Darley which contain material about tests, although manifestly of interest to guidance clinicians and directed to them, are considered of sufficient general interest to warrant referral when considering testing in general and are omitted in the later discussion of diagnostic procedures in guidance.

Clinical Prediction

Basic to the orientation of the clinician to the task of diagnosis is the attitude that he takes toward the problem of prediction. One way of stating the issue is that expressed by Sarbin, who contrasts actuarial prediction by regression equations with what he chooses to call clinical prediction on the basis of interpretation of case study data. He presents evidence that in the particular situation studied "clinical predictions add nothing to the actuarial prediction" (233, p. 597).[2] Since the skill of clinicians varies, as does the predictive efficacy of regression equations, this is not conclusive for all situations. In reference to the same problem Chein (48) cogently reminds us that the clinician is more interested in effecting change than in passive prediction. In stating his own point of view, Allport (3) forcefully presents the case for those who would hold that case study predictions are to be understood in terms of a comprehensive view of the personality in all of its individuality, with the implication that no series of regression equations can be more than a pallid partial substitute. Three articles appearing in Sociometry bear upon the issue of clinical prediction (Stouffer, 252; Cottrel, 54; Lundberg, 160) as do three others appearing in Character and Personality (Vernon, 277; Cattell, 45; Thomas, 263). A shift in emphasis occurred in the latter series in that the controversy centered on the

---

[2] Bibliography begins on page 428.

relative degree of reliability of case history (anamnestic) and test (psychometric) data. This discussion stimulated a study by Davis (65) in which he found that both biographical and psychometric data play an important role in the clinical judgments formed, but that whereas in cases involving children's adjustment problems biographical materials were more important, the reverse was found in vocational advisement cases. The general conclusion was that both are needed. Also relevant is the volume edited by Horst (121) on the prediction of personal adjustment. This includes a study on the prediction of individual behavior from case studies by Wallin, who also reviews the pertinent literature.

That there is diversity of opinion about the diagnostic implications of a case study is effectively demonstrated in the inquiry of Elkin (77), who gives a life-history report concerning a delinquent boy to a variety of psychiatrists, psychologists, anthropologists, and sociologists. Neither within a specialty group nor in general is there any agreement in interpretation of the meaning of either a behavior fragment or the significance of the case as a whole.

The Case Study

The case study is the means whereby the clinician is able to draw diagnostic inferences, relations, associations, and organizations from the raw data of which it is constituted. The clinical psychologist's skill in integrating the data is dependent upon individual factors of training and personality beyond the scope of this volume. However, considerable effort has been expended to aid clinicians as much as possible in this task. For example, the material of which the case study is made up has been organized systematically in order that the individual may more readily grasp its significance. Organization of the case study is, in a sense, similar in intent to statistical analysis because both are means of reducing an array of data to a form in which they can be grasped.

One of the more penetrating analyses of the preparation of the case study, although all too short, is presented in Allport's book on personality (3). Other valuable general discussions are offered in Louttit (156), Symonds (258), and Marzolf (171). Although designed for school teachers, the manual by English and Raimey (78) on the case study of the child brings together in a systematic fashion a considerable body of information which should prove helpful to the clinician irrespective of the age group with whom he is working.

Some discussion has occurred about the value of using prepared case study blanks. Louttit, preliminary to his description of the Indiana Psychodiagnostic Blank, summarizes arguments for and against the use of such devices (153). It is sometimes argued that in actual practice many clinicians do not use forms or other material guides. Their dispensing with these aids is probably due to such a degree of familiarity with some frame of reference that there is no necessity for a manifest guide in diagnostic sessions. Examination of case notes, however, will show that some form of organization is being used. A desirable goal for the psychologist to achieve is sufficient familiarity with the appropriate format to make possible guiding the diagnostic examination to bring out all the desired information in a natural fashion without direct reference to this format and without artificially forcing the session into a rigid formal and temporal mold.

After the examination it is necessary to report. The most exhaustive discussion of case reporting or recording of interest to the psychologist was prepared by a social worker for use in that profession. This author, Gordon Hamilton (107), deals with case recording in a number of its manifold aspects, including the purpose of recording; the organization of the record's contents; the recording styles of narrative, summarized, and interpretive recording; the various forms of a diagnostic statement; the recording prognosis; and the statement of treatment evaluation. The transfer to the work of the clinical psychologist is immediately apparent to the reader. Of less direct interest is a somewhat similar publication by Bristol (29), but her chapters on some fundamental problems of recording, accuracy, objectivity, brevity, and conciseness and clarity are worthy of examination.

The modern approach to the thoroughgoing case study owes much to the insight and effort of Murray and his co-workers at the Harvard Psychological Clinic. In the monumental *Explorations in Personality* (194), after proposing and developing a theory of personality, they present a series of procedures, many of them used for the first time in connection with the studies they report. A very elaborate case history of a single individual based on these procedures follows. However, for the person unfamiliar with this work the best introduction to the methodology is contained in an earlier article by Murray (193). A wealth of material as yet by no means fully exploited is offered in this article on techniques for a systematic investigaton of fantasy. After a description of what he conceives fantasy to be, Murray describes a considerable variety of what we would now call projective techniques, including questioning about fantasies, dreams and favorite themes, word association tests, induced visions, similes test ("as unhappy as . . ."), reveries induced by musical compositions, a word projection test, image projection by the Beta Ink Blots, a picture completion test, stories that were suggested by smelling various odors, elaboration of one or two sentence stories, elaboration of a short story, arranging a dramatic production from properties supplied, and the well-known Thematic Apperception Test. The way in which the results of this motley array were organized meaningfully, the general technique of interpretation, and some procedures of verification are then discussed. Later articles systematically growing out of and supplementing their studies in the *Explorations in Personality* include Murray and Morgan's clinical study of sentiments (195) and the article by White, Tomkins, and Alper (293) on a case study of an individual successfully adapted to his cultural needs and external reality. The account by Bellak and Jacques (15) of dynamic conceptualization in case studies is also relevant.

The Interview

The interview is a technique that has ramifications extending to the other aspects of diagnosis. An individual test, after all, is a standardized interview, as is a word association measure, whereas observations with or without ratings are made on the basis of information secured during its course. It is basic then to these other procedures. Obviously, much of what takes place during diagnostic procedures is based upon interviewing.

But it is likewise obvious that many interviews are not diagnostic in nature. The intent of many interviews is quite alien to the present consideration, e.g., public opinion polling and interviews used specifically for the collection of research data. Interviews such as those conducted by Landis and his associates (147) for securing information on problems of psychosexual development contained, as the investigators indicate, many questions that seem direct and brusque to the clinician. This directness, they go on to point out, was justified because they were not interested in the therapeutic value of the discussion. On the other hand, all diagnostic interviews may have a greater or lesser therapeutic effect, furthering treatment or hindering it.

Thus diagnostic interviews have therapeutic connotations. Interviews primarily therapeutic in nature, however, as well as those approaches in which diagnostic and treatment procedures merge imperceptibly will be considered in connection with treatment, e.g., non-directive counseling and play technique, even though the latter interview-observation approach is represented earlier in this section of the Readings by the article of Weiss Frankl.

Despite these and other complicating factors there is a considerable substratum of agreement about techniques of interviewing. Unfortunately this is more often agreement of opinion than agreement based on the data of objective studies of the positive aspects of the method, since these investigations are still few in number.

A variety of rather detailed general sources of information about the interview have appeared. Certain parts of Bingham and Moore (24) contain valuable material, especially the first four chapters concerned with general principles of interviewing, learning how to interview, interviewing students, and vocational counseling. Their position in regard to these issues is that of a traditional persuasive directive approach.

The two volumes of Garrett (93, 94), though with a case work and a personnel setting respectively, contain valuable information of an elementary sort. Influenced by the traditional approach, Miss Garrett has also integrated certain aspects of the relationship therapy associated with the work of Rank and Taft in her accounts. Another account of interviewing by a social worker is that of Young (306). She considers the nature of the objectives, the types, and the techniques of interviewing. Oldfield (201) examines at length the psychology of the interview, basing his account upon the premise that an interviewer's judgment is a judgment of the attitudes of the person interviewed. His account, therefore, follows this premise when dealing with the display and perception of attitudes, the setting of the interview, its conduct, and the observation and assessment of the interviewee. Still another general approach to the interview is given by Fenton (81) in a short manual. He presents his views with particular emphasis on interviewing the child, but many of his comments are applicable to other age groups. Other accounts of traditional interviewing useful to the clinician are given by Darley (64), MacFarlane (164), Paterson, Schneidler and Williamson (207), Strang (253), Watson (283), and Woodward and Rennie (303).

Psychiatrists naturally are concerned with problems of the interview peculiar to their diagnostic and therapeutic tasks. Whitehorn (294) has published a guide to interviewing and personality study of direct relevance to the psychologist. Valuable in itself, it also illustrates how the views held on psychodynamics directly influence the interviewing technique followed. This is likewise the case with Cobb (49) in his analysis of a technique of interviewing a patient with a psychosomatic disorder.

The literature on the interview is so vast that only a few other selections can be mentioned. They have been chosen as offering accounts of particular value to the clinical psychologist on as wide a variety of problems as possible. This, then, is the only trend of consistency in the account that follows. Certain issues basic to valid interviewing procedures are the sources of error (Neely, 199), the securing of rapport (Symonds, 259), the influence of the halo effect (Bingham, 23), the logical structure of the questions used (Martin, 169), the distinction between description and inference (Gaw, 95), the completeness and accuracy of interviewing reports (Covner, 55), and the psychological processes playing a part in the interview (Berdie, 19).

Tests

Limitation of space prevents dealing with the literature on specific tests of interest to the clinician. Since bibliographic sources list thousands of references, only material of a general nature can be mentioned here. Somewhat arbitrarily, then, articles and books devoted to a specific test will have to be excluded from consideration unless they illustrate some more general point.

The clinical tests used vary, of course, from agency to agency, but fortunately there is a certain degree of uniformity. From recent investigations it would appear that two patterns exist, one in college, psychiatric, and children's clinics in the narrow sense, and the other in counseling and guidance services. In 1947 Louttit and

Browne (157) reported on questionnaires mailed to 59 agencies representative of the first or "clinical" pattern asking them to indicate the tests they used. In 43 completed returns a total of 101 tests were mentioned at least four times. The nine most frequently used tests were, in order of popularity, the 1937 Revision of the Stanford Binet, the Wechsler-Bellevue, the Goodenough Draw-A-Man, the Rorschach, the Thematic Apperception, the Gray Oral Reading, the Arthur Performance, the Stanford Achievement, and the Strong Vocational Interest Test. The Veterans Administration Vocational Advisement Centers are presumably typical of counseling and guidance services in their choice of devices. Darley and Marquis, in their survey of these centers given earlier in the *Readings*, found the nine most popular tests to be the Kuder Preference Record, the various Otis intelligence tests, the Wechsler-Bellevue, the American Council Psychological Examination, the various Cooperative Achievement tests, the Strong Interest, the Minnesota Clerical, the Minnesota Multiphasic, and the Bennett Mechanical Comprehension Test. Similar findings are reported by Baker and Peatman (8). It will be noted that there is very little overlapping, the clinic group stressing the use of individually administered tests and the advisement units on the use of group tests. An individual clinical use is made, however, of the psychometric findings in both groups of agencies. Moreover, the inquiry of Baker and Peatman showed that practically all instruments used in clinics are also used in advisement agencies but that their usage occurs proportionately less often.

It is unfortunate that there is no one convenient source in which are brought together adequate summaries of such matters as the administration, the validity, and the diagnostic clues of even the most popular tests. Many test manuals are notoriously inadequate; some, such as those for the Wechsler-Bellevue and Stanford-Binet, are more useful and comprehensive. The clinical usage of many tests would be improved if manuals such as that which Darley (63) prepared for the Strong Vocational Interest Blank were available. There is an urgent need for comparable volumes. Just as there is no general volume on clinical methodology as such, there is no detailed, even partially exhaustive, discussion of individual psychological tests from the point of view of the clinician. Many accounts of clinical test methodology are either buried in journal articles primarily concerned with research problems and only incidentally methodological, or discussed in such a general fashion as to be almost useless.

The sources giving the best coverage for a preliminary survey of all kinds of tests are the psychological measurement yearbooks edited by Buros (36, 37, 38, 39). They are designed to give the prospective user the critical opinions of experts on the validity, reliability, and usability of the measures reviewed. They thus help to minimize the use of tests that cannot stand such scrutiny. On the other hand, once this is done, and a test decided upon as worthy of trial, the only help it gives the clinician is a non-annotated bibliography. It is unfortunate that limitations of space would permit nothing more, for the clinician needs information on administration and interpretation for diagnostic purposes. The bibliographies of Hildreth (116, 118) are of some value in locating tests but not in their evaluation, since they are only listings. The catalogues of the various test publishers are also convenient and valuable listing sources.

Two major journal review sources of material on psychological tests are available to the clinician: the *Psychological Bulletin*, which publishes reviews at irregular intervals, and the *Review of Educational Research* (e.g., cf. 198), which sponsors one triennially. The material included is apt to stress the results found by applying the test or tests under consideration to various populations, the derivation of reliability and validity indices, comparison with other tests, and so on. Such reviews, although valuable, are not necessarily useful in individual diagnosis.

Generally speaking, the many volumes published to be used in courses in tests and measurements are unsatisfactory to the clinical psychologist, covering, as they do, so much material irrelevant to his interest. Often written on a superficial level, they pay relatively little attention to the individual test. The book by F. N. Freeman (89) is a distinguished exception. The section on the criteria for the choice of tests and the chapters on the technique and theory of tests and interpretation of tests are especially valuable. Greene's lengthy book (101) on problems of measurement and the description of some typical tests has a certain value to the clinician. The chapters on the degree of control shown in various testing situations, the interpretation of scores, and the effect of practice on test scores are especially useful. The volume by Mursell (196) is also of value. Presentation in Paterson, Schneidler, and Williamson (207) and in Williamson and Darley (297) of material about tests in guidance has a utility for other than specialists in this field. Wells's *Mental Tests in Clinical Practice* (286), although published in 1927, is still of value because of its clinical orientation. In the same year Bronner and her associates (30) published a manual of individual tests on which the clinician must also depend.

A volume with which every clinician should be familiar is the *Mental Examiners' Handbook* of Wells and Ruesch (288). Designed for the psychiatric examiner, it contains a considerable variety of short, easily administered test questions, the answers to which are interpreted not so much by referral to psychometric norms as on the basis of the clinician's subjective judgment growing out of his experience. The use of the testing devices described therein drives home more than any other published source the fact that the test situation is to be used to study the patient, not to derive a score. It is especially useful for the examination of a large number of individuals in a short time, for the examination of the bedridden whose restricted energy does not permit extended examination, and for a preliminary examination to decide on the exact nature of the extensive battery to be used in a particular case.

Undue or unwise dependence upon the results of psychological tests has been the concern of some clinicians. Kent (136), drawing on her extensive clinical experience, has written very forcefully about the difficulties in depending upon psychometric instruments for valid information. Her article supplements the discussion by Doll in the *Readings* of psychometric pitfalls in clinical practice. The article by Kuhlmann (146) is somewhat in the same vein in that he shows a skepticism regarding certain trends in the use of tests which he considers retrogressive.

Books, monographs, and articles concerned with specific kinds of tests are so numerous that only a few can be mentioned here. Measures of personality, aptitude, intelligence, and interest will be considered. Vernon (278), writing on the assessment of psychological qualities by verbal methods, shows a thorough familiarity with both the American and the British literature on personality measurement by structured instruments up to the time of publication (1938). In the same area, Traxler (269), writing in a much simpler vein, gives information about specific tests suitable for an introduction to the field. Illustrative of a modern approach to problems in structured personality testing are the various papers published in the *Annals of the New York Academy of Sciences* in 1946 by Rapaport, Schafer, Scheerer, Wechsler, Weider, Wolff, and others (275). In the field of aptitudes and aptitude testing the book by Bingham (22), although published some time ago, is still the standard general reference. The term "aptitude" in this case is meant to include intelligence, and some consideration is given to group testing in this field. Measures of interest are also discussed. An account of manual and mechanical ability tests is provided by Bennett and Cruikshank (17). Some aspects of aptitude and achievement testing at the college level are very adequately covered by Crawford and Burnham (59), who promise other volumes on the same subject.

Most of the publications on projective methods are concerned with one or another of the specific instruments and hence are not discussed here. However, certain general discussions should be mentioned. What promises to be a distinguished contribution is the monograph of Frank (88) just published. In this he elaborates and extends the content of the article included in the *Readings*. The basic principles of projective techniques are the concern of Rapaport (211) who attempts to provide a rational basis for them, while Levinson (149) discusses the similarities and differences between projective and ability tests. General reviews of projective measures are offered by Sargent (234) and White (292).

Rating

Rating, strictly speaking, is a specialized aspect of the broader problem of observation, since a rating scale provides a means of expressing and ordering to a scale the observations directed to certain aspects of behavior, whether these be general or specific.

In any thoroughgoing treatment of rating and rating scales it would be necessary to discuss their general nature, construction, validation, and other characteristics, and then go on to describe and evaluate specific rating scales. Here, however, only some of the general literature will be identified and a bare mention made of a few instruments particularly appropriate to the interests of the clinician.

Not only are many rating scales omitted but also the voluminous literature on the validity of specific instruments must be disregarded. Reviewing and listing sources of standardized tests almost always include rating scales within their province. Consequently the general references mentioned in connection with testing devices are relevant.

In his discussion of the assessment of psychological qualities by the verbal method Vernon (278) presents a comprehensive and penetrating review of ratings and rating scales. Among the topics considered are the sources of error in rating and their correction, the kinds of rating techniques, the influence of extent of acquaintanceship on ratings, rating of various qualities of personality, the halo effect, the reliability and validity of ratings, and the factor analysis of ratings. In a volume devoted to psychometric methods, Guilford (103) devotes a chapter to the history, construction, sources of error, and a general evaluation of the rating scale technique. Other general discussions of value include those of Symonds (258), Strang (253), and Greene (101).

Two rating scales appropriate to the needs of clinicians in a variety of settings will be briefly described. Vernon (278) presents a general rating scale for testing and interviewing sessions that would be useful in many clinical situations. The characteristics to be rated are activity, movement, physique, personal appearance and expression, speech, personal care, self-assertion, cooperativeness, alertness and concentration, test reactions (planning) and emotional responsiveness. The same rating scale is reproduced in the volume by Greene (101). Wittman's test reaction scale (299) designed for use with mental hospital patients is of a sufficiently general nature to permit being used with non-hospitalized individuals in the testing situation. Attention, interest, willingness, social confidence, effort, motivation, volubility and relevancy of speech, emotional reaction, self-confidence, decisiveness, and autocriticism are the rating categories included.

Observation

Every clinician employs the method of observation, although all too frequently the observer makes no attempt to verbalize his use of the method. Unfortunately, however, he may have routinized it to the extent of depending both upon a certain number of personal clinical "clichés" that take the form of favorite expressions to describe the behavior of his patients, and upon certain favorite diagnostic clues uncritically accepted after a casual encounter or so in which there was an apparent connection between an observed behavior characteristic and a verified diagnostic construct. The article by Hunt in the *Readings* pleads for consideration of the testing situation as a sampling of behavior. An individual clinical testing instrument offers opportunity, as the literature on these instruments attests, for observational findings as well as quantitative scores. Too often the psychological clinician forgets to watch what the person does, so intent is his concentration on whether or not the test is performed correctly.

Observation of child behavior has received considerable attention in research through the development of time sampling techniques, check lists, and so on. As a consequence the reviews by Anderson (5, 6) of research methodology used with children are relevant since he discusses some of the extensive literature on these topics. In connection with time sampling technique the article by Olson and Cunningham (206) is especially instructive. The study by Lois Barclay Murphy (190) of social behavior in children is noteworthy both for the meticulousness and for the scope of the observations made and will repay careful reading for its methodological content. In her presentation of the Merrill-Palmer Scale, Stutsman (256) devotes a chapter to the discussion of observation of preschool children in the test situation. Gardner and Wollan (92) demonstrate the use of an observational approach to diagnosis in their discussion of the use for this purpose of club and athletic activities of a department of the juvenile court.

In the adult the observational methodology has been relatively neglected in so far as published accounts are concerned. The general discussions by Symonds (258) and Strang (253) applicable to both children and adults, although written some years ago, still have value. The article of Baumgarten (13) describing a check list for use in noting and interpreting behavior during the testing session is not acceptable in all particulars because one may disagree with certain specific interpretations, but it does bring out clearly the nature of the problem. It is especially noteworthy in showing how identically describable behavior may be subject to very different interpretations. For example, approaching a given test situation quickly may be interpreted as demonstrating quick comprehension, lack of foresight, or other characteristics.

Word Association

With the studies of Jung (130, 131, 132) the method of word association came into a certain prominence in American psychology. In 1910 Kent and Rosanoff (137) published their study which led to their well-known frequency tables (221). The early studies of the clinical use of word associations as complex indicators are summarized in a review published in 1914 by Kohs (142). Interest continued thereafter, but certain research studies unnecessary to review here cast doubt upon the value of the method and lessened interest for a time. Nevertheless, the use of word association as a clinical instrument continued even though the interest in it did not necessarily eventuate in publication, for it was then, as it is now, a diagnostic tool used by many clinicians, each in his own individual way. The literature before 1930 is clearly and comprehensively summarized both by Symonds (258) and by Wells (286). That the Kent-Rosanoff still possesses a clinical value is effectively demonstrated in the studies of Schnack, Shakow, and Lively (238) on its prognostic value in insulin and metrazol therapy. In 1945 Tendler (260) again reviewed the history of this instrument and offered a revised word association measure based on a selection of stimulus words from the original Kent-Rosanoff list that showed the highest sensitivity to certain scoring indices of pathological conditions previously found to have value. A somewhat new approach involving less emphasis on classification of content, length of reaction time, and use of frequency tables has been formulated by Rapaport and his associates (213). Schafer (236) gives an excellent introduction to this technique which is based on the conceptual closeness of the reaction word to or its distance from that used as a stimulus, disturbances being indicated by the patient either sticking too close to the stimulus word or wandering too far afield. Further details supplementing the article just referred to may be found in a study of the thought process in word association by the same writer (237).

Diagnostic Procedures with the Mentally Deficient

Diagnosis of mental deficiency is approached in various ways. The articles published by the two interested groups, psychologists and physicians, tend to stress differences of opinion, but careful reading will demonstrate a considerable substratum of agreement. Representative medical approaches are presented by Humphries (124) and Lurie (162). Doll's consideration of the social basis of diagnosis forms one of the previous *Readings*. The same authority has published other papers concerned with diagnostic criteria (66, 67) as have Yepsen (304), Werner and Strauss (289), and Starr (250). The concept of social adjustment, stressed by Doll, is criticized on various grounds by Crane (58). Another psychologist who pleads that psychometric data are not enough is Carl (41), who then proceeds to a discussion of what he considers the appropriate use of tests in diagnostic problems in this area.

An article by Hackbusch and Klopfer (105) supplements that by E. K. Sarason and S. B. Sarason appearing in the *Readings*. The presentation of the former is somewhat more specialized in that it deals only with the manner in which projective techniques aid in the understanding and treatment of children previously diagnosed by psychometric tests as feebleminded. S. B. Sarason (230) has also published on the use of projective techniques with the mentally deficient. Although concerned with a limited rather than a mentally deficient individual, the case study by Clarke (57) is illustrative of a thoroughgoing, clinically acute approach to diagnosis.

The problem of pseudofeeblemindedness due to language retardation is discussed in an article by Bijou (20) in the course of which he describes ways of recognizing this condition. The need for care in diagnosing mental deficiency is also the concern of Eaton, Gallico, and Campion (74), who refer particularly, however, to mentally defectives showing a high verbal I.Q. Stevens (251) presents a list of criteria for the selection of items to include in a cumulative case study record of the mentally retarded. Although oriented for the teacher, it has suggestions of value for the clinician.

A rating scale specifically designed for application by teachers and other personnel in institutions for the mentally deficient has been developed by Hegge (113). Statements are given concerning specific behavior items on which to base the ratings.

Diagnostic Procedures with Children

Psychologists working both clinically and experimentally with children have often been very conscious of and vocal about the methodologies they used. From the earliest use of the diary method, their techniques have often been such that they could be used for both research and clinical investigations. Accordingly, an excellent introduction to sources for diagnostic methodology with the child is the article on methods by J. E. Anderson (6) in the Manual of Child Psychology edited by Carmichael. Also still of value is his earlier article on the same subject in Murchison's Handbook (5). The volume edited by Lerner and Murphy (148) on the personality study of children contains more detailed methodological accounts with special emphasis on projective methods. Although research-oriented, it is provocative of clinical application. In an article appearing in 1935, Olson (205) presented a still useful description of the diagnosis of behavior disorders of children.

The approaches to diagnosis of various clinical psychologists who have specialized in the problems of children, such as Louttit, Rogers, and Porteus, are in many ways similar, but enough difference is discernible to make attention to their specific formulations a task well worth pursuing. The procedures followed by Louttit can be found in his Clinical Psychology (156) as well as in the various articles written concerning the psychodiagnostic blank by him and his collaborators (43, 158, 159). The blank is a carefully worked out case history blank tested in the clinical situation before general release. The article by Carter in the Readings on psychodiagnosis is a direct extension of this point of view. Rogers (218), introductory to his discussion of the treatment of the problem child, discusses critically four approaches to diagnosis, namely, personality testing, the egolibido method of Kenworthy, the evaluation of the case history by a weighting system, and his own component-factor method. Although today chiefly of historical value, the discussion does throw light on certain current issues, such as the actuarial-clinical prediction controversy, and offers various incidental points on method that are still appropriate. Porteus in his volume epitomizing his personal practice of clinical psychology (208) presents many chapters demonstrating his point of view toward diagnostic issues.

A problem especially relevant in the examination of children is the technique of introducing them to, and seeing that they maintain a satisfactory attitude toward, the diagnostic sessions. After all, a rational explanation of the necessity for the questions which they are asked and the antics which they are required to perform often fails even with adults. It is no wonder, then, that psychologists have written on these problems. Porteus, in the book just referred to, gives an instructive account of the first contact of parent and child with the clinic, conditions for testings, the child's emotional set, and the like. A vivid description of procedures followed for introducing both mother and child to the organization of the nursery group of the clinic of Child Development at Yale University is given by Washburn (282). She presents specific procedures for introducing the child to the testing situation, dealing with a recalcitrant child (and parent), and so on, which are of obvious transfer value to the usual clinical situation. Dwyer (73), Symmes (257), and Martin (170) also discuss methods for gaining rapport with children.

The Haggerty-Olson-Wickman (203, 204) Behavior Rating Scale, Schedule B, is a graphic rating scale for thirty-five intellectual, physical, social, and emotional traits that is often used with children showing behavior problems. Ratings of personal characteristics, both those of a behavior problem nature and those not so to be considered, are included. Each rating item is separately scorable and a total score derivable. Since in working with children information about the parents is important, Ricciardi (215) has developed a parent rating schedule for use in child guidance clinics. A scale developed for use with delinquents has been described by Harris (110).

It is natural, even inevitable, that the psychiatric approach to diagnosis in the child would show differences from that followed by the psychologist. Both the Preu (209) and the Lewis (151) diagnostic manuals devote some attention to the child. The former account is the more thorough of the two. Kanner's text (133) in child psychiatry, standard for many years, presents a short procedural description. An outline of diagnostic procedure followed at the Southard School of the Menninger Clinic is given by Ackerman and Menninger (1). Although somewhat out of date, it still has didactic value. Brown and his collaborators (33) offer an outline for the psychiatric classification of problem children that shows still another psychiatric approach.

Diagnostic Procedures in Guidance

Different points of view toward problems in clinical guidance activities exist among psychologists. Too well known to necessitate description in this brief review is the position identified with Williamson, Paterson, Darley, and other members of the University of Minnesota group (207, 296, 297). Several articles in the *Readings* are illustrative. The position of Fenton (80, 81, 82) deserves mention. He would have the clinical approach used more extensively by the school counselor, teacher, and other workers in the school system. It is his opinion that school case work, as he refers to the task, must be conducted even in the absence of the specialist. Unlike many other books ostensibly concerned with mental hygiene, Fenton's volume (82), *Mental Hygiene in School Practice*, contains much valuable methodological material. The case study, including diagnosis and the formulation of plans for treatment, is considered. Still another point of view toward guidance is exemplified by the work of L. B. Murphy (192) and R. L. Munroe (187), who depend more upon the intensive "depth" procedures of a dynamic psychology than most workers in guidance. They tend to stress the team concept, drawing both upon the fields of and workers in allied disciplines, such as psychiatry, social work, anthropology, sociology, and education. In their development of the dynamic factors affecting learning at the college level, Murphy, and Ladd (191) demonstrate implicitly many interesting methodological points. Over one-half of their volume is devoted to case history presentation. Also illustrative of this point of view is the study by Munroe (188) of three diagnostic methods—Rorschach, graphology, and appraisal of drawings applied to a normal typical college girl—to see not only whether these adequately described her but also whether they aided both in understanding her and in predicting her future college career.

In addition to the consideration of diagnostic problems by the aforementioned psychologists, some mention of the position of the educator and educational psychologist should be made, since their contributions are of obvious transfer value to the work of the clinician. The thirty-fourth yearbook of the National Society for the Study of Education was devoted to the problem of educational diagnosis (291). The articles by Tyler (272, 273) on the elements and characteristics of diagnosis are especially pertinent. The thirty-seventh yearbook also devotes some attention to guidance problems. The articles by Koos (143) and Eurich and Wrenn (79) are particularly useful. Good (98) has published an elementary account of educational diagnosis and its implications. Both general procedures and specific usages of diagnostic tests in the school situation are discussed by Traxler (268), who also presents an extensive bibliography on this topic.

The way one classifies the nature of the problems that face the clients coming to the clinical counselor affects the diagnosis made and the treatment attempted. Indeed, problem classification is a simple form of diagnosis. The article by Bordin in the *Readings* develops a set of diagnostic constructs which he contrasts with those developed by Williamson and Darley (297) and Williamson (296). Approaches other than these two include those depending more on psychiatric thinking. A representative illustration is contained in an article by Woods and Chase (302). After exclusion of those individuals who were psychopathic, neurotic, and psychotic, they classify the affective make-up of the college girls they saw as showing immaturity or childishness, overcompliancy, social inadequacy, nonconformity, lack of interest in study, worry or anxiety, and temporary perturbation. Although Margolis is concerned with but one "problem," his article (168) on "façade" in low scholarship students is instructive. By "façade" he means the initial statement made to the counselor by the student in attempting to explain his poor scholarship, e.g., noisy home, inability to concentrate, laziness, and the like.

Several of the previous articles in this section of the *Readings* dealt with the case study in guidance activities. The history, construction, and techniques of writing up the case study in the secondary and grammar schools are described by Traxler. In a setting of college guidance Darley gives a general description of the case study and Sarbin describes methods of arranging case notes, their functions, the characteristics of good notes, and a method of recording. More general discussions to supplement these are given in the texts of Strang (253), Williamson (296), and Williamson and Darley (297), and in the monograph of Traxler (267), the last of which includes a comprehensive bibliography.

The cumulative record maintained in most elementary and secondary schools with which the psychologist would come in contact is a variant of the case study. Depending as it does upon more of a piecemeal, temporally spaced recording of all pertinent facts that the institution has brought together, it might be regarded as the prolegomenon for a case study—the systematically collected material available when a thorough study is necessary. Traxler (271) describes the cumulative record in an article which serves as a companion piece to the one contained in the *Readings* regarding the case study. His volume on techniques of guidance (270) is especially valuable for his discussion of records and their maintenance. Three government publications (197, 227, 241) also give a thorough account of the cumulative record. A typical way in which these records are used is described in a monograph by Allen (2).

A technique of observation used in the school situation in connection with the cumulative record is the so-called anecdotal record, i.e., descriptions of factually reported behavioral incidents. Discussions by Traxler (266, 270), Wood (301), and Jarvie and Ellingson (128) are especially pertinent to the work of the guidance clinician.

Guidance forms to be partially filled out by the client and then used by the psychologist or other counselor provide a tool that deserves at least brief consideration. *The Aids to the Vocational Interview* developed by Paul Achilles and published by the Psychological Corporation was quite widely used for some years. In 1946 appeared an adaptation of this device prepared by Bennett and Orbach and called the *Guidance Summary Form*. It is typical of the various forms now in use. After requesting certain general information, it provides space for the recording of facts and opinions about education, work, health, family, interests, self-evaluation, occupational information desired, and vocational ambitions. Additional space for the use of the counselor in regard to psychometric results and other notes is also provided. Numerous similar forms both published and unpublished have appeared.

Revision B of the American Council on Education Rating Scale (27) is illustrative of rating scales used in guidance activities in schools. For its proper application it requires not only ratings on several items but also the recording of instances on which the judgments were based and, hence, partakes in addition of the characteristics of an anecdotal record. The clinician is not likely to complete this or similar rating scales personally, but since cumulative record files often contain such completed forms, an acquaintance with them is desirable.

A diagnostic tool specifically designed for use in guidance is the *Dictionary of Occupational Titles* (274). Unlike most sources of occupational information this comprehensive account of definitions and classifications of occupations is so organized as to be a diagnostic aid to the counselor in evaluating the client's previous occupational experience. Part IV of the *Dictionary* gives entry fields of work, placement, and training. Jobs to which individuals may be promoted are shown. Its use is described by Ward (281), Scott (239), and Shartle (245). Shartle's account is also valuable for its description of obtaining occupational information by job analysis and other methods of describing and classifying jobs.

Diagnostic Procedures in Severe Behavior Disorders

There is considerable diversity among psychologists in their approaches to diagnosis in severe personality and/or psychiatric disorders. The positions taken by Wechsler and Rosenzweig may be judged from previous articles in the *Readings*. Supplementing these is another case study published by Rosenzweig (223), and a general discussion by the same authority on the nature of psychodiagnosis (222). Several others are worthy of mention. The approach followed in the Menninger Clinic is made clear by several of its workers (140, 180, 213). Shakow and his collaborators (243) describe a method applied to a psychological study of a schizophrenic using a battery composed both of locally devised and of more commonly used instruments. Murphy (189), although not a clinician, presents a very penetrating and broad view in his discussion of the detection of personality imbalances. An approach probably typifying that of psychologists in a considerable number of psychiatric hospitals is described by Barten (11).

The neurological examination, as such, is naturally not the function of the psychologist. However, adjunct diagnostic procedures, particularly psychometric, fall within his province in dealing with this class of patients. Goldstein (97), a psychiatrist, deals, in the course of a comprehensive presentation of diagnostic problems in the injured brain, both with the psychiatric and with the psychological approaches. Benton and Howell (18), Ruesch (228), and Lynn and his collaborators (163) discuss the use of tests with the same category of patients. The psychological appraisal of neurological defects in children is the concern of Meyer and Simmel (182). Preliminary to a discussion of retraining aphasics Granich (100) discusses diagnostic considerations. Still another approach to the diagnosis of patients with organic defects is described in a case study by Kogan (141).

The volumes by Rapaport and his collaborators (213) concerned with a battery of tests including the Wechsler-Bellevue, the Babcock, the Goldstein-Scheerer Sorting, the Hanfmann-Kasanin, the Rorschach, Thematic Apperception, and Word-Association Tests run to over 1,000 pages and are a veritable gold mine of diagnostic inferences and clinical clues. But as in a gold mine, one must dig for the facts and also beware of "fool's gold." The lack of a really adequate summarization and the somewhat tortuous presentation interfere with the grasp of an already complicated subject. In some ways, the earlier and shorter manual (212) prepared by the same investigators and issued by the Josiah Macy Foundation, covering the Wechsler-Bellevue, the Babcock and concept formation tests, is much more usable. Although these volumes may be a very important contribution to clinical psychology, they have been subject to considerable methodological criticism. Very penetrating critical reviews by Brown (31), Lindner (152), and McNemar (178) should be read as well. As Rapaport and his collaborators urge, their findings should be used as clinical generalizations, not as laws. A desirable pragmatic approach by the psychologist would be to treat their generalizations as hypotheses to be verified or not, as the case might be in day-to-day clinical activities. Research, in the generic meaning of the term, is very much indicated.

Three rating scales designed for general use in psychiatric hospitals and showing promise of being useful, valid, and reliable instruments are described by Malamud, Hoagland, and Kaufman (166, 167), Wilcox (295), and Cohen, Malmo, and Thale (53). The first of these is the most involved, demands the most skill, and contains the greatest number of traits to be rated.

Two standard psychiatric diagnostic case outlines are those published by Preu (209) and Lewis (151). Both are widely used, and in many ways they complement one another. The one by Lewis is somewhat shorter and gives the impression of a more static approach. One-third of the volume is devoted to the presentation of the classification of mental disorders officially adopted by the professional associations. The book by Preu gives much more attention to explanatory material and a more thorough account of the case study of the child. The psychobiological approach to diagnosis stemming from the work of Meyer, although influencing case outlines such as those described above, is best exemplified in the psychiatric textbooks of Noyes (200) and Muncie (186). A standard text of clinical psychiatry, that by Strecker and Ebaugh (254), contains a section devoted to the psychiatric examination. Appel and Strecker (7) have also published a volume on this problem. Although not concerned with psychiatric cases, the volume by Dunbar (70) on psychosomatic diagnosis contains much of indirect interest to the psychologist. Kubie (144) also discusses an aspect of psychosomatic diagnosis in his consideration of detection of poor psychosomatic risks. Among other approaches to the case study which are by psychiatrists and with which the psychologist should be familiar are those of Chassell (46, 47) and Saslow and Chapple (235).

Bibliography

1) Ackerman, N. W., and Menninger, C. F. Treatment techniques for mental retardation in a school for personality disorders for children. *Amer. J. Orthopsychiat.*, 1936, 6, 294–312.
2) Allen, W. C. Cumulative pupil records. New York: Bureau of Publications Teachers College, Columbia University, 1943.
3) Allport, G. W. *Personality: a psychological interpretation.* New York: Holt, 1937.
4) Allport, G. W. The ego in contemporary psychology. *Psychol. Rev.*, 1943, 50, 451–478.
5) Anderson, J. E. The methods of child psychology. In Murchison, C. (ed.), *A handbook of child psychology* (2nd ed.). Worcester: Clark University Press, 1933. Pp. 3–28.
6) Anderson, J. E. Methods of child psychology. In Carmichael, L. (ed.), *Manual of child psychology.* New York: Wiley, 1946. Pp. 1–42.
7) Appel, K. E., and Strecker, E. *Practical examination of personality and behavior disorders: adults and children.* New York: Macmillan, 1936.
8) Baker, G., and Peatman, J. G. Tests used in Veterans Administration Advisement Units. *Amer. Psychologist*, 1947, 2, 99–102.
9) Baker, H. J., and Traphagen, V. *The diagnosis and treatment of behavior-problem children.* New York: Macmillan, 1935.
10) Balken, E. R., and Masserman, J. G. The language of phantasy: III. The language of the phantasies of patients with conversion hysteria, anxiety state, and obsessive-compulsive neuroses. *J. Psychol.*, 1940, 10, 75–86.
11) Barten, M. B. Psychometric methods in a mental hygiene clinic of a psychiatric hospital. *J. Consult. Psychol.*, 1944, 8, 286–290.
12) Bateson, G. *Naven.* Cambridge: Cambridge University Press, 1936.
13) Baumgarten, F. Approach in taking tests: a technique for studying the examinees behavior. *Occup.*, 1935, 14, 115–122.
14) Beck, S. J. *Introduction to the Rorschach method.* (Monograph No. 1 of the Amer-Orthopsychiatric Assoc.) New York: Amer. Orthopsychiatric Assoc., 1937.
15) Bellak, L., and Jacques, E. On the problem of dynamic conceptualization in case studies. *Character & Pers.*, 1942, 11, 20–39.

16) Benedict, R. *Patterns of culture*. Boston: Houghton Mifflin, 1934.
17) Bennett, G. K., and Cruikshank, R. M. *A summary of manual and mechanical ability tests (preliminary form)*. New York: Psychological Corporation, 1942.
18) Benton, A. L., and Howell, I. L. The use of psychological tests in the evaluation of intellectual function following head injury; report of a case of post-traumatic personality disorder. *Psychosom. Med.*, 1941, 3, 138–151.
19) Berdie, R. F. Psychological processes in the interview. *J. Soc. Psychol.*, 1943, 18, 3–31.
20) Bijou, S. W. The problem of pseudo-feeblemindedness. *J. Educ. Psychol.*, 1939, 30, 519–526.
21) Binet, A., and Simon, T. *The development of intelligence in children*. Baltimore: Williams & Wilkins, 1916.
22) Bingham, W. V. *Aptitudes and aptitude testing*. New York: Harper, 1937.
23) Bingham, W. V. Halo, invalid and valid. *J. Appl. Psychol.*, 1939, 23, 221–228.
24) Bingham, W. V., and Moore, B. V. *How to interview* (3rd ed.). New York: Harper, 1941.
25) Blumenthal, H. T. Effects of organismal differentials on the distribution of leukocytes in the circulating blood. *Arch. Path.*, 1939, 27, 510–545.
26) Bordin, E. S. A theory of vocational interests as dynamic phenomena. *Educ. Psychol. Measmt.*, 1943, 3, 49–66.
27) Bradshaw, F. F. American Council on Education rating scale, its reliability, validity and use. *Arch Psychol.*, 1930, No. 119.
28) Brewer, J. M., et al. *Case studies in educational and vocational guidance*. Boston: Ginn, 1926.
29) Bristol, M. C. *Handbook on social case recording*. Chicago: Univ. Chicago Press, 1936.
30) Bronner, A. F., Healy, W., Lowe, G. M., and Shimberg, M. E. *A manual of individual mental tests and testing*. Boston: Little, Brown, 1927.
31) Brown, A. W. Review of Rapaport, D., et al., Diagnostic psychological testing: Volume I. *Psychol. Bull.*, 1946, 43, 477–479.
32) Brown, R. R. The time interval between test and retest in its relation to constancy of the intelligence quotient. *J. Educ. Psychol.*, 1933, 24, 81–96.
33) Brown, S., Pollock, H. M., Potter, H. W., and Cohen, D. W. *Outline for the psychiatric classification of problem children*. Utica, N. Y.: State Hospitals Press, 1937.
34) Burks, B. S., and Jones, M. G. Personality development in childhood: a survey of problems, methods and experimental findings. *Monogr. Soc. Res. Child Developm.*, 1936, 1, No. 4.
35) Burnham, W. H. *The normal mind*. New York: Appleton, 1924.
36) Buros, O. K. (ed.). *Educational, psychological and personality*

tests of 1933, 1934, and 1935. *Studies in Education No. 9, Rutgers Univ. Bulletin*, 1936, No. 13.

37) Buros, O. K. (ed.). Educational, psychological and personality tests of 1936. *Studies in Education No. 11, Rutgers Univ. Bulletin*, 1937, No. 14.

38) Buros, O. K. (ed.). *The 1938 mental measurements yearbook.* New Brunswick, N. J.: Rutgers Univ. Press, 1938.

39) Buros, O. K. (ed.). *The 1940 mental measurements yearbook.* Highland Park, N. J.: Mental Measurements Yearbook, 1941.

40) Burr, H. S., and Northrop, F. S. C. An electro-dynamic theory of life. *Quart. Rev. Biol.*, 1935, 10, 322–333.

41) Carl, G. P. The role of psychometrics in appraisal of mental deficiency. *Nerv. Child*, 1942, 2, 29–36.

42) Carroll, L. *Complete Works.* New York: Modern Library, 1936.

43) Carter, J. W., Jr. Manual for the psychodiagnostic blank. *Psychol. Rec.*, 1940, 3, 250–290.

44) Cattell, P. Stanford-Binet I.Q. variations. *Sch. & Soc.*, 1937, 45, 615–618.

45) Cattell, R. B. Measurement versus intuition in applied psychology. *Character & Pers.*, 1937, 6, 114–131.

46) Chassell, J. O. *The experience variables: a study of the variable factors in experience contributing to the formation of personality.* Bennington, Vt.: The author, Bennington College, 1928.

47) Chassell, J. O. Experience Variables Record: a clinical revision. *Psychiat.*, 1938, 1, 67–77.

48) Chein, I. The logic of prediction: some observations on Dr. Sarbin's exposition. *Psychol. Rev.*, 1945, 52, 175–179.

49) Cobb, S. Technic of interviewing a patient with psychosomatic disorder. *Med. Clin. N. Amer.*, 1944, 28, 1210–1216.

50) Cofer, C. N. An analysis of the concept of clinical intuition. In Kelly, G. A. (ed.), *New methods in applied psychology.* College Park, Md.: Univ. Maryland Press, 1947. Pp. 219–227.

51) Coghill, G. E. Individuation versus integration in the development of behavior. *J. Gen. Psychol.*, 1930, 3, 431–435.

52) Coghill, G. E. Integration and motivation of behavior as problems of growth. *J. Genet. Psychol.*, 1936, 48, 3–19.

53) Cohen, L. H., Malmo, R. B., and Thale, T. Measurement of chronic psychotic over-activity by the Norwich Rating Scale. *J. Gen. Psychol.*, 1944, 30, 65–74.

54) Cottrell, L. S., Jr. The case-study method in prediction. *Sociometry*, 1941, 4, 358–370.

55) Covner, B. J. Studies in phonographic recordings of verbal material: III. The completeness and accuracy of counseling interview reports. *J. Gen. Psychol.*, 1944, 30, 181–203.

56) Covner, B. J. Studies in phonographic recordings of verbal material: IV. Written reports of interviews. *J. Appl. Psychol.*, 1944, 28, 89–98.

57) Clarke, H. J. The diagnosis of a patient with limited capacity. *J. Personality*, 1946, 15, 105–112.
58) Crane, H. W. The concept of social adjustment in relation to the defining and diagnosing of mental deficiency. *Proc. Amer. Ass. Ment. Def.*, 1939, 44, No. 2, 178–183.
59) Crawford, A. B., and Burnham, P. S. *Forecasting college achievement: a survey of aptitude tests for higher education: Part 1, general considerations in the measurement of academic promise.* New Haven: Yale University Press, 1946.
60) Darley, J. G. Tested maladjustment related to clinically diagnosed maladjustment. *J. Appl. Psychol.*, 1937, 21, 632–642.
61) Darley, J. G. Clinical predictions of student success or failure in professional training. *J. Educ. Psychol.*, 1938, 29, 335–354.
62) Darley, J. G. A preliminary study of the relations between attitude, adjustment, and vocational interests tests. *J. Educ. Psychol.*, 1938, 29, 467–474.
63) Darley, J. G. *Clinical aspects and interpretation of the Strong Vocational Interest Blank.* New York: Psychological Corporation, 1941.
64) (Darley, J. G.) *The interview in counseling: an outline of interviewing procedure for use of community advisory centers.* Retraining and Reemployment Administration, Washington, D. C.: U. S. Department of Labor, 1946.
65) Davis, F. P. Diagnostic methods in clinical psychology. *Train. Sch. Bull.*, 1945, 42, 113–120.
66) Doll, E. A. Current thoughts on mental deficiency. *Proc. Amer. Ass. Ment. Def.*, 1936, 41, 33–49.
67) Doll, E. A. Idiot, imbecile, and moron. *J. Appl. Psychol.*, 1936, 20, 427–437.
68) Doll, E. A. The Vineland Social Maturity Scale: revised condensed manual of directions. *Publ. Train. Sch.*, Ser. 1936, No. 3.
69) Doll, E. A. Annotated bibliography on the Vineland Social Maturity Scale. *J. Consult. Psychol.*, 1940, 4, 123–132.
70) Dunbar, F. *Psychosomatic diagnosis.* New York: Hoeber, 1943.
71) Dunbar, H. F. *Emotions and bodily changes.* New York: Columbia Univ. Press, 1938.
72) du Nouy, P. L. *Biological time.* New York: Macmillan, 1937.
73) Dwyer, F. M. A note on resistance and rapport in psychological tests of young children. *J. genet. Psychol.*, 1937, 51, 451–454.
74) Eaton, H. C., Gallico, M. W., and Campion, C. A. Care in the diagnosis of mental deficiency. *Amer. J. Ment. Def.*, 1945, 49, 450–452.
75) Edwards, A. L. Political frames of reference as a factor influencing recognition. *J. Abnorm. Soc. Psychol.*, 1941, 36, 34–50.
76) Edwards, A. L. Rationalization in recognition as a result of political frames of reference. *J. Abnorm. Soc. Psychol.*, 1941, 36, 224–235.

77) Elkin, F. Specialists interpret the case of Harold Holzer. *J. Abnorm. Soc. Psychol.*, 1947, 42, 99–111.
78) English, H. B., and Raimy, V. *Studying the individual school child: a manual of guidance.* New York: Holt, 1941.
79) Eurich, A. C., and Wrenn, C. G. Appraisal of student characteristics and needs. *Yearb. Nat. Soc. Stud. Educ.*, 1938, 37, Part 1, 31–87.
80) Fenton, N. *The counselor's approach to the home.* Stanford University, Calif.: Stanford Univ. Press, 1943.
81) Fenton, N. *The counselor interview with the student.* Stanford University, Calif.: Stanford Univ. Press, 1943.
82) Fenton, N. *Mental hygiene in school practice.* Stanford University, Calif.: Stanford Univ. Press, 1943.
83) Frank, L. K. The problem of learning. *Psychol. Rev.*, 1926, 33, 329–351.
84) Frank, L. K. Fundamental needs of the child. *Ment. Hyg.*, 1938, 22, 353–379.
85) Frank, L. K. Comments on the proposed standardization of the Rorschach method. *Rorschach Res. Exch.*, 1939, 3, 101–105.
86) Frank, L. K. Cultural coercion and individual distortion. *Psychiatry*, 1939, 2, 11–27.
87) Frank, L. K. Projective methods for the study of personality. *J. Psychol.*, 1939, 8, 389–413.
88) Frank, L. K. *Projective methods.* Springfield, Ill.: Thomas, 1948.
89) Freeman, F. N. *Mental tests: their history, principles and applications* (Rev. ed.). Boston: Houghton Mifflin, 1939.
90) Freud, A. *The ego and the mechanisms of defense.* London: Hogarth, 1937.
91) Freud, S. *Collected papers.* Vol. III. London: Hogarth, 1925.
92) Gardner, G. E., and Wollan, K. I. Activity-interview in the study of delinquency. *Amer. J. Orthopsychiat.*, 1941, 11, 143–150.
93) Garrett, A. *Interviewing: its principles and methods.* New York: Family Welfare Associations of America, 1942.
94) Garrett, A. *Counseling methods for personnel workers.* New York: Family Welfare Association of America, 1945.
95) Gaw, E. A. Case study techniques. *J. Higher Educ.*, 1943, 14, 37–40.
96) Gesell, A. *Mental growth of the pre-school child.* New York: Macmillan, 1925.
97) Goldstein, K. *After-effects of brain injuries in war; their evaluation and treatment: the application of psychologic methods in the clinic.* New York: Grune & Stratton, 1942.
98) Good, C. V. Problems and techniques of educational diagnosis and adjustment. *Sch. & Soc.*, 1938, 48, 261–267.
99) Goodenough, F. The measurement of mental growth. In Murchison, C. (ed.), *A handbook of child psychology* (2nd ed., rev.). Worcester, Mass.: Clark Univ. Press, 1933. Pp. 303–328.

100) Granich, L. *Aphasia: a guide to retraining.* New York: Grune & Stratton, 1947.
101) Greene, E. B. *Measurements of human behavior.* New York: Odyssey Press, 1941.
102) Gressey, O. L. Mental development as related to institutional residence and educational achievement. *Univ. Iowa Stud. Child Welf.*, 1937, 13, No. 1.
103) Guilford, J. P. *Psychometric methods.* New York: McGraw-Hill, 1936.
104) Guthrie, E. R. *The psychology of human conflict.* New York: Harper, 1938.
105) Hackbusch, R., and Klopfer, B. The contribution of projective techniques to the understanding and treatment of children psychometrically diagnosed as feebleminded: with sample case studies. *Amer. J. Ment. Def.*, 1946, 51, 15–34.
106) Hallowell, D. K. Stability of mental test ratings for pre-school children. *J. Genet. Psychol.*, 1932, 40, 406–421.
107) Hamilton, G. *Principles of social case recording.* New York: Columbia Univ. Press, 1946.
108) Hanfmann, E., Rickers-Ovsiankina, M., and Goldstein, K. Case Lahuti: extreme concretization of behavior due to damage of the brain cortex. *Psychol. Monogr.*, 1944, 57, No. 4.
109) Hapgood, H. *A Victorian in the modern world.* New York: Harcourt, Brace, 1939.
110) Harris, D. B. A play activities blank as a measure of delinquency in boys. *J. Abnorm. Soc. Psychol.*, 1942, 37, 546–559.
111) Harrison, R. Studies in the use and validity of the thematic apperception test with mentally disordered patients. *Character & Pers.*, 1940, 9, 122–138.
112) Hawkes, A. R. The cumulative record and its uses. *Educ. Rec. Bull.*, 1937, 21, 37–64.
113) Hegge, T. G. The significance of measurements of adjustment in the institutional and school situation. *Amer. J. Ment. Def.*, 1942, 47, 58–69.
114) Hertz, M. R. The Rorschach ink-blot test: historical summary. *Psychol. Bull.*, 1935, 32, 33–66.
115) Hildreth, G. H. Stanford-Binet retests of 441 school children. *Ped. Sem.*, 1926, 33, 365–386.
116) Hildreth, G. H. *A bibliography of mental tests and rating scales* (2nd rev. ed.). New York: Psychological Corporation, 1939.
117) Hildreth, G. H. Retests with the new Stanford-Binet Scale. *J. Consult. Psychol.*, 1939, 3, 49–53.
118) Hildreth, G. H. *A bibliography of mental tests and rating scales: 1945 supplement.* New York: Psychological Corporation, 1946.
119) Hill, A. S. The use of an objective type of case study in the analysis and prognosis of pupil maladjustment problems. *Educ. Admin. Superv.*, 1935, 8, 611–618.

120) Horowitz, R., and Murphy, L. B. Projective methods in the psychological study of children. *J. Exper. Educ.*, 1938, 7, 133–140.

121) Horst, P. *The prediction of personal adjustment*. New York: Social Science Research Council, 1942.

122) Hubbard, R. M. The use of psychological recommendations by social workers. *Family*, 1937, 18, 246–252.

123) Hug-Hellmuth, H. von. On the technique of child-analysis. *Int. J. Psycho-Anal.*, 1921, 2, 294–295.

124) Humphreys, E. J. The medical diagnosis of mental defect. *N. Y. St. J. Med.*, 1941, 41, 2041–2042.

125) Hunt, W. A., and Older, H. J. Detection of malingering through psychometric tests. *U. S. Nav. Med. Bull.*, 1943, 41, 1318–1323.

126) Huston, P. E., Shakow, D., and Erickson, M. H. A study of hypnotically induced complexes by means of the Luria technique. *J. Gen. Psychol.*, 1934, 11, 65–97.

127) Itard, J. *The wild boy of Aveyron*. (Trans. Humphrey, G., & Humphrey, M.) New York: Century, 1932.

128) Jarvie, L. L., and Ellingson, M. *A handbook on the anecdotal behavior journal*. Chicago: Univ. of Chicago Press, 1940.

129) Jersild, A. T., and Fite, M. D. The influence of nursery school experience on children's social adjustments. *Child Developm. Monogr.*, 1939, No. 25.

130) Jung, C. G. On psychological relations of the associative experiment. *J. Abnorm. Psychol.*, 1906, 1, 249–257.

131) Jung, C. G. The association method. *Amer. J. Psychol.*, 1910, 21, 219–269.

132) Jung, C. G. *Studies in word association*. (Trans. Eder, M.D.) New York: Moffat Yard, 1918.

133) Kanner, L. *Child psychiatry*. Springfield, Illinois: Thomas, 1935.

134) Kantor, J. R. *A survey of the science of psychology*. Bloomington, Ind.: Principia Press, 1933.

135) Kent, G. H. Oral tests for emergency use in clinics. *Ment. Meas. Monogr.*, 1932, No. 9.

136) Kent, G. H. Use and abuse of mental tests in clinical diagnosis. *Psychol. Rec.*, 1938, 2, 391–400.

137) Kent, G. H., and Rosanoff, A. J. A study of association in insanity. *Amer. J. Insan.*, 1910, 67, 37–96, 317–390.

138) Klein, M. *The psychoanalysis of children*. London: Hogarth Press, 1932.

139) Klopfer, B. (ed.). Rorschach research exchange. (Currently being issued since 1936.)

140) Knight, R. P., Gill, M., Lozoff, M., and Rapaport, D. Comparison of clinical findings and psychological tests in three cases bearing upon military personnel selection. *Bull. Menninger Clin.*, 1943, 7, 114–128.

141) Kogan, K. L. The diagnosis of a patient with organic defect. *J. Personality*, 1946, 15, 113–120.

142) Kohs, S. C. The association method and its relation to the complex and complex indicators. *Amer. J. Psychol.*, 1914, 25, 544–594.

143) Koos, L. V. The specific techniques of investigation: observation questionnaire and rating. *Yearb. Nat. Soc. Stud. Educ.*, 1938, 37, Part 2, 375–390.

144) Kubie, L. S. The detection of potential psychosomatic breakdowns in the selection of men for the armed services. *Ann. N. Y. Acad. Sci.*, 1943, 44, 605–624.

145) Kuhlmann, F. *A handbook of mental tests.* Baltimore: Warwick & York, 1922.

146) Kuhlmann, F. Retrogressive trends in clinical psychology. *J. Consult. Psychol.*, 1941, 5, 97–104.

147) Landis, C., Landis, A. T., Bolles, M. M., Metzger, H. F., Pitts, M. W., D'e Esopo, D. A., Molog, H. D., Kleigman, S. J., and Dickinson, R. L. *Sex in development.* New York: Hoeber, 1940.

148) Lerner, E., and Murphy, L. B. (eds.). Methods for the study of personality in young children. *Monogr. Soc. Res. Child Develpm.*, 1941, 6, No. 4.

149) Levinson, D. J. A note on the similarities and differences between projective tests and ability tests. *Psychol. Rev.*, 1946, 53, 189–194.

150) Lewin, K. *A dynamic theory of personality.* New York: McGraw-Hill, 1935.

151) Lewis, N. D. C. *Outlines for psychiatric examinations* (3rd ed.). Albany: New York State Department of Mental Hygiene, 1943.

152) Lindner, R. M. Review of Rapaport, D., et al., *Diagnostic psychological testing:* Volume II. *Psychol. Bull.*, 1946, 43, 479–481.

153) Louttit, C. M. A blank for history taking in psychological clinics. *J. Appl. Psychol.*, 1934, 18, 737–748.

154) Louttit, C. M. *Clinical psychology.* New York: Harper, 1936.

155) Louttit, C. M. The nature of clinical psychology. *Psychol. Bull.*, 1939, 36, 361–389.

156) Louttit, C. M. *Clinical psychology* (Rev. ed.). New York: Harper, 1947.

157) Louttit, C. M., and Browne, C. G. The use of psychometric instruments in psychological clinics. *J. Consult. Psychol.*, 1947, 11, 49–54.

158) Louttit, C. M., and Carter, J. W., Jr. The psychodiagnostic blank. *Ind. Univ. Publ. Psychol. Clin.*, 1939, Ser. 2, No. 7.

159) Louttit, C. M., and Waskom, W. B. *Manual for the Indiana Psychodiagnostic Blank.* Bloomington, Indiana: Indiana University, 1933.

160) Lundberg, G. A. Case-studies vs. statistical methods: an issue based on misunderstanding. *Sociometry*, 1941, 4, 379–383.

161) Luria, A. R. *The nature of human conflicts.* New York: Liveright, 1932.

162) Lurie, L. A. The medical concept of feeblemindedness. *Amer. J. Ment. Def.*, 1946, 50, 512–515.

163) Lynn, J. G., Levine, K. N., and Hewson, L. R. Psychologic tests for the clinical evaluation of late 'diffuse organic,' 'neurotic,' and 'normal' reactions after closed head injury. *Res. Publ. Ass. Nerv. Ment. Dis.*, 1945, 24, 296–378.

164) MacFarlane, J. W. Interview techniques. *Nat. Assoc. Deans Wom. J.*, 1943, 6, 61–66.

165) Maier, N. R. F. *Studies of abnormal psychology in the rat.* New York: Harper, 1939.

166) Malamud, W., Hoagland, H., and Kaufman, I. C. A new psychiatric rating scale. *Psychosom. Med.*, 1946, 8, 243–245.

167) Malamud, W., Hoagland, H., and Kaufman, I. C. A new psychiatric rating scale. *Arch. Neurol. Psychiat.*, Chicago, 1946, 56, 729–733.

168) Margolis, B. D. The problem of "facade" in the counseling of low scholarship students. *J. Consult. Psychol.*, 1945, 9, 138–141.

169) Martin, M. F. Logic in the informal interview. *Psychiat.*, 1940, 3, 535–537.

170) Martin, M. F. Gaining rapport in the school clinic. *Ment. Hyg.*, 1941, 25, 251–255.

171) Marzolf, S. S. *Studying the individual: a manual on the case study for guidance workers and psycho-clinicians.* Minneapolis: Burgess, 1940.

172) Masserman, J. H., and Balken, E. R. The clinical application of phantasy studies. *J. Psychol.*, 1938, 6, 81–88.

173) Masserman, J. H., and Balken, E. R. The psychoanalytic and psychiatric significance of phantasy. Part I. *Psychoanal. Rev.*, 1939, 26, 343–379.

174) Masserman, J. H., and Balken, E. R. The psychoanalytic and psychiatric significance of phantasy. Part II. *Psychoanal. Rev.*, 1939, 26, 535–549.

175) Mayer, B. A. Negativistic reactions of pre-school children on the New Revision of the Stanford-Binet. *J. Genet. Psychol.*, 1935, 46, 311–334.

176) McCallister, J. M. *Remedial and corrective instruction in reading.* New York: Appleton-Century, 1936.

177) McFadden, J. H. Differential responses of normal and feeble-minded subjects of equal mental age, on the Kent-Rosanoff Free Association Test and the Stanford Revision of the Binet-Simon Intelligence Test. *Ment. Meas. Monogr.*, 1931, No. 7.

178) McNemar, Q. Review of Rapaport, D., et al., Diagnostic psychological testing: Volume I. *Amer. J. Psychol.*, 1946, 59, 306–311.

179) Mead, M. *Sex and temperament.* New York: Morrow, 1935.

180) Menninger, W. C., Menninger, K. A., and Knight, R. P. The psychological examination: an outline of procedure in the determina-

tion of the mental status of the psychiatric patient. *Bull. Menninger Clin.*, 1941, 5, 97–110.

181) Merrill, M. A. The significance of I.Q.'s on the Revised Stanford-Binet Scale. *J. Educ. Psychol.*, 1938, 29, 641–651.

182) Meyer, E., and Simmel, M. The psychological appraisal of children with neurological defects. *J. Abnorm. Soc. Psychol.*, 1947, 42, 193–205.

183) Mitrano, A. J. The clinical interpretation of psychometric data. *Proc. Amer. Ass. Ment. Def.*, 1938, 43, No. 1, 156–160.

184) Morgan, C. D., and Murray, H. A. A method for investigating fantasies. *Arch. Neurol. Psychiat.*, Chicago, 1935, 34, 289–306.

185) Morrison, H. C. *The practice of teaching in the secondary school.* Chicago: Univ. of Chicago Press, 1931.

186) Muncie, W. *Psychobiology and psychiatry.* St. Louis: Mosby, 1939.

187) Munroe, R. L. *Teaching the individual.* New York: Columbia Univ. Press, 1942.

188) Munroe, R. L. Three diagnostic methods applied to Sally. *J. Abnorm. Soc. Psychol.*, 1945, 40, 215–227.

189) Murphy, G. The detection of personality imbalances. *Ann. N. Y. Acad. Sci.*, 1943, 44, 589–604.

190) Murphy, L. B. *Social behavior and child personality.* New York: Columbia Univ. Press, 1937.

191) Murphy, L. B., and Ladd, H. *Emotional factors in learning.* New York: Columbia Univ. Press, 1944.

192) Murphy, L. B., Lerner, E., Judge, J., and Grant, M. *Psychology in individual education.* New York: Columbia Univ. Press, 1942.

193) Murray, H. A. Techniques for a systematic investigation of fantasy. *J. Psychol.*, 1937, 3, 115–143.

194) Murray, H. A. *Explorations in personality: a clinical and experimental study of fifty men of college age.* New York: Oxford Univ. Press, 1938.

195) Murray, H. A., and Morgan, C. D. A clinical study of sentiments (I & II). *Genet. Psychol. Monogr.*, 1945, 32, Nos. 1 & 2, 3–149; 153–311.

196) Mursell, J. L. *Psychological testing.* New York: Longmans, Green, 1947.

197) National Committee on Cumulative Records. *Handbook of cumulative records.* Federal Security Agency U. S. Office Education. Washington, D. C.: U. S. Government Printing Office, 1944.

198) National Educational Association. Psychological tests and their uses. *Rev. Educ. Res.*, 1947, 17, 1–128.

199) Neely, T. E. *A study of error in the interview.* New York: Scribners, 1938.

200) Noyes, A. P. *Modern clinical psychiatry* (2nd ed.). Philadelphia: Saunders, 1939.

201) Oldfield, R. C. *The psychology of the interview.* London: Methuen, 1941.
202) Olson, W. C. *Problem tendencies in children.* Minneapolis: Univ. of Minnesota Press, 1930.
203) Olson, W. C. The clinical use of behavior rating schedules. *J. Juv. Res.,* 1931, 15, 237–245.
204) Olson, W. C. Utilization of the Haggerty-Olson-Wickman Behavior Rating Schedules. *Childh. Educ.,* 1933, 9, 350–359.
205) Olson, W. C. The diagnosis and treatment of behavior disorders of children. *Yearb. Nat. Soc. Stud. Educ.,* 1935, 34, 363–397.
206) Olson, W. C., and Cunningham, E. M. Time-sampling techniques. *Child Develop.,* 1934, 5, 41–58.
207) Paterson, D. G., Schneidler, G. G., and Williamson, E. G. *Student guidance techniques: a handbook for counselors in high schools and colleges.* New York: McGraw-Hill, 1938.
208) Porteus, S. D. *The practice of clinical psychology.* New York: American Book, 1941.
209) Preu, P. W. *Outline of psychiatric case study: a practical handbook* (2nd ed.). New York: Hoeber, 1943.
210) Raimy, V. C. The self-concept as a factor in counseling and personality organization, Ph.D. Dissertation, Ohio State Univ., 1943.
211) Rapaport, D. Principles underlying projective techniques. *Character & Pers.,* 1942, 10, 213–219.
212) Rapaport, D., Schafer, R., and Gill, M. Manual of diagnostic psychological testing: I. Diagnostic testing of intelligence and concept formation. *Publ. Josiah Macy Jr. Found., Rev. Ser.,* 1944, 2, No. 2.
213) Rapaport, D., Gill, M., and Schafer, R. *Diagnostic psychological testing: the theory, statistical evaluation, and diagnostic application of a battery of tests* (2 vol.). Chicago: Year Book Publishers, 1945, 1946.
214) Reavis, W. C. *Pupil adjustment in junior and senior high schools.* Boston: Heath, 1926.
215) Ricciardi, P. Summarizing the parent interview in a child guidance clinic. *J. Juv. Res.,* 1935, 19, 146–159.
216) Rickers-Ovsiankina, M. *Rorschach scoring samples.* Compiled from various sources for private circulation.
217) Rogers, C. R. The clinical psychologist's approach to personality problems. *Family,* 1937, 18, 233–244.
218) Rogers, C. R. *The clinical treatment of the problem child.* New York: Houghton Mifflin, 1939.
219) Rogers, C. R. *Counseling and psychotherapy.* New York: Houghton Mifflin, 1942.
220) Rorschach, H. *Psychodiagnostik.* Bern: Ernst Bircher Verlag, 1921.
221) Rosanoff, A. J. *Manual of psychiatry and mental hygiene* (7th ed.). New York: Wiley, 1938.

222) Rosenzweig, S. Clinical psychology as a psychodiagnostic art. *J. Personality*, 1946, 15, 94–100.

223) Rosenzweig, S. The dynamics of an amnesic personality. *J. Personality*, 1946, 15, 121–142.

224) Rosenzweig, S., and Shakow, D. Play technique in schizophrenia and other psychoses. I. Rationale. II. An experimental study of schizophrenic constructions with play materials. *Amer. J. Orthopsychiat.*, 1937, 7, 32–35; 36–47.

225) Rosenzweig, S., Simon, B., and Ballou, M. The psychodynamics of an uxoricide. *Amer. J. Orthopsychiat.*, 1942, 12, 283–293.

226) Rotter, J. B. Studies in the use and validity of the thematic apperception test with mentally disordered patients. *Character & Pers.*, 1940, 9, 18–34.

227) Ruch, G. M., and Segel, D. Minimum essentials of the individual inventory in guidance. U. S. Department of Interior, *Office of Education, Vocational Division, Bulletin No. 202*. Washington, D. C.: U. S. Government Printing Office, 1940.

228) Ruesch, J. Intellectual impairment in head injuries. *Amer. J. Psychiat.*, 1944, 100, 480–496.

229) Rust, M. M. The effect of resistance on intelligence test scores of young children. *Child Developm. Monogr.* 1931, No. 6.

230) Sarason, S. B. Projective techniques in mental deficiency. *Character & Pers.*, 1945, 13, 237–245.

231) Sarbin, T. R. The case record in psychological counseling. *J. Appl. Psychol.*, 1940, 24, 184–197.

232) Sarbin, T. R. Clinical psychology: art or science. *Psychometrika*, 1941, 6, 391–399.

233) Sarbin, T. R. A contribution to the study of actuarial and individual methods of prediction. *Amer. J. Sociol.*, 1942, 48, 593–602.

234) Sargent, H. Projective methods: their origins, theory, and applications in personality research. *Psychol. Bull.*, 1945, 42, 257–293.

235) Saslow, G., and Chapple, E. D. A new life history form, with instructions for its use. *Appl. Anthrop.*, 1945, 4, No. 1, 1–18.

236) Schafer, R. Clinical evaluation of a word association test. *Bull. Menninger Clin.*, 1945, 9, 84–88.

237) Schafer, R. A study of thought processes in a word association test. *Character & Pers.*, 1945, 13, 212–227.

238) Schnack, G. F., Shakow, D., and Lively, M. L. Studies in insulin and metrazol therapy: I. the differential prognostic value of some psychological tests. II. differential effects on some psychological functions. *J. Personality*, 1946, 14, 106–124; 125–149.

239) Scott, I. D. *Manual of advisement and guidance*. Washington, D. C.: U. S. Government Printing Office, 1945.

240) Segel, D. Prediction of success in college. U. S. Department of Interior, *Office of Education Bulletin No. 15*. Washington, D. C.: U. S. Government Printing Office, 1934.

241) Segel, D. Nature and use of the cumulative record. U. S. Depart-

ment of Interior, *Office of Education Bulletin No. 3.* Washington, D. C.: U. S. Government Printing Office, 1938.

242) Shaffer, L. F. *The psychology of adjustment.* New York: Houghton Mifflin, 1936.

243) Shakow, D., Rodnick, E. H., and Lebeaux, T. A psychological study of a schizophrenic: exemplification of a method. *J. Abnorm. Soc. Psychol.,* 1945, 40, 154–174.

244) Shakow, D., and Rosenzweig, S. The use of the tautophone ("verbal summator") as an auditory apperceptive test for the study of personality. *Character & Pers.,* 1940, 8, 216–226.

245) Shartle, C. L. *Occupational information: its development and application.* New York: Prentice-Hall, 1946.

246) Skeels, H. M., Updegraff, R., Wellman, B. L., and Williams, H. M. A study of environmental stimulation: an orphanage preschool project. *Univ. Iowa Stud. Child Welf.,* 1939, 15, No. 4.

247) Skinner, B. F. The verbal summator and a method for the study of latent speech. *J. Psychol.,* 1936, 2, 71–107.

248) Smithies, E. M. *Case studies of normal adolescent girls.* New York: Appleton, 1933.

249) Stagner, R. *Psychology of personality.* New York: McGraw-Hill, 1937.

250) Starr, A. S. The significance of qualifying factors in the diagnosis of borderline mentality. *Train. Sch. Bull.,* 1937, 34, 113–118.

251) Stevens, G. D. Suggested criteria for the selection of items for a cumulative case study record for the mentally retarded. *J. Educ. Res.,* 1945, 39, 201–209.

252) Stouffer, S. A. Notes on the case study and unique case. *Sociometry,* 1941, 4, 349–357.

253) Strang, R. *Counselling technics in college and secondary school.* New York: Harper, 1937.

254) Strecker, E. A., and Ebaugh, F. G. *Practical clinical psychiatry for students and practitioners* (5th ed.). Philadelphia: Blakiston, 1940.

255) Stutsman, R. *Performance tests for children of pre-school age.* Worcester, Mass.: Clark Univ. Press, 1926.

256) Stutsman, R. *Mental measurement of pre-school children.* Yonkers, N. Y.: World Book, 1931.

257) Symmes, E. F. Some techniques in securing rapport with preschool children. *Amer. J. Orthopsychiat.,* 1933, 3, 181–190.

258) Symonds, P. M. *Diagnosing personality and conduct.* New York: Appleton-Century, 1931.

259) Symonds, P. M. Securing rapport in interviewing. *Teach. Coll. Rec.,* 1938, 39, 707–722.

260) Tendler, A. D. Significant features of disturbance in free association. *J. Psychol.,* 1945, 20, 65–89.

261) Terman, L. M. *The measurement of intelligence.* Boston: Houghton Mifflin, 1916.

262) Terman, L. M., and Merrill, M. A. *Measuring intelligence*. Boston: Houghton Mifflin, 1937.

263) Thomas, F. C. Intuition or psychometry in the study of personality? *Character & Pers.*, 1939, 7, 309–317.

264) Thorndike, R. L. The effect of the interval between test and retest on the constancy of the I.Q. *J. Educ. Psychol.*, 1933, 24, 543–549.

265) Thorne, F. C. A critique of nondirective methods of therapy. *J. Abnorm. Soc. Psychol.*, 1944, 39, 459–470.

266) Traxler, A. E. The nature and use of anecdotal records. *Educ. Rec. Bull.*, 1939, Suppl., No. D.

267) Traxler, A. E. Case study procedures in guidance. *Educ. Rec. Bull.*, 1940, Suppl., No. 13.

268) Traxler, A. E. The use of test results in diagnosis and instruction in the tool subjects. *Educ. Rec. Bull.*, 1942, Suppl., No. 18 (Rev.).

269) Traxler, A. E. The use of tests and rating devices in the appraisal of personality. *Educ. Rec. Bull.*, 1942, Suppl., No. 23 (Rev.).

270) Traxler, A. E. *Techniques of guidance*. New York: Harper, 1945.

271) Traxler, A. E. The cumulative record in the guidance program. *Sch. Rev.*, 1946, 54, 154–161.

272) Tyler, R. W. Characteristics of a satisfactory diagnosis. *Yearb. Nat. Soc. Stud. Educ.*, 1935, 34, 95–111.

273) Tyler, R. W. Elements of diagnosis. *Yearb. Nat. Soc. Stud. Educ.*, 1935, 34, 113–129.

274) (Various) Dictionary of occupational titles, I. Washington, D. C.: Division of Standards & Research, U. S. Government Printing Office, 1939.

275) (Various) Non-projective personality tests. *Ann. N. Y. Acad. Sci.*, 1946, 46, 531–678.

276) Vernon, P. E. The significance of the Rorschach test. *Brit. J. Med. Psychol.*, 1935, 15, 199–217.

277) Vernon, P. E. The Stanford-Binet test as a psychometric method. *Character & Pers.*, 1937, 6, 99–113.

278) Vernon, P. E. The assessment of psychological qualities by verbal methods: a survey of attitude tests, rating scales and personality questionnaires. *Medical Research Council, Industrial Health Research Board, Report No. 83*. London: His Majesty's Stationery Office, 1938.

279) Vigotsky, L. S. Thought and speech. *Psychiatry*, 1939, 2, 29–54.

280) Wallin, R. Ego-involvement as a determinant of selective forgetting. *J. Abnorm. Soc. Psychol.*, 1942, 37, 20–39.

281) Ward, R. S. How to use part IV of the "Dictionary." *Occup.*, 1943, 22, 39–41.

282) Washburn, R. W. Re-education in a nursery group: a study in clinical psychology. *Monogr. Soc. Res. Child Develpm.*, 1944, 9, No. 2.

283) Watson, R. I. Interviewing. In Kaplan, O. (ed.), *Encyclopedia of Vocational Guidance*. New York: Philosophical Library (to be published).

284) Wechsler, D. *The measurement of adult intelligence* (3rd ed.). Baltimore: Williams & Wilkins, 1944.

285) Weiss, A. B. Qualitative intelligence testing as a means of diagnosis in the examination of psychopathic children. *Amer. J. Orthopsychiat.*, 1935, 5, 154–179.

286) Wells, F. L. *Mental tests in clinical practice*. Yonkers, N. Y.: World Book, 1927.

287) Wells, F. L. Rorschach and the free association test. *J. Gen. Psychol.*, 1935, 13, 413–433.

288) Wells, F. L., and Ruesch, J. (eds.). *Mental examiners handbook* (2nd ed.). New York: Psychological Corporation, 1945.

289) Werner, H., and Strauss, A. Problems and methods of functional analysis in mentally deficient children. *J. Abnorm. Soc. Psychol.*, 1939, 34, 37–62.

290) Whipple, G. M. The obtaining of information: psychology of observation and report. *Psychol. Bull.*, 1918, 15, 217–248.

291) Whipple, G. M. (ed.). *Educational diagnosis: National society for the study of education, 34th yearbook*. Bloomington, Ill.: Public School Publishing Company, 1935.

292) White, R. W. Interpretation of imaginative productions. In Hunt, J. McV., *Personality and the behavior disorders*. New York: Ronald Press, 1944, 214–251.

293) White, R. W., Tompkins, S. S., and Alper, T. G. The realistic synthesis. *J. Abnorm. Soc. Psychol.*, 1945, 40, 228–248.

294) Whitehorn, J. C. Guide to interviewing and clinical personality study. *Arch. Neur. Psychiat.*, 1944, 52, 197–216.

295) Wilcox, P. H. The Gardner behavior chart. *Amer. J. Psychiat.*, 1942, 98, 874–880.

296) Williamson, E. G. *How to counsel students: a manual of techniques for clinical counselors*. New York: McGraw-Hill, 1939.

297) Williamson, E. G., and Darley, J. G. *Student personnel work: an outline of clinical procedures*. New York: McGraw-Hill, 1937.

298) Willoughby, R. R., and Morse, M. E. Spontaneous reactions to a personality inventory. *Amer. J. Orthopsychiat.*, 1936, 8, 562–575.

299) Wittman, P. Psychometric efficiency levels for psychotic and age classifications. *J. Abnorm. Soc. Psychol.*, 1943, 38, 335–350.

300) Wittson, C. L., and Hunt, W. A. Three years of naval selection— a retrospect. *War Med.*, 1945, 7, 218–221.

301) Wood, B. D. Information for guidance: the anecdotal method of personal analysis. *Occup.*, 1935, 13, 795–803.

302) Woods, A. H., and Chase, G. Forms of personality obstructive to progress in college. *J. Soc. Psychol.*, 1937, 8, 411–431.

303) Woodward, L. E., and Rennie, T. A. C. *Jobs and the man*. Springfield, Ill.: Thomas, 1946.

304) Yepsen, L. N. Defining mental deficiency. *Amer. J. Ment. Def.*, 1941, 46, 200–205.

305) Yerkes, R. M. (ed.). *Psychological examining in the United States Army.* (Memoirs of the National Academy of Sciences, Vol. 15.) Washington, D. C.: U. S. Government Printing Office, 1921.

306) Young, P. V. *Interviewing in social work: a sociological analysis.* New York: McGraw-Hill, 1935.

IV

Methods of Treatment

MARION McKENZIE FONT

Tulane University School of Medicine

Therapeutic Aspects of the Psychological Interview[1]

Twice during recent months has this question been posed by interested social workers: "Do you do treatment—or testing?" And to each query the reply has been, "*I interview.*" Followed then an explanation of what the psychological interview contributed to findings obtained from testing procedure and observation of the patient, in the formulation of a diagnostic picture (71),[2] and how in certain instances the interview might take precedence over both testing and observation because of *therapeutic* as well as *diagnostic* implications. Explanation of one's functioning results in clearer perspective and verbalization brings to sharper focus that which was long implicit in one's thinking. The therapeutic implications of the psychological interview seem to have gone unnoticed by clinical psychologists, although the psychologist's contribution to individual diagnosis (through testing, observation and interview) is now an accepted fact not only in his own mind, but in the minds of psychiatrist and social worker who work with him as a clinic team.

Kamman (117), speaking of the Rorschach method as a therapeutic agent, makes a statement that psychologists might do well to ponder: "Since psychotherapy really begins when the patient is first examined, any diagnostic procedure (employed by the physician) becomes in reality a therapeutic agent." It is the purpose of this paper to discuss the psychological interview, a recognized diagnostic

[1] Reprinted from *Journal of Clinical Psychology*, 1946, 2, 84–87. Copyright 1946 by Frederick C. Thorne.
[2] Bibliography begins on page 719.

procedure, from the standpoint of its therapeutical implications, under the designation of "short service therapy"—a concept borrowed from the field of social work.

Social workers have for many years employed the term "short service case" to describe application of case work techniques in specific, usually acute, situations in which follow-up was not contemplated. Either an existing need is satisfied during short-service treatment or a gap is bridged between present crisis and referral to another agency equipped to handle the particular problem. Successful treatment of the short service case calls for both skill and experience, comparable to that necessary in successful work with the long-term or intensive case. The psychological interview, by bridging a gap between psychological examination and psychiatric appointment, and by satisfying existing needs as indicated by the following examples, thus qualifies as a form of "short service therapy" administered by clinical psychologists.

(a) Not infrequently an intelligent patient with marked anxiety and many perfectionistic trends has such need to release tension that a considerable portion of the time appointed for psychological examination is devoted to the interview. Sometimes the patient talks of his problems at length, and much more fully during his visit to the psychologist than during previous interviews with other clinic personnel. The recital often reveals the presence of guilt feelings, under guise of religious vows or self-imposed hardships. The interview in such cases comprises largely the art of listening on the part of the psychologist. Yet knowing how to deal with the patient's story so as to effect release of tension, forestall later guilt feelings because of having told too much, and give reassurance, satisfies an existing need of the patient to be accepted, and bridges the gap till his next appointment with the psychiatrist.

(b) Treatment of a neurotic can be initiated only when he recognizes an area in which he can accept help. Those whose anxiety finds expression in various bodily symptoms and complaints may for a long time deny that anything is amiss in family, home, or work relationships. One such patient was found during psychological interview to be greatly concerned over her complete inability to discipline and train an only child, and discussion revealed this recognized inadequacy to be an important source of patient's anxiety. Enabling this woman to verbalize her feelings regarding the child which she had repressed during previous visits to the psychiatric clinic, not only relieved tension but prepared the patient to accept help in an area where she herself asked for assistance—thus satisfying an existing need and bridging the gap till the next clinic visit.

(c) Many hyper-active children are insecure in their parent-child relationships in which unrecognized hostility and aggression may predominate. Psychological examination of such children is difficult, and formulation of results usually stresses the tentativeness of the conclusions drawn. Experience with such children has shown that testing procedure may be facilitated by allowing free play with two or three small toys (such as the doll and engine of the Binet test material when these are not used in the actual testing) before, during and after the examination. Focusing interest away from the examiner gives the situation a less tense and threatening atmosphere and renders the examiner more acceptable to the child, thereby enabling him to comply with an adult's requests. The free play itself is usually revealing of much aggression, which is released in a permissive environment, and leaves the child relaxed and quiet during the remainder of the examination. With these children, an existing need to relieve tension and express aggression has been satisfied and a feeling of security in an adult-child relationship established, that is of therapeutic value.

(d) Mathews (152), in discussing reading difficulties, mentions interpretation of the child's problems and formulation of plans as therapy, saying: "With certain children, treatment involved relatively simple procedures. Sometimes the interpretation of the child's limitations, his special interests, his reactions to success and failure, together with plans to meet these, was enough to permit the reading to progress. With other children the problem was more severe."

Interpretation of test findings on patients seen on consultation basis, to private physicians, parents, or interested agency, and recommendations for change of school, special instruction, or relief from pressure at home is a recognized phase of the work of most clinical psychologists. But some interpretation of test results to the patient himself, as part of the psychological interview, may also have definite therapeutic value and if carefully phrased will not encroach upon the field of the designated therapist (physician, social worker, or remedial teacher). The manifest, tearfully expressed relief of the child with a severe reading disability who has so often been scolded for stupidity, when the nature of his difficulty is explained to him, is but one example of therapy during psychological interview and has been known to initiate immediate improvement in social behavior and a new interest in school work even before the actual remedial reading program was begun. The increased self-confidence of the intelligent adult patient with inferiority feeling because of lack of educational opportunities, when the difference between intelligence and education is explained to him and his good abilities pointed out, is another example of "short-service therapy" during psychological interview. The patient himself may recognize the therapeutic aspects of the psychological interview, as shown by the spontaneous remark, "I feel so much better after talking with you."

The importance of clarifying the term "treatment" for the classroom teacher in order to make her part of an effective remedial reading program has long been stressed (19, 70). It is even more important to clarify the term for the clinical psychologist, who employs therapeutic techniques, yet who fears the formal designation of his work as "therapy." Clinical psychologists as a group, like the psychiatrists with whom they work as members of a team, know "only too well what the training to be a psychotherapist requires, and how few of the psychologists have it" (180)—if by psychotherapy is meant the intensive treament and highly specialized techniques of the psychoanalyst. Intensive and long-term therapy by a psychologist, however, is sanctioned by fellow-psychologists and psychiatrists alike when it includes remedial techniques in tool subjects, applied to the "educationally sick" child or adolescent. The clinical psychologist is considered peculiarly fitted to undertake therapy in such instances because of "his knowledge of the neuroses and the possible effects of these upon verbal and manual skills" (86). This "knowledge of the neuroses" can be employed to good use during the psychological interview, to make it more effective both from a diagnostic and therapeutic standpoint. While it is not believed that in every instance the psychological interview includes therapeutic aspects, the frequency of therapeutic implications should make the clinical psychologist increasingly aware of the necessity for highly developed skill in this important technique.

MARY C. ROLAND

Tri-County Child Guidance Center, Harrisburg, Pennsylvania

The Psychological Examination as a Beginning in Therapy[1]

Although child guidance clinics differ in policy as well as in their therapeutic approach, it is generally recognized that the psychiatric, psychological, and case-work areas are of optimum value in the understanding of children when they are synthesized in a process designed for the consideration and study of the individual child, and the factors contingent upon his maladjustments. The basis for this paper is the crucial place in which the psychologist finds herself in a child guidance clinic, or at least in those clinics which have, as part of their routine, a psychological examination preceding actual therapy.

There are representatives of clinics who consider this part of the child guidance process to be of exaggerated importance, as well as those to whom it is of minor significance. This paper represents neither extreme point of view. The material on which this paper is essentially based, has emerged from a clinic where there have been many children whose good intelligence would not be doubted, and for whom a psychological examination might be considered superfluous. We have, however, found it satisfactory and often advantageous, to have a psychological study preceding subsequent clinic contacts, so as to evaluate the child's approximate mentality, even though he was previously felt to be at least average in intelligence.

---

[1] Presented at the annual meeting of the American Orthopsychiatric Association, Hotel Pennsylvania, New York City, February 23, 1943. Reprinted from *Journal of Consulting Psychology*, 1945, 9, 171–177. Copyright 1945 by American Association for Applied Psychology.

In some children, the evidence from their day to day functioning, might even be suggestive of retarded capacities, although they are actually superior. The successful examination results depend principally upon the child's own attitude and participation, and the psychologist's recognition of the presence of possible emotional disturbances; these problems, which may be manifested in symptoms preceding advent to the clinic, sometimes distort the use of intelligence. Consequently, there are cases in which we would not presume to say that an examination would necessarily be revealing of the child's actual capacities. An understanding of a reciprocal dependence of intellectual functioning upon emotional stability is a part of seeing the child in his entirety. Herein we see the psychologist's work as complementary to that of the psychiatrist and psychiatric case-worker in a child guidance clinic.

The majority of cases treated at this clinic are first given a psychological examination; unless the specific case so indicates, comparatively few are deferred until the end of treatment. Other clinics may have ways of working more efficiently in their own situations but we have found, in most instances, that the child can be effectually introduced to the clinic by this procedure. When, therefore, the psychologist, representing the clinic's feeling towards the child, is the person with whom he has initial contact, it seems important that this time be used constructively as a part of the entire procedure, and that the first interviews, preceding or during a psychological examination, be understood and used dynamically by the psychologist, despite the necessity for more limitations and control than direct psychotherapy would impose. The child can then be helped to see the examination as a part of clinic procedure, yet as something distinct from what will follow. It seems apparent that the case-worker and mother also have therapeutic material from the psychological examination, which offers some reality in relation to what the child is doing in the clinic. At the same time the mother has, in the discussion of the material, something related to the child she has had to share with a strange person, yet which can concern only her and the case-worker. This can enable the mother to feel that she has a real part in the clinic and as a result, contributes toward helping the child to be freer in finding his own place.

A relationship of some kind inevitably arises when a child meets and works with anyone in a clinic. It is my point to emphasize that the elements which permeate this relationship ought to be utilized to every possible extent. If all the components of it are not given due consideration, or at least recognized, the psychological examination becomes nothing more than a psychometric examination, which is then a much less integrated part of the clinic procedure, contributing little as an introduction to therapy and possibly deterring it. A brief psychometric test is not a psychological study, nor is it an adequate substitute. The reality of tests being standardized neither permits inactivity on the part of the examiner nor requires that the interview be static. An attempt to be thoroughly objective may easily become indifference to the feelings the patient is expressing in his circuitous behavior or speech; the psychologist's eagerness to be unprejudiced may inadvertently depreciate into insufficient participation. If the child's feeling is left unrecognized because a psychological examination must be staid and standardized, the initial psychological interviews are of no advantage in enabling him to find his place in the clinic and do nothing to enlighten him about a situation which may already be baffling him.

The question may arise as to whether the psychologist may not complicate rather than facilitate the beginning of later therapy by becoming too involved with the child beforehand. The validity of any such question is readily conceded, and in some instances the answer lies in necessarily deferring the examination until treatment is ended. If the psychologist is equipped to handle the child's feelings in a therapeutic way she should certainly be able to recognize, however, those elements which arise as a relationship becomes too profound and which could be destructive to later therapy. Being aware of the depth of interplay between the child and herself is actually a part of showing the child the separateness of the different, yet complementary phases of child guidance procedure and of making them identifiable to him. Realizing the probability of fear or reluctance to his being in the situation at all, we have found that the psychological study is more satisfactory and of greater value in the child's continuing contacts, if it can be arranged for at least more than one time. In some cases an examination may not be possible until the patient has been seen for several interviews. Meanwhile, the parent may not have come to the point, with the case worker, of accepting aspects of the clinic, and, though having previously resigned herself to the psychological procedure for her child, may change her mind in fear of it. Other parents are relieved to find that here is an opportunity to actually learn the child's real capacities and not have to live any longer either with fear of his retardation or false hopes of his growing out of it. Although the possibility of the child's having two or more interviews with a person who may not carry the case later prolongs the contact with the psychologist, to limit this contact means sacrificing understanding that may be essential to the progress of the case. Negative feelings the child may show if transferred to another therapist can be used effectively as they provide another situation paralleling those which he may meet in everyday living: he has the opportunity to learn that giving up is a required part of all living, and can find himself more able to tolerate, and possibly even accept, what cannot always be changed in the more permanent relationships he has outside the clinic.

That a child who comes to a clinic for the first time may be fearful, uncertain, distrustful, or resentful, is not an original thought. Dr. Phyllis Blanchard has covered this phase quite adequately in a lecture which she presented at Smith College, "The Importance of the First Interviews in Therapeutic Work with Children." Although I am necessarily considering partially similar material, perhaps this will serve to point out that whether his introduction to the clinic be through the psychiatrist or the psychologist, the child can be made aware in much the same way that he is accepted at the clinic, that he will be changed only to the extent that he is willing to change himself, and can be made to feel more comfortable in his place there, not by the clinic's indifference to his requests and behavior, not by catering to his whims in an indiscriminate effort to establish rapport, but by a constructive use of the child's feelings in relation to the current situation.

We are all aware that new experiences may precipitate new problems. In a child guidance clinic we see this to be particularly evident, insomuch as it is a distinctive experience. There must be something formidable in a child's coming, for the first time, to a place where those he meets accept him with the feelings he has at the time, for what he is able to do in his new situation, and without reproach for that which has made him feel like a mortal enemy to many. He has usually been brought or sent for behavior which annoyed other people, and is met by a stranger whom he has no reason to trust or believe. It is a normal child's reaction to feel that adults are allied with adults, and this is one of the basic problems with which the child-guidance worker is forced to deal. If we, as adults, reminisce about having gone away to school at an early age, or having taught for the first time a class of students possibly older than ourselves, we have some examples of our own experiences in new situations, and perhaps have the right to feel that these were unparalleled traumatic experiences. Personal instances such as these might be analagous to and helpful in understanding the feelings of others, but few, if any of us, have had the opportunity of being subjected, as children, to a child-guidance situation, to a strange place where we were given over to unfamiliar people, and finally of allowing our mothers (sometimes equally apprehensive) to depart into unknown realms with someone whose ulterior motive was also unrevealing and cryptic. To have had no such personal experience would seem to put the child-guidance worker in the place of learning, from her own cases, the variety or complexity of feelings which must lie in the background of what is submerged or expressed by the child. We learn, at least, from our accumulation of experiences, that the ease or difficulty with which a child leaves his mother is dependent upon the reluctance or willingness of the parent to permit a separation; we also learn that feelings and attitudes are cleverly disguised, and the apparently passive child who comes for a first interview may be equally as negative or afraid as the aggressive, loquacious, and seemingly undisturbed one whose inner self demands a demonstration of the necessity of defending himself against and deluding the people his parents selected to change him.

The cases which follow are examples of how some children in our clinic have used and have been helped to use the interviews preceding the psychological examination and the examination itself, as a preliminary to therapy and a partial phase of a total experience.

Case 1. Instead of coming for an application interview, Mickey's prospective adoptive mother, Mrs. M., had her first direct contact with the clinic at the same time as he, because they came from a distant town. Her own uncertainty about the clinic procedure apparently tended to aggravate his problem in coming. Mickey was nine years old. He stood in the hallway with an expression of obstinacy, and his first reaction to the suggestion that he come into the office was a definitely negative one. There was no question that his attitude would have to become different before a situation conducive to testing could exist; this was more apparent as he became increasingly belligerent. Mickey remained with his head down, and the psychologist commented that he did not seem to want to come with her. He finally followed Mrs. M. down the hall but was told she would be in a different office. He pounded her arms, actively fought, and tugged at her body while she was unresponsive and displayed no annoyance. Mrs. M. tried to withdraw unobtrusively. Mickey immediately sped out another door to the porch, returning of his own accord shortly afterwards, and suddenly stopped as he noticed the toys which, in his excitement, had previously escaped him. Before long he began saying that he thought the clinic would be like a hospital where he had been taken without preparation, and agreed that he was afraid that we might do the same kind of thing to him and keep him with us. After he began to play he said he would not care if he would have to stay overnight. He was told that he would later be seeing a doctor at the clinic but it was not like a hospital, and he probably would not believe that this doctor was different from most doctors, and would not do the things to him that other doctors did. Mickey seemed better organized during the latter part of his hour, but had a brief moment of obstreperous behavior when warned that his time was nearly over. However, he was much more relaxed than when he had struggled with his foster mother. When he said he did not want to leave, a comment was made that he seemed to be feeling better than when he first came. He acknowledged this, and soon showed his wish to control the whole situation. In the waiting room he encountered a child who had been coming for some time, to whom he said, "You're supposed to come back this way. This is where you go." He also attempted to intrude on her interview before he left. He had already made the clinic his own. He was told that he knew he could come again the following week but he asked to remain in the outer office, and was reminded that no one had interrupted his hour.

In the interview that followed, Mickey came back to the office instead of going to the waiting room but accepted being told that he was early and would have to wait. His first comment referred to the toys' being different and it was recognized that he felt different about coming this time. He noticed some psychological materials, asked if he could play with them and was told that they were tests and not playthings, but could take the tests if he wished. In response to his questioning the examination was explained to him. He wanted to explore the materials but was told he would have to decide whether or not he would like to have any tests that day. He hesitated and acknowledged the comment that perhaps he was afraid he would not be able to answer all the questions. Distinction was made for him about the examination's being more controlled, and he was told that he could play more freely in his later interviews with the psychiatrist. When he commented "I don't think the teacher wanted me to come very bad today," this was verbally related to his own unwillingness to participate in something a little difficult. Mickey then began telling about his ride to the clinic and the pleasant time he had on his way. When suggested that it probably would be more fun to be somewhere else, he drawled, "Well, I didn't know this test would be so long."

Mickey seemed to gain sufficient understanding from these first interviews to realize that his seeing the psychiatrist would be something different for him. There were essentially similar elements in his working with the two people, insofar as he could feel accepted as a person in either situation. By the time he reached the psychiatrist, his initial struggle with the clinic was over and he could go into therapy without all of the confusion and negativism he first felt. This enabled him to express his need to control in a different and less negative way. Instead of remaining withdrawn, defiant and obstinate, he came into the therapist's office willingly, precipitated himself into play with the toys and immediately began building up a picture of his own strength.

Case 2. But, a six-year-old, infantile-appearing boy, was brought to the clinic by his mother who would not accept the school's test results indicating that her child was definitely of low intelligence. He refused to leave her and was reluctant to come into the office, even when she offered to accompany him. Mrs. E., his mother, began to discuss, in the child's presence, the school's report of him, and asked the case worker and psychologist to look at some of his school papers. At this point the psychologist asked Bud if he wanted her to see them. He began to explain what he had written, ignoring his mother's exit, but soon ran next door to see her. She tried to force him back to the office, despite the worker's suggestion that he might decide for himself. The worker had said this because it often happens that the child will spontaneously return to the psychologist's office, in a first interview, after he has made sure his mother has not left, and has found that no pressure is being exerted on him. Bud's mother, however, at first bribed him to return, then threatened him with not being allowed to go back to school. He struggled with her and was extremely negative and vehement in his cries that he only wanted to go home. When Mrs. E. returned to the worker's office Bud stood at the door in the hallway, screaming for her, without shedding tears, but made no attempt to follow her. When he was left alone he picked up some clay and began to play with it. He soon came in and asked the psychologist what she was doing. When the clay was offered to him, his answer was a definite, "No." He continued to scream and he was told that it seemed as if he didn't want to have anything to do with the place, but he was making sure we would all know he was here. As he stood outside the door, the psychologist commented that even if he did not feel like playing, it was probably a lot of fun to stand outside and cry. He looked in and said "Oh," at the recognition of his feelings. When it was mentioned that he was a little angry with his mother for not coming when he called her, he answered, "Uh huh." During his play, which he invited the psychologist to share, he suddenly ran out of the office, walked in to see his mother next door, but immediately returned of his own volition, only asking her to wait for him. The comment was made that he seemed a little concerned as to what she was doing and was worried that she would not wait for him. Some concept of Bud's intellectual level could be ascertained from his play, but only after three interviews was it possible to obtain an apparently valid psychological examination. He was enthusiastic about coming the second time and reluctant to leave. When his examination was completed he was able to understand in simple terms, that he could play more freely in subsequent interviews. In the meantime the social worker used, with the mother, our impressions from these first interviews, which prepared her to accept the later results verifying them. In his first interview in the brief period he was seen for therapy, there was one attempt to look for his mother but he readily accepted the therapist's suggestion that he talk to her by phone instead. Bud talked as if he had not seen her for a long time but told her that he would be coming again. In the interview which followed, he left his mother with only a goodbye and really began to consider his interviews as separate from hers and really his own.

Case 3. Seven-year-old Billy was hesitant about leaving the waiting room. As we walked by the worker's office he was shown where his mother would be. She had been eager to bring him, at the suggestion of the school principal. His infantile speech was only one aspect of a little boy who was having a hard time growing up. He did not know what kind of a place the clinic was, but associated it with his "not talking right." When asked if he wanted to talk so that people could understand him better he said he did not know. Looking at a high-chair in the psychologist's office, he questioned the clinic as being a place where babies are brought. In playing with the dictaphone his conversation disclosed a great deal of concern about having come. His attitude of uncertainty during his first interview reflected what was later learned from his mother. He had said he would come only once, told her she was reckless in her driving to the clinic, wondered whether the spare tire would work if they needed it, and thought she was taking the wrong road. While making some drawings in the first interview he showed fear of doing anything bad, and carefully collected eraser particles to dispose of them in the wastebasket. He was tempted to use the finger paints but did not want to get his fingers dirty. Before he left, the psychologist said that in knowing each other a little better they could try working together next week on some of the tests which other children do in the office. The explanation was then offered that he could then continue to come to the clinic to play, and have a special hour for himself each week. When the desirability of his returning was discussed with Billy, he was slow in deciding, but finally asked when he should come back. He was given some consideration in a choice of several appointments. In his second and third interviews Billy seemed more comfortable and he could proceed in the psychological examination.

In his first interviews at the beginning of therapy, following his introduction through the psychological examination, Billy was really able to be active, and to actually direct some of his aggression outward, as the clinic was no longer a totally strange place about which he knew nothing. He could feel free to test the therapist and bring out some of the badness he had previously had to deny. The psychological examination had provided a medium in which he could find his place in the clinic, and at the same time offered useful material for evaluation of him as a total person. We then knew that here was a child who not only needed therapy but could understand and make use of it.

In conclusion, we feel that a psychological examination for a child in a child guidance clinic can be extended to become of greater value than is sometimes assumed, if those persons on the staff who are concerned with using all resources of the clinic for the patient's greatest benefit can see the complete procedure as a therapeutic experience. Whether this type of study precedes or follows therapy must necessarily be related to each individual clinic but in our experience, we have felt than an awareness of the child's capacities beforehand provides the therapist with material which aids in understanding the dynamics of behavior and their relation to the use of intelligence. It assists in determining the extent to which the child will be able to use therapeutic interviews. For the child to enter the controlled situation of the psychological study after one or two interviews in preparation for it seems less complicated than to expect him to go from the much longer period of therapy and its freedom, despite its limitations, to a testing situation which would then be almost an isolated experience.

The psychological study can be considered a flexible therapeutic tool related to direct treatment in a child guidance clinic, yet differentiated for the child. If, however, the psychologist remains impervious to the dynamics which are so obviously a part of the relationship between herself and the child, she is not functioning as a part of the total therapeutic process evolved in child-guidance philosophy. If the child, in his first interviews in a clinic, can know that he is recognized and accepted with both his goodness and badness, we can anticipate that he can go into direct therapy with more security and greater possibility of receiving constructive help.

GRACE ARTHUR

St. Paul, Minnesota

Tutoring and Remedial Teaching as Educational Therapy[1]

From the standpoint of a child guidance clinic, tutoring and remedial teaching constitute a highly specialized service. They presuppose a psychological examination of the child to be taught, a diagnosis that is at least tentative, and a definite plan for therapy. They further presuppose a patient motivated to accept therapy in the form of teaching, and the cooperation of the family, the school, the physician and any social agency active on the case. Without the cooperation of every one concerned, no plan for therapy can be carried through to a successful conclusion.

They presuppose also a corps of intelligent tutors trained in the most modern teaching methods, and adaptable enough to take on new methods whenever these are indicated. They must be able to make accurate observations, and to report in detail any significant behavior of an emotionally disturbed child. Finally, they presuppose close supervision by a psychologist. On the basis of our experience, the last seems to be the most important from the standpoint of results.

The tutor selected for a given patient must not only have special training in teaching children of that age and grade, but must be able to meet the intellectual and emotional needs of that type of child. Of a long list of outstandingly capable tutors, not one is able to work effectively with all types of children. One who is invaluable

---

[1] Reprinted from *Journal of Consulting Psychology*, 1940, 4, 173–176. Copyright 1940 by American Association for Applied Psychology.

in dealing with extremely difficult adolescents, asks to be excused from tutoring young children. A fifteen year old boy throwing an ink bottle across the room in a temper tantrum does not upset her, but a shy six-year-old makes her nervous! Another tutor who has carried brilliant but undisciplined and unmotivated children through to recoveries that border on the miraculous becomes unhappy and discouraged when given a dull child to teach. Another is threatened by aggressive children of whatever age, while still another is baffled by vague, passive, generally ineffectual children although she can deal with any specific problem that is clearly outlined.

It sometimes happens that the tutor who can deal best with a child at one stage becomes less useful as his behavior is modified and passes into a different phase. One child who had been both over-indulged and over-managed without any consistent discipline was given to a gentle little tutor with instructions for the tutor to be as nearly passive as possible and still do any teaching. The child was in open rebellion against parents and school, took the lead. Her tantrums were ignored. Cause and effect had a chance to do their work. At the end of a year she had made considerable gain in reading, but not so much as a better integrated child would have accomplished. However, she had become aware of a personal need to learn. Although she made little attempt to control temper tantrums, she was not apologetic when one occurred. At this point a new tutor was introduced. This tutor was told, in the presence of the child, not to put up with any uncontrolled behavior. The child was told that she had gained so much during the previous year that it was no longer necessary for any one to make any allowances for her. She was now able to behave like other children. Temper tantrums came to a sudden end. Work habits improved, and progress became much more rapid. This child, today, is devoted to both tutors and realizes how much she owes to each.

The psychologist has to decide when tutoring can be expected to be of use, and when it has to be postponed until environmental adjustments can be effected. A little girl who had been seduced by an adult was preoccupied with memories of her sex experiences. It might have seemed logical to postpone tutoring until she had made a better emotional adjustment, but it was felt that increased intellectual activity could be useful in combatting the preoccupation with sex. This turned out to be the case. Starting with a new pride in school achievement made possible by an intensive program of remedial teaching, new interests began to develop that gradually crowded out the old habits of thought and helped her to develop into a normal little girl with wholesome interests and play activities.

Another child, however, who had been indulging in sex play was discovered and warned by an unwise adult that he would "lose his mind." When a severe reading disability interfered with school progress, he became alarmed. A real but manageable intellectual difficulty was converted through emotional conflict into an insuperable obstacle to learning. This child did not begin to learn to read until he had been interviewed by the psychiatrist and assured that many children indulge in the same kinds of sex play in which he had been involved, that it was not wholesome and had better be discontinued as it was making him very unhappy, but that it had not affected his brain and would not do so. At the same time, the emphasis in tutoring was put on arithmetic, in which he had no special disability. As he was older than the other children of his group, it was not difficult with daily help during the tutoring hour for him to become the best in his class in arithmetic. This demonstration that he could learn, re-enforced the assurances of the psychiatrist that he had not "ruined his mind" by sex play. He began to learn to read and soon was making normal progress in terms of his own intellectual endowment.

For still another child, school achievement is the most reliable index of emotional adjustment. It begins to drop when things go wrong in the boarding home, long before he is willing to admit that he is unhappy. Tutoring is useless until environmental discomforts are removed. He then responds quickly.

The WPA project that furnishes teachers to be trained in remedial teaching methods enables us to supply tutoring for children who are ill at home or who have to be hospitalized for long periods. This service is welcomed by the doctors and nurses as well as by the parents and the children themselves, as it helps the child escape from invalidism as rapidly as his physical condition permits.

One child had missed a year of schooling because of severe asthma. He was always tired, but did not rest well; undernourished, but did not eat well. A tutor was sent to him for an hour, one day a week. After his first tutoring period he ate a hearty lunch. He was tired from the unusual excitement and exertion, and slept soundly during his rest period. After his nap he worked for half an hour under the mother's supervision in the work books supplied by the Clinic. That night he fell asleep promptly. When tutoring was discontinued in June, standard achievement tests given at the Clinic showed his school work to be up to grade for a child of his age. He had gained in weight, and was reported by the physician to have made marked physical gain. He was able to play out of doors with the other boys of the neighborhood without excessive fatigue and in September returned to school on an equal footing with other children of his age.

Occasionally we are asked for help for a spastic child, too incapacitated to attend the special school for crippled children. These children, when tutored once or twice a week for a year are able to demonstrate their ability to learn. The regular visits of the tutor accustom them to responding to some one other than an over-protective mother or nurse, and they tend to over-react less to strangers. It is quite possible, also, that as the child begins to learn, the family unconsciously changes its attitude and begins to demand more, and to make fewer allowances for bizarre behavior. Some of these children have made enough improvement to enable them to attend the school for crippled children the following year.

Another group that has profited greatly by tutoring in the home is made up of epileptic children. When an epileptic child has to be excluded from school because of frequency or severity of seizures, a WPA tutor is sent to the home. Often, the child has been attempting work beyond his ability to perform, and the stimulation of group contacts has been greater than his nervous system could stand. Individual teaching at his own level once or twice a week, with a little work of the kind he enjoys most, assigned to be done each day elapsing between the visits of the tutor has been accompanied by reduction of seizures and increased academic achievement.

Our latest undertaking is to send a tutor into a maternity home to help girls illegitimately pregnant and there awaiting confinement, to complete the work of the school year they have begun. It is hoped that this will make it easier for them to return to school the following year and to resume normal habits of living.

Tutoring and remedial teaching, in this Clinic, are designed

1. To help the child with some special learning difficulty to keep,

through highly specialized help, his work in the difficult subject up to a level that will enable him to go ahead in other academic subjects at his own normal rate. It is aimed to prevent an intellectual idiosyncrasy from becoming a handicap.

2. To help the child who is reacting to daily class room failure by withdrawal or aggressive behavior, to work out a comfortable school adjustment that will make compensatory behavior unnecessary.

3. To help the child who is falling behind in school because of prolonged illness to make up, during convalescence, some of the work he has missed and to return to school able to do the work of his group.

4. To help children who are undergoing traumatic experiences in the home to learn under special instruction what they are too distracted to assimilate in the group. When these children are too much upset to be able to learn even under individual instruction, tutoring is postponed until the environment has become less disturbing. A pending divorce is peculiarly upsetting. The period preceding the institutionalization of a psychotic or feebleminded parent is another. The release of a parent from a penal institution or a psychopathic hospital, is often disturbing to children.

5. To provide indirect therapy to the child in need of help in meeting his problems of adjustment, but who is unable to accept direct psychiatric help.

6. To help toward normal adjustment the child who is debarred from regular school attendance by behavior resulting from some organic condition. This includes some spastic children, some epileptic, and some post-encephalitic, as well as an occasional case of extreme glandular imbalance.

In all cases the value of the individual instruction is supplemented by the new self-respect that comes to the child as a result of being liked and enjoyed by a kindly, intelligent adult outside the family group. The relationship is considered so important a part of therapy, that the tutors are expected to leave all unpleasant situations and decisions to the psychologist. This enables the tutor to be the unfailingly pleasant, kindly friend whose only interest is in helping the child to meet the requirements of a demanding world.

FREDERICK A. ZEHRER[1]

Harvard University

The School Psychologist as a Mental Hygiene Specialist[2]

The school psychologist is in a strategic position to perform a variety of functions of a mental hygiene nature. The fact that he is part of the school staff allows him many opportunities to carry on preventive as well as curative work in situations not usually available to psychologists in other community agencies. As a mental hygiene specialist his work ranges from that of a curriculum consultant to that of a participating guide in the process of making an individual case study of a problem situation.

Individual Case Study

The children who present problems of all types usually referred to a mental hygiene clinic are called to the attention of the school psychologist: the suspected mentally deficient; the academically handicapped; the socially maladjusted; and the emotionally unstable. As a specialist he is able to perform services extending be-

---

[1] Formerly Director, Department of Child Guidance, Greenwich (Conn.) Public Schools.

[2] All of the phases of the mental hygiene program described in this brief article actually have been carried on in the Greenwich Public Schools. This, the psychologist has done in addition to group testing, coordinating guidance in all of the schools, and related duties. Such a program is made possible through the assistance of a staff consisting of three visiting teachers; a speech specialist; a home teacher; an attendance officer; and four full-time adjustment teachers in the elementary schools. Reprinted from *Journal of Consulting Psychology*, 1942, 6, 218–222. Copyright 1942 by American Association for Applied Psychology.

yond immediate diagnosis and prescription. Just as treatment begins with the initial referral interview between a parent and a social worker in an agency so do the interpretation and related contributions start when a teacher or principal requests the psychologist's assistance in better understanding a child. The statement of the problem by the teacher, principal, nurse, or parent; the elicitation of pertinent data by the mental hygienist; and the summation of the facts at hand during the interview pave the way for broader understanding of mental hygiene principles in terms of specific, practical situations.

Using the case history material compiled by the visiting teacher plus the facts and observations developed during an examination a differential diagnosis is made. As frequently as is practicable a conference is then held in which all who deal actively with the child (except his parents) are included. Such an interpretive discussion always includes the child's teacher, the principal, the visiting teacher, and the psychologist. Frequently the child's previous teacher, the school nurse, or interested social or group agency worker is invited to participate in the oral evaluation.

In such a conference the tentative diagnosis is presented and a probable prognosis is made in areas where this is possible. The remediable elements and nonremediable factors are identified and considered. The activities of each professional person are considered and indicated to meet the needs of the case. Also, the groundwork is laid for follow-up work and future reconsideration of the situation to note the progress achieved and the responsiveness of the child. Again, the psychologist is interested beyond the immediate situation: he is making a conscious effort to weigh values and focus attention on the mental hygiene aspects of the problem in order that the school personnel may better comprehend the psychological implications of the situation and thus increase their understanding of the dynamics of behavior and methods of meeting the needs of the developing child.

Treatment: Direct and Indirect

The school psychologist has little available time for carrying a large case load for intensive individual therapy. Instead, he can better use his services by initiating, guiding, and supervising the activities of other individuals who can work to remedy the situation. The psychologist must determine at the time of the diagnosis the depth of the difficulties. If intensive treatment is indicated, referral to appropriate agencies are to be made. If the problems are of the types which can be treated satisfactorily under the psychologist's direction using available trained personnel, functions can be delegated to the visiting teacher, the classroom teacher, a member of a group agency, the adjustment teacher, the speech correctionist, or any other individual in the child's environment who can assist. The type of difficulty encountered determines which person on the school staff or in the community may best contribute to alter the remediable factors.

Follow-up and rechecks are made by the psychologist to find the extent of progress being made and to determine the kinds of specific modifications necessary to meet the changing needs of the child under consideration.

Provisions for Exceptional Children

The psychologist can make a vital mental hygiene contribution in the schools in the process of identification of exceptional children (gifted, mentally retarded, academically handicapped, socially maladjusted, and emotionally disturbed) and the prescription of educational and social adaptations to meet their specific needs. He is able to do much to encourage the establishment of necessary facilities and services. Also, he might train and guide the available teaching personnel in order to best deal with deviations from the average. His unique position allows an excellent opportunity to improve teacher and principal understanding of the psychological aspects of the adjustments of exceptional children. Again, the functions of the specialist extend beyond the immediate problem into the realm of preventive work.

If full-time adjustment teachers are available they can be used by the psychologist as liaison personnel to assist the classroom teachers daily in meeting social and emotional as well as academic needs of exceptional children.[3] Meanwhile, the visiting teacher carries on social case work whenever necessary. In a large school system the psychologist can assist the classroom teacher more specifically and concretely over a period of time through weekly or bi-monthly conferences with the adjustment teacher and visiting teacher. Where such

---

[3] Teachers with special training to instruct exceptional children.

a plan is utilized there need be no duplication of services on the part of the adjustment and visiting teacher. The one emphasizes the educational specifics in school; the other stresses the social and emotional factors in the home and school.

By supervising the education of all exceptional children, the psychologist is able to coordinate the contributions of all agencies in the community to meet special needs of children. The machinery of this procedure allows him an opportunity to interpret medical and psychological diagnoses to teachers in terms of school adjustments; to visit classrooms regularly; and to clarify the contributions of the school program to special cases being carried by community agencies.

In-Service Teacher Training

When we pause to consider the meager professional training of teachers in the area of mental hygiene and the extremely responsible part they play in the lives of growing children the need for in-service training is obvious. The school psychologist is equipped to carry on such work if he sets it up as an objective toward which to work. He must go beyond offering courses; suggesting professional reading; and lecturing. Rather, he must use all of these means as well as every opportunity with individual teachers, principals, and small groups of faculty members to make them aware of sound psychological principles and their applications to specific situations. If the case work approach is used consistently and the school faculty is encouraged and allowed to function actively in meeting problem situations cooperatively, many basic principles can be reviewed and clarified. This is a long, slow process but no one on the staff is in a better situation to head up this work and focus attention on practical mental hygiene techniques in the school environment.

In the same way, the psychologist can utilize the local promotion plan, marking system, and generally used classroom methods as practical means toward an end. By initiating, or actively encouraging, an evaluation of existing policies in the three areas mentioned the school psychologist can assist in the establishment of promotion policies, pupil reporting forms, and improved classroom methods in line with the accepted best professional practices. Using committee work and faculty meetings to bring about desired changes, the way is open for consideration of the mental hygiene aspects of the educational process and child guidance procedure. As teachers are assisted in terms of specifics in the understanding of their pupils; as the staff members see the administrative machinery in light of its effect upon children; and as children are helped to better comprehend their own adjustments the worth of the psychologist's contributions become apparent. So, regardless of the established practices in any community, this approach can be used effectively over a period of time.

In one town in which there are ten elementary schools and a senior high school, this technique has been applied. At the end of one year after the psychologist began his work cumulative record cards were set up, since none existed previously; at the conclusion of two years a system-wide promotion policy was established; at the completion of the third year new reports of progress (with teachers' manuals) replaced the traditional A, B, C, D report card; and throughout the five-year period adaptations of methods and materials have taken place in the classrooms in all of the schools. The purpose guiding these major system-wide alterations was not alone to "bring the schools up to date" but also to assist the entire teaching and administrative personnel to better understand children so that they might better guide and instruct them. There is still a tremendous task to be accomplished: by its very nature it can never be completed. However, the machinery has been set in motion: time and the products of such efforts can only determine the effectiveness of the contributions to the mental health of the children in the schools.

Relation to Community Agencies

The psychologist working in the public schools has an unparalleled opportunity to identify individuals and families who are in need of psychiatric help as well as social welfare assistance. Since the public schools serve the children of most of the people an alert child guidance department can recognize unusual conditions in their incipient stages and refer families to community or state agencies equipped to serve their needs. Serving as a selective agent, the psychologist is able to contribute greatly to the prevention of major social or emotional breakdowns.

When the school psychologist participates as an active member of the council of social agencies he is in a position to interpret the schools to the key people in the city and, in turn, bring to the school personnel a clear conception of the various agencies' functions. Any improvement in social and family relationships and living conditions resulting from such concerted efforts of the agencies represented make valuable additions (however intangible) to the emotional stability of the families in the community. The extent of the contributions of the psychologist to such groups may be limited only by the extent of his professional insight and willingness to co-operate.

Parent Enlightenment

Since we now recognize the importance of the preschool years upon the emotional and social development of children, it is essential that some assistance be offered parents if a valid mental hygiene program is to be effective. Functioning as a mental hygiene specialist, the school psychologist may carry on a parent education program. Such a plan might well take the form of parent-study groups; organized panel discussions; and published materials.

The parent-teacher organization can be a most effective means through which the psychologist may work. True, many of the parents who need such instruction the most may not be reached. However, those who do participate must certainly feel they need assistance so the offering can be justified.

In the community previously mentioned, parent study groups have been conducted under the psychologist's direction in each of the elementary schools with repeat requests from four of the ten. In five of the schools, particular interest was shown in the preschool level. All groups were concerned with positive mental hygiene principles.

The work along this line has brought out many direct requests from parents for child guidance assistance: many problem situations have been referred in their initial stages. In many of these parental referrals, the type of difficulty probably would not have come to the attention of school authorities until a much later date, if at all. The psychologist and his staff have been able to offer assistance at a time when it could do the greatest good.

Conclusion

In our democratic society we have a few mandatory provisions for the best interests of individuals. One such demand is compulsory education. It is for us to realize that this statute requires more than school attendance: it requires also the provision of equal educational opportunity for all children. In order to assist the school in meeting this responsibility, the school psychologist must interpret mental hygiene principles to school personnel and assist in the application of them. In order to perform this function, his work must not be confined to diagnosis and treatment of single situations; rather, it must permeate the entire school program and extend into the community. This requires working with, and through, all available services and agencies.

The emphasis of the efforts of the mental hygiene specialist must be upon the preventive aspects of child care and guidance: in and out of school. He must take full advantage of every opportunity to extend his work until he is recognized as a major contributing member of the school staff. To perform his duties effectively he must be a consultant, a diagnostician, an educator, and a director. Only then can he be in a position to initiate constructive change and assist in meeting the needs of all of the children.

PHYLLIS BLANCHARD
Philadelphia Child Guidance Clinic

Interpreting Psychological Data
to Parents[1]

In speaking of interpreting psychological data to parents, if what is meant is reporting and explaining all that we can learn from a study of the child, the first thing we might ask is what we hope to accomplish by so doing, in the case of the neurotic child or the child whose behavior difficulties arise from a neurotic basis. In educational and vocational guidance problems, reporting and interpreting the results of psychological tests and other data is indeed a suitable approach. But there is a very different situation in clinical work with neurotic and behavior problem children, so that the methods which are satisfactory in the educational guidance or vocational guidance fields are not applicable to this other clinical field. Here, there is a real question as to how much either child or parent can be helped by merely reporting and interpreting psychological data about the child to the parent.

There was a time, some fifteen years ago, in child guidance work, when we collected data about the child by means of a social history, medical, psychological and psychiatric examinations, then tried to explain the probable origin of the child's neurotic symptoms or his behavior difficulties on the basis of all these data. Certain of the data, together with our deductions concerning the causes of the child's symptoms or behavior, were reported and explained to his parents. This detailed interpretation of the case study findings presumably

[1] Reprinted from *Journal of Consulting Psychology*, 1940, 4, 120–123. Copyright 1940 by American Association for Applied Psychology.

was undertaken in the expectation that if only parents could acquire a psychological understanding of the child, this would in some magical fashion change their attitudes and behavior toward him. There was the further assumption that if changes in the external situation could be secured, the child's emotional responses would be unconditioned thereby and his neurotic symptoms or his behavior problems thus would be cured.

In retrospect, it seems surprising that we ever could have believed that environmental changes alone would have such extensive therapeutic effects, or that we could have expected parental attitudes to be influenced very greatly by formal interpretations of case study material. We now consider that the child with neurotic symptoms, and very often also the child with behavior problems, has more or less severe inner conflicts. This means that such children usually are in need of psychological therapy, in addition to any changes in the material or human environment. Moreover, the kind of therapy that is required is of the most highly skilled professional order; we cannot treat the child at second hand by trying to utilize the efforts of parents as amateur psychologists or therapists. Indeed, even if we could succeed in placing the parent in any such role in relation to his child, we should be making the child's situation worse, in certain respects, rather than better. The normal parent-child relationship is a very warm, human, personal and emotional relationship. It is, and it should be, quite different from the relationship of any professional person to the child.

In the last ten years of child guidance clinic work, the trend has been away from case study and report and toward a very different approach to the problems of parents and children, namely, the coordination of psychological therapy for the child and case work with the child's parents. This usually means that there are regular appointments for the child with a therapist and for the parent with a social worker, once or twice a week, for a period of several months. The actual length of time required for treatment of the child and case work with the parent varies with the individual case, but three or four months would usually be a minimum time for any case with once a week appointments.

In therapeutic work with the child, there is not merely study and observation, but a conscious utilization of the relationship with the child for therapeutic ends. The therapist does observe the child, of course, but with the chief interest in understanding the child's varied feelings and helping the child to bear these feelings in his own conscious experience. The child brings to the therapeutic relationship the responses, symptoms and behavior that he has developed elsewhere, in other relationships. In the relationship with the therapist, however, he has the opportunity to experience what he does feel, instead of repressing and denying certain feelings and converting them into neurotic symptoms or behavior.

While the child is having appointments with the therapist, the parent has the opportunity, in interviews with the social worker, to bring up questions about his own relationship with the child and to discuss problems with which he is concerned in their relationship. Case work with the parent does not mean that on the basis of the therapist's observations of the child, the parent will be informed or instructed as to what he must do. It is rather the material that the parent himself produces in his interviews with the social worker that lends itself to interpretation. The most effective method of interpretation, however, is that which can be worked out by the parent and social worker through their mutual participation in discussion.

Perhaps this participating kind of discussion may be illustrated from the case of a mother who brought her inhibited, fearful little boy to the clinic stating that she wished him to be cured of his fears. After a few interviews with the therapist, the little boy began to be somewhat less fearful, but also he became less docile and obedient. "He refused his spinach one day last week," said his mother. "He never did that before. I never even knew that he disliked spinach." She went on to question whether she could continue to bring the boy to the clinic, giving as a reason that the trip was too long and expensive. The social worker did not leave the question of the mother's continuing to bring the boy to the clinic on the basis of the trip, but inquired whether the mother might be worried over the changes in the boy and his being a little less obedient. The mother replied that he never had been disobedient before she brought him to the clinic, but then she was able to go on to talk of how she always had demanded docility and obedience of the boy. She ended this description with the query as to whether this way of bringing up the boy might have some connection with his having become such a fearful child. The social worker agreed that this was a real possibility and the mother decided that she would continue to bring the boy for treatment because she preferred him to be less fearful even at the expense of his being a little less submissive to authority.

Parents often have unconscious resistances to the very changes they have asked to have brought about in the child. They also may have unconscious resistances toward recognizing that they have any part in the child's problems. In working with parents, therefore, our chief concern is to understand the feelings that the parent may have in relation to his child and to help the parent recognize these feelings.

We cannot always help the parent to such recognition of his own feelings, for sometimes a parent's resistances are stronger than his wish for his child to be cured. Such was the case with one mother of a five year old boy, who insisted that mental deficiency must be the cause of his behavior difficulties. Although she described her dislike of this child and her preference for his younger brother, she was never able to see that her attitudes toward the two children could have any connection with the fact that one was a behavior problem while the other was not. To any suggestion of this possibility, she replied that she had never let the older boy know that she preferred his brother to him; she was sure that he must be mentally deficient and that the intelligence test must have been incorrect, for nothing but lack of intelligence could explain the way he behaved. By holding onto this explanation of his behavior, she was able to maintain her opinion of herself as a good mother, to protect herself from feeling guilty over her hostility to her son, and to avoid doing anything about her relationship to him.

If we have an understanding of human emotions, we shall realize that it is not just a parent's conscious intentions, but his deepest feelings about himself and his child that are involved when he seeks professional help. Hence, some unconscious resistances to taking that help are only to be expected. We need to have clearly in mind, in working with parents, that such unconscious resistances have the function of protecting the ego from more pain, guilt or anxiety than it can bear. We also need to be able to distinguish clearly between resistances and healthy impulses on the part of the parent toward solving their own problems with their children. Work with children or with parents requires all the professional skill that can be developed. It is one thing to know theoretically that people have feelings or resistances, but it is quite another matter to recognize their manifestations as they appear before us in our professional work with an individual. Perhaps it is even more difficult to be able to meet resistances without counter resistances of our own. It is possible that some of our counter resistances find expression in a wish to tell people what to do and how to do it, instead of holding to the purpose of utilizing our professional relationships with people in the more difficult task of helping them to find for themselves new ways of living. This task begins with accepting an individual as he is.

HARRIET L. RHEINGOLD

Rockford College

Interpreting Mental Retardation to Parents

A frequent and important task of the psychologist in the child guidance clinic is to give to the parents of a child an interpretation of his retardation. The interpretation is considered as much a part of the service rendered as is the determination of the child's retardation by examination. Often a guidance clinic's services are requested by parents solely to obtain an interpretation of the retardation, the examinations having been administered elsewhere. This suggests that school, court, and medical workers have limited their interviews with parents to reporting the diagnosis or to giving advice concerning commitment or special school placement. This practice too often injures the parents' feelings or arouses their antagonism. Neither attitude is a salutary one for the child or for his parents, for the antagonism causes them to dispute the findings, while disturbed emotions render them less able to consider the welfare of the child.

At the Institute for Juvenile Research it has been customary for the psychologist to interview the parents subsequent to the child's physical and psychological examinations. We are learning, however, that in many instances where other evidence of retardation is sufficient, we can render parents the assistance they need without complete psychometric examination of the child prior to the interview. What the parent wants is not only help in handling the child's

---

[1] Reprinted from *Journal of Consulting Psychology*, 1945, 9, 142–148. Copyright 1945 by American Association for Applied Psychology.

478

problems, but also the psychologist's understanding of his own emotional needs; he does not always require an accurate measure of his child's mental status in years and months. Psychometric and other examinations should be administered, not as a routine procedure, but to meet the requirements of each situation, to aid the psychologist, or to satisfy the parents' needs. This should not be understood to minimize the importance of actual observation of the child's behavior.

The purpose of the initial interview should be to guide the parents toward an emotional acceptance of the child together with his mental defect, since wise planning for such a child is impossible if the parents do not accept his retardation. There is little likelihood that they will act upon the advice given them until this goal is attained. Emotional acceptance in this sense may be defined as: sufficient agreement between the subjective facts (the parents' feelings) and the objective facts (the reality situation) to make wise handling and planning possible. Emotional acceptance of the child with his defect enables the parents not only to accept the psychologist's statements today, but also to feel a month from now that the conclusions are as wise as they appeared at the close of the interview. That is to say, they are able to change and adapt plans as the child or the situation changes. A realistic orientation of effort is a result of emotional acceptance. While this acceptance is the main purpose of the interview, the assistance rendered the parent in planning for the child is the chief by-product. The extent to which parents can utilize this assistance depends upon the success with which the primary purpose is achieved. Stating the diagnosis, answering questions about etiology and treatment, discussing habit training and educational plans are only the materials out of which the interviews are woven.

The interview, to be successful, should resemble closely any other therapeutic interview in which the gaining of insight is the objective. This means that the psychologist should not be, and should not allow himself to be, forced into the role of an authoritative person whose sole function is to give advice. As in all therapeutic interviews both persons—here psychologist and patient—must play active roles. The parent should feel not that he is being forced to accept what he has been told, but that he has worked in equal measure with the psychologist toward a solution of his problem. At least he should feel that having obtained a basis for action he can carry on independently.

This interview differs in some respects from the typical therapeutic interview. The psychologist possesses information which the parent needs. This means that the parent's questions cannot be turned back upon himself at every point, although at many points they need to be. The psychologist's role is therefore the more active one. Throughout the interview he should help the parent to clarify his own feelings about his problem, but if asked a question concerning test findings, private schools, and so forth, he should give a direct answer. The attitude of the psychologist should be that of any psychotherapeutic worker—interested, sympathetic, understanding.

From experimentation and experience we have found that a successful interpretive interview follows a sequence almost as orderly and regular as that of the psychometric examination itself. It possesses a logic of its own. Its development can be predicted. The content of the interview will vary, of course, according to the age and sex of the child, the degree of retardation, the physical symptoms, and the emotional needs of the parents, but this does not alter the sequence. Furthermore, each parent has been conditioned to some extent by the number of examinations his child has already had and by his own experiences with examiners. This, however, does not affect the orderly progression of the interview although it may increase the relative prominence of one step or reduce that of another, even to negligible proportions.

The writer finds that the therapeutic nature of the interviews can be facilitated by the character of the psychologist's opening remarks. As the first step, there should be a simple restatement of the problem: "You are worried about John's development, aren't you?" or, "I can see that Mary's care has been difficult for you." Such a beginning possesses several advantages. It assures the parent of the psychologist's understanding and sympathy from the first moment of the interview. It gives proper importance to the feelings of the parent, designates an active role for him, and makes him a protagonist.

Almost invariably the parent agrees that he has been worried about John for some time, or that Mary's care has been exhausting.

Thus, at the very beginning of the interview the simple restatement has secured an exposure of the parent's recognition of the child's problem and avoided antagonism which would hinder the therapeutic nature of the interview. This admission is necessary for the steps to follow; without it the parent's full co-operation cannot be secured. In contrast, if the interview is opened by giving a diagnosis, the parent's verbal admission that the child is retarded may never be attained, even up to the conclusion of the interview.

The admission itself stimulates the parent to take the next step, a description of the child's behavior. In this the parent can be assisted by the psychologist's asking, "What concerns you about Mary's development?" or, "Tell me more about John." In their descriptions parents find it easier to begin with the less serious and less stigmatizing symptoms; this is usual and should be accepted. One parent will begin with, "What bothers me most is that Anita is so clumsy. She's always falling down." Another will say, "I can't get Tom to chew his food." Other symptoms frequently given prominence at the beginning of the interview are: inability to play with other children, enuresis, day-dreaming, nervousness, lack of concentration, stubbornness, temper tantrums, and speech defects. As the psychologist verbally, and more importantly by attitude, shows his acceptance of these complaints as worthy of concern, the parent works through the less serious symptoms and finally arrives at the most serious, the child's inability to learn at a normal rate.

If the psychologist seems to reject the first symptoms as of minor importance, and if he presses the parents to describe the more serious ones, the parent may limit his recital to the less stigmatizing and never approach the more serious. The desirable progress of the discussion is insured by the psychologist's attitude of interest and sympathy at every point. No more is required of the psychologist by way of a verbal response than, "Yes," or "I can understand that." Only occasionally a more specific comment may be needed, such as, "That embarrasses you, doesn't it?" or "That worries a mother."

Throughout this sequence runs an evaluation of the child's development in terms of the achievements of other children of comparable age or of the parent's own older children as he recalls their behavior at the patient's age. While this comparison is usually spontaneous, in the few cases in which it is not, such questions as,

"Do any of your friends have a child about John's age?" or, "What was your older daughter like at his age?" serve to produce the evaluation for the steps to follow.

A few questions such as, "How was it from the time he was a baby?" or, "When did you first notice his slowness?" stimulate the parents to relate a history of the child's development. The gathering of a detailed history prior to the interview possesses no especial advantage for this type of interview; history taking has then become an integral part of the interview.

At this point the psychologist becomes more active and asks, "What age child do you think Margaret resembles now?" In our experience, parents then estimate an age very close to the mental age indicated by the tests. Surprisingly, underestimation is somewhat more common than overestimation. This occasionally may be an expression of parental rejection of the child.

At this point we may review the processes of this step. The parent himself has given sufficient material for a diagnosis. Since this has been given in terms of the development of other children, he has supplied a measuring rod which has meaning for him. He has been led a long way towards an understanding of the child's retardation; he will not now reject the psychologist's diagnosis. He has been forced to accept nothing; he has been allowed to evaluate the problem himself.

The parent will usually ask the psychologist at this point, "What do you think?" This leads to the third step in the sequence of the interview. The psychologist answers the question, but refrains from discussing the child's retardation in terms of future development or present planning. One should keep pace with the parent's progress in grasping the implications of the problem and avoid giving him more information than he can assimilate at the time. The results of tests should be presented to the parents in terms of mental age. In our interviews it has always been sufficient to give the mental age, not in years and months, but as "about four years," or, "between seven and eight years." The terms, "idiot," "imbecile," or even "high grade mental defective" are never used. The psychologist from now on usually talks about the child as one who is "slow to learn"; occasionally, as a "mentally retarded child."

How far it is wise to spare the parent's feelings must be considered, for sometimes parents ask, "But he isn't feeble-minded, is he?" One mother, seen at our clinic recently, decided to arrange for her son's commitment to a state school. The county clerk to whom she had to apply, asked her if the boy were feeble-minded. Although his I.Q. was 50, we had not reported this to the mother or used the term "feeble-minded" in our interview. She answered, "No, he isn't feeble-minded," whereupon the county clerk replied, "Well, then he doesn't belong there." Since then we have modified our procedure. We now tell parents who are thinking of commitment that "feeble-mindedness" is a legal term used by officials.

Parents will ask next about the child's future: "Will he be able to go to school?", "Will he ever learn to talk?", "How far can he go in school?", "Will he be able to get a job?" This we have recognized as the fourth step of the interview. The parent is asking now about the implications of the mental retardation; he is attempting to translate them into terms of future development. In general, the psychologist waits until the parent asks the question, and answers only the questions asked of him. He refrains from predicting the child's entire life history. For example, if the parent is worried only about the speech development of a young retarded child, the psychologist does not add that the child will never be able to support himself. In the manner suggested, the worker keeps pace with the parent's needs and feelings.

The parent next asks questions about etiology and treatment— the fifth step in the sequence. Parents are forever seeking a specific statement of cause. There are two reasons for this desire: first, that a definition of cause will relieve them of the responsibility for the defect; second, that a discovery of cause will indicate an effective method of treatment to correct the defect. In the discussion of etiology, the psychologist should encourage the parents to review verbally their own attempts to account for the retardation. Often they have sought to relate it to heredity, to accidents of birth, to prenatal or neo-natal experiences. If the explanation offered seems reasonable or constructive, the psychologist encourages the parent's belief. If it seems warranted the psychologist may offer a tentative diagnosis of Mongolism, Cretinism, or birth injury, to be checked by medical examination. More often, however, the psychologist can only point out the lack of definite etiologic knowledge, emphasizing points which tend to relieve feelings of responsibility, such as the many different causes advanced by medical science, the universality of the problem, the possibility of attributing it to fortuitous circumstances in the absence of more definite etiology. While the psychologist's statements in this area must be as accurate as possible, his attitudes and comments should be directed more toward allowing the parents an opportunity to bring out into the open their own thoughts on the subject rather than towards presenting them with a detailed review of medical knowledge.

The discussion of etiology leads directly into a consideration of treatment. Even if no specific statement of etiology is possible, parents hope desperately that somewhere a cure is available. They usually think of surgical measures first, then in order, other medical, educational, and social measures. Here again the parent should be encouraged to express the hopes he has cherished; again the psychologist should answer directly and as accurately as his knowledge and experience permits; for painful as it may be, most parents are seeking the truth.

For the most part parents of retarded children feel in some way responsible for the retardation. If the psychologist allows the parent the more active role during the discussion of etiology and treatment, the parent himself will raise the question of his responsibility. If he does not, the psychologist may say, "I suppose you sometimes wonder if you are to blame."

A sense of responsibility may stem from feelings of inadequacy or guilt, or both. Some parents feel that they are being punished for sins, real or imagined. The intelligent father of a very retarded child felt that he was being punished for his love of gambling. A mother may be haunted by her attempt to abort the child; another, by having entertained the idea; and still another fears that her ambivalent feelings about her pregnancy may have been the causative factor. A parent may feel that his own personal inadequacy as a man or as a woman is the cause of his child's retardation. Some parents blame themselves for not playing more with the child, or for not reading to him more often. In the latter instance, however, the self-reproaches usually mask more serious feelings of inadequacy or guilt. Associated with these feelings may be the fear of loss of status and prestige which seriously threatens the parent's emotional security.

The importance of encouraging the parent to express his feelings of responsibility can scarcely be overestimated, for the success of the interview may depend upon it. A parent does not parade these feelings; in fact, he struggles to repress them and hesitates to admit them, even to himself. But until he can obtain relief for feelings of guilt, inadequacy, or humiliation, he cannot view reality with sufficient objectivity to develop emotional acceptance of his child.

At some time during the discussion of etiology, treatment, and feelings of responsibility, the parent usually succumbs to an overt expression of his grief. Tears may come to his eyes; more often he weeps openly. This show of emotion need not disconcert the psychologist. It has cathartic value for the parent, while for the psychologist it is another indication of the successful progress of the interview. It requires no direct handling. Sometimes the psychologist need only wait until the parent gains control of himself; at other times he may say, "I understand how you feel." Frequently, following an emotional outburst, the parent will bring up what troubles him most: feelings of responsibility, fear of personal inadequacy, loss of status in the community. If the psychologist takes alarm at the show of feeling, or if he becomes too solicitous, the parent may retreat. Thus the psychologist may cut off an expression of the chief sources of the parent's anxiety.

At this point the parent usually returns to a consideration of the present situation. This is the sixth step. He asks, "What shall I do now?" He is attempting to express his clarified feelings in action. As a rule this question can be returned to the parent. The psychologist will ask, "What do you want to do?" or, "What do you think?" In this way the psychologist encourages the parent to plan for the child in accordance with the reorientation in thinking effected so far by the interview.

Since the purpose of this paper is to define the interview as a therapeutic process and to delineate its orderly progression, it is considered unnecessary to include here a discussion of the psychologist's thinking about the advantages and disadvantages of care at home vs. public institutional care; regular vs. special room placement; local resources; the tendency of most parents to press the mentally retarded child for academic achievement, at the same time requiring too little in social and emotional maturity; the possibilities for good personality development in spite of the mental defect. These are some of the considerations which arise at this point in the interview. The psychologist must be familiar with them for he will be called upon to answer questions. He should offer information freely; the decisions, however, must rest with the parent.

As the interview draws to its close, most parents begin to feel guilty because their objective discussion of the child seems to suggest their rejection of him. This attitude they express by an enumeration of the child's assets and especially of bits of behavior which seem to them bright and hopeful. They will say of a young child: "But he points out all the parts of an automobile," or of an older child, "But he can travel all over the city by himself." One should not feel at this point that the interview is of dubious success because this is only an expression of the parent's attempt to relieve his feelings of guilt. The psychologist in response verbalizes the parent's ambivalence. He may say, "You are afraid that you haven't been fair to your child," or, "It is natural for you to see that in some ways he is not as slow as in others."

Fear of seeming to reject the child becomes an even more serious matter when the parent considers committing the child to a state school. Moral censure arises both from within—his feelings of responsibility—and from without—his fear of community disapproval. Fear of loss of prestige and status arises here, too, for it is difficult for the parent to admit that he must resort to a state agency for the care of his child. Often a parent is unwilling to accept public assistance, and feels obliged to spend his own money on the child's care. When the parent can ill afford private care, and especially when the expense may be detrimental to the welfare of other children in the family, the psychologist should explain the meaning of this sacrifice as a compensation for the parent's feelings of guilt or inadequacy.

This type of interview leads to emotional acceptance of the problem and helps the parent plan for the immediate situation. His own personality needs, the severity of the retardation, the age of the child, the awareness and insight brought to the interview—these determine the extent of his acceptance. The psychologist may be skillful but he constitutes only half of the interview situation. While most parents can be carried through the interview with profit for themselves and the child, there are some who obtain only limited benefits. Occasionally a parent may seem to have arrived at emotional acceptance and to be able to plan more or less wisely for the child, yet at the end bring up his conviction that a tonsillectomy may still effect a cure. Sometimes this may represent no more than a temporary lapse into an earlier pattern of thought. At other times it may indicate that the parent is not yet able to plan wisely for the child's future. Occasionally one parent will leave the interview with apparent insight, but at home will be influenced by the other parent to return to the original hope that the child needs only speech therapy. These parents "shop around" from doctor to doctor, from clinic to clinic, seeking corroboration of their hopes. Some parents can only be regarded as untreatable.

Then, too, there are parents who, in one interview, achieve only partial emotional acceptance and objective insight into the needs of the child. The problem has proved too great and too damaging to the parent's ego, too bound up with feelings of personal inadequacy and guilt. For this reason we close each interview with an assurance of our interest and availability whenever the parent wishes to discuss any aspects of the problem. If the mother was interviewed, and it appears from her conversation that the father finds it difficult to accept the child's limitation, we offer an interview to the father and vice versa. Parents of young children are invited to return at six-month intervals for re-examination and interviews; parents of older children are invited to return at yearly intervals. Occasionally the parent's anxiety will appear disturbing enough to warrant our offering several interviews in succession. The general invitation is always given; more definite appointments depend upon his need and his desire for further help.

RALPH M. STOGDILL

The Ohio State University

Some Behavior Adjustment Techniques in Use With Mentally Retarded Children[1]

The mental hygiene and adjustment work at the Wayne County Training School is conducted under the direction of the medical department. In the capacity of clinical assistant, the mental hygienist is enabled to work with the cottage, school, and vocational staffs in an advisory and cooperative relationship. It is also his privilege to work with children directly in the solution of their problems. Since he has no administrative or disciplinary responsibilities, he is placed in a strategic position for helping boys who are in difficulty. The advantage of such an arrangement is apparent when we realize that many of these retarded boys, prior to their coming to the Training School, have had unpleasant experiences with individuals representing discipline and authority. Many of them have been unmanageable both at home and at school, and failed to adjust under probation to the juvenile court. Thus it is very essential that the mental hygienist should not be associated with discipline in the mind of the child.

Children are permitted free access to the mental hygienist's office. When a boy presents some problem or special need that cannot be handled by clinical methods, it becomes not merely the privilege but the duty of the mental hygienist to act in that boy's behalf until a satisfactory solution has been reached through proper administra-

[1] Reprinted from *Journal of Exceptional Children*, 1938, 5, 25–30, 45. Copyright 1938 by International Council for Exceptional Children.

tive channels. We maintain a constantly alert and active interest in the adjustments of our children.

It is our aim in adjustment work to enable each child to live happily at the Training School, and to enjoy a high degree of freedom and self-responsibility. In order to accomplish this aim, it is necessary to device practical, effective solutions to the child's problems as they arise, and as far as possible to anticipate probable difficulties. Practically, since our children are not merely preparing for life, but are *living here and now*, we must provide them with the means of solving their problems in terms of everyday realities.

There are no special types of problems to which our children are immune. They are subject to the same worries, fears, and tensions that affect all of us. If anything, they are more fearful and insecure than the average child, because many of them realize that their lack of insight and ability to evaluate situations has often led them to blunder into trouble unawares. Such a predicament is a powerful threat to a child's peace of mind. Our answer to this problem is a constant attempt to provide him with a stable, secure environment where he can learn through experience (trial and error, as well as directed behavior) what his advantages and limitations are. A child gains confidence as he eliminates compulsive, blundering, chance behavior through self-insight and the establishment of adequate habits.

We find it most helpful from a theoretical, as well as a practical, point of view to regard a child's maladjustments as responses to specific environmental situations. (I am speaking here of maladjustments that are functional in origin, rather than organic.)

We have found that the child's home situation is the most frequent and most potent source of emotional tension. Parents are permitted to visit and to correspond with their children. Children go home for week ends and vacations. An unstable home situation or any disturbance in parent-parent, or child-parent relationships reacts unfavorably on the child's adaptation to the Training School. A large proportion of the interviewer's time is devoted to problems of worry and emotional upset centering around the family. Many of our children feel rejected and abandoned by their parents. Should these inadequate parents seem to present favorable possibilities, the cooperation of our department of social work is requested. Through the efforts of this department, it is often possible to bring about such an improvement in parental attitudes that the home situation no longer serves as a source of disturbance. If the parents have definitely rejected the child and will have nothing further to do with him, then we aid him in evaluating his situation as objectively as possible. We assure him of our concern regarding his welfare, and of our ability to provide security and affectionate interest during his residence, and the necessary aid when he returns to the community to start life on his own responsibility.

In cases where the parents are over-protective or demand the child's return home, it is necessary to sell them on the value of the training in order that their discontent may no longer be communicated to him. We have had success with this method, especially when we have made special arrangements for the parents to visit the school to observe the activities in which their child participated.

On the Training School grounds, we find that tension inducing situations arise more frequently in the cottage and on the job than in the schoolroom or on the playground.

Adjustment methods, in order to be most effective, must be specific, clearly defined, and practical. The term *technique*, used in the title of this paper, suggests a higher degree of refinement and specificity than has yet been attained in adjustment work. However, it is a goal toward which we are constantly striving.

The interview is, of course, the essential technique in all adjustment work. We use the interview not only for gaining information about, and understanding of, the child's problems, but for influencing his behavior as well. We depend on this technique for aiding the child in gaining enough insight and understanding to relieve him of his conflicts, fears, and worries. Through discussing a child's difficulties with him, we are often able to assist him in deciding upon an advantageous course of action.

Behavior problems of the *mental conflict* or *emotional complex* type are handled by means of the analytic interview. Contrary to the popular belief that feeble-minded children lack sufficient intellectual development to permit them to have mental conflicts, we find that these children not infrequently exhibit such behavior. The neurotic conflicts of the retarded child differ very little in kind or complexity from those of the child with normal or superior intelligence. We have observed that many of our retarded children respond quite readily to analytic procedures.

We must be constantly on the alert for clues that will aid us in understanding the child's problems. If he is unable to verbalize his troubles, we employ subsidiary means through which the child may symbolize or dramatize his conflicts. The child can often reveal through picture drawing, poetry writing, making up stories, or telling about his dreams, things that are too painful to express directly in conversation.

We gained little insight into Thomas B's problem until we permitted him to use finger paints. Finger painting allows for freedom of expression without making great demands on energy or coordination. Thomas made painting after painting of ocean or under water caverns. The caverns were occupied by small, curled-up figures which we interpreted after talking with Thomas as representing a vague kind of fetus symbol. At first he would not discuss his paintings, but finally after many repetitions and elaborations of the theme he gave one of his drawings the title, "The Little People." He was somewhat startled when he heard what he had said, but he felt free at last to tell about his pre-occupation with the mysteries of birth and death, and the advent of a new baby into the family at home. Through his painting he was able to express an idea that he had been unable before to put into words. After he had given us a clue as to the nature of his phantasy conflicts, we were able to help him translate his ideas into words so that his misconceptions could be corrected and his emotional tensions reduced. Thomas still feels very insecure, but he no longer sits in a corner alone to daydream. He is gradually making friends and engaging in games and cottage activities.

Often it is necessary to employ some very concrete method, such as changing a child's environmental situation, in order to effect an adjustment. He may be transferred from one cottage to another, or from one vocational assignment to another. A child is more likely to develop favorably in an environment where he feels adequate and secure than where he is forced to strive and over compensate for his inadequacy. When we find a physically weak, retiring boy who cries, picks quarrels, and is negativistic with his cottage parents, we are often able to eliminate his behavior problem entirely by transferring him to a cottage where the boys offer him less competition, or where the cottage parents are more understanding of his particular kind of disposition.

Some children seek escape from responsibility and the pressing demands of everyday living by making frequent and persistent requests for transfers from one cottage to another or from one job to another. These cases require careful interviewing in order to determine the basis of the insecurity. Usually a double procedure is adopted. The child is called to the office for interviews over a period of time, and the cottage parents are given suggestions for any special treatment that may be required. In many cases an experimental attitude is adopted, in which the child is moved, as occasion demands, into new situations where he may feel more contented. Of course we must be on the alert in employing such measures, lest we permit the child to make a regressive adjustment. On the other hand, we must keep in mind that *facing reality* is not synonymous with being forced to do something that is beyond one's ability.

When we find a boy who is continually dominating other boys, or who has begun to lose interest and ambition, we can usually effect an adjustment by transferring him to a cottage where the boys are more active and aggressive and more mature in their interests.

Of a number of other adjustment measures that we might mention, I should like to discuss briefly a technique that seems to offer some promise for a worthwhile future development. This method might be called the *situational interview.*

We have observed that when a child comes for assistance in a state of extreme anger or emotional upset, it is possible to reduce his tension and solve his problem by returning with him to the location where his upset occurred and there talking the matter out with him in the presence of some individual associated with, or involved in, the incident.

If a boy has had a disagreement with his job supervisor, each is permitted to state his complaints to the interviewer in the presence of the other. These complaints are then evaluated by the interviewer and interpreted to each in simple terms. The interviewer maintains a dominant position throughout the discussion in order that there may be no doubt at the end that he expects this to constitute a final and permanent solution to the difficulty. In the same way, if two boys have had an open disagreement, they work out a solution with the aid of the interviewer. This has proved to be a very effective method of reducing tension in cases where the child is really upset.

The following case illustrates this method:

Lawrence S. is a fifteen-year-old boy who arrived here from an orphanage. Until the past two months he was a regular caller at the interviewer's office to make complaints about other boys not liking him, about having too much work to do, about the cottage parents' talking too loudly, and the like. Efforts to motivate this boy by talking to him and pointing out the advantages of his taking a more responsible attitude were of no avail. He resents having been rejected by his family, but is unable to make the connection between this and the general feeling of dissatisfaction and inadequacy that he constantly reveals. He does not gain insight readily. It appears at times as if he were creating situations in which he could dramatize his resentment. This all reached a climax when Lawrence came to the interviewer's office crying and enraged. He stated that his cottage father, Mr. Allen, was making him do his own work and other boys' too. He felt that he was not being treated fairly, and he wanted to go to a cottage with smaller boys. When Lawrence could see no merit in any of the arguments offered against such a move, it was suggested that he and the interviewer have a talk with Mr. Allen in an attempt to *iron out* the difficulty.

In the interview in which all three participated, the boy was asked to state his complaints. He was still somewhat angry and presented his case in very emphatic terms. Mr. Allen then pointed out Lawrence's inadequacies in regard to the work in the cottage. Although the discussion became quite heated, since neither of the participants hesitated to express his opinions, it was prevented from degenerating into an argument by the interviewer who interrupted whenever the boy and his cottage father started talking directly to each other. By keeping the conversation directed toward himself, the interviewer was able to act as interpreter between the boy and his supervisor. Whenever one said something that might offend the other, the interviewer rephrased the statement in such a way as to facilitate understanding and reduce tension.

For example, when Lawrence accused Mr. Allen of giving him "all the dirty work—pushing the old mop," the interviewer interrupted to point out to the cottage father that Lawrence felt that he had been in the cottage long enough for a change of work. The supervisor immediately replied that Lawrence did not want to work, but wanted a soft job where he could let the other boys do all the real work. He had not yet shown that he could do anything more difficult than mopping. The interviewer again interrupted, explaining to Lawrence that the boys of the cottage felt that he should do his share and do his work well before he should be trusted with a more responsible job. The interviewer continued, saying that he felt sure the supervisor would be glad to help Lawrence get a better job if he could do his work well for a few days. The tone of voice used encouraged Mr. Allen to say that this was acceptable to him. This apparent victory for the boy was enlarged upon with enthusiasm by the interviewer. Speaking for Lawrence, he assured Mr. Allen that this was exactly what the boy wanted—a chance to get a better job by doing his share. When Lawrence agreed to this, the interviewer stated that he expected the arrangement to work out satisfactorily, and the discussion was terminated.

The success of this method depends upon the interviewer's maintaining a dominant role, without assuming a dictatorial attitude that might arouse antagonism. He must speak with such an air of self-confidence and phrase his statements with such skill as to gain an assenting response whenever it is required. Any slight yielding to the interviewer's point of view is interpreted as whole-hearted co-operation.

The child gains self-confidence and security when he is in the presence of adults who feel confident and secure. In Lawrence's case, the usual analytic interview held in the mental hygienist's office had proved inadequate. However, with the situational interview, it was possible to give the boy a feeling of security in the very situation where he previously felt inadequate and insecure. As a result, he was able to make a much better adjustment and seemed happier than he had in any previous cottage situation.

There are several factors that appear to operate in the use of the situational interview. (1) The child feels that, in the mental hygienist, he has someone who understands his difficulty and who is willing to help him effect a legitimate solution to his difficulties. (2) His antagonisms, fears, and unfavorable reactions are deflected from their usual objects by the reduction of emotional tension in the situation. (3) The cottage parent, job supervisor, or teacher feels that his side of the matter is understood and considered fairly so that he is willing to cooperate to the child's advantage. (4) Both individuals are motivated by the fact that they feel their progress is being watched by a third person.

Some caution must be observed in using this method. The child must not be forced to face an individual who will later take advantage of him. We must not bring in other individuals except with the child's full cooperation and consent and when we are certain that the child's best interests will be served. One's loyalty must be with the child, and the child's confidence must be protected.

In conflict situations of the sort we have described, the conventional interview method (i. e., with the child only) is comparatively inadequate. When one treats the child only, he fails to alleviate the situational source of his difficulty. All too often the interview must be used for the solution of neurotic conflicts that have persisted in the individual's behavior, perhaps for years after the original conditioning occurred. We seek wherever possible to effect a satisfactory adjustment through reducing tension in the original situation at the time of the conflict and thus forestall a long continued maladaptation.

In all our work we attempt to provide our children with real-life solutions to their problems. The social habits the child acquires in the Training School must equip him for happy, effective living in the community.

DOROTHY W. BARUCH

Beverly Hills, California

Therapeutic Procedures as Part of the Educative Process[1]

Statement of Philosophy

To a greater or lesser degree, our culture impinges on the personality development of the individuals growing up in it. By the time a child is two he has already come in contact with many cultural impacts. By the time he arrives in nursery school or kindergarten he has already accumulated patterns of acting, of thinking, of feeling; and the patterns differ according to the social group with which his family has allied itself. These are truisms which need no elaboration.

Into the Nursery school and Kindergarten at the Broadoaks School of Education, Whittier College, come children from 18 months of age to 6 years. Their fathers are mostly of the two highest occupational levels.[2] Almost all the children have been under the care of a pediatrician from birth on. Almost all their mothers have tried hard to learn the "correct" methods of child-rearing and have attempted to carry through what they have learned to the letter of the law. The parents are an upper-middle-class social group of moderate means, typical of many another such group in the United States. In large part the children, when they enter the Broadoaks Preschool, show the effect of certain frustrating cultural impositions which have been almost universal in the group.

---

[1] Reprinted from *Journal of Consulting Psychology*, 1940, 4, 165–172. Copyright 1940 by American Association for Applied Psychology.

[2] During the past two years, 94.2% of the fathers' occupations fell into Groups I and II of the Sims Scale. (77% into Group I; 17.2% into Group II.) The remaining ones fell into Group III.

What, then, are the major cultural stresses to which these children have been subjected?

1. *Deprivation of cuddling experiences.* Few of the mothers have nursed their babies for any length of time. 37 of the 111 children who have attended the preschool during the past two years were not nursed at all. Only 5 were breast-fed for longer than six months. Of those babies who were nursed, almost half were breast-fed not longer than one month, and three-fourths not longer than three months. Those who were nursed were nursed by the clock for a limited number of minutes with either three or four hour intervals strictly adhered to. Night nursings were eliminated for most during the first few weeks of life. Thus, relatively few children have had much physical closeness to the mother supplied automatically, as it were, through breast-feeding during the first nine months of their lives.

In addition, most of the mothers have been strongly advised not to handle their babies. They are told to dress, bathe, and diaper them "with dispatch" and are warned against fondling and holding them. Thus, the lack of physical closeness due to lack of breast-feeding is not compensated for by substitute contacts with the mother.

2. *Too early toilet training and over-emphasis on cleanliness.* Toilet training is very important to the mothers. Two-thirds of the children had toilet training for bowel control begin under 6 months of age. For one-third, bowel training was begun under 3 months of age. With three-fourths of the children, training for control of urination was instigated under 1 year, and for approximately one-fourth of them under 6 months.

All along there has been a universal shutting off of outlets for normal interest in excreta and urine. And substitute messings also have been closed to these children since the matter of general cleanliness is continuously over-emphasized.

3. *Subjection to anger-producing situations without opportunities for release.* Not only have the children been forced into an early giving-up of their own desire to eliminate when and where they wish, they have also had to meet other regularizations involving frustration:

Feeding schedules have been rigidly adhered to. No attempt has been made to take into account differing metabolic rates, differing rates of utilization of sugar, differing degrees of tolerance for the pain of being left hungry until the hands of the clock have moved around to the feeding hour.

Sensory pleasures sought in the form of thumbsucking, or other oral or genital manipulations, have been vigorously curtailed.

Most of the children as babies were victims of the precept of "let them cry." When they were hungry or uncomfortable, when they sought response in the only primitive vocal way of which they were capable, when they cried, they were left to "cry it out." Each in his own way had had to bear whatever degree of anger he had felt against such frustrating environmental forces.

As they grew, most of the children were hemmed in by commands not to touch this or that object. They have lived in homes where many objects have been forbidden to curious, yet clumsy, hands.

When siblings have interfered with their possession of mother or father, there has had to be expression of nothing but brotherly love.

All through no protest or anger, no expression of aggression or hostility has been tolerated. There has been no chance for release of emotion against the adults who deprived, regulated and enforced, nor against the children who usurped attention or prestige.

In a society where such early frustrations are current, it is no wonder that admissions to psychopathic hospitals each year exceed the number of graduations from college. Patterns of maladjustment are formed early. Procedures are therefore needed early to help the personality meet cultural impacts without undergoing too serious hurt. Experiences are needed that will dilute the effects of too continuous and too great deprivations and thwartings. Early therapy aimed at easing personality stresses before too grave maladjustments result seems in order. This may be termed *Preventive Therapy*. It has two primary functions:

1. To supply satisfactions that will offset frustrations that are too painful for the personality to bear and yet remain healthy.
2. To give release to emotions which, if not released, would hold the germ of potential maladjustment.

The Preschool is in a strategic spot for meeting personality needs. The children come into it early. Their parents also come to school. It is quite possible to incorporate therapeutic procedures into the regular program as part of the educative process. This has been attempted in the Broadoaks Preschool. Procedures which are therapeutic in the preventive sense are an integral part of group guidance. All the children have opportunities for participating in them.

But for some children these are not enough. Some children have taken frustrations and deprivations with too great sensitivity. Onto some children impositions have been levelled with too great rigidity. For some children thwartings have been augmented and complicated by parents who are maladjusted with each other or with themselves, by illness or other handicaps, by divergence in physique, intelligence, or in other traits, from what is acceptable to the particular family in question. Some children come into the Preschool with personalities already warped. These children are in need of additional therapeutic opportunities in their play and in the experiences through which they move. And because their parents are so inseparable from them, so much part of the emotional life which they are now introjecting, work needs also to be done with their parents. Their parents need to be helped with their own problems of adjustment. What is done and labeled "therapy" is merely a portion of the total picture. Perhaps it is the total picture that should be called therapeutic instead. But for convenience sake, and for clarity and emphasis, a few procedures will be isolated and discussed.

Subjects

The present report deals with the 111 children who have been enrolled in the Broadoaks Preschool during the past two years. (September, 1938–June, 1940.) The type of home from which they come has already been described. Duration of their enrollment ranges from one to eleven semesters, with an average enrollment of three semesters. Their ages range from 16 to 61 months on entrance, and from 25 to 70 months on leaving. The average age on entrance being 36.6 months and on leaving, 50.6 months. I.Q.s range from 89 to 154 with a mean of 118. (Median 117, sigma 13.8.)

When the children enter, reports are received from the pediatricians who have cared for them and from their parents. These reports include developmental and health histories and information concerning the guidance and training the child has gotten in the home. During the entire period in which the child is in attendance, conferences are held with fathers and mothers separately. In these conferences any conditions that impinge on the child's adjustments may come under consideration. Parents are free to bring in their own personal problems since these affect their children. Each child is carefully observed and studied.[3] The full studies of each individual provide a broad setting in which changes and progress may be evaluated. Thus, the outcomes of whatever therapy is attempted can be interpreted in terms of observed movement in the development of any given child.

Types of Therapeutic Procedures

Certain experiences which may be designated as *Preventive Group Therapy* are provided for all children enrolled. For children who show signs of deeper maladjustment, additional opportunities are provided—the deeper the maladjustment, the more intensive the opportunities. Such opportunities can be given without removing the child from the group, in which case they may be placed under the heading of *Group Therapy*. Or they may be afforded the child in short, regular periods of time spent alone with a single teacher away from the rest of the group, in which case they fall under the term of *Individual Therapy*.

In every procedure termed therapeutic, there are opportunities for close contact with an acceptant, sympathetic worker. The provision of a sustaining, affectional, security-giving contact is therapeutic in itself, especially where it comes to children who have been deprived of close affectional contacts with their mothers. Thus one aspect of therapy in the preschool is that provided through affectional, warm contacts. As already stated, another aspect is that provided through opportunities for release of emotions. Therapy, to summarize, has been carried on in five different ways:

1. For the entire group through provision of general release and of normal affectional contacts.
2. For particular children through more than usual affectional, supporting contact within the group situation.
3. For particular children through opportunities for deeper individual, affectional contact away from the group in so-called "time alone" with a teacher.

---

[3] For a fuller account of general procedures with parents and children, of the type of conference held with parents, and the type of study made of the children, see: Baruch, Dorothy W., *Parents and Children Go to School* (23).

4. For particular children through provision of more than usual opportunities for release within the group situation.
5. For particular children through opportunities for greater release away from the group in "times alone."

Preventive Group Therapy Through the Provision of General Releasing Activities and Affectional Contacts

How are contacts and release provided for the entire group?

As concerns *contacts*, the child's entrance into the preschool is a crucial period. Always the mother is asked to stay until the child seems willing and able to let her go. With his mother still in the situation, one of the teachers also stays close. She helps his mother while his mother helps him. To the child she becomes associated with his mother. He is even told that she will be his "school-mother," and his "special teacher." Both these terms are used. When his mother finally leaves, his special teacher stays near.[4] For the time-being she makes her procedures as closely like his mother's as she can. She sees, for instance, that she uses the same toileting terms for a while, that she calls him by the same nick-name, that she hold his cup while he drinks if that is what his mother has done. At the same time she is very affectionate and outgoing to him. She takes him on her lap. She puts arms about him. Gradually, as he adjusts to the situation, her contacts are lessened. However, even as the months go by he receives daily focuses of some sort from her. She stands by with warmth when he is hurt or in distress. She accords him physical closeness as he appears to need it. Thus, some of the cuddling experiences that the child has needed are being supplied.[5]

As for the matter of *Release*. It has already been brought out that most of these children have been subjected to early toilet training and to curtailment of their natural interest in defecation and that they have been provided with no substitute outlets through messing of any sort. In the preschool, they have, in contrast, many such outlets. Finger paints, soft moist clay, muddy earth, soapsuds, water—all provide hands-in, delving-into, messing activities. Especially in-

---

[4] Each adult in the situation serves as "special teacher" for from three to five children. Since the "new" children are always in the minority (i. e. there is a large hold-over from semester to semester) it is usually feasible to arrange that not more than one new child needs to be under the wing of a single adult.

[5] In the meantime, through Parent Education, the mother is often being helped to allow herself greater affectional expressiveness so that the child's response life as a whole becomes less deprived.

teresting has been the fact that when given freedom to do what they wish, children over and over identify the clay as excreta. "It is big pieces like in my toilet." "Gooey, gooey, nice gronotty," from a child whose term this is for bowel movement. At first such remarks are made cautiously with suspicious glances at the teachers. A few children ask, "Can I? Can I," meaning, "Is it permissible actually to bring in these unmentionables?" One four-year-old even wondered, "Aren't you going to make me stop saying such nasty things?" It is only when the teacher remains non-condemning and acceptant that the children become free in this sort of play.

Aggression and hostility that have piled up as a result of the many anger-producing situations which the child has encountered also finds opportunities for release. A child with a particularly severe mother pounds nails with all his force into a piece of wood and mutters to himself, "Pound her. Pound her. Make her sick." There is always much savage hitting of punching bag and kicking of football. Clay may be broken and pinched and pounded. An indestructible doll can be spanked and put to bed, can be made to go "without dinner," can be "covered all over with sand so he can't breathe," can be put into an empty bucket while a child dramatizes that "she is being drownded all dead." In short, there are many materials in the environment that afford release for aggression. Release can come, too, within limitations, through a child's relationship with other children. "No, you stay 'way. You can't have the swing. You can't, you can't," and teachers have learned not to step in and induce too much "nice, polite" behavior. The outlets afforded by holding out against others, by good, round fist-fights, by calling others such names as "dope" and "you old wee-wee," all have therapeutic value, providing they do not go so far that actual hurt is done. For, an actual hurt—aside from the harm to another—would bring too much guilt in its wake for the child committing it and would throw him back against himself.

Still another set of facts serves a therapeutic purpose within the group situation. The preschool is equipped with materials which the child may utilize to his own ends. There is no need for the refrain of "don't touch" which he has heard so much at home. Blocks, wood, clay, paints, and other materials yield to his purposes. He can scale great heights on a jungle-gym. He can slide swiftly down inclined boards. Through his own body, through his own efforts, he can feel himself powerful, he can feel himself dominant. He can turn aggression into creative force.

Therapy Through More Than Usual Provisions of Affection Within the Group

In addition to the above, with nineteen of the 111 children who have been in the Broadoaks Preschool during the past two years, specific therapeutic procedures have consisted mainly in providing more frequent close contacts with the teacher who serves as a mother-substitute. Whenever a child is shy, timid, withdrawn, when he is lacking in spontaneity—the first move is to give him extra, close contacts.

At the same time, effort is made to see into his total life situation, to find out what is making his life particularly hard for him. For, when the school sees what factors lie behind his difficulties, it can more adequately adapt procedures to fit in with his needs. What is found out sometimes makes logical the continuance of warm, frequent contacts and sometimes suggests procedures of other sorts.

Ken, 2/10,[6] for instance, lost his mother[7] a year ago. He has a step-mother now of two months standing. She is young and frankly bothered by the acquisition of Ken and an older brother. She doesn't know what to do with them. Logically, then, Ken needs warmth from a mother-person, and a steady closeness. In school every day his special teacher sees that he gets it. To illustrate:

Ken comes into the door from the nurse's inspection. His special teacher sees him enter. Quickly she steps over, "Hello, Kenny." She smiles and puts arms around him. "Off comes the coat," she continues, but instead of letting him stand while he shifts from coat to sweater, she picks him up and holds him on her lap, managing several hugs during the process of changing. When the sweater is buttoned, Ken leans dreamily back against her, and sits, quietly resting, for several minutes; then climbs down and is off.

"Time Alone" for Contact

For some children, such contacts within the group do not seem enough. These children either do not show forward movement in

---

[6] Read: Two years, ten months.

[7] It is interesting to note that for the 7 children with one parent or the other deceased, these contacts appeared valuable in helping toward increased spontaneity and outgoingness.

their adjustment within a reasonable time, or they seem to want more contact than can comfortably be provided within the group. When this happens, the teacher sets aside fifteen or twenty minutes each day during which she leaves the group with the child, goes to a quiet place alone with him, takes a walk with him, or does something else of his own choosing. She says to him, "This is your time alone with me. You can have me all to yourself. You won't have to share me at all with the other children as you do have to sometimes when we're all together. And I'll save time alone just for you every day."

As illustration of what goes on during these "time alone" periods, come the following records:

Harry, 2/2, has a new baby brother at home. In school he has become much interested in a baby doll.

One day as he is playing, his teacher goes up to him. She tells him that he is to have time with her all alone and asks what he would like to do. He wants to take the baby doll and go to see the ducks in the kindergarten. Holding hands, they walk slowly toward the duck pond. As they walk, the teacher chants, "Harry and his teacher are going all alone, going to see the ducks, going all alone." She interjects that she thinks he's a nice boy. He climbs on her lap when they reach their destination and from that vantage point, while she cuddles him, they watch the ducks together.

Lindsay, 2/11, has an older sister who has been the center of focus. In his time alone he has chosen to go for a walk with his teacher. Always they must walk to the bus-bench at the end of the block and sit there and watch the cars go by.[8] The following is a typical record:

On arrival, Lindsay says, "I want to go for my walk." He wants exactly the same walk as before. When they get to the bench he says, "I want to sit on the bench." He sits on the teacher's lap. She sings to him. He asks for the same song over and over. He lolls against her and is most affectionate. Together they notice the bus and the passing cars. After fifteen minutes they get back to school, where Lindsay begins to play more spontaneously, it seems, than heretofore.

Besides children who are withdrawn and timid, most of the chil-

---

[8] At the date of writing, this same walk has been demanded 21 times, and interest in it is still going strong.

dren with speech problems are given time-alone-contact periods daily. Speech is, of course, one way in which the personality manifests itself externally. When a child stutters, when his speech is blocked, when his speech remains infantile, then usually emotional problems are found underneath. Sometimes close, supporting contact with one teacher seems to bring the security requisite for venturing forth both in activities and with language. Sometimes, after a child has come to feel secure in his relationship with the contact-teacher, he begins to reveal anxieties and conflicts. His contact periods then turn into periods which he uses to gain emotional release.

More Than Ordinary Provision for Release Within the Group

For 11 out of the 111 children who have attended the Preschool during the past two years, extra opportunities for release, and rather continuous ones, occurring here and there all through their play, have appeared useful. All of these children were overly aggressive. They were apt to be destructive and over-negative. They frequently bullied or attacked other children and upset objects for no apparent reason.

To illustrate: Robert, 4/4, comes from a family where father and · mother have been in conflict, and where, in addition, the maternal grandmother is dominant and dominating.

At rest time Robert pulls and tears the teacher's smock. The teacher says, "I know how you feel, Robert. You feel like being mean. You feel like pulling and tearing. So I'll get you an old towel and you can pull and tear it all you want." Robert comes back at her with, "I hate you because you make me do things I don't want to do." (Projecting from the home situation.) "I hate to do things. I hate you." The teacher gets the towel and gives it to him, saying sympathetically, "I know you don't like to do many things that you are asked to do." Robert takes the towel and tears it into pieces, saying, "I'll tear the old towel to pieces. I will. I will."

Lonny, 4/6, is an only child. His mother has been ill. The major tension for him, however, comes from an old and failing paternal grandfather who lives in the home and whose expectations are rigid and perfectionistic.

Lonny is using crayons at a table with Sara and Jane. For no apparent reason he reaches over and scribbles across Jane's picture. Then he throws a crayon at Sara. The teacher goes to him. "Lonny, it looks to me as though you were feeling mean. That's all right, Lonny, to feel mean, but we can find some other way of letting the meanness out. Come along with me and you can hit the punching bag as hard as you want. Sometimes punching the bag helps to get rid of those mean feelings." Together the teacher and Lonny walk over to the punching bag. Lonny hits it very hard. "I would like to hit it dead." He hits it ten times in all. Then announces he is through. He goes back and works happily and quietly at his crayoning, talking amicably with the two girls, until it is time to go to rest.

Marie, 3/6, has been brought up with more than ordinary emphasis on cleanliness. Her interest in messing is pronounced. So it is provided outlet.

She is given many opportunities to mess. She helps hose out the rabbit cage. She sweeps away the excreta. She helps the teacher wash cups in soapy water; mix the finger-paints; mix mash for the chickens; water the plants and moisten the clay. She helps clear the slime out of the aquarium. All the "dirtiest" jobs are hers, and all are thoroughly enjoyed.

Sometimes a fight between two children is encouraged as outlet. Peter, for instance, who is 4/1 and has been brought up with much emphasis on manners and external amenities, kicks at Tony.

Tony kicks back. The teacher steps in and laughingly comments that they look ripe for a good fight. She asks if the children wouldn't like to have a boxing match. They assent joyously. The boxing gloves are gotten and a three-round fight ensues.

In all these instances, and in many others like them in many schools today, the teacher simply stops the children and shuts off outlets to them. The point is lost sight of that such outlets are important for emotional release. Children who are overly-aggressive need extra opportunities for expression opened to them instead of having opportunities curtailed through premature demands for control. When such outlets are afforded, there must, of course, be limitations as in any therapeutic situation. Lonny may not, for instance, destroy Jane's picture or take chances of hurting Sara by throwing crayons at her. The limitations set have to do mainly with preventing hurt to other children—either physical or emotional. They protect the child from carrying his desires into directions that may create for him too great guilt and anxiety. A child may not, for instance, kill a duck, or drown a baby mouse, since such activities would hold the probability of bringing in their wake guilt that only creates further anxiety for the child to bear. Yet within such limitations, many outlets are still possible.

"Time Alone" for Further Release

For the children who appear seriously maladjusted, "time alone" is always provided. A start is made ordinarily by seeing that the child has the sort of experiences already described in connection with contact-time-alone. Then, as the child builds up confidence in the teacher, as rapport deepens, he begins in one way or another to seek release. His first steps toward release may be small ones, but the teacher is alert to them and follows up with opportunities for further release. One very introverted, withdrawn child, for instance, showed his first readiness for release by tapping on one key of the teacher's typewriter and in a giggly, silly, yet almost defiant way, repeating with every tap, "Pee-pee, pee-pee, pee-pee." Another, looking at a book with her teacher suddenly hit at the picture of a baby.

Release-time-alone may also grow out of the more general opportunities for release provided in the yard. Certain evidences of anxiety or disorientation, of hostility or of conflict come up and appear to be of a nature that can be dealt with alone more comfortably and with less danger of exposure to other children. One child, for instance, takes great blobs of wet clay, squeezes these between his hands and lets them drop onto the tin table-top. Obviously he is overly-excited as he does this and disturbed. He is flushed, his movements grow jerky, and he laughs shrilly. Another makes a penis out of clay and then viciously demolishes it. And so periods alone for release are begun.

These periods last for fifteen or twenty minutes. Twenty-three children out of the 111 have had such periods in the past two years. During these periods, dolls, representing the child's own family, have proven most productive. Frequently in the doll-play the child manifests points of conflict and freely expresses his feelings concerning family members. Productive also have been clay figures made crudely by the teacher. Clay, itself, manipulated by the child to his own ends has also been most useful. The teacher makes materials available. But it is the child always who initiates his own activities with them. In some cases he ignores them and turns to other forms of dramatization and play.

The activity launched by Royce illustrates the last point. Royce, 4/4, did little with any of the materials on hand. Instead, when alone with his teacher, he starts being a baby.

After saying that he'll pretend he's a baby, he lies down on the couch and makes a lot of baby noises. Then he says to the teacher, "Tell me that I *can't* get up." She says, "All right, if you want me to. You can't get up." He whimpers "I want to get up. I want to get up," and continues with his baby noises.

The next day he starts similar play:

He kicks his feet and makes crying noises like a baby. Then he demands, "You spank me hard and then I'll cry awfully hard." The teacher pats him lightly. "No," he begs, "spank me awfully hard like my mother does, and then I'll cry like a baby. I'll cry awfully hard."

Royce is a very disoriented child. His mother has been extremely bothered by circumstances in her own life. She is very flighty. When she is mad at him, and then only, does he have her full focus. Such contacts are apparently the most satisfying ones he has ever had with her. And now when he wants closer contact with his teacher, he seeks it in the same way. She suggests that they pretend she is spanking him "awfully hard." She follows his leads yet is careful not to hurt him, proving to him in this way that he can have comfortable, satisfying contacts with immunity from pain. And soon he begins to show her his deeper worries.

Time alone for release goes on day after day, usually for months, until the child seems ready to terminate these contacts.

One case sketched very briefly will serve to illustrate the sort of sequence that may occur.

Raymond was 4/2 when he came into the preschool. He remained for three semesters. On entrance he was extremely withdrawn. He did not talk. He did not play. He seemed impervious to what went on about him. There was no gross abnormality in physical health according to the pediatrician. His mother reported that at home he would sit and sit for hours without moving and that he seemed to be within a shell that no one could penetrate. She was worried about his lack of speech.

Chief among the items that might have caused such maladjustment, was the fact that the parents were in extreme tension in their relationship to each other. To the worker they avowed hatred of each other. They claimed, however, that they did not fight openly, that instead they "held things in." The mother drank for relief and thrashed the child, letting out onto him the antagonism she held against her husband.

To the worker the parents in their own separate conferences expressed their hostilities. They talked, they got mad, they ranted against each other. To her they let out many of their ranklings. And as they let out they apparently gained enough relief so that within approximately six months' time they were able to accept each other on a different basis—without such a weight of piled-up resentment.

They were able, too, to accept the child on a different basis. The mother no longer felt "red anger" against him. She could be more acceptant and have greater patience. But the child had introjected so much of her old emotion that he could not accept the new.

None-the-less, in school he did make some progress. He began to use materials manipulatively. He started to talk, but stuttered badly. He became more demanding of adult attention by getting silly and shrill. He remained tense, however. He continued to withdraw from contacts with other children, never attempted to defend his own rights, threw stones and sticks perpetually at the animals, and masturbated quite continually.

From the beginning he was given extra chances for contact within the group situation. But for the first months he was fearful of any but casual approaches. Releasing experiences were obviously impossible for him when he was not utilizing materials. However, the fact that demands were few and restrictions fewer, may have given him some sense of ease. Slowly observable trust in one of the teachers came, but this was deep enough to permit release in her presence only after he was in his third semester. Only then would he leave the group without near panic at being alone with an adult.

He was the child who began tapping a key of his teacher's typewriter, saying "pee-pee, pee-pee" with sly looks and great silliness, and a shade of defiance.

He ran the gamut of several distinct types of activity during his subsequent periods with her. He expressed aggression through bowel movements of clay. He even defecated on the linoleum floor several times in the room where these periods took place. He became exhibitionistic, showing his penis repeatedly to her and masturbating in front of her. Finally he attempted to make a very rude clay figure and demanded her help.

The figure became his mother to him. He would pound her, trample on her, urinate on her, poke his penis at her, pull her arms and legs and head off.

The teacher remained acceptant. She reiterated that children often do feel mean and mad to their mothers, that she understood how he felt, and that he could keep on telling her and showing her about it. A couple of times he attempted to hit and smear clay on her, but here she erected limitations, feeling that their relationship would be jeopardized if she permitted him to do to her what to him would symbolize harm. Hurting the one person whom he could thoroughly trust might lead into too great fear of desertion and into too great anxiety and guilt.

Finally, after an extreme orgy of biting and cutting and mashing of the mother figure, he became suddenly relaxed. For the first time his voice carried in it a sympathetic note. "Oh, she died, poor old nasty."

He then picks up the mutilated clay mother and very softly whispers, "Poor thing. She got runned over. Call the ambulance. Poor old nasty thing. She's dead all right." He pats the figure gently . . . "Let's see what she has inside her." He scratches the clay figure open. "Oh, there's blood. Blood is coming out. Put her in the ambulance." He picks her up again. "I don't want to hit you, mother." Then turning to the teacher he asks her to "fix the mother all right again."

She repairs the clay figure, and meanwhile interprets that it looks as if his old mean mother were dead and that perhaps this is a new mother whom he wants.

He picks up the figure. Calls it his new, good mother. One of the legs that the teacher had put hastily on, falls off. He picks it up and himself makes another leg and carefully moulds it back on. These are the first tender, caring-for, positive expressions toward his mother ever evidenced in his play. A short while later, when his time finishes, instead of demolishing the mother as on previous days, he places her carefully in the clay can, covers her gently with the oil cloth, saying gently, "there you are."

Apparently, through having let out hostility against the old mother, he has at last become able to accept a new mother.

Great changes are apparent in his behavior. He no longer stutters. He begins to defend his own rights. He becomes overly-aggressive to other children as a swing from earlier withdrawal and submission. He is less frequently silly or shrill, and more capable of demanding response through affectionate approaches. All in all, he is a much less tense and a much more open, natural person.

As a side comment, the child's intelligence test rating moved from an I.Q. of 76 to one of 106. This does not, of course, mean that intelligence increased, but that the child was no longer as blocked emotionally from showing and using what intelligence he had.

Evaluative Comment

Outcomes in the case just cited, as well as in others, have been vivid and striking. Oftener there is less extreme evidence of change but to the careful observer change is apparent in many children who have experienced the types of therapeutic procedures described.

What the outcomes are in any given case can only be seen as the development of the whole child is carefully evaluated. It is true that by far the greater number of children attending the Broadoaks Preschool do make progress in their total adjustment. They improve in the way they get along with other children, in the way they get along in their homes and they are freer and happier within themselves, more outgoing and more creative. They apparently achieve greater courage to meet life's demands. How large a part play therapy has in their development is, of course, impossible to determine under conditions where it is only one of many elements that enter into guidance. With human beings one can never say: You have this. Now you add that. And the result is as follows . . . There are too many complicating factors.

But when one child after another is watched as a growing entity, therapeutic procedures as described have appeared to serve them well, according to the staff's pooled judgments.

Preventive procedures apparently function best in cases where complicating stresses within the home are not too grave—where thwartings for the child have arisen out of the cultural patterns described earlier. When parents can reorient themselves so that some of these deprivations are relieved at home as well as at school, forward movement within the child becomes more noticeable. The more intensive procedures have appeared to serve a particularly effective role in such cases where major parental tensions have been relieved but where the child has so introjected the old situation that he needs augmented security and release before he can utilize the new. However, in a few cases these procedures have appeared to bring a measure of relief and reorientation to a child even when pressures and tensions within the parents have persisted. Never, though, under such circumstances, do they bring as great a measure of relief and reorientation as when parental tensions and anxieties clear, and when the home becomes a peaceful, harmonious, and secure place for both adults and children.

VIRGINIA W. LEWIS

Waterman, California

Intensive Treatment with Adolescent Girls[1]

The title of this paper needs a little definition or delimitation. Intensive is such a relative term when used in reference to number of contacts, and absolute time that it might better be discarded. None of the cases used were what might be called "deep" or interpretive therapy. The term "treatment" is limited to psychotherapy and for this group to the interview form. The paper presents the author's personal techniques with some attempts at analysis in psychological terms. The cases used were girls from 14 to 20 years, referred as delinquent, behavior problem, personality disorder; nevertheless, it is the author's belief that adjustment for these cases is a process of re-education although in the emotional realm with greater weight on the affective factors. Her aim has been to assist the girl in the analysis of her own feelings, their origin, the involvement of the past in her present experience, her real needs, techniques of satisfying these in the face of external pressures and limitations.

A girl is referred to a clinic because of observable behavior which is deemed unacceptable. This behavior is recognized by the clinician as an attempt on the part of the girl to relieve a situation which creates unpleasant tensions. The immediate question for the clinician is: Why does this girl behave as she does and to what extent is the behavior a response to pressures from the environment?

In considering the relation between the social history and the disturbing behavior, the clinician considers the presence of causal fac-

[1] Reprinted from *Journal of Consulting Psychology,* 1940, 4, 181–184. Copyright 1940 by American Association for Applied Psychology.

tors which are not related particularly to adolescence, both in the environment and within the girl. The most frequent external factors are poverty, membership in a minority group, frequent changes of residence or school, health, the cultural pattern. These external causes will rarely of themselves create behavior difficulties sufficiently serious to reach the clinic, but they increase tensions caused by internal situations due to deprivation or conflict in the area of basic satisfactions which the girl needs. For every child, there are certain basic satisfactions which she needs for normal development; emotional security, physical security, and opportunity for growth. In seeking terms to describe the operation of these basic needs, the best comparison seems to be that of the functioning of the endocrines. Similarly for normal emotional development interaction and balance in the basic satisfaction of needs is necessary.

At the period of adolescence the behavior is the result of the girl's attempt to solve the sense of deprivation or conflict by new methods of meeting external pressures. This problem solving process then takes on certain forms because of complications particularly due to adolescence: physical strains due to growth at this period, vacillation in the attitude and behavior of parent persons, vacillation in forms of expression in her own age group, conflicts in the cultural pattern which become apparent to her at this time. Each of the basic satisfactions is threatened or thrown out of balance. As a consequence of growing up in a complex culture which includes in its pattern many real conflicts, the adolescent girl in seeking satisfaction finds a state of conflict within herself and with the sources of satisfaction in her environment.

In seeking to diagnose the causes of the behavior, to determine the method of treatment, the clinician must consider the external pressures, adolescent strains, as well as internal conditions. Because additional data are revealed during interviews, the role of the therapist and the technique of treatment to meet a particular girl's needs cannot be rigidly set. There must be adaptability on the part of the therapist as there are changes in the patient during the course of treatment.

This psychologist in the initial contact administers psychological tests. Some people have felt that this is a handicap to the development of a therapeutic relationship; the writer has found the testing situation the most helpful approach. For the girl, it provides a safe situation with many familiar elements. It is true that therapy is hindered when during the testing the girl gets a consciousness of failure or when the pertinency of the testing to her problem is not apparent to her. Aside from the test results, the writer uses the situation to build in the girl a feeling of security; to observe the girl's characteristic muscular responses in gesture, expression and bodily movement to success, failure, and emotional blocking. When the testing is finished, if the girl asks for interpretation, it is given; or if the examiner feels it is needed at this point. There are cases where the interpretation is delayed until later in the treatment; occasionally it is never made.

Usually at this point the girl herself refers to her original statement of the problem, sometimes in the same form, more often in a new form. The interviews which follow are used by the therapist to give the girl a greater feeling of security so that she talks freely and honestly about what has happened, the meaning it has for her, the causes as she sees them. The method of giving her a feeling of security must be such that it enlists her effort in working on her problem, that it keeps the responsibility with her. She is encouraged to approach the problem by way of her feeling reactions. Freedom of expression and effort depends in part on the affectional relationship from the girl's standpoint. That relationship will depend somewhat on the genetic point at which deprivation took place, somewhat on the compensations the girl has worked out. The interviews give the girl emotional release, more understanding of herself and to the therapist more information. From the point of view of structure and progress in treatment the term "first interview" is a misnomer since it may include several contacts which as a group constitute the first phase of therapy.

The initial phase of treatment is closed by the girl when she herself shifts from dealing chiefly with the superficial problem and finding her place with the therapist, to a conscious effort to find the causes of her difficulty and a method of handling situations. Sometimes this second phase is dramatically introduced. A typical example:

> We haven't talked about this, but I get mad. It's been getting worse for three months. I want you to help me figure out why and what to do about it.

During this second phase the treatment becomes a cooperative project, recognized as such by both the girl and the therapist. During this period the girl talks more freely, going back over previous material; often she says, "Ask me some questions." The clinician listens, asks more questions, pushes the girl more to get below the surface. The questions, however, do not change in form; they are still: At that point how did you feel? What did you do and how did you feel then? What do you think it meant? What were you really thinking inside yourself?

The length of this second phase varies with the complexity of the problem, the duration and intensity of the problem behavior, the pressure of environmental factors, the quality of the emotional relationship between girl and therapist. During this phase there are interviews when the girl goes in circles over material previously given. It is necessary for the therapist to be sensitive to whether this circular movement is a necessary recapitulation period for the girl or whether it is perseveration in a track from which the girl must be helped to release herself. Each time she is able to break the circular movement, there is noticeably accelerated progress in therapy. This phase closes with a fairly clear recognition on the part of the girl of the etiology of her feeling and behavior reactions and a desire on her part to develop a new procedure. One girl said,

Why can't you be born grown up or stay little always? It hurts so to grow up. How can I grow up? How can we figure that out?

The third phase of therapy has been begun. During this the girl is less dependent upon emotional response from the clinician although the relationship continues. The girl now works on plans, new techniques of meeting internal and external pressures. She seeks reassurance from the therapist while she evaluates her work. Each time she returns she refers to the thinking, planning, and experimenting she has been doing. With some girls this is a very short period which each closes in her own manner.

The fourth phase is one of intermittent contacts sought by the girl for support. She comes for approval of her success, for re-evaluation of her techniques, for consideration of minor problems. The writer feels sure that this fourth phase must be provided.

In attempting to analyze the role of therapist with adolescent girls the author after study of her own case records, by introspective observation of her own emotional responses in the situation and later reports from the girls, has arrived at an hypothesis. In the situation therapist and girl constitute a private theater in which each person alternately and sometimes simultaneously is both actor and audience or director-coach. The emotional experience of the writer is clearly similar to experiences in amateur dramatics where as actor or coach she lived the part of the dramatic character, at the same time observing and evaluating the behavioral expression of the feelings of the character. The therapist in her empathic identification with the girl seems to take on for the girl the dramatic role of the girl herself; that is, the girl's other self. The treatment process then becomes a dynamic emotional experience, which duplicates in dramatic time value the developmental emotional experience, thus resulting in emotional growth. Case material gives some evidence of the validity of this hypothesis in that failure cases seem to have in common the element that the therapist was unable, doubtless due to causes within her own personality, of developing an empathic response to that particular girl. There are some successful cases where the girl had previously had contact with a therapist or counselor with no therapeutic result. The material seems to indicate that in some cases the previous worker gave sympathy to the girl to which she responded, but did not live through a dynamic emotional experience; in other cases, the previous worker, because of conflicts within herself, never escaped from her own ego to contribute empathy to the relationship. This hypothesis that the emotional relationship is an empathic one suggests an answer to the puzzling question: What is the role of the therapist? Statements by girls about the treatment experience indicate that the girls have some recognition of this:

I've been thinking about what you are to me. It's as though you were myself—a part of me. You're a balance wheel, you're not a person. It's almost as if I were talking to myself, but with someone listening in and trying to think on it. I'm not getting rid of anything but a lot of stored up feeling. I don't come for advice. No, sometimes I do. But then I'm conscious that I want advice. It really bothers me when you become a person. What you do is let a person talk and put in comments that keep it going instead of stewing in a circle. That's why I say you're a balance wheel. It's different now. When I first met you, you were a person, I disliked you because you were touching sore spots. Now, I know you'll be a person when I need you to be. Other times you're someone to blow off steam to and to talk to so I can make up my mind.

Success in treatment seems to depend upon the accuracy of the initial diagnosis as to the probable areas of difficulty, an open minded attitude as to the complete diagnosis, and a willingness to work toward the girl's making her own analysis in terms which she can implement. Equally important is the recognition of the limitations of the interview technique, of the girl's ability to generalize and apply, of the clinician's lack in ability to treat certain types of cases. It is not possible to exaggerate the importance in successful cases of the therapist's facility and willingness to assume the role which the girl and the situation impose, and her patience in permitting treatment to progress at the rate determined by the girl's ability.

In conclusion, it might be pointed out that only incidental case material has been presented, that there has been merely a generalized description of the author's technique of work. It might be characterized as groundwork for some psychological hypotheses. It is the author's conviction that psychology can make a real contribution by developing its own experience, examining processes and results out of its own frame of reference, and by expressing generalizations so as to discover the veracity of the premises by other means than "improvement in behavior." It is hoped that by the accumulation of such descriptions of experience psychological generalizations and hypotheses may be developed in this field.

CARL R. ROGERS

University of Chicago

Therapy in Guidance Clinics[1]

＝＝＝＝＝＝＝＝＝＝＝＝＝＝＝＝＝＝＝＝＝＝＝＝＝＝＝＝＝＝＝＝＝＝＝＝＝

In recent years there has been an increasing element of unity in the practice of therapy in the child guidance field. Treatment of the child and the parent, whether carried on in the child guidance clinic, by the school psychologist, by the visiting teacher, or by the case worker in child welfare, is likely to be carried on in certain rather well-defined ways and in pursuance of certain general principles. Furthermore, we are for the first time beginning to see the development of psychological research concerned with therapy, and this is a most fortunate sign for the future. It is as we examine therapeutic procedures with the tools of critical research that we can build on those elements which are proven to be sound and discard those which are shown to be unnecessary. The purpose of this paper is to picture some of the more important characteristics of present-day therapy as it is practiced in child guidance, and to indicate some of the significant psychological research in this field.

The basic principle which represents the core of all therapy with children and their parents is that we can help individuals only by promoting growth. There is no doubt that we are placing much more reliance upon the individual drive toward growth and maturity and adjustment than was formerly the case. The aim of therapy is not to change the individual in ways which we approve, but to release the normal processes of growth. More and more frequently in writings about therapy we find this view expressed, that therapy is aimed toward more independent, more responsible growth on the

---

[1] Reprinted from *Journal of Abnormal and Social Psychology*, 1943, 38, 284–289. Copyright 1943 by American Psychological Association.

part of the client, that it is a way of helping the individual to help himself. Such a viewpoint is built on the conviction that the resources of the individual for change and adjustment are far greater than the puny influences which we can bring to bear upon him. Our work becomes that of releasing constructive forces already present rather than the much more hopeless task of marshaling pressures which will bring about change.

One of the outcomes of this fundamental purpose is the increasing agreement among professional workers that the client is the one who is ultimately responsible for his own destiny, and that both parent and child have a very basic right to select their own solutions to their problems, whether or not these correspond to the aims and wishes of the therapist. The era of the reforming impulse is almost over in the child guidance field, and we are seeing instead the development of professional skills in the offering of assistance. Even the rather unfortunate word "guidance," which seems to imply the direction of the life of another, is coming to have new and less coercive connotations.

This change in emphasis—and it is a change, as will be evident from examining records of ten or fifteen years ago from any clinic—does not mean that workers no longer recognize social norms of behavior, or that they are becoming namby-pamby in dealing with behavioral maladjustments. It is based on a recognition that social behavior originates in a genuine desire to be social, that mature behavior grows out of the desire to be grown up, that affectionate behavior can come only from feelings of affection. We cannot make people social, or mature, or affectionate. We can, however, help parent and child to see themselves more clearly, to explore their own purposes more deeply, and to make a more clear-cut conscious choice as to the direction they wish to take and the behavior which is in accord with their own deepest purposes. Even when society steps in and lays its restraining hand on delinquent or asocial behavior, it is still the aim of the clinician to respect the integrity of the individual. It is recognized that the responsibility for choice still exists within the framework of social compulsion, and that growth can come only through the making of choices.

We already have evidence that the viewpoint which the counselor takes on this important issue sharply influences the type of counsel-

ing technique he uses. Porter (176),[2] in a study of psychologists carrying on counseling, found that those who tended to direct the
client, who took upon themselves the responsibility for solving the
client's problems, used techniques sharply different from the nondirective counselors. The directive group did most of the talking in
the interview, tended to ask many specific questions, gave a great
deal of information, frequently made suggestions, and often urged
a certain course of action upon the client. Nondirective counselors,
or the other hand, permitted the client to do most of the talking
and used primarily those techniques which reflect the attitudes the
client is expressing. These techniques will be discussed more fully in
a later section.

We might summarize this first basic aspect of therapy by saying
that it is based on a deep respect for the growth potentialities of the
individual and a corresponding desire to respect his right to make
responsible choices. This attitude is not a theoretical one, but has a
profound effect upon the type of approach used by the therapist.

Another characteristic of modern child guidance procedures is the
fresh emphasis which is placed upon catharsis. The value of "talking out," in the presence of an accepting person, all the defensive,
repressed, and conflicted attitudes which are troubling the client, is
recognized more than ever before. Our growing inventiveness in this
area accounts for the whole development of the concept of play
therapy, which is built on catharsis at the nonverbal level. As we
direct our counseling procedures toward helping parent and child
to release their feelings, we find that we are increasingly successful
in doing so. Lewis (140), in a study of the intensive treatment of
several cases, reported verbatim, found that 55 per cent of the client's conversation dealt with his own problems and the attitudes
which were related to them. Royer (194), making a somewhat more
detailed analysis of three counseling cases, arrives at a very similar
finding, with approximately 50 per cent of the client's conversation
falling within this definition. Clinicians are evidently becoming
quite successful in developing those therapeutic techniques which
enable the client freely to express his feelings.

Psychologists have gone further than this in their investigation of

---

[2] Bibliography begins on page 719.

the values of catharsis. Baruch (25, 27) has not only given an excellent description of catharsis as it exists in play therapy, and the methods used to promote it, but also reports on the high degree of success in the readjustment of 23 maladjusted youngsters of preschool age. Bixler (38) has also made a suggestive study in this same field, on a smaller number of cases. Allen (10) pictures the way in which expression is encouraged through play therapy at the Philadelphia Child Guidance Clinic. Haggard (101) has attempted a laboratory study of experimentally induced anxiety and finds that catharsis is the most effective of three therapeutic procedures in reducing the disturbance which had been aroused.

If, then, it is characteristic of child guidance treatment that the worker refrains from imposing patterns or goals upon the client, and if the initial aim of therapy is to promote the free expression of feeling, what is the role of the clinician? It seems clear, both from subjective descriptions given by psychologists and psychiatrists, and from more objective psychological researches, that the function of the therapist is to hold a mirror to the client's feelings. As the mother talks out her bitterness toward her son, criticizing, blaming, telling of his faults, the therapist does not argue, does not reproach her for these unmaternal attitudes, and does not agree with them. Instead the modern therapist recognizes and accepts these feelings as a part of the total situation, without blame, praise, or comment. The therapist may simply remark, "You feel your son is mostly bad," or, "You feel Johnny has a great many faults." The therapist who is working with the child adopts a similar attitude with the youngster, even though the attitudes may be diametrically opposed. As Johnny tells, directly through words, or indirectly through play, of his hostility toward his parents, the therapist recognizes his feelings. If he pounds a mother doll, and shows other signs of such hostility, the therapist may say, "Perhaps you would like to do that to your mother." Such a procedure is simple enough to describe, but exceedingly difficult for workers to put into practice, because it runs so deeply counter to our ordinary ways of behaving. It has several aims. In the first place, it continually brings into the client's consciousness the pattern of his own emotional attitudes, thus clarifying his picture of himself. Because it is completely noncritical, it does not arouse defensiveness or resistance and permits the client to view himself objectively. It enables the counselor to develop a satisfactory conversational relationship with the client, encouraging catharsis without intruding his own wishes, desires, or judgments.

Some of the research we have done at Ohio State University with phonographically recorded treatment interviews throws light on this process. Porter has shown, as mentioned before, that nondirective counselors use this technique of recognition of feeling more than any other type of response, contrasting most sharply in this respect with the directive counselors. Royer shows that 42 per cent of the nondirective therapist's responses are of this type, and another 9 per cent are simple acceptance—such responses as "I see," "M-hm," "I understand." These studies would indicate that more than half the time the therapist is introducing nothing new into the situation except clarification of the client's attitudes. Rogers (184) makes a detailed analysis of a number of phonographically recorded interviews, illustrating the way in which feeling is released, defensiveness is largely eliminated, and insight is encouraged, when the therapist sees his function as that of reflecting the client's emotionalized attitudes. Bixler has made the interesting experiment of conducting play therapy with six youngsters, limiting himself as completely as possible to this one type of response, simply clarifying the attitudes expressed. The results were very good in four cases, less satisfactory in two instances.

All of these studies indicate the trend which is clearly apparent in the child guidance field. The therapist is not trying to reform the parent or child. He is not trying to interpret the client to himself, an approach which often brings on resistance. He is not pouring out suggestions or advice. He is using procedures which reveal the client to himself, enabling him to see his own feelings clearly, without the defensive resistance which has always prevented this acceptance of himself. We find this approach typical of work both with the parent and with the child, and used in play therapy as well as in interviewing situations.

We turn now to another aspect of therapy which grows out of the steps thus far described. We find that this process of acceptance and catharsis leads to spontaneous and effective insight on the part of parent and child. Such insight is not the "parrot" type of verbal insight in which the individual has learned some verbal pattern to apply to himself, but it is genuine self-understanding, couched in the individual's own terms. The fact that this does come about spontaneously and is not forced by the therapist is shown in Royer's study of counseling interviews. She found that interpretation by the counselor was almost nonexistent—constituting 3 per cent of the responses as compared with 42 per cent of responses which simply recognize or clarify feelings—but that insightful statements on the part of the client constituted from 10 to 25 per cent of the client responses in some interviews. This study helps to confirm the viewpoint that if the client is enabled to see himself clearly, and to accept his "bad" as well as his "good" impulses and feelings, self-understanding develops without the intervention of the therapist.

It has long been recognized that the development of insight was an essential part of any successful child guidance. The rejecting mother must come to realize both her own attitudes toward the child and the effect these have upon his behavior. The oversolicitous mother needs to realize how satisfying it has been to her to live her child's life for him. Still another parent needs to see how the feelings of inadequacy which the family and the school have built up in the child have resulted in violent and perhaps delinquent compensations. In the past, as records show, the attempt has often been made, mostly unsuccessfully, to give such parents the insight they need. At the present time it is recognized in child guidance work that both parent and child need to *develop* such understandings themselves, and that the therapist's skill is best devoted to the creation of conditions in which insight can easily grow. In the adolescent or adult these insights are likely to be put in verbal terms. In the child such insights may never be clearly verbalized, but may be evident only in the changed goals and actions which result.

These new goals, the self-initiated actions which result from insight, are the crowning characteristics of modern therapy. Obviously there is no point to undertaking therapeutic procedures with either parent or child unless out of these experiences the clients are able to reorganize their lives in ways which are more satisfying, more mature, more socialized. They must undertake a positive redirection of their lives. Does this actually take place?

Again two researches, as yet unpublished, indicate that positive actions and steps do grow out of the sort of therapy described. Lewis, in the study of adolescent girls previously mentioned, shows that after the girl understands a number of the relationships between herself and others, and between various aspects of her own behavior, new plans are made, and actions are redirected toward more socialized and satisfying goals. Royer's study also gives striking confirmation of this fact. In early therapeutic contacts the client responses which are concerned with discussing plans of action, or with making positive decisions, are almost nonexistent. In the later therapeutic contacts, however, there are a significant number of such plans and decisions, and a number of responses which tell of constructive actions already taken. Responses of this sort constitute approximately 7 per cent of the client's responses during the last half of the series of interviews. Therapy clearly has its conclusion in a fresh choice of goal direction and the implementation of that choice in appropriate action.

The points which have been covered touch upon the outstanding features of therapy as it is carried on at the present time. We might, however, miss one important fact which underlies the material given. These various elements, taken together, constitute a definite and predictable therapeutic process, which does not, to be sure, operate satisfactorily in every case, but which does show a high degree of consistency from situation to situation. We are forced to realize that the field of child guidance effort has permanently left behind the opportunistic, well-intentioned attitude toward treatment which dealt with cases by intuition and has substituted a point of view in which a predictable process can be initiated by the therapist with either parent or child or both. The studies just mentioned, by Lewis and Royer, help to define in research terms the essential outlines of this process, while the books by Allen and Rogers describe it in more subjective terms. We may summarize these studies by saying that the skilled therapist now understands how to create a therapeutic relationship which will enable the client to embark on three major types of activity. First is the process of releasing pent-up feeling, the process of catharsis. This is followed by the development of self-understanding, of insight. Out of self-understanding comes the choice of more appropriate goals and the decisions and actions which lead toward those goals, the third step of self-initiated redirection.

Thus far the discussion has been kept on a somewhat abstract level, stressing some of the newer knowledge which we have gained about therapy. Let us take now the situation of Mrs. Jones and her son, coming to the modern child guidance clinic for help, and let us see how these characteristics of therapy express themselves in practical clinical procedure.

When Mrs. Jones arrives, the clinical worker does not take over responsibility for the situation. It is assumed that Mrs. Jones is coming because she feels some need for help, but it is also recognized that she is ambivalent about coming and may be unable to take help. The clinic does not coerce.

If, after explanation, Mrs. Jones decides to come in with her son for treatment help, the mother and son have appointments with different therapists. It may be possible for one person to work with both, but the likelihood of defensiveness, of trying to "put the best foot forward," is greatly increased.

Johnny, her son, in his contacts, is made to feel free to express his attitudes toward his parents, toward other persons and elements in his environment, and toward the clinic and the therapist. He is free to vent his angers by bitter talk, by shooting toy soldiers, by criticizing the clinic equipment, or in any other way which gives free expression to his feelings. The only limitation is upon destructive action which has social consequences. He can hate the therapist, if he wishes, and can destroy a doll which represents him, but he cannot attack the therapist directly. All of John's attitudes are recognized and clarified. The therapist shows his understanding, but he does not criticize, does not approve, does not try to meet the boy's needs himself. If Johnny feels unloved, the worker may recognize this ("You feel that nobody cares about you at all") but he does not try to become a parent substitute. Gradually, as Johnny begins to see himself in a certain way—for example, as a boy who feels very much unloved, and who in return hates his parents and torments them, but turns to others who will give attention—he finds that he has more control over his actions. He begins to see that there are some limited things he could do about his own situation. Perhaps he puts these into words. Perhaps he merely surprises his mother by offering to help her in her housework. A slight, but deeply significant, change takes place.

In her interviews, the mother goes through a parallel experience. For the first time in her life she finds herself able to talk of hidden attitudes which she has never admitted to herself. She does not know how the therapist makes this possible, but the dropping-away of the necessity of defending all her actions is something which is vividly experienced. Gradually she can admit how much she prefers her other child to John. Suddenly it occurs to her, and she can face the thought, that this is one of the reasons why John likes to do mean things just to annoy her. Because of her new understandings, her tone of voice changes when dealing with the boy at home, her discipline loses its slightly sadistic quality, and when John offers to help with the dishes, she is able to respond with a thoroughly sincere expression of her gratitude, and of her affection for him. Freed from the necessity of always being "right," she decides to discard some of the rigid methods she has devised for controlling him and to put their relationship on a more realistic and comfortable basis— a relationship in which each may express annoyance at the other, but in which there is also room for real affection. In her case, as in John's, a release of feeling leads to self-understanding, and this in turn leads to actions directed toward a more satisfying goal—a more genuine, more mature parent-child relationship.

Although these changes may seem small, we find that they are highly effective. As the relationship with his mother is more satisfactory, Johnny's troublesome behavior tends to diminish. As the mother has less need of punishing John to satisfy her own guilt feelings, she finds that he has good qualities, that she does enjoy him at times, and that she feels a real affection for him. The fundamental goals of both mother and child have been significantly altered, and satisfactions are found in constructive rather than destructive ways.

This is the process we call therapy. It develops spontaneously, providing the therapist has the skill to create conditions under which it can take place. To recognize that it is a process, that it can be studied and improved through the methods of scientific analysis and research, is indeed a heartening challenge to workers in the field, whether they be psychologists, psychiatrists, or social workers.

WILLIAM U. SNYDER

Pennsylvania State College

A Short-Term Nondirective Treatment of an Adult[1]

The criticism is frequently made, and justifiably, that articles discussing methods of psychotherapy deal in conceptual abstractions and wholistic interpretations and that they fail to demonstrate what processes actually occur during psychotherapeutic interviews. It is the opinion of the writer that much can be gained from an accurate reporting of the actual psychotherapeutic interview. Frequently interview reports contain such statements as "Said that we should construct a program for dealing with his problem, and he agreed," or "Patient is dissatisfied with his present situation and wishes to change." While such statements may reveal something about the interviews, they practically ignore the real dynamic interplay of ideas between the counselor and the client. Only a nearly verbatim record of the interview can approximate the recording of such processes. It is such a recording that we are presenting here. Of the five interviews, four are reported from notes made by the counselor during the interview; an attempt was made to approximate a verbatim account of the interview. In the other session, the fourth, without the client's knowledge, a phonographic recording was made of everything that transpired. The method of recording interviews is that described by Covner.[2] It was possible to record only this fourth in-

---

[1] Reprinted from *Journal of Abnormal and Social Psychology, Clinical Supplement*, 1943, 38, 87–137. Copyright 1943 by American Psychological Association.
[2] Covner, Bernard J. Studies in the phonographic recordings of verbal material, I and II (50).

terview in this manner. The writer believes, however, that as a result of the care used in taking notes little material of value was lost in the other interviews. All notes were transcribed *immediately* following the respective interview.

The method of therapy used in these interviews is the nondirective system of counseling described by Carl R. Rogers in *Counseling and psychotherapy*.[3] The present article is not an attempt to defend that method of counseling but rather to illustrate it with a record of a case in which the counselor made a very conscientious attempt to follow the system throughout the treatment. The information which the counselor had about the client when treatment began was very brief. He had been told only that his client was a 43-year-old insurance agent who had a problem which he believed was in need of immediate solution by psychological treatment. The case is here presented exactly as recorded by the counselor except where it was necessary to edit names and other identifying data.

Initial Interview (Reported from Notes)
Friday, February 13

Mr. M. started in by describing his problem as a lack of self-confidence which affects his business relationships. He said that the problem seems to be one of making initial interviews. He says that after an initial interview is made he has no trouble in doing a good job. He feels, however, that he is so resistant to the idea of making new contacts that he writes very few insurance policies. The situation is precipitated by its having been suggested that he may be dropped as an agent, even though he has been with the company for fifteen years.

It was recommended by a friend that he come out here, and the appointment was made. Mr. M. wondered whether this was the correct place, and whether we could do anything for him. I explained the setup and the type of nondirective interviews that would take place, and also their voluntary aspect, and the fact that they were

[3] The writer wishes to express sincere gratitude to Dr. Rogers for helpful discussion and criticism of this case, and for the much more important contribution of having first trained the writer in the nondirective method of psychotherapy. For a thorough description of this method the reader is referred to Dr. Rogers' book, *Counseling and psychotherapy* (184). See also an earlier book, *Clinical treatment of the problem child* (183). The writer is also indebted to Dr. Brent N. Baxter for very helpful criticism of the notes.

limited to an hour.[4] Since Mr. M. expressed himself as being in a hurry, I suggested that we could have as many as three interviews a week, although I recommended not more than that number. I asked him whether he wanted to go ahead with it and he said that if I approved he could try. He seemed surprised when I suggested that we begin at once, but went ahead willingly when I suggested that he start by telling me about the problem he had mentioned.

M. I feel that it is a problem of lack of confidence in making the first interview; once a contact is made I can do all right. Probably I do as well as anybody else, then. It is just this dread of starting the interview on the subject of insurance; it even keeps me from making contacts or from going out and looking them up. I resolve the night before that I will do it but I never do it the next day.

S. You feel that this handicap is really a lack of confidence in approaching people for the first time?

M. Yes. Even with friends, I hesitate to talk about life insurance. Sometimes I try to work the conversation about to the point where it would be appropriate to mention insurance, but then I don't go ahead.

S. It seems to be particularly with reference to life insurance that this blocking or fear takes place?

M. Yes. Only if I know they are sympathetic to the idea of insurance am I able to talk about it; otherwise not.

S. (After pause.) Would you care to talk more about that?

---

[4] Because this initial "structuring" or describing of the nature of the interviews was a fairly long speech by the counselor, it was difficult for him to record what he was saying. Some such statement as the following is what usually takes place. "Well, perhaps I ought to tell you what sort of thing we can do here. We can have a series of interviews in which we would talk over this problem and see what conclusions might be reached with regard to it. The things we talk about would be pretty much what you yourself thought was important. You would find that I wouldn't ask many questions and I wouldn't give advice. You see, the sort of thing to be worked out here is a solution which would fit your own problem because it represents your own feelings and attitudes. I can't give you a straightforward answer to your problems, partly because I don't know the answer and partly because what is true for me is probably not true for you. I would want you to feel that these interviews are entirely voluntary. If you feel we aren't solving your problems I want you to tell me so and we will discontinue our meetings. If I should feel that the interviews are unproductive I'll promise to tell you so. Do you think you would like to carry it out on that basis?" This introduction would be followed by a statement of the number of periods available each week for interviews, their limitation to an hour in length, and their confidential nature.

M.   It's a fear of ("rejection" was the idea, but notes are illegible at this part).

S.   Yes (*Pause*). Perhaps you'd like to carry that idea out a little further.

M.   You've really got me digging now. I can't seem to go any further.

S.   I wonder why it seems hard?[5]

M.   I haven't been able to figure that out. I've tried to reassure myself that the worst that can happen is for the fellow to tell me to get out. Or perhaps he just won't talk. But that doesn't do any good; I still might resolve to make the interview, but I'm always afraid to do it.

S.   You feel you've figured out a reasonable answer—that nothing terrible can happen—but that you can't accept the idea emotionally?[6]

M.   Yes. Of course I know other men don't like that job of opening the subject any better than I do. But I feel that those other men have the push and the zip to go ahead and do it anyway.

S.   You feel that others don't like it but they go ahead with it?

M.   Yes. I've discussed it with other people who feel the same way about it, but they go ahead and do it and get it over with. (Here Mr. M. told about a man, the one who sent him out here, who had the same problem in a slightly different aspect of the work. The problem was similar, however; and he seemed to understand Mr. M.'s situation.) Essentially he had the same problem, although the symptoms were slightly different.

S.   You feel that this inability to make contacts is a symptom of something else?

M.   I don't know what it is. I don't remember how I used the word.

---

[5] The counselor referred to the client's effort to make initial contacts, not to his inability to continue in this interview.

[6] The reader may wonder about this sort of statement. For those who are not familiar with the nondirective method of counseling it should be pointed out that one of the principal aims of the counselor is to recognize the feeling (rather than the intellectual content) which is being expressed by the client. Many responses of this type will be observed throughout this case. We propose that the speed of therapy is greatly dependent on the amount of just such recognition of feeling by the counselor.

S.   (*After long pause.*)[7] But you feel that it's puzzling you very much?

M.   Yes. Now when I set my mind to do something I can carry out a long program. Like setting-up exercises. I just decided to do that, and I *have*, every morning since. Then there's pinball machines. I decided I was spending too much time and money on them. So I decided to stop it. I did it positively—that is, it wasn't *stopping*, but walking *past* them that I tried. I can call what I'm going to do on that sort of thing, but when it comes to carrying out a selling campaign after making it up, I know I'm not going to do it. I know those plans aren't real, and won't take place.

S.   So you feel it's hard to visualize yourself really doing it after you plan it?

M.   I can visualize getting up courage, but I can't do it. I tried before and didn't get anywhere. I always know I won't. It's just too tough. It's happened too many times before.

S.   But you have thought about it a lot?

M.   Yes. I can realize how other fellows have the zip, but I don't. I think it may tie up with this. I can't get excited about anything but just getting by. Other people are ambitious and have goals for a lot of dough,[8] but I'm satisfied to be just comfortable. I've read that what you lack sometimes is the goal to drive toward. (Here he described sentiments such as found in Carnegie's book.)

S.   But you feel you are just lacking in motivation.

M.   Yes. So long as I can take care of my family fairly comfortably, that's enough for me. I just don't seem to care about getting lots of dough like most people do. I'd be satisfied to go to a football game any time. Or rather than go to a nightclub, I'd just sit home and read a book. It costs a whole lot less and it's just as much fun.

S.   Then you feel it's sort of a lack of desire on your part?

M.   I don't have the ambition to get anywhere in life.

S.   And you feel this lack of ambition keeps you from getting ahead?

---

[7] A "pause" was a silence lasting somewhere up to about 20 seconds. A "long pause" was any silence lasting from about 20 to 40 seconds.

[8] While this client uses many colloquialisms the reader should not be misled into underestimating his intellectual ability. He is probably a person of rather superior intelligence.

M. Yes. I just don't have any goal. I've read that's what you have to have. I'd like to have more dough, but it's not important.

S. You feel that lack of ambition is the basis of your trouble?

M. It could be. (*Pause.*) I don't know. (*Long pause.*)

S. I wonder whether you've thought much about the origin of your lack of ambition.

M. I haven't any notions.

S. . . . (Notes are confused here and on next statement.)

M. I wonder if it is . . . ?

S. Would you like to talk some about the origin of your problems?

M. Oh, it's my self-consciousness.

S. You feel it keeps you from having the right push?

M. Yes. Is it intelligent, what I'm saying? I never have before. (*Pause.*) Of course, I could talk to my wife about it, but I don't like to take business problems home. My wife's very nervous. Unusually nervous. She'd just worry.

S. You feel you have to work the matter out yourself?[9]

M. Yes. Those things are my problems. It's really not her problem. It's my job to provide the home, and hers to take care of it and keep it nice. She's too nervous for this. She can worry twice as much as I.[10]

S. You feel she would be too much upset by it?

M. Yes. She'd probably feel some worry if she didn't have any. But it's really my problem.

S. You feel you have to work out your own solution to your problem?

M. Which problem? Self-consciousness, or lack of goal and ambition?

S. Perhaps you'd like to talk about one of them; whichever seems more important.

M. I'm pretty near talked out on either of them.

S. You don't feel there's a whole lot to say?

[9] The counselor frequently finds it necessary to respond to a specific item in a statement, but at times he may feel he should respond to the general feeling of the entire statement. It was this last type of response which was used here.

[10] The counselor believed that the client was probably rationalizing his hesitancy to tell his wife about his difficulties. Note, however, that the counselor responded to this statement with a straightforward acceptance at face value.

M. I thought I'd said a lot. I'd like to know what advice you can give me.[11]

S. I think perhaps you'd like to have me give you some sort of cut-and-dried answer or method for solving this thing.

M. If there is one. (*Pause.*) I'm afraid it isn't that simple. No, it can't be figured out without some effort from me, I suppose.[12] I wonder if somebody can show me some way to get some more ambition or motivation? (*Pause.*)

S. Yes?

M. Or else if there's some way that when a person's mental makeup doesn't fit a certain job he can be changed. I know there's something wrong with my mental makeup. It must be mental for you have to think. If it can't be changed, tell me what it does fit me for.[13]

S. I think you sometimes wonder whether you're really in the right field, or whether you ought to switch over to something else.[14]

M. That's right. I've done everything I can to make a go of this job.

S. You feel you've worked pretty hard at trying to make it go . . . ?

M. At trying to make myself do a better job. I haven't tried to sell more; only to make myself get over this problem. That's it. (*Pause.*) It seems to be an insurmountable problem. Yes.

S. (*After long pause.*) But you feel you've tried every means you know of to understand it?

M. Yes, in the sense that I've tried to figure out all sorts of ingenious methods of avoiding this first contact. If I can have that arranged successfully I do a good job. I didn't realize that at first. I've tried to think of ways for pointing out that they should be interested. (Here he discusses a sale, his best one, where after contact-

---

[11] This is the first of numerous occurrences of the theme that the client has come for advice; it is a common one in almost all counseling situations. But the counselor does not take the most obvious course of giving some sort of advice. Neither does he meet the situation with an adequate restructuring of the nature of the interview, although such a procedure would have been appropriate at this point. It is not until the third interview that a fair restructuring takes place.

[12] Here the client himself gives the most adequate reason why the counselor should not drop the nondirective role and start to give advice.

[13] See footnote 11.

[14] This and the next three statements of the counselor are probably better-than-average recognitions of the deeper feeling of the client.

ing a man who became interested in Mr. M.'s little girl, he sold forty thousand dollars worth of insurance. He revised the man's whole program, much to the man's satisfaction.) I really do a lot of work on the problem of working out insurance programs. Most men sell one contact out of ten, but I think I sell half my contacts. Of course, my trouble is I don't make enough contacts, because I don't try to get new ones; I only contact those who are sympathetic to the idea of insurance. Also I've tried to read articles and force myself to do unpleasant things . . . (there follows a lengthy section of his early work as an industrial agent, selling by high pressure methods; he was made an assistant supervisor at that. But he didn't like it because of unfair methods. Also, he says, after the policy is worked out, he hates to deliver it to the people; but this is only because it's a boring detail.) Gee, you've got me worked around to the point where I'm doing a lot of bragging.

S. You feel, though, that when you can get out of this difficult initial interview your work is better than that of most agents.

M. At least as good. I did well because the sale was half made. The place was well picked. But you can't make any money if you only take the hand-picked ones. I've listened to other agents' tales about their high-pressure methods, but it doesn't seem possible.

S. You feel it isn't possible to believe such things?

M. No. That is, I can't imagine myself ever doing anything like that. I guess they're more forceful. They have to be really good, for they make the sales.

S. You feel you know pretty well what you should do, but you just can't see any results?

M. I don't understand your question.

S. You don't see how you'd be able to do the same thing.

M. I haven't been able to figure out a way, but there must be some way. (*Pause.*) That's why I'm here. (*Very long pause.*)

S. Perhaps you might like to discuss when you first noticed this problem of starting interviews.[15]

M. I've always had it as far as I know. (*Long pause.*)

S. You feel it's been with you pretty much your entire life?

M. I'm trying to think how far back I can remember it. I know

---

[15] It is questionable whether it would not have been better to recognize the feeling of the previous statement, rather than to use this directive attempt to probe for information.

I was that way in high school. For example, they tried to force me to be in a play, but I got conveniently sick. But when I did come back the teacher forced me to do it anyway. Then it went all right.

S. You feel that under compulsion you can do that sort of thing much better?

M. No, it doesn't seem to have much effect.[16] Perhaps I do better if I'm not pushed. But I've outgrown that now. I've made talks at conventions. That is, when I actually did a little selling. I was master-of-ceremonies at a high-school football banquet. I did pretty well, too, and I enjoyed it. But that was because I spent lots of time and prepared it well.

S. You feel that you have self-confidence when you know that you are prepared to give something people will appreciate?

M. Yes. *That* has something to do with my selling, *too*. When I'm prepared ahead of time, when I know it's going to fit the person's circumstances, then it's all right. I know the situation, then. I've had the time to work it out.

S. M-hm.[17] It's lots easier then, isn't it?

M. I just don't seem to think fast under pressure. I gotta have time to work things out. To reason it out. To satisfy myself about things. (*Long pause.*)

S. Well, I see that our time's up.[18] Normally I'd see you Tuesday, but since I'll be away part of next week, would you like to come in tomorrow, as I mentioned earlier?

M. I'll do whatever you want. Do you feel we've accomplished something?[19] Of course I know you shouldn't ask that the first day.

---

[16] A good example of the rejection of the counselor's interpretation. The interpretation may have been accurate or inaccurate, but the client was not in a situation where he was prepared to face the issue; the counselor had either missed the feeling or had interpreted it in a light which threatened the security of the client's self-esteem.

[17] Phonetic spelling of the sound made in accepting or agreeing with a statement.

[18] The counselor takes responsibility for bringing the interview to a close. At times this is met with resistance. How to respond to such resistance is a question of theoretical importance. For discussions of the significance of the time-barrier the reader is referred to Rank, Otto: *Will therapy* (179); Taft, Jessie: *The dynamics of therapy* (217); and Rogers, C. R.: *Counseling and psychotherapy* (184).

[19] Two significant occurrences: First, the client makes attempts to shift responsibility to the counselor; he wants to be told to come in for treatment. Secondly, the client attempts to force a statement of evaluation of the interview.

But I wonder how far we've gone.

S.   Let's talk about that the next time we meet. Do you want to come in tomorrow?

M.   Well, this is awfully important. I come in fifty miles,[20] but I'd like to get it done as fast as we can.

S.   Then we'll make it tomorrow at three.

Second Interview (Reported from Notes)
Saturday, February 14

S.   Well, I wonder how things have been going?

M.   How do you mean?

S.   I mean I wonder what you have been thinking about in the past twenty-four hours.

M.   I thought you might ask me that, and I've been thinking about a number of things. Perhaps I've come to some screwy conclusions. I thought you might expect me to say something about them so I wrote them down.[21]

S.   That's fine.[22] (*Mr. M. takes out two small pages of notes.*)

M.   I'll just read these off without doing much commenting. I believe it is not only first contacts which cause me this difficulty. It is new or strange elements in any situation, or any situation itself which is a new one. The only time when I don't feel this way is when I know in advance what is expected of me. It's not the fear. At least I can't analyze it as a fear. I just don't want to do the thing. For instance, I'll illustrate in something apart from business. Every year, you know, we have business conventions. Well, we usually have them at the ——— Hotel. But sometimes we have them some-

---

This lack of willingness to accept responsibility is sometimes thought to be especially common among certain neurotic persons. Note the response of the counselor. In a kindly manner he nevertheless refused to accept this responsibility. The value of this refusal will be seen later in this case, where the client actually recognizes that the clinician's refusal has therapeutic value.

[20] A statement which has significant bearing on the question of whether the client is in need of therapy.

[21] The client's making notes between interviews is not an uncommon occurrence with this type of therapy.

[22] An example of reassurance. It is probably a good thing, if held in proper discretion, to recognize and commend any real attempts of the client to proceed in the direction of accepting responsibility for his own treatment. Also, whenever he has made real progress toward self-understanding a little encouragement may be beneficial. It must be used with care, however, if the client is not to become dependent on this reassurance.

place else. Now I don't like it when they are held in other places. I don't like to go because it will be strange and I won't meet the same people in the same familiar places. Then here's another illustration. I love to go to baseball games up in ———— (city). But sometimes they hold them at the stadium, and then I don't like to go. I like it only when they hold it at the ———— (park). I feel at home there. There's a place for me to park, and I know just what to do. Another thing I do, I just realized this, I'm always trying to give a reason for the things I do so that it will sound acceptable to the other person. It's never a reason for myself, but one that will be satisfactory to others. For example, I told my wife . . . I decided I had to explain why I was coming down here . . . I told her about a certain manager in insurance, a very famous manager, who had some troubles and went to a psychiatrist and became much more successful because of it, or at least after it. But you see, that's really just an excuse. Don't you think so?[23]

S. That's a very good interpretation of it.

M. Yes, I think so. I didn't say that I really wanted to do it, that is come here. I made up a reason that would satisfy others. It was an alibi. It's funny, I wasn't going to bring these notes in with me.

S. I'm glad you did. (*M. goes on looking at notes.*)

M. I believe the only things I do are the things I enjoy, or those that I have to do because I'm afraid of the consequences of not doing them. It's a fear of what happens if I don't. (*Pause.*) No, that probably isn't true. I do some things to make myself look good to others.

S. You feel you do some things to get others to increase their estimate of you?

M. I often wonder if I make this special effort to be of service in my underwriting because I believe that it is something that the clients have bought and paid for, or because I think it makes me look smarter than the other insurance agents. I wonder, because I know it's my practice to put things off unless they absolutely have to be done. (*Puts notes in his pocket.*)

———————

[23] This entire statement seems to show that a good bit of careful thinking has been done by the client during the interval since the last session. He has achieved some insight into his own behavior. Note that the counselor again responds with supportive praise.

S.   Well, you seem to have been doing a good bit of thinking about this.

M.   Yes, I have. By the way, just as a question, I wanted to ask whether there is any chance of these records falling into other hands. I've assumed, of course, that it wouldn't be allowed to happen. But I know I'd be hesitant to talk if I wasn't sure. It would slow me up considerably.

S.   No, you won't have to worry about that.[24] These are just my personal notes, which I use to remind me of what we talked about. See (*showing them*) your name isn't anywhere on them. I fix it that way so that if they should be lost or someone would take them from my notebook, they still wouldn't learn anything about any particular person. As I mentioned yesterday, those notes are just for me, and for you to read if you feel inclined to do so. Any time you wish to do so, you have the privilege of going through them. Perhaps later you might find *that* a helpful thing to do. (*Long pause.*)[25]

S.   Well, you seem to have covered a lot of ground in your thinking. I wonder what sort of conclusions you have made about these ideas you thought out.

M.   I don't know. I seem to be confused. I've wondered if I know what I think. Yesterday I had my problems down pat, but today I'm not sure about them.

S.   You feel now you aren't sure just where you stand?

M.   I've wondered if it wasn't a foolish idea to try to think about it. It makes me all confused. I'm depending on you to get me out of it.[26] It doesn't mean much of anything to me. I don't see where

---

[24] There is, of course, an ethical issue involved in this statement by the counselor. Sometimes an agreement is made with a client that the use of such records by the counselor for research purposes is a part of the bargain offered in the free treatment. In this particular case it was felt that this understanding might affect rapport. On the basis of medical and other precedent, the counselor believed that, inasmuch as he was making a very conscientious effort to keep this client's identity confidential, he was not violating the client's trust by using these notes for research purposes, or for present publication.

[25] Letting the client read the notes is an interesting technique. A later statement by this particular client suggests that this procedure had a degree of therapeutic value in this case. It was for this purpose that the counselor had used this method. Such use required, of course, that the notes be restricted to a verbatim account of the interview.

[26] See footnote 19.

I'm further along. I can't reach any sort of conclusions. If I do I almost instantaneously change my mind. Perhaps it's because I'm afraid of the conclusions.[27]

S. Do you feel you sort of try to rationalize things?[28]

M. Yes. I didn't realize it till I started to think about it. I don't know why. It makes me wonder if I have enough courage to face problems.

S. I think perhaps you feel sometimes you're afraid to stand on your own feet.

M. I don't know. It may be so. At least I don't say anything except in trying to explain things so others will be satisfied.

S. Perhaps you feel you're overly dependent on their opinions?[29]

M. Well, I want them to feel that I'm doing things right. That's near to it. I say it in such a way that they won't criticize it.

S. Perhaps you're afraid somewhat of criticism or argument?

M. No. (*Pause.*) Not honestly afraid. Perhaps I worry a little though. Of course I really don't worry enough about things. Maybe not enough about this, either.

S. I wonder if you feel you worry less about this than other people do?

M. Yes, I do. (*Pause.*) Most of these things have occurred to me since I've been talking to you.

S. So it's sort of an effort to scrutinize yourself?

M. That's right. (*Long pause.*)

S. Perhaps you'd like to carry that point further? (*Long pause.*) Maybe it might be a good idea to work on some of the ideas you have in your notes you brought in.

M. (*Looks at his paper.*) Well, I'll tell you something about this first idea. This sounds absolutely nuts. I'm ashamed to tell you about it. I wouldn't tell anyone else. If you'd tell my friends I did this sort of thing, they'd call you a liar. Here's how it was.

----

[27] This seems to be another incident of very good recognition by the client of his possible weaknesses. See footnote 23.

[28] Although asked as an informational question, this was an attempt to recognize or interpret the preceding statement of the client.

[29] This is an interpretation which goes beyond the mere recognition of feelings. Similar interpretations occur throughout the rest of the case. Their theoretical significance is discussed in Rogers' *Counseling and psychotherapy.* It is probably true, in general, that interpretation borders on the directive method of counseling and should be used very judiciously if the counselor does not wish to arouse hostility or negativism on the part of the client.

Yesterday after the appointment was made I had to hang around for two hours till it was time to come to see you. So I thought I'd drop down to the —— (restaurant and bar) and read the papers or something. I've done that before. But when I got there I saw that they had a hat-check girl. They never had one before. Or rather, I'd always been staying at that hotel, so I didn't have a hat with me. But just the idea of having to check a hat was too much for me so I turned around and left. Then I came out here and wandered around the campus. Of course that was terribly silly. But it seemed so strange and new. You'll think I'm crazy. Or else that I never saw a hat-check girl before. But I really have been big places before, you know. (*Both laugh.*)[30]

S. Perhaps this little incident is symbolic of something?[31]

M. Maybe it's symbolic that I'm nuts. Not being able to do a simple thing like that.

S. I wonder how you might interpret it?

M. I *don't*.

S. How *would* you?

M. I don't know what it means. These things just seem strange to me.

S. You feel that something which is strange is more or less fearful?

M. It's just that *feeling* that I get. Other people wouldn't think I could do that sort of thing.

S. Perhaps you yourself even feel it's a strange sort of thing?

M. No, it's the way I do things. (*Pause.*) Oh, I don't know. I sometimes do things only because of fear of not doing them. Somebody else wouldn't lower himself that way.

S. You feel it's sort of a generalized reaction of yours?

M. Yes. I just don't usually check hats. I've been other places where you do, but not there before. That's where I get that idea that it's something new in an old situation.

---

[30] Here the symptom picture reaches its most serious stage. This last paragraph is offered as evidence of the severity of the neurosis.

[31] This and the counselor's next two responses seem to be a very injudicious effort to force a painful self-evaluation. Quite naturally it is strenuously resisted. The counselor was so much impressed by the significance of the previous revelation that he lost the nondirective focus. A more appropriate response might have been some such recognition of feeling as, "You feel that this was a pretty unusual sort of thing to do, is that it?"

S.   I think you feel more or less ashamed to admit that you do that sort of thing.

M.   Yes. That was the most exaggerated example.

S.   And you feel that it's typical of much that you do?

M.   Yes. I like ball games. It's just that when the place is different I don't like that trouble you have to go to.

S.   Perhaps it's not exactly fear you feel, but more or less of an anxiety.

M.   Well, yes. I'm sort of groping around here. I sometimes wonder if I don't want to appear natural. I don't want to show a lack of experience in new situations. Does that make sense?

S.   How do you feel about it?

M.   I believe I've got something here.

S.   I believe you have, too.

M.   Sometimes I wonder in my own mind if I'm not very much self-centered.[32] For instance, I always think other people are looking at me when I go anywhere, and wondering about me. But I know they're really not.

S.   You often feel people are interested in you, when you are in a strange group, but you really know that that isn't true.

M.   That's right. (Pause.)

S.   Perhaps you'd like to carry that idea a little further.

M.   I think it hooks up with my doing something, if someone's along, so as to make a favorable influence on their opinion of me. If no one is along I don't have to please anybody. Then I'm happy.

S.   I think you feel you are very sensitive to the criticism of others.

M.   Yes. I don't enjoy leisure or any sort of pleasure unless I can be doing things well. Maybe I like to show off.

S.   You feel somewhat frustrated by not appearing to the best advantage?

M.   I think that's true. (Long pause. S. was about to suggest that M. look at his notes.) Let's look and see if there's anything else here. (Looks.) I guess I do things to seem smarter than the other fellow. I'm not sure whether I offer these careful services to policyholders because I think it's right, or just to show off. It's hard to make an honest judgment of yourself that way.

---

[32] Another example of a willingness of the client to face personal weaknesses. See footnotes 23 and 27.

S.   You feel perhaps your idea of why you do things isn't always correct; perhaps sometimes you feel ambiguous about your motives.

M.   Yes. I like to think I'm not completely selfish. For example, on the ride down here my wife asked me—she came along for the ride—she asked me if I'd take her down town and let her do some shopping while I was up here. Now I got real pleasure from going out of my way to do that for her. So I wonder if I do things because I like to or because I'm unselfish; maybe it wasn't unselfish, but why did I do it? It made me very happy. Perhaps I'm not so bad.

S.   You feel perhaps your motives aren't too selfish, then.

M.   Well, they're self-centered. But I do things cheerfully for her and the kids.

S.   Perhaps you don't approve of one's being self-centered.

M.   Not if they're always selfish. I feel sorry for that sort of person. (Pause.) I'm not certain about this. It's hard to make an unbiased opinion, isn't it?

S.   Yes, I believe sometimes it is. Perhaps you sort of feel one can't always be sure about his own motives?

M.   I'm trying to dig it out, but I can't always decide. I think a person has a tendency to figure out excuses for himself. I might tell you uncomplimentary things about myself, and then I wonder if I'm trying to find excuses for myself.

S.   You feel you sometimes might protect yourself from honest judgments?

M.   Yes. I feel the same way in making excuses for my wife and kids. Maybe I'm just selfish. I don't know how honest a person can be in forming self-criticisms.

S.   Sometimes you recognize that you want to protect yourself?

M.   No. I might have a tendency to blame my troubles on others but whenever I see myself doing it I try to stop it. That is whenever I see I'm doing it.

S.   So you feel you try to be honest, and to avoid self-defense?

M.   Yes, I do. I can't help but think, here I am talking to you. Is it a way of putting something off, or am I really honest in being here?[33] Do I really want to find the answer? I wish I knew. My head gets in a whirl thinking about it.

---

[33] See footnote 4. The recognition which follows this statement seems to be a rather good one because it gets at the depth of the feeling.

S.   You feel coming in might perhaps be an effort to avoid facing your problems.

M.   Yes. I'm trying to throw it into somebody else's lap. I might have to do it myself. A lot of these things are questions. I don't know the answers. I try to figure it out. I think I'm honest. I've read enough, not in real psychology, but in popular books on applied psychology. I got my idea about visualization of ideas from a book back in 1916. Then I read it again last summer in *Reader's Digest*. I thought it must be out of date by now, but it's still being published. (*Long pause.*) I think I've read enough. I'm satisfied there's some merit in the scientific principles back of psychology. I should be able to get some help out of it.

S.   You feel perhaps psychology can help you to understand yourself?

M.   It can't help you to understand if you still feel yourself in some muddle after you've tried to analyze yourself. That's why I've come to you. You can help me where I can't do it myself. (*Pause.*)[34]

S.   You feel analyzing yourself has not been particularly helpful?

M.   Talking about yourself does help. You get further by doing something, even though the party you were talking about didn't know any more about psychology than you did yourself. But psychology would have the advantage of helping you to be honest with yourself.

S.   So you feel a technical knowledge is helpful in understanding your problems?

M.   On your side, but not on mine. It might help me but I couldn't do it alone, even if I did know it. You probably couldn't handle your own problems alone, though you have the technical training. It's having some one else to help work it out that counts. Don't you think that's pretty good philosophy?

S.   Yes, I think it's very good. Very well worked out.[35]

M.   I've often wondered. I believe I'd get a terrible kick out of studying psychology. (*Long pause.*) I seem to have run out of ideas.

S.   Perhaps you might look at your notes for some ideas.

M.   There's nothing more there. I've decided that it was all used up. (*Pause.*)

---

[34] The client again expresses his dependence on the counselor.
[35] Supportive praise. See footnote 22.

S.   Maybe we might talk about your problem.

M.   I'm not sure I know what it is. I knew when I came in. Now I don't know but that maybe it's just that I put things off. Even easy things, as long as I can.

S.   (*After pause.*) I wonder if you put pleasant things off?

M.   I put off getting ready for them.

S.   How do you mean?

M.   I wouldn't buy a ticket for anything in advance of when it has to be done. I don't do anything before it has to be done.

S.   . . . (Illegible notes.)

M.   I don't want to plan in advance. It ties me up. I never thought of it before.

S.   I wonder if you feel this has any bearing on your *problem?*

M.   Maybe the thing I said was the outgrowth of putting off most everything over a long period of years.[36] I haven't been able to get myself to do things I don't want to do. I've known that at least since I was fifteen years old.

S.   You feel perhaps this symbolized your real problem?

M.   Could be. I don't know. Yesterday I was confident of my problem. But that was the immediate one. It may be that the other one is really back of it. I've always done it since I was in high school. Even after high school. I had a job, but when the war came along I enlisted in the Navy. I wasn't called right away and my job started to go to pot. Maybe I'm getting right into something I don't understand. After I knew I wasn't going in right away my work just dragged along. Finally I got sick of it and went down to ————— (city) to the Marine Corps and asked them to get me out of the Navy and let me enlist with them so I could get started right away. That illustrates how I do things. Perhaps I was only trying to get away from my work, and not really to get into the Navy and do my duty.

S.   You think perhaps you were just trying to avoid your work?

M.   I don't know. It's too far back. I really can't say. I won't try to make conclusions unless I know the answer. That is, just to try to give you one. I'm commencing to wonder.

S.   You feel perhaps it's very confusing, and that you're more befuddled?

---

[36] The client is again recognizing his weaknesses; he has reached a point of rather good insight. It is carried further in the paragraph which follows the counselor's response to this statement.

M.   That's right. I wonder. How about you, do you feel I'm getting more confused?

S.   No, I don't think so. You've done some pretty deep thinking, I feel.

M.   I certainly hope you can see which way the answer lies.

S.   You feel perhaps you can't recognize the problem yourself?

M.   No. (*Pause.*) I don't know when I'm thinking the right thing. Sometimes my ideas are contradictory.

S.   I think sometimes it's a good idea to try to study out our motivations. When we're not sure what we think, that sometimes makes it easier to see the answer to our behavior.[37]

M.   But I don't seem to have any motivations. That's the trouble. They're just lacking entirely.

S.   I think it's an interesting debate whether it is true that anyone is ever really unmotivated.

M.   Yes, that's true. A person always has a decision to make. You have to do something. Either you *do* go, or you *don't*. I make too many negative answers. Well, that idea about too many negative answers isn't original with me. I read it in a book. But then, *nothing's* new. Like a puzzle I solved for a fellow. How to make "II=VI" a true equation by moving only one match-stick. I figured it out as "I=$\sqrt{\text{I}}$." Then later I happened to see a book I'd read once which gave the answer.

S.   That happens sometimes, doesn't it. (*Pause.*) I see our time's up. Shall we plan on next Tuesday?

M.   Well, since you're going to be away the latter part of the week, I wondered if we could make it Monday and Wednesday?

S.   I think perhaps that can be arranged. At least the first one on Monday. Let's make it Monday at three, and we'll see about Wednesday later.

Third Interview (Reported from Notes)
Monday, February 16

S.   Well, how have things been going?

---

[37] A very directive statement. The counselor at this point actually tries to hurry the therapeutic process by pointing out his own viewpoints on the subject. In his following statement he carries this technique far beyond the limits of a nondirective approach. Fortunately the client does not resist this attempt, so that the therapeutic process is not blocked by hostility as a result of this incident.

M. I don't know. I'm wondering when you're going to start doing the talking?[38]

S. How much do you feel I ought to say?

M. Nothing, I guess, till you feel I've given you something to talk about. Apparently you don't, for you don't say anything. Well, I thought about this thing a lot yesterday. I was busy today and didn't have much time. But I decided yesterday that I gave you three conclusions, and that none are exactly right. The first was that I have a tendency to put things off; everything, that is. Well, that can't be true, or it would end in complete inactivity. I don't want that. I have to have something to do. I can't just sit still. But I do have a tendency to put some things off. What I wonder is, what is it that makes up the things I tend to put off?

S. You feel that there is some sort of differential which causes you to put off certain types of things?

M. Yes. It can't be the physical activity, for I usually do the one that requires the most physical activity. And I don't think it's mental. No, I like to play around with mental problems. I like bridge better than to sit and talk. I like reading that makes me think. I don't know what the answer is. Apparently it's the things I think are going to be unpleasant. But the trouble is I don't know what it is that makes them seem unpleasant.

S. But you feel it's the fact that some things are unpleasant that makes you put them off?

M. Yes. I don't know. I can't analyze it. For example, such little things as delivering a finished policy. I'll put that sort of thing off for a long time when there's no real reason why I should.

S. You feel perhaps there's something unpleasant about it but you don't know what it can be?

M. I can't see how it would be. Maybe it's just a habit. But then how did I get into it? And when?

S. You feel perhaps it's something you picked up that you've just been unable to get over?

---

[38] A very open effort to shift responsibility of the interview. Presumably we may say that the situation has not been structured adequately for the client, who is still expecting the more usual type of directive treatment. The response to this statement is entirely inadequate. A much more adequate response would have been, "Perhaps I ought to remind you of my original description of what we can do here, etc." Then the counselor should repeat the fundamental elements of the "structuring of the interview," as outlined in footnote 4.

M.   I don't know. I can't get the answer. That's as far as I got on that. What was the second thing I told you? There were two or three other things I told you here. I can remember the third, but not the second. But they seemed to come in logical order.

S.   You said the first was that you have a tendency to put off unpleasant jobs.

M.   That's right. I remember. The second was that I shy away from new situations or new elements or new persons. But that isn't exactly true, because I like new problems. For example, in life insurance I like to have a man lay down his problem and then let me work out the best way of meeting it. These are all new situations that need to be handled separately.

S.   So you feel that it's not entirely true that you shy away from anything new?

M.   No, not exactly true. I can't decide. Exactly what type of strange things it is, I'm not sure.

S.   Perhaps there's some common characteristic that would fit the ones you avoid?

M.   I've tried to figure it out but I don't get any answer at all. Is this the kind of thing you want me to do?

S.   Yes, that's right.

M.   I'm trying to clarify my conclusions, but I'm not getting very far. It seems to leave me with a lot of loose threads.

S.   You don't feel you're getting it very well organized?

M.   No, not at all. There doesn't seem to be much daylight in it.

S.   You feel it's still pretty much confused to you?

M.   Yes, it's worse than when I started. I was terribly amazed when you said Saturday that perhaps we were getting someplace. (*Pause.*) The third thing was, I wondered whether—it was a conclusion first, then a question—whether I don't try to give people reasons to satisfy them for the things I do. What is my reason for doing these things? What's my motivation? Is it simply the hope of getting approval or the fear of getting disapproval? That has been answered since Saturday.[39] It answers itself. If it satisfied

---

[39] It might be interjected that a great deal of important thinking occurs in the interval between interviews. And this is one reason why it is quite possible that interviews should not be at too rapid a frequency. It seems probable that twice a week is frequent enough in most cases. See Rogers' *Counseling and psychotherapy.*

somebody, I wouldn't have to give reasons. I must have had some other reason. It answers itself.

S.   You feel perhaps the reasons you give only partly explain the actual reasons you have?

M.   Yes. I've tried to dig back into the things that have happened, as far as I can remember. In my own mind, I couldn't get any place. Do you want me to go over it?

S.   How do you feel about it?

M.   I don't know. I didn't get any place. I can remember things as far back—well, here's an example—when did I start putting things off? The last year in grade school I did my work pretty well; in fact they asked me to skip one grade, so I must have been doing things when I was supposed to. It musta' been in high school. It took me four and one-half years to do the high-school course. Though, when I graduated I was fourth in my class. Of course, there were only twenty. Maybe something happened in high school. I don't know. I had one year of college; University of ————. I was a straight "A" student. I must have been doing things when I should back then.

S.   You feel you have had times when things went well?

M.   I've been trying to figure out if this thing is inherited, or if I got it when I was too young to know any better, or later when I grew up. Perhaps not before I put in the first year of school. In between high school and college I put in twenty-two months in the Marine Corps. That went well.

S.   So you feel you must have been meeting your responsibilities pretty well, then.

M.   There's only one thing I can think of myself as an outside influence. I was the youngest boy in a large family. I had a younger sister. I was the only one who went in the service. Naturally, I became a little tin god around the house. Even with my father and mother. When I was in France my younger sister died. I came back the baby of the family. The rest were all married comfortably. My one brother was quite well fixed. And my sister married a well-fixed man. In fact, he paid all my expenses in college. Maybe that thing of being so important went to my head. Maybe having everybody waiting on me that way made me so spoiled that I haven't been able to get along since without that attention. Maybe I haven't been able to stand not having people insisting on taking care of me and looking up to me.[40] It might have affected my whole life.

S.   You feel that attention and extra consideration may have had a pretty marked influence on your life?

M.   It might have been the breaking-off point. I don't know whether that's what's broken me up or not. Here's what's happened since. I was an auto salesman for three years but I wasn't successful. In fact I was a flop. Then I became an accountant at ———— (corporation), and I did very well, there. That is, I did very well by the company, but not by myself. I had such poor relations with my boss that I lost the job. I made the auditor mad because I made suggestions, and didn't take him into consideration. He complained that he couldn't get along with me and since he had been there twenty years I had to go. But they took my suggestions about revising their setup there. I recognize that it was my own fault that I lost that job, although at the time I didn't think so. Then I had six months with an industrial life-insurance company. I was barely hanging on there and I didn't want to hang on. The superintendent insisted I try. Then I left that and got another job. Another agent helped me and I did very well. In fact I was the second largest producer in ———— (area). In fact, I got promoted to assistant superintendent. The first year I had the best record. The second year was a big bust. Maybe it's an alibi, but I blame that on the superintendent moving to ———— (city). I couldn't get along with the new one.

S.   You feel your personalities weren't compatible?

M.   I don't know. Probably it was my own fault. I was working for *him*. Although then I didn't think it was my fault. Then I had about—I'd been in life insurance for about fourteen years. Four years were pretty good, six I barely made a living, and four I didn't make a living. I haven't brought in much about this past part because I didn't think it was important. My trouble happened earlier.

S.   You feel that the course of your problems was determined at an earlier period?

M.   Seems so. I wasn't accomplishing anything some time ago. I can go to most anybody that wants a salesman and convince him I'm the man, and then after I get the job, I can't keep it.

---

[40] The client's insight here has become pretty clear. He will later relapse slightly, but only temporarily.

S. You feel there's some sort of blocking that keeps you from doing your best?

M. I don't know. That's what I'm trying to find out. (*Pause.*) Another illustration is this. Persuade some employer to take the premiums out of the pay checks regularly. I've sold four employers on that. There are ten other men in the agency and all the rest of them have only two all together. But I haven't got half as much business as any one of them could have.

S. You feel that there's something wrong that keeps you from getting ahead?

M. I can't seem to do the things they do without having very much trouble. Here's another example. One of these employers has 350 employees. I get $250 per month in premiums. But $160 all comes from one man. Why can't I get the other guys to take more? They're the ones really need it. But I don't do it. I sit around and tell myself these things, but I might as well admit I'm a failure.

S. You feel your experiences at selling have been pretty much a failure?

M. Can't be anything else. My education's better than these other guys, too. But some do more than I do. It's because they work harder.

S. You feel your trouble is that you just don't work hard enough?

M. That's right.

S. It makes you feel pretty much disgusted with yourself?[41]

M. I feel so helpless because I don't know how to make myself do it right.

S. You feel that to learn some way of forcing yourself is the answer to the problem?

M. I think so. (*Pause.*) I said my problem was in going out to see these people, but now I'm not sure that it is. If there is some way I can find of correcting my personality or disposition, or character; or had I better get out and get into something that I'm better fitted for? Frankly I don't know.

S. Sometimes you think maybe there is something that can be done to help you change, but sometimes you think the only way would be to get into some other line of work?

---

[41] Probably an erroneous interpretation; it was not accepted.

M. That's right. That's what I'm not sure of. I don't know enough about why a human mind or a man's personality works as it does. What is it that gives them push and zip? I can't decide if it's possible to change. Or whether I ought to have somebody tell me it's impossible. I'm asking for some reasonable answers from scientific and technical experience.

S. I think perhaps you're trying to throw it off onto me to decide what you ought to do.

M. No, I'm trying to get you to tell me what to do to fix myself. Just like if I went to a doctor. Tell me if it's something that can be taken care of. Perhaps it's incurable. Can a psychologist tell me what I ought to do to fix myself?[42]

S. Perhaps you feel that you really can't change yourself?

M. I wouldn't say I can't. Maybe there is no answer. I haven't reached any conclusions.

S. I think perhaps you want me to give you some cut-and-dried answer that will tell you what you can or can't do. I wonder whether the question isn't whether if I gave you such an answer you would accept it from me?[43]

M. Well, I guess you'd have to back it up a little bit.

S. I'd have to prove some way that I was right?

M. Not necessarily to prove. That might be very difficult to do. It might be necessary for me to take a course in psychology to understand you. But I'd expect you to explain your reasons. I don't think I'd believe it the way I should to have it do me any good, unless you did.

S. But when we first started I mentioned that you never would get any answer like that. That it was something that couldn't be given.

M. I thought you would say, "This is what I think is wrong with you." You would outline a general program or course I would

---

[42] At this point the counselor was offered a fine opportunity to "restructure" the counseling setup, i.e., to redefine the part he is to play in the interviews and the responsibility which the client must carry.

[43] The theory here expressed is good, but the expression is too abrupt. In previous cases it has been observed that the client seems to be unable to accept such advice, but it is not likely that he will understand this fact at the present stage of treatment. That he sees this point at least partially, however, is indicated in the discussion which follows about the necessity for proof. Herein is the major criticism of the giving of advice; such a procedure rests upon the prestige of the counselor and tends, apparently, to stimulate a negativistic reaction on the part of the client, i.e., an effort to show the counselor that he is wrong.

have to do to change my personality. Then it would be up to me
to decide whether it was worth while.

S.   But you want me to hold out an answer?

M.   Don't you feel it would do me good if you would tell me the
answer? Perhaps you already know it.[44]

S.   The reason that I can't tell you an answer is that I doubt if
you would be able to accept it. That's why I want to see the answer
come from you, yourself.

M.   It seems to me tough the way I might have to wander
around here. I keep wandering around in a circle.[45]

S.   I wonder why?

M.   I don't know.

S.   Is it perhaps an example of the sort of disguise you spoke of
before; where you do some things to avoid the real reason?[46]

M.   I can't seem to work that in in any way. What I said was
that I give reasons that may not be real reasons. I do do that. There
isn't any argument. What I can't get is the reason why I'll sit here
and lay out a whole day's work and then I'll figure all kinds of
reasons why I shouldn't do it.

S.   You feel you keep going around?

M.   Sure, but why?

S.   You feel, perhaps, in your thinking here you're groping
around and haven't covered any ground.

M.   I can't see any. I know people who are successful in some

---

[44] It becomes more and more apparent that the client feels the counselor
knows the answer but isn't willing to give it. The counselor himself, in his next
statement, further strengthens this impression. He would have done better to
say something to the effect that "Any answer I might give is the kind of thing
I would do, but it isn't probable that it would fit your problems, for you are a
different individual: that's why we have to work together until we find what
you yourself think is the best thing to do."

[45] The client's well-justified resentment is rather openly expressed here; he
feels he is being allowed to wander around alone. It is obvious that the situation
had not been adequately explained to him. The counselor's response to his last
statement is a very inappropriate sort of directive question which could not be
expected to assist the therapeutic process. It appears that the counselor has
allowed himself to be annoyed by the client's reproach, and is saying in effect
"Well, it's your own fault, isn't it?" Quite naturally the client is not going to
be taken in on such an implication.

[46] The counselor here actually makes a very direct implication although he
masks it in an innocent-looking question. Although perhaps the counselor is
quite correct, it is noteworthy that the client rejects the idea completely. That
is, we believe, very typical of the sort of response one may expect for the majority
of directive or coercive interpretations.

job. With the exception of one, they seem to have something to keep them going. There doesn't seem to be any difference except that I don't have it.

S. You feel you need to find that one thing that is lacking?

M. Maybe it isn't one thing. I don't know. All I know is, they work and I don't. When I was assistant superintendent I had a man working for me who was just like me. When I was pushing him he was the best agent. I was steamed up for a year. When I went to the dogs, he went faster. Now he's in a factory. But he *should* be selling insurance. He was a swell guy. And he knew insurance.

S. You feel that he had the same sort of thing stopping him that you have?

M. I don't know. They're two similar cases. He knew the business, but he just faded out. Nobody ever got the answer. There are two men that are more mystified about me than I am about myself. Well, one isn't mystified. He says I'm just plain lazy. But that answer doesn't seem adequate. Nobody is plain lazy. You do what you want to do, that's all.

S. That's a good point you have there.

M. There's nothing wrong with me physically either. I lost interest in active sports but it isn't a physical problem. I don't know.

S. You feel it isn't physical?

M. No. (*Long pause.*)

S. I see our time's up. Since you're in something of a hurry I'm going to suggest something I usually wouldn't.[47] In your thinking in the next two days you might consider two points. In what way were you different when you were successful from the way you are at the present time? Second: Think some more about the matter of your being a tin god to your family.

M. I wondered, since I'm in a hurry, if I couldn't come in tomorrow too. You said we made pretty good progress when I saw you Saturday, right after Friday. Of course, you're the doctor, and I'll do what you think is best. Perhaps you don't have the time.

---

[47] The theoretical aspects of this sort of suggestion are discussed in Rogers' *Counseling and psychotherapy.* The general feeling there is that such suggestions regarding the nature of the client's thinking between interviews should be used with great caution; it may perhaps serve certain legitimate interests if judiciously used.

S. I think it would be best not to do that. It wouldn't be good to hurry too much. Your thinking outside of here is very helpful. I know you'd like to progress as quickly as possible, but I think from your own point of view it would be best to skip tomorrow and come in Wednesday at three.[48]

M. O.K. That's all right, I guess.

(As we were going out Mr. M. asked me, "By the way, what is your position in the University? Do you teach?" I answered that I was clinical assistant and that I did part-time teaching. He asked me if I had a Ph.D., and I answered that I was still working for it.[49])

Fourth Interview (Transcribed from Phonographic Record)[50]
Wednesday, February 18

S. This is clinic day, so we have things kind of helter-skelter today.

M. I noticed it seemed more busy than usual.

S. M-hm. That's right.

M. Say, while I think about it—when we started—when we started this first day you said that at some time in the future it might be a good idea for me to, if I wanted to, to look at the notes you've taken.

S. M-hm. That's right.

M. I don't know whether you want to do that during the time that we're working here or whether you want me to look at them after we're through, or what, but I *would* like to see what you've written.

---

[48] The counselor meant this very sincerely. Already he believed that the interviews were taking place too rapidly. It is interesting to contrast the small progress made between the first two interviews with the marked progress made between the fourth and fifth, where the interval was a full week. Of course, these situations are not strictly comparable because they occur at different stages of the therapeutic process.

[49] The counselor interpreted this questioning as a hostility, or at least a resentment of the imposed authority. Or possibly the client has begun to wonder "Is he able to help me?" The counselor actually feared that the client might break the contact. Apparently, however, the counselor had managed to structure the situation enough that the client still felt he might have a chance of being helped. And it is rather significant that real progress occurred between this and the next interview.

[50] Except for obvious editing, this is a verbatim record of the interview.

S.   All right, well—yes, well, we'll arrange that. Now just whenever you would like to do that. It probably—we could either do it
sometime at the end of the period or something like that if you'd
just like to look over the—or—we could do it during a period—just
whichever way—

M.   Well, whichever way you want to take the time. I'd rather
like to look at some—

S.   All right, sure.

M.   I have been curious right along, but I've left it go, and you
said—(pause). Say, when, uh—when I get the answer to this thing,
is it liable to come to me just like that? (Snaps fingers.)

S.   (Laugh.) Uh—

M.   I got a reason for askin' that question.

S.   I think perhaps that might be more or less what will take
place. You may find that it works out fairly slowly, but I think
perhaps it's much more liable you'll begin to feel that way rather
quickly.[51]

M.   For an hour yesterday this thing was over, and— (laughs).

S.   M-hm. Go ahead and tell me some more about that.

M.   I had the answer to this thing just as clear in my mind for
an hour yesterday as anything you could imagine. Uh, I knew what
I had to do to take care of it. '

S.   M-hm.

M.   And I was just scared to death I didn't have the courage to
do it.

S.   M-hm. You felt like it was pretty big stuff.

M.   I'm telling you I never—I never had anything so clear in my
mind at any time—I was never so sure of anything as I was—and
it came to me just like—that's the reason I asked the question
"Will it come to a flash," because it came—something that I wasn't
thinkin' about at all—I was trying to—it was during the noon hour
yesterday, and I was trying to make some connection or do some-

---

[51] The counselor probably surmised that the client had reached a very sudden
insight into a possible solution of his problem. Also the counselor followed the
notion that one characteristic attribute of insight is that it seems to occur
suddenly. This depends on one's definition of course. Clinicians frequently speak
of "gradual insight," a term which would imply that they think of the word as
meaning "self-knowledge." Such a definition is admittedly more literal than the
counselor's.

thing about—oh, that period just after I got out of the service that you told me it might be desirable to think about.[52]

S. M-hm.

M. All of a sudden it just popped into my head—I've had this all my life—I've had a habit of hiding little things—I don't mean—I mean little things that I've done.

S. M-hm.

M. And as a result of it, this was—I could have just raved on about this for an hour yesterday[53]—right now it's hard to put it into words.

S. M-hm. You felt pretty much stewed up about it, uh—

M. Yeah, I really did. And as a result of hiding these things—little things that I've done that weren't really important at all, and probably if I'd just told somebody about them why they'd never think anything of it—uh—I've got into the habit of uh—of just hidin' too many things and of—when I'm not hidin' what I did why my reasons for doin' it—(pause) and the result of the thing is that I've got so many things that I'm worried about somebody findin' out—probably don't amount to two raps if they do find them out, most of 'em—

S. M-hm.

M. That I just, well, I don't like to see anybody for fear those things are goin' to come up.[54]

S. M-hm.

M. I thought—why heavens, I remember sayin' to Mr. Snyder that I don't tell my wife my troubles because I don't want to bother her, and the—probably the real reason I don't tell 'em is because I don't want her to know I have any.

S. M-hm.

M. I'm too smart to have troubles.

S. M-hm.·

M. I figured the first thing for me to do, to get this mess

---

[52] Perhaps this indicates that the counselor's "advice" at the end of the last interview was helpful in this case. It is rather frequently observed, however, that clients tend to ignore these last-minute directions, and to follow their own line of thinking.

[53] It is not unusual to find this insight producing a strong pleasurable feeling. This would seem to favor the basic tenet of nondirective therapy, that the client wishes to improve.

[54] A new level of self-recognition or insight.

straightened out, is to go home and to lay the whole thing right out on her lap.[55]

S.   M-hm.

M.   And the next thing to do is to go around and see a lot of other people and tell them a lot of things. (*Laughs.*)

S.   M-hm.

M.   And from here on never to hide anything from anybody. Do what I want to do when I want to do it and if it steps on anybody's toes, why let it step on 'em.

S.   M-hm.

M.   I was thinkin' about all this for about an hour. I was so—I was so enthusiastic about the thing right at the time that I almost took the telephone to call up to see if you were down here, so I could come down and talk to you about it.[56] (*Laughs.*)

S.   M-hm.

M.   Yesterday afternoon. That's the way I was feelin' right then.

S.   You really thought you'd come across something that meant something to you?

M.   Yeah. Then I had to—I had something I had to do, so I went ahead and did it and never thought about it. I had to keep busy the rest of the afternoon with other things. Last night I was alone—my wife was out to a club. After the kids went to bed, why I started thinkin' about the thing and didn't get the same (few words missing, needle stuck) . . . It was just like some of the other things that I've talked to you about—maybe it's so and maybe it isn't, but I was just all burning up with that thing for about an hour.

S.   M-hm. Well, how do you feel about it now?

M.   Just as I tell you—my—I *think* I've got *something*. I mean there is something that I have to take care of.

S.   M-hm.

M.   I'm not sure right now like I was for a little while yesterday that that's *the* thing. I'm not so sure that just because—yesterday

---

[55] The beginning of a positive program for self-treatment. Experience suggests that if the client had been told to do this he would have found a hundred reasons why he should not comply.

[56] It is, of course, only speculative, but we wonder, because of the frequency of this sort of thing, whether it doesn't represent the client's determination that he should have had his way about being given an appointment on the preceding day.

I just felt all I had to do was go on with my work and everything's goin' be all right.

S. M-hm.

M. That's the feeling I had. Now I'm not so sure.[57] I am—I do rather feel that the analysis was right—I mean that I do do those things and I've got to quit doing them, and that I've got to quit kiddin' myself that I'm tryin' to protect somebody else when actually I'm runnin' away from the results of my own actions and sidesteppin' things—that's what it amounts to. I've got to quit doin' that—but I'm not so sure that that's the whole answer to the thing—I'm not so sure that I can just do that and then everything's automatically going to take care of itself.

S. M-hm.

M. I did feel that way for a while yesterday.

S. M-hm. For a while you felt that you had really gotten the answer to everything and now you feel—while you're not sure it's the answer to everything, you know that it's something.

M. It's part of the answer.

S. M-hm.

M. It's part of the answer—there's no question about it. (Pause.) In other words, though—that's been goin' on over a long period of years, and the result of it is that I have—well, rather a sneaking feeling about it.

S. You feel that you sort of have to hide away from things— or hide things?

M. Yeah. Darn little things that don't amount to a rap. (Long pause.) As a result of it, I don't believe I know when I'm being honest—with myself or with anybody else.

S. You think that this tendency to hide things keeps you from really knowing what your real attitudes are—what your real feelings are?

M. That's right. (Long pause.) I wouldn't be surprised if basically that's the—this particular thing is at the back of this whole situation.

S. M-hm. You feel this might be what is actually causing you this particular situation?

---

[57] A slight relapse takes place. He has seen the solution but, as he has already asked, is he going to have the courage to carry it out? Quite naturally, that prospect is not going to be so exciting.

M.   Yes. M-hm. I mean that's what—at least that's what—that was the origin of it, and it's grown up now to where I'm not so sure that takin' care of one thing is goin' to solve the problem.

S.   M-hm.

M.   As I say, I'm not even sure I've got the courage to do the one thing.

S.   M-hm. You feel it's a pretty—pretty difficult job to try to change that after such a long period.

M.   Listen—the only way I can see to do it and do it right—well, I suppose there are two ways to do it when you really think about it. I could change my disposition and my characteristics so that I— oh, I don't—I'm absolutely indifferent to what anybody should think about me. I should convince myself that—what's the difference if they do find out what I've been like in the past. Maybe I can go along from here on that basis, but from here on I would do—that is, I would not attempt to hide anything but I wouldn't attempt to do anything to cover up—to rectify the condition as it exists right now, do you know what I'm drivin' at?

S.   M-hm.

M.   Well, that's one way and I'm not so sure that that way would be satisfactory—that is, I think it probably takes a stronger character than *I* am to do that. The other way is to go to Mrs. M—— (wife)—and this is most important of all—and say to her something like this.[58] "That I've been a pretty darn weak sister over all these years and I've been havin' troubles of all kinds which I haven't told you anything about—kiddin' myself all the time that I was doin' it for your benefit so that you wouldn't have anything to worry about, when actually I was hidin' the thing from you—to protect my own pride so that you wouldn't know that I was in any difficulty. I am in tough shape and I need some help." (*Nervous laugh.*) That's the other way, and it takes some courage to do it, Mister, don't think it doesn't. (*Laugh.*) Whether I got it or not I don't know.

S.   M-hm. You feel that would take a good bit of force to do something like that.

M.   It's been goin' on with her for fifteen years. (*Pause.*)

----

[58] This was not spoken lightly, but slowly and with very deep feeling. Even the contemplation of this course of action seemed to be a rather frightening prospect.

S.   You feel that that last solution would be really the best way to handle the thing?

M.   I don't think there's any question there, sir.

S.   M-hm.

M.   Now will you tell me something?

S.   Well, I—

M.   Do you think—do you think I've been honest in my thinking about this thing—just what we've been talking about here so far, and do you think that my second way to handle that thing is the best way? Or don't you want to tell me?

S.   Well, I'd rather not, because I'd rather have you figure it out for yourself.[59]

M.   All right. (*Pause.*)

S.   You did do pretty well by yourself this time, really, didn't you?

M.   I think maybe I did. (*Pause.*) Peculiar thing about the way it happened, too. I mean—it just came like that, and after I—I have been strugglin' around over this thing. I've done a lot of thinkin'—hustlin' back and forth from one thing to another seeming to get no place. I think I have got something to hang on there—I mean something to tie to, and I don't think I have had before.

S.   (*After pause.*) You think that perhaps this is offering you a real solution—a real thing that you might be able to use?

M.   Uh, I'm not sure it's the solution to the whole thing. And, uh—maybe this is going back to my— (*laughs*) previous methods of finding false reasons for things—I don't know. I wish I did. But I don't think I have to say *anything* to her about this until I'm convinced that I've got the whole answer to the problem, so that I can say "Here's what I've done, here's what I think I can do from here on, here's what I think's the answer to this thing." Maybe that's just a lack of courage, maybe it's alibi-ing for myself again, but I honestly believe that this is thinkin' of her.[60]

S.   M-hm.

M.   If I'm anywhere near—if I'm anywhere near to a complete

---

[59] The counselor was unduly cautious in his use of praise, because of his feeling that this client depended rather heavily upon it. He realized immediately, however, that he was being niggardly and tried to make amends in his following statement.

[60] Already the client is beginning to recognize his motivation in wishing to evade the obvious course of action.

answer to my problems there's no use in worrying her about 'em for even a few days until I get the answer—or a few weeks or whatever it may be. I *think* that's honest.

S.   M-hm. You're not absolutely certain that you're being honest there, but you feel that you're trying to be, and that it looks that way—best that way as far as you can see it.

M.   Yeah, I really do. (*Long pause.*) I know how I felt yesterday, now. I just felt that if I go do that with her—just lay that thing out the way I told you—not that that girl hasn't got every confidence in the world in me because she has—but if I'd just go lay all that out to her I'd feel so good when it was over that I could do every—anything.

S.   M-hm.

M.   Whatever else it took to do the job I could do it after that was done once. That was gonna be so darn tough to do that other things'd be easy by comparison.

S.   M-hm.

M.   Now, I don't—I'm not so sure about that now.

S.   At first you felt if you more or less unburdened yourself about this it would clear up a great deal of that weight that was bothering you there.

M.   That's right. (*Long pause.*) Well, that really is—is all that I've got done and the only thing that's—all my thinkin' since then's been along the same line of tryin' to get myself back in the same mood I was in for an hour yesterday, and I haven't done it.

S.   M-hm. It's a—

M.   You know if I could—if I could uh—maintain that feeling that I had there yesterday it wouldn't make any difference whether that was really the answer to the problem or not—it would do. (*Laugh.*)

S.   It really was an exciting or encouraging sort of feeling, wasn't it?

M.   Yes, it was. It really was. I say, whether it was really the right answer to what's been botherin' me or not, it would'a served.

S.   M-hm. (*Pause.*) So you feel now you'd sort of like to recapture some of that—that early—

M.   Enthusiasm.

S.   Enthusiasm. M-hm.

M.   If a man could feel convinced all the time of any one thing as I did of that for a little while yesterday, he could do anything.

S. M-hm. (*Pause.*) It really must have been something that had a good bit of bearing to your problem to give you that—that amount of pep and strength.[61]

M. It must, and yet I—I can't uh—well, I suppose it could be. (*Pause.*) You know, when I really get—I don't know—one reason for losin' that enthusiasm or whatever it may be, may be that I'm more—I think I am, more analytical if (word blurred)—I don't know whether that's the word I want to say or not—or logical, uh—in my—that is, when I consciously think about things I am more than I am when I act by emotion.

S. M-hm.

M. Oh, I want—I want to know in my own mind definitely that —uh, I've got the answer to anything.

S. M-hm.

M. Well, for instance—I've worked a little bit—just a couple times—cases with a man . . .

(Here there takes place a five-minute discussion of a case which Mr. M. used to illustrate his own conscientiousness. He refused to take advantage of a situation where he could have written a $30,000 policy, because he was not sure but that the arrangement under which it was being offered was something of a misrepresentation. He went to great pains to analyze the situation, and finally explained to the client that the policy would only save him money if interest rates remained at their present low level, and if income-tax rates continued to increase for the next four years.)

. . . That's what I say—I—I always have to convince myself in my own mind before I can say anything to anybody else, or before I can act on it myself. I'm not—it took an awful long time to explain to you what I'm talkin' about, but I—I couldn't think of anything else right then that would do it. I'm not convinced thoroughly in my own mind that I have the whole answer to the problem but I don't suppose I will until I can figure out some way for myself to—if it's possible for me to do it—figure out some way how this very definitely—I don't know whether—I don't know whether it does explain everything or not, but at least I'm not convinced that it does.

---

[61] This statement by the counselor is a projection of his own opinion rather than a simple recognition of feeling. The client is very uncertain, however, about whether it should be accepted.

S.   M-hm. So you feel that while this is partially in the right direction it isn't the whole answer and you're not going to be satisfied until you see every point very logically?

M.   Well, I just don't know whether it's the whole answer—It may be. (*Long pause.*)

S.   You feel you're going to . . . (defective line) . . . or have this worked out as the whole answer, or else something else?

M.   That's right. (*Pause.*) I could go at this a lot better if you could explain one thing to me. This is—this is a mental problem— right? (*S. nods.*) Yet I'm gonna get the answer to this and know I got the answer to it, when I don't understand the—my own mental processes, any more than I could get the answer to some physical ailment when I don't understand physiology. (*Laugh.*)

S.   So what you're really wondering—[62]

M.   How—how—how am I gonna do this? Is—is—you're sure that it's possible for me to do it? That's what I am getting at.

S.   M-hm. Yes, I feel very sure of that. That you'll be able to work this out and you'll be able to work it out yourself.[63]

M.   You know the mental processes. I don't. That's what I'm sayin'. I don't see how I do this when I don't under—in fact I was wonderin' when it would be a good thing for me to start gettin' ahold of a book on the basic psychology—principles of psychology, and start readin' it, so I know what I'm workin' at here—if I got to work this thing out for myself. I was wondering that. But if you're —you say that the answer will come if I keep strugglin' around, why, I'll keep strugglin'.

S.   (*Laugh.*) All right. (*Pause.*) You feel a little bit puzzled to understand how it's gonna' come through when you don't feel you understand the route yet. You wonder just what—

M.   Why—

---

[62] The counselor was about to say, "So what you're really wondering is how you're going to solve this problem without advice from me?"

[63] This is not strictly true. The counselor is overemphasizing the necessity of independence of the client. If the client could work out the problem without the help of a counselor he would not have come in for treatment. Obviously neither counselor nor client believes that therapy will occur without a mutual working-out of the feelings. The counselor knows that he is not going to be put in the position of giving advice, but he is not careful enough to explain the significance of his role in the uncovering of the client's true feelings. He might well have reviewed for the client the counselor's position in the therapeutic interview.

S.   What is going to be the—

M.   I don't understand the instrument that I'm—or the organ that I'm dealing with in this things. After all, why—I don't understand it. I probably know a little bit more about my body than the average person because I've studied some of it in order to know how to take care of my kids—I've always been very much interested in that, but at the same time I wouldn't try to doctor myself. Sometimes my wife thinks I do a little bit too much with the kids, but I wouldn't—anything serious, I wouldn't try to doctor myself. I don't know how I'm gonna' work out my own answer to this thing. (*Pause.*)

S.   It's still a little bit puzzling because it's the first time somebody's—has told you that they wouldn't—wouldn't give you advice or an answer, and that you would get the answer or advice yourself.

M.   No, I wouldn't uh—I wouldn't say that that's the reason. That—uh, just because you said you wouldn't give me advice. I'm willing to go along on this thing. If you say I can do it—it's a mystery to me how I'm going to get the answer—(*pause*), any more than how I would know how to start my automobile motor if something goes wrong with that motor—within certain very limited things—that is, I can look to see if the spark-plug wires are on there, and I can—I can know if the battery's down or a few—I can tell whether it's getting gas, but, beyond that—why I'm lost. Well, I feel the same condition exists here. I'm tryin' to find out something —what's wrong with my mind when I don't understand the processes of mind—if it's a mental problem and I don't— (**Pause**). While we're talkin' about mental problems the thought popped into my head—it's a question—in real, modern psychology—is the brain and the mind the same thing?

S.   Well, for an actual te—if you want an actual technical answer to that, I would have to say that probably we don't know, because neither one of the—well, the term "brain" has been very well defined, but the term "mind" has never been very well defined. So— even when you ask me a simple basic question like that I can't give you a very good answer. (*Laugh.*) (*Pause.*) The term "brain" refers to a physiological structure.

M.   H-hm.

S.   And the term "mind" is generally used to refer to a thought process.

M.   Well, in other words, it is considered now, or is it (laughs) —I should say, is it considered now that the brain doesn't just function of its own accord—that there is something that makes the brain go around? Is it—is that, uh—

S.   That's about right, m-hm.[64]

M.   Which you can call a mind, or—

S.   M-hm. (Pause.)

M.   Well, darn it, if all that's uh—I'm—I been askin' you these questions for a—I had a reason (laugh) back of askin' some of these things.

S.   M-hm.

M.   And so far if—if what I've asked you here is right, this—this book on applied psychology which I told you I've read off-and-on for the last ten years—it isn't a book—it's a small set of books—apparently is still sound. The methods they give in there ought to work. (Pause.)

S.   You feel that seems more or less consistent with—with any ideas I've suggested and probably it would have an answer.

M.   I tell you, I made it work in a couple small things but I can't make it work in big ones, and I wonder if I jumped into the big ones too fast.

S.   M-hm. (Pause.)

M.   Whoever—whoever wrote that book must have been pretty sound at the time he wrote it. (Pause.) It's a—was a very well-reasoned-out thing except that—darn, what I should have done with that thing a couple of years ago was to get ahold of a book on basic psychology, or the phases of it, a good modern book and studied it and found out if what was in the real newer books was—agreed with what was in that one—if it was I could have probably convinced myself that I ought to keep on with that thing.

S.   M-hm. (Pause.) You feel perhaps in one of these technical books you're going to find enough about mental processes that it'll lead you to a way to answer your own problem?

M.   Well here—when I read—when I read this—listen, if the—

---

[64] The counselor did not feel, of course, that this was a very adequate representation of his view of the body-mind problem, but he was reasonably certain that a technical discussion of that issue would scarcely contribute to therapeutic progress. Quite obviously the psychological background of the client would not justify a very careful explanation, either.

if the methods of handling your life, making your character, that are laid down in that book are sound, a man can do anything with himself that he *wants* to do.

S. M-hm.

M. Of course within the limits of his own mental capacity, because I presume some people do have higher—are more highly intelligent than others. But my old—this analytical mind that I'm tellin' you about a while ago, I—I follow this thing through—I follow all their arguments, and I can't find anything wrong with 'em. But I know that he knows more about his subject than I do. So maybe there are flaws in there that I can't find. And maybe because of the flaws that are in there are the reason that the methods that worked for me on little things weren't good enough to work on big things.

S. M-hm.

M. The chances are the reason that they didn't work for me was because I wasn't sold enough.

S. M-hm. You feel maybe that the reason this didn't work for you on bigger problems was that you didn't have enough actual confidence in it to try to carry it over to these.

M. Well, I tried to carry it over but I probably didn't have enough actual confidence to make it work . . . (about one sentence is blurred). . . . You know—what I think—what I think maybe I'm gonna do, if you think it's a good idea—I believe it would help—there are twelve basic laws that are laid out in that set of books. Next time I come, I'm—I'm gonna write those twelve things down. I can—I can—I learned them off by heart once, and I know the first four or five of them right now—bring all twelve of 'em down; and ask you that, so far as modern psychology knows, those things are true.[65]

S. M-hm.

M. I believe I can make some use—I believe I—I'd have more confidence that—after that—that this darn—that these darn things ought to work for me. If—if they work a fellow can do any darn things with himself. Now I don't know whether psychologists now believe that that's true or whether they don't, but if what this has

---

[65] The client makes a final effort to obtain advice. He goes to considerable trouble to work out a scheme for accomplishing this.

laid out here is true, why you can, now that's—you just make any-thing out of yourself that you set out to do.

S.   M-hm. So you feel if you could bring those in and I were to say—yes—

M.   There isn't any—there isn't any—if you would say to me that so far as—well, these things were written about 1918—if you would say to me that "So far as I know from all my study of psy-chology everything that's down there is the truth," I think I could believe that they are the truth—and uh—of course if they're not, why after all they're so much water over the dam and I can forget about them and get another thing out of my way that I've been foolin' around with. If they are, why they're certainly a good thing for anybody to know and to make use of.

S.   You feel that would give you a good bit of confidence in them, if I were to back them up and say they—those are two good principles—they still hold.

M.   Yeah. As I say I can't uh—be absolutely certain in my own mind. I read and studied those books. Everything that they put down is reasoned out by a man who knows his subject so much better than I do that he could be slippin' one over on me. Also he could be—he could have been perfectly honest in what he was put-ting down there, and since that time things have been discovered that make the things that he wrote absolutely untrue.

S.   M-hm.

M.   I don't know who it was wrote that book. Believe his name was Hilliard. Don't know why that pops into my head, but it does. Don't know who wrote it. Don't know what purpose he had in writing it. May have been just to make some money. I don't know. I don't know whether he was a good man in his field or not. The books were given to me by my brother—an older brother. I didn't have any interest in them at the time, whatever. There's no par-ticular reason why I should have any confidence in what I read in those books except what I can figure out for myself to be the truth.

S.   M-hm.

M.   *But,* I came *here* because I had confidence that I would find honest—people—, and up-to-date in their theories and practices. I would certainly have much more reason for believing what you would tell me than I would for believin' what I read in that book.

S. You feel there's no real reason why you should have confidence in them—in the books, uh—except in what actually appears logical to you yourself.

M. That's right.

S. M-hm. But you feel that if I were to stand back of the book, that would seem to have a lot more legitimacy then because of—you expect me to be more up-to-date and more modern in the field.

M. Sure. Not only that, but as I say, I came here with every expectation of finding—after all at a state university, a good institution of learning—you don't come in here expectin' to find a quack or a crook or something like that. You come in expectin' to find an honest man that's uh—interested in the thing that he's doing and, well I don't know—just uh—I just feel that I have a right to be used the way I ought to be used here and (laugh) I expect to be used that way.

S. You're looking for someone you can have trust or confidence in, I feel, in trying—in supporting you on this—this uh—on whether or not these principles are true.

M. You know I think you got something there—I didn't know it till you said it, but I think that's so. (Laugh.) (Pause.) That darn thing must have been around the back of my mind here all the time—I've mentioned it two or three times since I came in here. (Laugh.) (Pause.)

S. You feel that by logical processes I'm the sort of person you should be able to have confidence in because I have a position in a reliable institution where people are assumed to be more or less honest and dependable, and therefore you want to bring it to me to find out whether I'm in accord with what they say in the book.[66]

M. That's right. And on top of that—besides the—besides the reasons that you gave for expecting to find somebody honest here—this isn't a place where you're just out to get some practice and make some money.

S. M-hm.

M. There can be only—there can be only two reasons for you doin' all this that you're doin' here; one of them is to help me and the other one is to learn something for yourself.

[66] The counselor continues to recognize the client's feeling, even when it is directed toward the counselor himself.

S.   (*Pause.*) So you feel—

M.   And you can't learn anything by bein' crooked with me if you wanted to, I don't see how you could. And—

S.   So you feel you have pretty good reason to be sure of my motives, but you don't know whether you could really be very sure of this other fellow's motives—the fellow who wrote the book.

M.   That's right. (*Pause.*) That's right—and I don't know anything about him. He—for all—well as I say, the thing was so well reasoned—that is, it was logical to me, so logical that I imagine he was a good man, but for all I know he may be a crackpot that uh—could reason well. Some of them can. (*Laugh.*)

S.   M-hm.

M.   He knew more about his subject than I did. (*Long pause.*) Well, do you think that's a good idea?

S.   How do you feel about it?

M.   Well, I do. I think that I'd like to do that. But you've been very backward here about wantin' to do anything that —well it looks to me as though you've even been backward about wantin' to do anything that would even encourage me to come in here. (*Laugh.*) Now you *know*—you know your job and you probably know a lot more right now about me and my mental processes than I do about myself. If you say that—if you still want to hang back and not give me any advice, why that's still all right with me—I'll still be back here. (*Laugh.*)[67]

S.   Well, I might do one of two things—I might have you bring the book in and I might look at it and say, "Well, this looks like a good book to me, or this looks like it fits my ideas," and I might— or I might say, "Well, this doesn't look so very good to me." Now that's one—that the one alternative I might do, or I might have—I might say, "No, I'd rather not do that," and my reason for doing either one or the other would be—I would do the thing that would bring you nearest to the solution of your problem. Now I'm not just sure what—which I should do in that case, uh—so it's sort of a question of whether you're wanting to bring them in has any relationship to your problem. That's my reason for questioning whether I should do that or not. Perhaps I ought to say that I'll

---

[67] The client is here recognizing the nature of the nondirective counseling and is accepting it, on the counselor's authority, but he also frankly admits that he does not understand why it is being used.

put that up to you—if you bring the books in I'll look at them and give you my frank opinion of them.[68]

M. Well, I wasn't—I didn't intend to bring the books in—there's twelve of the darn things—

S. Or—well, you mean the—

M. I mean they got twelve principles that they lay out there for —as a—uh, method of—oh just of *shaping* your *life*, that's all.

S. M-hm.

M. The first of them don't have anything to do with that, but they logically lead up to that—for instance the first thing that they—I can quote it for you[69]—the first one says all human achievement is a result of some form of bodily activity. Then they go into great detail and establish that that's so—that, uh—there must be bodily activity or there is no achievement, and the second thing is—all uh—bodily activity is caused, controlled, and directed by the mind, and uh—the third one is that the mind is therefore the instrument you must use in the accomplishment of any object—the accomplishment of any purpose. The fourth one is that—I don't remember the exact wording of this now—or whether I can quote it or even get the gist of it, but the mind is made up of two parts, the conscious and the subconscious—I forget just how that goes on, but anyway by a logical process, why, it may lead you up to a point where by uh—using the affirmation and picturing things in your mind in the right way and at the right times that you want to do why they just—you just gotta be able to do 'em.

S. M-hm.

M. Well, as I say it was by this—by this method that I started to do one thing and stopped another—the one thing that I thought was undesirable I stopped, and the desirable one I started. But it makes a very—seemed to me very logical case for itself, but there just isn't any answer to it. If you believe this thing and do it and do it the way they tell you to, why, darn, you're going to do anything you want to do, within the limits of your mentality.

---

[68] The counselor here finally structures the interview sufficiently that it gets across to the client in its full significance. The counselor's decision is, of course, a compromise between his policy of not giving advice and his desire to let the client direct the interview. In making the compromise, however, he gets across the point that his own motive is to reach the solution of the client's problem.

[69] The client is still going to make an effort to get this advice upon which he really feels quite dependent.

S. You'd like to find someone who would give you an answer, carefully written out—do this, do this, and do this, and—that you could follow and that you could have confidence in.[70]

M. Oh, I don't—I don't know—I don't know that that's exactly the thing or not. Now understand even, I know now that even if I find that thing is absolutely true—there's something else—well, I got a job to do in order to make the thing work, because the thing that you have to do first is to know where you're goin' and why, and you get yourself a name, and I haven't got one. I sat down the other day and tried to think, "Well, suppose I had enough dough that I didn't have to work—what would I do?"

S. M-hm.

M. And I didn't know.

S. You felt you just couldn't answer that problem. It wasn't— you didn't know just exactly what you would do if you had plenty of money.[71]

M. If I could just keep on doin' the thing that I been doin'—the things that I been doin' in the way that I been doin', and uh—if I could make just a few hundred dollars a year more doin' it, why I think I'd be just as happy—the way I am right now, I'd be just as happy as anything I can think of. (Pause.) So that's another thing —yes, that's one of the things that makes me worry—well I say that's one of the things; that never occurred to me till right now. (Laughs.)

S. M-hm.

M. I said that's one of them as though I'd been thinkin' of it before, but I haven't been at all.

S. M-hm.

---

[70] This is an interpretation which the client does not accept. In a sense it is as near as the counselor ever comes to making a diagnosis—that is, it represents his own notion of what the client's trouble really is, *i.e.*, his dependence on others for guidance. Note, however, that this interpretation is rejected by the client.

[71] Some people have expressed interest in the way in which the counselor permits the client to change the direction of the discussion. This is, however, a consistent aspect of nondirective counseling. It is assumed that the client changes the direction for a reason; he wants either to bring up a new aspect of it or to avoid any insight which is painful to him. That the former type of change leads to progress is probably not doubted by many people. In the case of the latter type of change the reader is referred to *Counseling and psychotherapy* for a discussion of the rationale which determines the counselor's refusal to force the client to face the unpleasant insight.

M.   (*Laugh.*) It popped into my head right now. I should say that it's something else—a reason why I wonder if my ideas yesterday is an answer to the whole darn thing, because (pause) a fellow can't go any place unless he knows where he's goin'. (*Pause.*) Sure, I get daydreams occasionally—wouldn't it be swell to be doin' this, or wouldn't it be swell to be doin' that—I've even thought since I've been down here talkin' to you—I've been thinkin' "Well, wouldn't it be a swell idea if I get this situation of mine cleared up—if I get this cleared up so that I know where I'm goin'—if this —(pause) if Mr. Snyder helps me to that point, wouldn't it be swell if I could study psychology myself and run around and help a lot of other poor insurance agents in the same boat I am, and probably do the job for 'em.[72] (*Pause.*) There's a lot of good to be done in the world on that, too, I'm telling you. There's just all kind of insurance agents runnin' around that ought to be doin' fifty per cent more business than they are, and don't know why.

S.   Well, it looks like our time is just about up. How did you feel about the notes?

M.   Well I'd like to look at 'em but I don't—I don't want to take your time to do it.

S.   Well, suppose I just left them here with you, and came back in a little while and picked them up—how would that be?

M.   That's all right.

S.   Is that all right with you?

M.   Yeah. I can't take more than ten or fifteen minutes to it right now anyway.

S.   Well, suppose I come back in fifteen minutes, then.

M.   All right.

S.   I *would* suggest this; that we don't talk about them after I come back.

M.   All right. We're through talkin' for today.

---

[72] Experience suggests that this is one of the first signs that a client is reaching the end of the therapeutic process. The idea of perhaps becoming a psychologist himself frequently occurs to a client when he begins to see daylight on his problem, and starts to contemplate the process by which his transformation has occurred. Other general signs of the approaching end of the therapeutic process seem to include an interest on the part of the client in the personal characteristics of the counselor, a statement by the client suggesting that he is pleased with or enjoys the therapeutic process, and interest in the theory of the therapy, a spontaneous statement indicating a reluctance to break off the interviews, a very markedly improved affective tone in general.

S.   That's right.

M.   If we do any talkin', why we'll do it next time.

S.   That's right. All right. Let me see. That's right. (*Looking through notes.*) All right, I'll pick 'em up in about fifteen minutes.[73]

M.   All right. Thank you, Mr. Snyder.

Fifth (Final) Interview (Reported from Notes)
Tuesday, February 24

S.   Well, it's been quite a long time since we had a talk, hasn't it?

M.   Yes, it's almost a week. (*Pause.*) I haven't been doing much thinking, but I've been doing plenty of acting.[74]

S.   I see.

M.   First I cleared up several matters with my wife. Then I cleared up matters with a man from—(city)—that I've been doing some work with. Then I made a trip to—(city)—and saw a couple of people there. I laid myself out in front of a number of friends. And I found out I had a number of friends that I didn't know about, either.

S.   M-hm.

M.   I really don't think it was necessary for me to come down today.[75]

S.   You feel you have things pretty much in hand?

M.   Yes, that's right. The only thing that's been wrong with me all this time is I haven't had any real purpose in life. I've just drifted along. I've let myself be pushed around from one thing to another without any real ambition from myself. All I need, really, is to decide what I finally want to do. Nobody but me can decide that;[76] if I decide that, then the situation's taken care of. If I don't decide then I'll continue to be pushed around the way I always have been.

---

[73] The notes which were left were a typed copy of this account (without footnotes) through the first three interviews.

[74] We consider self-initiated remedial activity a true sign that therapy has occurred.

[75] Also a sign of therapeutic success is the client's feeling of being cured, or of being independent.

[76] We feel that this statement is justification enough for the effort to keep the therapy nondirective. We believe that if the counselor had said this in some directive manner the client would not have been able to accept it with the assurance with which he now states it.

S. You feel that it's really your own problem and you have to make up your mind for yourself about what you want to do?

M. That's right. I've just got to not let myself be influenced to do something else. I haven't decided what I'm going to do. But I have to decide for myself and nobody can do it for me. Of course I think my wife has a right to help me.

S. You really feel you've worked this through to where you're standing on your own feet? You feel you'd be able to figure out the answer for it, and then go ahead? You feel it's pretty much cleared up.

M. As far as it can be cleared up without having me go ahead and do the things I have to do. I haven't got that just exactly clear in my mind, but I realize that I'm the one has to make the decision. (*Pause.*) I would like to ask you one question. I suppose there are tests you can take to determine whether you're in the right profession, or what you're more fitted for. What do you think of those tests? Would I learn anything from taking one?

S. Well, there's a test you might take which would study your interests and then say, "Now here's what you're interested in. People who are interested in these things usually make good in the following professions."

M. So it really doesn't tell much, because I'd probably settle on the thing I'm able to do anyway?

S. That's probably right.

M. Well, as far as the solution to this thing is concerned, I think that's it and there's nothing more to it. I would like to ask you two questions, aside from this business, but bearing on what I read in your notes. First, do you think my English is poor? The way it read, it seemed pretty bad to me, although I always thought I was fairly good. Not like a college professor, of course, but at least average.

S. I think it is perhaps better than the average. Of course you wouldn't expect it to be like a college professor's. Perhaps the reason it seemed poor is that in taking notes one has to record ideas, and the material will seem a little choppy because every word hasn't been recorded.

M. The other thing I wondered. Is it common for people to be so confused when they come in for help. I think I was in a terrible frame of mind. In fact, reading what you indicated I had said was the thing that made me decide I ought to get out and do something.[77] Are many people that confused?

S. I don't think you were any more confused than most people are when they come for help.

M. Then, so far as that's concerned, I think the thing's done.

S. You feel you have a grasp of the situation, and that you can handle it yourself?

M. Yes, it was really the flash that did it. That told me to go ahead. That's the flash I told you about the last time. Of course reading what I had said is really what forced me to do something about it.

S. And you feel, now, there's little reason for us to continue with these sessions?[78]

M. Right now I don't think there is any point in it. Unless you think I should continue. So far, you've stalled from giving me any advice. That was a good thing.[79] Now I think I can do it myself. Unless you feel I ought to continue coming. I'd take your advice because you've been right in the things you've done here. Do you feel there can be any object in my continuing?

S. By now perhaps you can guess what my answer will be.

M. No, I can't. I do feel I've had help in coming here.[80] So if you said I should continue I would be glad to do it. Of course I don't really know the answer yet. But I feel I can get it now, myself.

S. You feel that you're independent and able to work on your own?

M. Yes. And the problem's a lot tougher than you know about. There's a lot of things to be done.[81] But I know now that I've got to do it myself. That's what I needed. You've done well in insisting

---

[77] A suggestion that, for this case at least, reading the notes was helpful to the therapeutic process.

[78] The counselor is giving the client the responsibility for the closing of the interviews. Even at this stage it seems advisable to remain nondirective. For discussion of the theory on this point, see Rogers' *Counseling and psychotherapy*.

[79] The client has accepted the nondirective method and recognized its appropriateness in his case.

[80] See footnote 79.

[81] The client recognizes that everything is not settled. But he knows now that problems are things that people face rather than cover up. He sees that he can work out the details of re-aligning his life habits. This, we believe, is the most helpful value which he will carry over from this therapy into other life problems.

on my thrashing this out for myself, and in resisting every effort I made to get you to tell me what I should do. I'd be glad to come back, but I feel it would be just a waste of your time and mine.

S.   Perhaps then we should leave it that way.

M.   It'd probably be an enjoyable conversation, but it wouldn't get us anywhere.

S.   Yes, I think that's right. Let's say that we consider this the last interview. Of course, if at any time you felt you had to come in, you would be welcome to do so, but it would be on a new basis, and entirely voluntary, like it was before.

M.   That's right. Now could I ask you something? This has nothing to do with the matter we've talked about. But I would like to read some decent psychology. Would you tell me some books I could read that would actually be good modern psychology? You see, I've thought there are a lot of people in insurance who don't actually know why they're selling the stuff. And the companies don't help you. They give you a lot of stuff, but it really isn't true. For example, they say the way to serve your community is to sell as much insurance as possible. They appeal to a man's feeling that he is serving people and therefore a great person. But anybody knows you really sell insurance to make a living. Why shouldn't they tell the people the truth in the beginning? Why do I try to sell big policies? Anybody knows it's the little people who need it most. The answer is that I want to make more money. (*Pause.*) Well, I wonder if you would give me the names of some books that would help me to understand the principles of psychology, and how people think?

S.   Perhaps I could mention a couple that would give you a start. If you are interested in general material, I'd suggest the *General psychology*, by Gardner Murphy. If you want to know something about how people get into problems, you might try Laurance Shaffer's *Psychology of adjustment*. Here, I'll write that down for you. (*Writes.*)

M.   Thank you Mr. Snyder. I guess that's about all. (*Puts on coat.*) Well, thank you very much for doing all this for me. I still can't understand your part. You just seemed to listen, and yet you were doing a lot more, I think.[82]

---

[82] See footnote 79.

S.   Let's call it part of my job.

M.   Yes, it's your trade-secret. (*Shakes hands.*) Well, I hope I won't see you again, Mr. Snyder. (*Laughs.*) Not here, I mean, and in this manner.

S.   I hope not, too, Mr. M——. Good-bye.

FREDERICK C. THORNE

University of Vermont

A Critique of Nondirective Methods of Psychotherapy[1]

The development by Rogers (*183, 184, 185*)[2] of nondirective methods of counseling and therapy should be clearly recognized as a new contribution of major significance to the methodology of clinical psychology and psychiatry. Although many of the theoretical foundations and methods of nondirective psychotherapy derive from antecedent sources, Rogers is the first to integrate and coordinate the basic principles into an internally consistent system. Nondirective psychotherapy is more than just a synthetic regrouping of methods borrowed from older schools of thought and constitutes a genuine contribution to the armamentarium of psychiatry.

The historical development of nondirective methodology is perhaps best understood from a consideration of the evolutionary forces operant in the field of clinical psychology. For the last twenty-five years clinical psychology has suffered a progressive decline in vitality as it passively suffered encroachments into its field of operations by other sciences. Although the first child study and mental hygiene clinics were organized under the auspices of university psychology departments, these movements were quickly taken over by the medical science of psychiatry. Except for a few individuals who succeeded in establishing themselves as consulting psychologists, the field of psychotherapy was largely preempted by psychiatrists and

[1] Reprinted from *Journal of Abnormal and Social Psychology*, 1944, 39, 459–470. Copyright 1944 by American Psychological Association.
[2] Bibliography begins on page 719.

579

psychoanalysts who relegated the clinical psychologist to the relatively subordinate position of laboratory technician whose major contribution was psychometrics. Clinical psychologists also found themselves most seriously handicapped by being cut off from the study of clinical materials which had largely come under the control of psychiatrists operating as administrators of mental hospitals and other institutions where case material was available for study. In the absence of systematized training programs and other opportunities for working actively with large quantities of clinical materials, the clinical psychologist has too often operated in an intellectual vacuum in which he was forced to acquire experience through the second-hand study of textbooks and whatever fortuitous informal contacts he could manage to negotiate for the study of case material. With this limited and unsatisfactory background of training it is easy to understand why clinical psychologists have varied so much in clinical ability and have progressively lost prestige in competition with psychiatrists who have enjoyed much more standardized and intensive educational opportunities. Clinical psychologists have also been forced to contend with the legal aspects of the situation in the sense that their activities were so unorganized as to fail to secure recognition as one of the healing arts. It has been necessary to exert considerable caution in limiting their activities to avoid malpractice suits in the event that the patient's condition suddenly changed for the worse while under treatment by the clinical psychologist.

The practical result of this situation in interprofessional relationships has been that the clinical psychologist has limited himself to psychometrics and borderline counseling activities in areas where psychiatric resources are not available. The strengths and weaknesses of the nondirective method may be partially understood in terms of the professional background of the clinical psychologist who has developed a technique to fit the limitations of the clinical situation in which he has been forced to operate. Nondirective methods are relatively simple to master, require relatively little clinical experience with which to obtain results, and involve relatively small dangers of worsening the patient's condition by inept bungling. Since the patient works out the solutions to his own problems, it follows that the clinician is relatively free from the possibility of being charged with malpractice. These comments have been intended to apply to the total situation in clinical psychology and not specifically to Dr. Rogers, who is one of the few clinical psychologists who have maintained clinical contacts to a sufficient degree to make possible intensive study of case material. As utilized by Dr. Rogers, nondirective methods open new vistas of clinical activity to psychologists and others who understand their limitations. It seems wise to reemphasize Dr. Rogers' statement that the new nondirective techniques will have more widespread usefulness in the guidance and counseling fields than in the treatment of mental disorders.

Positive Factors in Nondirective Therapy

Patient-Clinician Relationships. Nondirective methods emphasize "client-centered" approaches to the study of personality. The therapist submerges his own emotional needs and intellectual prejudices as completely as possible in the attempt passively to guide the patient by methods of indirection to a more comprehensive self-understanding. The major responsibility for the direction and conduct of psychotherapy is subtly displaced from the clinician to the patient, who learns to gain insight into life situations and manipulate them actively for himself. Instead of exhorting, arguing, urging, or persuading the patient to adopt some suggested course of action, the clinician tactfully and indirectly leads the patient to express, recognize, and transform his own attitudes with a minimum of regulation or interference from without. Instead of being "told" what is the matter, the patient is led to discover it himself. There can be no doubt of the value of client-centered therapeutic techniques. One of the major criticisms of psychoanalysis is that preconceived theories of personality structure are foisted onto each individual case regardless of their applicability, *i.e.*, the analyst discovers in each patient the same stereotyped mechanisms which are postulated as universal in Freudian theory. In all fairness to modern psychiatry, however, it must be admitted that a reorientation to the problems of the clinician-patient relationship has been occurring in all branches of psychotherapy and that this is not an exclusive contribution of nondirective technique. Nondirective methods have been in general use by many experienced psychiatrists for many years even though no systematic formulation was attempted.

Autonomous Regulation of Personality. In contrast with such directive techniques as psychoanalysis in which the patient puts himself in the hands of the clinician who actively analyzes, tears down, rebuilds, and resynthesizes the personality, nondirective methods recognize the advantages of allowing the patient to resolve his own problems with a minimum of outside interference. Psychoanalysts in general are characterized by the blitheness and confidence with which they omnipotently assume the responsibility of reorganizing the personality of another human, and unbelievers may be forgiven if they express questioning doubt concerning the omniscience and psychiatric infallibility of the analyst who presumes to revise the works of God after communing briefly with the works of Freud. Nondirective methods may be regarded as a reaction against the dangers of extreme overregulation and psychic reconstruction as carried out by those who are overenthusiastic about the infallibility of some prevailing school of thought.

It is of great value to assist the client to explore and resolve his own problems personally and autonomously with the clinician minimizing active direction and interfering as little as possible with existing patterns of personality integration.

The Growth Principle. Newer methods of psychotherapy emphasize that effective adjustment is the result of normal processes of growth and maturation operant within the individual as an infinite number of forces and stimuli interact and resolve themselves during development. Therapy is directed toward releasing normal growth potentialities so that the individual gains more control over the forces within himself by acquiring more comprehensive insights. In contrast with psychoanalysis, in which the transference between analyst and patient results in a father-son relationship with the patient more or less passively submitting to analysis and reeducation from without, nondirective methods utilize the clinician as a catalyst of growth for which the patient himself is actively responsible. Growth occurs by resolution of forces from within instead of by reconstruction from without.

Releasing Expression and Achieving Insight. These chapter headings from Rogers (184) summarize two of the important therapeutic objectives of the nondirective method as well as all other treatment. By encouraging free expressions of feeling, mirroring the client's feelings and attitudes, and failing to impose arbitrarily patterns and goals, the clinician provides an ideal situation in which there is the fullest opportunity to ventilate and restructure the feelings and attitudes which have caused maladjustment. The client is subtly led to recognize and reconsider his feelings in new patterns or configurations which result in better insights into the total situation.

Avoiding Hostility and Undesirable Personality Reactions. Rogers (183, 184, 185) emphasizes the general principle that therapy proceeds most effectively when the clinician maintains a rigorously detached and objective viewpoint and avoids any critical or regulatory action which might stimulate undesirable emotional reactions in the client. Nondirective procedures operate to produce objective and impersonal therapeutic relationships and thereby make therapy less complicated and upsetting by avoiding hostility and negativism in the patient who senses emotional or critical attitudes in the therapist. Almost all psychotherapy is to some degree disturbing to the patient because it is deflating to the ego to be so maladjusted that it becomes necessary to place one's self in the embarrassing position of having to admit failure and seek help from others. Any method which makes it easier for the patient to express himself freely and without danger of arousing critical or condemnatory attitudes marks a great therapeutic advance.

It is also important, however, to express the opinion that the therapist should not endanger his effectiveness by being too cautious and timid about doing anything which might arouse hostility and negativism. There are clinical situations in which the patient needs to be acquainted with critical attitudes and to face unpleasant realities. It has been said that one of the major values of institutional psychiatric treatment is that it forces the patient to mobilize all his resources in the effort to regain enough integration so as to leave such an unpleasant environment. Some patients may be benefited by judicious shock and punishment.

The Method of Controlled Associations. One of the interesting variations of analytic technique is the method of distributive analysis outlined by Diethelm (60) in which the clinician skillfully directs the trends of the patient's associations and productions into areas which seem profitable of exploration. There is similar value in the nondirective technique of putting subtle pressure on the client to verbalize his own attitudes progressively and thereby to ventilate his feelings under controlled conditions where the therapist skillfully guides the client to better insights. By repetitious and leading questions, the client is indirectly led to achieve new orientations and structurings of his problems. The nondirective treatment reported by Snyder (206) provides an excellent example of how a patient can be subtly drawn out along the lines of his own feelings and attitudes. This technique will be of value not only in counseling but also in the treatment of all types of mental patients.

The nondirective technique utilizes controlled associations to explore any desired area of attitudes. Use of the questions "Why? Where? When? How?" makes it possible to uncover significant material and to force the patient to evaluate certain sequences of behavior for himself. Another most valuable question is, "What do you think about that yourself?" All these questions are completely nondirective and the patient's attention is directed to causal relationships which had formerly been unrecognized and which he can quickly perceive now for himself without the embarrassment of having to "take it" from another person. Through skillful questioning it is possible to implant any desired idea in the client's mind in such a manner that the client thinks he thought of it himself and is therefore more ready to accept it. Nondirective methods are the foundation of the modern psychology of leadership by indirection instead of force.

Self-Initiated Goals and Actions. Mental health is generally considered to involve internally consistent attitudes, unified goals and integrated personality. The objectives of all therapy are to bring these conditions about as smoothly as possible with the patient himself striving to become adjusted and independent. Lecky (132), another experienced clinical psychologist, taught as far back as 1936 that mind was an organization of mutually consistent ideas the nucleus of which was the person's conception of himself. Using nondirective methods to lead the client to restructure his conception of himself, Lecky led his patients to acquire new attitudes and self-initiated goals which resulted in a transformation of their actions. Nondirective methods are very effective in demonstrating inconsistent attitudes, conflicting goals, and disintegrating forces to the client in a painless manner.

Inadequacies of the Nondirective Method

The value of any new method of therapy is not to be determined by the seeming brilliance or rationality of its theoretical foundations but by a careful critique and evaluation of the results of its use. It is perhaps more difficult to objectify the results of psychotherapy than of any other type because each case is unique and it is never possible to determine what might have happened if no treatment at all had been given or if the results would have been different with slight variations in procedure. No one can refute the claim that the patient would have been better or worse if another method had been used. The therapeutic situation is so complex that there are unlimited possibilities concerning what might happen with different techniques or therapists. A method which is very effective in one situation may be very unsatisfactory in the hands of another because of the different personalities involved. The publication by Snyder (206) of a verbatim recording of what took place in a short-term nondirective treatment of an adult makes possible a detailed analysis of the technique in terms of what has been learned about psychiatric methods in general. A number of specific comments may be made concerning various inadequacies which seem to detract from the effectiveness of this form of counseling as used in this case.

Inadequacy of Case History. Throughout the five sessions reported by Snyder (206) only the barest outline of a case history was obtained. Little attempt was made to secure the background case material which a psychiatrist would consider absolutely essential for even a limited understanding of the total situation. How does the counselor know that he uncovered the major problems of the patient? The experienced clinician knows that the presented complaint frequently involves only a minor aspect of the total problem and that it is necessary systematically to explore the total personality to obtain a comprehensive understanding. Directive techniques are very valuable in obtaining a good case history. When properly utilized, the patient accepts the directive technique without question and in fact derives considerable reassurance from the fact that the therapist is making such a careful investigation of the situation.

Failure to Obtain Corroborative Evidence. The patient's evaluations of himself have been accepted at face value in Snyder's nondirective treatment. No effort was apparently made to interview the patient's wife or business associates to elicit further evidence from objective sources and to evaluate the situation as a whole. One of the basic rules in treating mental patients is to obtain corroborative evidence since these cases are notoriously deficient in insight concerning the magnitude of their maladjustment.

Inelasticity of the Method. In our opinion it is undesirable to limit one's self to any one therapeutic technique rather than to utilize all available methods according to needs of each individual clinical situation. Rigid adherence to nondirective techniques may prevent the clinician from giving adequate treatment in cases where directive methods would be more effective. This criticism is not inherent in the method itself but rather in the use made of it. We mention it in this critique because Snyder in his footnotes commentaries on the treatment seems to imply that any deviation from the nondirective method would be very undesirable and even dangerous. Ideally, the clinical approach should be individualized and a judicious utilization of both directive and nondirective methods may be more effective than either alone.

Superficiality of Contact with Patient. One of the most serious criticisms of this short-term nondirective treatment is that it never proceeded beyond the most superficial grappling with the patient's problems. The entire treatment limited itself to "surface" phenomena as contrasted with the "depth" analysis which has proven so fruitful in analytic psychiatry. The patient browsed along the edges of his problem, coming to grips with it only in terms of a few partial insights which would doubtless have been achieved as easily with other forms of therapy. There are indications that the patient himself recognized the superficiality of the therapeutic approach and was vaguely dissatisfied with the conduct of the interviews. The therapist did a good job of "structuring" or selling the method he was using and the patient finally acquiesced to its use. It would have been interesting to have followup studies after several months to discover whether any lasting improvement occurred and whether Mr. M was still satisfied with the results.

Failure to Evaluate the Total Personality. Summarizing the failure to obtain an adequate case history and to secure corroborative evidence, it may be concluded that the superficiality of contacts with the patient precluded any comprehensive evaluation of the dynamic mechanisms operant in the total personality. This entire treatment of five interviews was limited to the consideration of one small area or part-functioning of the total personality. Even though one or two dynamic mechanisms are elaborated, one gets the impression that the counselor is dealing with symptoms rather than underlying causes. It is true that Mr. M did get a "flash" of insight concerning what he might do about one aspect of his problem in the last two interviews but it might be questioned whether he developed any genuine insight into the dynamic mechanisms. The fact that the patient gives expression to feelings of satisfaction over the way the interviews were conducted (pp. 574–577) and utters a few platitudes about the necessity of working out one's own problems cannot be accepted as evidence that genuine insights were attained. The partial insights which Mr. M relates on pages 556–561 are on surface levels and do not indicate any genuine understanding of underlying personality mechanisms. How did this man get to be as he now is? Why did he develop this particular type of personality reaction? Do we really know much about Mr. M at all at the end of five interviews? There are many questions to which no answer is available from a perusal of the course of treatment and which could reasonably be expected from the orthodox directive treatment of equivalent length.

Conduct of the Interview. It is very important that any therapeutic interview should be conducted in a natural facile manner which puts the patient at ease and quickly establishes the rapport which is so necessary for effective treatment. With good rapport the patient is usually cooperative enough to carry the treatment through to completion even though parts of it may be unpleasant. There are no variable and established rules concerning how most effectively to conduct an interview and this is an individual matter which each therapist must determine for himself. Most important, the counselor must try to discover what the patient has come to obtain; *i.e.*, to satisfy the needs of the patient. Some needs of the patient may be satisfied by nondirective methods but other needs may require more aggressive directive techniques.

A valuable insight may be obtained into one of the inadequacies of nondirective technique as utilized by Snyder (206) by reading aloud the remarks of the counselor in the verbatim reports of the five interviews. When reread aloud, many of the therapist's interjections seem stilted and inane. In his attempts rigorously to limit himself to nondirective comments, the counselor frequently goes to excessive lengths to remain neutral and avoid interpretative statements. It becomes very monotonous to hear the counselor conscientiously summarizing each of the patient's statements in order to produce recognition of feeling. At some points we sense wonderment and dissatisfaction on the part of the patient and wonder how many revisits he would have made had the treatments been costing $20 per session.

Failure to Follow Up Significant Leads. One of the values of directive methods of therapy is that they enable the experienced clinician actively to explore the various areas of personality in which maladjustments appear to arise. During the interview the patient frequently makes an apparently innocuous remark which may be the key to much significant material the importance of which the patient himself is unaware. It is often of prime importance to utilize directive methods in overcoming the patient's resistances to uncover repressed material which may be of critical importance in understanding the case. At least six times during the five sessions conducted by Snyder, the therapist failed to follow up significant leads which Mr. M produced spontaneously and seemed anxious to elaborate upon. It would not have interfered with effective therapy in any way to have inquired further into the childhood illness (p. 536), why it was necessary to satisfy himself about things (p. 536), more about his worries and neurotic behavior (p. 540), childhood experiences and the reasons for losing many jobs (pp. 549–550), his lost interest in physical sports (p. 554), and more about his preoccupations and conscientiousness concerning the insurance business (pp. 563, 577). Even with the most skillful nondirective handling, there is some question whether all the responsibility for carrying on the continuity of discussion can be placed on the patient. One of the major contributions of Freudian psychology is that some behavior must be interpreted in terms of unconscious conflicts or complexes which are normally repressed and can be uncovered only through the methods of depth analysis. In his attempts to limit himself to neutral nondirective comments, the counselor frequently blocks the patient's continuity of expression when a more positive approach would probably uncover additional significant material.

On Advice and Counseling. From time immemorial people have gone to the wise men for information, advice, and clarification of their problems. The dictionary defines counseling as to give advice or to recommend, as an act or course. The advice is usually critically evaluated by its receiver and then accepted or discarded according as it seems consistent or untrue on the basis of past experience. Even though advice may be verbally rejected at the moment that it is given, there is good evidence that it is usually assimilated and later acted upon after the shock of facing unpleasant reality has worn off.

In commenting on his technique, Snyder explains his intention of refusing to give his client any advice (footnotes 11, 12, 13) because he feels it best for the client to work out his own solution to his problems. In footnote 46, Snyder states his belief that the client can be expected to reject completely the majority of directive or coercive interpretations. Although admitting the validity of these conceptions in some situations, it may nevertheless be suggested that there are also many situations where advice and counsel are not only extremely valuable but are gratefully accepted by the patient. Considering the fact that it probably takes many years to become a wise man (even though one has a doctorate in clinical psychology), the counselor who consistently finds his advice being rejected might well reflect upon his own powers to determine whether his advice is indeed valid and whether he is personally impressive enough to exert any real influence over the client.

Suitability for Various Types of Patients.   Rogers (184) has indicated the limitations of the nondirective method and emphasizes that the technique is most effective with essentially normal people who have enough personality integration to resolve their own problems with a minimum of direction from the counselor. It is less effective with patients who have lost personality integration to the degree that they are no longer capable of self-direction and rational thinking. The more serious psychiatric disorders require a more or less intensive manipulation of the patient's entire life situation, often in the face of intense resistance from the patient himself. Even with disturbed patients, however, there are many clinical situations where the nondirective method may be utilized to fit the needs of the individual situation. The question is not so much whether the nondirective method is or is not applicable to different types of patients, but whether it should be used solely to the exclusion of other methods. Some doubt may be raised whether the treatment of Mr. M might not have been more effective if a judicious combination of directive and nondirective techniques had been used. Snyder admits that Mr. M has a severe neurosis (footnote 30) and is perhaps overoptimistic concerning the permanent benefits to be expected from this short treatment (footnotes 75, 81).

Nondirective Methods: Technique or System?   There is no question concerning the validity or applicability of nondirective methods in selected clinical situations. There is some question whether they are the complete and final answer to all problems of counseling to the degree that they constitute a new system or school of thought. It usually requires a period of years before new contributions of methodology become evaluated and assimilated into the body of existing knowledge. It is unfortunate that too often these newer methods are worked to death by enthusiastic converts as in the history of the psychoanalytic movement.

Probably as the result of partisan adherence to currently popular schools of thought, there has arisen an attitude that education and therapy are matters of extreme delicacy and that the slightest error or deviation from the rule might result in grave damage. Human living is not as delicate and exacting a proposition as some assume. Children are not ruined for good inevitably by traumatic episodes early in life. Most people are singularly successful in spite of insuperable odds of stupidity and error. In fact most doctors admit that patients will get well in spite of anything they do for them. It seems profitable to suggest that clinicians should desensitize themselves concerning the elaborate rituals which they come to feel are absolutely necessary for effective treatment. Most therapeutic methods are not precision instruments which must be administered according to a rigid technique in order to be successful. There is opportunity for the effective use of many methods with numerous variations in technique. Our regard should be focused on goals of therapy rather than on dogmatic adherence to specific methodology.

Summary

Nondirective methods of psychotherapy constitute a valuable new technical tool for use in appropriate clinical situations, but they are definitely not the complete answer to all therapeutic problems even in mild personality disorders. Nondirective methods will take their place along with older directive techniques in the therapeutic armamentarium and the clinician will learn to choose his method to fit the needs of the individual situation. It is gratifying to note that clinical psychology has at last made a noteworthy contribution consistent with trends in modern psychiatry.

WILLIAM U. SNYDER

Pennsylvania State College

Dr. Thorne's Critique of Nondirective Psychotherapy[1]

In a recent issue of *The Journal of Abnormal and Social Psychology* Dr. Frederick Thorne (222)[2] presented a critique of nondirective methods of psychotherapy which, while it makes many good points, seems in our opinion to justify a reply by way of defense of the nondirective technique. In particular Dr. Thorne makes frequent reference to a nondirectively treated case (206) which was previously published in this same journal by the present writer. Our desire to reply is not as much in defense of the specific case, which admittedly has its strong and weak points, but rather in defense of the method which we believe this case to be illustrating. There are criticisms in which we feel that Dr. Thorne fails to recognize basic tenets of the nondirective technique, and others in which he defends criticisms of the technique with some "commonly recognized" facts which are the same principles that persons interested in nondirective counseling are attempting to disprove.

It would seem best to discuss Dr. Thorne's criticisms in a chronological order, so that the reader may refer to the original source if he wishes to do so. We agree with the introductory section of the critique. The discussion of the background in the history of clinical psychology which may have brought about the rise of nondirective theories is sympathetic to the problems of the clinical psychologist.

[1] Reprinted from *Journal of Abnormal and Social Psychology*, 1945, 40, 336–339. Copyright 1945 by American Psychological Association.
[2] Bibliography begins on page 719.

Naturally, also, we do not find much with which to disagree in the second section of the critique, which discusses positive factors in nondirective therapy. We find most of the points similar to those which Rogers (184) makes in his published exposition of this method. However we believe Thorne misses a basic tenet of the nondirective method when, under his discussion of the method of controlled associations, he states that "use of the questions 'Why? Where? When? How?' makes it possible to uncover significant material and to force the patient to evaluate certain sequences of behavior for himself." Dr. Thorne states that these questions are "completely nondirective," and he implies they are frequently used by the nondirective counselor. There are occasions when they may be so used if the counselor is attempting to help the client reveal an attitude or feeling, but in general these words are carefully avoided by the counselor who is nondirective. In a detailed study (207) by the writer it was found that in six carefully evaluated nondirective treatment cases by four different counselors these "direct question" leads constitute only 5.8 per cent of the remarks made by the counselors in verbatim recorded interviews, as contrasted, for example, with approximately 40 per cent of the statements classified as "clarification of feeling," and approximately 30 per cent of the total number of statements as "simple acceptance" ("yes" or "I see"). The same study also reveals that these "direct question" leads seldom are followed by a client's statement of his problem, or by his insight into its causes. Essentially we believe that questions which start with "why, where, when, or how" are directive in character. Thorne appears to recognize this fact when he says that such questions "force" the client to face certain facts. Although he states that "through skillful questioning it is possible to implant any desired idea in the client's mind in such a manner that the client thinks he thought of it himself," we believe that the concept of "implanting" is foreign to the spirit of nondirective counseling, which is "client-centered" and attempts to help the client bring out the problem which *he* feels is important.

Turning to the third part of Dr. Thorne's article, or that which comprises the criticisms of what he considers to be inadequacies of the nondirective method, we disagree with numerous points. As Dr. Thorne states, in the case of Mr. M the counselor did not attempt to compile any material similar to that traditionally understood to comprise a case history, "which a psychiatrist would consider absolutely essential for even a limited understanding of the total situation." Dr. Thorne questions how the counselor can know that the major problems have been uncovered and states that the experienced clinician considers the presented complaint frequently to be not too significantly related to the total problem. With regard to the point of presented complaints, we recognize the fact and would point out that throughout the series of five interviews the client goes into his deeper problems as he develops insight into their significance, and as he is able to accept the fact that he possesses various weaknesses. Again the nondirective counselor does not himself try to determine the problems, but helps the client to determine them through clarifying *his* feelings.

Having taken many case histories himself, the writer is aware of the importance which they frequently have in a certain type of case. It is the contention of clinicians who employ the nondirective method that in many adult cases the taking of a case history is injurious to the outcome of treatment, because it places upon the counselor the responsibiilty for pointing out the solution to the problem. Dr. Thorne states that "when properly utilized the patient accepts the directive technique without question and in fact derives considerable reassurance from the fact that the therapist is making such a careful investigation." We disagree, for we feel that many times patients do not accept a directive technique without question, no matter how skillfully it may be used, but actually resent and evade the exploring into their personal history. As Dr. Thorne indicates, some clients may take reassurance from this process, but in turn we feel that they must thereby automatically place on the counselor responsibility for giving them advice.

We should point out that in the nondirective technique reassurance is handled very carefully in order to keep it from becoming a crutch. While it is perhaps a minor point, we have so frequently leafed through pages of social case history relating to the fortunes and idiosyncrasies of relatives located in a distant city that we wonder how significantly related this material is to the problem of the patient. The reader is referred to a discussion of this topic in Rogers' book *Counseling and Psychotherapy* (184), pages 80 to 84.

We recognize that there are times when case histories are important, particularly when one is treating a child, but in the case of an adult client, we feel that the damage which may be produced by this information-getting attitude on the part of the counselor can be a very significant matter.

If the criticism is made that the counselor is perhaps overlooking some serious personality deviations in the client, we would reply that in our opinion a good part of the training of counselors should be in the recognition of the various types of psychoses. In this regard it can be mentioned that Rogers in his book excludes psychotics from his group of persons for whom this method seems adaptable. Rogers more recently expresses the feeling that after the psychotic is placed in the "controlled environment," the nondirective approach "might be definitely feasible and would enable him gradually to accept responsibility for the limited segment of life which is within his control."[3] Rogers admits this is still a hypothetical possibility.

In criticizing the inelasticity of the nondirective method, Dr. Thorne feels that "ideally the clinical approach should be individualized and a judicious utilization of both directive and nondirective methods may be more effective than either alone." As Rogers has indicated in chapter five of *Counseling and Psychotherapy* (184), it is clearly recognized that there are situations in which a nondirective technique is not applicable, but we disagree with the belief that the clinician can waver between directive and nondirective methods as he pleases. Experience with many cases has shown that once a clinician has assumed an authoritative or directive attitude he cannot then suddenly shift his point of reference to the other approach and expect the client to follow. Therefore if a nondirective technique is desirable in a case, it seems that it would be necessary to follow it consistently throughout the treatment. Since Dr. Thorne makes a point of indicating that nondirective techniques require relatively little skill, we would in turn make the point that much of the skill of the clinician is to be evidenced in his use of the initial interview to determine whether he does or does not intend to follow nondirective methods, and we believe that until he has made that decision it would be best for him to remain as nondirective as possible.

---

[3] Recent correspondence from Dr. Rogers.

The case of Mr. M is criticized on the basis of superficiality of contact with the patient. Dr. Thorne feels that this is one of the most serious criticisms of the method. The method is criticized because it contrasts with the "depth analysis which has proven so fruitful in analytic psychiatry." One of the tenets that Rogers indicates in his book is that repressed attitudes have been overemphasized in psychotherapy and that, if given a chance, problems which are significant in determining the patient's behavior will come to the surface. Mr. M did bring up items which he recalled from his youth, and the clinician considered these matters important and recognized them. The clinician did not probe into areas which the client did not at the time wish to discuss. We doubt whether Mr. M's "vague dissatisfaction" resulted from the superficiality of the interviews, and are inclined to think it was because he was being required to accept responsibility which he clearly wished to avoid.

In the critique, Dr. Thorne also criticizes the writer's "failure to evaluate the total personality." We see little difference between this criticism and the suggestion that the treatment did not go deep enough. With regard to Mr. M's "insight into the dynamic mechanisms" we feel that such a criticism might be more valid if Mr. M had been a deeply disturbed person. We would be more likely to accept Dr. Thorne's dismissal of Mr. M's development of insight as being only a "few platitudes about the necessity of working out one's own problem" if it were not a common insight reached by many clients who have undergone more directive psychotherapeutic techniques without obtaining a satisfactory outcome. Furthermore, the writer has frequently encountered clients who have contrasted favorably the nondirective method to their previous directive treatment.

Regarding the criticism of failure to follow up significant leads, we should like to point out that any counselor must decide at the end of a client's statement which element he wishes to respond to. This is part of the judgment and training which the experienced counselor possesses. The writer selected for response the feeling which appeared to him to be most significant. If some six times during the five sessions the counselor is thought to have made a poor choice, he would probably not be doing any worse than average for clinicians using other methods.

A further study of Mr. M's case (207) shows that a total of 103 clarifications of feeling were made. To these 103 clarifications the client responded with 238 ideas, subsequently classified as follows:

Statement of a problem 48
Asking for advice 30
Acceptance of clarification of feeling 53
Rejection 10
Showing insight 60
Discussion of future plans 16
Ending the contact series 1
Unrelated material 12
Unclassified responses 8

The predominance of *growth* experiences on the part of the client is quite apparent in the high percentage of responses classified as showing development of insight, acceptance of the counselor's clarification of the client's feelings, and further efforts of the client to state his problem and to make plans for the future.

With regard to the criticism favoring advice in counseling, we emphatically disagree with Dr. Thorne. His citing of a dictionary definition of the term "counseling" as "giving advice" is not adequate grounds for keeping the clinician from using the procedure which he considers to be best. In a nondirective technique the clinician desires to help the client grow in the shortest time possible. If the client is seeking information in a technical sense, he may go to various sources for such information, but it has been our experience that personality problems are seldom the result of lack of information. If the clinician merely had to tell the client the thing he ought to do, counseling would be a simple procedure.

We wonder whether in most cases a client is in a position to accept or discard advice on the basis of his "critical evaluation." Usually it is found that it is not the *advice* the individual wants, for he already knows what he *should* do, but his problem is that he does not *wish* to do it. Action which is fortified by the prestige and forcefulness of the counselor is not far removed in nature from the conversion following religious exhortation, and perhaps just about as enduring. We feel that it is very basic to the whole theory underlying the nondirective technique that there is no place for advice in the satisfactorily conducted treatment. We disagree with Thorne's statement that rejection of advice is usually a reflection on the ability or impressiveness of the clinician. We believe such rejection is the result of the client's need to find his own best solution to the problem.

We are a little dismayed by Dr. Thorne's inference that therapy is a process which may be approached somewhat casually and that patients will get well "in spite of" what is done for them. It is our feeling that, if psychotherapy is to become a tool that can be taught, every effort should be made to make it as clearly as possible "a precision instrument." In treating an illness a physician does not prescribe just any treatment according to his whim. But he does have a number of treatment methods available and uses the appropriate one.

We accept whole-heartedly Dr. Thorne's statement that the skillful clinician needs to know more than this single method of psychotherapy. As a matter of fact, we are pleased with Dr. Thorne's acceptance of the nondirective technique as one method of psychotherapy.

EMILY L. STOGDILL

The Ohio State University

Techniques of Student Counseling[1]

It would be difficult to describe techniques of student counseling in mental hygiene in college without reference to two fundamental factors in the situation: the wide range in emotional maturity represented by the clients, and the high level of intelligence likely to characterize the large proportion of those who can be referred to legitimately as "treatment cases."

The term "student counseling" as here employed will refer to the treatment of the total personality of the student rather than to the eradication of symptoms or isolated bits of behavior. It will connote more than merely adjusting the individual academically or vocationally, although these areas may be important ones in the entire picture. The importance of academic maladjustment as a presenting problem should not be overlooked, however, as has been pointed out in a previous report (215).[2]

The problem stated by the student is not always the problem needing clinical analysis, but indicates the student's insight into his own difficulty, and what problem he is willing to recognize himself as presenting. The most popular stated problems are: grades, educational guidance, nervousness and discouragement.

During a ten-year period of work with college students, a change was noted in the nature of the presenting problem in the "increase in concern over poor social adjustment, a decrease in the use of vocational guidance as an excuse for consulting the psychologist about other personal problems, and fewer instances in which a purely emo-

[1] Reprinted from *Journal of Consulting Psychology*, 1940, 4, 176–180. Copyright 1940 by American Association for Applied Psychology.

[2] Bibliography begins on page 719.

tional reason such as general discouragement was given for the consultation."

In the above study, four clinical problems were found associated as a group in a large number of cases, regardless of what problem had originally been stated by the student as his reason for seeking counsel. These were personality defects, difficult home adjustment, chronic sub-acute physical conditions, and social strain. This finding is in accord with published reports of other clinicians showing that students come for help, not because of some one major acute difficulty, but as a result of a number of minor chronic problems, any one of which, alone, might presumably have been dealt with successfully by the student unaided, or in cooperation with his previous advisers.

The methods used in solving student difficulties should be described as essentially educational in character—education applied directly to the needs of the individual, in a personal-contact situation. The student enters voluntarily into the counseling situation without pressure from authority or expectation of academic credit. Educational therapeutic processes have been variously described by a group of psychologists and psychiatrists in a recent panel discussion[3] on "The Area of Agreement in Psychotherapy." Robert Waelder described therapy as "training and reconditioning, persuasion, encouragement, moral support, relieving from anxiety and guilt by means of assurance and reassurance, guidance in important decisions or in the conduct of life—i.e. partisanship in the student's inner conflicts." Joseph Chassell suggested the importance of the opportunity to learn "in a secure setting . . . that it is safe to accept one's spontaneous self, (and later to learn to take responsibility for it)." Goodwin Watson pointed out:

> Psychotherapy reassures the individual; sometimes by offering facts to correct maladjustments born of ignorance; sometimes by developing new insights which enable the client to accept as reasonable and natural what had seemed strange and frightening; sometimes by relieving his sense of peculiarity and isolation. . . . No psychotherapy presumes to remove all conflict.

At the present time there would seem to be considerable value in listing what might be called "types of techniques," for there are

---

[3] Panel discussion at the American Orthopsychiatric Association meeting at Boston, Mass., February, 1940. (Quotation from mimeographed sheets.)

many well recognized and useful procedures, the details of which are relatively obvious once they are called to the attention of the trained clinical worker. Such lists pave the way for further formulation by others of unique or personally characteristic methods of accomplishing therapy. This article is conceived as an attempt to set forth certain principles and methods of approaching the study of techniques as well as to describe therapeutic devices that have proved useful in actual practice. More specifically stated in terms of work with college students, these general principles are represented in the outline which follows.

A. Techniques providing the student opportunity for free expression of emotional tensions

  1. The student may be encouraged to give an unhurried and uninterrupted verbalization of his present feelings concerning his stated problem and other relevant material such as

    a. early experiences

    b. parent-child relationships

    c. tabooed behavior, attitudes or topics

    d. his attitudes toward himself, or of others toward him

    e. fears and worries

    f. various individuals in their relationship to his situation.

  2. The student may be encouraged to write out additional autobiographical material between interviews. This may include connected written accounts of such things as dreams or reveries, or lists of various kinds such as

    a. wishes or goals

    b. points of superiority or inferiority in himself

    c. types of situations in which he feels adequate or inadequate

    d. individuals who add to or detract from his feeling of effectiveness.

  3. The clinician may act as a source of temporary emotional security for the student during the period of emotional readjustment by

    a. accepting him uncritically as a worthwhile individual with unfulfilled possibilities which can be realized

    b. giving him complete attention during specified times

    c. reading carefully any written material submitted, and discussing it with him objectively

    d. making him understand that his confidences are respected

    e. being intellectually and emotionally consistent in behavior toward him throughout the contacts

    f. standing between him and certain immediate consequences of his ill-advised behavior

    g. acting as mediator between him and other individuals involved, such as parents, faculty or administrative officers

    h. assisting him in analyzing his conflicting obligations and loyalties.

B. Techniques providing the student the opportunity for securing information and for gaining better interpretation of relationships

  1. Information may be furnished through books, lectures, and personal discussions on topics about which the student is confused or deeply concerned such as sex, marriage, heredity, insanity, ethical standards, or religious viewpoints.

  2. The student may be guided through personal discussion to clarify his interpretations of

    a. inter-personal relationships such as those between
      (1) student and student
      (2) student and faculty members
      (3) student and his family
      (4) men and women

    b. differences of viewpoints on such matters as race and religion as they may represent areas of confusion in his parental home or in his choice of friends or mate

    c. desirable attitudes to adopt in view of such situations as
      (1) parental expectation of unreasonably high grades
      (2) parental pressure for early or financially advantageous marriage
      (3) parental insistence on a vocational choice in a field in which the student is uninterested or incompetent
      (4) undue parental self-effacement or self-sacrifice
      (5) previously unverbalized resentment toward some member or members of his family because of early experiences such as punishment felt to be too severe or unmerited, unfair comparison between children, or lack of parental affection
      (6) parental disharmony or separation.

  3. Realistic attitudes toward self-evaluation may be encouraged through such methods as

    a. pointing out to gifted or to unusually emotionally mature students the reason for their apparent difference from the majority of their fellows

    b. pointing out that the attitude of the clinician is one of tracing causal relationships, not one of praise or blame, and encouraging the student to adopt the same viewpoint

    c. interpretation of scores on "mental" and personality tests. Retesting in cases of wide discrepancy with observed behavior

    d. pointing out by means of concrete illustrations, from the student's own behavior, abilities or disabilities overlooked or incorrectly evaluated by him

    e. observation by the student of the clinician's unperturbed reaction to his recital of his "sins and shortcomings" and guilty feelings

    f. tracing with the student the developmental history of various types of his behavior in order to help him realize their essential modifiability.

C. Techniques involved in the planning of specific activities for the student between interview periods

  1. The clinician can judge the student's adequacy more objectively if he can arrange to observe him first hand outside the consultation situation, rather than being entirely dependent on his self-reports which may be very misleading. The mistake of entering into a social relationship with the client must, however, be avoided. It is possible to use reports from disinterested persons in the student's environment as partial substitutes for observation, provided they can be secured without invading the confidential nature of the relationship, or making the student the object of scrutiny.

  2. The student may be assisted in giving a more accurate picture of his own behavior to the clinician and to himself by the use of various recording charts and written lists. Some of these methods are

    a. keeping a time schedule for a stated period and then comparing his distribution of time with tabulated results of similar studies

    b. keeping a financial account and facing it objectively with the aid of the clinician

    c. keeping a chart for recording instances of behavior which the student desires to develop or to free himself from, for example a chart of ascendant or of submissive behavior

    d. listing a number of things for which he would feel insulted to be praised (like knowing the letters of the alphabet or washing his face), and comparing it with another list of things for which he finds himself demanding approval.

  3. The clinician may find it necessary to assist the student or to ask the help of other responsible individuals in arranging modifications of his client's situation such as

    a. finding him a different room or roommate

    b. securing him employment, loans or outright gifts of money

    c. arranging a more reasonable scholastic program

    d. getting him into various social groups in which he may broaden his contacts

    e. assisting him with problems of personal appearance, posture and speech.

D. Techniques involving contacts with parents, faculty members or administrative officers with regard to the student's problems

  1. The clinician may need to present a somewhat generalized statement concerning a student's difficulties to faculty members or administrative officers in order that they may deal with him more adequately in the light of such knowledge. There are cases, how-

ever, in which it is inadvisable to call the student to the attention of any school official.

2. Contact with parents is frequently essential to the successful handling of a student's problems. In other cases it is definitely detrimental for the parent even to learn that his child is consulting a clinical psychologist. A single unfavorable report about the student's school adjustment, sent out as a routine matter by some college office, may undo months of work on the clinician's part. Often the clinician needs to be able to secure special handling of school situations pertaining to his client's welfare.

3. Contact with parents may take the form of interpreting the student and his difficulties to them, of getting their point of view about his situation, or of enlisting their cooperation in granting him needed freedom or encouragement. Sometimes it is necessary to assist parents in adjusting to problems of their own, as well as to reassure them about their children's development.

It has been necessary to make quite an arbitrary selection of techniques in order to present a wide range of material, and yet remain within the limits set for this paper. The inclusion of some methods and the omission of others has not been based on any one rigid criterion. No extensive mention of a testing program has been made, for example, because it has been assumed that clinicians in colleges have access to the scores of all student-clients on adequate tests of "intelligence." Referral to other campus agencies for medical diagnosis and treatment, remedial instruction in study methods and reading, speech correction, vocational and educational guidance, has been merely mentioned, although it is one of the important aspects of the service which a clinician renders his clients. This paper has been written to stimulate further professional discussion of the techniques of mental hygiene counseling for college students.

RALPH F. BERDIE

University of Minnesota

Judgments in Counseling[1]

Vocational counselors in student personnel programs attempt to assist students make judgments about their own capacities, potentialities, and personalities. The counselor supplies the student with two things. Primarily, he gives the student information about himself and his relationship to his surroundings. The student is told how his various abilities and interests, as estimated by test scores and past achievement, compare with the abilities and interests of people in different jobs, schools, and curricula. The counselor then helps in the use of this information so that the student can make a sound judgment regarding plans for the future.

Techniques for estimating abilities and interests have been discussed by many writers and summarized by others (37).[2] Methods of assisting students in arriving at judgments have been discussed by Williamson, Rogers, and others (184, 239). Before a student can understand his situation and plan for the future, he must make comparisons and discriminations. Information that has been analyzed and evaluated results in judgments, which in turn lead to decisions, which in their turn lead to action.

An attempt to adopt methods of clinical psychology and psychiatry in vocational counseling has led to a difference of opinion regarding underlying philosophies and techniques. One group of workers emphasizes the judgments that the counselor must make.

---

[1] This article is adapted from *Factors Associated With Vocational Interests*, by Ralph F. Berdie, a Ph.D. thesis on file at the University of Minnesota Library. Professor D. G. Paterson was the author's major advisor. Reprinted from *Educational and Psychological Measurement*, 1944, 4, 35–55. Copyright 1944 by Science Research Associates.

[2] Bibliography begins on page 719.

Another group expresses the opinion that it is not only unnecessary but also undesirable that the counselor make judgments. The counselor, according to the latter group, functions only to assist the student in arriving at judgments and does not provide judgments of his own which the student can accept or reject.

The view of the group deeming the counselor's judgment essential is expressed by Williamson (239, page 118):

It should be repeated that in vocational counseling the counselor collects data about the student's potentialities and then proceeds to compare these data with the requirements of the student's expressed occupational choice. In this way he arrives at a diagnosis of aptitude and a judgment as to the wisdom of that choice. *This comparison of potentialities with preferences is the important step in diagnosis.*[3] Following this step comes the interpretation to the student of the counselor's diagnosis and the cooperative planning of next steps.

The judgments studied in this investigation were judgments made by counselors about students, and the results are therefore most relevant for those counselors subscribing to the school represented by the quotation from Williamson.

When a student seeks vocational counseling, he usually is considering one or more possible vocations and he is attempting to make a judgment regarding the relative appropriateness of the considered vocations before deciding to enter one. The large number of factors serving to attract a student to various vocations results in one vocation usually being more or less preferred over others. Students seldom are considering two or more vocations all of which seem of exactly equal attractiveness. They have preferred vocations and they want to determine if they should enter those vocations. To assist in this determination the counselor and the student organize information based upon school grades, aptitude and ability tests, achievement tests, interest tests, personality scales, hobbies, and work experience. This organization usually results in both the counselor's and the student's making judgments about the appropriateness of vocational choices. The counselor's judgments may be the most effective force in molding the student's judgments.

This study sought to determine how consistent different counselors were in making judgments about vocational choices and what factors were instrumental in their arriving at these judgments. The

---

[3] Italic is the original author's.

judgments were all based upon the same material, i.e., case folders, and the counselors all had gone through a series of training clinics that supposedly supplied them with a common knowledge of the relevancy of the tests used and the data collected.

Methods

Twenty case folders of pre-college men were selected from the files of the Testing Bureau of the University of Minnesota. The vocational choice of each of these students had been judged in the first counseling interview as either appropriate or inappropriate by the counselor. The case notes were then reviewed by a case reader who verified the judgment of the original counselor. A duplicate folder was then prepared for each of the cases and all identifying data, such as name of student, name of father, etc., were removed. The following material was contained in the folder in this order:

1. The preliminary interview report—containing the student's stated problem, his high-school record, and observations made by the receptionist.
2. The summary profile of test scores—containing the names of the tests, the raw scores, the percentile scores, and the norm groups. Tests given at the Testing Bureau include tests of scholastic aptitude, scholastic achievement, special abilities, and personality.
3. The Strong *Vocational Interest Blank* profile. Scores were recorded for twenty-eight occupational scales and two non-occupational scales, masculinity-femininity, and occupational level.
4. The Kuder *Preference Record* profile, unrevised form. These profiles were not available for all of the twenty cases.
5. The University Testing Bureau *Individual Record Form*—a questionnaire covering family background, work experience, recreational activities, occupational plans, health history, etc.
6. A short statement of factual information obtained by the original counselor in the first interview with the student. No interpretative statements were included.
7. A rating form—containing the three following statements:
     The student comes to you and says, "If you say 'yes,' I will attempt to become a(n) (*insert occupational choice*). If you say 'no,' I will not."
     In this case you are forced to make a judgment. On the basis of the contents of this folder alone, would you say:
           Yes ...... or No. ...... (check one)
     1. If you think someone might disagree with you on the above judgment, what do you think his basis for disagreement would be?

2. Why do you think this basis insufficient to change your judgment?

The folders were then arranged in numerical order and given to each of the five counselors with the following instructions:

This is a necessary step in determining how judgments regarding the appropriateness of students' vocational choices are made and how consistent these judgments are. Will you please read through the twenty folders in the order in which they are given to you and after you have obtained the necessary information as you do in the interview or prior to the interview, answer the questions which are on the mimeographed sheets in each folder.

It is impossible to duplicate the exact interview situation without the student, but in order to provide as much of the interview atmosphere as possible, the data observed and recorded by the original counselor have been included in the folder. Regard these observations as factual rather than interpretive, i.e., they are exact statements of description rather than what the observer thought. Please be sure to answer all the questions.

After each counselor had rated the twenty cases, a procedure requiring from two to four hours, the folders were checked and put in their original order. New rating forms were inserted and the folders were given to the next counselor.

Results

Table 1 shows those cases judged by each counselor as having appropriate vocational choices and those having inappropriate choices. The check after the number of a student indicates that the counselor judged his choice as appropriate. The absence of a check indicates that the counselor judged it as inappropriate.

Of the 100 judgments, fifty-five were in the direction of appropriateness and forty-five in the direction of inappropriateness. Of the twenty students, ten had been judged by the original counselor as having appropriate vocational choices and ten as having inappropriate choices. Eighty-one of the 100 judgments made by the five counselors agreed with the judgment previously made by the counselor who originally interviewed the student. Analysis of the data in Table 1 yields a tetrachoric coefficient of .86 between the judgments made by the original counselor and the judgments later made by the five counselors. The results indicate that in judging the appropriate-

TABLE 1.   Judgments of Counselors Concerning Appropriateness of the Vocational Choices of Twenty Students

Cases Judged as Having Appropriate Choices by Original Counselor	Counselors Who Later Made Judgments of Appropriateness				
	1	2	3	4	5
13755	x	x	x	x	
13972	x	x		x	x
14095	x	x	x	x	x
14124	x	x	x	x	x
14178	x	x	x		x
14377	x	x	x	x	x
14423	x	x	x	x	x
14442	x	x	x	x	x
14485	x	x	x	x	x
14642				x	

Cases Judged as Having Inappropriate Choices by Original Counselor	Counselors Who Later Made Judgments of Appropriateness				
	1	2	3	4	5
13885					
13964	x	x	x		
14081	x			x	
14142		x			x
14396	x	x			
14445					
14486				x	
14600	x			x	
14640					
14749					

ness of the vocational choices of groups of students, trained counselors are able to agree.

Of the decisions originally made in the direction of appropriate choice, 14 per cent were later judged as inappropriate. Of the decisions originally made in the direction of inappropriate choice, 24 per cent were later judged as appropriate. This suggests that counselors tend to agree more upon judgments when students' choices are appropriate than when they are inappropriate. Counselors are perhaps more willing to put their stamp of approval on the student's plans than they are to discourage him. If a doubt exists in the mind of a counselor regarding the appropriateness of a student's vocational choice, he is more apt to decide the choice warrants a tryout than to decide it does not. These generalizations spring from clinical experience and the above data tend to substantiate them.

The judgments of the majority of counselors (three or more) agreed with the original classification of appropriateness-inappropriateness in eighteen of the twenty cases. The only people who considered the choice of case 14642 appropriate were the original counselor in both his first judgment and later judgment, and the case reviewer. One counselor besides the original counselor and the case reviewer considered the choice of case 13964 inappropriate, but three counselors considered it appropriate. The results do indicate that in the great majority of cases, judgments of the five counselors agreed with the decisions reached by the original counselor and the case reviewer.

Fourteen of the twenty cases had originally been interviewed by counselors who later served as judges in this study. It is doubtful if the original counselors remembered the cases, as all identifying data were removed at second presentation and a period of several months had elapsed since the original interview. Of these fourteen judgments, not one disagreed with the original decision. Even those two cases on whom the majority of counselors disagreed with the original counselor were consistently judged a second time by the original counselor. Here is evidence that a period extending from two to four months does not alter the judgments a counselor makes regarding the appropriateness of vocational choices and that counselors tend to arrive at the same judgment in the interview as they do by merely reviewing the case data and never seeing the student. These are essentially the results found by Super and Brophy (216), and it seems safe to generalize from them in the area of vocational guidance.

Up to this point, the analysis of judgments concerning appropriateness and inappropriateness of vocational choices has provided information regarding the consistency of these judgments. Little has been shown regarding the actual judgment-making processes themselves, however, and the factors considered in these judgments have not been discussed. A more complete understanding of these judgments will be obtained through a careful consideration of some of these cases themselves and the comments made by the counselors as they were making the judgments. Limitations of space prevent presentation of this material for all of the twenty cases.

Case number 13755 was a seventeen-year-old boy who graduated from high school one month after he came to the Testing Bureau. His occupational choice was chemical engineering, his father was dead, he had one eleven-year-old brother, and he said he would have to work about twenty-four hours a week while attending college.

Test scores were as follows:

Test	Percentile Score	Norm Group
High-school scholarship	42	
A.C.E.	77	University freshmen
Ohio Psychological	61	U.T.B. cases*
Cooperative English	46	University freshmen
Iowa Math. Training	57	Engineering freshmen
Iowa Chemistry Training	87	Engineering freshmen
Cooperative Physics	47	National—1 year high-school physics
Cooperative Social Studies	88	S.L.A. freshmen†
Minnesota Clerical—Numbers	54	General population
Names	94	General population
Finger Dexterity	54	General population
Tweezer Dexterity	33	General population
Spatial Relations	99	General population
Revised Paper Form Board	88	Engineering freshmen
Chapman-Cook Reading Test	64	S.L.A. freshmen
Minnesota Personality Scale—		
Morale	14	S.L.A. freshmen
Social	52	S.L.A. freshmen
Family	90	S.L.A. freshmen
Emotional	60	S.L.A. freshmen
Economic Conservatism	17	S.L.A. freshmen

* University Testing Bureau cases.
† Freshmen in the College of Science, Literature and the Arts.

Strong Test scores were A on keys for chemist, farmer, carpenter, printer, mathematics and physical science teacher, forest service man; B+ on keys for dentist, engineer, Y.M.C.A. physical director, social science high-school teacher, office man; B on keys for production manager and accountant. *Masculinity-Femininity* percentile— 82; *Occupational Level* percentile—2. Percentile scores on the Kuder *Preference Record* were: Scientific, 98; Computational, 30; Musical, 8; Artistic, 86; Literary, 8; Social Service, 9; Persuasive, 44.

The following statement of factual information was obtained from data contained in the interview notes of the counselor who originally counseled the student.

He is a husky, rather ordinary appearing young man. He is a little crude in his approach but very friendly. His father is dead and he lives with his mother and younger brother.

He will be totally self-supporting. He has saved about $100 from his paper route in the last three or four years and will continue to have a morning and evening route while going to college.

He says he took his first two years in high school as a joke and as compulsory education. Then he realized he must work harder but was unable to fully compensate for his previous loafing. He seems well motivated.

The original counselor and the case reviewer originally decided that the boy's choice of chemical engineering was appropriate. In making the later judgments, four of the five counselors agreed that this choice was appropriate; one decided it was not.

The dissenting counselor's response to the first question concerning the basis for disagreement was as follows:

They would stress the adequate ability and high-school achievement factors, together with the A and B+ scores on the chemist and engineering key on the interest test. They would then suggest that the boy be given a chance to show what he could do. They would also stress the good tests of background in mathematics and chemistry.

In response to the second question, concerning his reasons for considering the above inadequate to change his judgment, he wrote:

The discrepancy between H.S.R. and A.C.E. or *Ohio* seems to indicate under-achievement of long standing. The extremely low *Occupational Level* score and the problem of complete financial support are not hopeful signs of staying power. The block of skilled trades interests on the *Strong Test* is vitally important, partially because of their rarity.

Three of the other counselors mentioned the low high-school rank but did not appear to give it enough weight to have them change their judgments. One counselor thought a basis for disagreement might be found in the fact that it was too early for the boy to make a choice as specific as chemical engineering. Two counselors specifically mention the boy's motivation and appear to think that the fact that his achievement tests are better than his high-school rank improves his chances in the university.

One counselor, rating the occupational choice as appropriate, recognized these negative factors:

1. Average mathematics test score
2. Low high-school rank
3. Low *Occupational Level* score—"interests evidently immature"
4. C on mathematician key of *Strong Test*
5. Totally self-supporting
6. Low grades in high-school mathematics

We thus have two counselors who considered and listed the same factors, and yet one decided the choice was inappropriate, while the other wrote:

The above is strong evidence to question his choice, but because of the positive factors which are also clearly indicated, I'd be inclined to give him the benefit of the try-out.

The above counselor's note concerning the *Occupational Level* score gives a suggestion concerning one possible source of this disagreement. This counselor evidently interprets the *Occupational Level* score as an expression of interest maturity which therefore might change as the student ages, while the first counselor vaguely interprets it as an index of academic motivation.

Only one of the counselors approving of the occupational choice mentioned the financial problem, and none of them emphasized it as being important. The original counselor recognized the financial problem in the interview and took steps to meet it. Although he realized the importance of this problem, he did not consider that the boy should stay out of engineering.

This boy completed the first two quarters in the Institute of Technology with an honor point ratio of .42. His grades were:

College Algebra	D
Chemistry	C, C
Composition	D, I (incomplete)
Drawing	D, D

He dropped out of school at the end of his second quarter and has not returned.

Case number 13972 was an eighteen-year-old boy who graduated from high school six months before coming to the Testing Bureau and who was completing six months of post-graduate work in high school. His occupational choice was mechanical engineering, his father was crippled with arthritis and unable to work, he had two younger sisters, sixteen and eleven years old, he had work experience drafting on an N.Y.A. job, and would be totally self-supporting.

Test scores were as follows:

Test	Percentile Score	Norm Group
High school scholarship	98	
A.C.E.	76	University freshmen
Ohio Psychological	78	U.T.B. cases
Cooperative English	70	University freshmen
Iowa Mathematics Training	97	Engineering freshmen
Iowa Chemistry Training	17	Engineering freshmen
Minnesota Clerical—Numbers	74	General population
Names	96	General population
Chapman-Cook Reading	20	S.L.A. freshman
Minnesota Personality Scale—		
Morale	10	S.L.A. freshman
Social	31	S.L.A. freshman
Family	66	S.L.A. freshman
Emotional	57	S.L.A. freshman
Economic Conservatism	26	S.L.A. freshman

Strong Test scores were: A on keys for chemist, production manager, farmer, carpenter, printer, mathematics and physical science teacher, accountant, office man; B+ on keys for engineer, forest service man; B on keys for dentist, personnel manager, social science high-school teacher, purchasing agent. *Masculinity-Femininity* percentile—76; *Occupational Level* percentile—22.

The following statement of factual information was obtained from data contained in the interview notes of the counselor who originally counseled the student.

The boy does not have much money. His father is disabled because of arthritis. The boy has been working part-time for five months on a N.Y.A. job doing drafting work and making about $100 a month. He has had other odd jobs from time to time.

He is intrigued with mathematics and doesn't know much about the work of an actuary. He does not know that the training for this type of work is essentially through business and not through mathematics.

He has applied for a scholarship open to sons and daughters of World War veterans.

He is socially retiring.

The original counselor and the case reviewer decided that the boy's choice of mechanical engineering was appropriate. In making the later judgments, four of the five counselors agreed that this choice was appropriate, one decided it was not.

The dissenting counselor wrote:

This is a loose judgment. It would actually depend upon a judgment of which field (Institute of Technology or actuarial) the boy wanted most. He would be handicapped by lack of chemistry [in high school].

Three of the other counselors recognize the boy's expressed and measured interests in the business field and two of them suggest possible combinations of business and engineering. One of these two "mildly objects" that the boy hasn't quite the personality type for executive or management work. Two of the counselors indicate that the financial problem might serve as a basis for someone disagreeing with their judgment of the choice as appropriate. Both say, however, they think the problem can be satisfactorily managed. One counselor mentions the low *Occupational Level* scores but thinks this is overbalanced by the excellent achievement in high school. This is the same counselor who in the last case interpreted the *Occupational Level* score as an index of maturity. He is apparently using it here as an indicator of potential achievement! This counselor also recognizes the low score on the chemistry test but discounts it because the boy has not had chemistry in high school.

In general, there are no fundamental disagreements among the counselors regarding this case. They all tend to recognize that the boy has several potentialities and is a good college risk. Although one counselor indicates he would not encourage the occupational choice, he later qualifies this.

This boy completed the first year in the Institute of Technology with an honor point ratio of 2.11. His grades were:

Algebra	A
Trigonometry	A
Analytic Geometry	B
Chemistry	B, B, C
Composition	A, B, B
Drawing	B, B, C

He is now making satisfactory progress in his engineering course.

Case number 14095 was an eighteen-year-old boy who graduated from high school the same month he came to the Bureau. His vocational choice was business, the occupation of his father. His test scores were as follows:

Test	Percentile Score	Norm Group
High school scholarship	30	
A.C.E.	53	University freshmen
Ohio Psychological	45	U.T.B. cases
Cooperative English	49	University freshmen
Iowa Mathematics Aptitude	64	University freshmen
Iowa Mathematics Training	8	University freshmen
Cooperative Natural Sciences	24	S.L.A. freshmen
Cooperative Social Studies	87	S.L.A. freshmen
Minnesota Clerical—Numbers	94	General population
Names	89	General population
Mechanical Assembly	56	General population
Finger Dexterity	40	General population
Tweezer Dexterity	86	General population
Spatial Relations	86	General population
Chapman-Cook Reading	70	S.L.A. freshmen
Minnesota Personality Scale—		
Morale	93	S.L.A. freshmen
Social	96	S.L.A. freshmen
Family	31	S.L.A. freshmen
Emotional	84	S.L.A. freshmen
Economic Conservatism	53	S.L.A. freshmen

Strong Test scores were: A on keys for personnel manager, real estate salesman; B+ on keys for social science high-school teacher, accountant, office man, sales manager, life insurance salesman; B on keys for production manager, Y.M.C.A. secretary, purchasing agent. *Masculinity-Femininity* percentile—76; *Occupational Level* percentile—66. Percentile score on the Kuder *Preference Record* were: Scientific, 42; Computational, 79; Musical, 10; Artistic, 7; Literary, 62; Social Service, 60, and Persuasive, 99.

The following statement of factual information was obtained from data contained in the interview notes of the counselor who originally counseled the student.

He is a young man of short stature, not too neatly dressed, has a rather informal manner in the interview. He is rather ordinary in appearance. He would like to be self-supporting while going to school. He has about $250 saved now and might earn enough before starting at the University to continue without working while in school. His father would help him but he dislikes asking his father for help.

The father and mother were divorced about three years ago. The father is the president of a business. There are no other children in the family and the boy lives with his mother and gets along well with both parents.

In high school he says he studied just enough to get by but says he realizes now that that was not so smart.

The original counselor and the case reviewer decided that the boy's choice of business was appropriate. In making the later judgment, all of the five counselors agreed that this choice was appropriate. Four of the five said they did not think the boy's chances of graduating from the University were good but their attitude is expressed by this counselor.

I can't see any basis for disagreement since the job is waiting for him when he is through with school. However, I do not think he'll graduate from the University.

Again in this case there is general agreement among the counselors. It is doubtful if the boy's plans would have been influenced differentially by the counselors as they were all ready to approve of his vocational choice. This case is quite clear-cut.

This boy entered the College of Science, Literature and the Arts and at the end of his first quarter had an honor point ratio of .oo. It is doubtful if his academic "flop" will seriously interfere with his vocational adjustment. His grades were:

> Composition—cancelled
> Economics   D
> Political Science   C
> History   F

He did not return to the University after his first quarter.

Case number 13885 was an eighteen-year-old boy who came to the Testing Bureau the month he graduated from high school. His father was a salesman. The boy had one younger sister. The family was going to finance his college education. He had no work experience outside of working for his father and his vocational choice was advertising.

The test scores were:

Test	Percentile Score	Norm Group
High school scholarship	30	
A.C.E.	8	University freshmen
Ohio Psychological	10	U.T.B. cases
Cooperative English	2	University freshmen
Iowa Mathematics Aptitude	7	University freshmen

Test	Percentile Score	Norm Group
Iowa Chemistry Aptitude	19	University freshmen
Cooperative Natural Science	62	S.L.A. freshmen
Cooperative Social Studies	28	S.L.A. freshmen
Minnesota Clerical—Numbers	63	General population
Names	42	General population
Mechanical Assembly	24	General population
Finger Dexterity	29	General population
Tweezer Dexterity	46	General population
Spatial Relations	32	General population
Manual Dexterity	13	General population
Revised Paper Form Board	15	Engineering freshmen
Chapman-Cook Reading	4	S.L.A. freshmen
Minnesota Personality Scale—		
Morale	30	S.L.A. freshmen
Social	9	S.L.A. freshmen
Family	10	S.L.A. freshmen
Emotional	3	S.L.A. freshmen
Economic Conservatism	9	S.L.A. freshmen

Scores on the *Strong Interest Test* were: no A ratings; B+ on keys for farmer, purchasing agent, real estate salesman; B on keys for personnel manager, office man, president of a manufacturing concern. *Masculinity-Femininity* percentile—57; *Occupational Level* percentile—40. Percentile scores on the Kuder *Preference Record* were: Scientific, 57; Computational, 45; Musical, 1; Artistic, 58; Literary, 15; Social Service, 17; Persuasive, 52.

The following statement of information was obtained from the data contained in the interview notes of the counselor who originally counseled the student.

He is a very immature boy and his mother came with him the first day. He gives the impression of not knowing much about anything. He doesn't react favorably to General College.

The original counselor and the case reviewer originally decided the boy's choice of advertising was inappropriate. In making later judgments, all of the five counselors agreed that this choice was inappropriate. Three of the judges could see no reason why anyone would disagree with them. Two of the counselors suggest he might be able to handle a lower level job of advertising.

They might think he could do a low-grade type of advertising (show card writing, window displays) which may be what he means by advertising man. . . . He could never get the degree from the advertising sequence in the Business School because of various reasons. I doubt whether he'd be much good even at a low level of advertising in view of the poor manipulative skills and ability to work in spatial relationships.

The judges appeared to have very little difficulty in arriving at a decision on this case. He entered the General College and at the end of the first year took three comprehensive examinations, receiving a C in Social Civics, an F in Vocational Orientation, and an F in Individual Orientation. His course grades were:

Individual Orientation	C		
Current History	B	C	B
Government Studies	B	B	
United States in World Civilization	B	C	
Vocational Orientation	D		
Human Biology	C	C	
Oral Communication	C		
Psychology	C		
Physical Science	B		
Human Development	C		
Economics	C		

Case number 13964 was a seventeen-year-old boy who came to the Bureau the month he graduated from high school. His father was a car and truck mechanic and there were two younger brothers and a younger sister in the family. He had no unusual work experience and his vocational choice was architecture. Test scores were as follows:

Test	Percentile Score	Norm Group
High school scholarship	99	
A.C.E.	53	University freshmen
Ohio Psychological	67	U.T.B. cases
Pressey Classification	84	General population
Cooperative English	23	University freshmen
Iowa Mathematics Training	91	University freshmen
Iowa Chemistry Aptitude	80	University freshmen
Meier-Seashore Art	86 (exceptional)	
Minnesota Clerical—Numbers	73	General population
Names	47	General population
Revised Paper Form Board	83	General population

Test	Percentile Score	Norm Group
Chapman-Cook Reading	13	S.L.A. freshmen
Minnesota Personality Scale—		
Morale	13	S.L.A. freshmen
Social	69	S.L.A. freshmen
Family	42	S.L.A. freshmen
Emotional	99	S.L.A. freshmen
Economic Conservatism	32	S.L.A. freshmen

Scores on the *Interest Test* were: A on keys for printer, mathematics and physical science teacher; B+ on keys for farmer, personnel manager, accountant, office man; B on keys for carpenter, forest service man, Y.M.C.A. physical director, Y.M.C.A. secretary, social science high-school teacher, *Masculinity-Femininity* percentile—30; *Occupational Level* percentile—22. Percentile scores on the Kuder *Preference Record* were: Scientific, 50; Computational, 65; Musical, 63; Artistic, 90; Literary, 35; Social Service, 3; and Persuasive, 30.

The following statement was obtained from the data contained in the interview notes of the counselor who originally interviewed the student.

There is a financial problem here, to some extent. He has applied for N.Y.A. assistance. He claims he enjoys art very much and has done a great deal of poster work and layout work. He has a chance for a scholarship at the Institute of Art but will not accept it.

The original counselor and the case reviewer decided the boy's choice of architecture was inappropriate. In making the later judgments, two of the counselors agreed that the choice was inappropriate, three decided it was not. All the counselors rating the choice as appropriate noticed the absence of measured interests but made the following statements.

"No confidence in Strong for architecture." "Kuder tests shows 'artistic'; has art skills; has necessary ability. The Strong test may be in error." "The Strong is against me but his experience (making posters) is good enough to lead me to let him try it. The other interest test supports his choice."

One of the counselors rating the choice inappropriate cited in support the great concentration of skilled trades interest, the low *Occupational Level* score, the poor home and cultural background, and the financial problem. The superior high-school rank was discounted in light of the relatively poor school the boy attended. The other counselor rating the choice as inappropriate admitted the boy probably had enough ability to get the degree and that the choice might be appropriate from the standpoint of job opportunities. He added, however:

He probably is not outstanding enough in ability to make his living in this field, which offers limited opportunities to all but the very exceptional person. In view of the lack of Strong's measured interests, the low level of occupational aspiration, I'd say he should probably get mechanical drafting training or commercial art training.

This counselor, who is now interpreting the *Occupational Level* score as a measure of occupational aspiration, is the same one who previously interpreted it as a measure of interest maturity! This boy did not enter the University.

In this case, the basis for disagreement is quite clear-cut. Two of the counselors, chiefly on the basis of the interest test, would discourage the boy from entering architecture. The other three would discount the lack of measured interests and not discourage the boy. A tendency has also been found for some of the counselors to consider some of the keys of the *Strong Test* valid and some not. The factors which help the counselors determine which keys are valid have not been identified.

Case number 14081 was a nineteen-year-old boy who came to the Bureau one year after graduating from high school. He will have to help finance his college education. His vocational choice was metallurgical engineering.

The test scores were as follows:

Test	Percentile Score	Norm Group
High school scholarship	13	
A.C.E.	47	University freshmen
Miller Analogies, Form B	68	Education freshmen
Ohio Psychological	21	U.T.B. cases
Cooperative English	3	University freshmen
Iowa Mathematics Aptitude	34	University freshmen
Iowa Mathematics Training	32	University freshmen
Iowa Chemistry Aptitude	68	University freshmen
Iowa Chemistry Training	65	University freshmen
Cooperative Social Studies	85	S.L.A. freshmen
Cooperative Contemporary Affairs	57	S.L.A. sophomores

Test	Percentile Score	Norm Group
Minnesota Clerical—Numbers	34	General population
Names	29	General population
Chapman Cook Reading	5	S.L.A. freshmen
Minnesota Personality Scale—		
Morale	22	S.L.A. freshmen
Social	47	S.L.A. freshmen
Family	66	S.L.A. freshmen
Emotional	57	S.L.A. freshmen
Economic Conservatism	49	S.L.A. freshmen

Scores on the *Strong Test* were: A on keys for engineer, chemist, farmer; B+ on no keys; B on keys for architect, mathematician, printer, mathematics and physical science teacher, purchasing agent. *Masculinity-Femininity* percentile—65; *Occupational Level* percentile—66. Percentile scores on the Kuder *Preference Record* were: Scientific, 70; Computational, 91; Musical, 50; Artistic, 55; Literary, 5; Social Service, 9; Persuasive, 60.

The following statement of information was obtained from the data contained in the interview notes of the counselor who originally interviewed the student.

He lives with his mother and sister, both of whom are working. His father is dead. He applied for admission last year but was referred to the General College. He did not wish to go there so he did not come to school. He has an unusually strong vocational fixation.

The original counselor and the case reviewer decided the boy's choice of metallurgical engineering was inappropriate. In making the later judgments, three of the counselors agreed with this decision while two counselors judged the choice as appropriate. Two of the counselors rating the choice as inappropriate said they would expect no disagreement. The other counselor rating it as inappropriate said that, in the light of the boy's apparent strong drive for engineering, and "with the equivocal results on the Strong's," some might claim he should be given an opportunity in engineering. This counselor does not expound the mentioned equivocalities of the *Strong Test*. He decides, however, that, without an interview, the above factors cannot be given much weight. Both counselors rating his choice as appropriate recognize the boy's limited abilities and one mentions his relatively weak background in mathematics and chemistry. One of the counselors writes:

They would question his ability. His vocational choice has changed since he left high school. That might help him to work to capacity. Then I think he could make it. . . . I would improve his motivation, I hope, and if so, he'd make it. He lacks verbalistic skills. This would not be such a handicap to him in the Institute of Technology.

This boy did not register in the University.

In this case the basis for disagreement is again quite clear. The boy has interests congruent with his choice but abilities and a background that are not encouraging. All the counselors apparently recognized these factors, but three of them decided engineering was not a satisfactory choice, while two of them decided to take a chance, not place too much weight on the ability factor, depend on the interest and motivational factors, and let the boy try it.

Summary of Analysis of Judgments

The preceding discussion has covered much territory and many inferences have been drawn. Inferences drawn from the six cases discussed and the fourteen remaining cases are not conclusions based upon experimental results but are generalizations based upon observations of only a few cases. Often they are merely clinical hypotheses that should be investigated. Some of them are nothing more than verbalizations of conditions generally known to exist but often not explicitly recognized.

1. In making judgments regarding the appropriateness of students' vocational choices, trained counselors agree with the original judgment 84 per cent of the time. The tetrachoric coefficient between judgment made by different counselors is .86.

2. The majority of five trained counselors agreed in making judgments regarding the appropriateness of students' vocational choices upon the basis of the case notes with the decisions of the counselor who originally counseled the student and the case reviewer 90 per cent of the time.

3. In fourteen out of fourteen cases, the counselor who originally counseled the student and judged the appropriateness of his vocational choice at that time made the same judgment from the unidentified case folder several months later.

4. Counselors tend to approve of vocational choices oftener than they disapprove of them.

5. The Occupational Level score has been interpreted as a

measure of interest maturity, as a measure of motivation, as an index of occupational aspiration, and as a cause for poor achievement in high school.

6. Some counselors are reluctant to have a student of high ability enter business even if other factors suggests the advisability of such a choice.

7. When both measured and expressed interests are in business, counselors will seldom discourage a student from entering business. They may disagree on the level of training desired.

8. If ability and interest factors indicate success in an occupation, counselors tend to think meager informational backgrounds can be compensated for.

9. The appropriateness of a student's choice cannot easily be agreed upon when the occupational requirements, duties, and status are poorly defined.

10. The greater the apparent contradiction between the student's test scores, the greater will be the disagreement regarding the appropriateness of his vocational choice.

11. Some counselors interpret more rigorously scores on some scales of the *Strong Test* than they do scores on other scales.

12. Counselors do generalize results of the *Strong Test* to occupations for which there are no keys. Often they disagree upon the probable pattern people in a given occupation would obtain.

13. Lack of ability and absence of measured interests in an occupation almost always lead counselors to disapprove of a student's choice of that occupation.

14. If a student's aptitudes are too low, a counselor will disapprove of his vocational choice even if he has measured interests in that occupation.

15. Relatively little attention was paid to personality test scores in judging the appropriateness of vocational choices. Much attention was given to tests of ability, information, interests and high-school achievement.

16. Interest tests are used in determining occupational areas; ability and information tests and high-school achievement are used in determining levels of training.

17. Counselors make decisions regarding the appropriateness of vocational choices based upon generalizations which are often without support.

18. Sometimes when counselors consider the same evidence in making judgments on the appropriateness of vocational choices, they will not reach the same conclusion. They sometimes place different weights upon tests at different times, interpret them differently, and disagree with each other regarding these interpretations.

Evaluation of these results might cause one to question if counseling based upon such judgment can be more than systematic guess-work. In light of the statistical results, however, it must be concluded that regardless of the discrepancies in interpretations and regardless of some of the peculiar logic used by the counselors, the final outcomes at which they arrive do agree. We must remember that in the above cases the counselors were forced to make a decision. In many actual interviews, the counselor can suggest try-outs of various kinds that provide additional information in terms of actual success or failure before a decision has to be made. Often the counselor cannot make a decision and does not have to put himself on a limb as he did here. The student is also an important factor in arriving at a final decision in the actual counseling situation. The responsibility for making the decision is eventually his, and counseling which is more "non-directive" in character may not force the counselor to make a decision at all. As long as the counselor is to present test data to the student, however, he will most likely have to interpret it as either supporting or not supporting the student's choice or else interpret it as being completely irrelevant.

PETER BLOS

Brooklyn College

Psychological Counseling of College Students[1]

Our increasing insight into personality disturbances and the increasing recognition of the need for services equipped to deal with these problems have both brought to the fore a new field of therapeutic endeavor which I will call "psychological counseling." In this paper, attempt is made to differentiate its scope, function, and technique from other well established counseling services, such as vocational, educational, and others.

Psychological counseling deals with individual problem situations which are largely due to irrational factors, where rational solutions (talking it over) or cathartic expression (talking it out) prove inconsequential and of little help. Of this group, only those individuals will gain from psychological counseling who have not yet established a rigid, repetitive, neurotic pattern, but are rather acutely overwhelmed by inner or outer pressures. Unprepared or inadequate to cope with such pressures, the individual resorts to protective reactions. Such reactive conditions are most frequent when maturational strains, instinctual as well as environmental, are the rule rather than the exception; namely, during early childhood and puberty. Obviously, maturational conflicts and crises are crucial periods for the onset of neurotic difficulties, especially during adolescence.

Among the older adolescent, the college student is in a position

[1] Presented at the 1946 Annual Meeting. Reprinted from *American Journal of Orthopsychiatry*, 1946, 16, 571–580. Copyright 1946 by American Orthopsychiatric Association.

peculiarly his own. He has postponed, either willingly or under moral or social pressures, the attainment of adulthood for the sake of educational advantages or social prestige. This protracted adolescence, with its unavoidable effects on the psychic economy of the individual, is still a stepchild of psychiatry and mental hygiene. The problems created by the artificial prolongation of a maturational period affect almost every student at one point of his college career. Most students can cope with this situation, but an appreciable number undergo personality disturbances, some of which are at this time amenable to correction. As described in the foregoing, this group represents a strategic area where preventive psychiatry might well concentrate its efforts.

With such considerations in mind, five years ago Brooklyn College undertook to organize a counseling service for this specialized task. It had become evident that the student body—like any student body—presents personality disturbances which interfere with college work. This became of particular concern when the student of promising intellectual ability was unable to function adequately and was doomed to academic mediocrity or failure. To become acquainted with the run-of-the-mill student, I devoted part of my time to routine counseling work related to dropping of courses, excessive absences, change of programs, mid-term warnings, etc. I came to realize how often such situations are indications of a remote disturbance, and how effective counseling could be if it concentrated on minor symptomatic difficulties as soon as they appeared.

Since the psychological counselor is dependent on referrals, it is necessary that others understand his work, his function, and his responsibilities in order to make use of his services. For this purpose I gave seminars to the faculty and to the members of the Department of Student Personnel over a period of one year. Case presentations illustrated better than anything else which students should be referred and what could reasonably be expected from psychological counseling in terms of change or improvement. While some students show improvement within weeks, other require years to show any signs of growth. The discussions with the faculty were rewarding. Today psychological counseling is an established service in the College, and the medical office, the Deans, and the faculty request advice from the psychological counselor in all cases which lie within his province. Records are kept confidential; they are not included in the student's folder and are not available to anyone except the counselor.

Cases which come to the attention of the psychological counselor are as diversified as might be expected. Gross mental disturbances are referred to clinic or psychiatrist with the help of the family. Neurotic conditions are, if possible, also referred for psychotherapy or psychoanalysis. This leaves us with a bulk of disturbances which do not fit into any of the customary classifications of personality disorders. In fact, when I tried to classify 387 cases, I was appalled to find that classification would indeed be fitting them into a procrustean bed, for the sake of typology. I began to realize that I was dealing with case material which was basically different from cases seen in a mental hygiene or child guidance clinic; the difference being that no definite symptom complex had developed in these cases. A dysfunction had made its appearance in a limited field of the student's life, which rendered college an unsatisfying or unsatisfactory experience.

Complaints of this kind rarely come to the attention of psychiatric or mental hygiene services outside the college, because the individual is still in the state of seeking solutions by managing the environment or by isolating his conflicts in the process of symptom formation. It is precisely in this state of personality disturbance, when a maturational conflict is acted out rather directly in a displaced form, when the symptom has not yet crystallized into a symptom complex, that psychological counseling is called for. This type or state of personality disturbance is, in fact, the legitimate field of psychological counseling.

In an attempt to group the problems which had come to my attention over the years, I could use none of the customary classifications based on the dynamics of the disturbance, but had to resort to the overt complaint or difficulty as presented by the student. The following types of problems were met with regularity: 1) The student who cannot study, who complains of inability to concentrate. 2) The student who is lonely, who cannot make friends. 3) The student who is afraid of examinations, who is unable to speak in class. 4) The student without any purpose or vocational aim. 5) The habitual evader, obstructionist and complainer. 6) The student in acute conflict with his family. 7) The student with a physical defect. 8) Special problems of veterans.

Cases in this state of limited dysfunction can necessarily only receive remedial attention where psychological counseling services are intramural; that is, available within the educational institution. Only then are referrals made early and easily before too many faculty members have tried their latest reading in psychology on the student. Wherever such services are made part of a medical office or a student health service (which is primarily for physical attention), a psychological barrier is erected which tends to eliminate those cases which could profit most from psychological counseling. In addition, it must be recognized that referral to clinic or psychiatrist is for the college a drastic step, and for the student a frightening one. No one in any educational institution will take the responsibility for it except where the need is obvious. If states of limited dysfunction, if diffuse disturbances of concentration, memory, interpersonal relations, etc., received remedial attention at the time they become observable and were scrutinized as to character, the preventive effect of such services would undoubtably be worth the effort and many times the cost.

An additional advantage of intramural service lies in the ease with which the contact with the counselor can be renewed at any time. In most therapeutic situations we are accustomed to think in terms of time limitations, of termination of contact at a given point of therapeutic achievement. The cumulative process of psychological counseling as described here represents technical problems and therapeutic possibilities which have not yet been fully explored. The fact that the contact with the counselor can be renewed easily at any time has a direct influence on technique. Difficulties can be met progressively: one semester the overt problem might be academic, the next semester sexual, later vocational, etc. Counseling at each time lays the foundation for the progression to the next step of insight.

My experience with this type of counseling has impressed me with the fact that the resolution of an acute conflict (e.g., "I can't do my homework because I can never be as good as my father thinks I am") stimulates an integration of the new insight or growth experience which renders the personality capable of moving to a higher level of self-differentiation. This gain in "affective mobility" (*mobilité affective*) as the result of new insight emphasizes conflicts of which the individual was totally unaware. This might lead to resuming counseling again. The time which an individual needs to integrate therapeutic or growth experiences varies from months to years and often counseling is suspended for as long a period as that. The fact that the counseling process as here described is never ended but can be resumed at any time seems particularly adapted to counseling which gravitates around maturational conflicts as is the case in most of the work with college students. So unorthodox a technique immediately raises the problem of the transference and how it operates in a cumulative counseling process. This problem will be taken up later in detail.

Let us examine a case illustration which presents some typical aspects of psychological counseling.

Stanley, an upper sophomore, age 18, was referred by his class counselor to the psychological counselor, because he complained of feelings of apathy and inability to concentrate. Stanley ranks as a student of superior intelligence; his record is good but uneven; his work had declined of late. He is very eager to receive help.

Stanley doubts his intellectual abilities and any decision he makes. He compares himself almost compulsively with others, and asks himself if he is normal. Following the wishes of his family, he started college with the intention of taking over his father's successful business. After he had failed in essential courses prerequisite for the planned career, he decided against it. Now, a year later, Stanley has found a field of his own interest, but feels he cannot be sure that his decision is valid and wonders whether he should not give up his own desires and again follow his father's wishes. Apathy, distraction, absent-mindedness, and apprehensiveness are at the moment dominant. He asks himself, what shall I study? On what shall I concentrate? In what am I talented?

As a child, he was promising, intelligent, and greatly admired by his parents. He stated he was an only child, but admitted after four months that he has an older sister who has been in a mental institution for a number of years. His mother overpowered him with loving possessiveness and inhibited his masculine development. Passive and submissive tendencies were overcompensated by hyperactivity, but he derived no pleasure from it. Of late this hyperactivity was replaced by a feeling of having no purpose and no future. The desire and fear of taking over his father's business resulted in a state of indecision and apathy. A factor in intensifying this fear is the mental breakdown his sister suffered when she was his present age. At that time she decided, against her parents' wishes, to enter a career of her own choosing. Stanley's and his sister's careers have the common factor of being in artistic fields. The fear of insanity as a natural consequence of disobeying parental wishes contributed to the state of indecision. Shortly before he started being counseled, he read books on abnormal psychology until this reading became too disturbing and he "put it all out of his mind."

Stanley's disturbance is the result of an inner conflict which has as its conscious and unconscious components the fear of taking over the father's role. The desire to do so represents in its ambivalence the typical recrudescence of the oedipus conflict on the adolescent level. But it must not be overlooked that passive and submissive tendencies were equally strong. As a defense against these tendencies, he forced himself into masculine self-assertive behavior which, consequently, was not wholly genuine in its quality. For his weakness in the present struggle Stanley blamed his mother because she had not been strict enough with him when he was a child. The parents', especially the mother's, boundless trust in him as a child had given him a feeling of omnipotence which helped him in being successful in school without exerting real effort. In his present crisis he lost this feeling of unquestionable competence, and with it, his self-confidence. His present attitude of ignoring his mother, his apparent indifference to both parents' concern about his future; in brief, his lack of any feeling tone at home, but his intense, almost frantic preoccupation with his normality and vocational choice, indicate that he has displaced his conflict with the family into the sphere of academic problems and college life.

Conscious material which he had carefully kept isolated became linked together; for example, the fear of insanity in relation to an autonomous choice and his seeking of reassurance with regard to his normality were brought into awareness. The transference, then, was instrumental in loosening up emotional rigidity and provided a new affective experience which had a twofold effect; it helped to strengthen a weak masculine identification and lent support to his inadequate ego in regaining a position of control and objectivity. He could, for example, for the first time in two years inform the family of his vocational desires. Eventually he pursued his newly gained interest with less anxiety, became freer in making contacts with people, and finally began to recognize his sexual problems. While this process was going on the difficulties in concentration decreased (he passed the semester with B average), he became more active and felt less apathetic; the compulsive comparison of himself with others, and doubting his decisions, gradually declined though did not disappear completely.

This process of counseling can be summed up as follows. An emotional stalemate was broken even though the basic conflict continued to exist. What was achieved was the regained capacity to act, to make decisions, to be less morbidly introspective and therefore receptive to new experiences, and to give free play to inhibited affects. The student was seen 39 times over the period of three semesters.

A follow-up after ten months showed that Stanley had retained his ability to act, to make contacts with people, to pursue his interest, and he had made a very good academic record. Inadequacy feelings in relation to heterosexual adjustment continued, but the self-doubt and the indecision in relation to vocational choice, interest, and ambitions were markedly reduced. His activities still bear the stigma of earlier compensatory hyperactivity and still contain compulsive features, but his activities are better organized, are more realistic and stable, and are socially integrated. Among other things, he founded an active club in the field of his creative endeavor.

Why was this case considered suitable for psychological counseling? In answering this question I will simultaneously clarify some of the theoretical concepts related to psychological counseling. To start with, we have to remind ourselves that each personality disturbance has different layers in terms of which it can be described and evaluated.

In Stanley's case there was at the bottom of his disturbance an emotional conflict which interfered with adequate ego function. When faced with the necessity for emancipation from the family his ego was too weak to stand up in the ensuing struggle. Two characteristic ego reactions to a maturational crisis can be observed; namely, ego-restriction and ego-regression. Both reactions are protective measures: ego-restriction to ward off anxiety through inhibition of function, and ego-regression to master anxiety through archaic ego expression. Ego-restriction became apparent in his failure in the courses prerequisite to entering his father's business. (He failed despite the fact that he scored in this particular field in the tenth decile on the scholastic aptitude test administered at college entrance.) Ego-repression became apparent in Stanley's mistaking similarity for identity (sister's illness) and in his use of will power and thinking power (magical thinking), to mention only a few.

While reality factors such as his sister's breakdown at his age, and the father's tireless wooing for his son's submission were responsible for the reactive state as described; these factors could not be made solely responsible for Stanley's condition. The recrudescence of infantile conflicts, clearly the oedipus complex, determined his reaction to a disturbing present. The condition in which the student found himself contained, besides infantile, also maturational, conflicts in relation to adolescent psychosexual development. While he was able to maintain an outward equilibrium up to late adolescence, the increasing pressure of instinctual and environmental demands finally proved to be stronger than his ego. His ego inadequacy was the point where the counseling effort concentrated, and not the infantile conflict which was the source of the present predicament.

Psychological counseling does not attempt to resolve unconscious infantile conflicts; in fact, it carefully avoids entering this sphere which is the realm of psychoanalysis. Psychological counseling deals with the derivatives of these conflicts in terms of ego reactions. In its interpretive aspect it restricts itself to the realm of the ego. In Stanley's case it brought to awareness the relatedness of isolated facts, some of which come only very slowly to the surface. While dissociated conscious material could be related, an insight into ego defenses was gained through the interpretation of omissions, contradictions, denials, forgetfulness, etc. All these efforts would have been fruitless without a purposeful use of the transference. Here the unconscious conflicts which were recognizable during the counseling process found a mode of expression and communication where the direct verbal expression would obviously have been inadequate.

In this connection I should like to mention that every personality disturbance is related to unresolved relationship conflicts. It is obvious, therefore, that the relationship in psychological counseling which with adolescents can hardly escape from developing into a transference in the proper sense of the term, is a most valuable, if delicate, instrument in dealing with adolescent personality disturbances. Depending on the case, either interpretation or mere manipulation of the transference as an affective experience is used to better advantage.

In the case here reported, the counselor had to steer away from a repetition of the parental pattern. During the first months, for example, Stanley showed an eagerness to understand himself, an objectivity in looking at the problem, a seemingly mature attitude which might well have been mistaken as a favorable sign. In its rigidity and detachment, this attitude betrayed its defensive character. It was his way of warding off passive and submissive tendencies in relation to the counselor. Situations such as the counselor discussing with Stanley rather critically the products of his creative efforts instead of accepting them indiscriminately as attempts at independence strengthened his ego by lessening the fear of passivity which loomed dangerously in any situation of unconditional and complete acceptance. The transference experience provided an opportunity to express positive and negative emotions without re-experiencing the family situation which he tried naturally to repeat. In this respect the relationship to the counselor was different from any in his past. It was an extension of the past into the present which, through the medium of the counselor, exerted a modifying influence on an emotional pattern still in flux.[2]

This use of the transference differs in principle from the use of the transference in psychoanalysis. As is well known, the latter transference serves as a screen on which infantile relationship conflicts are projected. The development of a transference neurosis is in fact the precondition for psychoanalytic therapy. Psychological

---

[2] Dr. Clara Thompson expressed a similar idea about the limited use of the transference, which I quote: "For example, a person who has been dominated by a forbidding father presents without insight a submissive attitude to the therapist, probably based on fear. The fact that the therapist is actually more permissive and tolerant means that the patient finds himself in a more favorable milieu and can develop to a certain point, although nothing is done about his tendency to be dominated. He is still a submissive person, but he has, as it were, put himself under the guidance of a benevolent tyrant, and in his efforts to please the new father he may achieve some worth-while growth for himself. He will probably never become independent, but he will be able to have more freedom under this authority than under the old one." "Transference as a Therapeutic Instrument," (221).

counseling, on the contrary, prevents at all cost a transference neurosis from developing, because it is not prepared to cope with the consequences. It is well to remember that transference phenomena will become manifest during psychological counseling regardless of the counselor's doings. He cannot escape from becoming involved. It is often questioned whether active or passive, directive or nondirective counseling is preferable. In the light of the foregoing, the attitude of the counselor ceases to be a matter of principle, but becomes a variable dependent on the affects in operation and the counseling purpose dominant at the moment. These factors alone determine to what degree and in what manner the counselor participates in the counseling process.

As has been said before, not every personality disturbance which comes to the attention of the psychological counselor is *eo ipso* a psychological counseling case. There are counterindications which are of particular importance because their recognition will prevent both waste of counselor's time and, even more important, a negative therapeutic experience of the student which might make therapy unacceptable to him for some time. In an appreciable number of cases, therefore, psychological counseling consists solely in making some form of psychotherapy acceptable to the student rather than the counselor participating in the student's maneuvers which aim at depreciating an existing difficulty. Such maneuvers which simulate progress and improvement are often striking, as, for example, the student who overcame her depression and hysterical conversion symptom as soon as the counselor mentioned psychiatric help. Evaluation of a complaint or symptom is necessary before psychological counseling can prognosticate its adequacy. This evaluation must take into account the transitory and permanent elements of the given symptom complex or, to state it differently, it has to assess the maturational (instinctual) and environmental as well as the neurotic or psychotic components of the maladjustment. Where symptoms have assumed neurotic rigidity and repetitiveness, psychological counseling will bring about no fundamental improvement. Where, however, the conflict has not been fully internalized, and the so-called symptoms are to a large measure due to acutely menacing and aggravating pressures from without (environment) and within (id, superego), there psychological counseling will prove effective. At no point is it overlooked that unconscious conflicts play their part in any personality disturbance, a realization which determines the limited objective with which psychological counseling approaches its task.

The following case will illustrate a situation where psychological counseling was contraindicated. David was referred by the medical office because he impressed the examiner during a routine check-up as tense, nervous, and apprehensive. David talked freely to the psychological counselor, in fact, he enjoyed the interview "more than he had anticipated" and readily arranged a time for his return. David considers himself an introvert who has little contact with people, nor does he desire such contacts. He lives in ideas, feels that he is superior to others and will not share their "base and primitive interests" like movies, sports, or girls. He has become so used to imaginary company that he can easily dispense with real people. The kindred spirits in whose close company he moves include Nietzsche, Rimbeaud, Baudelaire, Kirkegaard, Proust, and others. He argues that "*they* all lived in a shell." His only complaint is that he feels "totally unproductive." He is not concerned about his social isolation, his disinterest in and remoteness from people. He feels misunderstood at home. "I am an anomaly in my family."

David is an only child. Overprotected by his mother, was never allowed to play unsupervised with other children until the age of eight. He can still recall standing behind the front gate of the family house, with clean hands and creased knee pants looking at the outside world and the free children. While David liked to talk to the counselor, his attitude remained the same through several interviews: distant, colorless, friendly but slightly condescending, verbal and repetitive. He had to convince the counselor that he, David, is like one of those many "misunderstood and neurotic geniuses." "I am like them" was the stereotype explanation. His isolation was his distinction and proof of superiority. Academically he succeeded extremely well.

This case was considered unfit for psychological counseling because the conflict was totally internalized and fantasy constructions had replaced any interpersonal relationship. The student's history and present symptoms indicated a serious neurotic disturbance (compulsion neurosis), possibly with schizoid trends. Through periodic follow-up interviews the counselor kept an eye on the student, waiting until he would express the need of psychiatric help which had been explained to him on several occasions.

The line of demarcation which separates the field of psychological counseling from bordering therapeutic disciplines is not as neat and clear-cut as one would desire. In the first place the field is new and still undefined; in addition, it should be remembered that adolescents present symptom complexes which would be considered far more serious if they appeared at another age level. Adolescents show reactions to maturational strains which are often difficult to differentiate at first sight from neurotic or even psychotic conditions.[3] However, information about the student's life, the duration of the overt conflict or the symptom, the degree of alloplastic ego activities in conjunction with transference phenomena will aid in an evaluation of the acute problem for which the student seeks help and will determine whether psychological counseling is indicated or not. This decision can usually not be reached before a number of exploratory interviews have taken place.

Psychological counseling as presented here is based on the application of Freudian psychoanalytic psychology. With its special technique, it must be based on a coherent psychological system or theory which provides the counselor with the conceptual tools for the understanding of the dynamic and economic problems involved in each case. The fact that the counselor must differentiate between those problems which belong in his domain of competence and those which need other types of help and therefore are better off without any psychological counseling, raises many questions with regard to training and supervision. Besides the technical training in psychology, I believe that the psychological counselor should have undergone psychoanalysis as a professional prerequisite for this type of work. Extensive supervision on the job is another essential phase of the training in this field. This cursory statement requires elaboration, but the purpose of this paper lies in another direction and therefore the problem of training can only be mentioned in passing.

In summarizing, it might be said that protracted adolescence of

---

[3] Sylvan Keiser. *Severe Reactive States and Schizophrenia in Adolescent Girls* (121, p. 25). "We believe that many benign psychopathological reactions of the adolescent period are incorrectly diagnosed as schizophrenic. A good number represent reactive states dependent on the recrudescence of infantile conflicts occurring during adolescence."

college youth tends to precipitate personality disturbances of the reactive type, which interfere seriously with the successful life, academically and socially, of the student. Such maturational disturbances are detected at an early stage only where psychological counseling services are intramural and a simple but effective referral system is set up. Psychological counseling as a discipline is still in its early stages, lacking clear demarcation of the field as well as definition of its function and elaboration of its technique. The purpose of this paper is to stimulate the discussion of these three problems: namely scope, function, and technique of psychological counseling.

DOROTHY W. BARUCH

Beverly Hills, California

Description of a Project in Group Therapy[1]

Since group therapy is becoming an increasingly important adjunct to individual therapy in a war and postwar period, and since techniques and procedures are still in a great state of flux, it is hoped that the present paper will hold some value even though it is an informal report rather than controlled research.

Twelve sessions of *therapeutic group discussion* which were held as part of a college course in techniques of therapy are described. The course also included a sampling of psychodrama and of creative writing used as a therapeutic tool. During the discussion sessions an attempt was made (1) to keep record briefly on what took place, (2) to analyze techniques of leadership, and (3) to tap the effects of the process through the expressed reactions of the group members.

Therapeutic group discussion might be likened to counseling with a group. The basic orientation of the therapist bears a major influence on the process, which accordingly becomes directive or nondirective, persuasive, suggestive, permissive, or what not.

Orientation in the present instance was to a type of group discussion characterized above all by permissiveness and acceptance.

Creation and maintainance of a climate where these qualities can function, involves not only the therapist's—or group leader's—own attitudes but also the interacting attitudes of the group members.

[1] Reprinted from *Journal of Consulting Psychology*, 1945, 9, 271–280. Copyright 1945 by American Psychological Association.

The therapeutic relationhsip is not on a one to one basis, but on a basis of manifold and shifting inter-relationships. The resistance and guilt factors that need to be dealt with are not those of an individual counselee but of many. The all-important problem of maintaining acceptance involves not alone the therapist's feelings, but the feelings current among group members. As discussion proceeds, subleaders rise in the group and the therapist's own attitude toward giving up leadership as well as the attitudes of group members toward having one another assume leadership—all enter in. The very complexity in these inter-relationships is what makes the group process so subtle, and the so-called leadership techniques so difficult both to analyze and to convey.

Subjects

The present group was composed of twenty-three members, both men and women. Ages ranged from eighteen to forty-nine years, with a mean age of thirty-five ($\sigma = 6.9$). The members included a school administrator, a physician, a business secretary, a psychiatric social worker, an industrial counselor, an administrator and several group workers from the Los Angeles Youth Project,[2] and teachers from the nursery through high school. Education included a medical degree, three masters', eleven bachelors'. Eight people had not completed college. The majority were Protestant-Anglo-Whites, although there were five Jewish members, one Catholic, one Negro and one Mexican. Sixteen were married, two were single and five were separated or divorced. (See Table I.) Eleven had attended a mental hygiene course given by the group leader.

Process and Analysis of Techniques

On the assumption that undergoing therapy themselves would best clarify and point up techniques for them, the group members spontaneously elected to have such an experience.

In the first two sessions, the therapist—or group leader—took a more active role than at any later time. She assumed major responsibility for establishing a warm friendly feeling in the group, for using first names, for seating members informally in circular arrangement. She saw to it that the process of therapy was briefly introduced and that her own non-advisory role was defined. She brought

---

[2] An interagency project focusing on the prevention of delinquency.

out that the major function of the group members was to talk about matters that were troublesome, but that talking was not essential

TABLE I.   Face Data

Total Enrolled......................................	23
Age Range...	18 to 49
Mean Age..	35 ($\sigma = 6.9$)
Education	
High school graduate.............................	1
High school and some college......................	6
College graduate.................................	2
College and post graduate.........................	9
Master's degree..................................	3
M.D..	1
Business School..................................	1
Occupation	
Students...	2
Teachers[a].......................................	13
School Administrator..............................	1
Group Workers (Youth Project).....................	2
Youth Project Administrator.......................	1
Psychiatric Social Worker..........................	1
Industrial Counselor..............................	1
Secretary..	1
Physician..	1
Marital Status	
Single...	2
Married..	16
Separated..	2
Divorced[b].......................................	3
	23
Religion	
Protestant.......................................	11
Catholic...	1
Jewish...	6
None[c]..	5

[a] Teachers were from the following levels:

Nursery School..	2
Elementary...	8
Junior High..	2
Senior High..	1

[b] This face sheet information was collected at the middle of the term. At the end of the class two of the divorced members were married to each other.

[c] Three of the members listing themselves under "none," indicated backgrounds of religion, i.e., one baptized Protestant and converted to Judaism on marriage, one baptized Methodist, and one Congregational-Presbyterian. One member (Methodist) emphasized his deliberate withdrawal, at the age of fifteen, from the church where he had received complete indoctrination, in contrast to those whose withdrawal was due to "drifting," or to those who had "no religious background."

unless they felt like it. She stressed the fact that material would need to be kept in strictest confidence and defined some of the mechanics for carrying on group discussion, such as avoidance of asides, not stopping to raise hands, not waiting to be called on, and the like.

Some members felt that it would be difficult to discuss any real problems in a group. The leader accepted this initial resistance, nodded and restated, simply: "You feel it will be difficult." Several concurred but went on to say that they would nonetheless like to try it out. In consequence, the leader asked that those who wished to do so, cite some of their problems. Fifteen members presented problems which the leader then grouped under larger, more collective headings—as marital problems, problems with parents, etc. . . The majority chose the latter to begin on.

As the various individuals talked and as it became clear to them that the hostilities they felt toward their parents were common and acceptable, they spontaneously brought up other items. Several were still bothered by sibling rivalry or by feelings of having been rejected. Several were having marital problems. Some were involved in the difficulties presented by continence and some by concern over extra-marital affairs. Several felt that their disappointments in marriage, such as lack of orgasm, and difficulties in understanding and accepting their partners, were directly tied up with earlier attitudes. Important among these, they felt, were the conflicts that had arisen from parental reactions to masturbation and bodily exploration.

After the twelfth session, leadership techniques were discussed and analyzed by the group and were later summarized into a written schedule by the leader. (See Listing of Techniques of Leadership in Group Discussion.)

Two members went over the running records made during the therapeutic sessions and separately categorized each leadership technique recorded. Out of the sixty-six paired judgments made in the assigning of categories, there were sixty agreements, yielding an extremely high percentage of agreement—namely 91 per cent; and a difference of 9 per cent—with a significantly small standard error of .01.

The records clearly indicated that major techniques had to do with *bringing resistances, embarrassment, guilt feelings, and other* emotions into sharper focus, to clarify them, to make collective meanings appear and to facilitate working them through. Many times the leader would do this simply by restating feelings that had been expressed verbally or by putting into words feelings that were indicated by non-verbal cues, as psychomotor tensions, evasiveness, breaks in discussion, etc.[3]

The following excerpts from the seventh session illustrate this restatement technique.

One of the men (2M)[4] brought up that punishment received for having masturbated had made him feel cheap, unworthy, soiled. . . The leader accepted this, restating: "You felt that your body was cheap and unworthy; so the whole of you seemed cheap and unworthy" . . . Others came in with experiences that had affected them similarly. One (13F) had been punished for playing under the bed clothes with her brother; another (3F) had witnessed her parents having sex relations and had absorbed a recoil attitude from her mother. The first (2M) said: "They put pepper on my penis to keep me from masturbating. . . Made me feel horrible and guilty. . ." Another (20M) said, "Being good was being non-sexual. I had a feeling of being wicked. The devil had me by the tail because I enjoyed masturbation and necking" . . . and later, "Sex was one thing; you were another. Sex then couldn't be a part of any love relationship that you were involved in. . . What chance for marriage?" . . . The leader synthesized these various contributions, restating in terms of their collective meaning by saying, "Attitudes toward sex . . . were put in the dark isolated without regard for the human relationships involved."

She continuously *put observed tensions into words*, thus: "It is hard to talk about these things. They're usually taboo. I'm wondering if you've felt, in consequence, that some of the group were non-acceptant?" Several were then able to come out with feelings of disapproval or of having been disapproved of.

Another of the important techniques was *to keep the focus on emotional content* either by pointing out frankly when the group began to intellectualize or by calling for concreting with such

---

[3] This is similar to the restatement technique used by Rogers in individual counseling.

[4] M = male; F = female.

phrases as "Tell us what you mean" . . . "Can you give an example?" "Can you remember what you did and how you felt?"

Other techniques included *keeping the discussion dispersed* so that no one person monopolized it, and *keeping it geared, also, to majority focus,* thus facilitating identification, acceptance and increased ease in emotional release. Questions such as: "How do the rest of you feel about this? Or, again, restating in such a way as to make a point collective served to effect this end.

Important, too, appeared the *increasing passivity of the therapist,* her willingness to turn leadership functions over to group members and her matter-of-fact acceptance of growth for its emotional value to the individual rather than in judgmental or moralistic terms.

Probably, the most important aspects of leadership, however, were the *permissiveness, acceptance* and *empathy* that the therapist continuously expressed. In the words of one of the group members, "It was her warm and sincere interest in each one of us, and a kind of real affection, that made it possible to go on."

LISTING OF TECHNIQUES OF LEADERSHIP IN THERAPEUTIC GROUP DISCUSSION

I. *Sets up situation suitable for release*

1. Shows empathetic, permissive attitude (sincere and warm interest in each individual)

Expresses warmth and empathy actively, though not necessarily verbally (i.e. does it through facial expressions, gestures, etc.)

2. Establishes informality

Seats group in circular formation in not too large a circle; comfortable chairs where possible; no double row of chairs but sitting on floor instead

Refreshments beforehand with opportunity for exchange

Asks group members to take on various responsibilities, as turns at bringing refreshments, setting up chairs, opening door, taking enrollment, fees, etc.

Uses first names

3. Introduces therapeutic process

Concept that all people have troubles

Value of release (what it does)

Value of talking as means of release

Value of listening in a therapeutic group as another means of release until ready to talk

4. Defines relationships

Brings up confidential nature of group therapy and the consequent necessity for each person to assume professional attitude toward material and to keep it inviolate. Calls on group for discussion and mutual agreement

a. Leader's role

Major function to remain acceptant (non-advisory, non-condemnatory, non-judgmental)

b. Group Members' role

Two fold:

(1) To gain release by talking of own

troubles or by listening if not ready to talk

(2) To help others gain release by remaining acceptant—not probing, questioning, or interpreting

5. Welcomes initial resistances to discussing personal problems in a group situation	Restates any resistance that is expressed verbally	"You feel it will be hard to voice your real feelings in public, as it were . . ."
	Brings into open apparent resistances shown by psychomotor tensions	"You look doubtful about something."
	If no resistance is voiced or shown, calls on group for expression of how they actually feel; or states that many people are at first concerned over the idea of discussing troubles before others	"I'm wondering how you are feeling about telling about your troubles in front of others . . ." "At first, it's often hard for people to believe it can be done . . ."
	Pauses for group expression and response	
	Shows by acceptant attitude that it is permissive to bring into group of this sort, the negative feelings not ordinarily directly expressed	
6. Introduces a few essential mechanics for	Stresses free participation; not raising hands or waiting to be called	

carrying on discussion method	on; "talk when feel like it," give-and-take idea	
	No asides, whisperings, notewriting, etc. Desirability, instead, of bringing out into open whatever comes into mind	
7. Helps group locate a common problem and to begin on it	Calls on group members to name some of their troubles	
	Places individually mentioned problems under larger categories so as to make them collective (as: problems with parents, husband-wife problems, etc.)	
	Asks group which type of problem appeals to most	
	Calls on group to begin talking about experiences and feelings along line of problem selected	"Imagine we're ready to start now on our troubles . . . Perhaps A would like to go on with hers . . ."

II. *Facilitates release*

1. Keeps discussion focused on emotional-content vs. action-content or theory	Calls for specifics (i.e. for concrete experiences) and for feelings about these	"Tell us what you mean . . ."
		"Can you give an example?"
		"Remember what you did and how you felt?"
		"How did you feel when that happened?"

	Points out frankly that group is theorizing or escaping into other peoples' problems vs. working through their own	"There we go again talking in vague terms . . ." "We're not staying with ourselves and with how we feel. . . ."
2. Establishes and seeks to maintain mutual, interactive ACCEPTANCE (i.e. both leader's acceptance of group members and their acceptance of each other)		
a. Clarifies) what) group ex-) presses so) that it be-) comes) more un-) derstand-) able to all)	*** *Restates feelings that have been expressed verbally*	"You felt very irked . . ." "You felt antagonistic . . ."
b. Relates) what vari-) ous peo-) ple ex-) press so) that col-) lective) meanings) and appli-) cability) appear)	*Puts into words feelings that have been expressed non-verbally (i.e. through psycho-motor tensions, eva-siveness, breaks in dis-cussion, etc.*	"Some of you are looking both-ered. . ." "It's hard to bring out things like this. . ." "We're usually hesitant over talking about such things."
c. Helps) bring ten-)		

*** This section includes the major and most important techniques that the leader uses in group discussion. They come in over and over again as discussion advances. (See also Sections I 5 and III 3.)

sions and) inter-) group hos-) tilities) into the) open so) that they) may be) worked) through)	Pauses for group to let out these feelings	
d. Helps) bring dis-) comfort,) embar-) rassment,) guilt-feel-) ings out) so that) they may) be worked) through)	Occasional calls on group for how they are feeling Again, restates etc.	"I wonder how you are feeling now?"
3. Keeps discussion dispersed (i.e. so that no one person talks too long, especially at first, thus avoiding too fast exposure with too great guilt resulting and closing up on release or self-accept-ance; also avoiding any one person becoming a target for criticism and rejection by others before they have learned to be suffi-	Turns point in question to group	"How do rest of you feel about this?"

ciently accept-
ant; reducing
also, the
chances for
shutting off re-
lease of more
timid ones by
more aggres-
sive group
members

4. Keeps discussion geared to majority focus (thus facilitating identification, acceptance and increased ease in emotional release)	Reiterating, when pertinent the necessity for keeping together, for avoiding asides, etc. Letting side-lines run on if related to majority focus; but stopping them if unrelated by brief acknowledgment of sideline content and then restating what was under focus at point where majority focus was lost
5. Occasionally brings in a relieving type of information	

III. *Facilitates self-direction*

1. Recognizes sub-leadership roles in group as these develop	Is aware of fact that group members tend gradually to assume sub-leadership functions and that this is a sign of movement toward self-direction
2. Is willing to relinquish own	Remains acceptant and non-defensive as

leadership role to sub-leaders	this occurs (i.e. does not feel need to cling to any supposed prestige value in role)	
	At first, at least in some instances, shows recognition by reiterating what sub-leader says	"As R says, we do seem to feel embarrassed . . ."
	Brings in fewer and fewer restatements or other techniques; relies more and more for these on the group members	"As B just brought up, we're escaping again into generalizations . . ."
3. Accepts reports of progress, of new actions, of help gained in the course, of new insights and other types of forward movement, keeping emphasis still on emotions, and on feeling values to the person himself	Again, restates what members bring in, still remaining acceptant rather than judgmental (i.e. Does not, by voicing approval or gratification, put person in a position of having done this for leader; but, by simple acceptance, emphasizes that person has done this for himself, which, in turn implies that having done it, he can continue to help himself grow)	"It felt good to have done that . . ." "It made you feel stronger . . ." "You felt clearer and more free . . ." "Many of you feel that you could talk more readily because of having heard that others had similar problems. As result now, your own problems feel less heavy."
	Accepts growth for its emotional value to the person rather than in moralistic or judgmental terms	

Group Members' Statements as to Effects of the Therapeutic Experience

At the end of the course, the group members were asked to write informal statements as to what they felt they had gotten, if anything, from the therapeutic experience. The necessity for honesty was stressed in view of the research purpose underlying the request. In addition, the group-records were examined for statements made verbally during sessions. Thirteen of the twenty-three members turned in written statements while verbal statements of eighteen appeared in the records. Five failed to indicate reactions. (See Table 2.)

TABLE 2.   Indications of Growth, as Expressed by Group Members[5]

Easing of Personal Problems	No. of Cases	Gains in Personal Adjustment	No. of Cases	Professional Growth	No. of Cases
Sense of increased ease and reduction of guilt, hostility and in feelings of being different	11	Increased understanding of self and gains in insight and ability to face and accept own problems	14	Understanding of the value of group therapy and clarification of techniques	11
Reduction of conflict in family relations	3	Increase in emotional capacity and expressiveness	5	Improved practices with children	3
Reduction in speech handicap	1			Improved practices in working with adults	2
		Increased understanding of other people and increased ability to accept them	7	Increased confidence in own work and in methods utilized	2
		Increased energy and better ability to direct it	2		

[5] This table is based on information from group members turned in on informal individual written reports and in oral statements made during group sessions and shown in the running record. Five members did not make either a written report or an oral statement (e.g.—1F, 8F, 9F, 17F, and 21F).

Among the outcomes was an increased understanding of self and gains in insight and in ability to face problems. (Mentioned by fourteen people.) As example, one person (13F) said, "I think part of my illness was caused by bottling up my hostility. It had to come out in some way so it came out through my body." Another said:

"I began masturbation at three. Now I realize the relation of my guilt over this to my shyness." . . . (18M)

A sense of increased ease and reduction in guilt, hostility and in feelings of being different—was cited by eleven people. "I haven't talked much" said one, "but I've gotten a lot of relief out of hearing feelings like my own expressed." (12F) Another: "I could remember hating my brothers but it was a guilty hate. Now I can face the fact that such feelings are normal . . . (15F) Another: "It makes me feel better to know that others don't have orgasm either," . . . (3F)

Seven mentioned having acquired an increased understanding of other people. Three mentioned a reduction of conflict in family relations, and one—improvement in a speech handicap. Professional growth was mentioned by twelve. This included not only an extension of insights and understandings but a carry-over into improved practices with children and adults.

Seven mentioned an increase in emotional capacity and expressiveness: Said one, "I can feel more. I can express my emotions. Before I was a passive kind of person" . . . (13F) Another, "I can feel things now. I never used to. . . . I never used to feel . . ." (23F) Another: "The experience has helped me throw off a little of the restrictiveness in my emotional life and has allowed greater interplay of my personality with others, especially in the more intimate situations where restrictions and pressures exert a serious block." (3F)

This new acceptance of emotions in a culture which so restricts expressiveness that various neurotic patterns result was nicely illustrated by the freedom shown in some of the therapeutic writing done after the group discussion-sessions were over. One person wrote:

> "If I start to let the mad things through,
> There's no telling where I'll stop.
> There's the man whose car I pushed across the street just now
> And got my grill bent in, for thanks;
> And the folks who made me grow up
> Burdened down with heavy guilt—
> So a sense of fun was something new to learn.
> There are lots of things, too, in between
> Enough for several other poems." [17F]

Another said:—"My mother's house is a mess . . . looks like a crazy house . . . good furniture . . . but dirty. Looks like a museum, disarranged and ugly . . . Now—I'm the same. B (her husband) said, 'You're always trying to excuse yourself; I'm not going to help you rationalize any longer . . .' This made me mad . . . He went on . . . 'I give up! I never dreamed that I'd be glad to get back to a lousy job just to get away from this house. I never knew anyone who could ruin a weekend like you do.' I said, 'Well, if you'll just shut up, I'll get this work done.' My energy began to come up with my hate . . . I started the dishes. God, I hate them! . . . [But] he seemed in a decent mood for the rest of the evening; and I ended up feeling pretty good myself!" (13F)

It was the subjective impression of the leader, supported by a similar impression of three members, that all but two people had received help, and a kind of "freeing," from the therapeutic experience in the group.

JEAN STEWART ANDREWS

Middlebury, Vermont

Directive Psychotherapy: I. Reassurance[1]

In terms of psychotherapy, reassurance means to restore confidence in another by assuring him of certain facts which were previously uncertain or unknown to him. Reassurance is a natural psychological antidote for the negative emotions of fear, worry, doubt and uncertainty. Through reassurance a person reestablishes confidence by being made sure or certain of facts which operate to remove fear and feelings of insecurity. To reassure is to restore faith and once more make possible confident living.

The art of reassurance has been so extensively practiced by physicians, clergymen, teachers, friends and relatives that it hardly deserves designation as a special technique in guidance unless it is so skillfully utilized as to go beyond ordinary common sense. Historically, reassurance is one of the oldest psychotherapeutic methods, since men have attempted to reassure each other since time immemorial. No one would question the efficacy of the loving mother who reassures the distraught child by rocking it to sleep with soothing words. It is a most comforting experience to be reassured with love and hope whether one is a frightened child seeking protection of its parents or an uncertain adult seeking help in wartime against the uncertainties of existence. One of the values of religion is the reassurance it gives its followers that they are the children of God and will receive protection and help in times of need. Any technique of reassurance which restores courage and confidence must be

---

[1] Reprinted from *Journal of Clinical Psychology*, 1945, 1, 52–66. Copyright 1945 by Frederick C. Thorne.

considered valuable even though its effects be only transient and operative only on superficial levels of treatment.

Unfortunately, objective studies of reassurance are lacking in psychological literature and little attention has been given to the technique and indications for its use. The method of reassurance is perhaps the simplest of psychotherapeutic techniques and has recently come into some disrepute because of the unsatisfactory results obtained by poorly trained therapists using it crudely and without appreciation of its limitations. The method of reassurance has a valuable place in the psychotherapeutic armamentarium and need not be discarded because it is sometimes misused. It is the purpose of this study to analyse the technique of reassurance and to indicate its uses and contraindications so that it may be more effectively and objectively utilized in counselling and guidance.

The Technique of Reassurance

Reassurance may be communicated from one person to another in many ways other than words. Reassurance is most effective when it is given on both verbal and behavioral levels, i.e., when actions support and reinforce the effect of words. Too frequently reassurance fails because verbal formulations are discovered to be erroneous by the patient who quickly learns to disregard words which do not speak louder than actions. Reassurance is most consistently effective where the total environment is manipulated in such manner as to restore self-confidence and give feelings of security. It is usually most effective to support verbal reassurance on the intellectual level with behavioral reassurance on the affective level in order to reach both rational and emotional levels of personality. For example, the rejecting parent may give the unhappy child repeated verbal assurances of love but fail to be convincing because of failure to reinforce the words with kisses and caresses which the child emotionally craves.

A basic consideration in giving effective reassurance is the degree of positive rapport which exists between counsellor and client. The client must have sufficient confidence in the counsellor to unhesitatingly accept what reassurances are given. Any conditions or circumstances which enhance rapport will operate to reinforce the effect of reassuring words or actions. The client-counsellor relationship has begun to be successful when the client gains enough confidence in the counsellor to begin to accept and act upon reassurances given.

The Needs of the Client. It is perhaps not generally enough recognized that most patients have a genuine psychological need for reassurance that they are receiving the best medical or psychiatric treatment. Since financial cost is usually regarded as a most reliable index of the value of anything, it follows that most patients are prepared and indeed demand to pay any reasonable sum to obtain the best treatment possible. Many patients appear to value and derive benefit from treatment in direct proportion to what it costs them. Free or inexpensive treatments are frequently unconsciously or consciously depreciated by the patient, while the sacrifice of paying heavily appears to give genuine satisfaction and reassurance. Psychoanalysts have recognized this principle in their general refusal to conduct gratuitous analyses even for students. Financial sacrifice inclines the patient to regard the whole matter more seriously and to improve motivation, because most patients wish to secure as much as possible for their money.

A psychiatrist was called in consultation to a little rural hamlet 75 miles away by the relatives of a 15-year-old girl. A local physician had previously made a diagnosis of schizophrenia and recommended commitment but the family refused to cooperate and insisted on obtaining consultations with other physicians, osteopaths, chiropractors, etc. On examining the patient, the psychiatrist quickly verified the correctness of the local physician's diagnosis and made the same recommendations. The relatives showed little inclination to accept this advice and fell to debating among themselves what to do next. Somewhat irritated, the psychiatrist announced that his fee was $50. A dramatic change occurred in the family's attitude immediately. They seemed convinced that the $50 diagnosis was certainly more correct than the $2 diagnosis of their own family physician and proceeded to carry out the advice without further debate.

Similar comments may be made concerning anything which enhances the personal prestige of the counsellor. In proper taste, effective use may be made of suggestion, pomp and ceremony in enhancing the effects of reassurance. The *ethical* conscientious clinician frequently looks askance at the impressive office, elaborate equipment, dramatic professional manners and high fees which are utilized by some ultra-successful colleagues who are sometimes regarded as charlatans. These devices are effective because they subtly reassure the patient and his relatives that the utmost is being done and they are therefore satisfied with the results because regardless of the outcome they can always reassure themselves that everything humanly possible was done. In spite of the critical attitudes of their professional colleagues, the ultra-successful practitioners have learned to minister to the psychological needs of their clients who seem to get value received for money spent.

It is commonly recognized in medical practice that the mere presence of some physicians is highly reassuring to their patients. There are many clinicians who though extremely well-trained scientists are nevertheless ineffectual because they are unable to inspire enough confidence in the patient to get him to come for treatment. It is not the purpose of this paper to consider the factors contributing to an impressive professional manner but it may be suggested that effective personality and a quiet, dignified mode of speaking and acting are very reassuring to most patients. Successful clinicians inspire such utter confidence that their clients are reassured that they are receiving the best possible treatment. Conversely, extreme youth or unprofessional conduct on the part of the clinician will very seriously impair the effect of any reassurances which he may attempt to give.

Similar comments may be made concerning the use of devices which keep the patient coming for treatment even though they are not a part of the counselling technique. A frequently encountered problem in therapy is the patient who considers himself cured and discontinues treatment as soon as superficial improvement or symptomatic relief occurs. It may be completely ethical to avoid premature termination of treatment by utilizing such devices as repeated injections or treatments which reassure the patient by presenting material evidence that something is being done for him and that it is therefore desirable to continue treatment. Perhaps more in psychotherapy than in other specialties is there a danger of terminating treatment prematurely because the client becomes discouraged over the lack of immediate improvement and does not understand the necessity of patiently undergoing long and sometimes superficially unproductive periods of treatment. Even though reassurance has no direct effect upon the therapeutic outcome it may be very valuable in persuading the client to continue treatment long enough to allow other techniques to operate. These considerations may be particularly important when it becomes necessary to persuade reluctant friends or relatives to continue cooperating with a long expensive treatment.

Factual Reassurance. Psychiatric studies of reassurance have emphasized that it is most effective when it involves a factual presentation rather than expressions of opinion or mere consoling terms. Diethelm (60) points out that the patient's own statements may often be reformulated or interpreted in such manner as to provide reassurance by yielding new insights. As the client is led to reevaluate the total situation, it is appropriate for the counsellor to emphasize reassuring facts or aspects which may give the client new orientation.

Levine gives a number of interesting examples illustrating how neurotic anxiety may be lessened by giving reassurance through intelligent conduct of the course of treatment. The experienced clinician is frequently able to present new facts to the patient which logically contradict his anxieties and also provide emotional support in the sense that the patient derives a feeling of security from being treated by one who is recognized and respected as a competent personage. The client usually derives considerable reassurance from authoritative statements that he is not insane, not going to die, has a known disease and will probably recover with proper care.

It is interesting to compare the efficiency of reassurance as given with varying amounts of factual support. A common situation is the one where the client turns to the clinician at the end of an interview and asks for reassurance concerning his progress.

C. Is there anything else you wanted to ask about today?
S. Yes. . . . Do you think I am getting any better? It seems as if we are just where we started. Sometimes I get very discouraged.
C. Oh, I think you are much better. You should be congratulated on the progress you have made.

Obviously this example represents the crude and probably ineffectual technique of reassurance which has brought discredit and disillusionment to the use of the method. Unless the patient is very suggestible and uncritical, reassurance of this type will probably produce nothing more than a momentary feeling of well-being, since no amount of persuasion will cause genuine difficulties to disappear. It will be noted that the counsellor gave the client an opportunity to uncover any further problems and then effectively blocked further exploration of the causes of discouragement. In actual practice, however, it frequently seems desirable to give crude reassurance of this type particularly to patients with profound feelings of insecurity who constantly demand reassurance during early stages of therapy. Judiciously administered, words of encouragement and cheer are probably not harmful and may give just enough symptomatic relief to enable the patient to carry on through moments of despondency and despair.

The next example illustrates a situation where the clinician is able to offer a logical factual interpretation which produces a reorientation of attitudes and offers effective reassurance on a symptomatic level. Miss W. is a 23-year-old single college graduate who came to the clinic in an acute anxiety state after the circumstances of a previously well-concealed pregnancy had been discovered. Situations of the following type appeared repeatedly during the first three interviews:

S. Last night I had the most awful feeling. I thought I was going to die. I suddenly felt that I couldn't breathe. My breath would suddenly stop so long I didn't know whether it would ever start again. (*Cries*) I can't go through that again. You've got to do something for me.

C. I think I understand how you felt. What you have is well known in medicine. I can assure you that these symptoms are alarming but not dangerous.

S. But doctor, you simply can't understand how terrible these feelings are; not to know whether you are going to take another breath. There must be something the matter with my lungs. I want you to listen to them again.

(At this point S became so agitated that it seemed wiser to reexamine her lungs. During the examination she gradually quieted down.)

C. Did you ever hear of anybody dying of such a condition?

S. Well, yes. My girl friend told me about an aunt of hers who died in a spell where she couldn't get her breath.

C. How old was this aunt?

S. I don't know exactly. I guess she was about 60 or 65.

C. The chances are she died of heart trouble which you definitely do not have. You are a young girl and your heart and lungs are all right. In fact, I want you to try something. Just try holding your breath and see if you can do it for more than a few moments. You can't do it. Nobody ever died that way.

This interview illustrates a situation where the client produces a question or complaint which is so subjectively upsetting that effective action must be taken if the client is not to break off treatment or become even more agitated. The patient was very much frightened about symptoms which she knew nothing about and which demanded attention even before the underlying dynamic personality mechanisms were explored. The counsellor gave immediate reassurance that the symptoms were annoying but not dangerous and then went on to uncover the origin of the fears following which further reassurance supported by a logical explanation was given. This example illustrates how the physical examination or any other diagnostic technique may be used to give reassurance, particularly when the results of the examination are known to be favorable. Contrary to recent suggestions by Rogers (184) that adequate nondirective therapy may be undertaken without intensive case study, it is our opinion that intensive case studies and complete diagnostic examinations are essential not only to evaluate the total situation but also to reassure the client that every possible thing is being done to solve the problem.

Mr. F. is a 27-year-old medically discharged veteran with a long history of social maladjustment and neurotic behavior. He was referred to the clinic because of inability to hold a job and failure to cooperate with unemployment agencies. He opened his eighth weekly interview as follows:

S. I'm pretty discouraged this week. It doesn't seem I'm any better. Maybe I'm going crazy.

C. Why do you say that?

S. Well here it is six months since I left the army and look where I am. I'm all shot.

C. What do you mean?

(S went on to give a long résumé of all his physical disabilities and then stated he thought the government should give him a higher rating for percentage of disability. He also expressed paranoid ideas of persecution against the entrenched greed of the home front which kept him from getting a "soft" job.)

C. Which would you rather do, live on a government pension or earn your own living?

S. I guess I would rather earn my own way but how can I the way I am now? I think the government owes me something, don't you?

C. Well, let's see. You haven't been in bed a day since you left the army, have you?

S. No. But . . .

C. And you are back living with your wife again even though things aren't perfect. And you seem to be earning some money working for your brother-in-law. The best thing is that you look and act better. Tell me the truth now. How do you feel compared with when I first saw you?

S. Well, maybe things ain't so bad after all. If only I knew I wasn't going crazy that would make some difference.

C. Well, I can tell you that you are not. I've had a pretty good chance to study your case and I can say that you are better, not worse.

It is apparent that Mr. F. came to this interview looking for sympathy concerning his disabilities, hoping to receive support for his plan to request a higher disability rating from the veterans' bureau, and perhaps genuinely worried about the possibility of losing his mind. This fear of insanity dated from a short mental hospital commitment eight years ago and was reinforced one year ago when an exasperated army doctor told him that he was a "psycho." No sympathy or support for obtaining a larger pension was given him but an attempt was made to reassure him concerning his general condition and the possibility of insanity by reviewing certain facts indicating that he was gradually getting back to a useful existence. This reassurance did not materially influence the dynamic mechanisms of his psychoneurosis but it appeared to provide sufficient symptomatic relief to enable him to overcome his gravest doubts, temporarily at least. It seems important to stress that giving symptomatic relief may facilitate the progress of treatment even though the underlying psychopathology is not modified. The temporary relief from distressing symptoms facilitates the treatment as a whole, in that the patient sees some progress, gains confidence in the therapist, and becomes accessible for more intensive depth analysis.

Affective Reassurance. In the impersonal contacts of modern medical center practice the affective needs of the patient are easily overlooked. Too often the clinician becomes irritated at the exasperating client who makes excessive demands for attention because of deep-seated needs for security, love and protection. An astoundingly large number of patients have an acute need for reassurance that they are loved and important to someone in the world. Usually their selfish exasperating behavior may be understood as a protest against the rejecting attitudes which they have encountered in life.

R.A. is a 10-year-old deaf, mute boy who was committed to the state school for mental defectives after he had become an impossible behavior problem at a privately endowed orphanage. At the orphanage he was very aggressive and cruel to other children, generally disrupting their play by starting fights, kicking, biting and breaking up toys. The matron and attendants could do nothing with him, as all forms of punishment had no effect.

The day of his arrival at the state school he had to be dragged out of the car by three adults. On entering the dispensary he struck the nurse a hard blow in the chest immediately after which he was given a light slap on the head at which he burst into tears.

Operating on the theory that his misbehavior was a protest against previous rejection and lack of affection, R.A. was quietly but firmly handled. He was greeted with smiles and brief masculine caresses such as having his hair ruffled up or his shoulder squeezed. Good performances were rewarded by pats on the back and praising gestures. In short he was given to understand that he was a valued member of the group. His aggressiveness and overactivity rapidly disappeared and were replaced by an almost pathetic desire to learn and be useful in the school community.

This case is cited as an example of how affective reassurance can be given solely by non-verbal means of communication. This child received affective reassurance for perhaps the first time in his life and this proved to be a major therapeutic tool. Even though this child did not at first understand anything which was being said, he did understand the non-verbal reassurances which were given. For the first time in his life he received signs of security, friendship and affection from an important personage in his world and this was all that was needed to stimulate his latent potentialities for civilized living.

It is difficult to formulate in verbal terms those factors of personality which stimulate a positive affective response in other people. Almost all socially effective personalities have the ability to communicate positive affective attitudes to other persons who in turn respond positively and favorably. The clinician who assumes a smiling, friendly, non-critical manner has taken an important step in reassuring the client that here is an understanding person who will listen to one's troubles in an affectionate sympathetic manner. Psychoanalysis is correct in perceiving the value of strong positive emotional rapport which induces the patient to go through with the treatment, supported by mutual affection. Most patients are quick to sense a lack of brotherly love or negative emotional attitudes in a counsellor and this recognition destroys rapport and interferes with effective treatment.

Indications for the Use of Reassurance

Mental Deficiency. Much of the hopelessness which is typically associated with the care of mental defectives is related to a lack of understanding of the psychology of the subnormal constitutionally inadequate personality. It has not been recognized universally enough that many mental defectives suffer from profound feelings of inferiority, developing as a personality reaction to their inability to compete effectively against their superiors. Unable to compete physically or intellectually and tormented in many little cruel ways which only children can devise, these unfortunate individuals revert to primitive regressive behavior which only increases the degree of maladjustment because of its asocial nature. After having once escaped from discipline, the mental defective secures his share of attention in many socially undesirable ways such as clowning, aggressive behavior, stubbornness, delinquency, etc. As their behavior becomes increasingly difficult for the community to assimilate, they encounter increasingly rejecting and condemnatory attitudes which result in the establishment of a vicious chain of events in which each successive asocial act results in an increase in repressive measures.

Reassurance is a form of psychotherapy which is particularly effective in dealing with persons who are mentally defective or very suggestible. The subnormal respond to crude forms of reassurance which would be questioned or rejected by the more intelligent. They are usually starved for affection, praise and recognition, consequently they react most positively to anyone who reassures them of their worth and expresses affection. Those who have worked with mental defectives in daily contacts will know how important it is to maintain a friendly, cheerful attitude, praising constantly even when undeserved, and frequently reassuring the child that his work is valued and appreciated. It is possible to surround the dejected resentful mental defective with such a massive barrage of reassurance as to transform him almost overnight into a well-adjusted individual operating up to the limits of his ability.

The following excerpt illustrates a short conversation between the school psychiatrist and 13-year-old D.T. who was committed to the school following a succession of aggressive acts against superior schoolmates.

D.T. How'm I doin' Doc? (*As he putters around clipping grass.*)
C. Fine! Haven't heard any bad reports about you in a long time.
D.T. When do you think I'll be goin' home?
C. Don't see how we can consider that now. How do you think we would get along here without you?
D.T. Gee, I don't know, Doc. I guess I'm one of the best boys around here, ain't I?

For the first time in his life, D.T. is experiencing some of the satisfactions of being liked and feeling he is some good to the world. In the beginning of his treatment reassurance was laid on thick and fast even in situations where he did not really earn it in order to build up a more positive and less defensive attitude. As his self-confidence grew with the passage of time, he showed less need for reassurance and less was given.

Combating Anxiety. It is frequently possible to allay simple anxiety states by giving the client factual reassurance designed to correct misinformation and to counteract ignorance or superstition. Assailed with unsettling doubts, worries and anxiety over circumstances which are disturbing because poorly understood or seemingly unsurmountable, it is normal for people to feel discouraged and depressed over the trend of events at certain times in life. In psychotherapy, treatment has begun when the patient recognizes that he has psychological problems and derives confidence from the fact that a trained clinician is taking the case in hand. It is reassuring to know (1) that one is suffering from a known condition, (2) that other people have been so involved and have recovered, (3) that one is not insane and about to die or become worse, and (4) that the best available therapist has been obtained and is competent to treat the case. Reassurance of this type operates to relieve feelings of isolation and hopelessness in the face of the unknown.

It is particularly important to give factual reassurance concerning matters about which the client cannot possibly be expected to have information and reach a solution by himself. Two brief case summaries will indicate the type of situation which frequently arises where a suggestible patient develops intense anxiety concerning facts which are misunderstood or misinterpreted.

Case 1. A young boy was admitted to a general hospital for an appendectomy. The operation was a complete success but the boy became listless and seemed to fail rapidly during the first 72 hours postoperatively.

Finally his mother elicited the statement that he thought he was dying. The physician got the boy to talk and discovered that just at the end of the operation the surgeon had said: "There's still a little bleeder there but I can't get it now." Coming out of the anaesthesia the boy heard this remark and thought it to mean that he was slowly bleeding to death internally.

Case 2. A 19-year-old college sophomore was referred to the clinic because of a sudden unexplained seclusiveness and failure in her work. She seemed happy only when by herself and even avoided the young man to whom she was engaged. It was discovered that she had had illicit relations for some time over which she had never felt much guilt until she heard a male classmate state that a man could always tell by looking at a girl whether she had ever had relations. She suddenly developed anxiety and strong feelings of guilt over the idea that everyone knew her secret. She responded well to simple reassurance and shortly afterwards began a happy married life.

Superficial mild anxieties frequently respond well to skillfully given reassurance which provides symptomatic relief and makes possible the treatment of underlying complexes by other methods.

Feelings of Inferiority and Inadequacy. In spite of the teachings of Alfred Adler it is not generally enough recognized among successful professional men how widespread profound feelings of inferiority are. Particularly during periods of stress such as depressions or war, large masses of the population experience severe frustration accompanied by feelings of inadequacy and despair. Relatively few people have any real taste of wealth, luxury, happiness or true love such as they read about in books or see in the cinema. Life can be bitterly cruel and every little bit of reassurance helps in reestablishing morale and self-confidence.

F.R. is a 21-year-old college senior whose academic career has been marked by extreme variations in grades and achievement. Although scoring an I.Q. of 145, his high school record was extremely spotty with grades ranging from failures in languages to almost perfect in mathematics. He barely passed the work of the first college year and failed 4 out of 5 subjects the first semester of the second college year. Without benefit of outside counselling, his marks jumped to honor levels during the 3rd and 4th college years and he went on to become a promising graduate student.

Up until the 3rd college year, F.R. had never really tasted success. Never really happy because of poor physical development and an unprepossessing appearance, he had gone along without ever developing adequate motivation and frequently so tied up in his own conflicts as to be unable to devote proper attention to school work.

The turning point in his academic career came when a sociology instructor became interested in him and indicated his belief that F.R. was a potentially brilliant student. F.R. was so stimulted by this surprising evaluation that he extended himself to do excellent work and secure an A grade for the first time in his college career.

The case of F.R. is cited as an example of how even relatively gifted people may be so burdened with feelings of inadequacy over actual or fancied inferiority that they are unable to achieve up to the limits of their potentialities. A little tactfully given reassurance concerning native ability serves to keep motivation at a high level during periods of discouragement or apparent defeat.

It is intriguing to reflect how many misfits could be salvaged if more effective methods for discovering talent were available on the level of secondary education. Biographical studies (such as the life of Hitler) reveal how frequently great ability matures very slowly, being obscured for long periods by the more sensational exploits of others, and blooming only in late adulthood after periods of ineptness, frustration and discouragement. In how many instances is the opinionated teacher or professor wrong when he blithely asserts that this student will never amount to anything? It is a basic rule of psychometric technique that the child should be praised and given every reassurance that he is doing well on the test in order to stimulate maximum motivation and performance. If optimal conditions of motivation are so important in psychometrics, why are they not equally so in other life situations? Tactful and appropriate reassurance does much to improve motivation and build up self-confidence.

Many people have barely enough self-confidence to adjust well under optimum conditions, and they become completely demoralized in difficult situations. An example of this type is the case of Mr. C., a 26-year-old young man who suffers from alternating feelings of guilt, humiliation and relief over being classified 4F in the draft because of psychoneurosis. After his principal neurotic symptoms were relieved by psychotherapy and he had accepted the fact that he was inadequate for military service, he continued to have periodic upsets whenever his draft classification was reconsidered or attention was otherwise directed to his status. The following excerpt illustrates what took place in a typical interview:

S.   I thought I'd better come in and see you because I've been upset this week. I had to give up my job because I missed so much sleep.

C. What has been bothering you?

S. This. (*Showing an anonymous letter he had received in the mail taunting him for being a slacker.*)

C. You feel pretty bad about this don't you?

S. Yes, I guess it is bothering me. I thought I would take it to the postmaster and find out who sent it. It's against the law to send letters like that. They ought to be punished.

C. You feel somebody ought to be punished for doing such a thing.

S. Yes. It's getting so I can't look people in the face any more. I never know but what he might be the one who is sending these letters. I don't feel easy when I go out.

C. Do you think it would be wise to actually go to the postmaster?

S. Yes, I do. This has got to stop.

C. Well, I don't know. Seems to me that would make matters worse. I think the best thing might be to simply ignore the whole business. Let's see now, you have been getting along pretty well until this happened, haven't you?

S. Not too bad if this thing hadn't set me back.

C. I don't think anybody ever gets completely over a thing like this without some setbacks. The important thing is whether the main trend is forward. You have gone a long ways in the last year. . . . Well, the important thing is not so much what has happened but what you are going to do about it. Have you given that any thought?

S. I thought I might leave town and get a job somewhere where they don't know me. My girl friend has a job in. . . . (*Goes into a long discussion about how he would like to live near his girl who has a very reassuring attitude toward him.*) I thought I would come down here today and talk this over and see what you thought I ought to do.

C. Is there any reason why you shouldn't leave town?

S. I can't see as there is. I know you told me once I ought to try and face my problems and not run away from them. But I've thought it over and that's what I'm going to do.

C. Well, you will have to decide that for yourself. There are many ways to skin a cat. If one doesn't work you can try something else.

S. I want to tell you just what I plan to do. (*Interview goes on with S. outlining his plans in detail. C. assumes a neutral, non-directive attitude during the remainder of the session.*)

It is apparent that Mr. C. requested this consultation to gain reassurance for a projected course of action which he had little intention of altering. Even though the major portion of the treatment had been completed, he continued to return every few weeks, seemingly to get reassurance that he was holding his own and to talk to someone who would listen to his troubles in a friendly uncritical manner. This situation where patients are satisfied to relate their progress and do not want or ask for active treatment is commonly encountered in counselling practice. Sensing what the patient wishes to hear, the therapist gives the desired reassurance and the patient goes away contented until the next visit.

Child Guidance. Reassurance is a valuable technique in psychotherapy with children in inverse proportion to the child's age and intelligence. The younger and more suggestible the child, the more effective is reassurance intended to allay anxiety and feelings of insecurity. Even the crudest forms of reassurance which would be instantly rejected by an adult are usually effective in building up the rapport which is so necessary. Reassurance may be given either verbally or in the form of friendly affectionate behavior which the child instantly recognizes as offering protection and non-critical acceptance. Even though performance or behavior may not be of high quality, children do their best when amply praised and led to believe that their work is excellent. The lesson taught by the use of reassurance in psychometrics can be transferred to many other life situations. People enjoy what they think they do well. Free use of reassurance is not hypocritical even though undeserved if it enables a person to function with highest efficiency.

It has been stated that one difference between good parents and bad is that the former love and protect their children through periods of maladjustment while the underprivileged child is rejected and allowed to take the rap with all its undesirable consequences. Giving a child reassurance that he is loved, even while being punished, is very valuable psychotherapeutically. Freud was correct in his insight that the transference mechanism provides valuable emotional support for the client who is undergoing unpleasant corrective experiences. Not all children need reassurance of this type, but when indicated there should be no hesitation in giving it.

It is not always recognized how overwhelmed a child may become by never-lifting feelings of inadequacy and frustration. Because of inarticulateness and repression resulting in symptom formation, the child himself is unable to express his needs and too often becomes involved in a vicious chain of maladjustments which reinforce each other and conceal the roots of the difficulty.

J.S. was a poorly developed, rather unattractive little boy who came to the clinic because of dishonesty and stealing over a period of 3 years. Although very bright in other respects, he did not seem able to learn the

Ten Commandments even though punished in every conceivable manner. Home conditions appeared good, both parents being college graduates and seemingly conscientious in trying to do what they considered best.

Two dreams elicited early in treatment gave partial insight into the dynamic mechanism operative. In the first dream, Johnny would feel himself lying in bed trying to go to sleep. His body would begin to feel numb as if turned to wood, the room would seem to get bigger and bigger while he grew smaller and smaller; finally he would wake up crying in a nightmare. In the second dream he would be sitting in the rear seat of a car at night. Looking out the back window he would see another car catching up with headlights which looked like eyes. No matter how fast his car went, the other car would always catch up and a bad witch would get out and catch Johnny.

The first dream was interpreted to symbolize an acute inferiority complex in which Johnny would feel himself becoming progressively less able to cope with life. The second dream represented the never-ceasing regulation of an over-conscientious mother who tried to control his every movement. This child was carried along for several interviews with the therapist taking no active role except to provide reassurance through word and action that Johnny's worth was appreciated and that he could do as he pleased.

Contraindications

The method of reassurance has been depreciated by some, not because it is considered harmful or dangerous but on the negative grounds that it is operative only on superficial symptomatic levels and does not appreciably influence underlying dynamic mechanisms. Rogers (184) has expressed the opinion that the use of reassurance is rarely indicated, but this may be considered an extreme view. Many of the criticisms have been directed more against its crude unskilled use rather than against its value as a basic psychotherapeutic tool.

False Reassurance. Reassurance has too often been used harmfully in misguided attempts to conceal the truth in situations the nature of which the patient dimly recognizes. Particularly in the case of dreaded or deadly disease, efforts are made to conceal or evade the truth in order to protect the patient from knowledge which it is assumed he would not be able to stand. This false reassurance and assumed cheerfulness does more harm than good when the patient senses the truth and often bitterly resents not being taken into the confidence of the doctor. While no general rule can be set up, it is usually wise to tell a patient only as much he as demands to know. Those patients who don't want the truth generally do not ask, while at the other extreme are some for whom the truth is less terrible than uncertainty. Efforts to distort the truth, however well meant, can only result in disillusionment and loss of confidence when the facts become known. Similarly, hush-hush attitudes may only succeed in arousing deeper anxiety in a patient who feels that the situation must be indeed serious if such precautions are necessary. It is rarely justifiable to conceal facts which a person desires and has a right to know.

Crude Reassurance. Fortunately it is rarely possible to do irreparable harm by giving reassurances unskillfully or inappropriately. Crudely given reassurance is ineffectual in the sense that the patient senses the irrelevancy and loses confidence in the counsellor. The most serious complication is that the counsellor loses prestige and the rapport is impaired to the point where the efficacy of other methods is threatened. It does no good for the counsellor to contend that everything is fine and nothing is the matter when the client knows only too well that nothing has been solved.

The method has come into disrepute largely because it was the main tool in trade of well-intentioned but untrained uplifters who go about proclaiming that all will be well if only the client perseveres. Such shopworn platitudes as "A man may be down but he is never out" and "Every cloud has a silver lining" are singularly sterile to the person wallowing in trouble. The use of reassurrance in this manner is not only ineffective but it wastes valuable time and confidence when other methods should be utilized.

Attempts to Shift Responsibility. Many clients seek to obtain reassurance and the counsellor's approval for indefensible actions or dubious plans for which the client desires to shift or evade responsibility. A typical situation of this type is faced by the marriage counsellor called upon for advice concerning divorce. Mrs. A. came to the clinic apparently on a shopping tour to find someone who would side with her in her search for justification and support on going ahead with a divorce. After a long discussion of the mental cruelties which she claims her husband inflicted upon her, Mrs. A. reached the crux of her problem as follows:

Mrs. A.   You do feel I'm right about leaving George don't you? Even his own Aunt will tell you he's a brute.

C.   Well . . . Truly now, how do you feel about it yourself?

Mrs. A. (*after a long pause*).   I don't know. Everybody says it's the only thing to do . . . After what he's done to me I just can't stand it any longer. Sometimes I cry all night. (*Cries.*)

C.   What would you do if you left him? Who would take care of the children?

Mrs. A.   I don't know. George says he has just as much right to them as I have. We just can't seem to agree on anything . . . (More about quarrels.)

C.   I can't tell you what to do. If I do and it comes out wrong you will blame me for the rest of your life. This is something you will have to decide yourself. I can help you a little but you must fight it out yourself. . . . It does seem though that things are not as bad as they look. Part of the time you get along O.K., don't you?

Mrs. A.   Yes, if he would only treat me better we'd get along. Now you take his drinking. During the week he's all right but Saturday night he goes down to the club and spends more than we can afford. He is so stubborn. He knows I'm killing myself trying to pay off our house but he keeps right on doing it.

C.   Let's see now. As I understand it George gets $34 a week and only spends 75¢ or a dollar on himself. Is that right?

Mrs. A.   Yes.

C.   And you've paid off almost $500 on your mortgage. That's not so bad.

Mrs. A.   Yes, but we'd have it all paid off if he would stay closer to business and not get drunk every week. I think it is terrible for a man to do that.

C.   I understand George has been working steady on this job for 12 years hasn't he? He says he never misses a day.

Mrs. A.   I guess I'll have to admit that's true. You have me there. If only he wouldn't beat me up. You ought to see my body black and blue.

C.   When did George beat you last?

Mrs. A.   About two weeks ago. He grabbed me by the wrist and my arm was all black and blue for a week afterwards. I went to the police about it.

C.   Why did he grab you?

Mrs. A.   I guess I said something. (George had previously made the counterclaim that Mrs. A. had been seeing another man and had taunted him about it.)

C.   What was it?

Mrs. A.   I guess I told him I would go out as I pleased if he got drunk all the time.

C.   Well maybe George had a reason for getting mad. Every family has quarrels like this. Do you think yours are worse than other family's?

Mrs. A.   I would say so. Other people don't fight like this all the time.

C.   There are a good many good things about the situation aren't there? I think you have done pretty well to have bought a house and made that many payments on what George gets. He has worked steady for 12 years on one job and I hear that he is considered a good man. Maybe he'd stay home if things went smoother at home. After all it takes two to make a fight. If one of you would keep quiet while the other is mad, it would soon blow over. As I see it the most important thing is your 3 little boys. Why don't you go home and sit tight for a little while. I always say, don't do anything until you are positive you know what you want to do.

Mrs. A. was a constitutionally inadequate person whose ideals were higher than anything she had yet managed to wrest from life. Disillusionment over the failure of her marriage to live up to her fondest dreams had embittered her and she became so emotionally disturbed that she was contributing more than her share to family quarrels. For at least six months she had been going about telling her troubles to anyone who would listen and had finally worked herself up to the point of divorce. She was denied the reassurance she asked for and instead the facts of her situation were presented in a manner designed to reorient her to the total situation.

Attention-Seeking Behavior.   Occasionally a client seeks repeated reassurances where the need is a symptom of neuroticism or emotional parasitism. Unable to secure attention and emotional outlet in conventional manner, the client keeps returning on the pretext of needing help with his problems but actually because of the gratification secured from the attention given and intimate contacts with the counsellor. If allowed to go unchecked, these clients make a business of obtaining professional advice usually from the most attractive young male available. When one counsellor loses patience they move to another, buying the attentions they cannot secure from normal sources.

Overconfidence.   The giving of reassurance appears to be contraindicated with individuals who are already too aggressive and self-confident in their attitudes toward others. The counsellor will frequently encounter patients whose difficulties appear to originate in a pathological *lack* of conflict rather than excessive conflict. Such persons are frequently extremely extroverted, aggressive, rigid and lacking in appreciation for the sensitivities of others. They ride roughshod over all opposition, seemingly unaware of the problems created by their bluntness and uncontrolled egoism. These personalities require repressive handling intended to limit and discourage behavioral excesses. In such instances it becomes the obligation of the counsellor to indirectly, or if necessary forcibly, call attention to the crudeness of the client's asocial behavior. There is urgent need for objective research directed to techniques for arousing normal conflicts in persons with excessive egoism where the self-centered attitudes derive from uncontrolled excess in one direction or another.

Every experienced clinician has experienced the situation where a client accepts a suggestion too literally and uses it as a rationalization for behavioral excesses. When faced with the consequences of extremist behavior, the client smugly blames it on the counsellor stating that he is merely carrying out what he thought he was told to do. The use of reassurance is better saved for clinical situations where there are deep and genuine feelings of inferiority or inadequacy.

Summary

Reassurance as a method of psychotherapy includes all those techniques which operate to restore confidence and self-assurance in the client. Reassurance operates on superficial levels of personality and its effects are frequently only temporary; however, it is a valuable therapeutic tool when used to bolster confidence and carry the patient through periods of insecurity or uncertainty. The simplicity of the technique and the relative freedom from harmful effects even when unskillfully administered make it a valuable addition to the therapeutic armamentarium. Its use is particularly indicated with mental defectives, young children and other immature personalities in combating feelings of inferiority and anxiety.

ROBERT I. WATSON

Washington University School of Medicine

Treatment as an Aspect of the Clinical Method: A Review[1]

On surveying the contributions of psychologists to treatment as exemplified in the preceding readings, one can be proud of the auspicious beginnings made by members of the profession working with this aspect of the clinical method. Some vistas are opened or further explored in these articles. Other contributions included are of such a nature that it might be difficult to distinguish the professional background of the author, so closely do they follow the terrain previously explored by others. Nevertheless, the published works of psychologists, who have entered the realm of treatment in some numbers only in recent years, obviously do not dominate the field. Most, if not all, the distinctively great contributions to psychological treatment have originated in the work of professional personnel trained in other disciplines, particularly medicine. Without in any way meaning either to decry or to commend the work done by the psychologist, it may be said that many of his contributions have certain points in common. His contributions to therapy as expressed in the literature show that so far, at least, the pattern has been more drab and more limited than the rich tapestry woven by some psychiatrists. Stated another way, he has been perhaps more objective, more cautious, and less intuitive in his approach. Coming from a scientific rather than a clinical tradition, he has characteristically insisted upon careful control and experimentation.

---

[1] Prepared especially for this volume.

However, limitations set for the present account do not permit further development of these points and must therefore rest here merely at the level of opinion.

Whether or not psychologists actually apply certain of these methods to be described is irrelevant. As Font and Roland show in their articles included in the *Readings*, it is impossible to separate sharply diagnosis and treatment. Even if it were possible to do so and the psychologist never directly engaged in therapy, it would still be essential that he be conversant with all phases of the clinical method if he is to use his professional background and clinical acumen to their fullest extent. Diagnostic interpretations and recommendations are dependent upon the understanding of their implications for treatment on any level of psychological clinical practice.

The status of knowledge of treatment procedures among psychologists is curiously uneven. A certain provincialism in thinking in regard to the variety and the scope of therapeutic methods available is readily observable. Occasionally the suspicion may arise that some less well informed members of the profession consider psychotherapeutic points of view as encompassing merely the non-directive approach, the directive approach of Thorne, psychoanalysis, and common-sense advice.

On the basis of the foregoing discussion, it is apparent that a synoptic review of the literature on all major treatment methods prepared especially with a psychological audience in mind is not out of place. Limitations of space make impossible anything but the briefest non-critical statement. As in discussing the literature on diagnostic methodology, only enough will be presented about an article or book to allow identification of material discussed. Even with this restriction only a small fraction of the published reports can be considered. Hypnotherapy alone, for example, has a bibliography of over 1,200 titles published during the last 50 years (41).[2]

The major criterion applied in the selective process to arrive at the relatively limited number of references was the validity and clarity of the selection in representing the position or method described. In so far as possible, the writer's personal opinions about the merits of the position or method are minimized.

In introducing such selection it was decided to ignore therapies

---

[2] Bibliography begins on page 719.

depending directly upon pharmacological, physical, or surgical procedures. Accordingly, there is no discussion of hydrotherapy, shock treatment, operative procedures, or drug therapy, even though many, if not all, these procedures have aspects in which psychological phenomena form an integral part.

At this point it is relevant to consider the various methods for the classification of literature on treatment, since classification in itself introduces further selective factors. Scrutiny of the literature revealed that psychological treatment procedures were described from a variety of different positions. The most obvious orientation is that in which a theory of dynamics is integrated with a system of treatment considered appropriate in the light of that theory—e.g., psychoanalytical, relationship, non-directive, and psychobiological approaches. Another way of discussing therapeutic procedures is to relate them to syndromes, disorders, reaction patterns, and areas of maladjustment—e.g., therapy in schizophrenia, treatment of alcoholics, and treatment procedures with the mentally deficient. Still another method of organization centers around the age of the patient—e.g., child psychiatry. The number simultaneously in the treatment situation makes possible still another way of dealing with the topic—e.g., group therapy. Organization of therapeutic accounts in terms of mechanisms also appears—e.g., persuasion and catharsis. Other accounts use an historical or chronological approach to developments in therapy—e.g., history of psychiatric therapy. Still another method of presentation centers around the type of organization supplying the therapeutic services described—e.g., child guidance clinics and college counseling centers. Unlike the aforementioned orientations which operate through the direct interpersonal relation of therapist and patient, there are others indirect in nature which are dependent upon mediating adjuncts to therapy—e.g., books, music, or persons other than the therapist and patient. It is almost needless to add that articles using various combinations of these orientations have appeared. Although no article on an historical account of psychoanalytically oriented approaches to transference in the group treatment of mothers of compulsive children in a child guidance clinic is recalled, such a title embracing all these orientations is at least conceivable.

It is possible then to classify treatment procedures by dynamic approach, syndrome, age, number, mechanism, history, agency, and directness. Certain of the articles included in the preceding readings serve to illustrate these orientations. The articles by Snyder illustrate a systematic approach referred to as the non-directive, Stogdill deals with the mentally deficient, Zehrer with children, Baruch with groups, Andrews with reassurance as a mechanism, Berdie with college students, and Rheingold with the parents of the patients.

Since it would be impracticable to utilize all these orientations in this review, it became necessary to select those which permit survey of the published materials without too many important omissions and with as little distortion or artificiality as possible. It was decided to dispense with the historical, the agency, the mechanism, and the syndrome approaches. As a consequence of the omission of an historical approach, certain earlier publications of the great therapeutic pioneers are not mentioned unless they can still serve as introductory readings to methodology. The works of Janet, Jung, Meyer, Dubois, Adler, Dejerine, and Bernheim, to mention but a few, are neglected for this reason. The failure to use the orientation which presents therapeutic methodology in terms of the particular kind of agency in which it is applied is not particularly serious except that it has resulted in somewhat less attention to treatment activities in college guidance bureaus, institutions for the mentally defective, and homes for delinquent children. The publications organized around mechanisms such as suggestion and catharsis in most instances are readily subsumed under the various systematic approaches, while the articles and books dealing with specific syndromes are less fundamental generally and of less consequence to the psychologist than those concerned with the systematic approaches that give rise to application with particular kinds of patients.

Turning now to the classifications utilized, it was decided that a major subdivision could be made between direct and indirect methods of treatment. Within the direct methods further distinctions were made between individual, group, and play orientation. The fundamental distinction made, however, was in terms of the more prominent systematic approaches—namely, the eclectic, psychobiological, relationship, non-directive, and psychoanalytic. While individual and play orientations are each discussed in terms of all these points of view, it was necessary to add two others in reviewing group therapy, specifically activity group therapy and psychodrama, and to eliminate the psychobiological approach. The indirect methods are subdivided into those which utilize some mediating adjuncts to therapy, specifically play materials, occupational and recreational therapies, psychological tests, educational procedures, bibliotherapy, audio-visual aids, and hypnotherapy on the one hand, and those which depend upon influencing the environmental milieu of the patient, specifically environmental manipulation and modification. In both direct and indirect methods distinctions between treatment procedures used with children and those used with adults are made whenever relevant.

Before considering the various approaches to therapy it is appropriate to describe certain reviews of treatment procedures and to mention expositions of the common factors in all therapy.

General Reviews. The general reviews of therapy to be considered have been limited to those either written by psychologists or addressed to a psychological audience. Perhaps the most documented review of psychotherapy is that by Snyder (209). He confines himself to psychotherapeutic counseling, which he defines in terms of face-to-face relationships of therapist and client, using verbal methods to modify emotional attitudes. As a consequence so-called non-verbal therapies, such as music, foster-home placement, occupational therapy, shock therapy, and play therapy, are excluded. Traditional therapy, hypnosis, psychoanalysis, psychodrama, relationship therapy, non-directive therapy, and group therapy are considered. The literature since 1940 is examined in terms of five aspects of each approach: (1) methodological descriptions including case material, (2) theoretical considerations, (3) research studies, (4) evaluative studies, and (5) special modifications of the approach. A general introduction to therapy is offered by Appel (17). After an historical review, he discusses treatment as symptomatic (hypnosis, suggestion, reasoning, and persuasion); as physical (rest, relaxation, physiotherapy, medication, shock, and surgical); and as involving reorganization of the personality (psychobiology, reeducation, explanatory-interpretive, bibliotherapeutic, psychoanalysis, and dynamic growth). Sections on therapeutic approaches with children are also given, divided into the therapies in which the child's role is minimized (authoritarian, environmental manipulation, and social interpretation) and those in which his role is maximized (release, play, relationship, and psychoanalysis). A section on some statistical analyses of the effects of therapy follows. The general discussion in a textbook of abnormal psychology by Maslow and Mittelmann (151) is of some value as an introductory account. After presenting the aims and nature of psychotherapy, they describe specific techniques including release therapy, group therapy, institutionalization, suggestion and hypnosis, and psychoanalysis. Louttit in his volume on clinical psychology as applicable to children (144) gives still another general account of treatment procedures. He discusses environmental manipulation, environmental treatment by changing parental attitudes, and personal manipulation which includes authoritarian, educative, interpretive, expressive, and relationship methods.

Common Factors in Therapy. A symposium of the American Orthopsychiatric Association in 1940 (235) demonstrates very well certain areas of agreement in psychotherapy. The chairman summarizes the symposium as showing agreement that objectives are similar, broadly increasing capacity to deal with reality, work, love, and meaning; that therapy exists in a relationship between therapist and client; that responsibility rests with the client; and that good therapy involves an enlargement of the patient's understanding of himself.

An analysis of the implicit common factors in diverse methods of psychotherapy has been the concern of Rosenzweig (191, 192). His accounts are extremely valuable in that they tend to offer a needed corrective to the tendency to be overimpressed with differences in method when many points of similarity, if not identity, exist. Among the features that he points out are the cathartic effect, faith in the therapist, the indefinable effect of the personality of the therapist, the reconditioning of social relationships, and what he refers to as the function of interpretation. This last common factor needs further elucidation. He says in effect that if a personality disorder is the result of a conflict of personality constituents, then a system formally consistent, regardless of its specific nature, would be a prerequisite for successful therapy, since its consistency gives the patient a scheme for bringing about personality organization.

Direct Methods of Treatment

INDIVIDUAL THERAPIES

Eclectic Approaches. The great majority of therapists of whatever professional background hold to no one distinctive school of thought in regard to psychotherapy. Instead there is a selection from among the contributions of various points of view according to the personality of the therapist, his education and clinical experience, the particular sort of patient to whom he is exposed at the moment, and the like. It is hardly surprising that he seldom judges it necessary to write about his methods. When he does so, it is often in a setting of a particular agency or institution, an orientation not utilized in the present exposition. Consequently, exposition of characteristic eclectic views is somewhat difficult.

ECLECTIC APPROACHES IN GENERAL. Eclectic approaches in general may be appropriately illustrated from the contributions of certain psychologically trained therapists. Characteristic of many eclectic approaches to treatment has been a greater emphasis on the direction by the therapist of the activities, thoughts, and emotions of the patient. Psychobiology, closest to an eclectic spirit and viewpoint among the distinctive approaches described later, is also the most directive in nature.

It is because his approach is directive in character that Frederick Thorne refers to what is essentially an eclectic view by this distinguishing term. He and his associates have stated their views in a series of articles appearing in the *Journal of Clinical Psychology*. Illustrative of his point of view is the first in this series, the article by Andrews on reassurance which appears in these *Readings*. Characteristic of Thorne's approach (226) is the stressing of the contention that a worthwhile technique is the giving of information about psychological matters to maladjusted individuals whose insight is not severely impaired. Therapy is a learning process—learning of the causes and then learning of some more suitable patterns of behavior. In this process the therapist thus is essentially a teacher. Intellectual factors are also stressed by Thorne (228). In considering the importance of the world view taken by individuals as a factor in adjustment and maladjustment, he conceives emotional instability in certain instances to be a secondary phenomenon occurring because of failure to solve problems with one's intellectual resources. He differentiates a number of causal sequences comprising those in which the individual's *Weltanschauung* (1) is too rudimentary to permit facing a crisis, (2) is such that it contains so much misinformation that adjustment is impossible, (3) is now outdated and ineffectual, (4) is so limited by insufficient personality resources of an intellectual or emotional sort that he is frustrated by a world he can never comprehend, and (5) is adequate but presents so many adverse circumstances that the individual loses confidence. Thorne suggests that the best way of handling the maladjustments centering around such problems, once the affective disturbance coincident with the original presentation of his difficulties by the patient has subsided, is to conceive of treatment fundamentally as education directed toward reorienting the individual's *Weltanschauung*. Assistance in developing a new point of view must be offered which is both directive and educational. Thorne (227) conceives that maladjustment is frequently caused by a pathological absence of conflict especially among the very young, the mentally defective, immature individuals of whatever age, extrovert personalities, and psychopathic personalities. He offers as a therapeutic technique the confronting of the patient more or less forcibly with factual information which might cause him to reevaluate his attitudes. Indications and contraindications are discussed. In keeping with this eclectic directive approach Thorne (224) lays considerable emphasis on the case history both as a method of clinical examination and as a therapeutic aid. In therapy it helps in establishing rapport and allows opportunity for desensitization, catharsis, reassurance, sharing the burden of trouble, and the induction of insight. In other articles Thorne describes the nature and treatment of simple maladjustments (223), various methods of reducing intensity of symptoms thus allowing palliation (225), and the use of the psychological antidotes and prophylactics (229).

Hathaway and Harmon (108) present by case studies an avowedly eclectic approach in which they stress the shifts in therapeutic method dictated by their formulations of the dynamics of the matter at each particular period of therapeutic development. At one point or another in these case studies they refer to the methods used as reorientation of attitude, relaxation, hypnosis, automatic writing, post-hypnotic suggestion, suggestion, encouragement, and catharsis.

A patient in whom compulsive eating was the most prominent symptom forms the basis for an analysis of the therapeutic techniques used, as reported upon by Crider (51). The principal techniques appeared to be structuring (statements to help the patient realize that psychic events have causes), interpretation (explanation of personal characteristics heretofore not understood or realized), clarification (succinctly summarizing what the patient already knew), and asking for information.

Two articles included in the *Readings*, that by Berdie on judgments in college counseling and that by R. M. Stogdill on mentally retarded children, involve an eclectic approach. The approach of most guidance counselors is of eclectic origin. Frequently, but not necessarily superficially, such an approach puts more emphasis on intellectual than upon emotional factors. The volume by Williamson (239) is both representative and definitive. In advising or planning a program of action, he speaks of advice, persuasion, and explanation, the last being considered the most satisfactory. Discussion of specific counseling techniques centered around problem areas, the major ones being described as personality problems, problems of educational orientation and achievement, and problems of occupational orientation. Within these major areas there are more specific problem areas, such as social maladjustments, ineffective study habits, and discrepancy between vocational interests and aptitudes, to mention one from each.

ECLECTIC APPROACHES WITH CHILDREN. Paradoxically, perhaps, through eclectic discussions of adult treatment or of treatment applicable to both child and adult, psychologists have made some significant contributions, but one searches the literature in vain for significant original eclectic contributions by psychologists to the direct individual treatment of the child, as distinguished from environmental manipulation. Accounts by psychiatrists which might serve to introduce eclectic approaches to direct treatment of children include contributions by D. M. Levy (138), Hartwell (107), Potter (175), and Kanner (118). Levy discusses in an introductory fashion both environmental manipulation and more direct methods of treatment or "pure" psychotherapy, with the latter divided into insight and release therapies, although the two actually blend one into the other. Release therapies include restoration of traumatic situations, controlled play situations for the purpose of modifying social attitudes, and various forms of release approaches. Levy considers that pure insight approaches generally have been a failure and that affect approaches are usually combined with them. An elementary general discussion of therapeutic practice with children is given by Hartwell, centering on such admonitions as knowing the child's emotional attitudes, using the child's vocabulary, not being disgusted or shocked by the child, and so on. In an account of psychotherapy in children, Potter considers the aims and techniques of psychotherapy to be, first, the establishment of a contact or relationship; second, a release of emotional tension and, along with it as therapy progresses, an analysis of behavior and neurotic symptoms in terms of the child's emotional conflicts, followed by an explanation of behavior symptoms in terms of the child's problems; and lastly helping the child to live in a real world. Although the section in the volume by Kanner on child psychiatry specifically concerned with the principles of treatment is very short, it is important because it is representative of the thinking of many medical men. According to Kanner, treatment embraces work with the child, the family, and the community. Secondary therapeutic aids include the pharmacological, habit training, and suggestion, but emphasis is placed on active changes to bring about readjustment in the child-family-community constellation.

A distinctively important contribution to psychotherapeutic work with children has recently appeared under the editorship of H. L. Witmer (241). Ten cases drawn from the experience of eight therapists are presented in order to illustrate the techniques whereby they deal effectively with typical problems encountered in child guidance work. Originally planned with the hope of differentiating the various psychiatric schools, the general result ultimately obtained, however, as is explicitly recognized by them, is the appreciation of the general unity underlying the therapeutic processes of various dynamic points of view. The cases are presented in detail, with explanatory, theoretical, and evaluative comment in the form of footnotes. In addition to the editorial syntheses, Witmer herself supplied a history of the development of child guidance therapy, an analysis of the dynamics of therapy, and a summary of general conclusions. To be sure, certain of the case studies show clearly the influence of one or another of the specific theoretical orientations to be discussed later, particularly the psychoanalytic, but in an integrated catholicity of approach they are eclectic in the most desirable sense of the term.

The Psychobiological Approach. The psychobiological position is, of course, associated with and has gained recognition through the work of Adolf Meyer. A more eclectic, "common-sense" point of view than many of those discussed later, it stresses the interrelatedness of the physical-psychological attributes of the organism. Indeed a unity is postulated; attitudes, for example, are not psychological alone but are attitudes of the entire organism—psychobiological responses (128). Meyer himself unfortunately did not offer a complete statement of his position. One of the best statements of the psychobiological orientation to treatment is given in a text by Muncie (169). The task of the physician is to give relief from suffering by disentangling and redirecting forces. After hearing the patient's complaint in his own words, the therapist by questioning directs the subsequent account so as to obtain a complete picture. Then the physician restates the problem for his own guidance, notes the gaps in information, and formulates steps to be taken as a means of intervention. Simultaneously the physician reformulates the problem to the patient as much as possible in the patient's own terms. Further steps depend upon the particular nature of the pathology present. In addition to symptomatic (part-function) therapy, which is recommended if it does not introduce the possibility of adverse sequelae, there is need for basic therapy which takes the form of personal therapy. By this is meant the attempt to bring security and ease through understanding of personal functioning. Specific methods are the illumination of the present as a product from the past, and ventilation and redirection of effort through persuasion, re-education, suggestion, and the development of the positive assets of the individual. Since emotional factors arising in the complaint cause difficulty in the understanding and attainment of sensible measures, attention is directed by the therapist to alternate hypotheses, this practice being an expansion of the complaint problem to see a balance of liabilities with assets. This, called distributive analysis by Adolf Meyer, is one of the characteristics of the psychobiological program.

Illustrative of another psychobiological approach is Kraines' volume on the therapy of neuroses and psychoses (128). He attempts to offer specific practical suggestions, the majority of which are presumed to be within the competence of most physicians. The threefold aim of psychotherapy is considered to be to remove stress, to eliminate immature traits, and to substitute mature ones. Analysis of social pressures producing stress is conducted with the aim of removal of stress, removal from stress, and advice on adjusting to stress. The psychological factors are treated by making the patient aware of attitudes to be changed, by removal of emotional tone, and by retraining. A thorough physical examination and resulting physical therapy are essential. Thus a socio-psycho-biological analysis and treatment is conducted. How psychobiological principles may be applied by the average physician to many neurotic patients is the concern of an article by the same writer (127). Psychotherapy is conceived to be the replacement of unhygienic psychobiologic attitudes by those that are healthful and efficient.

A somewhat more theoretical account is given by Rennie (182) in which psychobiological therapy is shown to be concerned with every level of personality organization including detailed personality study or distributive scrutiny following any scientifically established methods that offer melioration.

Relationship Therapies. Strictly speaking, there is not a relationship therapy; rather there are several more or less related views which emphasize the therapeutic effectiveness of the patient-therapist relationship and build their procedures around this. These points of view include those we associate with Rank and Taft, Allen, and John Levy. Regardless of what it is called, in the treatment situation the patient has a relation with another human being to whom he has come or has been sent for help with certain of his problems. Naturally, then, other points of view take some cognizance of this relation: witness rapport and transference as used in eclectic and psychoanalytic views, and the so-called non-directive point of view. However, other factors are considered more or equally fundamental in these approaches.

Historically, Rank (179) was one of the earliest to utilize the procedure both of emphasizing to the patient that the analytic hour provided an opportunity to relive the past experiences of life (actually an affective reliving of birth trauma), and that this present therapist-patient relationship is the essence of therapy. Bound inextricably with certain far-reaching complicated theoretical modifications of Freudian psychoanalysis, his book is less valuable as an introduction to this form of relationship therapy than that in which Taft (217) explains her modifications emphasizing the therapist's goal as providing a relationship which the patient can experience as a new and unique role.

Allen (10), working primarily with children, emphasizes less the reliving of the past and more the new experience that is the therapeutic session. Indeed he specifically disclaims interest in knowing what the problems mean in terms of the past (8). The patient's being able to live with himself today is more important than either the patient's or the therapist's understanding the origin of his feelings. Interpretations offered are in terms of the feeling the child experienced, not in terms of historical or external situations. The relationship with the therapist comes to have value in and for itself as a present clarifying experience of the moment. In this relationship the child behaves as he does toward others, bringing into play his attempts at control of the situation, his likes and dislikes, his anxieties and his fears. The experience in the therapeutic session is a new present relation. Characteristic reactions enter with the child's separation from the mother at the first session, they occur in the relationship during the hour, and they even manifest themselves at the closing of the session at a fixed time. Understanding the child, the therapist can deal with the feelings of dislike the child manifests without threatening him with his own dislike; he can allow expressions of aggression without retaliation. The therapeutic objective then is determined primarily by the feelings the patient has toward the therapist. Free expression is permitted, but there is an imposition of barriers to certain ways of gratifying the feelings, physical violence or property damage being forbidden. Allen's book (10), previously referred to, discusses various phases of the problem of psychotherapy in children beginning with a presentation of the nature of the normal psychological growth process, since the therapeutic process is itself a form of growth. A general description of the therapeutic process follows. Separate chapters are then devoted to the beginning phase of therapy, the child's participation with special reference to play as a medium of expression,[3] a case presentation of a fearful child, problems associated with aggressive behavior, factors that interfere with the therapeuic process, the ending phase, and the broader implications of the whole approach. Two articles by Allen (8, 9) give earlier, less fully developed expressions of his views, both valuable, however, for their clarity, and the second paper for the vividness of the case material presented.

Another approach stressing the relationship between therapist and patient is that described by Lewis both in an article included in the Readings and in a later, more lengthy publication (140). Since definite educational and directive procedures are used, it

---

[3] The value and characteristic use of play in Allen's approach will be discussed later in connection with this topic.

would be a matter of debate whether this could not be regarded with equal appropriateness as an eclectic approach.

Some slight idea of the nature of relationship therapy according to John Levy can be obtained from a short article by him (139). However, as it is in connection with group and play therapy that work inspired by him is best known, further attention to this approach will be deferred until discussion of these topics.

The Non-Directive Approach to Therapy. For a variety of reasons the account of the non-directive approach will not be given in as great detail as present interest among psychologists might seem to justify. Indeed, this great interest and consequent greater general fund of information constitute one of the reasons for the relative shortness of the review. In addition, the inclusion of articles in the *Readings* by Snyder, previously referred to, covers the field comprehensively. As a consequence no attempt will be made to give a general description; general familiarity will be assumed.

It is important to remember that the non-directive approach is in a state of rapid but healthy change. Rogers' volume on counseling and psychotherapy (184), although published as recently as 1942, is no longer representative of either his own thinking or of those associated with him.[4] It is most objectionable apparently because in certain sections it gives approval, in part, to supportive suggestive directive counseling that now would be rejected. Nevertheless, his present critics occasionally are guilty of writing as if this volume represented the final word on his point of view.

It is the purpose of the present brief review to mention a very few carefully selected references that may be said to supplement those included in the *Readings*. Perhaps the most general and significant recent statement from Rogers himself is contained in a paper primarily concerned with those aspects in which non-directive therapy differs most sharply from other procedures (187). He feels that these distinctive elements include the predictability of the process taking place in the form of a pattern, the discovery of the constructive forces residing in the client, and the client-centered nature of the therapeutic relationship. It is this last point which makes him prefer the term "client-centered" over "non-directive"

---

[4] A revision is promised soon.

as more descriptive of the present view. Another article by Rogers (186) that is particularly instructive is concerned with the place of insight in counseling, especially the use of simple acceptance and recognition and clarification of feeling. For illustrations of case material to supplement the case by Snyder given in the Readings, undoubtedly the best source is the casebook edited by the same writer (208). Five cases, exhibiting a variety of problems, are described with large sections quoted verbatim from the recorded materials. Footnote annotations commenting on the counselor and client responses add enlightening information. Curran's volume (53) on personality factors in counseling includes a detailed account of a single case for which all twenty interviews had been phonographically recorded. He makes an analysis of their content and compares the results with other studies. A shorter illustration is given by Madigan (150).

Two articles appearing too late for inclusion in Snyder's review but offering certain criticisms of this approach are especially worthy of mention. In a thoughtful and temperate account Wrenn (245) makes the point that client-centered counseling is part of a continuum of emphasis of client centeredness–counselor centeredness, not a dichotomy, and that the essence of skillful counseling consists in knowing when to use the varying procedures available along the continuum. This seems to be in substantial agreement with some of the remarks of Hahn and Kendall (102), who also consider certain other issues raised about the present conflict between so-called directive and non-directive schools of thought.

Psychoanalysis. Psychoanalysis is at one and the same time a theory of the dynamics of human nature, a method of research, and a method of treatment. More than any other method of treatment it can be properly understood only through knowledge of its theoretical superstructure, the dynamics of the personality as it is seen by the psychoanalyst. Understanding of dynamics must precede understanding of procedure, and the account which follows presupposes this understanding.

The major sources parenthetically referred to in the description to follow appear in the collected papers of Freud (76, 77, 78, 79, 80, 81), his volume on the interpretation of dreams (82), a book on psychoanalytical technique by Lorand (143), and articles by Alexander (2), Bergler (35), French (73), and Thompson (220, 221).

The aim of psychoanalytic therapy is to bring into consciousness the emotions and motivations of which the patient is unaware and thus to extend his conscious control over them. To give a short account of how this process is conducted is the present aim.

Classical psychoanalytic procedure involves four to six hourly visits a week, extending generally from about one to two years. During the sessions the patient usually lies on a couch with the doctor sitting behind him at the head of the couch (79). The patient proceeds by engaging in what is known as free association, saying whatever comes to mind without regard to relevance, merely giving his mind free play (79). Free association is something never experienced before the psychoanalytic sessions—the patient is learning to speak, behave, and think in a way unique to this situation. He is encouraged by the analyst to describe and to express feelings which are hidden under ordinary circumstances, to speak without shame or embarrassment. The freely associating state reveals memories, fancies, accusations, feelings, and reproaches, apparently in a disordered jumble. As the sessions roll on, meanings and connections related to the main problems facing the patient begin to appear first to the analyst, who interprets the material to the patient either when first grasped or more commonly somewhat later as dictated by his estimation of the patient's ability to stand the interpretation. Forcing interpretation too fast when the patient cannot assimilate it must be avoided. Before interpretation ego analysis is necessary—that is, an analysis of the patient's conscious attitudes and behavior toward repressed mental contents—since such materials cannot be brought into consciousness unless preceded by an analysis of the ego's defense against them (73). The meaning of these free associative outpourings centers upon ungratified infantile tensions long buried from conscious recognition.

A valuable source of material for association is that supplied by dreams (77, 82, 143). Dream analysis is in itself a technique of helping along the analytic procedure, for dreams, according to Freudian thinking, are attempts on the part of the mind to live out wishes and to solve its conflicts. The elements of the dream after their recounting are used as starting points for further free associative activity.

During these sessions two important dynamic phenomena considered basic to psychoanalytic doctrine by Freud (76) are revealing themselves: transference and resistance (78, 81, 143, 220, 221). The unique situation in which the patient finds himself leads to the development of an emotional relationship from the patient to the analyst, based upon emotional attitudes from childhood which are transferred to the current situation. This is the phenomenon of transference. Transference is not mere liking. It is essentially a repetition of the dependent attitudes of the child with relation to its parents in all of its irrational aspects. This transference may be one in which he regards the analyst with love, admiration, respect, or other positive feelings, or it may be one in which he exhibits hostility, anger, embarrassment, or other negative feelings. These feelings toward the analyst too are called to his attention and analyzed as to their meaning. The analyst, of course, must avoid reciprocal feelings or counter transference (143). The concept of resistance might be said to be operationally defined; the interpretation which is offered the patient meets with his disagreement and he struggles against it, trying to prove the analyst wrong, or lapses into silence or talks about insignificant topics. The resistances themselves are then analyzed. As the process of free association continues, the patient gradually increases his ability to verbalize unconscious materials and gradually works back to materials hidden by infantile amnesia.

In psychoanalysis, three aspects of a curative process may be said to be taking place: emotional abreaction or discharge, intellectual insight or understanding, and the appearance of conscious awareness of formerly repressed memories particularly infantile (2). All three are necessary for cure, but the degree to which they are necessary forms the basis for deviations within the ranks of psychoanalysts, one stressing abreaction, another insight, still another the awareness of infantile memories. They are all intertwined. All must be "worked through"; that is, a deepening of insight is given by relating the newly uncovered material to the conscious and present experiences of the patient (35, 80).

Analysis, contrary to popular opinion, does not make the patient dependent upon the analyst. The latter takes pains to see that by analyzing the bond of transference itself with the patient, he will be free and independent (143).

MODIFICATIONS OF PSYCHOANALYTIC THERAPY. Departures from psychoanalytic therapy have arisen from differing theoretical con-

ceptions, from the age of the patient, from the nature of the difficulty facing the patient, from the use of adjuncts to psychoanalysis,
and from attempts to find a less time-consuming procedure, to
mention a few of the more important considerations.

Although explicitly concerned with psychoanalytic therapy in
a mental hospital, an article by Knight (125) forms an excellent
introduction to some forms of modified psychoanalytic technique,
including changes introduced in the analysis of children, of psychotics, of severe neurotics, and of the use of brief psychoanalytically
oriented therapy. Illustrative of the adaptability of the psychoanalyst today is the report by the same writer (126) of his therapeutic efforts with a mute adolescent catatonic schizophrenic.
Because of the presence of mutism he combined directive and
relationship elements in his endeavor to establish contact, a far cry
from classical psychoanalytic procedure.

A very interesting and lucid historical account of recent advances
in psychoanalytic therapy is given by Frieda Fromm-Reichmann
(84). These advances, according to her, include (1) changing
conceptions of the nature of drives, departing in various ways from
the erotic-destructive duality postulated by Freud, with Horney
and Sullivan given as illustrations, (2) changing of the Freudian
conception of objective reality simply because the "real" worlds
about us are changing, (3) changing attitudes toward interpretations offered the patient as to timing and content and quantity, and
(4) changing conceptions about choice of patients, with an ever-
widening circle of conditions being found amenable to some form
of psychoanalytic approach.

A short account of the therapeutic differences among the various
schools of psychoanalysis has been given by Waelder (234). He
discusses the positions of Jung, Adler, Rank, Abraham, Horney, and
others. Illustrations of differences due to variation in theoretical
formulation with a consequent variation in practice are given in the
work of Karen Horney. Believing that orthodox analysts have devoted too much attention to unconscious fantasies and childhood
experiences and not enough to the patient's current experiences,
rivalries, insecurities, and cultural restrictions, she and her associates
emphasize study of the methods whereby the ego deals with current
external challenges. Author of several books, Horney is most explicit
regarding methodological problems in a volume entitled *Self Anal-*

ysis (*115*). This volume is recommended not so much for her account of self-analysis, the validity of which has been seriously challenged, but because it contains the most complete statement of her analytic therapeutic approach. In another book she devotes some attention to therapy (*114*). A critique of her position has been given by Alexander (*3*).

Descriptive of variations from standard psychoanalytic procedures, the volume by Alexander and French and their collaborators (*6*) is one of the most important publications on psychotherapy for psychologists to appear in recent years. It was not written particularly with psychologists in mind, but because it is addressed to an audience wider than the psychoanalytical practitioner, it is particularly appropriate for the members of the psychological profession not well versed in regard to treatment procedures. In a sense the title *Psychoanalytic Therapy* is misleading since it is concerned with a variety of what Alexander referred to in a short paper (*4*) as "practical and flexible psychoanalytic techniques." A variety of modifications are proposed, including brief psychotherapeutic procedures, manipulation of frequency and interruption of treatment sessions, the manipulation of extra-therapeutic experiences, a variety of forms of manipulation of the transference relationship such as choice of a therapist according to age, sex, and personality considerations, and the planning of a preliminary dynamic outline of strategy to be followed. Brevity, interruption, manipulation of the environment and the advance outline, all are different from classical psychoanalytic procedure but perhaps are not alien to Freud's own conception of a continuing expanding advance. It is perhaps too little known that Freud considered deserving of the name "psychoanalytical" any method of therapy acknowledging both transference and resistance (*76*). A shorter account of some of these modifications is given in an article by Alexander (*5*).

The article by Blos included in these *Readings* is an interesting and valuable attempt to use psychoanalytical insight not in the realm of unconscious infantile conflicts, but at the level of the ego. Awareness of isolated facts and tendencies on the part of the student was brought about by utilization of transference phenomena.

It is not surprising that for both theoretical and practical reasons psychoanalytic procedures are modified when applied to children. Probably the two chief exponents of child analysis are Melanie

Klein and Anna Freud, whose views show definite contrasts. Melanie Klein (124) believes that play activities are of the same significance and value as the free associations of the adult. Behind every playful action she endeavors to find its significance, direct interpretation being offered immediately in order to allay anxieties. A transference situation is considered to be developed as in adults with its consequent transference neurosis. Her aim is the development of the child's ego through this process so that the child can meet the vicissitudes of his environment without any kind of educational influence or direct modification of the environment. Anna Freud (74, 75) offers a different approach to child analysis. Actual analytic work is preceded by a period aptly called courtship in which she woos the child to a position of positive transference by a variety of techniques showing that she is powerful, trustworthy, or useful. In her opinion, the positive attachment is not such that a real infantile transference neurosis develops. Dreams, daydreams, and drawings are the associative materials used for interpretation, whereas play technique, so important to Klein, is of considerably less symbolic value according to Anna Freud precisely because she believes it is not always symbolic. In addition to the pre-non-analytic period she also insists there is a non-analytic educational role to be played with the children to assist them in adjusting to the environment.

A detailed and highly illuminating account of a child analysis conducted by Gerard (88), adherent of the Vienna School of Anna Freud, is one of the best reports obtainable. Little or no interpretation is given to the child even though the symbolic material is clear to the analyst. Interpretation comes only when the child can express feelings in direct instead of disguised form. Gerard's case study, presented without theoretical evaluation, is ably supplemented by a discussion which followed its presentation at a meeting of the American Orthopsychiatric Association (89). An extraordinarily vivid and clear statement of treatment by analytic methods of a 12-year-old boy is presented by Vander Veer (177).

Another variant of psychoanalytically oriented therapies is hypnoanalysis, whose history is briefly sketched in Brenman and Gill's review of hypnotherapy in general (41, 42). The most exhaustive account of hypnoanalysis is undoubtedly that of Wolberg (243), who not only presents a case in detail but also discusses the theoretical psychoanalytical background. Two papers by Gill and Brenman

(90) and Gill and Menninger (91) present in a very clear and much shorter fashion both case material and theoretical discussions of their combination of certain significant features of hypnosis and psychoanalysis. They consider hypnotizability to be essentially a transference phenomenon and thus properly to belong within the framework of analytical principles of psychodynamics. Interpretation of dream material and free association are used in a manner not substantially different from that followed in classical psychoanalysis. The work of a psychologist, Lindner, with this technique should be mentioned (141). After a brief discussion of his use of hypnosis he describes in detail forty-six hourly sessions that made up his therapeutic efforts with a criminal psychopath. He would use the technique of free association until serious resistance was encountered and then turn to deep hypnosis in order to obtain the withheld material. Theoretical discussion is almost completely neglected.

GROUP THERAPIES

An article by a psychologist, Luchins (148), serves as an excellent introduction to the nature of the various kinds of group structure that develop during the course of group therapy. He concludes that they may be described as a mere assemblage of patients, as an audience of passive spectators with no apparent interaction, as a participating audience, and as an interacting group among themselves. In his own experience he found that no session was precisely one or the other and that the groups did not necessarily proceed consecutively through all the various types of structure; some groups skipped or reverted or became fixed at one or another of these levels. Solomon and Axelrod (212) distinguish four levels of group work, the most superficial being recreational and educational wherein the major focus is on the activity itself and the next a planned program in which the individual members have opportunity to express their needs. The third level might be termed social group work, comparable to group work in case work and superficial therapy in individual therapy, with the program being completely oriented to the use of the individual participants. The fourth level, group psychotherapy, then occupies their attention.

The use of children's behavior in a group with emphasis on the diagnostic possibilities is discussed by Redl (181). Not only is diagnostic group work a means for saving time but it also supplements interviews, providing material not otherwise accessible. Furthermore, it serves in cases in which the verbal interview is not as successful, as with those children whose ability to verbalize is underdeveloped or so overdeveloped as to create an elaborate system of verbal defense.

Pointing out that the types of relationship among people is important for the therapist to understand because they are major tools in treatment, Slavson (202) proceeds to discuss various types of relationships. He differentiates domination-submission, parasitic, symbiotic, anaclitic (where one person puts forth another to handle for him the actualities of life and to protect him against them), supportive, transference, and equipodal (equal give and take). When relationships are used as tools we have (1) transference, (2) supportive, (3) unilateral (emotional flow in one direction—e.g., psychoanalysis and activity group therapy), (4) bilateral (case work, interview group therapy), and (5) multilateral (both aim and tool of group therapy).

Certain general articles should be mentioned before discussing the differing approaches. A review of the literature on group therapy through 1942 is offered by Thomas (219), and an historical account through 1944 is given by Klapman (122), while a bibliographic listing up to 1946 has been prepared by Slavson and Meyers (205). A critique of group therapy is one of the contributions of Harms (106). The interrelation of group and individual therapy, concretely illustrated, is the concern of both Baruch and Miller (28) and Shaskan (199).

To some, group therapy is a necessary evil brought about by the presence of too many patients and too few therapists. To others, it is a technique uniquely valuable in its own right, offering something that individual psychotherapy cannot or at least does not do so directly and so readily. Thus it is assumed to have an heuristic value with specific indications and contraindications. These values accruing from the use of group therapy are, of course, stated in terms of the theoretical positions which their protagonists espouse. Presentation hereafter will take the form followed with individual direct methods of treatment, with the omission of the psychobiological approach, and with the addition of two other theoretical positions, activity group therapy and psychodrama.

Eclectic Approaches. Group psychotherapy is regarded by some as primarily an educational procedure to effect in the individual participant an understanding of his personality and the mechanisms which cause him to behave as he does. For example, an article aptly entitled "Pedagogical Group Psychotherapy" by Klapman (123) gives a short, clear statement of his own position. This same writer (122) presents a rather comprehensive discussion of group therapy in a book devoted to the topic. For an account of his own position it is of considerable importance. A representative article by Hadden (100) concerned with the treatment of the neuroses by class technic is characteristic of his work. He too stresses the role of explanation. It would be misleading, however, to leave the impression that this is all that is operative in their approaches to group therapy. Klapman speaks of a living-through process, and Hadden refers to the relaxing, the inspirational, and the cathartic effect.

Although group therapeutic methods involve both insightful and cathartic elements in varying degrees, it is interesting to note that the extent to which either is used varies even under the direction of one therapist. For example, Teicher (218) used the lecture type of approach with individuals in whom anxiety traits predominated, but those exhibiting hostility and resentment were best treated by meetings in which ventilation was stressed.

Eclectic in spirit, though rooted in psychoanalytic experience, the analyses of the dynamics of both group and individual therapy by Ackerman (1, 146) are especially penetrating. He considers group therapy an independent method with its own unique dynamic characteristics. Still another eclectic point of view has been presented by Rome (189). Although concerned with the description and analysis of a group therapy program in the Navy, he gives a clear picture of the dynamics involved.

Relationship Therapies. An application of relationship therapy to several people at one time in an approach customarily associated with the work in individual therapy by John Levy is described by several writers (67, 94, 147). Levy's emphasis was on having the patient work out actively with the therapist, through his relationship with him, the interpretation and understanding of existing attitudes and conflicts. In the group the line of treatment relationship is from each individual to the therapist. Group interactions are of a decidedly secondary consequence. This approach is therapy *in* the group, not therapy *by* the group. Durkin, Glatzer and Hirsch (67) and Lowrey (147) describe its use with a group of mothers of patients.

Non-Directive Approach to Therapy. That non-directive therapy is of some value in the group situation is demonstrated in a research study of Peres (174). For the present purposes, however, the article is of particular value in showing how this approach may be used with groups.

Psychoanalytically Oriented Approaches. Various writers have used psychoanalytic formulations in their accounts of work in group therapy. Schilder (196) describes a psychoanalytic method of group therapy using an autobiographical technique combined with free association and dream interpretation. Sarlin and Berezin (195) speak of three major forms of psychotherapy, group therapy included: spiritual, intellectual, and uncovering or analytic. The spiritual approach is based on exhortative emotional appeal and depends upon suggestion and transference; the intellectual approach through the application of reasoning is one in which the patient is told of the nature and meaning of his symptoms so that understanding may develop; and the uncovering approach is based on the belief that neurotic conditions are the result of unconscious conflicts, and therapy is directed toward recognizing and making conscious these conflicts. Sarlin and Berezin reject the first two approaches and describe a method of therapy based on a modification of the psychoanalytic approach which they applied to a group of eight soldiers. Detailed concrete descriptions of the eighteen sessions are given. A method of group therapy in a mental hospital is described by Wender (236), who conceives the functions of group therapy to include intellectualization or comprehension of emotional reactions; patient-to-patient transference which is used to facilitate the transference to the therapist through the identification of one patient with another who is already in rapport; catharsis, or more strictly, catharsis-in-the-family in which the patient may react to the group as one would to a family; and group interaction arising from the fact that since he hears from others in the group the patient can evaluate his own problems against those of others. Wender considers his approach to be analytically oriented although different from Freudian analysis, especially in the much greater activity of the therapist. A very illuminating account of the use of

drama in therapy is given by Solomon and Fentress (213). Originally stimulated by the work of Moreno, they put considerably
more emphasis on preparation before the dramatizations, including
individual therapy and the writing of an autobiography, which are
used by the therapist to select the scenes to be played and to instruct the supporting players. Examples and interpretations are
offered which are psychoanalytically oriented with emphasis on
the value of this approach in obtaining abreaction, insight into unconscious material, and modification of over-strict or weak super-
egos.

Activity Group Therapy. Therapy is considered to be possible
only in a world of action, hence the name "activity group therapy"
as used by Slavson (201) to describe his work in a setting of a case
work agency. Group therapy is used with children judged in need
of it after diagnostic exploration, most often with accompanying
individual therapy. The group organized ostensibly as a club decide
and carry out their activities with no direction and interpretation
offered by the therapist who plays a neutral role. Permissiveness
is encouraged, but not uncritically, some groups having more limitations placed upon them than others. Even those without restrictions on fighting and destructiveness are permitted such activities
only in the early stages, since participation in everyday activities
demands restraint. Permissiveness, however, within these broad
limits is very important in that it is a means of breaking down resistances to the world as it is. Complete freedom in idiosyncratic behavior is allowed. Thus activity catharsis or expression of feeling
through actions analogous to play therapy is considered to be important. Materials similar to those used in play therapy are supplied
along with arts and crafts materials, refreshments are served, and
outings to movies, museums, and the like, if the group wishes it,
are made possible. According to this account, group therapy as thus
used encourages security of unconditioned love, ego-development,
leisure time interest, and acceptance by the group. The group is
presumed to be a substitute family with the therapist a parent sur-
rogate. With this adult and with other children the child establishes
relations which make possible a transition toward a more realistic
balanced perception of the world and its demands upon him. Insight is gained by the child in the situation, not through interpretation. Two considerably shorter accounts of his approach to group

therapy are given by Slavson (146, 203). A study of a small group of girls attending a much larger day camp by Hewitt and Gildea (111) supplies excellent concrete illustrations of what occurs in the permissive atmosphere akin to that described by Slavson.

In addition to activity group therapy Slavson (201) reports on other variations of group treatment including conducting interviews in the general activity setting, and the leading of discussion groups, especially with older patients, in which treatment *in* a group is more important than the treatment *through* a group previously described. He has also written on the differential dynamics of activity and interview group therapy (204).

Psychodrama. Parallel with and related to Moreno's development of psychodrama was the sociometric approach to the interaction of individuals in groups referred to later in connection with environmental modification. Although they may be separated for the sake of presentation, many of psychodrama's explanatory concepts are rooted in sociometry. A psychodramatic session consists of the enactment of a spontaneous dramatic incident. This particular situation is either selected by the director (therapist) as relevant to the person's difficulties based on a prior private interview, or suggested by the patient himself as an area in which personal problems lie. Immediately before the session the incident is briefly outlined. The background merely is given—e.g., the wife has told the patient she is leaving him. How he is to handle the situation is not described, it being essentially self-directed with the person reacting as he sees fit. Supporting players called auxiliary egos are used to play the roles of absentee members of the patient's network of interpersonal relations. They do not know the patient and are dependent upon clues given by the director prior to the session and upon the patient's description of the scene and how he reacts to it. They act only as suggested. Variations of procedure from that outlined above are encouraged and adopted when they seem indicated. For example, if rapport between patient and therapist is weak and the patient does not respond spontaneously to the situation presented, a variety of warming-up techniques are used. In this momentary situation on the stage the patient is presumed to show basic aspects of his personality, his striving, and his conflicts. Thus diagnostic material is obtained, but what is more important, a process of catharsis is taking place by the acting out of conflicts and by the analysis later in a post-dramatic interview with the director. Training in spontaneity is offered both in regard to remeeting past situations and in meeting situations not heretofore faced. This factor of spontaneity is considered to be the core of psychodramatic therapy. A mobilization of personality characteristics on the spur of the moment on the psychodramatic stage creates a resourcefulness in meeting life's situations which, if sufficiently developed, increases the individual's adjustive capacity.

Perhaps the best single source for a relatively short account of psychodrama as a technique is certain sections in the first of three volumes by Moreno entitled *Psychodrama* (164), especially the material beginning on page 177. Another excellent introductory source is an article by Moreno appearing in the first issue of *Sociometry* (163). The organization of a psychodramatic unit is the concern of two of Moreno's associates, Del Torto and Cornyetz (57). They also have written on the relation of the projective aspect of psychodramatic methodology to other projective techniques (58). The application of psychodrama in various fields is illustrated by Herriott's publication (110) on its use in diagnosis, Franz's analysis (72) of its interrelationship with interviewing, and Greenhill's description (96) of its use as a means of play therapy with children. Snyder's general review (209) mentioned previously gives an account of psychodrama to which Moreno has recently taken exception (166). The relationship of psychodrama to group therapy in general is the concern of Meiers in an historical account (153). Moreno (165) and Lawlor (131) also discuss this same relation.

PLAY THERAPIES

In working with children the conventional question-answer interview method has been judged unsuitable by many clinicians. It is not surprising then that play, often said to be the child's natural means of expression, has been utilized for diagnostic and therapeutic purposes. The term "play therapy" is somewhat confusing in that it might be construed that play, as an activity in itself, is the only therapeutic element which is far from the truth. Free play, in itself, or play not understood by the therapist, may well be merely another traumatic experience to the child, since nothing is done to allay the child's anxiety and guilt which might arise in such situations.

Amster (14) makes the point that play is a medium of exchange comparable to words. No more than words can it be a therapy in itself. Play used for diagnostic and therapeutic purposes is what is meant by play technique. Amster goes on to discuss the uses to which play may be put, namely, for diagnostic understanding, to establish a working relationship, to reestablish different ways of playing, to help the patient verbalize certain materials, to help him act out unconscious material, and to develop an interest in play useful in other settings.

Included in the previous section of these *Readings* is an article by A. Weiss Frankl which illustrates the diagnostic use of play technique. Before discussing play therapies it might be well to mention some reviews. A review of the literature, diagnostic and therapeutic, through 1939 is given by Kanner (119) who is highly critical of the analytic approach. Preliminary to an account of his method of play therapy, Rogerson (188) also gives an historical summary. Other reviews have been prepared by Bender and Woltman (34), Whiles (237), and Traill (231).

In an evaluation of play approaches Newell (173) distinguishes between controlled or standardized play illustrated by the work of David Levy, Conn, and Solomon, and spontaneous play exemplified in the work of Allen, Blanchard, Gitelson, Gerard, and Rogerson. The essential difference, he indicates, is the activity of the therapist. In the former situation he is active, choosing the materials and suggesting a scene, whereas in the latter he remains in the background, giving the child free rein in choice of materials and form of play. He then goes on to discuss the advantages and disadvantages of these contrasting methods. This, then, is one way of viewing the various play therapies.

Still another orientation, the one adopted here, is through the various theoretical points of view previously discussed—eclectic, psychobiological, relationship, non-directive, and psychoanalytic. The distinctions, however, among the various methods of play therapy in terms of systematic approaches is not as clear as in the case of either the individual or the group method. There is a healthy blurring, fostered at least in part by the orthopsychiatric spirit and movement, which makes such a simple schematization tenable only for the purposes of expositions such as this one. For example, in this presentation David Levy's release therapy is considered to be eclectic, although with some justification it could be considered psychoanalytically oriented. The work in play therapy by Conn and Solomon is associated with and shows enough kinship to the psychobiological approach to be so classified, but no great violence could be said to have been done to the facts if the eclectic rubric had been chosen. The problem is further complicated by the fact that both group and individual play therapy are employed and may be accompanied by either group or individual non-play treatment. For example, the article by Baruch included in the Readings is concerned with group play therapy accompanied by individual treatment.

Eclectic Approaches. In 1938, under the chairmanship of Gitelson (92) a section meeting of the American Orthopsychiatric Association on play therapy was held. The discussants representing a variety of points of view included Helen Ross, Erik Homburger, Frederick Allen, Phyllis Blanchard, Hymen Lippman, Margaret Gerard, and Lawson Lowrey. The extent and nature of the similarities and differences in point of view are especially noteworthy. An admirable account of an eclectic-dynamic approach to play therapy is given by Gitelson (93) himself, with special emphasis on the initial reactions to the situation on the part of the children, the tendencies exhibited which suggest therapeutic progress, the preparation (if any) given the child before treatment, the aims of treatment, and the evaluation of the results obtained with forty cases.

In describing his use of so-called release therapy, David Levy (137) indicates that it is an affect therapy aimed at the release of feelings of the child, no attempt to produce insight being made. Interpretation is reduced to the minimum. Play therapy in general he considers as a blend of release and insight factors, and his emphasis on the former is for purposes of clarity of exposition. He uses other forms alone or in combination with release therapy when indicated. Criteria of selection of suitable cases is determined by the presence of a definite symptom picture precipitated by a specific event of not too long duration and problems uncomplicated by family difficulties. He would use it for the restoration of traumatic situations, for controlled play situations aimed at modifying social attitudes, and for simple release of aggression and of infantile pleasures, this last being used with children too conforming, orderly, and neat. Sometimes situations are set up for simple release, e.g., throwing objects, spilling water, sucking water out of a nursing bottle, sometimes arranged in a standard pattern depicting sibling rivalry and so on, and sometimes individually in a situation set up to resemble a specific life experience. The same author (136) has also written a shorter account of release therapy in which he differentiates between two forms: specific release therapy, in which the situation giving rise to the anxiety and accompanying symptoms is restored by "playing" about it, and general release therapy, utilized typically when symptoms have arisen because of early or excessive demands or prohibitions. Another contribution (135) concerns the use of a specific doll play situation framed so as to permit the study of sibling rivalry.

Baruch (24), a psychologist, describes the use of a family of dolls whom the child readily identifies as members of his own family. Her account shows the revealing nature of the diagnostic clues thus obtained. Another article by the same author (26) demonstrates some of the material in regard to aggression that is obtained by the same method. Although certain aspects of her approach are in keeping with the spirit of the non-directive orientation, it was developed independently and avowedly contains definite interpretive elements.

An admirably restrained account of play therapy is given by Rogerson (188). Although somewhat influenced by psychoanalytic thinking, his point of view is perhaps closer to that of Allen in that he stresses the contention that the changes which take place in play therapy are probably in large measure due to the development of a relationship with another individual who accepted the child with understanding and without criticism.

The Psychobiological Approach. Illustrative of the use of play therapy arising in the atmosphere of a psychobiological orientation are the procedures developed by Conn (47) at Johns Hopkins. The emphasis is upon planned play procedures in which the needs of the child determine the "sets" arranged by the physician. They are arranged so that the child can express his feelings and thoughts as if the dolls, not he, were responsible. The specific use of this way of handling the situation is illustrated by the same writer's description of the treatment of fearful children (49). This approach is more directive than others, as is aptly brought out in still another account (48).

Solomon (210) refers to his approach as active play therapy, which is in keeping with Newell's analysis given earlier. The method centers on restricting the child to a play situation, using dolls representing individuals from his own environment and with which he reenacts situations from his own life. In a later article the same investigator (211) presents a case study in which a doll representing the therapist is added to the scene so that the child can work out his relationships with him in the play situation. Solomon considers his work akin to the Levy release approach and to that of Conn. Emotional conflicts are worked through by bringing to light all suppressed feeling the child has toward people.

Relationship Therapies. Allen (10) makes the distinction between a purposive and controlled use of play such as that described previously and the fact that without play activities no relationship could be established. The important issue is the use made of play. He would center it not on the particular play or its content but on the spontaneous responses of the child as he relates himself to the therapist, drawing him into it, shutting him out, bossing him, and so on. For example, whether he does or does not play is much less important than the fact that he is permitted a choice. Play materials are provided which may or may not be used. Spontaneous choice, not the particular activity, is the more important. Play activity in itself has a therapeutic significance secondary to the relationship the child is building.

Durkin (66) applied relationship therapy to a preschool summer play group. Inspired by the work of John Levy, therapy is regarded as a growth process arising from the unique nature of the relationship between therapist and patient. The pivotal factor is the interpretation of the relationship between therapist and patient. Instead of responding to factual material, the therapist tries to see its significance in terms of the feeling behind it on the assumption the patient will try out his typical attitudes on the therapist. Illustrative material is given and the possibilities and limitations are discussed.

The Non-Directive Approach to Therapy. The non-directive approach with children has been applied in a setting of play. The most complete account is contained in a volume written by Axline (21). Responsibility and direction, she claims, are left to the child. What are considered to be the fundamental principles of such counseling are given, but lengthy excerpts and complete case transcriptions make up over half the book. Desirable situations for the application of this approach and suitable materials are described. No attempt is made to review the literature. Indeed, the book is remarkable in that not a single reference to other literature is cited. An article by Axline and Rogers (22), the gist of which is contained in Axline's book, may serve as a shorter introduction to non-directive play therapy. An account of a treatment of a reading problem by Bixler (39) is also noteworthy.

Psychoanalysis. In the psychoanalysis of children, play technique is also used with play materials substituted in varying degrees for other associative material. Anna Freud (74) finds it valuable chiefly in its diagnostic revelations, but not particularly useful for direct interpretation. Klein (124), on the other hand, uses play material in the same way as free association, offering immediate interpretation to the child. Illustration of an actual detailed psychoanalytic approach to certain play therapy experiences is presented by Homburger (112). Emphasis is on the interpretation of the actual arrangement in space that the child (or adult) makes with the play materials. The spatial configurations are considered to be the important characteristic which differentiates the psychological material obtained through play from that communicated by words. Illustrative drawings of these arrangements of play materials add clarity. In a more general article the same writer (113) describes in detail findings in play technique in which the mechanisms of resistance, transference, and regression are found to appear in social, verbal, spatial, and bodily forms of expression. Fries (83) also discusses play techniques in the analysis of young children.

Indirect Methods of Treatment

Heretofore, presentation has centered upon the various approaches to therapy—eclectic, relationship, and the like. This survey, however, would not adequately convey the more outstanding contributions to psychological treatment without some attention being devoted to indirect methods of treatment embracing the devices used to carry out the therapeutic aims and the utilization of environmental manipulation and modification. In the literature now to be reviewed the writers may well espouse one or another of the approaches discussed earlier, but at the moment emphasis on the devices used and the manipulative procedures utilized is paramount. The writings concerned with the media of play therapy will be seen to make this change of focus from that previously presented.

MEDIATING ADJUNCTS TO THERAPY

Play Materials. Certain of the contributions to play therapy deal with specific media, such as dolls, puppets, clay, finger paints, and art productions. Bender and Woltmann (33) describe the use of non-hardening clay (plasticine) in work with children. Once the plastic object is created, the child not only considers it as more or less an image similar to the object, but also imbues it with a function. For example, it may be passive and played with, or it may take on an aggressiveness. The child creates a world, and consequently these activities constitute a means of emotional release. Photographs of some of the creations add further realism to this account. They also describe (32) puppet plays using hand puppets especially adapted for a free expression of infantile aggression in young children. Two fundamental problems in childhood they consider to be aggression *by* the child with consequent anxiety, or aggression *against* the child with consequent apprehension; and, secondly, the problem of the child's relationship with his father, mother, and siblings. Through puppets he can give expressions of aggression without anxiety or fear and also free expressions of love. Woltmann (244) in another publication describes the use of puppets in helping the child to understand and to solve his emotional problems.

The use of specially selected toys with which the child is encouraged to build a "world" is described by Lowenfeld (145), Traill (231), and Whiles (237). In this procedure the child constructs a scene from a wealth of supplied properties. A metal tray is the locus of activity, with sand and water supplied to form the fields, hills, rivers, and other geographical formations, while small figures representing adults, children, soldiers, and animals are available along with toy houses, fences, cars, aeroplanes, construction bricks, and so on.

Expressions of feeling through art creations is the concern of Alschuler and Hattwick (11) in a very thorough investigation using nursery school children. It is their thesis that these art productions are meaningful and expressive and may be related to the experiences that the child is undergoing. Easel painting is the most prominent medium in which the factors of color, line, form, and space usage are investigated for the light they throw on understanding the child in relation to his experiential changes. Although primarily diagnostic in nature, this study also demonstrates certain therapeutic values in art productions, particularly through its release functions. An article by Brick (43) is likewise illustrative of an attempt to sketch interpretive conclusions concerning children's graphic art work. She indicates certain findings in regard to the color, subject matter, size, approach, and the like in the art material projected by the child which are considered indicative of emotional states such as aggression or anxiety. Bender (31) holds that the therapeutic values of graphic art production are to be found in the following factors: It is a means of establishing rapport with children who are rather inexpressive or withdrawn, have speech problems, or are reluctant to discuss their difficulties; it is a means of obtaining insight into a child's unconscious life; it allows expression of aggressive impulses; it serves as a socializing force; and it gives opportunity to express impulses to motor activity. Naumberg (172) describes in considerable detail the art work of behavior problem children. Since she regards such drawings as satisfaction of wishes with a manifest and latent content, spontaneous choice and execution by the child were encouraged.

Ruth F. Shaw, a psychologically untrained person, originated finger painting as a form of play and as a medium for self-expression, but was quick to recognize its diagnostic and therapeutic value, appreciating that it permitted a certain freedom in expressing fantasy life (200). Although its use as a hobby has been emphasized, and continues to be, others have now become aware of its clinical usefulness (170). Finger painting is, in a sense, a misnomer since the hand and arm are often used. Specially prepared harmless non-staining paints are used on previously dampened paper. Preceding actual use there is a demonstration by the administrator of the many ways in which the hands and arms may be used and of the variety of movements that may be made. Although actual manual help may be given when asked for, it emphatically is not an art lesson, and criticism or suggestion is out of place. Very complete historical and procedural descriptions are given by Napoli (170). In this same monograph and in a later article (171) he offers a diagnostic analysis of results obtained with this method. Other workers have concerned themselves with its therapeutic value. Arlow and Kadis (18), for example, after general discussion and case presentation of its use in children, summarize by concluding that finger painting facilitates the emergence of phantasies; is a means whereby an individual may be confronted with trends in his own creations which he perforce accepts since they are embodied in the paintings; and is a record of the progress of treatment.

Occupational and Recreational Therapies. No essential distinction between occupational and recreational therapy really exists. However, although the two merge, the publications to be discussed sometimes show an emphasis on one or the other. If this be the case, the distinction made is that occupational therapy stresses handicrafts while recreational therapy emphasizes games and sports.

Recreational-occupational therapy may be distinguished from recreational activities and occupational training on the basis of the intent of the activity. Therapy is prescribed in the sense that activities are selected or omitted for their therapeutic values with the needs of the individual patient considered as primary. A settlement house recreational program directed to the group as a whole is not organized in this fashion and is not therapy.

Recreational-occupational therapies and play therapies show many points of similarity. Despite the differences in ages of the patients, many of the therapeutic features are present in both: the release value, the relationship with the therapist, interpretive possibilities, and so on. Methods and even materials may be essentially the same. An example of similar materials is found in the use of puppets. While the work of Bender and Woltmann previously described falls properly in play therapy, Lyle and Holly (149) apply it with adults. They point out that puppetry is extraordinarily versatile; building the puppets may satisfy a creative urge in one, the complete control of the puppet's mechanism may give a feeling of mastery to another, and the manipulation of puppets may provide outlets for exhibitionistic or aggressive strivings in others. The media of finger painting, too, has been used with adults; Fleming (69), for example, presents a series of observations concerning its use with older persons, while Mosse (168) introduces the technique of asking the patient for his free associations with the pictures, thereby increasing the diagnostic material available. Others who have stressed its diagnostic possibilities include Rosenzweig and Durbin

(193), who used a somewhat simplified form of finger painting technique in a study of hospitalized psychotic patients, comparing patients in the various diagnostic categories in regard to planning of production and what colors were used.

Music also has been used as a therapeutic agent. Therapies either stimulate or repress, and since music produces such effects, it becomes evident that properly used it is a therapeutic tool, especially for symptomatic treatment. Altshuler (12), an authority on this mode of therapy, indicates in an article which might well serve as an introduction to the subject that much research remains to be done before it can be used with entire effectiveness. This is in agreement with Van de Wall (233), who states that as a means of treatment it is still in its infancy, at the stage of opinion and debate. In his volume he presents a discussion on the use of music in a considerable variety of hospitals, including those concerned with psychiatric problems.

Articles and books dealing with other aspects and media of recreational therapy have appeared. Apparently designed to serve as a text, a volume by Davis (54) contains some interesting and valuable material relating specifically to recreational therapy. His discussion of education and reeducation, interest and effort, and his classification of activities, physical education, and the aims and objectives of recreational therapy form a comprehensive introduction to recreational media. Individualized recreational therapy—i.e., therapy prescribed to meet the individualized needs of the patient —is described by Menninger and McColl (157). They contend that it allows resocialization, makes reality more pleasant, forms an outlet for aggression, permits phantasy expression, and gives an opportunity to create. In a presentation of occupational-recreational measures used in a mental hospital, Bellator (30) indicates some specific therapeutic values served by horticulture, bibliotherapy, dramatics, music, homemaking, sports, and calisthenics. Anderson (16) presents the thesis that informal social gatherings provide certain benefits to the mentally ill. Reality situations thus created offer opportunities for encouraging initiative and cooperation. That there is kinship with group therapy is obvious.

The most comprehensive modern statement of the principles and practices of occupational therapy is given in a volume edited by Willard and Spackman (240). Of particular interest to the psychologist are the chapters describing its history, its scope and aims, the activities pursued, and its uses with mentally ill patients and with children. A text on occupational therapy as used with the mentally ill has been prepared by Haas (99). He first reviews its history and its aims, and then discusses methods of receiving patients and beginning occupational therapy. Brief case studies are presented which are illustrative of the adaptation of this form of therapy to counteract depression or excitement, to restore confidence, to provide outlets for aggression, to give training in cooperation, and to prepare for new occupations. He goes on to discuss the organization and management of the department and to describe the crafts best suited for occupational therapy. The problems attendant upon the prescription by the therapist of specific occupational therapy activities are the concern of Dunton (65). He sketches its general nature and then devotes attention to its special applications with mental and physical disorders. The nature of the special problems associated with the use of occupational therapy with children is the theme of a short paper by Krider (129).

Tests and Testing Sessions. That the handling of the psychological examination has therapeutic effects, good or bad, is fairly well established. Indeed, one of the *Readings* by Roland discusses the psychological examination as a beginning in therapy. Not so fully appreciated is the fact that specific psychological tests, as such, have definite therapeutic value. Deabler (56), for example, has used the Thematic Apperception Test near the beginning of contacts because it lends itself very well to establishing rapport. The client, hesitant to talk about personal matters, is given the measure so that he can speak without feeling that he is talking about himself. Afterwards he may feel more free to do so. As used by Deabler it also allows the patient opportunity to vent his emotions and to arrive at his own insights by arranging ample time after the stories are given to express his feelings and attitudes with regard to them. With this same instrument Bettelheim (36) found that some students also showed evidence of increased insight in regard to their personality problems on completion of the measure. The Vineland Social Maturity Scale has been used in substantially the same manner among prisoners by Doll and Brooks (64). Catharsis and self-analysis were found to result. The Rorschach Test may also be employed as a therapeutic agent. Kamman (117) finds it helpful in establishing

rapport and in showing concretely to relatives and to the patient
something about the patient's disturbances. The value of this measure in certain specific psychiatric conditions is also discussed. Steinmetz (214) has also written on the subject of the therapeutic value
of tests, showing how they may be used to produce psychological
understanding. This last approach is implicit in the work of many
guidance counselors who emphasize the interpretation of test results
with their clients.

Educational Procedures. That educational procedures are treated
here as a medium of therapy rather than as an aspect of treatment
itself is not to be construed as implying that educational elements
do not enter into other approaches to therapy—perhaps with greatest emphasis in the eclectic and the psychobiological approaches.
Of necessity, all psychological therapies are educational in aim since
each in its own way attempts to teach the patient to live more effectively. However, present consideration is focused on pedagogic instruction as such, individual or class, used for therapeutic purposes.
Informational sources, however, such as occupational pamphlets
and remedial techniques used in specific school subject disabilities
and with aphasics, are not discussed. Bibliotherapy will be reviewed
subsequently in a separate section.

The psychologist writing most persuasively on the utilization of
individualized teaching or tutoring as a means of therapy is Grace
Arthur, one of whose articles appears in the *Readings*. She has published a volume on tutoring as therapy (20) in which she emphasizes the role of the psychologist as the planner of such tutoring,
which is carried out, however, by others. The finding of the appropriate kind of person to serve as tutor is cogently discussed, as is the
organization of a tutoring program. Case histories illustrate graphi-
cally the far-reaching effects of subject matter failure on the child's
adjustment and show how even serious behavior problems may be
solved by removing the causes of the insecurity and hostility. An
earlier shorter account is given in an article by the same writer (19).

Another approach to educational therapy by a psychologist is
shown in the contributions of Baruch, one of which is included in
the *Readings*. Her emphasis is on the incorporation of therapeutic
procedures directly into the process of education itself. A follow-up
report supplementing this article has appeared (27).

Some forms of educational therapy bear close resemblance to

occupational-recreational therapy described in one of the previous sections. The work of the Menninger Clinic, described in the publications of Ralston (178) and W. C. Menninger (156), is illustrative of this similarity. In her discussion of educational therapy, Ralston states that resocialization is its primary aim. Attempts to accomplish this are made through adapting educational endeavors to the individual's personality requirements, by providing an atmosphere that allows an individual to test his progress, by finding new outlets, and by filling out actual deficiencies in academic education which if unfilled might be a handicap to the person when outside the institution. Specific illustrations of how these devices operate are given. The article by Menninger describes the organization of the educational program, the directorate, instructors and subjects, type and duration of classes, prescription of class work, and the results obtained.

Bibliotherapy. Books may be used for therapeutic purposes in either of two ways: as more or less specific attempts to introduce further understanding of psychological or physiological factors, to increase contact with reality, to allow opportunity for identification and compensation and the like; or in a more general way as part of the mobilization of all forces making for healthful adjustment. On occasions of its use in the first manner, specific readings are apt to be assigned with some particular reason in mind; in the second, general exposure to a library is arranged, accompanied by encouragement to use it.

There is no one major source for work in bibliotherapy of the guided-reading sort. Perhaps the person who used this approach to a greater extent than any other was T. V. Moore. In his text (160) he devotes some attention to an evaluation and description of guided-reading. He found it most effective in connection with behavior disorders and problems of childhood and adolescence. In a later discussion (161) he described in detail its application in the case of a delinquent boy. The presentation of Bradley and Bosquet (40) is valuable not only for its discussion of the therapeutic uses of literature but also for the lengthy list of books they consider appropriate for use with children.

Although some of the sources mentioned above indicate the use of bibliotherapy with psychotics, the most valuable direct source is an article by W. C. Menninger (155) in which he deals with the therapeutic prescription of reading material for psychotic patients. A concrete account of how books are used in a psychiatric hospital is given by Allen (7).

An analysis of the present status of bibliotherapy is the concern of Bryan (45). She feels that at present it is at an anecdotal stage and awaits experimental study of its effectiveness. An article by Schneck (197) is the most thorough review of the publications concerned with this method of treatment.

Audio-Visual Aids. Although nothing prevents their utilization with individual patients, audio-visual aids are generally employed in the group setting and consequently are to be considered as an adjunct to group therapy. The various films found useful are reviewed by Katz (120). A typical use of battle sounds phonographically recorded and used to induce the reliving of a battle scene is described by Kupper (130). The rationale of the application of motion pictures in group therapy as one aspect of this approach is considered in papers by Rome (189, 190).

Hypnotherapy. Hypnosis in its former guise of a means for forcing the disappearance of symptoms followed by a closing of the therapeutic sessions has now almost completely disappeared. Modern usage emphasizes its adjuvant character as in the alleviation of acute symptoms which prevent other therapies being utilized, the establishment of initial rapport, the creation of confidence in the therapist, the resolution of resistances, and the like.

LeCron and Bordeaux (133) present a very valuable modern treatment of hypnosis—in fact, the only thorough general introductory account that has appeared in years. After a historical survey, they discuss methods of inducing hypnosis, the place of suggestion in creating the phenomena of hypnosis, the phenomena themselves, and theories of hypnosis. Roughly half the book is devoted to hypnotherapy; after placing it in a setting of other psychotherapeutic methods, they discuss it in some detail and then proceed to a presentation of hypnoanalysis.

For a review of the literature on hypnotherapy that has appeared during the last fifty years, an excellent source is the monograph prepared by Brenman and Gill (41). After briefly summarizing its historical vicissitudes, they consider the remaining material under the headings of methods of induction, susceptibility to hypnosis, therapeutic applications, and the theory of hypnosis. This monograph has been republished in book form (42) with supplemental case studies, some of which are referred to in the discussion of hypnoanalysis.

ENVIRONMENTAL MANIPULATION AND MODIFICATION

Two aspects of indirect treatment yet to be considered may be distinguished: environmental manipulation or outright removal of the individual from his present environment and placement elsewhere, and modification of certain aspects of the environment without removing the individual. Foster homes and institutional placement are characteristic means used when the former is the method chosen; modification of parental attitudes toward a child is a characteristic approach in the latter.

Indirect treatment by environmental manipulation and modification can be expected to produce some beneficial results in a child even though he himself is not treated, since his patterns of behavior have not crystallized, being still in a process of growth. With the adult, however, with environmental manipulation there is apt to be merely a change of the nature of complaints expressed, precisely because he is not as plastic. To be sure, institutionalization is often indicated with adults, but frequently this is not because institutionalization per se is considered of any considerable therapeutic value but because environmental change is indicated for the purposes of allowing other forms of therapy to be used expeditiously or for custodial or protective reasons. However, even with adults there is some therapeutic benefit from the neutral environment, the protection afforded, the regularity of regimen, and, on occasion, the isolation from relatives. However, in keeping with the emphasis found in the literature, work with children will predominate, although attention will be drawn to methods used with other age groups.

For the psychologist, the most important general discussion yet to appear concerned with environmental manipulation and modification is that by Carl Rogers (183). He covers substantially the topics mentioned above and, in addition, discusses the school's part in changing behavior and the use of clubs, groups, and camps.

A collection of clinical case records has been prepared by Towle (230). Although primarily directed toward the student social worker, it contains several specific case studies illustrating both environmental manipulation and modification as well as direct treatment.

Environmental Manipulation. The literature, although showing in varying degrees the influence of various systematic approaches to treatment, tends to stress the method almost to the exclusion of the dynamics. Consequently, in the mention of some illustrative examples respectively of child placement, adult foster family care, institutionalization, and summer camps, the practice of describing the setting in which it is used will be followed.

Social workers, often the supervisors of environmental manipulative procedures, have written voluminously on the subject of child placement. Garrett's account (87) of case work treatment of the child is illustrative of the combination of child placement with social work and individual therapy. For a lengthier account of child placement in general, the volume by Baylor and Monachesi (29) is probably representative. A discussion of trends in child placement is given by Lippman (142), including the selection of foster homes, institutional placement, and the placement of aggressive children. Healy and his associates (109) describe its use with delinquents. Indicative of the sort of problems faced in child placement is Deming's analysis (59) of the needs of the child when home and group placement are considered. The use of boarding homes in connection with day attendance at the Southard School of the Menninger Foundation is described by Wright (246). An excellent general discussion of the basic factors and the therapeutic considerations in parental substitution is offered by Harms (104).

A variant of environmental manipulation occasionally used with hospitalized or institutionalized mentally ill or defective adults is foster family care. Generally those selected for this form of treatment are individuals for whom hope of full recovery is slight. When a patient responds to institutional treatment to the point of showing a possibility of his profiting from the individual atmosphere of family life, this form of custodial service is used. Not infrequently, however, this custodial intent of making him reasonably comfortable at a more or less static level of malfunctioning is, on occasion, happily contravened by an actual improvement. Sometimes family care is used deliberately with this thought in mind; individuals are so placed with the purpose of hastening recovery. The most comprehensive modern discussion of foster home care has been prepared by Crutcher (52), who surveys its administration, the results obtained, selection of patients and homes, methods of supervision, and its rationale as a therapeutic procedure. Particularly noteworthy for the purpose of understanding the therapeutic value of foster home care are the vivid case histories included.

Discussions of institutionalization as a means of treatment are typically presented in terms of the patient group concerned. The accounts by Dybwad (68) and Doll (61, 62) are illustrative of a copious literature that has developed in regard to institutional placement of mental defectives. *The American Journal of Mental Deficiency* and the *Training School Bulletin* in which they appear include many articles on this and related topics. Institutionalization of mentally and emotionally disturbed children is discussed by Wolberg (242). He stresses the therapeutic influence of the hospital environment in terms of the demands placed upon the child to reorient himself in his relations with people found in that environment. An account of unfortunately atypical institutional procedures in the treatment of delinquency is given by Grossman (98).

A summer camp directed by and associated with a psychiatric children's clinic used for treatment purposes is described by Young (247). After enumerating the dangers of a blanket prescription of a camping period, he describes criteria of selection and the kinds of children most benefited and illustrates by case presentations. Another description of a summer camp under psychiatric auspices is given by Amsden (13), while actual procedures followed are stressed by Galkin (85). It should be obvious that environmental manipulations such as these are separated from group therapy only by temporal discontinuity and the more general nature of the camp prescription.

Environmental Modification. Environmental modification, most often actively carried out by social workers, takes many forms. Physical changes in the home may be arranged, e.g., a boarder may be asked to leave, or a change to another dwelling may be suggested; child management and health advice may be offered; but most important and relevant is the attempt at modification of parental behavior by interpreting the child's behavior to the parents, particularly the mother. The child's personality, his needs and difficulties, may be interpreted to the parents and other adults in his environmental milieu in an effort to introduce changes in their ways of dealing with the child. The articles by Blanchard and Rheingold appearing in these *Readings* are illustrative of interpretation with parents.

Many of the functions in a consultive capacity of child guidance and psychoeducational clinic personnel and school psychologists involve their making recommendations to parents, teachers, and others at the level of social interpretation which this method of treatment represents. The article by Zehrer included in the *Readings* is concerned essentially with this indirect approach. Further illustrative is an article by Cason (46) in which are offered some suggestions on the interaction between the school psychologist and the classroom teacher designed to aid in the task of his cooperating with teachers in helping pupils solve their problems. Recommendation for change in grade placement is indicative of the methods utilized.

It is common practice for both the parent and the child to be seen by the personnel of a child guidance clinic. At the outset, however, it is important to point out the fact that because a parent is involved is no reason for making deviations from accepted therapeutic practices. The only unique feature is that the child was brought for treatment first; any of the individual or group methods described in previous sections of this chapter might be appropriate for the adult. However, certain therapeutic endeavors arising directly from this problem will be indicated.

The treatment directed primarily toward the mothers of child patients is the concern of Moore (158, 159). She describes as attitude therapy an authoritative pedagogical method of modifying those attitudes of the mothers which affect the child. In a later article David Levy (134) also describes attitudes therapy in the treatment of mothers in which the objective is given as the elaboration, definition, and tracing to their early sources the social responses typical of a given individual. The mothers are encouraged to talk of their experiences, thus bringing about an emotional release and also giving information about their attitude patterns useful for interpretive purposes with them. Wichman and Lanford (238) in a discussion of their work with the parent in the children's psychiatric clinic focus interest on her feelings in familial relationships because they consider this to be the area which limitations of time would suggest as the most advantageous to select. Security in being a parent is looked upon as the goal of this work. An account by Johnson and Fishback (116) of a collaborative treatment serves to emphasize the fact that parent and child may be equally in need of intensive treatment instead of relatively to minimize the treatment of the adult because the child was the reason why therapeutic help was sought. Dawley (55) calls attention to what she considers a neglected basis of therapy, namely, the interrelationship of the shift and change in both parent and child as the therapeutic experience progresses for both of them.

In her discussion of the social worker's role in a child case work agency, Hamilton (103) devotes a chapter to the problem of treatment of the members of the family. In the volume edited by Witmer (241) the case worker's notes included in the accounts of therapeutic work with children illustrate some of the procedures followed when working with parents.

Although sometimes regarded as a means of group therapy, the sociometric approach fostered by Moreno can for present purposes be regarded as a form of environmental manipulation. Sociometry is a method of study of the interrelation of feeling patterns toward one another existing among people. The so-called sociometric test is used for disclosing the feelings which individuals have in regard to one another in respect to membership in the group in which they are at the given moment or in which they may later be placed. It is emphatically not a mere friendship test; it may be used for all sorts of groups—e.g., in a schoolroom in which a child may be asked to select those other schoolmates whom he wants to sit beside, or in a home for delinquents in which the girls may be asked which particular cottage mother they would like to live with. In situations where there is an official leader, choice preferences are also made by this leader. Many other criteria of sociometric attraction-repulsion have also been worked out and are applied in sociometric analysis, with final selection based on the evaluation of all criteria by the analyst. When a class, cottage residents, working group, club, or other group is actually selected or reconstituted on the basis of the results of such testing, we have a form of environmental manipulation. The basic source for information in regard to this method is a volume by Moreno (162).

Bibliography

1) Ackerman, N. W. Some general principles in the use of group psychotherapy. In Glueck, B. (ed.), *Current therapies of personality disorders.* New York: Grune & Stratton, 1946, pp. 275–280.
2) Alexander, F. The problem of psychoanalytic technique. *Psychoanal. Quart.,* 1935, 4, 588–611.
3) Alexander, F. Psychoanalysis revised. *Psychoanal. Quart.,* 1940, 9, 1–36.
4) Alexander, F. Practical and flexible psychoanalytic techniques. *Digest Neurol. & Psychiat.,* 1945, 13, 283.
5) Alexander, F. G. The indications for psychoanalytic therapy. *Bull. New York Acad. Med.,* 1944, 20, 319–332.
6) Alexander, F., French, T. M., and others. *Psychoanalytic therapy: principles and applications.* New York: Ronald, 1946.
7) Allen, E. B. Books help neuropsychiatric patients. *Libr. J.,* 1946, 71, 1671–1675; 1693.
8) Allen, F. H. Therapeutic work with children: a statement of a point of view. *Amer. J. Orthopsychiat.,* 1934, 4, 193–202.
9) Allen, F. H. Discussion of case. *Amer. J. Orthopsychiat.,* 1934, 4, 323–358.
10) Allen, F. H. *Psychotherapy with children.* New York: Norton, 1942.
11) Alschuler, R. H., and Hattwick, L. B. W. *Painting and personality: a study of young children* (Vols. I & II). Chicago: Univ. of Chicago Press, 1947.
12) Altshuler, I. M. Four years experience with music as a therapeutic agent at Eloise Hospital. *Amer. J. Psychiat.,* 1944, 100, 792–794.
13) Amsden, R. L. The summer camp as a behavior clinic. *Ment. Hyg.,* 1936, 20, 262–268.
14) Amster, F. Differential uses of play in treatment of young children. *Amer. J. Orthopsychiat.,* 1943, 13, 62–68.
15) Amster, F. Collective psychotherapy of mothers of emotionally disturbed children. *Amer. J. Orthopsychiat.,* 1944, 14, 44–52.
16) Anderson, M. The role of prescribed social gatherings in the treatment of the mentally ill. *Bull. Menninger Clin.,* 1941, 5, 56–60.
17) Appel, K. E. Psychiatric therapy. In Hunt, J. McV. (ed.), *Person-*

ality and the behavior disorders. New York: Ronald, 1944, pp. 1107–1163.

18) Arlow, J. A., and Kadis, A. Finger painting in the psychotherapy of children. Amer. J. Orthopsychiat., 1946, 16, 134–146.

19) Arthur, G. Tutoring as therapy. Amer. J. Orthopsychiat., 1939, 9, 179–185.

20) Arthur, G. Tutoring as therapy. New York: Commonwealth Fund, 1946.

21) Axline, V. M. Play therapy: the inner dynamics of childhood. Boston: Houghton Mifflin, 1947.

22) Axline, V. M., and Rogers, C. R. A teacher therapist deals with handicapped child. J. Abnorm. Soc. Psychol., 1945, 40, 119–142.

23) Baruch, D. W. Parents and children go to school. Chicago: Scott, Foresman, 1939.

24) Baruch, D. W. Doll play in preschool as an aid in understanding the child. Ment. Hyg., 1940, 24, 566–577.

25) Baruch, D. W. Therapeutic procedures as part of the educative process. J. Consult. Psychol., 1940, 4, 165–172.

26) Baruch, D. W. Aggression during doll play in a preschool. Amer. J. Orthopsychiat., 1941, 11, 252–260.

27) Baruch, D. W. Incorporation of therapeutic procedures as part of the educative process. Amer. J. Orthopsychiat., 1942, 12, 659–666.

28) Baruch, D. W., and Miller, H. Group and individual psychotherapy in the treatment of allergy. J. Consult. Psychol., 1946, 10, 281–284.

29) Baylor, E. H., and Monachesi, E. D. The rehabilitation of children: the theory and practice of child placement. New York: Harper, 1939.

30) Bellator, N. S. An educational therapy program in a mental hospital. Occup. Ther., 1938, 17, 147–152.

31) Bender, L. Art and therapy in the mental disturbances of children. J. Nerv. Ment. Dis., 1937, 86, 249–263.

32) Bender, L., and Woltmann, A. G. The use of puppet shows as a psychotherapeutic method for behavior problems in children. Amer. J. Orthopsychiat., 1936, 6, 341–354.

33) Bender, L., and Woltmann, A. G. The use of plastic material as a psychiatric approach to emotional problems in children. Amer. J. Orthopsychiat., 1937, 7, 283–300.

34) Bender, L., and Woltmann, A. G. Play and psychotherapy. Nerv. Child, 1941, 1, 17–42.

35) Bergler, E. "Working through" in psychoanalysis. Psychoanal. Rev., 1945, 32, 449–480.

36) Bettelheim, B. Self-interpretation of fantasy: the Thematic Apperception Test as an educational and therapeutic device. Amer. J. Orthopsychiat., 1947, 17, 80–100.

37) Bingham, W. V. *Aptitudes and aptitude testing*. New York: Harper, 1937.

38) Bixler, R. Non-directive play therapy. Unpublished M.A. thesis, Columbus, Ohio: Ohio State Univ., 1942.

39) Bixler, R. H. Treatment of a reading problem through non-directive play therapy. *J. Consult. Psychol.*, 1945, 9, 105–118.

40) Bradley, C., and Bosquet, E. S. Uses of books for psychotherapy with children. *Amer. J. Orthopsychiat.*, 1936, 6, 23–31.

41) Brenman, M., and Gill, M. M. Hypnotherapy. *Josiah Macy Jr. Found., Rev. Ser.*, 1944, 2, No. 3.

42) Brenman, M., and Gill, M. M. *Hypnotherapy: a survey of the literature*. New York: International Universities Press, 1947.

43) Brick, M. Mental hygiene value of children's art work. *Amer. J. Orthopsychiat.*, 1944, 14, 136–146.

44) Brown, J. F., and Rapaport, D. The role of the psychologist in the psychiatric clinic. *Bull. Menninger Clinic*, 1941, 5, 75–84.

45) Bryan, A. I. Can there be a science of bibliotherapy? *Libr. J.*, 1939, 64, 773–776.

46) Cason, E. B. Some suggestions on the interaction between the school psychologist and the classroom teacher. *J. Consult. Psychol.*, 1945, 9, 132–137.

47) Conn, J. H. The play-interview: a method of studying children's attitudes. *Amer. J. Dis. Child.*, 1939, 58, 1199–1214.

48) Conn, J. H. The child reveals himself through play. *Ment. Hyg.*, 1939, 23, 49–69.

49) Conn, J. H. The treatment of fearful children. *Amer. J. Orthopsychiat.*, 1941, 11, 744–751.

50) Covner, B. J. Studies in the phonographic recordings of verbal material. I & II. *J. Consult. Psychol.*, 1942, 7, 105–113.

51) Crider, B. Psychotherapy in a case of obesity. *J. Clin. Psychol.*, 1946, 2, 50–58.

52) Crutcher, H. B. *Foster home care for mental patients*. New York: Commonwealth Fund, 1944.

53) Curran, C. A. *Personality factors in counseling*. New York: Grune & Stratton, 1945.

54) Davis, J. E. *Principles and practice of recreational therapy for the mentally ill*. New York: Barnes, 1936.

55) Dawley, A. Inter-related movement of parent and child in therapy with children. *Amer. J. Orthopsychiat.*, 1939, 9, 748–754.

56) Deabler, H. L. The psychotherapeutic use of the Thematic Apperception Test. *J. Clin. Psychol.*, 1947, 3, 246–252.

57) Del Torto, J., and Cornyetz, P. How to organize a psychodramatic unit. *Sociometry*, 1944, 7, 250–256.

58) Del Torto, J., and Cornyetz, P. Psychodrama as expressive and projective technique. *Sociometry*, 1944, 7, 356–375.

59) Deming, J. Foster home and group placement. Amer. J. Ortho-psychiat., 1940, 10, 586–594.
60) Diethelm, O. Treatment in psychiatry. New York: Macmillan, 1933, pp. 111–133.
61) Doll, E. A. Boarding-home care of mental defectives. Train. Sch. Bull., 1938, 36, 1–10, 35–40.
62) Doll, E. A. Foster care for mental defectives. Train. Sch. Bull., 1940, 36, 193–205.
63) Doll, E. A. A preparation for clinical psychology. J. Consult. Psychol., 1944, 8, 137–140.
64) Doll, E. A., and Brooks, J. J. The therapeutic uses of the Vineland Social Maturity Scale in its application to adult prisoners. J. Crim. Psychopath., 1942, 3, 347–358.
65) Dunton, W. R. Prescribing occupational therapy (2nd ed.). Springfield, Ill.: Thomas, 1945.
66) Durkin, H. E. Dr. John Levy's relationship therapy as applied to a play group. Amer. J. Orthopsychiat., 1939, 9, 583–598.
67) Durkin, H. E., Glatzer, H. T., and Hirsch, J. S. Therapy of mothers in groups. Amer. J. Orthopsychiat., 1944, 14, 68–75.
68) Dybwad, G. The problem of institutional placement for high-grade mentally defective delinquents. Amer. J. Ment. Def., 1941, 45, 391–400.
69) Fleming, J. Observations on the use of finger painting in the treatment of adult patients with personality disorders. Char. & Pers., 1940, 8, 301–310.
70) Font, M. McK. Orientation in clinical approach through remedial reading instruction. Amer. J. Orthopsychiat., 1942, 12, 324–334.
71) Font, M. McK. Psychological techniques applied to selective service cases. Amer. J. Orthopsychiat., 1943, 13, 130–137.
72) Franz, J. G. The psychodrama and interviewing. Amer. Sociol. Rev., 1942, 7, 27–33.
73) French, T. M. Ego analysis as a guide to therapy. Psychoanal. Quart., 1945, 14, 336–349.
74) Freud, A. Introduction to the techniques of child analysis. (Trans. by L. P. Clark.) Nerv. Ment. Dis. Monogr., 1928, No. 48.
75) Freud, A. The psycho-analytical treatment of children. London: Imago, 1946.
76) Freud, S. On the history of the psycho-analytic movement. In Collected papers (Vol. I). New York: International Psycho-analytical Press, 1924, pp. 287–359.
77) Freud, S. The employment of dream-interpretation in psycho-analysis. In Collected papers (Vol. II). London: Hogarth Press, 1924, pp. 305–311.
78) Freud, S. The dynamics of the transference. In Collected papers (Vol. II). London: Hogarth Press, 1924, pp. 312–322.
79) Freud, S. Further recommendations in the technique of psycho-

analysis. In *Collected papers* (Vol. II). London: Hogarth Press, 1924, pp. 342–365.

80) Freud, S. Further recommendations in the technique of psychoanalysis: recollection, repetition and working through. In *Collected papers* (Vol. II). London: Hogarth Press, 1924, pp. 366–376.

81) Freud, S. Further recommendations in the technique of psychoanalysis: observations on transference-love. In *Collected papers* (Vol. II). London: Hogarth Press, 1924, pp. 377–391.

82) Freud, S. The interpretation of dreams. In Brill, A. A. (ed.), *The basic writings of Sigmund Freud.* New York: Modern Library, 1938, pp. 179–549.

83) Fries, M. E. Play techniques in the analysis of young children. *Psychoanal. Rev.*, 1937, 24, 233–245.

84) Fromm-Reichmann, F. Recent advances in psychoanalytic therapy. *Psychiatry*, 1941, 4, 161–164.

85) Galkin, J. The treatment possibilities offered by the summer camp as a supplement to the child guidance clinic. *Amer. J. Orthopsychiat.*, 1937, 7, 474–482.

86) Gardner, C. E. Future therapeutic role of the clinical psychologist. *Amer. J. Orthopsychiat.*, 1942, 12, 383–387.

87) Garrett, A. M. *Case work treatment of a child.* New York: Family Welfare Association of America, 1941.

88) Gerard, M. W. Case for discussion at the 1938 symposium. *Amer. J. Orthopsychiat.*, 1938, 8, 1–18.

89) Gerard, M. W. The 1938 symposium. *Amer. J. Orthopsychiat.*, 1938, 8, 409–435.

90) Gill, M. M., and Brenman, M. Treatment of a case of anxiety hysteria by an hypnotic technique employing psychoanalytic principles. *Bull. Menninger Clin.*, 1943, 7, 163–171.

91) Gill, M. M., and Menninger, K. Techniques of hypnoanalysis illustrated in a case report. *Bull. Menninger Clin.*, 1946, 10, 110–126.

92) Gitelson, M. (chm.). Play therapy. *Amer. J. Orthopsychiat.*, 1938, 8, 499–524.

93) Gitelson, M., and collaborators. Clinical experience with play therapy. *Amer. J. Orthopsychiat.*, 1938, 8, 466–478.

94) Glatzer, H. T., and Durkin, H. E. The role of the therapist in group relationship therapy. *Nerv. Child*, 1945, 4, 243–251.

95) Gramlich, F. W., and Stouffer, G. A. Functions of the psychologist in the neuropsychiatric unit at the Farragut Naval Training Station. *J. Consult. Psychol.*, 1943, 7, 211–215.

96) Greenhill, M. Psycho-dramatic play therapy in disorders of childhood. *Proc. Inst. Child. Res. Clin. Woods Schs.*, 1945, 12, 107–122.

97) Grigg, A. E. The concept of levels in orthopsychiatry. Amer. J. Orthopsychiat., 1943, 13, 147–149.

98) Grossman, G. The role of the institution in the treatment of delinquency. Amer. J. Orthopsychiat., 1938, 8, 148–157.

99) Haas, L. J. Practical occupational therapy for the mentally and nervously ill. Milwaukee: Bruce, 1944.

100) Hadden, S. B. Treatment of the neuroses by class technic. Ann. Intern. Med., 1942, 16, 33–37.

101) Haggard, E. A., and Murray, H. A. The relative effectiveness of three therapy procedures on the reduction of experimentally induced anxiety. Psychol. Bull., 1942, 30, 441.

102) Hahn, M. E., and Kendall, W. E. Some comments in defense of non non-directive counseling. J. Consult. Psychol., 1947, 11, 74–81.

103) Hamilton, G. Psychotherapy in child guidance. New York: Columbia Univ. Press, 1947.

104) Harms, E. Substitution therapy: dogmatic or differential? A report on incomplete symposium. Nerv. Child, 1944, 3, 36–47.

105) Harms, E. The arts as applied psychotherapy. Occup. Ther., 1944, 23, 51–61.

106) Harms, E. Group therapy—farce, fashion or sociologically sound? Nerv. Child, 1945, 4, 186–195.

107) Hartwell, S. W. The treatment of behavior and personality problems: A. the psychiatrist. Amer. J. Orthopsychiat., 1931, 1, 3–20.

108) Hathaway, S. R., and Harmon, L. R. Clinical counseling in emotional and social rehabilitation. J. Clin. Psychol., 1946, 2, 151–157.

109) Healy, W., Bronner, A. F., Baylor, E. M. H., and Murphy, J. P. Reconstructing behavior in youth: a study of problem children in foster families. New York: Knopf, 1929.

110) Herriott, F. Diagnostic examination of mental patients on the psycho-dramatic stage. Sociometry, 1940, 3, 383–398.

111) Hewitt, H., and Gildea, M. C. L. An experiment in group psychotherapy. Amer. J. Orthopsychiat., 1945, 15, 112–127.

112) Homburger, E. Configurations in play: clinical notes. Psychoanal. Quart., 1937, 6, 139–214.

113) Homburger, E. Studies in the interpretation of play: clinical observations of play disruption in young children. Genet. Psychol, Monogr., 1940, 22, No. 4.

114) Horney, K. New ways in psychoanalysis. New York: Norton, 1939.

115) Horney, K. Self-analysis. New York: Norton, 1942.

116) Johnson, A. M., and Fishback, D. Analysis of a disturbed adolescent girl and collaborative psychiatric treatment of the mother. Amer. J. Orthopsychiat., 1944, 14, 195–203.

117) Kamman, G. R. The Rorschach method as a therapeutic agent. Amer. J. Orthopsychiat., 1944, 14, 21–27.

118) Kanner, L. *Child psychiatry.* Springfield, Ill.: Thomas, 1935.
119) Kanner, L. Play investigations and play treatment of children's behavior disorders. *J. Pediat.,* 1940, 17, 533–546.
120) Katz, E. Audio-visual aids for mental hygiene and psychiatry. *J. Clin. Psychol.,* 1947, 3, 43–46.
121) Keiser, S. Severe reactive states and schizophrenia in adolescent girls. *Nerv. Child,* 1945, 4, 17–25.
122) Klapman, J. W. *Group psychotherapy: theory and practice.* New York: Grune & Stratton, 1946.
123) Klapman, J. W. Pedagogical group psychotherapy. *Dis. Nerv. Syst.,* 1946, 7, 205–208.
124) Klein, M. *The psychoanalysis of children.* London: Hogarth Press, 1932.
125) Knight, R. P. The place of psychoanalytic therapy in the mental hospital. In Glueck, B. (ed.), *Current therapies of personality disorders.* New York: Grune & Stratton, 1946, pp. 59–69.
126) Knight, R. P. Psychotherapy of an adolescent catatonic schizophrenic with mutism; a study in empathy and establishing contact. *Psychiatry,* 1946, 9, 323–339.
127) Kraines, S. H. Brief psychotherapy. *Ment. Hyg.,* 1943, 27, 70–79.
128) Kraines, S. H. *The therapy of the neuroses and psychoses: a sociopsycho-biologic analysis and resynthesis* (2nd ed.). Philadelphia: Lea & Febinger, 1943.
129) Krider, A. Some special considerations in occupational therapy for maladjusted children. *Bull. Menninger Clin.,* 1940, 4, 23–27.
130) Kupper, W. H. Observations on the use of a phonograph record of battle sounds employed in conjunction with pentothal in the treatment of 14 cases of severe conversion hysteria aroused by combat. *J. Nerv. Ment. Dis.,* 1947, 105, 56–60.
131) Lawlor, G. W. Psychodrama in group therapy. *Sociometry,* 1946, 9, 275–281.
132) Lecky, P. Unpublished doctoral dissertation. Columbia Univ., 1938.
133) LeCron, L. M., and Bordeaux, J. *Hypnotism today.* New York: Grune & Stratton, 1947.
134) Levy, D. M. Attitude therapy. *Amer. J. Orthopsychiat.,* 1937, 7, 103–113.
135) Levy, D. M. Studies in sibling rivalry. *Res. Monogr. Amer. Orthopsychiat. Assoc.,* 1937, No. 2.
136) Levy, D. M. "Release therapy" in young children. *Psychiatry,* 1938, 1, 387–390.
137) Levy, D. M. Trends in therapy. III. Release therapy. *Amer. J. Orthopsychiat.,* 1939, 9, 713–736.
138) Levy, D. M. Psychotherapy and childhood. *Amer. J. Orthopsychiat.,* 1940, 10, 905–910.

139) Levy, J. Relationship therapy. Amer. J. Orthopsychiat., 1938, 8, 64–69.
140) Lewis, V. W. Changing the behavior of adolescent girls: a description of process. Arch. Psychol., N. Y., 1943, No. 279.
141) Lindner, R. M. Rebel without a cause: the hypnoanalysis of a criminal psychopath. New York: Grune & Stratton, 1944.
142) Lippman, H. S. Newer trends in child placement. Family, 1941, 21, 323–328.
143) Lorand, S. Technique of psychoanalytic therapy. New York: International Universities Press, 1946.
144) Louttit, C. M. Clinical psychology (Rev. ed.). New York: Harper, 1947.
145) Lowenfeld, M. The world pictures of children: a method of recording and studying them. Brit. J. Med. Psychol., 1939, 18, 65–101.
146) Lowrey, L. G. (chm.). Group therapy: special section meeting, 1943. Amer. J. Orthopsychiat., 1943, 13, 648–691.
147) Lowrey, L. G. Group treatment for mothers. Amer. J. Orthopsychiat., 1944, 14, 589–592.
148) Luchins, A. S. Group structures in group psychotherapy. J. Clin. Psychol., 1947, 3, 269–273.
149) Lyle, J., and Holly, S. B. The therapeutic value of puppets. Bull. Menninger Clin., 1941, 5, 223–226.
150) Madigan, V. E. An illustration of non-directive psychotherapy. J. Clin. Psychol., 1945, 1, 36–52.
151) Maslow, A. H., and Mittelmann, B. Principles of abnormal psychology: the dynamics of psychic illness. New York: Harper, 1941.
152) Mathews, W. M. Scope of clinical psychology in child guidance. Amer. J. Orthopsychiat., 1942, 12, 388–392.
153) Meiers, J. I. Origins and development of group psychotherapy. Psychodrama monographs, Beacon House, 1945, No. 17.
154) Menninger, K. A. Clinical psychology in the psychiatric clinic. Bull. Menninger Clin., 1943, 7, 89–92.
155) Menninger, W. C. Bibliotherapy. Bull. Menninger Clin., 1937, 1, 263–274.
156) Menninger, W. C. Experiments with educational therapy in a psychiatric institution. Bull. Menninger Clin., 1942, 6, 38–45.
157) Menninger, W. C., and McColl, I. Recreational therapy as applied in a modern psychiatric hospital. Occup. Ther., 1937, 16, 15–23.
158) Moore, M. U. The treatment of maternal attitudes in problems of guidance. Amer. J. Orthopsychiat., 1933, 3, 113–127.
159) Moore, M. U. Attitude therapy. Amer. J. Orthopsychiat., 1940, 10, 681–696.
160) Moore, T. V. The nature and treatment of mental disorders. New York: Grune & Stratton, 1943.

161) Moore, T. V. Bibliotherapy in psychiatric practice. In, Glueck, B. (ed.), *Current therapies of personality disorders*. New York: Grune & Stratton, 1946, pp. 132–153.

162) Moreno, J. L. Who shall survive? A new approach to the problem of human interrelations. *Nerv. Ment. Dis. Monogr.*, 1934, No. 58.

163) Moreno, J. L Inter-personal therapy and the psychopathology of inter-personal relations. *Sociometry*, 1937, 1, 9–76.

164) Moreno, J. L. *Psychodrama*. Vol. I. New York: Beacon, 1946.

165) Moreno, J. L. Psychodrama and group psychotherapy. *Sociometry*, 1946, 9, 249–253.

166) Moreno, J. L. Discussion of Snyder's "the present status of psychotherapeutic counseling." *Psychol. Bull.*, 1947, 44, 564–567.

167) Morris, C. A. Psychological service or mental testing. *Amer. J. Orthopsychiat.*, 1941, 11, 493–497.

168) Mosse, E. P. Painting-analysis in the treatment of neuroses. *Psychoanal. Rev.*, 1940, 27, 65–82.

169) Muncie, W. *Psychobiology and psychiatry*. St. Louis: Mosby, 1939.

170) Napoli, P. J. Finger-painting and personality diagnosis. *Genet. Psychol. Monogr.*, 1946, 34, No. 2.

171) Napoli, P. J. Interpretive aspects of finger-painting. *J. Psychol.*, 1947, 23, 93–132.

172) Naumberg, M. Studies of the "free" art expression of behavior problem children and adolescents as a means of diagnosis and therapy. *Nerv. Ment. Dis. Monogr.*, 1947, No. 71.

173) Newell, H. W. Play therapy in child psychiatry. *Amer. J. Orthopsychiat.*, 1941, 11, 245–251.

174) Peres, H. An investigation of nondirective group therapy. *J. Consult. Psychol.*, 1947, 11, 159–172.

175) Potter, H. W. Psychotherapy in children. *Psychiat. Quart.*, 1935, 9, 335–348.

176) Porter, E. H., Jr. The development and evaluation of a measure of counseling interview procedures. Unpublished Ph.D. thesis, Columbus, Ohio: Ohio State Univ.

177) Preston, G. H. (chm.). Symposium: psychotherapy for children. *Amer. J. Orthopsychiat.*, 1945, 15, 1–46.

178) Ralston, P. Educational therapy in a psychiatric hospital. *Bull. Menninger Clin.*, 1940, 4, 41–50.

179) Rank, O. *Will therapy and truth and reality*. (Taft, J., Trans.) New York: Knopf, 1945.

180) Rapaport, D. The psychologist in the private mental hospital. *J. Consult. Psychol.*, 1944, 8, 298–301.

181) Redl, F. Diagnostic group work. *Amer. J. Orthopsychiat.*, 1944, 14, 53–67.

182) Rennie, T. A. C. Psychobiological therapy. *Amer. J. Psychiat.*, 1940, 97, 611–622.

183) Rogers, C. R. *The clinical treatment of the problem child.* New York: Houghton Mifflin, 1939.
184) Rogers, C. R. *Counseling and psychotherapy: newer concepts in practice.* Boston: Houghton Mifflin, 1942.
185) Rogers, C. R. Therapy in guidance clinics. *J. Abnorm. Soc. Psychol.,* 1943, 38, 284–289.
186) Rogers, C. R. The development of insight in a counseling relationship. *J. Consult. Psychol.,* 1944, 8, 331–341.
187) Rogers, C. R. Significant aspects of client-centered therapy. *Amer. Psychologist,* 1946, 1, 415–422.
188) Rogerson, C. H. *Play therapy in childhood.* New York: Oxford University Press, 1939.
189) Rome, H. P. Group psychotherapy. *Dis. Nerv. Syst.,* 1945, 6, 237–241.
190) Rome, H. P. Therapeutic films and group psychotherapy. In (Anon.), *Group psychotherapy: a symposium.* New York: Beacon House, 1945, pp. 247–254.
191) Rosenzweig, S. Some implicit common factors in diverse methods of psychotherapy. *Amer. J. Orthopsychiat.,* 1936, 6, 412–415.
192) Rosenzweig, S. A dynamic interpretation of psychotherapy oriented towards research. *Psychiatry,* 1938, 1, 521–526.
193) Rosenzweig, L., and Durbin, L. A. Finger painting as an investigative approach to therapeutic techniques. *Occup. Ther.,* 1945, 24, 1–12.
194) Royer, A. E. An analysis of counseling procedures in a nondirective approach. Unpublished M.A. thesis, Columbus, Ohio: Ohio State Univ., 1942.
195) Sarlin, C. N., and Berezin, M. A. Group psychotherapy on a modified analytic basis. *J. Nerv. Ment. Dis.,* 1946, 104, 611–667.
196) Schilder, P. Results and problems of group psychotherapy in severe neuroses. *Ment. Hyg.,* 1939, 23, 87–98.
197) Schneck, J. M. Bibliotherapy and hospital library activities for neuropsychiatric patients: a review of the literature with comments on trends. *Psychiatry,* 1945, 8, 207–228.
198) Sears, R. R. (ed.). Clinical psychology in the military services. *Psychol. Bull.,* 1944, 41, 502–579.
199) Shaskan, D. A. Must individual and group psychotherapy be opposed? *Amer. J. Orthopsychiat.,* 1947, 17, 290–292.
200) Shaw, R. F. *Finger painting.* Boston: Little, Brown, 1934.
201) Slavson, S. R. *An introduction to group therapy.* New York: Commonwealth Fund, 1943.
202) Slavson, S. R. Types of relationship and their application to psychotherapy. *Amer. J. Orthopsychiat.,* 1945, 15, 267–277.
203) Slavson, S. R. The field and objectives of group therapy. In Glueck, B. (ed.), *Current therapies of personality disorders.* New York: Grune & Stratton, 1946, pp. 166–193.

204) Slavson, S. R. Differential dynamics of activity and interview group therapy. *Amer. J. Orthopsychiat.*, 1947, 17, 293–302.

205) Slavson, S. R., and Meyers, G. (comps.). *Bibliography on group therapy.* New York: American Group Therapy Association, 1946.

206) Snyder, W. U. A short-term nondirective treatment of an adult. *J. Abnorm. Soc. Psychol., Clin. Suppl.*, 1943, 38, 87–137.

207) Snyder, W. U. An investigation of the nature of non-directive psychotherapy. *J. Gen. Psychol.*, 1945, 33, 193–224.

208) Snyder, W. U. *Casebook of non-directive counseling.* Boston: Houghton Mifflin Company, 1947.

209) Snyder, W. U. The present status of psychotherapeutic counseling. *Psychol. Bull.*, 1947, 44, 297–386.

210) Solomon, J. C. Active play therapy. *Amer. J. Orthopsychiat.*, 1938, 8, 479–498.

211) Solomon, J. C. Active play therapy, further experiences. *Amer. J. Orthopsychiat.*, 1940, 10, 763–781.

212) Solomon, J. C., and Axelrod, P. L. Group psychotherapy for withdrawn adolescents. *Amer. J. Dis. Child.*, 1944, 68, 86–101.

213) Solomon, A. P., and Fentress, T. L. A critical study of analytically oriented group psychotherapy utilizing the technique of dramatization of the psychodynamics. *Occup. Ther.*, 1947, 26, 23–46.

214) Steinmetz, H. C. Directive psychotherapy: V. Measuring psychological understanding. *J. Clin. Psychol.*, 1945, 1, 331–335.

215) Stogdill, E. L. A survey of the case records of a student consultation service over a ten-year period. *Psychol. Exch.*, 1934, 3, 129–133.

216) Super, D. E., and Brophy, D. A. The role of the interview in vocational diagnosis. *Occupations*, 1941, 19, 1–5.

217) Taft, J. *The dynamics of therapy in a controlled relationship.* New York: Macmillan, 1933.

218) Teicher, J. D. Experiences with group psychotherapy. *U. S. Nav. Med. Bull.*, 1945, 44, 753–756.

219) Thomas, G. W. Group psychotherapy: a review of the recent literature. *Psychosom. Med.*, 1943, 5, 166–180.

220) Thompson, C. Transference as a therapeutic instrument. *Psychiatry*, 1945, 8, 273–278.

221) Thompson, C. Transference as a therapeutic instrument. In Glueck, B. (ed.), *Current therapies of personality disorders.* New York: Grune & Stratton, 1946, pp. 194–205.

222) Thorne, F. C. A critique of nondirective methods of psychotherapy. *J. Abnorm. Soc. Psychol.*, 1944, 39, 459–470.

223) Thorne, F. C., Directive psychotherapy: III. The psychology of simple maladjustment. *J. Clin. Psychol.*, 1945, 1, 228–240.

224) Thorne, F. C. Directive psychotherapy: IV. The therapeutic implications of the case history. *J. Clin. Psychol.*, 1945, 1, 318–330.

225) Thorne, F. C. Directive psychotherapy: VI. The technique of psychological palliation. *J. Clin. Psychol.*, 1946, 2, 68–79.

226) Thorne, F. C. Directive psychotherapy: VII. Imparting psychological information. *J. Clin. Psychol.*, 1946, 2, 179–190.

227) Thorne, F. C. Directive psychotherapy: XI. Therapeutic use of conflict. *J. Clin. Psychol.*, 1947, 3, 168–179.

228) Thorne, F. C. Directive psychotherapy: XII. The client's Weltanschauung. *J. Clin. Psychol.*, 1947, 3, 277–286.

229) Thorne, F. C. Directive psychotherapy: XIII. Psychological antidotes and prophylactics. *J. Clin. Psychol.*, 1947, 3, 356–364.

230) Towle, C. *Social case records from psychiatric clinics.* Chicago: Univ. of Chicago Press, 1941.

231) Traill, P. M. An account of Lowenfeld technique in a child guidance clinic, with a survey of therapeutic play technique in Great Britain and U. S. A. *J. Ment. Sci.*, 1945, 91, 43–78.

232) Trow, W. C. Psychologists report their training needs. *J. Consult. Psychol.*, 1943, 7, 27–40.

233) Van de Wall, W. *Music in hospitals.* New York: Russell Sage Foundation, 1946.

234) Waelder, R. Present trends in psychoanalytic theory and practice. In Lorand, S. (ed.), *The yearbook of psychoanalysis.* Vol. I, 1945, pp. 84–89.

235) Watson, G. (chm.). Areas of agreement in psychotherapy. *Amer. J. Orthopsychiat.*, 1940, 10, 698–709.

236) Wender, L. Group psychotherapy: a study of its application. *Psychiat. Quart.*, 1940, 14, 708–718.

237) Whiles, W. H. Treatment of emotional problems in childhood. *J. Ment. Sci.*, 1941, 87, 359–369.

238) Wichman, K. M., and Lanford, W. S. The parent in the children's psychiatric clinic. *Amer. J. Orthopsychiat.*, 1944, 14, 219–225.

239) Williamson, E. G. *How to counsel students: a manual of techniques for clinical counselors.* New York: McGraw-Hill, 1939.

240) Willard, H. S., and Spackman, C. S. (eds.). *Principles of occupational therapy.* Philadelphia: Lippincott, 1947.

241) Witmer, H. L. (ed.). *Psychiatric interviews with children.* New York: Commonwealth Fund, 1946.

242) Wolberg, L. R. Child institutionalization as a psychotherapeutic procedure. *Psychiat. Quart. Suppl.*, 1944, 18, 167–178.

243) Wolberg, L. R. *Hypnoanalysis.* New York: Grune & Stratton, 1945.

244) Woltmann, A. G. The use of puppets in understanding children. *Ment. Hyg.*, 1940, 24, 445–458.

245) Wrenn, C. G. Client-centered counseling. *Educ. Psychol. Measmt*, 1946, 6, 439–444.

246) Wright, D. G. The role of the social case worker in the boarding home plan of the Southard School. *Bull. Menninger Clin.*, 1944, 8, 211–215.

247) Young, R. A. A summer camp as an integral part of a psychiatric clinic. *Ment. Hyg.*, 1939, 23, 241–256.

Bibliography

Index

Adjustment, see Behavior adjustment
Adler, Alfred, 288
Admissions procedures, 147–148
Adolescent girls, treatment of, 513–518
Affective reassurance, 661–662
Agencies, rehabilitation, 171–172
    social, 334–348
Alexander, F., 692
Allen, F. H., 522, 685–686, 704
Allport, G. W., 406
Alschuler, Rose H., 386 n.
American Association for Applied Psychology, 3, 14
American Board of Examiners in Professional Psychology, 46–47, 79
American College Personnel Association, 117
American Council on Education, 67
American Psychiatric Association, 36, 80
American Psychological Association, 3, 10–11, 29–30, 34, 36, 44, 80, 117, 402
Analytic interview, 490
Andrews, Jean S., 654–673
Anxiety, relief of, 664–665
Appel, K. E., 678
Armed Services, 30–32
Army, U. S., 66, 309, 311–312
Arthur, Grace, 461–465, 711
Arthur Point Scale, 322
Associations, controlled, 583–584
Audio-visual aids, 713
Axline, V. M., 704–705

Baruch, Dorothy W., 496–512, 522, 638–653, 703, 711
Baumgarten, F., 417–418
Baxter, Brent N., 529 n.
Beers, Clifford W., 8

Behavior adjustment, 488–495
    analytic interview in, 490
    environmental change in, 491–492
    finger-painting in, 491
    situational interview in, 492–495
Behavior disorders, 425–427
Berdie, Ralph F., 604–624
Berezin, M. A., 697
Bibliotherapy, 712–713
Binet, Alfred, 330, 349
Binet-Simon scale, 6
Bingham, Walter V., 66
Bisch, L. E., 12
Bixler, R., 522 f.
Blain, Daniel, 40
Blanchard, Phyllis, 349–365, 454, 473–477
Blos, Peter, 625–637, 692
Bordin, Edward S., 229–243
Broadoaks Preschool, 496–512
Brooklyn College, 626–627
Brotemarkle, R. A., 9–10
Brown, R. R., 354
Burnham, W. H., 361

Campbell, Helen M., 106–114
Carnegie Institute of Technology, 66
Carter, Jerry W., Jr., 183–186
Case histories, diagnosis of feeble-mindedness, 317–324
    in psychological counseling, 629–633, 635–636
    in vocational counseling, 610–622
    nondirective treatment of adult, 528–578, 585
    of interviews preceding examination, 455–460
    of psychotic ex-soldier, 299–313
Case loads, 119–121
Case notes, 217–218
    characteristics, 221–223

733